Landmarks of Britain

Landmarks of

CLIVE ASLET

Britain

THE FIVE HUNDRED PLACES THAT MADE OUR HISTORY

HODDER

For C.E.M.A.
and his brother adventurers in history

First published in Great Britain in 2005 by Hodder and Stoughton
A division of Hodder Headline

The right of Clive Aslet to be identified as the Author
of the Work has been asserted by him in accordance
with the Copyright, Designs and Patents Act 1988.

A Hodder & Stoughton trade paperback

3

A CIP catalogue record for this title is available from the British Library

ISBN 978 0 340 73511 4

ISBN 0 340 73511 2

Designed by Nicky Barneby @ Barneby Ltd.
Maps by Reginald Piggott
Picture research by Josine Meijer

Typeset in Quadraat and Monotype Grotesque by Hewer Text (UK) Ltd, Edinburgh
Colour repro by Radstock Reproductions, Frome, Somerset
Printed and bound by Butler & Tanner Ltd, Frome, Somerset

Hodder Headline's policy is to use papers that are natural, renewable
and recyclable products and made from wood grown in sustainable
forests. The logging and manufacturing processes are expected to
conform to the environmental regulations of the country of origin.

Hodder and Stoughton Ltd
A division of Hodder Headline
338 Euston Road
London NW1 3BH

Contents

Introduction

THE WORD 'LANDMARKS' in the title of this book needs explanation. I am using it in the sense of 'places where things happened'. As a nation, we are bound together by the land that we inhabit and the history that we share. My landmarks are the sites – whether found in cities or towns, villages or fields – where great events have been played out. They range from battlefields to laboratories, from scenes of industry to homes of poets, from the garden where Elizabeth I sat as she heard that she would ascend the throne to the Grand Hotel in Brighton where Mrs Thatcher was nearly assassinated. Each entry tells a story, and each story is in some way an episode in the nation's story.

If you were to visit all five hundred landmarks, you would find the whole panorama of British history laid open before you, from Cheddar Man in Gough's Cave to the Millennium Bridge across the river Tyne. Some of them, such as Shakespeare's birthplace in Stratford-upon-Avon, have achieved the status of national shrines: Sir Winston Churchill's Chartwell is rapidly becoming one. But shrine-visiting is not generally the British way. We have no equivalent of Gettysburg in the United States, no Mount Vernon or Monticello.

An information board is all that the modern visitor can find at the battlefield of Naseby to interpret the decisive conflict of the Civil War. So far from being protected, this most important of historical sites was, not long ago, compromised when the A14 was pushed through part of it. What a contrast this makes with attitudes in the 19th century. In 1823, a local family erected a stone monument to the battlefield, outside the village of Naseby (on land that had in fact paid little part in the fighting). They saw the battle as having helped to forge the world in which they lived, and furthermore it pointed a useful moral. Visitors were reminded by an inscription that Naseby 'terminated fatally the Royalist cause and led to the subversion of the Throne, the Altar and the Constitution, and for years plunged the nation into the horrors of anarchy and civil war, leaving a useful lesson to British Kings, never to extend the bounds of their just prerogative, and to British Subjects, never to swerve from the allegiance due to their legitimate monarch'. History meant something to such people. We may smile at the sententiousness, we may question the interpretation of events, but we should applaud the spirit that lay behind it.

I mention Naseby in particular because it was where this book started. For some years, my weekend route often took me past the battlefield and made me wonder why more was not made of this titanic conflict, involving Prince Rupert's headstrong cavalry charge on the one hand, and Cromwell's steely New Model Army on the other. Not only was the outcome momentous, but also the lead characters could hardly have made a stronger contrast, in terms of personality and belief. What a story! To stand on the very ground where the Parliamentary pikemen prepared to form into their 'hedgehogs', and stare across at the ridge where brave, dithering little King Charles stood, on the aptly named Dust Hill, was a communion with the past. Thinking about neglected Naseby one day made me consider battlefields in general. Once, virtually every clash of arms would have been marked by crossed swords on road maps, but modern map-makers prefer to highlight leisure destinations. On the ground, the Battle of Towton in Yorkshire – the bloodiest ever to have taken place in Britain – has no memorial at all.

Battles are out of favour. None of our great national victories is celebrated with a bank holiday: even in 2005, the two-hundredth anniversary of Nelson's death, children still went to school on Trafalgar Day. The Americans celebrate Independence Day, the French Bastille Day, but British public holidays have no such resonance. Few children know what famous event took place on 18 June (a clue: the Duke of Wellington was involved). Royal Oak Day is similarly forgotten – and yet was there ever a tale to equal that of Charles II's escape after the Battle of Worcester, when he spent a day wedged into the bushy crown of an oak tree at Boscobel? That question is not entirely rhetorical. It invites the unexpected answer, yes. This book is full of extraordinary tales.

Battlefields are among the most obvious, and most neglected, of historical sites, but they represent only one of many groupings among the landmarks of Britain. Julius Caesar landed on the shingly beach at Walmer in Kent. George Frideric Handel composed the *Messiah* in a house in Brook Street, London. Edward Jenner deduced the principles of vaccination, which led to the global eradication of smallpox, in a Gloucestershire village. (Just a mile away, over four centuries earlier, a king had been horribly murdered in Berkeley Castle.) Alexander Fleming discovered penicillin in St Mary's Hospital, Paddington. Edward VIII signed his abdication papers at Fort Belvedere. Five hundred landmarks have produced five hundred stories – many highlighting exceptional achievement, some triumphs against the odds, others turning points in history.

Some landmarks chose themselves. William of Normandy defeated Harold II at Hastings. King John signed Magna Carta at Runnymede. Mary Queen of Scots was imprisoned in Loch Leven Castle, and Charles I had his head chopped off outside the Banqueting House in London. William of Orange landed at Brixham Harbour, soon supplanting James II on the throne. The Jacobite cause perished at Culloden, and Admiral Nelson fell, victorious in death at Trafalgar, on the deck of HMS *Victory*. In the 20th century, Rutherford split the atom at the Cavendish Laboratory in Cambridge and, in a Eureka moment twenty-one years later, Crick and Watson astonished lunchtime drinkers in a pub in the same city by exuberantly announcing that they had just discovered the 'secret of life', or the structure of DNA.

These are palpable events, palpable places, but not all landmarks can be pinned to a single moment. Nearly all the prehistoric landmarks are memorials of a marathon of work as opposed to a 100m sprint. We do not know precisely what happened at Stonehenge, but we know that its construction evolved over millennia. Its very mystery reinforces its role as a national icon, since it has been regularly re-interpreted according to the preoccupations of the age. Bede lived and worked at St Paul's Monastery in Jarrow, his achievement there being the sum of his life rather than any sudden flash of inspiration; he would no doubt have been intensely distrustful of sudden flashes, other than visions. Darwin's *On the Origin of Species*, written in Down House in Kent, was published twenty-eight years after he had set sail in the *Beagle*. Gertrude Jekyll created a wonderful garden at Munstead Wood, which, being her own house, perfectly expressed her strikingly original ideas; nevertheless, like any garden, it did not sprout overnight. The Second World War was won from Churchill's Cabinet War Rooms underneath Whitehall. These are landmarks that record continuous endeavour, hard slog or, in the Churchillian phrase, 'blood, toil, tears and sweat'.

Some landmarks have been included because they are firsts. The first arrival of a Viking longship on British shores; the first British saint; the first British castle to fall to artillery; the first lighthouse to be built at sea; the first Methodist chapel; the first British pillar-box; the first British mosque; the first drive-through safari park outside Africa; the world's first nuclear power station and the world's first 'in vitro' baby . . . these are pioneering examples that have, in one way or another, affected national life.

I tried to resist landmarks whose only claim on history is that they are the oldest of their type, although I do not pretend to have been entirely successful or consistent in this. The discovery of Cheddar Man, the oldest complete skeleton found in Britain, was itself an event, but the real importance of the entry lies in the antiquity of the bones; known British history starts with Cheddar Man because he is the first person of whom evidence exists. I have similarly weakened in favour of the extraordinary contraption in Salisbury Cathedral that is the oldest clock in the country and, maybe, the world. I found the little church at Bradwell-on-Sea, with its wading birds and mudflats, equally remarkable; it is the oldest church of any size in Britain, and was made the more special for me by the Good Friday ceremony that was taking place there when I arrived. I have also included the country's oldest parliament; the oldest Norman castle; the seat of Britain's only remaining medieval dukedom; and the oldest shop still to be selling the same product (tea, naturally).

The building of some landmarks was an historical occasion in itself. The Pictish standing stones at Nigg are, so to speak, their own event, rare pieces of evidence testifying to the lives of the mysterious people who made them. Similarly, Rosslyn Chapel near Edinburgh is an amazing structure that remains, architecturally and iconographically, an enigma. The Royal Botanic Gardens at Kew is important simply because it exists, as the greatest botanic garden in the world. The bridges over the Menai Strait and the river Tamar were marvels of construction, which provided the last link in the chain of vast civil engineering achievements – Telford's road from London to Holyhead and Brunel's Great Western Railway respectively. Similarly, the digging of the Channel Tunnel ended millennia of physical isolation from the Continent.

I have tried to avoid too many birthplaces. Shakespeare's must qualify, if only because of the layers of association that it has acquired since his death; Robert Burns's cottage for the same reason; Lloyd George's Llanystumdwy and Nos. 1–3 North Parade in Grantham, the grocer's shop where Margaret Thatcher grew up, qualify as being so much a part of the legends of those politicians.

Occasionally I have included landmarks just because they have survived. The Bowthorpe Oak is one of them: I defy anybody who sees it not to be in awe of its venerable antiquity. The swannery at Abbotsbury is another. In these cases, survival must be treated as an event in itself. If pressed, I would admit that a small number of landmarks are really relics, rather than places; among them are the Mappa Mundi in Hereford Cathedral, the 1st Marquess of Anglesey's trouser leg at Plas Newydd, and the head of Lord Cardigan's charger at Deene Park. I crave the reader's indulgence. I have tried to be as comprehensive in my selection as possible, but I also wanted to share the stories that appeal to me. I am, in my approach, an antiquarian, in the tradition of William Stukeley (see Primrose Hill, page 164) rather than a PhD student. I like the thought that the name of Hotspur, the late 14th-century warrior, survives in the name of Tottenham Hotspur Football Club. I enjoy the coincidence that the bowmen who secured Henry V's victory at Agincourt came from near the future king's birthplace at Monmouth.

Because my landmarks are the physical record of the history that made Britain, I hope this book will be of use to any freshly landed Martian wishing to understand the British character and tradition. I have furthered that end by embracing a selection of landmarks that strike me as being particularly distinctive to this country – such as red telephone boxes, Worcestershire sauce, the BBC, cricket, church music, Winchester and Eton, Marks and Spencer, English mustard, whisky and Druidism.

The British have always enjoyed visiting stately homes, to admire and wonder at the beauty with which the aristocracy were able to surround themselves. But we do not so often go on pilgrimage to the places where our history was made and I hope that this book will inspire and stimulate the interest to do so. I freely confess myself to being stirred and moved to wonder by the contemplation of the giant figures that crowd the past. In this book I have tried to introduce them through the medium of the places where they lived, loved, fought and died.

Clive Aslet
London, April 2005

AUTHOR'S NOTE

There are many different ways of arranging a book of this nature – strictly alphabetically, regionally or by individual counties. I chose to have regions, both for practical reasons and because I feel they have strong local identities. Within each region, the landmarks again could be compiled chronologically or alphabetically, and I chose the latter system – but perhaps you would not think so. Although South-West England begins with Abbotsbury, the next entry is Roman Baths. The Home Counties begins with Shaw's Corner. That might not seem very alphabetical, so a word of explanation is in order.

The order is alphabetical by the location. Thus Abbotsbury is followed by Bath (which is where the Roman baths are), and the Bath entries (which appear chronologically) are followed by the Bovington Tank Museum. Where the entry is under the name of a house (like Shaw's Corner), the order is designated by where Shaw's Corner is – in this case Ayot St Lawrence. However, where the name of a landmark is 'near' a town or village rather than 'in' it, then the entry goes under the name of the landmark and not the location: therefore, Stowe Gardens near Buckingham is under S and not B. The index will, however, lead you directly to an entry no matter how it appears within the text.

There is a small difference in the typeface used for the headings; those in a sans serif face are modern – or, at least, 20th century.

The cross-references are there to lead you either to other entries about the same general subject (as in the case of the battles of the Wars of the Roses and the English Civil War), and these appear at the end of the entry; or to read more about a specific person or thing mentioned elsewhere in the book but not in the context of the same subject (for example, more information about the Order of the Garter or Samuel Pepys), and these appear within the text of an entry. Very occasionally, there is a cross-reference at the end of an entry that does not have an * referring to it within the entry; these refer to unrelated but similar entries.

Finally, some acknowledgements. Just as Sir Nikolaus Pevsner dedicated one of his *Buildings of England* volumes to the inventor of the ice-lolly, so I must salute the makers of satellite navigation. Criss-crossing Great Britain would have been laborious without it. (I say Great Britain to denote the geographical scope of the book, not the British Isles: I did not think the story of Northern Ireland could be told through its landmarks without any from the Republic of Ireland, and to have included the whole of Ireland was beyond the spatial limits of one book.) I have other thanks to render: to my publisher Richard Atkinson; to the incomparable Jenny Dereham; to Esther Godfrey and Emma Flatt; to my colleagues at *Country Life*; to my agents Zoe Pagnamenta and Tracy Bohan; and to Naomi and my children for inspiration.

Landmarks of Britain
A CHRONOLOGY

PREHISTORIC

ROMAN BRITAIN

ANGLO-SAXON/VIKING BRITAIN

THE NORMANS

1066–1087: William I

1413–1422: Henry V

1415	Battle of Agincourt	Portchester Castle, page 84

1422–1461: Henry VI

1439	Richard Beauchamp, Earl of Warwick dies	St Mary's Church, page 347
1440	Eton College founded	Eton College, page 215
1455–1485	The Wars of the Roses	
1455	The Earl of Warwick defeats the Lancastrians	First Battle of St Albans, page 240
1460	Richard, Duke of York killed	Battle of Wakefield, page 403
1461	Henry VI rescued from the Yorkists	Second Battle of St Albans, page 241
1461	Edward, Earl of March, seizes crown for Yorkists	Battle of Mortimer's Cross, page 332

1461–1470: Edward IV

1461	Richard Neville, Earl of Warwick helps destroy Lancastrian army	Battle of Towton, page 402
1464	Edward IV meets Elizabeth Woodville	Queen's Oak, page 324
	The first British castle to fall to gunpowder	Bamburgh Castle, page 383

1470–1471: Henry VI

1471	Prince of Wales dies on the battlefield	Battle of Tewkesbury, page 346
	The King is murdered	Battle of Barnet, page 204

1471–1483: Edward IV

1476	William Caxton arrives in London	Fleet Street, page 138

1483: Edward V

1483	Two princes murdered in the Tower	Queen's Oak, page 324

1483–1485: Richard III

1485	Defeat and death of the King	Battle of Bosworth, page 309

THE HOUSE OF TUDOR

1485–1509: Henry VII

1485	Henry Tudor lands in Britain	Milford Haven, page 426
1487	Lambert Simnel challenges for the throne	Battle of Stoke, page 342
1488	Death of James III of Scotland	Battle of Sauchieburn, page 480
1497	John Cabot discovers Newfoundland	St Mary Redcliffe, page 10
1502	Death of Prince Arthur, heir to the throne	Worcester Cathedral, page 349

THE HOUSE OF STUART

1820–1830: George IV

1830–1837: William IV

1837–1901: Victoria

1859	*On the Origin of Species* published	Down House, page 67
		Museum of Natural History, page 233
	Great Western Railway completed	Royal Albert Bridge, page 36
1860	Florence Nightingale's institution for the training of nurses founded	St Thomas's Old Operating Theatre, page 181
1861	Death of Prince Albert	Balmoral Castle, page 443
	William Morris founds Morris & Company	Red House, page 51
1862	The International Exhibition	Elkington's Factory, page 305
	Royal holiday home acquired	Sandringham House, page 284
1863	World's first underground railway	Arnos Grove Station, page 112
1865	Lord Palmerston dies	Broadlands, page 53
1868	The world's first traffic lights	Bridge Street, page 118
1872	The Royal Parks and Gardens Regulation Act	Speakers' Corner, page 187
1873	Foundation of the Kennel Club	Swimbridge, page 42
1874	The greatest Rothschild house begun	Waddesdon Manor, page 245
1877	First lawn tennis championship held	All England Lawn Tennis Club, page 111
1878	Frederic Leighton becomes President of the Royal Academy	Leighton House, page 155
1879	Blackpool is illuminated	Blackpool Pleasure Beach, page 355
	Marx and Engels escape death	Tay Bridge, page 486
1880	The first domestic house to have electricity	Cragside, page 385
1881	Death of Disraeli	Hughenden Manor, page 223
1882	Site chosen for new Catholic cathedral	Westminster Cathedral, page 194
	The fourth Eddystone Lighthouse	Eddystone Lighthouse, page 21
1884	First public telephone kiosks	Broad Court, page 123
1885	Queen becomes patron of a dogs' home	Battersea Dogs' Home, page 115
1890	Mr Marks meets Mr Spencer	Kirkgate Market, page 394
	Model village created	Port Sunlight, page 374
1895	The trial of Oscar Wilde	Central Criminal Court, page 131
		Reading Gaol, page 236
1896	National Trust acquires its first building	The Clergy House, page 48
1897	Charles Rennie Mackintosh designs art school	Glasgow School of Art, page 463
	The rules of golf are laid down	Royal and Ancient Golf Club, page 479

South-West England

THE WEST COUNTRY is an ancient and mysterious region. The first man in Britain with whom it is possible to make historical acquaintance was discovered in Gough's Cave in Cheddar Gorge, our oldest complete skeleton. Stonehenge continues to taunt archaeologists with its secrets: we know that it was in use for two millennia – longer than Christianity has been practised in this country – but what for? More certain is the purpose of the village street around which the 1st- or 2nd-century BC dwellings of Chysauster are organised. Mystery returns with Cadbury Castle – was this the site of King Arthur's Camelot? It continues at Glastonbury: Joseph of Arimathea may or may not have planted his staff into the earth there, but faith sufficiently fortified the last abbot of the monastery to defy Henry VIII – with predictably grisly results.

Cornish tin attracted traders. In 325BC, one of them, Pytheas of Massila, thought it worth mentioning in a travelogue, and for the first time Britain enters written history. It is an appropriate debut: Britain is a trading nation, surrounded by the sea. Nowhere is this salty, mercantile, buccaneering character more prominent than in the West Country. Devon claims Sir Francis Drake, while Sir Walter Raleigh seated himself, at ruinous expense, at Sherborne in Dorset. The extraordinary Henry Winstanley built the first offshore lighthouse on the Eddystone rocks in 1703 before it was washed away, and him with it. Bristol built its fortune on trade, including slavery, but saved its soul through Methodism.

There is elegance here, and has been since the first elaborately coiffed Roman lady visited the spa at *Aquae Sulis*, later known as Bath. Elegance produces surprises, however: John Wood's Circus in Bath was inspired not by the Coliseum in Rome but by Stonehenge. We return thus to the mystery. The enigmatic figure of T. E. Lawrence at Clouds Hill perpetuates it. With Judge Jeffreys at Wells and the development of battle tanks at Bovington Camp – called 'mechanical monsters' by Churchill – we encounter moments of savagery on the way.

South-West England

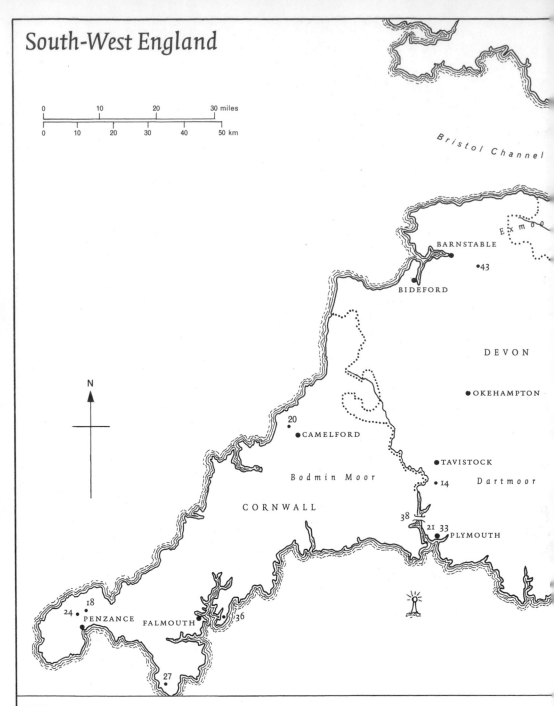

Bristol Channel

Exmoor

BARNSTABLE

•43

BIDEFORD

DEVON

•OKEHAMPTON

20
•
•CAMELFORD

•TAVISTOCK

Bodmin Moor

• 14   Dartmoor

CORNWALL

38

21 33
•PLYMOUTH

18
•
24 •
•PENZANCE   FALMOUTH   •36

27

N

0   10   20   30 miles
0   10   20   30   40   50 km

WALES

River Severn

BRISTOL
8 9 10 11

CHIPPENHAM
26   7

BATH
2 3 4 5

Mendip Hills

Salisbury
Plain

16

45
WELLS

22

WILTSHIRE

42   41

28

30 25
GLASTONBURY

32
37
SALISBURY

BRIDGWATER
39

SOMERSET

River Parrett

TAUNTON

15

YEOVIL

40 SHERBORNE

TIVERTON

DORSET

44
DORCHESTER

POOLE   17

EXETER

LYME REGIS

1   29   WAREHAM

19 6
13   BOURNEMOUTH

3

31
WEYMOUTH

Lyme Bay

34

BRIXHAM

12

English Channel

ALDERNEY

FRANCE

SARK

GUERNSEY

JERSEY

CHANNEL
ISLANDS
on smaller scale

35
ST HELIER

ABBOTSBURY

The only surviving medieval swannery

The monks of the Benedictine monastery of St Peter at Abbotsbury were greatly blessed. They passed their life next to the thin sliver of heaped-up rocks known as Chesil Beach or Bank, which runs for about 10 miles from Abbotsbury to Portland. The rock debris was deposited in Lyme Bay by the melting waters of the last ice age, and then beaten back onto a bed of clay by the waves of the Atlantic. There it rests, 35ft high and, in places, over 150yds wide, protecting the strip of shallow water known as the Fleet that lies between it and the land. Reeds grow in the lagoon, providing the thatch with which the houses in the village of Abbotsbury are sometimes still covered; so do great quantities of eelgrass. To the berry-like eye of a swan, the Fleet looks like a huge larder overflowing with food. To the monks, the swans were themselves a delicious dish and source of income. The first record of a flock having been managed here dates from 1393.

When the Abbotsbury abbey was dissolved in 1536, Sir Giles Strangways, who had administered the monastery's surrender for Henry VIII, bought its lands, buildings and swannery. His descendants, who became Earls of Ilchester, have operated the swannery ever since. In the Tudor period, roast swan was considered such a delicacy that the monarch assumed ownership of all the swans in England that did not belong to a recognised swannery. Some nine hundred swanneries existed under licence during Queen Elizabeth's reign. Abbotsbury is a rare survivor.

The colony of swans, which does not migrate, numbers between 600 and 1,000, each being marked by a nick in the webbed foot to distinguish it from the wild swans that are still owned by the Queen. On the Thames, the annual ceremony to mark the birds claimed by the Vintners' and Dyers' companies is known as swan-upping (see page 214).

Swans not only made a spectacular dish for feasts, but their feathers played an incalculable role in England's cultural development. It was from them, hardened in hot sand, that quill pens were cut. No swans, no Shakespeare.

ROMAN BATHS

The pragmatic Romans make the most of a Celtic cult

Around AD100, elegant Roman women wore their hair in a kind of thick sausage across the tops of their heads. There is a monumental female head of this type at Bath, originally on a tomb; from it we can deduce that, within half a century of the Roman invasion of Britain in AD43 (see page 89), the sacred springs at Bath were being visited by people of quality – women, to boot.

The power of the hot springs had been known before the Romans came. Legend has it that Bladud, the son of a British king, contracted leprosy on his travels, upon which he was exiled from his father's court to become a swineherd. The pigs also became leprous, until one day they rooted their way among the bubbling waters of a reddish spring, over which a mist of steam hung on cold days. As though by a miracle, they were cured; so was Bladud, and he went on to reign and beget King Lear. Since this story was first recorded in the Middle Ages, it is almost certainly without foundation. The Celts did, however, believe that the smoky water had curative properties, thanks to the deity Sulis. To the pragmatic Romans, Sulis sounded very like their own Minerva, and the two became conflated in a pagan goddess whom they sometimes called Sulis Minerva. In their temple, the centrepiece of the pediment was a round head, carved of stone. His luxuriantly curling beard and hair resemble snakes (perhaps a memory of the Gorgon on Minerva's shield) and an owl peeps from a corner (the owl is Minerva's attribute). They called the town that they built – dominated by baths and temples – *Aquae Sulis*, or Waters of Sulis.

Romans, or Romanised Britons, came to make sacrifices here, to offer up prayers and to formulate curses (mostly against thieves). Like the lady with the coiffure, they sometimes died here: those who were rich enough had their passing commemorated on monuments. The waters also had their lighter side, for bathing was an important social activity in Roman life, and for the conquering legions, the discovery of hot springs in Britain's uninviting climate must have been particularly welcome. Once they had put lead-lined walls around the spring to form a basin, and driven piles into the surrounding marsh, they set about constructing baths. The baths must have astounded local tribespeople who could never have seen structures of this size before – with their barrel-vaulted roofs, they came to occupy the space of a modern football pitch. No doubt the Romans' elaborate water rituals, which involved a succession of baths of different temperatures, followed by massage with aromatic oils, astounded them too. A baffled barbarian chieftain is supposed to have asked a Roman governor why he bathed once every day. Because, replied the Roman sadly, he was too busy to bathe twice a day.

BATH ABBEY

SOMERSET

Imperial coronation of King Edgar

In the Heritage Vaults of Bath Abbey is what looks like a little Saxon window; originally, it would have been set next to the altar to hold sacred vessels. Did it look down on the coronation of Edgar, King of the English, in 973? Edgar was king of Mercia, Wessex and Northumberland – the three most important areas of England. Bath lay on the edge of Wessex and Mercia, and he probably chose it for his coronation to demonstrate power over both kingdoms. He had left his coronation a little late, given that he had already been on the throne for fourteen years. Earlier in 973, he had staged a water pageant when no fewer than eight kings of Scotland and five Welsh princes had rowed him along the river Dee: another symbolic demonstration of his supremacy. By his accumulation of kingdoms, he had united most of England north of the Thames; he issued laws that extended to Northumbria, parts of which were under the Danelaw, and since five of his aunts had married foreign rulers, he managed to keep his increasingly united realm – looking more and more like the geographical England that we know today – free of invasion.

Bath Abbey had been founded by Offa, England's mini-Charlemagne (see page 428), in the mid-8th century. During his coronation there, Edgar prostrated himself before the altar in an act of humility, for which he won praise. He was a pious man. One of his first acts on becoming king in 959 was to bring the austere former abbot of Glastonbury, Dunstan, back from exile to be Archbishop of Canterbury, and it was he who performed the coronation ceremony. Under Edgar's patronage, Dunstan reformed monastic life throughout the country. The Normans replaced the Saxon abbey at Bath, and no trace of its Saxon heritage may be seen above ground. All that remains, putatively, from that abbey are a few pieces of carving that had once been part of stone crosses, and the little window. Henry VII replaced the Normans' church with the present abbey, with its fan-vaulted ceiling. The walls are now lined with monuments to Georgian visitors for whom the water did not prove efficacious.

QUEEN SQUARE
BATH, SOMERSET
Triumph of English town planning

In 1727, John Wood hit upon an idea that was to revolutionise the appearance of British cities. He built Queen Square in Bath. There was nothing new in building terraces of houses around squares: Inigo Jones had done so, creating the *piazza* of London's Covent Garden, a century before. Wood's innovation was to design a terrace so that it looked like one very grand building, rather than a string of individual dwellings joined together. The north side of the square looks like a palace, with a central pediment, end pavilions and giant columns. Few subsequent terraces were as grand as this, until John Nash built those around Regent's Park in London (see page 163). But the principle that terraces could be composed to architectural effect was profound, giving order and architectural style to streets that would otherwise have lacked presence. Edinburgh, Brighton, London's Belgravia and many other Georgian and Victorian developments were beneficiaries.

As the son of a builder, Wood, who was born in Bath, was first apprenticed to a carpenter. He seems to have had a strong sense of Bath's history, since Queen Square re-creates some of its Roman glory. At first sight, you might think that his next development, the King's Circus (now simply known as the Circus), was also inspired by the classical world. Well-travelled contemporaries would immediately have been put in mind of the Coliseum in Rome. Wood's inspiration, however, was Stonehenge (see page 39), to which he intended the dimensions of the circus to correspond. Because the curative properties of the hot springs had supposedly been first discovered by Prince Bladud, cast out for leprosy and temporarily working as a swineherd (see page 5), the top of the parapet is adorned with stone acorns. These allusions would have had no meaning for people who lived other than in Bath, but the idea that fashionable urban developments could unfold as a sequence of geometrical spaces shaped the Georgian town.

Wood died in 1754, just as work on the King's Circus was beginning. Its completion was left to his son, John Wood the Younger, who introduced another geometrical form to Georgian building in the shape of the Royal Crescent. Development in Bath had now moved from the low-lying marsh around the springs and had spread up the hill. Wood, responding to the contemporary taste for the landscape of the Picturesque, used this to his advantage, by turning his new crescent towards the view. A leafy park spills down the hillside: whereas Queen Square and the King's Circus were enclosed urban spaces, the Royal Crescent opens itself towards nature.

Between them, father and son Woods formed fashionable Bath, with its ever-changing cast of wealthy visitors. It was not just their vision as architects that achieved this, but their energy as developers. Most of Bath, so harmonious in its classical proportions and unified through the use of creamy stone supplied by Ralph Allen's quarries at nearby Combe Down, was a speculative development, whose grand architecture must have been completed piecemeal as different builders finished houses for different clients. Like other speculative developers before and since, John Wood the Younger was unable to stay ahead of the game, and died heavily in debt. He left behind the most beautiful planned town in England.

LANSDOWN TOWER

BATH, SOMERSET

Beckford's tower – the one that didn't collapse

In December 1825 the tower of Fonthill Abbey in Wiltshire collapsed, leaving the house that William Beckford had begun a quarter of a century earlier in ruins. Fonthill was an extreme building, even by Romantic standards. As 'England's wealthiest son', as Byron called him, Beckford – sophisticated, literate and ostracised by society for his homosexual tastes – could give his imagination free rein. He built a tall fence around his estate to keep out fox-hunting neighbours, and created a house whose front door alone was 35ft high; to increase the drama, Beckford employed a dwarf to open it. By the time of the collapse, however, he had sold Fonthill and moved on. Although the Jamaican sugar plantations from which his fortune derived were badly managed, and his income had declined, he had already begun another fanciful project – a tower outside Bath, from which he could take in the spectacular views. It is said that his first intimation of the disaster at Fonthill had come when he noticed a gap in the horizon where the tower should have been.

Bored by politics and shunned by the county, Beckford lived as a recluse. As a young man, he had written a novel set in Arabia called *Vathek*, greatly admired by Byron. His own physical surroundings were no less remarkable, since, in an age of great connoisseurs, Beckford was perhaps the most remarkable collector. He loved rich effects, extraordinary workmanship, the weird and the exotic. Paintings of his *objets de vertu* show baroque pearls next to Chinese vases, lapis lazuli cups beside enamel reliquaries. Some of these were kept in Lansdown Tower, others at his house in Lansdown Crescent in Bath. After his death, they were inherited by his daughter Susan who had married the 10th Duke of Hamilton; a number found their way to the Hamiltons' summer home of Brodick Castle on Arran.

After Beckford's death in 1844, the Duchess sold Lansdown Tower, and it became a beer garden briefly. She then bought it back, and the land surrounding it was turned into a cemetery. The Regency cult of the exotic was thus overtaken by the Victorian fascination with death.

BOVINGTON TANK MUSEUM NEAR WAREHAM, DORSET
The 'mechanical monsters' that ended the stalemate of trench warfare

Before the autumn of 1914 was out, just weeks after the start of the First World War, the Germans retreated to the river Aisne and, in order to hold on to the French and Belgian territory they still had, dug trenches. The Allies were unable to break through, and dug their own trenches. Soon a line of trenches extended from the northern French coast to Switzerland. Impasse had been reached. The machine gun meant that unprotected infantry could only advance at colossal cost, if at all. While increasingly ferocious artillery bombardments were supposed to shatter enemy defences, the guns could not be brought forward over the moonscape that their shells had created, leaving the infantry once more exposed when they pushed forward beyond the guns' range. Arras and Ypres were the scenes of the first battles during which horrifying numbers of casualties were inflicted, for little perceptible gain to either side.

The journalist Maurice Hankey and his friend Colonel Ernest Swinton were convinced that another weapon was needed to counteract the machine gun. The caterpillar track had been invented as long ago as the late 18th century. Steam-powered tractors, using tracks, had been effective in the Crimean War. A motor war-car, armed with machine guns in turrets, had been developed by a British inventor in 1899, but not taken up by the War Office. Hankey and Swinton envisaged an armour-plated vehicle on tracks, driven by a petrol engine. Their idea captured the imagination of Winston Churchill, the First Lord of the Admiralty, who set up a Landships Committee to investigate its development. He and the Minister of Munitions, David Lloyd George, had already seen a tractor on tracks demonstrated at Wormwood Scrubs. The new vehicle was code-named the 'tank'. First used in the Battle of the Somme in 1916, tanks offered the hope of a breakthrough in the appalling war of attrition in which the Allies and the Central Powers had become locked.

They were described at the time by Churchill as 'mechanical monsters . . . spreading death from armour-plated sides, and crushing everything which barred their passage like veritable juggernauts'. The French quickly introduced the Renault tank; the Germans never succeeded in developing an effective tank of their own during the First World War.

Before leaving for the Front, the new British tanks were tested on a secluded area of Dorset heathland around Bovington – the sort of countryside familiar to us from the novels of Thomas Hardy. Here crews from the élite Machine Gun Corps were trained to drive and maintain them. When the war ended, hundreds of tanks were brought back from France and parked around Bovington, until being taken for scrap. A few were spared, in recognition of their role in history. The suggestion that they should form the basis of a museum was made by the author Rudyard Kipling (see page 55), when he visited Bovington in 1923.

BOWOOD HOUSE
NEAR CHIPPENHAM, WILTSHIRE

Joseph Priestley discovers oxygen

In December 1772, Lord Shelburne, who later became 1st Marquess of Lansdowne, appointed Joseph Priestley as his librarian, literary companion, and the tutor to his two young sons. Priestley was an ordained non-conformist minister, and had radical political views. However, his scientific researches already made him an ornament for any nobleman's household. Born near Leeds in 1733, he had written a book about electricity and studied a gas which he called 'fixed air', now called carbon dioxide. Priestley wrote a second book explaining how this could be impregnated into water, to make what would later be known as soda water. At Lord Shelburne's Bowood House, he was given an ante-room to the Library to use as his laboratory.

It was here that, on a sunny 1 August 1774, Priestley took a 12-inch glass lens and focused the heat from the sun on some red mercury oxide. He had expected this solid to be inert but, on the contrary, a gas was given off. Having succeeded in collecting some of it, he was astonished to discover that 'a candle burned in this air with a remarkably vigorous flame'. A mouse, which had suffered when being confined in fixed air, became lively when it breathed the new gas. Priestley called it 'dephlogisticated air', air that was free of a substance called 'phlogiston', which Priestley believed to be given out when substances burnt. He believed that the gas could be both administered to the sick, and also used to ventilate places where air was bad. Later that year he published *Experiments and Observations on Different Kinds of Air*. It was left to the French chemist, Antoine Lavoisier, whom Priestley visited in France, to continue the experiments, and coin the term 'oxygen' for the gas.

In 1780, Priestley left Bowood for Birmingham, attracted by the scientific investigations of the Lunar Society to which many industrialists belonged. However, this brilliant mind was diverted by politics – of such an unpopular hue that a mob ransacked his house, smashing his laboratory. He spent the last ten years of his life in America.

ST MARY REDCLIFFE BRISTOL
Whalebone brought back by John Cabot

St Mary Redcliffe is celebrated as a great work of architecture, on the scale of a cathedral. Even the 16th century recognised it as 'the fairest, goodliest, and most famous parish church in England', according to no less an authority than Queen Elizabeth. One of its less regarded treasures, however, is a whalebone, believed to have been brought back by John Cabot (aka Giovanni Caboto) as a thanksgiving for a safe return from his voyage in 1497 when he discovered Newfoundland. It rests in the church near a model of his ship, the *Matthew*.

Cabot had arrived at the court of Henry VII shortly before. He had already failed to interest the kings of Spain and Portugal in his proposed expedition, which was intended to open a new trade route to Asia. Although Henry VII was no romantic he thought it worth sponsoring him. Cabot's high-sterned, square-rigged caravel the *Matthew* touched the New Founde Landes at a place he named Bonavista. He and a party rowed ashore but stayed no longer than to plant flags, returning at once to the ship. They then sailed 900 miles down the coast of North America, coming home with geographical knowledge, strange tales but no great wealth. The next year Cabot mounted another expedition, from which neither he nor the crew of his five ships returned.

THE NEW ROOM

The first Methodist chapel

John Wesley's 'New Room in the Horsefair', built in 1739, is the oldest Methodist chapel in the world, and was associated with Wesley during the span of his preaching life. Wesley was born in Lincolnshire in 1703, studied at Oxford, and preached throughout England, but his style of religion found its warmest reception in what were then the industrial areas of the West Country and Wales. He was invited to Bristol by his friend from Oxford days, George Whitefield, a fellow clergyman. It had been Whitefield who first preached to miners in the open air – scandalising Bristol merchants, who feared that 'enthusiasm' could engender unrest. Wesley followed Whitefield's example. About 3,000 people came to his first open-air sermon, held on a brickfield (situated at what is now the junction of Old Bread Street and Kingsley Road) on 2 April 1739. 'With the voice of praise and thanksgiving,' as Wesley recorded, the foundation stone of an enclosed structure was laid ten days later.

Wesley always referred to it simply as 'the room'. Although focused on a three-decker pulpit (which is reached from the room above), with altar table and altar rails in front of it, this plain space was intended to serve as more than a chapel, doubling as a school-room and dispensary for medicines. As a result, the congregation sat on simple benches (without backs) rather than pews, since these could be easily rearranged. Wesley held eighteen of his annual conferences here, including the last in 1790. Above the chapel were lodgings for preachers and a book room.

In 1791, Wesley died, still preaching, at the age of eighty-seven. Since then, the New Room has survived much as he left it. In 1808, the Methodist congregation had grown to such a size that it required a much larger space, and the New Room was sold to the Welsh Calvinistic Methodists, who installed box pews. The relatively few other changes that they introduced were reversed when the Welsh Calvinistic Methodist congregation dwindled and the New Room was sold back to the Wesleyan Conference in 1929.

THE GEORGIAN HOUSE

The slave trade at home

Bristol's 18th-century wealth was founded, in large part, on slavery*. John Pinney, for example, inherited estates on the small Caribbean island of Nevis which he went out to run in 1765. Although he was shocked to see 'human flesh for sale', he had soon bought nine blacks. For, as he wrote in a self-justifying letter, 'surely God ordained 'em for the use and benefit of us otherwise his Divine Will would have been made manifest to us by some particular sign or token'. As a shrewd businessman, he knew better than to drive his slaves too hard, because illness reduced productivity. Nevertheless, he conquered his scruples sufficiently to sell out to a notoriously cruel neighbour. When he returned to England in 1783, he established himself in Bristol, the principal port for the West Indies, and began trading in one of the commodities produced by slave labour – sugar. It was run from the back of his elegant, though not ostentatious house which he had built in Great George Street and where he lived with his family; the servants included a slave called Pero. His business partner, James Tobin, wrote pamphlets against the abolition of the slave trade.

Bristol is peppered with uncomfortable memories of its slaving past. Blackboy Hill and the Blackboy Inn speak for themselves. Guinea Street presumably took its name, like the coin, from the Guinea coast in Africa (gold was one of its products, slaves another). Sea captains involved in the slave trade once occupied the city's best houses. The genteel inhabitants of Queen Square, Bristol's handsomest Georgian development, lived on fortunes tainted with slavery. Bristol craftsmen made the trinkets which were used to buy slaves in Africa. Its bankers funded the trade. Its manufacturers processed the products that came from it, such as sugar and tobacco. Bristol's historians are now staring these uncomfortable facts in the face.

*See St Andrew's Church, page 263, and Wilberforce House, page 392

SS GREAT BRITAIN BRISTOL
The first propeller-driven transatlantic steamship

The SS *Great Britain* was the world's first propeller-driven, ocean-going passenger ship – a precursor of the luxurious liners that would ply the Atlantic between the two world wars. Launched in 1843, the *Great Britain* was intended to attract a prosperous clientele: Queen Victoria admired the looking-glasses that made the First Class Dining Saloon 'appear almost boundless'. Isambard Kingdom Brunel's design was revolutionary: no other ship of this size had been built with an iron hull, or equipped with a propeller.

Six years earlier, Brunel's *Great Western* had steamed across the Atlantic without refuelling. This fulfilled Brunel's dream of extending the line of his Great Western Railway from Paddington to New York, but she had to rely on her sails for much of the journey since paddle-wheels cannot work in heavy seas. Furthermore, the material of which she was built – wood – limited her size. A great quantity of wood had to be used to withstand the stresses and strains caused by steam. When the Astronomer Royal, Sir George Airy, devised a compass that would work on iron-built ships, Brunel seized on it. Similarly, he immediately saw the potential of Francis Pettit Smith's screw-propeller, demonstrated by the *Archimedes*: as soon as this ship appeared in Bristol in 1839, Brunel chartered it for six months in order to study it at close quarters. By then the keel of the *Great Britain*, originally designed to support the world's largest paddle-wheel, had already been laid. Brunel unhesitatingly changed the design.

With its tall funnel flanked on either side by three masts, the *Great Britain* was a wonder. Crowds were astounded by her ability to sail backwards. She was fêted when she reached New York after a crossing that lasted 14 days and 21 hours, but later a series of navigational problems culminated in her running aground off Northern Ireland and in 1850 she was sold to Gibbs, Bright & Co. of Liverpool for a fraction of the development cost. After modification, the *Great Britain* became a sailing ship assisted by steam, rather than a steamship assisted by sail, and she was used on the route to Australia, then in the grip of a gold rush. A farmyard of animals was loaded to feed over 700 passengers, the poorest of whom were packed tightly together in what would become baking conditions – in the Tropics, the iron hull heated up like an oven. Six cannons were fitted to protect consignments of gold.

Following an epic conservation programme, the ship has now returned to the dry dock in Bristol that was originally built for her construction.

BRIXHAM HARBOUR   DEVON
Landing place of William of Orange

In June 1688, Mary of Modena, James II's queen, gave birth to a longed-for son. To the Protestant establishment, this was a disaster. It was bad enough that James should have come out as a Catholic, having married a Catholic princess as his second wife; he was already favouring Catholics over Protestants. Now he had a male heir who would be brought up as a Catholic, too. The rumour was put about that the young prince was not really James's son but a changeling, smuggled into the supposed birth chamber in a warming pan. James's fiercely Protestant daughter, the future Queen Anne, was one of those behind this ugly and implausible story.

Until now, William of Orange, the Dutch Stadtholder who was married to James's elder daughter Mary*, had resisted calls for him to curb his father-in-law's Catholic excesses. The new birth, however, threatened Mary's inheritance. His gentle, pious wife, relying on Anne's letters, believed the tale of the warming pan; William was probably too shrewd to do so, but he put any scruple on that score aside and raised an army of 15,000 men. They set sail from Holland on 19 October but a gale wrecked the fleet and it had to turn back. A second attempt was made on 1 November. This time the bad weather

William encountered acted to his advantage since the English fleet was unable to leave port. He sailed along the Channel in full view of crowds watching from Dover. James sent urgent word that Portsmouth should be fortified. It was not, however, there that William chose to land, but at the fishing harbour of Brixham in Devon. It was low tide and William was rowed ashore in a fishing boat. On the harbour side, he unfurled his standard, with the motto *Libertate et Religion je Maintiendray* (Liberty and Religion I shall maintain).

William and his supporters moved to Exeter from where he waged a propaganda campaign against the King. James left London to confront him and reached Salisbury but, unable to make up his mind to fight, he withdrew, against the advice of his officers, towards Reading. His most senior officers slipped away in the night. In London, Princess Anne was thrown into a panic by the prospect of her father's return, and fled. 'Even my daughter has deserted me,' said James in tears. He now concentrated his efforts on arranging his own escape and that of his queen and the young Prince of Wales to France.

The momentum caused by William of Orange's landing toppled James from the throne without a battle. Bloodshed would come later. William's navy fought Louis XIV's fleet, which supported James, in a ferocious battle at La Hogue. James attempted a comeback from Ireland but was defeated at the Battle of the Boyne in 1690, and the measures that followed fomented centuries of sectarian hatred. Later, historians called this period the Glorious Revolution since it was achieved without a long civil war. The position of Parliament was strengthened; the country remained Protestant; the coinage, debased under the Stuarts, was redesigned and its value maintained; the army was reorganised, with the formation of many famous regiments. Immediate results of this were the building of Devonport Dockyard and the King's Quay at Brixham. It is on this quay that William III's statue – a particularly bad one – now stands; it was erected on the two-hundredth anniversary of his landing.

*See Kensington Palace, page 152, and Royal Naval Hospital, page 172

BROWNSEA ISLAND   DORSET
The birth of the Scout Association

In July 1907, Major-General Robert Baden-Powell established the first Boy Scout camp in the world. He was already famous for his exploits in South Africa. According to Winston Churchill, the British public regarded him as the 'outstanding hero of the [Boer] War', for his command of the 1,000-strong garrison at Mafeking against a siege by 9,000 Boers. By daring, bluff and jaunty defiance, he inspired the town to resist for 217 days: on hearing the news of the relief of Mafeking in 1900, the streets of London went wild. After the Boer War, Baden-Powell began his mission to encourage the Empire-building qualities of pluck, dash and initiative in the youth of Britain – particularly those from the industrial towns.

To achieve this, Baden-Powell wanted to expose boys from all backgrounds to the kind of adventurous, open-air existence he had known in the *veld*. A desert island would have been the ideal setting for his first experimental camp since, as a figure of media interest, he wanted it to take place away from the gaze of newspaper reporters. There was no desert island anywhere near the shores of Britain, but he knew some people – the van Raaltes – who owned Brownsea Island in Poole Harbour. They were happy to provide a camp-site near the sandy beach. Baden-Powell arrived with twenty-one boys, bell tents, a flagpole, an army marquee, a pigsticking lance from India to fly the flag that had fluttered over his headquarters in Mafeking, and an African koodoo horn (its unfamiliar note woke the boys at 6am). Each boy was expected to know how to tie a reef knot, a sheet bend and a clove hitch on arrival.

The name of 'scout' that he was to give them the following year, when he founded the Scout Association, derived from his experience as Colonel of the 5th Dragoon Guards in India; there he combined the need to develop reconnaissance skills with that of training raw recruits. By the time of his death in 1941, the Boy Scout movement had become an international phenomenon.

BUCKLAND ABBEY
NEAR YELVERTON, DEVON

Sir Francis Drake spends some of his treasure

In 1581, Francis Drake* was knighted on board the *Golden Hind*, the ship on which he had just circumnavigated the world. He was born the eldest of twelve brothers of a farming family in Devon. As an outspoken Protestant, his father had been forced to leave Devon because of his religious beliefs, taking the family to live in a hulk near Chatham in Kent, and much of Drake's childhood had been spent in poverty. Now, however, he was not only famous for his feat of navigation but also vastly wealthy, having stopped to plunder the rich Spanish and Portuguese territories in South America along the way. The Spanish regarded him as a pirate. In England he was a hero, and the city of Plymouth elected him mayor on his return home. It was time, he decided, to buy a country house appropriate to his status.

His choice settled on Buckland Abbey. It was an unusual rather than beautiful house, having been created out of the church of a Cistercian monastery. Even for Devon, it had not been a particularly rich abbey, although the great barn, built about 1300, is on a majestic scale. After the Dissolution (see page 133), Buckland was sold to Sir Richard Grenville, and it was his son,

Sir Roger, who was the first to live there, presumably in the old domestic ranges, after the departure of the monks. For a time, an attempt was made to establish the name Buckland Grenville, but local people would have none of it, stubbornly sticking to Buckland Monachorum – Buckland of the Monks. (This distinguishes it from the equally picturesquely named Eggbuckland and the many other Bucklands – 'lands held by book' – in Devon.)

When Sir Roger went down in the *Mary Rose* in 1545 (see page 86), Buckland was inherited by his son, Sir Richard, forever to be remembered as commanding the *Revenge* in its last desperate fight off the Azores in 1591. Sir Richard turned the church into the present house, putting the date 1576 over the hall chimneypiece. He was at home more than he might have liked at this time since Queen Elizabeth, placating the Spanish, had blocked his plans to establish a southern route round the Americas. The house was fashioned out of the church by inserting two floors and the necessary partitions to make rooms. Otherwise, alterations were kept to a minimum. As a result, carved details are prone to appear unexpectedly – for instance, the carved ox of St Luke can be seen, aptly enough, in the corner of the Georgian dining room.

Only weeks after Drake's triumphant return from his circumnavigation, Grenville left the orbit of Plymouth, withdrawing to an ancestral seat in Cornwall. Was he piqued? To Drake, a social upstart, the idea of acquiring Grenville's own mansion, so recently created, may have seemed particularly sweet. He had sixteen years in which to enjoy Buckland, most of them in the company of his beautiful second wife, Elizabeth Sydenham, but almost as soon as he acquired the house, he was anxious to get to sea again; even for the period that he was on land, we do not know how much time he spent at Buckland and how much at court in London. Nevertheless, despite later changes of ownership and architectural alterations, some iconic Drake objects can still be seen in the house: most prominent among them is Drake's drum, which is supposed (thanks largely to a poem by the tub-thumping Victorian Henry Newbolt) to beat by itself at moments of national danger.

*See Plymouth Hoe, page 32

CADBURY CASTLE
Is this the site of Camelot?

Is this hill fort, rising above the tussocky landscape of south Somerset, the site of King Arthur's Camelot? As you walk up the shady lane, its banks dancing with pink campion, a rope left by children who had perhaps been playing 'castles' hanging from a branch of one of the trees, it is a bewitching idea. Furthermore, it is possible.

The antiquarian John Leland recorded the belief that this was 'Camellate, sumtyme a famose toun or castelle', in 1542. He notes that many ancient coins and artefacts, including a silver horseshoe, had been found. It might seem implausible that the nearby villages of Queen Camel and West Camel, and the river Cam, could be linguistically related to the Arthurian capital, but in the 1960s Leland's identification received support from archaeology. What had originally been a Bronze Age settlement, in occupation 2,000 years before the Romans arrived in Britain, was cleared by the Roman legions around AD70. In the 5th century, however, after they had gone and the Roman town of Ilchester was deserted, it was refortified. This was the period in which the historical Arthur would have existed. A Celtic king, he and his warriors were able to halt (for a while) the advance of the Saxons westwards across England, defeating them decisively in the battle of Mons Badonis, the site of which is unknown.

Behind the dry-stone walls that were erected around the perimeter of Cadbury Castle lay a wooden hall. Pottery shards form a memory of the feasting that took place there. Since the vessels from which these came had been imported from the Mediterranean, the society occupying Cadbury must have been wealthy and sophisticated. The castle could have housed a war band of 800 warriors, which would have been very big for that time. These days, banks that are yellow with buttercups do not evoke either the splendours or the military prowess of a 5th-century king, but they help make this a place of mystery, enchantment and wonder. Did Merlin walk here? Half close your eyes and it is possible to imagine so.

GOUGH'S CAVE CHEDDAR GORGE, SOMERSET
Discovery of Britain's earliest known man

It was Christmastide 1903 and the owners of Gough's Cave in the Cheddar Gorge, already a tourist attraction, were blasting a hole for a drain. When the dust settled, they discovered the bones of a man – the oldest complete skeleton ever found in Britain.

Nine thousand years ago, in the Middle Stone Age, Cheddar Man had been buried in the cave where he lived. He and his contemporaries had not been its first residents. It had been used 3,000 years before, but a drastic fall in temperature drove the inhabitants southwards, and the cave was abandoned. Then, when the world suddenly got warmer, the melting ice flooded the cave, so the precursors of Cheddar Man would have needed to clear its mouth of resulting debris before occupying it. Although the cave now consists of a spectacular series of interconnecting vaults, Cheddar Man was buried near the entrance. Stone Age people would not have ventured far beyond the reach of daylight.

Archaeology and tourist attractions do not mix. Enlarging the mouth of the cave destroyed the record of how Cheddar Man lived. We can imagine him, however, nursing fires against the cold, putting up wattle screens to keep out animals, and sleeping on a bed of moss. He may have caught fish using wicker traps, killed game with a bow and arrow, and worked with others to drive wild horses over the precipitous cliffs of the Gorge, where they fell to their death, providing much-needed flesh. His children would have gathered berries from the woods. They in turn grew up to have their own children, who continued the succession, conservatively yet loyally staying in the area where they were born.

In 1997, a comparison of Cheddar Man's DNA with that of living Cheddar residents showed that one of them – a history teacher called Adrian Targett – seemed to be his descendant.

CHRISTCHURCH PRIORY DORSET
The merry bells of England

Pealing bells are one of the most evocative sounds of England, associated with every great national celebration, as well as many personal ones. A number of the bells are ancient, two of the oldest still in use being at Christchurch Priory. They date from 1370, having been cast by King Edward III's bellfounder, John Rufford.

When they were new, they would not have been rung in 'changes', the numerical sequences which are special to England. Until the Dissolution (see page 133), the monks of the Priory would probably have tolled them singly, with a different bell chosen for different times and services. Then came the Dissolution, and English belfries fell into disrepair; at Christchurch, two of the seven bells were taken away for the 'King's use', presumably to be re-cast into cannons. The practice of ringing bells in orderly patterns seems to have been developed in the 17th century. Bells in England were not hung in the same way as on the Continent; they were attached to full wheels, rather than half or quarter wheels, so that the bell makes a complete rotation each time the rope is pulled. When the mouth of the bell is uppermost, the wheel is stopped; the bell descends in the opposite direction the next time. This method allowed ringers to control the sounding of the bell in a way that was not possible under the Continental system.

Change-ringing was originally regarded as an intellectual exercise, reserved for the educated classes. Fabian Stedman, the 'father' of bell ringing, dedicated his *Tintinnalogia* of 1668 to the Noble Society of College Youths. The permutations that can be made to the order in which the bells are rung are described as 'hunting' (changing position one place forward or backward), 'dodging' (suddenly changing direction in the hunt) and 'making a place' (retaining the same position while the other bells change place). A 'peal' describes a full ring of all the possible variations that a given number of bells can provide, and can last several hours. At Christchurch there are seven bells giving an amazing 5,040 permutations.

CHYSAUSTER ANCIENT VILLAGE
Arguably the oldest village street

The English village is ancient beyond memory. Chysauster, a settlement of eight dwellings, has possibly the oldest village street in the country, built in the 1st or 2nd century BC. Only the lowest stones of the walls survive now, but it is easy to make out the house plans. In the depths of the immensely thick walls were a number of separate chambers, each of which had its own conical roof, probably made of thatch or turf, slotted onto a central pole. Apart from the one nearest the entrance, which is oblong, these rooms are always round. The walls enclose courtyards which were presumably used to pen animals. These courtyard houses are only found around Land's End, in the Scilly Isles and in Wales. The residents could enjoy wide views since the village stands towards the top of a gentle hill, on the edge of moorland. However, the brow of the hill shelters it from northerly winds, while the courtyard entrances face away from the prevailing south-west wind. The villagers tilled a system of small fields which the expert eye can still distinguish. If they also panned tin, they were probably relatively well off. Roman occupation would have made little difference to them, since the legions did not remain west of the river Tamar for more than two or three decades in the 1st century.

The settlement may once have been bigger than the surviving houses, and it may also have been older. One mystery typical of the area is the *fogou*, or underground chamber. The best surviving *fogou* is at Trelowarren, near Helston. Nobody knows what these caves were used for.

CLOUDS HILL
Lawrence of Arabia's retreat from the world

On 13 May 1935 Thomas Edward Lawrence was riding his Brough Superior motorcycle from Bovington village to the spartan cottage that he kept nearby, when he swerved to avoid two boys on bicycles, and was pitched over the machine's handlebars. Six days later he died, aged forty-six.

As Lawrence of Arabia, T. E. Lawrence had become a legend for his part in helping the Arab revolt against the Turks during the First World War. This preceded the British capture of Damascus in 1918. Afterwards, he worked to refashion the political landscape of the Middle East, serving as adviser to Winston Churchill, then Secretary of State for the Colonies, at the Cairo conference of 1922. At the same time he was completing the text of *The Seven Pillars of Wisdom*, which describes his war career. Overwork and fame were, at this point, acting on latent feelings of inadequacy which unbalanced Lawrence. He sought to stave off mental collapse by enlisting as a humble airman in the RAF, under the false name of J. H. Ross. Within a few weeks, the Daily Express had exposed him; he re-enlisted as a private in the Tank Corps, this time under the pseudonym T. E. Shaw. He acquired Clouds Hill as a bolt-hole where he could write.

The building reflects his austere, monkish nature. Upstairs, he created a music room, where he played his gramophone and wrote. Next door, a simple iron bedstead for guests was later replaced by bunks: aluminium foil lines the walls against damp. Downstairs, the one furnished room was dominated by a large leather divan. The walls were covered with bookshelves to accommodate a remarkable library. Lawrence had been fascinated by book production since his days at Oxford; he published the first edition of *The Seven Pillars of Wisdom* as a sumptuous printing of one hundred copies for subscribers. There was no kitchen, Lawrence eating direct from tins, stores of which he bought in bulk. He usually ate and slept at Bovington Camp. Royalties from a translation of the *Odyssey* later enabled him to remodel the cottage, where he was intending to live when his army enlistment expired. This brought Lawrence's one concession to comfort: a bathroom with hot water.

DELABOLE WIND FARM *NEAR CAMELFORD, CORNWALL*
A first try at green energy

In 1991, Britain's first wind farm began generating electricity at Delabole. Environmentalists had become increasingly concerned by the rate at which man was depleting the earth's reserves of fossil fuels; the most highly developed alternative, nuclear power, seemed to present an equal danger to the planet, through the generation of toxic waste. As yet, few people had awoken to the possibility that the amount of carbon dioxide and other gases that had been thrown into the atmosphere since the Industrial Revolution might be artificially changing the world's temperature. An early champion of this view was the prime minister Margaret Thatcher – in other respects, a zealous advocate of the free market. As a trained chemist, she persuaded President Reagan that the United States should be one of the 165 nations that signed the United Nations Convention on Climate Change at the Rio Earth Summit in 1992.

After the Kyoto Earth Summit in 1997, Britain, under the premiership of

Tony Blair, committed itself to stretching targets for renewable energy. It was decided that 10 per cent of the nation's energy should come from renewable forms by 2010 and 20 per cent by 2020. Following the example of Continental countries, particularly Denmark, wind energy seemed the best means of meeting the challenge. Britain is, after all, the windiest country in Europe.

As a result, the turbines that seemed a novelty at Delabole have become an increasingly common sight, although modern turbines are, at over 300ft tall, more than double the height of the originals. There is increasing concern that this method of producing 'green' energy contradicts the principles of sustainable development, because of the impact each turbine makes on the environment (foundations contain enough concrete for an Olympic-sized swimming pool), the visual damage wind farms of a hundred or more turbines cause to the landscape, and the suffering they impose on local communities who object to the noise and the bad effect on property values. Since the wind only blows at the right speeds for a third of the time, their efficiency is questioned.

Often sited in remote, hilltop locations, wind farms generally require long power lines to connect with the national grid. It has been suggested that wind farms are better sited at sea than on land, preferably near existing power stations where the infrastructure of the national grid already exists. They will remain an alien presence in the landscape long after more serviceable green technologies have been developed.

EDDYSTONE LIGHTHOUSE
First lighthouse to be built at sea

PLYMOUTH HOE, DEVON

The Romans built the first lighthouses in Britain: the stump of one tower, octagonal, survives at Dover. After the Romans left, mariners had to wait until the Middle Ages before priests and monks helped steer them off the rocks by putting lights in church belfries. The practice of erecting purpose-built towers was revived in the early 17th century, with examples at Dungeness and North and South Foreland on the English Channel, at the Lizard in Cornwall and elsewhere. They stood on the coast. The first lighthouse to be built at sea was on the notorious Eddystone Reef, 14 miles off Plymouth Hoe.

It was the work of the extraordinary Henry Winstanley in 1696–9. The son of the steward of Audley End House in Essex, he came to own five merchant ships, one of which, the *Constant*, was wrecked on the Eddystone rocks in 1695. Trinity House, the body responsible for lighthouses around Britain, gave permission for a toll of a penny per ton of cargo to be levied from ships passing the lighthouse Winstanley planned to build, making it not just an act of revenge on the reef but a commercial speculation. Waves lashed the rocks as Winstanley and his men drove in their spikes and attached their stones. Work was halted temporarily at one point when he was captured by French privateers. Slowly, however, a tower arose, to a fantastic polygonal design 100ft high and topped by a weather vane. The twenty-four tallow candles were first lit in 1698, and Winstanley celebrated the work by commissioning the handsome silver salt that is now in Plymouth Museum. Alas, the tower was washed away, with Winstanley inside it, by a great storm in November 1703. Two days later, the reef claimed its next victim, a merchantman laden with a cargo of tobacco.

A new lighthouse was built in 1706, this one 92ft tall, but it burnt down in 1755. The tower that replaced it was engineered by John Smeaton, who took four years to complete the work, and would influence all subsequent lighthouse design. Smeaton, a Yorkshireman, was the sort of practical man who could equally run a mill as make instruments or dig a canal. He gave his lighthouse – the only one that he built – a slightly tapering silhouette, to lower the centre of gravity. The stone blocks (granite on the outside, Portland stone within) were bound together by special quick-drying cement that he devised, as well as interlocking joints. Once again, twenty-four candles provided the light. Only in 1810 were the candles replaced by oil lamps backed by reflectors; these in turn gave way to lenses in 1845. Each lens gave a light intensity that was more than three thousand times that of a candle. Whatever the light source, the lighthouse keeper slept in a small wooden cot, and made himself snug in tiny circular rooms, equipped with curving furniture made especially to fit the walls. Space was limited and, ultimately, it was the size of the lighthouse that caused its replacement. During a heavy sea, the tower, which was 85ft high, could be completely engulfed by the waves that broke over it, obscuring the light and thus rendering the lighthouse useless when it was most needed.

The fourth Eddystone Lighthouse, set 133ft above the sea, was built in 1882 by J. N. Douglas. This was not the end of Smeaton's tower, however: having provided such good service, it was taken down and re-erected on Plymouth Hoe (see page 32). The 1882 lighthouse survives, much altered, but there is no longer a lighthouse keeper. Since 2001, all the lighthouses in Britain have been controlled from the land.

BATTLE OF EDINGTON   SALISBURY PLAIN, WILTSHIRE
King Alfred fights the Danes

At the battle of Edington, on the edge of Salisbury Plain, King Alfred of Wessex began the fight back against the Danes, which ultimately led to the return of London to Mercia and the confinement of the Danes to the Danelaw, that part of England which lies east of Watling Street. Alfred came to be known as 'the Great', the only English king to be awarded the honorific. His greatness lay partly in a quality always admired in Britain, dogged determination.

With his brother, King Ethelred, Alfred had won the Battle of Ashdown in 871 but, having succeeded Ethelred as King when still in his early twenties, he suffered a series of reverses. He withdrew to a fastness in the Somerset Levels, the Isle of Athelney, with a small band of personal followers, and brooded. It was here that he is supposed to have been asked to look after some cakes baking in the oven; such was his preoccupation with the plight of his kingdom that they burnt. Naturally, military success is a necessary attribute of greatness, and this came at Edington in 878. In the depths of winter, the Danes had seized Chippenham, from where they harried Wessex. After Easter, Alfred emerged from his fortress, rallied the men of Somerset and assembled an army at somewhere called Egbert's Stone. In a ferocious battle, they defeated the Danes so comprehensively that they promised to leave Wessex; in addition to which, their king, Guthrum, converted to Christianity.

Alfred is also called Great because of his rule during the peace that eventually followed. One daughter was married to an earl of Mercia, another to the Count of Flanders, a particularly desirable ally because of his navy. The fighting capability of Wessex was reorganised, with a militia that served in rotation, so that there was always a body of men under arms. Across southern England, towns were fortified – a memory of which survives in place names ending in -burgh (burh in Saxon means fortress). Deeply religious, Alfred founded an abbey at Athelney (it vanished after the Dissolution, see page 133), and was dismayed by the loss of learning caused by the pillaging of monasteries by the Danes. He saw that the decline of the international and legal language of Latin inhibited good governance, and promoted education. He himself learnt Latin when in his thirties. Alfred was truly the Great, although he might just as well have been known as the Wise.

EXETER CATHEDRAL DEVON
The glory of English church music

In Exeter cathedral – as in Norwich cathedral, Lincoln cathedral, King's College Chapel, Cambridge, and elsewhere – the organ stands proud in the centre of the building. Made by John Loosemore in 1663–5, it was installed, in a splendid case, over the choir screens, soaring up in the very centre of the church. This organ was needed to replace an instrument dating from 1513 – a very good one – that had been dismantled during the Civil War, when the Puritans banned music in church services. According to one account, the soldiers, having contemptuously broken down the organ into its constituent pipes, 'went up and down the streets piping with them'. During the

Commonwealth, the religious differences that rent the country were personified in the partition of the cathedral: Independents worshipped in the eastern half, Presbyterians in the west – with unfortunate results when both factions wished to do so at the same time.

The Restoration of Charles II in 1660 signalled the return to the old, richer style of service, including the music that so much delighted the diarist Samuel Pepys. It is thought that most of the 1513 organ was destroyed when the cloisters, where it was stored, were demolished in 1655 and turned into a market. However, certain parishioners were able to produce pipes which they had hidden for safe keeping.

The first reference to organs in the cathedral had been in 1286. Now, after the interruptions, the ancient tradition of organ playing as an accompaniment to choral music was resumed, and has been maintained to this day. This tradition is so integral to the worship in many cathedrals and churches – to the point of being regularly broadcast on Radio 3 – that British congregations accept it without a thought. It is, however, unique to this country. Nowhere else does the Church sustain, as a matter of course, professional adult choirs which sing alongside child choristers. The choristers come from schools attached to the cathedrals or college chapels, and from the age of eight lead lives that are focused on their musical duties. While their friends are opening their Christmas presents or Easter eggs, they will be singing music by Thomas Tallis or William Byrd. If they belong to successful choirs, their school holidays will partly be spent recording or touring. Whatever may be said about the decline of the Church of England, this is one aspect of its contribution to national life that continues undiminished.

At Exeter, the organ is mounted sideways, so that the sound is shared equally between the nave and the choir. Only the case dates to the Restoration. The instrument itself was replaced by one made by the great firm of Willis in 1891, although it is said that some of the old pipes were re-used.

GEEVOR TIN MINE   NEAR PENZANCE, CORNWALL

Mines that first put Britain on the map

In 325 BC the Phoenician Pytheas of Massila (Marseilles) sailed round Spain to Cornwall. His account of the journey provides the first recorded mention of Britain in literature; although the original text has been lost, its content has come down to us through a summary by the Greek historian Diodorus Siculus. Pytheas was not the only Phoenician to make the journey: the wild coast of Cornwall was then the tin capital of Europe, and tin was a precious commodity – so much so that it was later used for making coins. Mixed with copper it formed bronze. Pytheas describes how the tinners would beat the tin that they had

panned into sheets the shape of ox-hides and take them to the Isle of Ictis –
the present-day St Michael's Mount, from where Phoenician traders would
come and buy them.

There is more cassiterite – the mineral from which tin is extracted – around
Land's End than anywhere else in the world. Since it occurs in almost vertical
seams or lodes, it has to be mined if it is to be extracted in quantity. Towards
the end of Elizabeth I's reign, the topographer John Norden described the
village of Botallack – near what became Geevor Tin Mine – as being 'most
visited with tinners, where they lodge and feed, being nere theyre mynes'.
These miners could not dig very deep, because the shafts were liable to flood.
Thomas Newcomen's invention of a drainage pump in the early 18th century
made it possible to mine more deeply, and eventually mines ran out for miles
under the sea. The ruins of engine houses, with their tall brick chimneys,
scatter the peninsula.

Geevor Tin Mine, which closed in 1990, is the biggest tin mining site to
survive. Although there had been a mine here in the 18th century, Geevor was
not opened until 1911. By this date, ore was blasted from the lode by means of
gelignite, then taken to the lift shaft by electric locomotives. The ore, containing about one per cent tin, was then crushed, ground and shaken to produce a
concentrate of particles which could be sent away for smelting. The International Tin Council succeeded in keeping the price of tin artificially high until
the mid-1980s, when the price collapsed. Cornish tin mining collapsed with it.

GLASTONBURY ABBEY · SOMERSET
Mysteries of a sacred site

In 1539, Abbot Whyting of Glastonbury was strapped to a hurdle, dragged up
to Glastonbury Tor, which overlooked his abbey, and hanged, together with
the abbey treasurer and another of his monks. His body was then taken down
and dismembered, his head to be stuck on top of the abbey gateway and
quarters of his body dispatched to Bridgwater, Ilchester, Bath and Wells. He
had been one of the few abbots to resist Henry VIII's determination to disband
their monasteries. Henry, of course, succeeded. In a five-year period, from
1536 to 1540, he reduced the number of religious houses from 800 to zero (see
page 133).

Glastonbury Abbey was a particularly rich prize. Glastonbury Tor had been a
sacred site before the arrival of Christianity. There was a sacred well, fed by a
spring which never ran dry; in Christian times this came to be called the Chalice
Well. Legend has it that Joseph of Arimathea, who owned the tomb in which
Christ was buried, came to what was then an island surrounded by rivers and
marsh. With him he brought two cups that contained drops of Christ's blood

and the chalice used by Him at the Last Supper. The chalice, or Holy Grail, disappeared: the search for it became a prime object of the Arthurian knights. What did visibly exist, at least until the 18th century, was an ancient thorn tree, said to have sprouted from the staff that Joseph of Arimathea had stuck into the ground. (Puritans who attempted to cut it down found that their axes turned against themselves.) It was Joseph of Arimathea who founded the original wattle-and-daub church around which a glorious abbey would later grow.

Or so the legend says. An alternative account credits the building of the church to missionaries who arrived from Rome in the 2nd century. Either way, the foundation of church and abbey came very early in the history of Christianity in Britain. King Arthur is supposed to have been buried there. In the mid-10th century, St Dunstan energetically reorganised the monastery, using Cluny in Burgundy as his model and building the first cloister in England. By the time of the Norman Conquest, it was England's richest abbey. The Normans, with their policy of stamping their own image on their new territory, pulled it down and rebuilt it. This church burnt down in 1184, prompting half a century of rebuilding work.

At the time of the Dissolution, the abbey could vie in scale with Canterbury; only Westminster Abbey was richer. An idea of the sumptuous life that the abbots enjoyed can be gained from the 14th-century kitchen that was built to feed them. It is an extraordinary work of architecture in its own right, free-standing to limit the risk of fire and surmounted by an eight-sided roof which is topped by an octagonal lantern, allowing smoke to escape through a central vent in the vault. In the 15th century, an inn was built to serve pilgrims (now the George and Pilgrims Hotel), which has an architectural richness to rival the Angel and Royal at Grantham (see page 271).

After Abbot Whyting's execution, the glories of the abbey vanished with what, only a few years before, would have seemed impossible rapidity. Everything of value was either carted off to London or sold. The stone of which the abbey was built was plundered by the townspeople, and can still be seen incorporated into walls around Glastonbury. In the early 20th century, the abbey ruins were re-bought by the Church and remain a centre of pilgrimage, as well as an occasionally noisy focal point for New Age belief.

LACOCK ABBEY
NEAR CHIPPENHAM, WILTSHIRE

Subject of the world's first photograph

The earliest surviving paper negative shows an oriel window at Lacock Abbey, then the home of William Henry Fox Talbot. Talbot was a scientist whose brilliant mind ranged from microscopy to classical archaeology. In the autumn of 1833 he was travelling on the shores of Lake Como, unsuccessfully attempting to draw pictures with the aid of a *camera lucida* (a box with a prism which could project an image onto a glass screen, which could then be traced using dampened paper). He tried again using a *camera obscura*. 'It was during these thoughts,' he later wrote, 'that the idea occurred to me . . . how charming it would be if it were possible to cause these natural images to imprint themselves durably and remain fixed on the paper!' At home, he experimented with various types of sensitised paper. The negative of the oriel window was taken in August 1835.

Talbot was stimulated by Louis Daguerre's publication in 1839 of his work that produced pictures on an iodised silver plate. Talbot was nettled at the attention the Frenchman was given, and soon announced his own discovery of 'photogenic drawing' to the Royal Institution (see page 171). The next year, while trying to re-sensitise some paper that had failed to expose, he discovered the latent image, which can lie invisibly in film until chemicals are applied to develop it. This greatly reduced exposure times. In 1844, Talbot published *The Pencil of Nature*, the first commercial book illustrated entirely by photographs.

Talbot called his method of photography 'calotype', after the Greek *kalos* meaning beautiful. The fact that it never became as popular as the daguerreotype can be explained partly by the high fees that Talbot expected for rights. In the 1850s it was superseded by the collodion process: Talbot lost his legal claim that this was covered by his own patents.

MARCONI WIRELESS STATION *THE LIZARD, CORNWALL*
First wireless transmission across the Atlantic

In 1900, Guglielmo Marconi came to the south-western extremity of England, the Lizard in Cornwall, and built a radio transmitter at Poldhu, supported by two black-painted wooden huts a little further down the rocky coast. Marconi, whose father was an Italian aristocrat and whose mother came from the Jameson whiskey family, had come to Britain, the world's leading maritime nation and imperial power, after failing to interest the Italian Ministry of Posts and Telegraphs in his wireless wave experiments. At Poldhu, he filed the world's first patent for a wireless telegraphy system, much to the chagrin of Oxford's Professor Oliver Lodge, who had already succeeded in making a rudimentary radio transmission. Marconi, however, was the one who foresaw the practical application of the science. From the Lizard he hoped to send Morse code signals to the United States – the first time that radio signals would cross the Atlantic.

There was some scientific scepticism about the viability of this aspiration. The world's surface is curved; it was deemed that radio signals travel in a straight line. In 1901, Marconi suffered a practical setback when his mast at

Poldhu, 200ft high, blew down, as did its pair in Cape Cod. A new mast was built at Newfoundland, being nearer to Britain, and another mast was built at Poldhu, this time 150ft high, and kept upright with the aid of a kite. The first attempt to transmit a signal was made on 11 December 1901, but the wind was so strong that the kite broke loose. The next day, another kite was launched, and a faint dot . . . dot . . . dot – Morse code for the letter S – was received on the other side of the Atlantic. From that moment on, communication between continents no longer relied on fixed cables. Marconi had leapt the Atlantic; within a century, man would be able – by means of radio waves sent from earth to spacecraft and satellites – to leap between planets.

Although the historic transmitter at Poldhu no longer exists, the black huts survive beside wild Kynance Cove as monuments to what was hailed as Marconi's 'great miracle'.

See also Broad Court, page 123

LONGLEAT HOUSE *NEAR WARMINSTER, WILTSHIRE*
The first drive-through safari park outside Africa

Like most country houses, Longleat – one of the greatest of Elizabethan prodigy houses – had suffered during the Second World War, having been taken over by a school. In 1946 the 5th Marquess of Bath died, leaving massive death duties. His son Henry, the 6th Marquess, although unable to get into Eton and written off by his headmaster at Harrow as 'a moron beyond reach', found a means of keeping the house alive, and in family ownership. He opened his house to the public. Longleat was the first stately home to go into the entertainment business.

Dressed in old corduroy trousers, Lord Bath would personally act as car park attendant. As he sprayed weedkiller from a container on his back, he would, in P. G. Wodehouse tradition, be mistaken for the gardener. It was an image he cultivated, for he had a flair for showmanship and publicity – helped by studiously off-hand comments favouring right-wing dictators. This was the spirit in which he responded to the circus owner Jimmy Chipperfield's suggestion that he should turn the park into a game reserve. The first dozen lions arrived in 1966, to be joined by rhinos, giraffes, chimpanzees and other wild animals. This was the first drive-through safari park outside Africa. At a time when British fashion and music were throwing convention to the winds, it caught the *zeitgeist* with its mix of the exotic, freedom from the cage, and populism. To local people who feared that dangerous animals might escape, Lord Bath replied that he understood lions to be temperamentally lazy, and likely to remain docile for as long as they received their rations: half a bullock's head a day, except on Sundays: 'I suppose that's a throwback to when they ate Christians once a week,' he concluded.

In order to pay the death duties, the Marquess had sold much of his land. With what hindsight has shown to be greater prudence than he could have realised at the time, he did not sell works of art, which have soared in value since 1947. As a result, Longleat remains a spectacular ensemble of parkland, architecture, art and decoration – in which the extensive murals painted by the 6th Marquess's son, Alexander (now the 7th Marquess), ebulliently portray the Thynne family, who first came here 1541, as still being very much present.

MAIDEN CASTLE
The greatest Iron Age hill fort but no match against the Romans

There is mystery to Maiden Castle; perhaps there always has been. That was part of its defensive strategy. The gently sloping ridge on which the great earthworks were constructed is evident enough, just as those making their way across the plain below, on their way to attack it, would have seen it. But attackers would have had no idea what lay in store on the further side of the crest until they reached it. This first slope was followed by another and then another, each separated by a deep ditch. The entrance to the site, where the slope of the land was shallowest, was protected by a kind of maze, at any twist of which hidden defenders could spring out, while other defenders standing above could rain down pebbles from their slings. The attackers could only guess what obstacle was coming next.

The first earthwork was constructed 5,000 years ago. However, Neolithic man deserted the site, only returning, some hundreds of years later, to use it for burials. The present complex was redesigned and improved towards the beginning of the 1st century BC. Dorset was then home to the Durotriges tribe; from its size, Maiden Castle may have been the stronghold of their chieftain. It was a settlement as well as a fort, with a variety of artisans – such as potters, blacksmiths, jewellers – living among the tribesmen responsible for maintaining the defences. Beyond that, the cloak of mystery descends. It was up to the Roman legionaries who bravely attacked the earthworks in AD43 or 44 to pierce through it. Under the efficient generalship of the future Emperor Vespasian, they probably attacked the end opposite the main entrance, fought their way over the terraced ramparts, set fire to some huts and, under the ensuing smoke screen, stormed the fort, killing indiscriminately. Once the castle had been subdued, the traumatised survivors were left to bury their dead, interring with them the food and trinkets that would help them in the next life.

The Romans dismantled the fort and built a new town, Dorchester, on the plain. By about AD70, Maiden Castle was abandoned and mystery descended once more.

MEARE FISH HOUSE

Essential source of food for the monks

Adam de Sodbury, Abbot of Glastonbury, liked fish. His appetite is commemorated in an elegant stone building which now stands in a flower-filled meadow on the edge of the village of Meare. When Abbot Sodbury built it in the early 14th century, it overlooked the Meare Pool, a lake that was five miles in circumference.

The Meare Pool (something of a tautology, since Meare itself means pond) had developed from a low-lying landscape which had always been half underwater. In the Iron Age, villages were created on the raised areas that formed islands, reached by dug-out canoe or wooden trackways (the latter have been found preserved in the peat). When the marshes were in due course drained at the end of the 18th century, the Meare Pool disappeared, but the Fish House survived. The water bailiff who lived and worked here undoubtedly would have received olfactory reminders in his first-floor living quarters of the salted fish that was stored below.

Because travel was slow and expensive, very little food came in from outside the immediate region. Fresh produce either had to be eaten when killed or newly harvested, or pickled in order to preserve it. This made 'living larders', in which animals or fish could be kept alive until wanted, particularly valuable. Rabbits were kept in warrens, pigeons in dovecotes and fish in ponds of various sizes; the Meare Pool was unusual only because of its size. Nearby, wild fowl were netted in a duck decoy. The wetlands also provided timber, reed for thatch and peat for fuel. After the Dissolution of the Monasteries (see page 133), the economy changed and later generations were unable to live in the same style of the medieval abbots.

MELCOMBE REGIS

Where the Black Death entered England

The old port of Melcombe Regis is almost impossible to find, having been so fully incorporated into Weymouth that it exists only in a couple of street names near the seafront. Nobody in the town council wants to remember its name, since its fame rests in having let the Black Death into England in July 1348.

Ironically, the plague – or, more accurately plagues – which originated, amid portents, in the Orient, very probably arrived from Calais. Calais had only just been retaken for England by Edward III, following the Battle of Crécy. All that summer, grand ladies dressed themselves in the luxurious textiles that had been looted from France, in order to attend the tournaments that had been organised to celebrate the newly instituted Order of the Garter (see page 249). As many hostesses have discovered subsequently, no outdoor social event in Britain is immune from bad weather, and in 1348 it rained almost every day for six months. Crops failed and people's resistance against infection was lowered. Bubonic plague is borne on the bodies of fleas which live, among other places, on rats. The Black Death spread from seaport to seaport, and from there up the rivers. The toll was dreadful; it could not be explained to the medieval mind except in theological terms; it exercised an awful democracy by killing the great as much as the lowly. Between one third and one half of the country's population died.

Bristol was reduced to a wasteland, with grass growing several inches high in the main streets. Parishes were left without clergy; whole monasteries were wiped out. The Bishop of Bath and Wells urged the dying to make confession to a layman – even, if absolutely necessary, to a woman – if no priest could be found. Nearly half his clergy died. Life in towns was at the best of times so fetid that a high rate of mortality was inevitable. But towns were few; England was still a country of villages, and here the effects were radical. Not only were some villages abandoned as the survivors moved to 'clean' ground, but the old manorial system began to collapse as peasants found that they were in a sellers' market for their services. One result of the consequent social change was the Peasants' Revolt (see page 185).

OLD SARUM   NEAR SALISBURY, WILTSHIRE
A town abandoned, though it kept its MP

Within the impressive earthworks of an Iron Age hill fort, a Norman castle was built. A cathedral was begun in 1075, rebuilt almost immediately when a storm brought down the tower, then rebuilt again by Bishop Roger in the early 12th century. Bishop Roger was one of the most significant men of his day. He controlled Henry I's treasury, introducing a system of auditing based on a chequerboard: this lent its name to the Exchequer. It is fair to say that in the bishop's importance lay the seeds of Old Sarum's decline. As long as Henry was alive, the bishop was in control of the castle as well as the cathedral; in the next reign, however, his castle was confiscated by King Stephen. From then on, castle and cathedral – King and Bishop – never saw eye to eye at Old Sarum.

As the community on the hilltop expanded, so water became ever more scarce. It was time to move. Bishop Richard Poore abandoned the cathedral at Old Sarum in 1219, and began a new one the following year beside the river Avon, in the place that is now Salisbury. This new cathedral would become the most elegant in Britain, constructed (except for the famous spire) within the relatively short time span of sixty years, as a result of which it is stylistically consistent. Life in the old settlement meandered on, its dwindling band of inhabitants no doubt conscious of glories that had once been.

The fact that Old Sarum barely existed was not, however, noticed at Westminster. It became one of the 'rotten boroughs' – a borough able to elect an MP though having very few voters. Old Sarum had the distinction of returning William Pitt, later 1st Earl of Chatham, as their MP from 1734–47, his grandfather having bought the site at the end of the previous century. By then, there were only two nominal electors who solemnly cast their votes at an elm known as the Parliament Tree. 'Rotten boroughs' were abandoned by the Reform Act of 1832.

PLYMOUTH HOE

Where Drake awaited the Spanish Armada

Plymouth Hoe, now a park under the eye of Plymouth's 17th-century citadel, is forever associated with Sir Francis Drake*. He was playing bowls there in 1588 when the Armada was sighted, and is said to have coolly finished his game before joining his flagship, the *Revenge*. It is a curious story to pin on Drake, who was not renowned for patience and had already been holed up in Plymouth, awaiting action, for many months. Later historians, knowing the outcome of the conflict, may have been tempted to amplify the contempt for the Spanish fleet that the tale implies, but it is unlikely to have been shared by Drake and his crews, sailing out in their nimble ships to meet the most powerful fleet that the world had ever seen. Perhaps Drake knew that the tide was coming in, and that he would be unable to sail until it turned.

The year before, Drake had displayed his intrepidity and astounding seamanship by sailing into Cadiz harbour and devastating the Spanish fleet. He had dispensed with the quaint tradition of offering a challenge to combat, and the Spaniards were hopelessly unprepared. Dozens of enemy ships were destroyed, and six captured. This gave him an eye-witness view of the Spanish preparations for their assault on England. When he returned home, he urged Queen Elizabeth to allow him to undertake another raiding mission. Instead, she listened to peace overtures from the Duke of Parma.

Drake was sent to Plymouth with fourteen of the Queen's ships to guard the western approaches to the Channel. Lord Howard of Effingham, recently appointed Lord High Admiral, brought his fleet to join him and, in the middle of summer, word reached them that the Armada was making its final preparations. The fleet raced to Spain hoping to stop the Armada in its tracks, but the wind was against them, and they returned home. On 19 July, it was reported that Spanish ships had been sighted off the Scillies. The following day, Howard and Drake saw a vast Spanish fleet, sailing towards England in a great and impregnable crescent. There were 132 Spanish ships while their own fleet numbered sixty-two. On 23 and 24 July, the English fought the Spanish off Portland Bill and the Isle of Wight. They continued the running fight towards the French coast; their ships were more agile than the Spanish galleons, but as yet the result was a stalemate. The Spanish hoped to load soldiers from the coast but the English sent in fireships to force them into open water, where Drake bombarded them.

This reverse for the Spanish was followed by the first of the bad weather that would be their undoing. The role of the English fleet now was to prevent the Spanish from re-entering the English Channel, forcing them to sail north-wards round Scotland. The Spaniards were poorly equipped for such a journey; already damaged by fighting, many ships were unable to withstand the ferocious gales that lashed them. Only half of the most powerful fleet that had ever been assembled limped back into Santander harbour.

It was from Plymouth that Drake set out the next year to destroy what remained of the Armada. Although he inflicted some damage on the Spanish navy, he did not return with the booty that the Queen had hoped for. He died of yellow fever at Panama in 1596, whilst leading his last privateering raid.

*See Buckland Abbey, page 15. See also Eddystone Lighthouse, page 21

ISLE OF PORTLAND DORSET
The site of the first Viking raid

In 789, the King of Wessex's representative, Beaduheard, heard that three ships had landed on the Isle of Portland. Coming from the east, they had probably drawn up on the beach of Church Ope Cove or on what were then the salt marshes that faced the mainland. Beaduheard, as a competent official, bustled off to meet the visitors, whom he assumed to be traders, intending to ensure that their presence should be properly notified to the royal authorities. But the foreigners were of a different mind, and murdered him.

There is some dispute as to whether these Vikings came from Denmark or, as more often in the early period, Norway. It little mattered to the Anglo-Saxons whose villages they raided. The sudden appearance of the longships, whose shallow draught allowed them to be rowed right onto a beach, was terrifying. *The Anglo-Saxon Chronicle* describes the Norsemen as 'stinging hornets [and] fearful wolves [who] robbed, tore and slaughtered not only beasts of burden, sheep and oxen, but even priests and deacons, and companies of monks and nuns', including, in 793, the monastery at Lindis-farne (see page 395).

Like the Huns and Goths, these Viking raiders were pagans, with no regard for civilised culture and tradition that the monasteries followed. Their achievement was to travel further than Europeans had ever previously done, discovering America, establishing trade routes with Byzantium and Arabia, and colonising rich commercial centres from York to Kiev. Attacks on Britain continued into the 11th century, the last Danish attempt to conquer England being in 1085. Quite why it was that they first appeared in Dorset is not known; they usually attacked the east coast of England, being closest to Scandinavia.

The Normans, who came in 1066, were themselves originally Vikings, and William the Conqueror's victory at Hastings (see page 49) was made easier by the diversionary attack by the Norwegian Harald Hardrada in the North (see page 401).

ST HELIER

JERSEY, CHANNEL ISLANDS

Britain's first pillar-boxes

In Anthony Trollope's *He Knew He Was Right* (1869), Miss Jemima Stanbury did not think much of pillar-boxes. She 'had not the faintest belief that any letter put into one of them would ever reach its destination', and thought a walk to the post office was preferable to shovelling letters into what she called 'an iron stump . . . out in the middle of the street with nobody to look after it'. It was a subject close to Trollope's heart. As Post Office surveyor, he had introduced the first pillar-boxes to the British Isles, erecting four around St Helier in November 1852 – at David Place, New Street, Cheapside and St Clement's Road. It was an idea he had seen in France. The Jersey boxes, or 'receivers' as the *Jersey Times* called them, bore the royal arms, and Trollope scored another first by painting them red. Elsewhere in Britain early boxes were painted green. In 1853, a further three pillar-boxes were installed in St Peter Port, Guernsey, the one in Union Street now being the oldest pillar-box in Britain still in use.

The pillar-box could not have evolved without Rowland Hill's earlier invention of the postage stamp. The penny black came into existence in 1840. Until then, sending a letter had been exorbitantly expensive, the charge increasing the further it was carried. Postage was paid by the recipient. This was time-consuming and costly. The new stamps, paid for by the sender, saved the expense of collecting money at the other end. A letter with a stamp on it could simply be dropped into a pillar-box (the name of which derives from the fact that some early boxes were shaped like a classical column). Hill argued that the penny post would not cause the Post Office to lose revenue because the number of letters would multiply fivefold. In time, he was proved right. During the year of 1839, 76 million letters were posted; by 1870 that number had soared to 863 million. Today, despite the telephone and email, an average of 81 million items is posted each day.

See also Bridge Street, page 118, and Broad Court, page 123

ST MAWES CASTLE NEAR FALMOUTH, CORNWALL

After the Dissolution, Henry VIII puts his defences in order

Internationally, King Henry VIII was unpopular following his divorce from Catherine of Aragon and self-promotion to head of the Church in England. By 1540, the Pope – who had awarded Henry the title of Defender of the Faith at the beginning of his reign – wanted him off the throne of England, and was egging France and Spain to take action. Fearing invasion, Henry looked to his defences, and found them in bad order. Fortunately he now had the money – plundered from the Dissolution of the Monasteries (see page 133) – to put them right.

Architecturally, St Mawes is the finest of the forts he built along the south coast. It was erected in concert with Pendennis, on the other side of the Fal estuary, to protect the port of Falmouth, always strategically sensitive in its position on the south-western approaches to the English Channel. Cornwall was then a far-away province of which the court in London knew little, but the vulnerability of Falmouth had been graphically demonstrated when a Spanish fleet randomly attacked some French ships in 1537, driving them aground. A request was made for blockhouses but they were probably hurriedly and inadequately erected and soon afterwards the king demanded the forts be built.

St Mawes was splendidly constructed, with the degree of architectural enrichment appropriate to a military building. Inside, it was comfortable; outside, it demonstrated the latest thinking on defence. This was now the age of gunpowder; as a result, the fort's profile is low, to minimise the target that it presented to the guns of an enemy ship standing off the harbour (which would have been additionally handicapped by the movement of the sea). Around the central tower are three segmental bastions, designed as intersecting circles; this was where the long-range guns were stationed. The curving walls would have deflected any cannonball that struck them.

At the end of the Civil War, St Mawes surrendered to Parliamentary forces without firing a shot, its governor Hannibal Bonython realising that it could not be defended against a land attack. Across the estuary, Pendennis withstood a five-month siege, the hopelessness of which was apparent after King Charles himself had surrendered to the Scots in May 1646 (see page 342); the garrison, half-starved, was allowed to march out to the sound of drums and trumpets, each soldier having a bullet in his mouth as a last show of defiance.

SALISBURY CATHEDRAL

Perhaps the oldest piece of machinery in the world

In 1386, the Dean of Salisbury sold the lease of a shop, the income from which funded a clock in the (then free-standing) bell tower of the cathedral. When the bell tower was demolished in the 18th century, the clock was relocated in the cathedral tower. In 1884, a new clock was installed, and the old one dismantled. Fortunately, the bits were not thrown away; they were rediscovered in 1929 and can now be seen displayed in the north transept of the cathedral. It is thought to be the oldest clock in Britain, perhaps the oldest in the world. The clock was restored to working condition in 1956.

According to T. R. Robinson, who rediscovered the clock and wrote a booklet about it, it 'is almost certainly the most ancient piece of real machinery – apart from crude mechanical devices – in original condition, still at work anywhere on earth, a point of great distinction in this increasingly mechanised world.' It is fair to say that all modern engineering developed from clock making.

It is not a clock of the familiar type. There are no hands or dial. Only the hours are marked, by the striking of a bell. Power is supplied by two weights attached to ropes wound around drums; the rate of fall of the weight is controlled by an escape mechanism. In the early morning, before worshippers or visitors have arrived, the tick-tock reverberates throughout the length of England's most elegant cathedral, a reminder of the temporal world amid the celestial 13th-century architecture.

ROYAL ALBERT BRIDGE

Isambard Kingdom Brunel completes the Great Western Railway

The Royal Albert Bridge over the river Tamar at Saltash, outside Plymouth, was the last major piece of the Great Western Railway to be put in place by its engineer Isambard Kingdom Brunel*. It was completed in 1859, the year of Brunel's death. Since the GWR was the greatest of all Brunel's projects, it is fitting that this last work should be the king of his bridges – a symbol of the visionary quality of his genius.

Brunel first stepped onto a railway train in 1831. Two years later, aged twenty-seven, he was appointed to engineer the GWR, then as yet unsurveyed, unfinanced and unprovided with the necessary parliamentary legislation to see it built. Many railway ventures were being talked up in the mid-1830s. Generally, their promoters seem not to have imagined the far-reaching effects that the new mode of transport would produce. Engineers such as George Stephenson, with a background of working in the collieries of the north-east, imagined that they would principally be used to move goods around at low speeds. Brunel grasped the huge opportunity that the railways offered – to carry people. To do this successfully, journey times had to be kept to a minimum. Consequently, Brunel persuaded his directors to engineer a track that would allow trains to run at speed. In this, he struck upon the principle of the revolution that would transform British life at every level, economic as well as social. There was to be no cost cutting; the GWR – sometimes thought to stand for God's Wonderful Railway – was to be 'the finest work in England'.

In order to achieve better speeds, Brunel successfully persuaded his directors to adopt a wider gauge of track than that used by Stephenson and other engineers. Stephenson's 4ft 8½-inch gauge, laid on stone blocks, might be adequate for trundling coal trucks around; set on baulks of timber, the 7ft gauge advocated by Brunel allowed the centre of gravity of the rolling stock to be lowered, larger wheels to be adopted and friction to be reduced. After Brunel's death, his insistence on the 7ft gauge was shown to have been an error. Even the mighty GWR, dominating the south-west, needed to connect with other railways.

To the west of Exeter and the Welsh border lies hilly terrain over which it was difficult to lay track. Brunel sought to avoid it as far as possible, by choosing routes along the coast. But there remained deep gorges at the mouths of rivers which needed bridges to cross them. The most formidable were at Chepstow over the Wye, and at Saltash over the Tamar. To span them, Brunel decided to use cast iron. This was a difficult and controversial material, very strong in compression but weak in tension. To overcome its weakness, Robert Stephenson had a decade earlier pioneered the box girder, made up of wrought-iron plates, triumphantly demonstrated in his Britannia Bridge over the Menai Strait – a principle recently revived for road bridges. Brunel's solution was to create tubes of wrought-iron plates that could be used as trusses, from which the bed of the bridge could be hung. In the Royal Albert Bridge, two arched trusses are fixed either side of a tall central column. As the weight of a train presses down on the bridge, it tends to push the supporting piers apart; the trusses, being arched, counteract this effect, pulling them together again. In addition, the bridge is suspended from chains hung from the piers.

The Royal Albert Bridge is not conventionally pretty, but beauty lies in the engineering imagination that created it, which seems to be complemented by the extraordinary drama felt by every train passenger with a soul who passes over this most spectacular of gateways to Cornwall. Alas, it was, in engineering terms, a dead end. Lattice girder construction (already used by Brunel in some of his smaller bridges) was found to be just as safe and much cheaper.

*See The Brunel Engine House, page 124

BATTLE OF SEDGEMOOR

Downfall of the Duke of Monmouth

'The most skittish, leaping gallant that ever I saw,' wrote Samuel Pepys, 'always in action, vaulting or leaping, or clambering.' This was the attractive side of the Duke of Monmouth, the eldest of Charles II's illegitimate children, when he was aged sixteen. He was always a charmer, and devastatingly successful with women. The King was fond of his illegitimate son and gave him many favours, but Monmouth did not repay him kindly; he was implicated in the Rye House Plot to kill the King and his brother, the future James II, in 1683.

There was a strong rumour that, at the age of nineteen and in exile, Charles had married Monmouth's mother, the bewitching, chestnut-haired Lucy Walter. Although not impossible, this was probably untrue – certainly it was unsubstantiated. Still, rumour alone was enough for Monmouth's hot-headed companions to persuade him to claim the throne after his father's death. James II, Charles's brother and Monmouth's uncle, had, unlike the wily Charles, openly declared his conversion to Roman Catholicism. Monmouth upheld the Protestant cause.

Coming from Holland, Monmouth landed at Lyme Regis on 11 June 1685. By 5 July, he and his ragged army had reached Bridgwater. A local boy called Richard Godfrey, who had been minding cattle on the Levels, ran to tell him that the royal army was camped outside Westonzoyland. From the tower of St Mary's Church in Bridgwater, Monmouth was able to see them through a spy-glass. Given that his troops were untrained and poorly armed, the desperate decision was made to mount a night attack, relying on Godfrey's knowledge of the area. The royal army was protected by a deep and seemingly impenetrable ditch called the Bussex Rhyne. On a dark and foggy night, Godfrey was unable to find all the 'plungeons', or plank bridges, across this and other ditches. A pistol shot rang out, nobody knew from whom: it signalled that they had lost the crucial advantage of surprise. Monmouth's raw cavalry, unable to get across the rhyne, were fired upon, and their inexperienced horses galloped away from the action, to the considerable dismay of the rest of the troops. The infantry fought bravely but their position was hopeless. Monmouth, having attempted to flee with the rest of his commanders, was caught hiding in a ditch.

On Tower Hill in London, it was only at the fifth stroke of the axe that Monmouth's head was cut off. His followers were treated equally barbarously at the Bloody Assizes held by Judge Jeffreys (see page 44).

SHERBORNE CASTLE

Sir Walter Raleigh's fanciful castle

In 1589, Sir Walter Raleigh was working to secure the manor of Sherborne in Dorset as a seat commensurate with his status as a leading figure at the court of Elizabeth I. Born the son of a tenant farmer, his tall, curly-haired figure had first caught the royal eye as a soldier in Ireland, where his brutalities are best overlooked. Now in his mid-thirties, he shone as a poet, scholar and the promoter of American colonies, who had enriched himself through monopolies and won royal gratitude for his energy in preparing England's defences in the face of the Spanish Armada. The manor of Sherborne belonged to the See of Salisbury. By keeping the See vacant for three years, then appointing an amenable Bishop, Elizabeth was able to detach the manor from the church, as a reward for her favourite.

Raleigh took receipt of it just in time. His worship of Elizabeth as the chaste moon goddess, with whom all male courtiers were supposed to be in love, had been compromised by his relationship with Bess Throckmorton, one of the Queen's maids of honour, who became secretly his wife and pregnant, not necessarily in that order. He entered a period of prolonged disfavour, during which he built a curious new house a short distance away from the original castle – not large, but tall, proudly sited on top of a hill and crowned with heraldic beasts – and elaborately ornamented the grounds.

Although Raleigh regained Elizabeth's good graces, Sherborne was to ruin him. Having sunk his fortune into it, he allowed a mistake to creep into the conveyancing, which gave James I, who imprisoned Raleigh, the chance to bestow it on his favourite, Robert Carr. It spurred Raleigh to make a last desperate expedition in search of El Dorado; his failure to return with the promised gold led to his execution in 1618.

STONEHENGE

An ancient and constantly inspiring mystery

Stonehenge is one of the great buildings of the world: the sight of it, massive and alone in its bare landscape, evokes wonder at its antiquity, at its survival, at its beauty, at the feat of will and organisation necessary to create it. The circle of stones appears simple enough as a design; and yet the monument presents us with a 4,000-year-old mystery to which nobody has yet found the key. By far the oldest ceremonial building in Britain, it has inevitably become a national icon, whose power over the national imagination is, if anything, enhanced by the ability of every age to find a different meaning in it.

Stonehenge evolved over a period of 2,000 years, longer than Christianity has been practised in this country. We cannot know for certain that the purpose of Stonehenge was religious (although since it cannot have been built for shelter or defence, it seems likely that it was). Assuming that religious rites took place there, they surely changed over time. Even so, the site's sacred associations must have been extraordinarily long lived, and still have the power to move some people. What was worshipped here, or how, remains impossible to tell.

For the first 800 years of its existence, Stonehenge looked quite different from the ring of great standing stones and lintels that is so familiar today. Inside a ditch, archaeologists have found some fifty-six post holes, but do not know what sort of structure they contained. The only thing that can be said is that it formed a circle. The first stones, eighty of them – were erected around 2300BC. Each weighing approximately 5 tons, these 'bluestones' originated in the Preseli hills in west Wales. Unless they were carried here by the action of glaciers, it is assumed that they must have been dragged to Stonehenge.

It is not known how or why this extraordinary feat was achieved, but in 2004 some light was shed on the sort of people who might have been responsible. Workmen laying a water pipe on Boscombe Down near Stonehenge discovered the grave of seven Bronze Age skeletons, three adults, a teenager and three children. Analysis of the enamel on their teeth shows that they came from the same area as the stones. Two years earlier, the grave of the so-called Amesbury Archer was found during building work three miles away: the Archer originated from the Alps and was clearly a man of high rank since he was buried with richer goods than any other known contemporary in Europe. Together, these discoveries suggest a society which travelled more extensively than had been thought, perhaps searching for copper. It is significant that Preseli would have been on the trade route to Ireland.

The great ring of upright sarsen stones joined by lintels, which forms the popular image of Stonehenge, came some centuries later. Sarsen occurs naturally in chalk outcrops, and must have been a source of wonder to early man. Originally it seems they were highly coloured, but the lichen that has built up over centuries makes them look greyish – hence the alternative and more homely name of grey-wethers, meaning 'old grey sheep'. Those at Stonehenge were hauled from the Marlborough Downs, eighteen miles away. Although extremely hard, the stones were carefully and cleverly crafted so that the lintels fitted into the uprights; the flanks of the stones were also shaped, presumably for aesthetic effect.

Why did they do it? Each generation finds a new explanation, according to the preoccupations of the time. In the medieval period, it was thought that Stonehenge must have been whisked from Ireland by the magician Merlin. To the 17th-century architect Inigo Jones, entranced by the ancient architecture he had studied in Italy, it was a complex geometrical monument bequeathed to us by the Romans. In the great 19th-century age of faith, the religious purpose of the structure seemed paramount. With its New Age expectations, the 20th century chose to emphasise Stonehenge's supposed Druid history, whether or not it actually had one (the Druids generally worshipped in shady woods, not on open plains). The idea that Stonehenge might have been a gigantic prehistoric observatory attracts a generation which, having witnessed space travel for the first time, looks at astronomy with new eyes.

STOURHEAD NEAR WARMINSTER, WILTSHIRE
Greatest example of a Picturesque landscape

Stourhead, a landscape park begun in the 1740s, is a landmark of beauty. It has sometimes been said the Picturesque movement, associated with gentlemen's enhancement of their parks, was Britain's greatest contribution to the visual arts of Europe. Stourhead is possibly its greatest surviving example.

The garden was created by the banker Henry Hoare*. As a young man, Hoare had lived a fashionably dissolute existence; to distinguish him from the others in his family called Henry, he was nicknamed The Magnificent, on account of his art collections and patronage – in contrast to his father who was known as The Good. He was well travelled, well read and devoted to his family. In 1743, his second wife died. He never remarried; instead, he began the landscape garden which occupied him for the remainder of his life.

In the 18th century, Picturesque meant, literally, like a picture. Until the beginning of that century, the object of gardening had been to create a sense of order: man demonstrated his power over Nature by taming it. Then a number of English architects and writers began to formulate a different approach. Sir John Vanbrugh argued that the Duchess of Marlborough should preserve Old Wood-stock Manor because it stirred the imagination. The essayist Joseph Addison objected to trees being clipped into topiary shapes, wanting them to be allowed to grow freely. The poet Alexander Pope extolled the *genius loci*, or spirit of a place, which 'Paints as you plant, and as you work, Designs.' His choice of words prefigures the desire of gentlemen returning from a Grand Tour to re-create the landscapes they had seen around Rome – or to be more exact, acquired in the form of paintings by Claude Gellée and Gaspard Dughet, otherwise known as Claude Lorrain and Gaspard Poussin (brother-in-law of the more famous Nicolas Poussin) respectively. Hoare was in this camp. He owned two large paintings by Poussin, and took them as the yardstick for the creation of his own landscapes. 'The view of the bridge, village and church altogether will be a charming Gaspard picture at that end of the water,' he wrote.

The route that visitors took round his lake, formed by damming the local river, was strictly controlled to provide a series of views of buildings that Hoare had erected to make the landscape more suggestive. Like paintings, Hoare's views were intended to inspire uplifting thoughts, whether about the natural qualities of the spot (a grotto invokes water deities), about the classical world (the Temple of Flora, the Temple of Apollo, the Pantheon), about British patriotism (Alfred's Tower celebrates the king who saved England from invasion) or about the nation's mercantile prosperity (Bristol's medieval High Cross was brought here in 1764). Hoare even employed a hermit to inhabit the grotto in order to highlight his own desires for an ascetic life.

*See Hoare's Bank, page 151

SWIMBRIDGE
NEAR BARNSTAPLE, DEVON
Birthplace of a very English breed of dog

At Swimbridge, the name of the 19th-century vicar is perpetuated in that of the pub. The picture on the inn sign, however, shows the dog that was, in turn, named after the vicar: Parson Jack Russell. As a breed, this feisty little terrier, which seemingly runs on three legs and refuses to conform to any regular specification, is close to the British heart, perhaps because it is more akin to a mongrel from Battersea Dogs' Home (see page 115) than a pampered show dog.

The Jack Russell was bred to work. The parson had a passion for hunting. He had discovered the joys of hunting while at school, and was nearly expelled for keeping foxhounds there. Later, he devoted a considerable part of his modest income to running a pack: it was a source of friction with his bishop who was particularly distressed that the parson's curate went hunting with him as well. Religion, to the Rev. Jack Russell, was a personal affair, not to be the subject of too much ceremony. His kindly, frank manner and country ways made him much loved by his flock.

Russell bought his first terrier, Trump, from a milkman in Oxford when studying there as an undergraduate. Since Russell's stud books have disappeared, quite how he developed Trump's progeny is uncertain, but he succeeded in breeding a terrier of personality which could take on a fox, nipping him bravely but not actually fighting to the death. The parson did not want a terrier that would kill foxes; in the same spirit, he fought vigorously against country people who sought to destroy foxes by means other than hunting them. The terriers were bred to have a predominantly white body in order to make it easy to tell it apart from the fox; the caramel patches are never the same on any two dogs.

Russell, who had helped found the Kennel Club in 1873, died at Swimbridge a decade later. It is said that children wept as they threw wildflowers into his grave.

TOLPUDDLE

Milestone on the journey towards workers' rights

In 1834, the harsh treatment of six farm workers from the thatched village of Tolpuddle became a cause that defined future relations between employees and their bosses. Ten years earlier, a law had been passed to legitimise trades unions; the case of the Tolpuddle Martyrs showed that new laws do not necessarily change social attitudes, or the willingness of domineering interests to cede some of their power over other people.

In the 1830s, agriculture was in the doldrums. The wage of a farm worker in Tolpuddle in 1830 was nine shillings a week; by 1834 it had been reduced to seven shillings. This was barely enough for those who received it to feed their families, and George Loveless, a farm worker who was also a Methodist preacher, led his colleagues in an effort to protect their livelihoods. Nothing practical came of the approaches that were made to the employers through the local vicar, so contact was made with Robert Owen's (see page 476) Grand National Consolidated Trades Union, whose membership was rapidly growing in industrial towns. Two delegates arrived at Tolpuddle, and the Friendly Society of Agricultural Labourers – comprising Loveless and five other local men – was born. Rightly fearing repression, they cemented their bond by swearing an oath of loyalty and secrecy.

Farmers and landowners feared that the new union would be another expression of the social disorder which had already caused local riots and the burning of hay ricks. At Dorchester Assizes, Loveless and his friends were tried for having taken an illegal oath, under a law which had been intended to prevent mutiny in the armed forces. The men were found guilty, and the judge passed a sentence of seven years' transportation as an example to others. Even by the standards of the time, this seemed grossly inhumane. When the Tolpuddle Martyrs, as they soon became known, were sent to the penal colony in Tasmania, the agitation to free them swelled. More than 30,000 people met on Copenhagen Fields, near the site of what is now King's Cross Station in London; over 800,000 names were gathered on petitions. The Home Secretary, Lord Melbourne (see page 209), whose advice had been sought by the Dorset magistrates before the Martyrs were tried, was implacable but his successor, Lord John Russell, realised that he had to give ground. In 1836, two years after the trial, he agreed to a full pardon.

Very slowly, the men began to come home but the last Martyr did not come back until 1839. Their supporters raised enough money to settle them as tenant farmers in Essex. When their tenancies ran out, one of them found his way back to Tolpuddle and the other five emigrated to Canada. Meanwhile, the name of Tolpuddle became an unlikely rallying cry for the growing trades union movement.

MARKET PLACE, WELLS

Judge Jeffreys shows no mercy to rebels

George Jeffreys, Lord Chief Justice of England, was chosen in 1685 to preside over what became known as the Bloody Assizes, during which some 2,600 of the rebels who had fought with the Duke of Monmouth, Charles II's illegitimate son, against his uncle James II* were tried. Jeffreys suffered from excruciating kidney stones, which no doubt encouraged the sarcasm with which he habitually mocked the defendants before him. Even before Jeffreys opened his makeshift court at Wells, created out of the old market hall (now demolished), on 23 September, he was anxious to finish his job. Of the 542 men that came before him on that day, all but one pleaded guilty, as they had been advised to do on the grounds that their sentence would be commuted to transportation. The one who maintained his innocence was executed the same afternoon.

As a firm Anglican who believed blindly in royal authority, Jeffreys set out to make an example of the rebels – with the full approval of a merciless king. Rather than being executed where Jeffreys had sat, the condemned were distributed around the region to be hanged, drawn and quartered, their putrefying body parts being displayed on poles as a grisly warning to others. In all, about 200 were put to death. Others died of smallpox in the filthy, overcrowded prisons, while the majority were effectively sold into slavery in the West Indies at between £10 and £15 each.

One of the reasons Jeffreys was in a hurry to get back to London was that the Lord Chancellor was ailing. He duly died, and Jeffreys succeeded him. At the age of forty, he was the youngest holder of that office in its long history. When William of Orange landed in 1688, Jeffreys was one of those who stuck by James II, and his advice, if the vacillating King had adhered to it, might have averted revolution (see page 13). When, one morning, Jeffreys discovered that the King had fled, he shaved off his bushy eyebrows to avoid detection, and hurried to Wapping, disguised as a seaman. However, he was spotted and thrown into the Tower of London where, after more internal agonies, he died shortly afterwards.

*See Battle of Sedgemoor, page 38

South-East England

SOUTH-EAST ENGLAND: the wedge of Britain that jabs towards the Continent. Proximity to France made it the first target of invaders – invasion successful, invasion rebuffed. Julius Caesar's legions sprang ashore onto the shingles of Walmer Beach; nearly a century later, their successors built a great triumphal arch at Richborough fort, and some one thousand years after the Romans, the Norman Conqueror defeated King Harold at Battle.

For the next millennium, the story was one of hurried preparation to repulse attacks that often never happened. Instead, the coastline saw the embarkation of the nation's armies to fight at Agincourt, and the building of the concrete Mulberry Harbours essential to the D-Day landings, the start of the end of the Second World War. Nelson sailed from Portsmouth, and HMS *Victory*, on which he died, now rests there. It was from airfields such as RAF Tangmere that young pilots in their Spitfires and Hurricanes threw themselves against the Luftwaffe during the Battle of Britain. Among those who came in peace was St Augustine, and seeking peace was Sir Winston Churchill at Chartwell. Eventually the Channel Tunnel punctured the balloon of British insularity, but no mere engineering achievement can supplant the White Cliffs of Dover as an iconic national image, a gleaming defensive wall arising, as it were, from the moat formed by the English Channel.

And yet, for all the fighting and foreign infiltrations, there is nowhere so cosily, mistily English as the South-East. This is the England of the Rev. Gilbert White, minutely chronicling the seasons at Selborne; the England of myopic Gertrude Jekyll's garden harmonies at Munstead Wood; the England of cricket, of Poohsticks and *The Pickwick Papers*; of seaside holidays, of the Prince Regent at Brighton and the architect A. W. N. Pugin at Ramsgate. Here is that part of England in which Rudyard Kipling chose to make his home. Here that exemplary English charity, the National Trust, acquired its first property, an oakily Wealden house near the Cuckmere valley. To Churchill, 'a day spent away from Chartwell', with its soothing views, was 'a day wasted'.

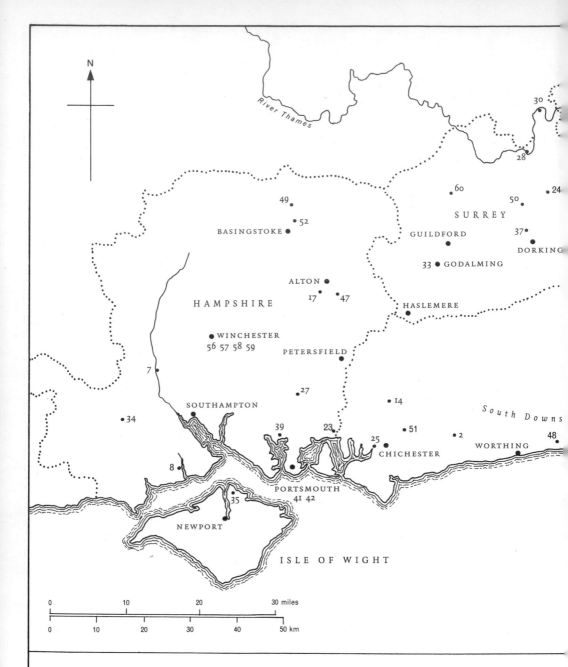

N

River Thames

30

28

24

49

60

50

SURREY

52

BASINGSTOKE

GUILDFORD

37

DORKING

33 GODALMING

ALTON

17   47

HASLEMERE

HAMPSHIRE

WINCHESTER
56 57 58 59

PETERSFIELD

7

27

14

SOUTHAMPTON

South Downs

34

39   23

51

2

48

25

CHICHESTER

WORTHING

8

PORTSMOUTH
41 42

35

NEWPORT

ISLE OF WIGHT

0	10	20	30 miles
0	10	20	30	40	50 km

River Thames

Thames Estuary

LONDON

• 4

GRAVESEND • 26

• 21

45

16 CHATHAM

55

MARGATE

• 32

43

North Downs

• 18

MAIDSTONE •

CANTERBURY •
10 11

44

DEAL • 53

• 15 54

K E N T

• 29

ASHFORD •

DOVER •

20
19

12

TUNBRIDGE WELLS •

40

EAST GRINSTEAD
• 38

S U S S E X

9 •

RYE 46

• 3

LEWES • 31 13

HASTINGS •

BRIGHTON •

36

5 6

1

22

EASTBOURNE

English Channel

South-East England

THE CLERGY HOUSE ALFRISTON, EAST SUSSEX

The National Trust's first building

The Clergy House at Alfriston was the first building acquired by the National Trust, in 1896. The National Trust grew out of the work undertaken by Octavia Hill and others to improve life in the slums of Britain's major cities: people who lived in squalid urban conditions should, they said, have the chance of visiting the beautiful countryside, preserved on their behalf. Hill was greatly influenced by John Ruskin (see page 356), for whom social improvement and beauty went hand in hand; she endured a public falling out with the sage when she (quite rightly) alluded to the impracticality of his vision.

Since 1865, the Commons Preservation Society had been campaigning against the illegal encroachment of common land so that it could remain available for the public to enjoy. The National Trust was a body that could actually own the landscapes, places of historic interest and old buildings that it sought to protect.

The Clergy House was exactly the sort of building that appealed to Octavia Hill and her friends. It was modest in scale, beautifully positioned on the edge of an old village, overlooking a river. It is said to date from as early as 1350 – an unusual time for building, coming soon after the decimation of England by the Black Death (see page 30). Although on the edge of the South Downs, it is a type of house usually called 'Wealden' – timber-framed, with a central hall flanked by two side bays, the upper floors of which project over jetties. (One of the Clergy House's bays was rebuilt after a fire in the 16th century.)

When the National Trust acquired the Clergy House, part of the hipped roof was covered by a threadbare carpet of thatch and the rest had been boarded over. Architects had been alive to the charms of vernacular buildings like the Clergy House since the 1860s. Gertrude Jekyll, champion of the cottage garden style (see page 79), was among the people concerned to record the crafts, traditions and music of the English countryside which were fast disappearing in the face of industrialism and growing prosperity. Picturesque old buildings such as the Clergy House were valued for being, in Hill's words, 'rich in memories of England as our ancestors knew it'.

By 1885, the Clergy House had become such an embarrassment to the vicar of Alfriston that he sought to demolish it. It was then occupied by an old woman who pleaded to be allowed to end her days there. She died in 1888, and when a new vicar arrived the next year, he began a vigorous, though only partially successful, campaign to restore the building. It was the Society for the Protection of Ancient Buildings, founded by William Morris (see page 51) in 1877, that recommended he should approach the newly formed National Trust.

48 LANDMARKS OF BRITAIN

ARUNDEL CASTLE

Seat of Britain's only remaining medieval dukedom

Arundel can be seen for miles: a French Gothic cathedral beside a mighty castle, standing as aloof and glorious as a picture in a fairy tale. It is an image which owes as much to the 19th century as to the Middle Ages, but that does not diminish its romance. Arundel is the seat of the Dukes of Norfolk, the oldest dukedom in Britain and the only one of medieval foundation that still exists. It is therefore a symbol of dynastic survival. While, in much of the rest of Europe, the *Code Napoléon* (the French Civil Code) ensured that family fortunes were divided equally between siblings, and therefore dispersed, the British principle of primogeniture – however unfair to younger children – allowed great families to retain great possessions. As Roman Catholics, the Norfolks were unable to take part in public life until the Catholic Emancipation Act of 1829; in addition, before the 20th century they had to endure a history of tragedy, something of a setback for a family of vaulting ambition. On the other hand, they have the advantage, probably unique among the British aristocracy, of having a saint as an ancestor.

The 1st Duke, initiating the family tradition of adherence to unfashionable causes, died fighting for Richard III at Bosworth in 1485 (see page 309). The 3rd Duke would have been beheaded had Henry VIII not died on the day the sentence was due to have been carried out. Previously, he had ruthlessly succeeded in putting two attractive nieces – Anne Boleyn and Catherine Howard – the King's way, and they became wives two and five; both were beheaded. It was the eldest son of the 4th Duke, Sir Philip Howard, who became the saint, having died in custody after a long imprisonment in the Tower. In Charles II's reign, the 5th Duke was effectively exiled, having lost his mind. Through all these vicissitudes, however, the family patrimony was somehow preserved, until, in the late 19th century, the 15th Duke devoted his energy and income to church building and the re-creation of Arundel as an exemplary ducal seat: whilst far from homely, perhaps, it trumpets the values of a great Catholic gentleman. And so it stands, in the words of the family's historian John Martin Robinson, as the 'Valhalla of the Fitzalan-Howards'.

BATTLE OF HASTINGS

One in the eye for King Harold

The Battle of Hastings on 14 October 1066 imposed a new dynasty on the English throne, one that brought with it new laws, new systems of organisation, new ways of building and a new language. Seized in the Norman fist, England was forced to become more centralised and united than at any time since the Romans had left. Its future was now inextricably yoked to that of mainland Europe, forging connections of not only trade but also warfare.

The Normans had landed a fortnight earlier, at the end of September, at Pevensey Bay (see page 82). It was not unexpected, and for many weeks the English army, under their commander, Harold, son of Earl Godwin, had been camped near the south coast, waiting for them. However, an invasion by the fearsome Norwegian King Harald Hardrada meant that Harold's army had to march north, surprising the Vikings at Stamford Bridge*. William's failure to take advantage of Harold's absence by advancing on London, or some other prize in the south of England, has never been properly explained. However, once Harold's forces had begun to assemble, he quickly moved out to engage them in battle.

The English army must have been weary after hurrying southwards from Yorkshire, but they were able to choose a strong defensive position along Senlac Ridge just outside Battle. From the terrace walk that was created here in the 1820s, it is easy to imagine how daunting their shield wall – not to mention the huge Anglo-Saxon axemen, swinging their two-handed axes – must have seemed to the Norman army, as it contemplated an attack uphill. Against this, the Normans had the advantage of more bowmen and cavalry. Harold's men used horses for travel but fought on foot. It has been calculated that the armies were of roughly equal size; about 7,000 men each. They wore similar suits of heavy chain mail (hauberks), with conical helmets and long, tapering shields.

Harold had already demonstrated his generalship in the north; his rapid journey southwards, and his ability to keep together an army that was largely composed of the *fyrd* (a militia made up of farmers), showed an impressive degree of control and organisation. William, the illegitimate son of Robert, Duke of Normandy, was a highly successful and ruthless commander. His followers came from a landless warrior caste which needed victories outside Normandy in order to obtain riches and estates. Defeat at Hastings would almost certainly have meant death.

William first ordered forward his archers, then his infantry, and finally his cavalry. The horsemen on the left wing, attacked by Harold's javelin throwers and axemen, broke and retreated down the hill. There was a rumour that William had been killed, but the Norman raised his helmet to show that he was still alive, rallying them. Harold's force resisted the temptation to take advantage of the disorganisation and advance: it has been said this was a lost opportunity for Harold. Instead, some Anglo-Saxons were taken in by a series of attacks and staged retreats that William mounted. The sight of the Norman cavalry retreating proved irresistible, and the Anglo-Saxons left the security of the shield wall and ran down the hill after them. The Norman's ploy was successful and, having regrouped, they turned and charged into the disordered ranks of foot soldiers.

At dusk, William led a final assault on the English line. The line broke, and soldiers threw off their heavy hauberks in their attempt to flee. The Bayeux Tapestry shows Harold being killed by an arrow through his eye, and the next day his mutilated body was recovered.

William refused to allow him a Christian burial, and he was buried on the seashore. It is believed that his remains were later taken to Waltham Abbey in Essex (see page 292).

*See Stamford Bridge, page 401

RED HOUSE
BEXLEYHEATH, KENT

Where William Morris became a decorator

In the spring of 1859, William Morris began building Red House at Bexley-heath, to the designs of his friend Philip Webb. Morris was then twenty-five, and newly married to a beautiful young wife. His new house breathed romance, its turrets having first been conceived during an architectural tour of the Seine valley in France. Although the style, combining red brick, pointed arches and sash windows, was similar to that of some Gothic Revival parsonage houses, a unique feature was a porch that Morris imagined might be a resting place for pilgrims en route to Canterbury (the road to which passed nearby).

It was the need to furnish this house that inspired Morris to found his own decorating firm, Morris & Company – the fountainhead of Arts and Crafts decoration. Idealistic and bohemian, he had hoped that Red House would become the focus of a colony of artists; another house nearby was designed for Edward Burne-Jones. This was not to be, but the artist friends who stayed with the Morrises – including Ford Madox Brown and Philip Webb – were pressed into service painting murals and decorating furniture on Arthurian themes. They designed stained-glass windows and hangings, and made tiles. Every-thing in the house was thought out from first principles. The result was not always comfortable, but the ebullience of Morris's personality – he was a prodigious host – made up for it.

The dream did not last. Although not very large, Red House, with its stables, was inconvenient and expensive to run. When the income from Morris's investments fell, the family had to move, but its memory survived in some of Morris & Company's most famous wallpaper patterns, inspired by the plants and birds that Morris could see from his studio window. Although the ideal of a community of artists and craftsmen, working together, was never realised by Morris himself, it lived on as the goal to which his many Arts and Crafts followers aspired.

ROYAL PAVILION

The Prince Regent builds, decorates and collects

As a monument of extravagance and Eastern promise, the Prince Regent's Royal Pavilion at Brighton is one of the most extraordinary buildings in Europe. The Prince, later George IV, was the greatest collector in the history of the monarchy after Charles I. In 1787, his health was already faltering and his doctors suggested that sea-bathing would improve it. In need of a marine pavilion, he employed Henry Holland to remodel what was a modest farmhouse in the neo-Classical style; from 1810, the year that George became Prince Regent, Holland's austere building was engulfed in a tide of minarets and onion domes by John Nash (see page 163). Inside, the predominantly Chinese decoration was rich, exquisite, colourful and fantastic – gas lamps were placed behind stained glass to make it glow at night.

The Pavilion was not only remarkable for its style. As the gout that would cripple him grew worse, the Prince came to crave greenhouse temperatures, which were provided by underfloor central heating. Although regarded as highly uncomfortable by visitors, the heat enabled the Prince to sleep under a sheet that relieved the pressure of bedclothes on his inflamed joints. When not in bed, the Prince made his way around his apartments in a wheeled Merlin chair, as a result of which there are no steps. It was thus the first Royal palace created for disabled access.

In the kitchens, mostly now demolished, the great French chef Antonin Carême produced his astonishing food extravaganzas. There were steam tables and hot cupboards for keeping food warm. As one thing inevitably leads to another, the Pavilion was also ahead of its time in its provision of water-closets: no fewer than thirty of them, at a time when the French were lampooning British men for their unsavoury negligence in where they relieved themselves after dinner. The parties of dandified men and *décolleté* women – presided over by the King's mistresses, Mrs Fitzherbert and Lady Jersey – have gone, but the Pavilion itself remains, as fabulous as ever.

GRAND HOTEL, BRIGHTON

Margaret Thatcher narrowly escapes death

It was nearly three o'clock in the morning of 12 October 1984. The Tory Party Conference in Brighton was about to enter its last day, and Mrs Thatcher* was working on her speech. She sat in an armchair in the Napoleon Suite, in the white-fronted Grand Hotel. Outside, people still on the seafront at that late hour saw a piercing flash of light as a bomb tore open the front of the building, hurling masonry into the air. A 5-ton chimneystack plunged down through the hotel, collapsing floors into the basement. Five people died. Others, such as the Trade and Industry Secretary Norman Tebbitt, were only winched from the wreckage hours later; his wife Margaret was paralysed for life. In the manner of Guy Fawkes, seeking to blow up James I and the House of Lords, the Provisional IRA had sought to murder the whole Cabinet. It was a miracle, aided by the Grand's robust Victorian construction, that the death toll was not much higher.

That morning, at Mrs Thatcher's insistence, the Conference opened at 9.30 as planned. She delivered her speech, redrafted, declaring: 'This attack has failed. All attempts to destroy democracy by terrorism will fail.' The IRA issued a chilling statement that read: 'Today we were unlucky, but remember, we only have to be lucky once; you will have to be lucky always.'

The Brighton bomb, demonstrating that terrorism will sometimes evade even the tightest security, was the IRA's worst atrocity on the British mainland. Paradoxically, it turned Mrs Thatcher into a media heroine, for her indomitability and sang-froid. The bombers later claimed that this strike at the head of government hastened the Good Friday Agreement of 1998, whose power-sharing could be interpreted as a first step on a British retreat from Northern Ireland. If so, they were fortunate not to have killed more senior politicians, which would have made such a *rapprochement* unthinkable for a generation.

The 30lb bomb, hidden behind bath panels in room 629, had been planted several weeks before by Patrick Magee. He was identified after a palm print on the registration document was matched with fingerprints he had given for a teenage driving offence years earlier. Of the thirty-five years to which he was sentenced, he served only fourteen, being released in 1999 under the terms of the Good Friday Agreement. Within two years of the 1984 explosion, the hotel had been rebuilt, but there is no longer a room 629.

*See North Parade, Grantham, page 272

BROADLANDS NEAR ROMSEY, HAMPSHIRE
The Prime Minister who loved gunboats, women and shooting

Queen Victoria never liked the 3rd Viscount Palmerston. Despite her disapproval, he was one of the constants of British politics for more than half a century. He became an MP at the age of twenty-two, serving a succession of Prime Ministers, both Tory and Whig, as War Secretary, Foreign Secretary and Home Secretary, before himself becoming Prime Minister aged seventy. His name is forever associated with the use or threat of military warfare as part of political negotiation – so called 'gunboat diplomacy'. His single-mindedness on this issue was one source of conflict with Queen Victoria, who feared that some of her relations would lose their thrones if their governments were unseated. He was also notorious for his irrepressible womanising: nicknamed Lord Cupid, Palmerston's morality belonged more to the era of his Queen's dissolute uncles than of her own reign. Handsome, fiery, implacably anti-democratic but a popular figure, he preferred the image of a sporting squire to that of a career politician.

Born in 1784, Palmerston inherited Broadlands, along with the Irish estates from which his title was taken, at the age of seventeen. The house had been built by his grandfather, the 1st Viscount Palmerston, in the first half of the 18th century, then remodelled by the 2nd Viscount in the 1760s and 1770s for the display of his treasures from the Grand Tour; it took a heavy toll on his finances. The 3rd Viscount had a taste for the country. He kept a ferret while at Harrow, and he always loved shooting, tramping for hours through his woods. He was sufficiently kind-hearted to seek to commute the death sentence passed on a local poacher who had wounded one of his gamekeepers, to no avail. He hunted with the New Forest Foxhounds into his seventies.

The arrival of the railway in 1840 made it easier for him to come down for weekend house parties, where politics would be discussed in an unbuttoned atmosphere. In his library, which he had enlarged, he installed a desk at which he could work standing up. Palmerston died two days before his eighty-second birthday, still Prime Minister.

BUCKLER'S HARD
Where Mulberry Harbours for D-Day were built

By the Second World War, the maritime heyday of Buckler's Hard, on the sleepy Beaulieu river, had long passed. Once, the shipyard had built ships of the line, three of which – including Nelson's favourite, HMS *Agamemnon* – fought at Trafalgar. Memories of its naval past were revived during the First World War with the construction of Fairmile motor launches, but in the years that followed, the only sailors to frequent the yard had been yachtsmen. In 1943, however, the peaceful oyster beds south of the village were transformed into a building site: wooden shuttering was erected for a series of reinforced concrete structures which would form part of the Mulberry Harbours destined for the Normandy coast.

On 30 May 1942 Winston Churchill (see page 128) sent a typically un-compromising memo to Lord Mountbatten, Chief of Combined Operations Command, under the heading 'Piers for use on beaches'. It instructed: 'They must float up and down with tide. The anchor problem must be mastered. Let me have the best solution worked out. Don't argue the matter. The difficulties will argue for themselves.'

Britain and America had begun to plan the invasion of Europe which took place in 1944. Churchill foresaw the difficulty of capturing intact a harbour in German-occupied France, and ordered two Mulberries to be built which would create prefabricated docks and breakwaters. The pier sections had to float, so as always to be within reach of ships, whatever the tide. Each was about a mile in length, and over two million tons of steel and concrete went into them. On the eve of D-Day, tugs towed the Mulberries towards France. An armada of over 2,700 ships soon joined them. Operation Overlord had begun. The Mulberry concept was sounder in theory than practice. Freak storms struck the Channel on 18 June, putting Mulberry A out of action. Mulberry B, however, continued in service, landing 9,000 tons of material a day, until the Allies took Antwerp and Cherbourg in August.

The techniques developed for the landing were to revolutionise shipping after the war, through the introduction of the roll-on, roll-off principle, aided by containerisation and the forklift truck.

BATEMAN'S
BURWASH, EAST SUSSEX

Kipling's own image of England

By 1900, Rudyard Kipling was the most famous author in England, having published *Plain Tales from the Hills*, *Soldiers Three* and the first and second *Jungle Books*, among numerous other titles. The next two years saw the appearance of his novel *Kim* and the *Just So Stories*. By 1902, aged thirty-seven, he was rich enough to buy the home that was his image of England, a stone house in the Weald called Bateman's.

Born in Bombay, the son of an artist, he was deeply affected by the beauty of the scene that surrounded Bateman's. He made a garden there but the social organisation of the countryside held little appeal for the mouthpiece of the common man. 'England is a stuffy little place, mentally, morally and physically,' he wrote to the great imperial adventurer Cecil Rhodes. Living in Sussex gave him a new horizon to explore. 'Puck's Song' from *Puck of Pook's Hill* (1906) evokes the people who had worked the land, fought battles and built now-vanished towns around Bateman's since prehistoric times.

Kipling wrote on a French walnut table which is still in the study. It was, and is, crowded with what he described as 'fetishes' such as pen trays, boxes of paperclips and pins, a paperweight that might have belonged to Warren Hastings, an inky foot rule and 'all manner of unneeded essentials'. He hummed as he worked, and was so wrapped up in the process of creation that he could not be interrupted. When he had finished writing each day, he had time for teasing and joking with his family and the constant parade of visitors who passed through the mellow, oak-panelled rooms: writers, journalists, publishers, politicians – above all, his cousin the Prime Minister Stanley Baldwin. His life darkened after the death of a daughter aged six and the loss of his son John at the Battle of Loos. Bateman's gave consolation.

ST AUGUSTINE'S ABBEY   CANTERBURY, KENT

Fostering the re-conversion of Britain

Christianity, whose followers had been persecuted in its early days, became tolerated from the early 4th century, when Emperor Constantine himself was converted. However, the fall of Rome in 476 withdrew protection for Christians in Britain. The invading Saxons, Angles and Jutes brought with them new gods that are still commemorated in place names (for example, Wootton, named after Woden), and Christianity fled with the romanised Britons into their last fastnesses of Wales and the west. At the very end of the 6th century, word reached Pope Gregory that parts of England might be sympathetic to hearing the Gospel. The King of Kent, Ethelbert, had married Bertha, a daughter of the King of Paris, who was a Christian. Gregory targeted Ethelbert as a conversion prospect, sending the monk Augustine, supported by a small band of other monks, to preach to him. They arrived at Canterbury in 596 and Ethelbert was converted later the same year.

Ethelbert gave Augustine an old Roman church in Canterbury from which to preach; it became Canterbury Cathedral. Beyond the city walls, the monks built a monastery, whose first abbot was Peter, one of the monks who had come to England with Augustine. There was not, in fact, one church to serve the monks but four: they were small buildings, strung out in a line from east to west: this was a practice Augustine would have seen on the Continent. In due course, the church of St Mary and the church of St Peter and St Paul were joined by an octagonal tower; then, in the great period of monastic building after the Norman Conquest, the single church that this had created was demolished to make way for a much grander church, built on the same alignment but spreading to either side of the old plan. The new church, of which little now remains above ground level, was once as big as Canterbury Cathedral.

St Augustine's Abbey continued to evolve. Like other monasteries, it was able to entertain the monarch when he travelled to this part of his kingdom. Henry VIII found its hospitality so convenient that he converted part of it to a palace after the abbey was dissolved in 1538. The great library was scattered, and all that remains of the treasure is a single silver-mounted coconut, now in Canterbury Cathedral. The monastery had been in continuous use for 940 years.

CANTERBURY CATHEDRAL

Murder of Thomas à Becket

When Chaucer's band of pilgrims set out from the Tabard Inn in Southwark in his late 14th-century *Canterbury Tales*, their destination was the shrine of Thomas à Becket in Canterbury Cathedral. Becket had been murdered two centuries before. The persistence of the Becket cult that followed shows the enormous impact that the slaughter of an archbishop in his cathedral had on the medieval imagination – particularly when the man who had been killed stood as a symbol of opposition to royal authority. Canterbury cathedral was an indirect beneficiary of the interest excited by the drama within its walls. The money rolled in.

In Thomas à Becket's day, Canterbury Cathedral was a Norman structure – magnificent by the standards of the time, although not nearly as magnificent as what was to come. Becket's career had been spectacular, built on a genius for administration, noticed by King Henry II who made him his chancellor. At this period of his life, Becket's tastes were nothing if not worldly. He enjoyed the friendship of the King, and lived in luxury.

To Henry, Becket seemed a mischievously suitable appointment as Archbishop, when the see fell vacant in 1162; a friend who could surely be relied upon to help him regain some of the royal authority that had been lost during the reign of his father, Henry I. What happened next took the King and everyone else by surprise. As soon as Becket became Archbishop, he repented of his past life and resigned the chancellorship. He punished his body by wearing a hair shirt which he never changed: it was found to be crawling with lice when he died.

Relations between the King and his archbishop quickly deteriorated and Becket spent six years in exile in France. He returned to England in 1170 when an uneasy truce had been established between the two men. Earlier that year, Henry had sought to secure the succession by having his eldest son crowned by Becket's rival, the Archbishop of York, an office that should have been performed by the Archbishop of Canterbury. Becket had the Archbishop excommunicated and vigorously pursued those people who had profited by his absence in France to usurp his estates. Their complaints reached Henry's ears in France. With his territories both in England and in France threatened by neighbouring powers, the last thing he needed was more trouble from the Archbishop of Canterbury, his own unwise appointment. He turned to his knights, wondering how he could have nurtured so many miserable drones and traitors 'who let their lord be treated with such shameful contempt by a low-born clerk'. Four of them slipped away and took a boat to England. They found Becket in his cathedral. The first blow from the long, two-handed sword sliced off the top of his head.

Miracles were immediately associated with Becket's body, and pilgrimages began. In 1174, the eastern part of the cathedral burnt down. In a way, this was providential since it allowed the choir to be rebuilt handsomely as a setting for Becket's shrine, which was plated in gold and thickly encrusted with jewels. Under Henry VIII, the Church suffered what, in business parlance, might be called a hostile take-over, followed by asset-stripping on the grand scale. Becket's shrine was swept away, his bones were scattered, and the gold and jewels gathered up by the royal treasury. The crown had won; but it had taken 366 years to do so.

CHANNEL TUNNEL   KENT

Bienvenu, wilkommen . . . the end of Britain's geographical isolation from the Continent

On 1 January 1973, Britain became a member of what was then called the Common Market and is now the European Union. Europe was sold to the British public as principally a free-trade zone, but since then the hidden intention of the founding fathers to create an ever more integrated Europe has been steadily implemented – not always to the joy of those who value Britain's long tradition of independence. In the 1980s, having imposed hard-won economic reforms on Britain, Margaret Thatcher did not want to allow her work to be undone by a predominantly socialist Europe. In 1992, however, Britain signed the Maastricht Treaty with its provisions for closer union between the twelve member states, although it secured opt-outs from the Social Chapter and moves towards a single currency. The Labour government that came to power in 1997 adopted the Social Chapter and signed up to the European Convention on Human Rights.

The physical symbol of Britain's new relationship with its Continental neighbours is the Channel Tunnel. Previous generations may have celebrated Britain as a jewel 'set in a silver sea', whose waters had protected her from invasion since 1066, but in the new European reality Britain's position as an island on the western extremity of the Union was an economic disadvantage. Visionaries had dreamed of connecting Britain and France by tunnel since the age of Napoleon. An attempt at tunnelling had actually been made in 1880, when a boring machine began digging on either side of the Channel. In 1940, when Britain's High Command waited daily for Hitler to launch a seaborne invasion, there was general relief that a tunnel did not exist. By the mid-1950s, however, it was deemed that the military objection to a tunnel was obsolete. Plans were drawn up in the 1960s and launched in 1973. It was not an auspicious year: a sudden rise in oil prices threw the economy into confusion and the project was abandoned. A cross-Channel bridge, or Europont, was examined, but rejected on grounds of cost.

In 1984, the French and British governments at last showed that they were serious about a tunnel, although they wanted private money to pay for it. Eurotunnel made the successful bid, for two rail tunnels with a service tunnel linked to them in between. As built, the tunnel is 31⅓ miles long; 8 million cubic metres of soil had been removed at a rate of 2,400 tonnes per hour; a total of nine billion pounds had been spent. When it opened in 1994, Britain felt itself to be a little less an island than it had been before. Suddenly, Paris and Brussels were, in time, rather closer to London than Liverpool or Carlisle. Among the many hitherto unnoticed qualities in the French to which British eyes have been opened is the superior state of their railway track, as passengers, comparing the bullet-like speed of the train on the French side of the 'Chunnel' with the slow, spasmodic progress between Dover and Victoria Station, remain all too acutely aware.

CHARLESTON FARMHOUSE   *NEAR LEWES, EAST SUSSEX*
The Bloomsbury Group en campagne

The economist John Maynard Keynes wrote his book *The Economic Consequences of the Peace* – prophetically criticising the harsh terms imposed on Germany by the Treaty of Versailles after its defeat in the First World War – at Charleston Farmhouse, on the seaward side of the Sussex Downs. Keynes was no country-man, and would wear his dark suit and Homburg hat even when picnicking in the fields. But the farmhouse was hardly a conventional agricultural dwelling, having been occupied by Vanessa Bell, Duncan Grant and Roger Fry, with intermittent visits by Vanessa's husband Clive Bell, since 1916. It was Vanessa Bell's sister Virginia Woolf who had spotted it, when staying with her husband Leonard at their own farmhouse four miles away. Other regular visitors included Lytton Strachey and E. M. Forster. Many of them met at Cambridge and went on to live and gather in Bloomsbury, from where they took their collective name.

During the First World War, core members of the Bloomsbury Group were conscientious objectors, and were given work on the land close to Charleston, which they were able to use as a base. Since many of them were also artists, the farmhouse became an object that could be enriched by decoration – much as Picasso came to decorate ceramics. The place itself appealed to a generation whose outlook was coloured by the Arts and Crafts Movement, with its rejection of overblown stylistic pretension. 'It is really so lovely,' rhapsodised Vanessa Bell in a letter to Roger Fry in the autumn of 1916, '. . . very solid and simple with flat walls in that lovely mixture of brick and flint that they use about here – and perfectly flat windows in the walls and wonderful tiled roofs.' Household effects came from the Omega Workshops, which had been founded by Fry in 1913 to produce furniture and decorated plates in the Post-Impressionist taste. Wall surfaces, fireplaces and even antique furniture were covered in patterns and bold, stylised images, generally of nudes, in a style which translated Mediterranean hedonism into earth colours that were not out of place in the English countryside.

For the children – Quentin and Julian Bell, and later Angelica Garnett (Vanessa's daughter by Duncan Grant) – it was heaven. They were allowed to do just what they wanted. Meanwhile, the grown-ups did just what they wanted, too: painting, writing, lolling around in the garden and talking about anything that interested them, irrespective of social taboos. They rose above domestic catastrophe and icy temperatures. The unsung heroine of the house was Grace Germany, the housekeeper, whose presence allowed Vanessa the freedom to paint and talk.

In European terms, the painters of the Bloomsbury Group were a backwater, just as the Sussex Downs were a backwater, but the creative collision between these highly talented, cosmopolitan individuals and the rural setting of the Sussex farmhouse produced a unique, yet characteristically English result. The preservation of room settings that were almost as ephemeral as the conversation that took place in them is in itself a minor miracle.

FOX HALL

CHARLTON, WEST SUSSEX

The first pack of foxhounds in Britain

Until the 1670s, the fox had been considered vermin that should be exterminated by any means possible, and was beneath the dignity of gentlemen to hunt. Around 1675, the Duke of Monmouth founded a pack of hounds which, for the first time, would have only the fox as its quarry. The Duke was unable to take much pleasure from his institution when he had to flee the country in 1683. Two years later, his defeat at the Battle of Sedgemoor (see page 38) and his subsequent execution meant that he would never hunt with earthly hounds again, but the Charlton Hunt went from strength to strength.

At one point, half the Knights of the Garter were among its subscribers. Travel being difficult, these grand men would – once they had made the journey to Charlton – remain to hunt over several days. Some of them built hunting boxes in which to stay, and Fox Hall was one of these, built in 1730 for the 2nd Duke of Richmond. Tall, narrow and unexpectedly severe, given the purpose, the lodge largely comprises a great communal dining room in which the hunt members would meet for dinner. It says much for the elevated standing of the hunt that Fox Hall's architecture was supervised, if not designed, by the Earl of Burlington, better known for Chiswick House (see page 134).

In the late 17th century, the light chalky land of the South Downs must have been more exciting to ride across than the boggy Shire counties of the east Midlands. In the 19th century, however, the situation changed when agricultural improvements created a new and even more exhilarating landscape comprising small fields and stout hedges made by farmers who were fattening bullocks. Sussex lost the palm to Leicestershire and Northamptonshire, although the need to increase food production during the Second World War meant that much of the springy old pasture which connoisseurs loved to feel beneath their horses' hooves was ploughed up.

In 1885, the Duke of Beaufort, in the introduction to his hunting volume in the famous Badminton Sporting Library series, wondered how much longer fox hunting could continue, 'when the brutality of field-sports is being denounced with so much eloquence and energy'. In 2004 the Duke's pessimism finally proved justified, and the sport of fox hunting was banned. Foxes were now to be exterminated by any other means possible.

CHARTWELL
Sir Winston Churchill at home

Winston Churchill at home is almost as big a subject as Winston Churchill in politics*. To some extent, the two are inseparable, because Churchill's home embodied his idea of what was most important about English life, and it was at home that he wrote his speeches, formulated his strategies and cultivated people of importance. That home, for forty years, was Chartwell, bought for its views of woods and hills that seemed to typify England. With characteristic self-belief, he acquired it in 1922, after he had lost his seat in Parliament, when the Liberal party to which he belonged was breaking apart, and without telling his wife, Clementine. Clemmie, as she was invariably known, never loved the place, but made it the domestic theatre in which he could both shine and relax.

Relaxation for Churchill involved keeping busy. The house he bought had been a Victorian frenzy of gables and chimneypots. The architect Philip Tilden, who had worked for Churchill's friend Philip Sassoon at Port Lympne (see page 85), was asked to remodel it, improving the plan, calming the architectural effect and making the most of the views. Churchill threw himself into the project, just as he threw himself into the making of the garden and lake. (Sassoon sent black swans as a present.) Famously, Churchill laid bricks, becoming an adult apprentice of the Bricklayers' Union. He tried his hand at farming, but without much success. He was a vigorous painter and Chartwell was one of his favourite subjects.

Chartwell was the solace that comforted Churchill during his years out of office, giving his frustrations a practical outlet. It was at Chartwell that he wrote the cascade of books and newspaper articles that kept his name before the public and his finances afloat. It was not a grand or large house, nothing like Blenheim Palace (see page 206) where he had been brought up. Weekend guests were confined to an inner circle, and Chartwell's position only an hour from London made it easy for guests to run down for luncheon. Visitors included political friends and acolytes, newspaper magnates, scientists and – to the delight of the children – such figures of popular myth as Lawrence of Arabia (see page 19) and Charlie Chaplin. Above all, it was a family home. Churchill adored his parents, but they had been distant figures. His own style of parenting was robust but warm; in the nursery, he would imitate a gorilla, in the garden he built tree-houses.

During the Second World War, Chartwell was too easily identifiable a target from the air for Churchill to continue to live there. Afterwards, a group of political friends bought Chartwell for the nation, on the understanding that Winston and Clemmie could continue to live there during their lifetimes. This eased some of the financial anxiety which had clouded Clemmie's pleasure in it. Churchill's last years were spent at Chartwell painting, playing bezique with Clemmie or feeding his fish.

*See Cabinet War Rooms, page 128

CHATHAM DOCKYARD
Where HMS Victory *was built*

Every sailor in Nelson's navy had to know the ropes. With its 37 sails, HMS *Victory**, Nelson's flagship at Trafalgar, was rigged with 26 miles of rope, in 17 different thicknesses – the biggest of which was 19ins in circumference. Sailors prided themselves on their ability to knot and splice the tarry hemp. Rope was not only indispensable but ubiquitous. It was used to haul the guns about the gun deck. It stung the backs of sailors when the bosun wielded his rope 'starter', or lashed them when the cat-o'-nine-tails was produced. Rope extracted the ultimate penalty from a condemned sailor by forming a noose.

Chatham was one of four dockyards that supplied rope to the navy. The building in which the rope was made was said to be the longest in Europe: today, a reasonably long-sighted individual cannot discern from one end what lies at the other. But rope-making, which employed 300 people there, was only one of the many activities required to make or refit a wooden-walled man-of-war. Shipbuilding was Chatham's speciality. Founded in the Tudor period, the dockyard became the navy's most strategic base during the Dutch wars of the mid-17th century, being the port closest to Holland. It was here that Charles II's best ships were laid up when the royal finances were exhausted after the

Great Fire of London – leaving them vulnerable to being caught unawares, to Britain's shame, by a daring Dutch raid in 1667. When France became enemy number one in the 18th century, the English Channel and the Atlantic replaced the North Sea as the prime centres of activity. As a result, Chatham lost its importance as a station for warships to Portsmouth and Plymouth. Instead, it was developed as a yard where ships were constructed and equipped. Between 1700 and the end of the Napoleonic Wars, over a hundred ships for the Royal Navy were launched onto the Medway at Chatham.

In the next century, Chatham was the first of the Royal Navy's dockyards to build an ironclad, the *Achilles*. Dickens, who knew Chatham well, his father having been a clerk here (see page 72), recorded the sight and, above all, sound of the 1,200 men hammering on its hull in *The Uncommercial Traveller*. ('Ding, Clash, Dong, Bang, Boom, Rattle, Clash, Bang, Clatter, Bang Bang BANG!') The biggest ship made at Chatham was HMS *Africa*, launched in 1905, and it was the last of consequence. The Medway was not deep enough to take the enormous Dreadnoughts being built in the arms race against Germany that preceded the First World War, and so Chatham's sun was again eclipsed. Nevertheless, the dockyard acquired expertise in the building of submarines, and the scale of its importance in the refitting of warships can be gauged by the 1,360 that were serviced during the Second World War. Plans to close Chatham were announced in 1981; ironically, the very next year a large naval task force set sail for the Falkland Islands. This late triumph for the Royal Navy was not enough to save the dockyard, which ceased activity in 1984.

*See HMS *Victory*, page 87, and Tilbury Fort, page 290

JANE AUSTEN'S HOUSE   CHAWTON, HAMPSHIRE
The tripod table at which Emma *was written*

It is a truth universally acknowledged that the son of a clergyman who has seven brothers and sisters must be in want of a good fortune. In the case of Richard Austen, brother of the novelist Jane, one arrived with the death of a childless cousin of his father, who had adopted him as his heir. He acquired two good country seats – at Godmersham in Kent and Chawton in Hampshire – preferring to live at the former and settling his mother, two of his sisters and one of their friends in a modest house near the latter. To Jane, arriving in 1809, it was heaven. Since her father's retirement as vicar of Steventon in Hampshire, she had lived in Bath and, following his death, Southampton.

Now, at last, she had a settled home, with her sister Cassandra to look after most of the housekeeping while she oversaw the dispensing of precious tea, and wrote. She sat at a diminutive tripod table, covering small sheets of paper in lines of tidy script. A creaking door would warn her that someone was coming – whereupon she would hide her work away. In this manner she revised the novels she had written in her early twenties, *Sense and Sensibility*, *Northanger Abbey* and *Pride and Prejudice*, and wrote *Mansfield Park*, *Emma* and *Persuasion*. She had only eight years to complete this oeuvre. Addison's disease, which affected her kidneys, was diagnosed in 1816, and she died in Winchester the next year.

CROYDON AIRPORT
First purpose-built airport

SURREY

Built from 1926–8, Croydon Aerodrome was the world's first purpose-built airport*. Churchill used Croydon regularly: as Minister of Munitions during the First World War, he frequently flew to France from the old airfield that preceded it. A galaxy of film stars and society figures gave it their seal of approval, and it was to Croydon that Amy Johnson returned amid celebrations after her solo flight to Australia in 1930.

Beddington airfield had been established a little to the west of the present Croydon terminal in 1915. Beddington was originally used by the Home Defence Squadrons of the Royal Flying Corps, as one of a ring of airfields around London to combat Zeppelin raids. Prince Albert, later George VI, won his wings there in 1919. Edward VIII, as Prince of Wales, also learnt to fly at Croydon: until expressly forbidden by his father, he performed aerobatics with a one-armed VC, Major W. G. Barker. In 1920, the airfield was amalgamated with the adjacent Waddon aerodrome, a test flying ground, and officially designated Croydon Aerodrome, the customs airport for London. By 1935, the local paper could say that the fame of Croydon Airport (as it had become known) was 'world-wide', being 'a gateway to the Empire'.

Navigation in the early days was hazardous; pilots guided themselves at night from Croydon to Paris by following a trail of fifteen beacons, flashing in Morse code. It may not be a coincidence that the international distress call 'mayday' (*m'aidez*) was invented by the Croydon radio operator, F. S. Mockford. As late as 1931, a white line was chalked onto the grass runway to help pilots orient themselves when taking off in thick fog; this was regarded as an innovation of major importance. The time taken flying to Le Bourget by the Imperial Airways fleet of eight Handley Page biplanes (all given heroic names such as *Hannibal*, *Heracles*, *Hanno*) depended on the weather; if it were very inclement, they would have to turn back when halfway across the Channel. One passenger described the experience of flying: 'They put you in a box, they shut the lid, they splash you all over with oil, you are sick, and you're in Paris.'

As the first building of its kind, the Croydon terminal presented some features – the through-baggage hall, for instance – that were widely imitated; a similar control tower was built at Moscow. The imperial classicism of the building did not, however, set a precedent for subsequent airport architecture in Britain. Airports in the decade after Croydon – Heston, Brooklands, Shoreham, Ramsgate, Birmingham, Jersey – favoured smooth concrete walls, cantilevered balconies and wrap-around windows to give an impression of modernity, appropriate to the new mode of travel. The Croydon buildings looked safe and respectable: 'One gets the immediate impression,' wrote Captain Norman Macmillan, describing them in *The Air Travellers' Guide to Europe*, 'that civil aviation in England has been established on a sound basis, that it is reality and not a toy played with by enthusiasts.'

The airport closed in 1959, superseded by Heathrow† and Gatwick.

*See Shoreham Airport, page 93. †See Heston Aerodrome, page 221

WHITE CLIFFS OF DOVER KENT
A natural landmark that resonates with English patriotism

The White Cliffs of Dover are an iconic landmark for the English. Over the centuries, they have come to symbolise 'home'. Julius Caesar wrote about the cliffs when he invaded Britain in 55BC: he did not land his legions there because of the tribesmen 'fully armed and drawn up all along the cliffs' (see page 97). To troops leaving for war overseas, the cliffs have often been the last morsel of homeland that could be seen from the departing ships; equally, they were the first intimation of homecoming for soldiers and travellers coming back from the Continent. It is now possible, of course, to leave England, or return to it, by air or via the Channel Tunnel under the sea (see page 58), but from the top of the cliffs, cross-Channel ferries, cargo ships, fishing boats and pleasure craft can still be seen performing their endless ballet in the sea around the port of Dover. To some of the English aboard those ships, the cliffs are so rich in association and cultural meaning that they will bring a lump of patriotic sentiment to the throat.

The White Cliffs stretch for ten miles between Folkestone in the west and Walmer in the north-east. Their geology and unique ecosystem have been researched by the National Trust, which owns six of the cliffs. The chalk of which they are made belongs to a bed that is some 270ft deep. Eighty million years ago, the process of forming them began as an infinite number of plankton and other organisms died and floated down to the bottom of the warm sea which then covered Europe. In the course of a million years, the shells of these tiny creatures would combine to form chalk. The water level dropped and the chalk was exposed. An unimaginably vast torrent of water gouged out the English Channel at the end of the last ice age. The pebbles on the beach are made from the hard flints that are found embedded in the soft chalk; they were made from the shells of other sea creatures which contained silica.

Although the White Cliffs may seem a creation of nature, they have, in the course of history, been intensively utilised. The primeval forest of trees that would have covered them, as the rest of England, was cleared; the grasses that grew up in place of the trees were grazed by sheep. From Roman times, ships sailed into and out of Dover harbour, and lighthouses were built to guide them. With France only 21 miles away, the natural fortification provided by the cliffs was enhanced, so that the cries of seagulls were joined by the shouts of men and the rumble of machinery. The cliffs may have shrunk back from the sea, retreating perhaps as much as 300yds from the line that greeted Julius Caesar, but they endured all the human activity, smiling. The plants that grow on the cliff top thrive on very thin soils; the tracks and abrasions left by man have only encouraged them to flourish. The tapestry of flowery turf represents one of the most diverse plant ecosystems in Britain. Among the orchids, salad burnet, carline thistle, wild thyme, bird's-foot trefoil and horseshoe vetch can be found the wild cabbage brought to Britain by the Romans, from which our own familiar green vegetable descends.

DOVER CASTLE   KENT
England's greatest fortification under siege from the French

Dover has been recognised as one of England's most strategically important sites ever since a hill fort was built here during the Iron Age. The English Channel is pinched to a narrow waist, only 21 miles wide at its narrowest point, allowing English guns to shell the French coast during the Second World War and German guns based around Calais to attack Dover. Ten miles of tall chalk cliffs (see above), rising almost vertically from the sea, are broken only by the estuary of the River Dour as it empties into the sea. This is where the port of Dover came to be built. Above it, the Romans used the site to erect a tall lighthouse, with walls of flint layered with tile; this was later attached to the Saxon church, St Mary-in-Castro, as a sort of bell tower. Ever since William the Conqueror, marching to Dover after the Battle of Hastings, ordered that an earth mound and timber palisade be erected around the lighthouse and Saxon church, there has been a castle up above the cliffs to defend it.

Henry II spent a colossal sum in constructing a new keep, with walls that were nearly 21ft thick in places. Not only that, but his engineer, Maurice, built towers to the inner bailey, and began work on the walls of an outer bailey, beyond which was a further perimeter wall. This made Dover the first castle in Europe to be defended by concentric rings of high wall studded with towers, a principle of military architecture that was to endure until artillery forced the adoption of new defensive techniques in the 16th century. But Henry II's work was left unfinished on his death in 1189. When King John lost Normandy in 1204, France suddenly seemed very close. The construction work was completed swiftly.

This was just as well, since in the autumn of 1216 the castle was besieged by Prince Louis of France who had come to the aid of the barons. Although the French stone-throwing catapults were not able to make much impression on the strong walls, the barbican collapsed when Prince Louis's men mined underneath it. The King's men were unable to stop them by counter-mining, or digging their own tunnels. One of the gate-towers subsided. The King's knights fought bravely and managed to secure the breach, and the castle withstood the greatest threat in what would be a near 900-year history of military use.

King John's death towards the end of 1216 took some of the sting out of the siege. When the army of the new king, John's son Henry III, defeated the French at Lincoln in 1217, the attackers set their sails for France. Henry III learnt well from that siege and turned Dover Castle into the indomitable fortification that remains one of the first sights to greet foreign visitors arriving at Dover from across the Channel.

DOWN HOUSE NEAR ORPINGTON, KENT
Where Darwin wrote On the Origin of Species

Like Florence Nightingale (see page 212), Charles Darwin was one of Victorian England's eminent invalids. His illness, which was never identified, had the effect of making a secluded home, close to London, important to him. Here, working in short bursts, with three walks taken in his precious garden at the same time every day, he wrote *On the Origin of Species by Means of Natural Selection* and carried out research on earthworms (some of which were put on top of his wife's piano to see if they could hear).

As a young man, Darwin had been the despair of his doctor father – not given to medical study, unwilling to become a clergyman, prone to gambling and other dissipations. The one subject that captured his imagination was natural history; at Cambridge, he collected beetles along the Backs. He was encouraged in fieldwork by the Rev. Prof. John Henslow, who was instrumental in finding Darwin a passage with Robert Fitzroy, captain of the *Beagle*, on a voyage to survey Tierra del Fuego and the East Indies. His role was partly that of unpaid naturalist, partly of companion for the depressive Fitzroy, who, after a distinguished career, eventually killed himself. The ten-gun brig sailed in December 1831, visiting the Cape Verde Islands, the South American coast, the Strait of Magellan, the Galápagos Islands, Tahiti, New Zealand, Australia, the Maldives and Mauritius before its return five years later. The cramped conditions on board ship were exacerbated by the fossils, insects, animals and birds that Darwin collected.

Darwin moved to Down House in 1842, and it was in his study here – with its shipshape filing drawers, microscope by the window and furniture on wheels – that he analysed his collection. In the course of this patient analysis, Darwin's species theory took shape. The fossils showed him that creatures had not always been as they are now; the differences between examples of the same species living in isolation of each other – such as on the hot, black islands of the Galápagos – showed that they had adapted to their environment. He deduced that the means that effected these changes was reproduction; individuals who were best suited to their conditions were likely to win the healthiest mates. The implications of this theory for a society which believed that all life had been divinely ordained were obvious to him; his wife was deeply religious and feared for his soul. It was twenty years before he could be persuaded by scientific friends to publish his conclusions.

When *On the Origin of Species* was published in 1859 and the storm of controversy broke*, the domestic routine of Down House became more important than ever. Having already spent eight years classifying every known type of barnacle, he went on to study orchids and facial expressions, as well as the logical extension of his species theory in *The Descent of Man* (1871) – for the first time using the word 'evolution' in its modern sense, arguing that man is descended from apes.

*See Museum of Natural History, page 233

THE REDOUBT, EASTBOURNE

EAST SUSSEX

Defensive system to repel Napoleon's threatened invasion

Towards the end of 1803, Napoleon camped an army of 130,000 men outside Boulogne and assembled a fleet of over 2,000 flat-bottomed boats. The previous year, the Peace of Amiens had brought a short-lived truce but hostilities had resumed in May 1803. The Bayeux Tapestry was taken to Paris for inspiration; Napoleon was getting ready to invade Britain.

Britain had not been successfully invaded since 1066. Indeed, invasion had come to seem such a remote possibility that the south and east coasts were virtually undefended, except by a small number of ancient forts. The government rushed to make good the deficiency by building a chain of over

Abbotsbury, page 4. A flock of swans has been managed here since at least 1393, when the fowl formed a part of the diet of the monks of the nearby abbey.

Roman Baths, page 4. For the conquering Romans, with their love of bathing, the hot springs at Bath will have been a welcome respite from Britain's intemperate climate.

Lansdown Tower, page 7. William Beckford,
'England's wealthiest son' and one of the most remarkable
Regency collectors of fine art, had a penchant for towers;
this is the one he built that didn't collapse.

Clouds Hill, page 19. T. E. Lawrence, otherwise Lawrence of Arabia, bought this spartan cottage as a bolt-hole where he could write.

Top: Lacock Abbey, page 26. The photographic pioneer William Henry Fox Talbot used his house as the subject of the earliest paper negatives.

Above: Bowood House, page 9. In 1774, the non-conformist radical Joseph Priestley discovered oxygen in his laboratory in Lord Shelburne's country house.

Chysauster Ancient Village, page 19. This street runs through a hamlet dating from the 1st or 2nd century BC.

Maiden Castle, page 29. The defensive rings of the castle were stormed by the Romans, under the future Emperor Vespasian, in about AD43.

Glastonbury Abbey, page 25. Thanks to the legend of Joseph of Arimathea, pilgrims flocked to Glastonbury; how rich the abbey became is shown by the scale of the Abbot's kitchen.

Above: Stourhead, page 41. Begun in the 1740s, this landscape park is perhaps the greatest surviving example of the Picturesque movement.

Top right: Geevor Tin Mine, page 24. From the 4th century BC, tin put Cornwall on the map and provided the first reference to Britain in literature.

Right: Royal Albert Bridge, page 36. Completed in 1859, Isambard Kingdom Brunel's bridge over the river Tamar was the last important section of the Great Western Railway to be built.

Canterbury Cathedral, page 57.
The murder of Thomas à Becket in
1170 established Canterbury as
Britain's foremost pilgrimage site.

Exeter Cathedral, page 23. The dominating
central position of the organ case reflects the
primacy of music in the Anglican tradition.

Top left: Battle of Hastings, page 49. This colourful 15th-century illumination depicts the famous battle that established the Normans in Britain.

Top right: Portchester Castle, page 84. Henry V's army embarked for Agincourt from this fort that had been built by the Romans some 1,100 years earlier.

Above: The *Mary Rose*, page 86. The attempt to adapt Tudor ships to carrying cannons proved too much for the *Mary Rose*, which sank in 1545.

Royal Pavilion, page 52. John Nash's extraordinary building of 1811 is a monument to the extravagance of the Prince Regent.

The Grange, page 88. The architect A. W. N. Pugin attempted to revive the glories of
the medieval church at his home at Ramsgate.

Above: Charleston Farmhouse, page 59. Bloomsbury in the country: a portrait of Vanessa Bell at Charleston by Duncan Grant.

Left, top: Down House, page 67. Charles Darwin and his wife. At one time Darwin kept earthworms on the piano to test if they could hear.

Left: Chartwell, page 61. Winston Churchill was an enthusiastic painter, and his beloved Chartwell provided many subjects.

Above: Broadlands, page 53. Viscount Palmerston, lover of women and gunboats, entertains guests at his country house, 1859.

Top right: Margate Beach, page 78. Margate was one of the first seaside resorts for mass tourism; the crowds originally came from London by boat.

Opposite: Munstead Wood, page 79. Gertrude Jekyll's soft, cottagey borders – recorded in this picture taken by herself – reinvented English gardening.

Fishbourne Roman Palace, page 71. This mosaic of Cupid riding a dolphin shows the sophistication of the largest Roman building north of the Alps.

a hundred squat towers to protect vulnerable beaches. The idea of these towers came from a fortified tower on Cape Mortella, on Napoleon's home island of Corsica. In 1794, this tower, armed with only three small artillery pieces, had fought off two of the Royal Navy's ships of the line, inflicting heavy casualties: it only surrendered when, after two days of bombardment, an internal fire drove the defenders out into the open. The British Martello towers, as they were called, were designed on the principle that a stout tower, thicker on the seaward side than the landward, could control a beach with only one gun.

At Eastbourne, Hythe and Harwich, the Martello towers were supplemented with redoubts. Ironically perhaps, all the terminology used in their construction was French: redoubt, deriving from the French word for shelter, in this context means a circular fortress, armed with ten cannons and garrisoned with 350 soldiers. Artillery had improved since the days of the star-shaped fortress, of which the most complete British example is Tilbury (see page 290). There was more long-distance pounding, less fighting at close quarters. The Eastbourne redoubt, built directly onto the shingle of the beach, crouched behind a deep, shelving earth bank (or glacis), on the far side of which lay a dry moat. Attackers would have been sprayed with grapeshot from the guns as they tried to scramble up. The moat could not be allowed to fill with water or the walls would have collapsed; but to give extra protection they contained five covered ditches (or caponiers) from which the defenders could fire. As yet the town of Eastbourne did not exist (it was developed in the middle of the 19th century): the site was strategic because of its position between the marshy Pevensey Levels, which could be artificially flooded, and the cliffs.

Begun in 1804, the Eastbourne redoubt was not completed until 1810. By then, the threat of invasion had long passed. It could not have taken place without French control of the English Channel. Napoleon, frustrated by what he regarded as the under-performance of his navy, abandoned the plan, and marched off to invade Russia instead. The British victory at Trafalgar in 1805 put the last nail in the French navy's coffin. We cannot know how effective the redoubts and Martello towers would have been in repelling the French. We do know, however, that the Eastbourne redoubt quickly became obsolete. Guns mounted on parapets were shortly to be replaced by ones protected by tunnels. By the 1860s, the redoubt had lost military credibility – although it was pressed back into service, to shelter stores and men, before the D-Day landings of 1944 (see page 54).

EMSWORTH

Breeding ground for comedy of genius

In the annals of English comic literature, Emsworth has a cherished place. It provides the title of the absent-minded, pig-besotted earl, whose seat is Blandings Castle. The quest, among P. G. Wodehouse aficionados, for the model upon which Blandings was based equals that for the Holy Grail. It eludes capture. A striking number of the *dramatis personae* of the Wodehouse tales, however, owe their names to the spell (relatively short) during which the author lived in the oyster-fishing town of Emsworth near Chichester. The house he rented and then bought was called Threepwood. Freddie Threepwood, Lord Emsworth's son, would have been bereft without it.

Threepwood stands in Record Road. This was originally called Beach Road; Beach is the name of Lord Emsworth's butler. From Emsworth, Wodehouse on one occasion bicycled the 65 miles to London – a feat replicated, in other circumstances, by Bertie Wooster. Not far away is Hayling Island, where a policeman was once thrown into the harbour. Surely this sowed the seed for all those unfortunate incidents with officers of the law which are a leitmotif of the Wooster stories.

Wodehouse first came to Emsworth in 1903. He rented Threepwood from 1904–07 and bought it in 1910. He was by now shuttling between London and New York, as well as up and down to Sussex. Threepwood was sold some time before the First World War, but it was typical of Wodehouse that, though his best books were written in the 1920s and 1930s, he should have reverted to names he had encountered in the Edwardian era. In some ways, the world he created around Bertie Wooster glowed with the nostalgia of a long Edwardian afternoon; in other ways, it is timeless.

EPSOM RACECOURSE

Scene of the tragic 'Votes for Women' protest

King George V's horse Anmer was never going to win the 1913 Derby, held – as it had been since the Earl of Derby first organised the race in 1780 – on Epsom Downs. The horse was lying third to last as the field came out of Tattenham Corner. Emily Davison, ducking under the rails with a shout of 'Votes for Women', probably misjudged the speed of the tightly bunched front-runners thundering past her. Without even knowing that Anmer belonged to the King, she darted forward to seize its bridle. The horse ploughed into her, fell and threw its jockey. An early cinema film captures the incident: the heads of most top-hatted racegoers were still turned the other way, watching the finish of the race. Emily Davison never regained consciousness. The suffragettes had a martyr.

The reaction of the British public was not all that she might have hoped for. In a maddeningly British way, the Press showed more concern for the harm to the jockey, Herbert Jones (fractured rib), and even the horse (bruised shins), than the fatally injured crusader. By now, they were used to suffragette outrages. Led by Emmeline Pankhurst, the Women's Social and Political Union had concluded around 1905 that peaceful argument was not, by itself, enough to win women the vote, turning instead to a campaign to inconvenience the male leaders of the Establishment – and shock society. They discovered that the hunger strike was an effective weapon against prison sentences. After Emily Davison's death, they attempted to burn down houses belonging to politicians (partially succeeding in the case of Lloyd George), as well as such male preserves as cricket pavilions, golf clubhouses and race-course stands.

When the First World War was declared, the WSPU suspended hostilities against the government, demanding a different form of equality instead of votes – the right to serve their country by doing war work. It was a shrewd move. War gave the nation a practical experience of equality, as women showed their competence in jobs that would previously have been done by men. Afterwards, they could no longer be denied the vote. First, by an overwhelming House of Commons majority in 1918, the vote was granted to women of property over the age of thirty, then the Representation of the People Act finally gave women the same voting rights as men in 1928.

FISHBOURNE ROMAN PALACE
Biggest Roman building north of the Alps

NEAR CHICHESTER, WEST SUSSEX

In 1960, the water board was cutting a trench across a field near Chichester when a mass of old rubble was encountered. In due course, this led to the excavation of a palace, built towards the end of the 1st century AD, of extraordinary size – bigger than that in Rome of the Emperor Nero. It is, in fact, the biggest Roman building to have been discovered north of the Alps.

The site, near the village of Fishbourne, was an obvious one for a settlement, since it lies on the edge of a sheltered natural harbour to the south coast, convenient for trading with Gaul. It seems to have been used as a Roman supply base soon after the Roman invasion of AD43 (see page 89); a granary and other wooden structures were built at this time. In the 60s, a fairly substantial villa with a bath house was erected – a sign that the Romans had decided to stay, having found Britain to be worth some investment.

This building, however, was eclipsed by the great palace that was begun around AD75. Entered by deep porticos and built around a big central courtyard, it could have come straight from the Mediterranean. The most elaborate of the luxurious mosaics, from the middle of the 2nd century AD, shows a cupid riding on a dolphin – hardly the sort of scene much observed from the shingly beaches of the Sussex coast. The owner of the villa may have been used to the harsh climate since archaeologists believe that he could have been the local British chieftain Cogidubnus, who sided with the Romans and was perhaps being treated with great favour as an example to others. Since the workmen who constructed the villa must have come from Gaul or Italy, it is likely to have been ordered by Emperor Vespasian. Vespasian, who had been the military commander in Britain, would have known Cogidubnus.

But we cannot be sure. Whoever the owner was, a guess may be made at his family life. A girl's gold ring suggests that he had a daughter. A marble fragment of a boy's head may mean that she had a brother. Did they run around the gardens of the courtyard, hiding among the box hedges and running in and out of the fountains? In later centuries, the villa was too big to be maintained in the sumptuous manner of the early owners. Only parts were lived in. Towards the end of the 3rd century, a fine underfloor central heating system, or hypocaust, was built, but seems never to have been used. Before it was ready, a disastrous fire had consumed the palace. Rivulets of lead ran from the roofs and formed puddles on the ground. It was the end of Fishbourne, until Professor Barry Cunliffe led the excavations of the 1960s.

GAD'S HILL
NEAR ROCHESTER, KENT
The world of Charles Dickens

Charles Dickens's first words as a novelist, in Pickwick Papers, evoke Rochester, and Rochester is the subject of the last words that he wrote, in his unfinished novel The Mystery of Edwin Drood. Dickens was born near Portsmouth in 1812, but spent the five happiest years of his childhood around Rochester, when his father, John, had worked as a naval pay clerk at Chatham Dockyard (see page 62). When Dickens was ten, the debt-ridden John Dickens moved the family to London, and the surroundings of the insalubrious dockyard (full of sailors and low life), the cathedral city (struggling to maintain its respectability) and the Medway landscape (like a Dutch painting, where the mood changes with the light) were replaced by the alarming alleyways of a great city. Two years later, John Dickens was arrested for debt and confined, with his wife and youngest children, in the Marshalsea prison (see page 199). Dickens spent thirteen months working in a shoe polish factory, pasting labels onto tins. It was as though childhood had been snatched away and education denied him. His earlier happiness in Kent took on a still-rosier glow.

In those fondly remembered days, his father would take him to see a mellow Queen Anne house some three miles from Rochester, on the Gravesend road.

This was Gad's Hill. Young Charles thought it 'the most beautiful house . . . ever seen', and said to his father that 'if ever I grew up to be a clever man perhaps I might own that house'. He did grow up to be a clever man, and he bought it in 1856. To look at today – with its Victorian bay windows filled with plate glass, and its pimple of a cupola – Gad's Hill is not, in all respects, as beautiful as it appeared to the young Dickens, but it formed the setting for a rollicking family life, the social focus of which were the amateur theatricals that Dickens loved. One of the first guests was the writer of fairy tales, Hans Christian Andersen, whose Nordic propensity to gloom did not chime well with Dickens's irrepressibility. A card was placed above the looking-glass in his bedroom to read: 'H.C.A. slept in this room for five weeks. To the family it seemed like AGES.'

To pay for Gad's Hill, however, Dickens began to undertake readings from his own works, a task which exhausted him. The strain did not help the harmony of his married life: his wife Catherine was already finding his genius and celebrity too much to keep up with. Within a couple of years, he had developed an infatuation for the young actress Ellen Ternan, which ended his marriage. Catherine left him to Gad's Hill, and an increasing sense of estrangement from the world.

Rochester and its surroundings are described, whether or not by name, in several of Dickens's works, including *David Copperfield* and *Great Expectations*. It is only fitting, therefore, that Rochester has acquired one landmark that belonged originally to Gad's Hill: this is the Swiss chalet, given to Dickens in kit form by his disreputable actor friend Charles Fletcher in 1865, which immediately became his writing room. 'Most delicious' was how Dickens described its situation in his garden, and here he wrote *Our Mutual Friend* and launched into *The Mystery of Edwin Drood*.

Worn out from a lifetime's overwork, Dickens died at Gad's Hill in 1870.

BROADHALFPENNY DOWN   HAMBLEDON, HAMPSHIRE
Thwack of leather on willow

On a shoulder of the Downs outside Hambledon, cricket came of age. It would be an exaggeration to say that cricket was born here. Boys played a game called cricket in the middle of the 16th century. Its development was particularly associated with the Weald of Kent and Sussex, perhaps because of the ironworkers there. A game was played under 'articles of agreement' at Goodwood House in Sussex in 1727. A further set of rules was drawn up in 1744. The Hambledon Club was established in 1750. Fielding a team that was for a time invincible, it developed several aspects of the game that became standard; above all, it played with style.

Its prime mover was the Rev. Charles Powlett. A son of the 3rd Duke of Bolton and the actress Lavinia Fenton, he recruited players from the local countryside, as well as the gentry: the secretary, Richard Nyren, kept the Bat and Ball Inn, overlooking the cricket field. It seems to have been at Hambledon that the modern form of the bat, a straight blade with sloping shoulders, was evolved, in preference to the hockey-stick form that had been used previously. This innovation is associated with the gamekeeper-cum-champion batsman, John Small, who devoted all his spare time to making bats and balls. The modern style of batting, with defensive strokes as well as slogs, developed in response to the bowling of legendary figures such as the great David Harris, a potter by trade, who, despite the under-arm style of the age, was able to make the ball lift quickly towards the wicket.

With the founding of the Marylebone Cricket Club (MCC) in 1787, the Hambledon Club was eclipsed. From here on, Lord's Cricket Ground in London would become the game's most hallowed turf. In its day, however, the Hambledon side could take on All-England and win.

HAMPTON COURT SURREY
Another palace for Henry VIII

Magnificence: the word sums up Henry VIII's aesthetic philosophy and explains, in part, why he seemed to do so many things to excess. At a feast, the sideboards would groan with the gold plate on display; these were vessels that may have been a stylistic mix but served as a very visible expression of royal liquidity (they were the first things to be melted down in times of crisis). In the same spirit, Henry came to own no fewer than sixty-three houses. Even by Renaissance standards, it was an exceptional number: indeed, he was the most prodigious acquirer and builder of houses that England has ever known.

His first architectural mentor was Cardinal Wolsey. After Wolsey's fall from grace (see page 328), following his failure to secure the annulment of Henry's first marriage to Catherine of Aragon, Henry showed his enthusiasm for the Cardinal's taste by seizing his three houses.

The greatest of them was Hampton Court, conveniently situated on the river Thames which, in Tudor England, was the equivalent of a motorway, linking the most important royal residences. Gaily caparisoned oarsmen rowed the royal barge up and down the river, sometimes to the accompaniment of music. One of the virtues of the elaborate astronomical clock which Henry installed over a gate at Hampton Court was that it told the time of the tides.

Houses became something of a hobby to Henry VIII. He took considerable personal interest in the improvements of those that he owned, and at Hampton Court Anne Boleyn (see page 75) seems to have joined in the fun. In moving between his large number of residences, Henry was following the practice of all English monarchs since William I. The King would descend upon his far-flung properties, as well as the houses of his courtiers, during the summer, as part of a progress around his realm to show himself to his people. In the winter, the royal Court shifted between the different houses around London, of which Hampton Court was one. There were various reasons for this, not least to clean thoroughly those that had been recently vacated. The winter movements followed a previously prepared timetable known as the gist. The King had a great dread of the plague and the Court would decamp as soon as an outbreak occurred in the vicinity of where they were staying, or alter course if any case had been found near their intended destination.

A Tudor palace was essentially a theatre. When Henry and his Court were not there to people the rooms, they would have stood empty, almost bare of decoration. The King's rich furniture, brightly coloured tapestries and opulent household effects preceded him from house to house. Again like a stage production, all Henry's building projects were characterised by their extreme urgency. Wolsey's palace had been built quickly: he began it when appointed Archbishop of York in 1514; eleven years later (not much time in view of the scale of the undertaking) the royal apartments that he created for King Henry and his queen, Catherine of Aragon, were completed. It was constructed from the material that had come into vogue since England became settled after the Wars of the Roses: brick. When Henry VIII got his hands on the palace in 1528, he at once began to reorganise it, so that his lodging was not on top of the Queen's (by then Anne Boleyn) but next door. While Wolsey kept a household of 600, the King's was of 1,500. Naturally, this meant that the kitchens and sculleries required to service the Great Hall had to be greatly extended.

While Greenwich had been the palace of Henry's athletic youth, Hampton Court was designed to satisfy his corpulent middle age, so there was less provision for jousting and tournaments, but what might now be termed a leisure complex was formed out of Hampton Court's real tennis courts and bowling alleys. Perhaps we would have a different image of Henry VIII if it had been Greenwich rather than Hampton Court which survived. As it is, Hampton Court stands as his pre-eminent memorial.

HEVER CASTLE
Childhood home of Anne Boleyn

NEAR EDENBRIDGE, KENT

Anne Boleyn* grew up at Hever Castle in Kent. The castle had been built at the end of the 14th century, square, strong, moated but not very big, and later modernised, with Tudor window and chimneys, by Anne's grandfather, Sir Geoffrey Bullen, a former Lord Mayor of London. Anne was probably born in

1507, on the Bullens' other estate of Blickling in Norfolk. Her father, Sir Thomas Bullen, had married Lady Elizabeth Howard, eldest daughter of the Duke of Norfolk, and it was after her death in 1512 that the family moved to Hever, using it as their principal home. Hever was more convenient to London and the Court where Sir Thomas was a Gentleman of the Bedchamber. None of the Bullens, however, enlarged the castle to a scale appropriate to a family with high ambitions.

Anne's education was completed at the French Court, but at the outbreak of war she was recalled home in 1521, becoming one of Catherine of Aragon's ladies-in-waiting. It is said that she changed her name to Boleyn following her return from France. She withdrew to Hever at moments of crisis: after the frustration of her love affair with Lord Henry Percy, to avoid plague, at delicate moments during Henry's divorce from Catherine. In the days of their court-ship, Henry would write her ardent letters there, and even visit. The dainty castle and its setting, still remarkably peaceful, must have made a powerful contrast to the dazzle, pomp and intrigue of Court life, where she was a notorious and very public figure.

Perhaps she thought of Hever when putting on the grey damask robe, ermine cape and white cap that she wore to the scaffold.

*See Hampton Court, page 74

ROYAL BOTANIC GARDENS KEW, SURREY
A great scientific institution is formed by a king and a gardener

As a scientific institution, the Royal Botanic Gardens at Kew owe their existence to two men: George III and Sir Joseph Banks. George III had an especial affection for Kew because he had made it his family's private retreat – a new concept for the monarchy, which had hitherto lived largely in the public gaze. His mother, Princess Augusta, had an estate here, which she had employed the architect Sir William Chambers to landscape: he built the chinoiserie pagoda that was completed in 1762. A botanical garden was created under the eye of Lord Bute – who made a far better botanist and patron of the arts than he did a prime minister – and tended by William Aiton, previously of the Chelsea Physic Garden. On his mother's death in 1772, George III united this estate with an adjacent one that he had inherited from his grandfather George II. Having greatly admired Bute for his knowledge of botany, he fell out with him over politics. At the very time that he needed to find someone to develop the garden, Sir Joseph Banks came within the royal orbit.

Banks was already a celebrity. The son of a wealthy Lincolnshire landowner, from whom he inherited at the age of twenty-one, he had accompanied

Captain Cook on his voyages of exploration in the *Endeavour* (see page 400). In developing Kew, Banks was able to call upon the many scientific contacts he had made around the world. In addition, the King's name could be invoked to encourage ambassadors and the East India Company to help in collecting plants and seeds. Banks was a systematic man. Hoping to rival and surpass similar institutions in Paris and Vienna, he organised a programme of plant collecting that would be as comprehensive as possible. Gardeners from Kew were sent to southern Africa, the Canaries, Australia and South America. They not only sent back plants, but details of the soil in which they grew and the conditions in which they flourished. Two gardeners from Kew were on the *Bounty* when Captain Bligh sailed to Tahiti to collect breadfruit plants, to be raised and transplanted as a source of cheap food in the West Indies. This particular consignment never reached the West Indies since they were thrown overboard during the famous mutiny.

Today, the Kew Gardens that visitors enjoy do not resemble the gardens as Banks left them. After his death in 1820, they declined for a short time before being rescued by Sir William Hooker who, in 1841, became the first full-time director. Hooker worked in collaboration with – and sometimes in opposition to – the architect Decimus Burton and the landscape architect William Andrews Nesfield; together they created the main landscape features (the Broad Walk, the Pond and the Arboretum), as well as the great Victorian glass houses. However, the principle of universality that Banks established – and was most recently embodied in the Millennium Seed Bank, which seeks to store seeds of every species around the world – provides the basis on which the international fame of the Royal Botanic Gardens now rests.

BATTLE OF LEWES EAST SUSSEX
Simon de Montfort defeats the King

When Simon de Montfort* came from France in 1230, he was a virtually penniless younger son, seeking to reclaim some family estates. Not only did he succeed in persuading Henry III to grant him the estates but he also married Eleanor, the King's sister. Eleanor, who had already been married to the Earl of Pembroke, one of the greatest of Henry's magnates, was regarded as a very big prize indeed – one that should have been reserved, the Court generally thought, for some diplomatic alliance. The marriage incensed many of Henry's supporters, who saw de Montfort as an upstart. De Montfort's problem was that he did not have enough estates to support his mighty position as well as set up his five sons; most of Eleanor's riches were only hers for life.

Under Henry, England was becoming crippled by taxes and famine. The King was unpopular with his nobles, a feeling brought about by the cost of rebuilding

Westminster Abbey, a foolish campaign to make one of his sons King of Sicily, and his insensitive advancement of foreigners. De Montfort became leader of the mighty barons who rose up against Henry, incensed that the King was not adhering to the provisions of Magna Carta. In 1258, Henry was forced to accept the Provisions of Oxford, which subjected his decisions to approval by a council of barons. When the King reneged on these obligations, rebellion broke out.

At the Battle of Lewes in 1264, Simon de Montfort succeeded in taking Henry by surprise. Before dawn, he made his men prostrate themselves before God and put on the white crosses of crusaders: he came from a crusading family and was deeply religious. Then he led them onto a crest of the Downs, below which the King's army was encamped. The King and his followers hurried out from the security of the castle and priory, where they had been lodging. On one wing, Prince Edward (later Edward I), fighting for his father, broke de Montfort's cavalry, but his own charge carried his troops too far from the battlefield. De Montfort's men attacked downhill. Another of the King's sons, Richard of Cornwall, was captured, and the King himself, having had two horses killed underneath him, fled back to Lewes where he and his commanders locked themselves in the priory.

De Montfort realised that any destruction caused by a frontal attack would be damaging to his cause, while a long siege would allow other royalist forces to come to the King's rescue. He therefore negotiated a treaty called the Mise of Lewes, in which Henry promised to abide by the Provisions of Oxford. The deal was cemented by a Parliament called in 1265. To widen the base of de Montfort's support, the assembly included knights of the shires and burgesses, this being the first time commoners had been represented. Although the barons soon tired of 'Simon the Righteous', who was killed at the Battle of Evesham later the same year, the commoners were retained as an element of later Parliaments, and their presence soon became standard. Thus our modern idea of Parliament owes much to this complex, bewitching but despotic man.

*See Kenilworth Castle, page 327

MARGATE BEACH   KENT
Did it give birth to the seaside?

Your holiday began here. Margate was among the first-ever seaside resorts at a time when sea-bathing was equivalent to taking the waters of a spa: medicine rather than frolic. In 1736, an announcement was placed in the *Kentish Post* advertising the 'very convenient bath', which Thomas Barber had constructed, allowing bathers to submit themselves to sea water without the risk of having to 'expose themselves to the open Air'. In time, this contrivance was joined by other bathing apparatuses, so that when Zechariah Cozens wrote *A Tour through the Isle of Thanet and some other parts of East Kent* in 1793 he could 'behold between thirty and forty of these curious machines in a morning hovering on the surface of the water . . . continually revolving in their course, either returning with their cleansed guest or going out with a freight of, perhaps, jolly citizens preparing to wash off the dust and care of a six-month attendance to their counting houses.' In point of strict historical precedence, Margate may have been beaten to the first bathing machine by Scarborough, where one appears in a print of 1735, but Margate was certainly the first resort town to attract a wider range of society than the genteel element, pursuing fashion as well as health. The seaside had at last become fun.

At the beginning of the 19th century, Margate was an easy boat journey from London. It was a much cheaper method of travel than carriage. Soon so many people made the journey for pleasure that in 1810 the *Morning Chronicle* reported that Margate had become a kind of 'epitome of that vast metropolis'. The amusements included a *camera obscura*, a shell grotto and what would become the established seaside tradition of donkey riding along the sandy beach. Among those who came by the steam packet was the world's greatest painter of sea and light, J. M. W. Turner: he first visited the town in the 1780s, when he was eleven, perhaps staying with a relative of his mother's who was a fishmonger. It may have been Margate that fostered his love of the sea; another draw was his landlady Mrs Booth, whose house (now demolished) stood near the pier completed by John Rennie in 1815: on her husband's death, Turner would refer to himself as Mr Booth.

The advent of the railway in the Victorian era brought even greater crowds. Holidays, when they became the norm, were invariably spent at the seaside (rather than in rural areas) because that is where the railways went. Car ownership, which became standard during the beginning of the second half of the 20th century, combined with the rise of package holidays abroad, sent the old seaside towns into decline. Margate was no exception.

See also Blackpool Pleasure Beach, page 355

MUNSTEAD WOOD   NEAR GODALMING, SURREY
Cradle of a gardening revolution

Gertrude Jekyll reinvented the English garden. She rescued it from the showiness and artificiality of the Victorian parterre, gaudily bedded out in geometrical patterns formed out of thousands of plants that had been grown in greenhouses. Her goal was a natural-seeming harmony, achieved by means of woodland walks, daffodil drifts, primula banks and mixed flower borders.

She revived old-fashioned features such as the pergola, smothered, perhaps, in the small, scented blooms of a rambler rose – which she preferred to the big, brightly coloured Victorian hybrid roses. A sense of place was important. Her gardens were the reverse of *arriviste*: they were intended to look mellow and, if anything, more cottagey than they were.

Like Octavia Hill (see page 48), remembered as the founder of the National Trust but equally dedicated to a range of other social causes, Miss Jekyll was more than a gardener. Born in 1843, she trained as an artist, enrolling – unusually for a young Victorian lady – in the Kensington School of Art. She was not only a painter and an embroideress; she might have developed a career as an interior decorator, long before that term had entered the language, but her eyesight failed her and she was forced to give up close work. The garden became her new canvas. She brought to it the taste of an artist.

In 1883, Miss Jekyll bought the 15 acres that would become her own garden of Munstead Wood. It was not until 1896 that her house was completed. The architect was the young Edwin Lutyens (see page 131), who had also been brought up in Surrey and formed his early style from sketches of the old country buildings that he saw there (made using a piece of sharpened soap on glass). At Munstead Wood, these observations are distilled into low-sweeping roofs, tall ribbed brick chimneys, walls of honey-coloured Bargate stone and, flush with them, casement windows in oak frames.

Lutyens was twenty-five when he began to work for Gertrude Jekyll, building first what was known as the Hut, a cottage where she could entertain her friends. This early meeting with Miss Jekyll was the making of him. He became her protégé, and it was she who made the introduction to Edward Hudson, the proprietor of *Country Life*, for which she was the gardening correspondent; his magazine thereafter missed no opportunity to 'boom' Lutyens's career. Lutyens was called upon to design the architecture around which many of Miss Jekyll's most famous gardens (Hestercombe in Somerset, Folly Farm in Berkshire) were created. The thin young architect and the cottage-loaf-shaped, middle-aged gardener made an unlikely looking pair, as Lutyens acknowledged in the sketches that accompanied his letters to his wife: with typical irreverence, his nickname for Miss Jekyll was Aunt Bumps. It was, however, an artistic partnership that lasted until her death in 1932.

RUFUS STONE
NEW FOREST, HAMPSHIRE

William Rufus is killed by an arrow

In the summer of 1100, William Rufus, second surviving son of William the Conqueror, was hunting in the New Forest. Thirteen years before, on his father's death, this stocky, red-faced man had become King of England:

William I had left Normandy to his oldest son, Robert Curthose, and England to his second son. William aggressively sought to oust his elder brother from the dukedom of Normandy. In order to pay for his campaigns, he raided monasteries – in signal contrast to the devout Conqueror, who had been their patron. Architecturally, he is to be remembered for building Westminster Hall, a colossal building for the age (see page 195). The army loved him, but his savage temperament was not the sort to win hearts.

With William Rufus on the hunt that day were the brothers Gilbert and Roger de Clare, along with Walter Tirel, their relation by marriage. Tirel was known to be a fine archer and an arrow from his bow struck the King in the chest, quickly killing him. Was it an accident? Hunting was a dangerous sport. Tirel did not risk being tried but jumped on his horse and rode straight for France. William Rufus's younger brother, Henry Beauclerc, raced to Winchester to seize the Treasury, which represented the most practical form of royal power. He was later crowned Henry I. The de Clares were showered with valuable appointments.

A stone marks the spot where William Rufus's body supposedly lay, little mourned, in the New Forest, before it was taken to Winchester cathedral for burial. After being damaged, the stone was encased in iron in the 19th century.

OSBORNE HOUSE
NEAR COWES, ISLE OF WIGHT

Queen Victoria's children are amused

Prince Albert was at his best with children. Visitors who were privileged enough to enter the royal nurseries could hardly believe the change that came over this stiff, aloof man as he played hide-and-seek. Queen Victoria, although less wholly at ease with her offspring and unable to conquer her distaste for childbirth, nevertheless produced nine children. The royal family offered a model of happy home life to the nation. Osborne House, bought by the Queen with her own money as their holiday home, was the setting for the best of it*.

The nurseries were in Queen Victoria's private wing. As yet, there were none of the nursery wallpapers that appeared at the end of the century; the decoration was not very different from any other country-house bedroom of the period. However, a member of the Royal Household observed that 'all round the room are literally stacks of toys'. Recreations usually had to be morally improving, and little time was to be wasted: Prince Albert, a natural student as a boy, deplored anything that smacked of rowdiness or mindless games. The children had their own little gardening tools with which to raise vegetables. They could play at 'houses' in the Swiss Cottage, especially imported in 1854; its kitchen was fully equipped and the royal children were expected to cook there. Prince Arthur – the future soldier Duke of Connaught –

was allowed to build a model fort, known as Albert Barracks. When Victoria and Albert were a young couple with a growing family, Osborne House rang with the shouts and laughter of childhood. After Prince Albert's death in 1861, Osborne became indelibly shrouded in the cult of his memory that the Queen perpetuated.

*See Balmoral Castle, page 443

PEVENSEY CASTLE
EAST SUSSEX

Roman Britain protects itself against the Saxons

When William the Conqueror (see page 50) jumped ashore onto the shingles of Pevensey Bay in 1066, he must have been grateful for the husk of a castle overlooking the beach. It had been built by the Romans about 775 years earlier, at the end of the 3rd century. Even today, it is an impressive structure, with walls that are 30ft high in places, embracing a site that is the size of a village. Perhaps it was being used as a fishing village when the Norman force landed; if so, it is easy to imagine the inhabitants' terror as they had their homes requisitioned by the invading army. It had not been used for military purposes for over 500 years.

Pevensey became one of a chain of nine forts, known as the 'Saxon Shore' forts, which were built or rebuilt along the south coast. They must have been intended to defend Britain from raids by the Saxons: each was at the mouth of a river, to prevent the interior of the country being penetrated, and they may have had fighting ships stationed alongside them. The castle would have provided a formidable obstacle to invading Saxons. It stood on what was then a promontory, connected to the mainland by a causeway; the marshes of the Pevensey Levels provided further protection. The two most exposed walls are equipped with D-shaped towers – newly introduced to Roman military architecture when the castle was built. The irregular oval plan, rather than rectangular or square, reflects the shape of the promontory. These defences, left by the Romans when they withdrew from Britain in the early 5th century, were not enough to protect the local population from a Saxon raiding party in 491; according to *The Anglo-Saxon Chronicle*, every last one of them was slaughtered.

For centuries, the castle seems to have been deserted. The Normans, having made it their bridgehead before the Battle of Hastings, later built their own keep within the Roman walls. Those ancient walls were once more pressed into service during the Second World War, when Pevensey Bay again seemed to offer a possible landing place for an invasion. Pillboxes were built inside the Roman west gate, and the Home Guard camped within the Norman inner bailey. Happily, Pevensey's preparations were never put to the test.

POLESDEN LACEY

'The nicest place, within a prudent distance of town, in England'

When the playwright and politician Richard Brinsley Sheridan died in 1816, his beloved house at Polesden Lacey was in ruins. He had begun to pull it down, intending to rebuild it, but he was far too deeply in debt. Prospects had looked very different in the 1770s when he was starting out. Before he was thirty, he had eloped to France with Elizabeth Linley, fought a duel, studied law, written *The Rivals* and *School for Scandal*, purchased the Drury Lane Theatre and set himself up in a richly furnished London house, turned to politics, and been elected MP for Stafford. In 1802, he refused a peerage in return for supporting the Tories, saying that he had 'an unpurchasable mind'.

Sheridan bought Polesden Lacey in 1797, five years after the death of his first wife. The purchase was made possible by the dowry of his second wife. Together they extended the elegant terrace walk overlooking the medieval landscape of Ranmore Common, which had been begun by Admiral Geary in the 1750s. He adored playing the squire at Polesden, calling it 'the nicest place, within a prudent distance of town, in England'. His problem, however, was cashflow. His wife's family were not excessively rich, and his principal asset, the Drury Lane Theatre, had to be rebuilt twice, once because it was unsafe and once because it burnt down. After his death, Polesden Lacey's new owner pulled down the house that Sheridan had loved, but the terrace walk survives.

POOH BRIDGE

Adventures of a stout, helpful and immortal Bear

Alan Alexander Milne was a Londoner. With his young son, Christopher, he and his family would go down to a farmhouse at Hartfield at the weekends. This was 1925, and Milne, a prolific writer for *Punch* and the stage, was enjoying the runaway success of a book of verses called *When We Were Very Young*. Accompanying the family in the car would be Christopher's teddy bear, initially called Edward but renamed, more exotically, Winnie, after a real bear in London Zoo. It has never been properly explained how this bear acquired the suffix of '-the-Pooh'.

In the Milne nursery, Winnie-the-Pooh's friends included a piglet and a droopy-necked donkey, both presents from friends. When Milne was pressed to produce another children's book, he made these toys into characters (Piglet and Eeyore), inventing two others, Owl and Rabbit. In search of further inspiration, he and his wife made a special visit to Harrods, where they found Kanga and Roo. The setting for the stories in *Winnie-the-Pooh* and *The House at Pooh Corner* was the surroundings of the farmhouse, with its stream, ditches and woods. The Hundred Acre Wood has its origins in the Five Hundred Acre

Wood outside Hartfield. The bridge from which Christopher Robin played Poohsticks is still there, although it has been rebuilt a couple of times.

The Winnie-the-Pooh books instantly became children's classics in the tradition of *The Wind in the Willows* by Kenneth Grahame and the books by Beatrix Potter (see page 363). Their peculiarly British humour, with its wordplay and classical references, has been carried by many readers into adulthood. In a later age, its characters acquired a new – if to traditionalist admirers, grotesquely unsubtle – life as Disney cartoons, earning those to whom Milne left the copyright – Westminster School, the Garrick Club, the Royal Literary Fund, and his descendants – tens of millions of pounds. The one person to whom Milne's writing brought little pleasure was Pooh's owner, who later told a reporter from the *Sunday Dispatch* that he had always 'hated being Christopher Robin'.

PORTCHESTER CASTLE
Henry V embarks for Agincourt

HAMPSHIRE

For many weeks in the early summer of 1415, Henry V stayed at Portchester Castle, supervising the embarkation of his army at Southampton. A fort had been built in the late 3rd century, as one of the defences of the 'Saxon Shore' (see page 82). The walls, which still stand, enclosed a rectangle that was the size of a large village. For three decades in the 12th century, they were occupied by a priory, which left its church behind when it moved elsewhere. In one corner of the Roman walls, Richard I built a castle, which Richard II turned into a small palace, although he was killed before having the opportunity to stay there.

Assembling the invasion force was an elaborate logistical achievement, for which Henry had been prepared by earlier campaigning in Wales. There were ships of all sizes – as many as 1,500 according to some sources – a few belonging to the King but mostly commandeered. They had to be filled with enough bread, dried fish, salted meat and other rations to sustain an army in the field. The munitions that Henry had been amassing since he came to the throne two years before included siege engines, tubby bombards, elegantly tapering culverins, gun-stones, gunpowder and thousands of arrows. Once they were stowed, hundreds of warhorses needed loading (which, as anyone who has urged a horse up the ramp of a horse lorry will know, is an unpredictable business). The army that gathered consisted of about 2,000 men-at-arms, drawn from the lesser gentry and therefore sufficiently well off to afford the heavy, exhaustingly hot armour in which they fought. They were joined by some 8,000 archers, carrying longbows: having learnt their skills at the archery butts that stood next to every parish church, these anonymous, agile yeomen were to prove England's deadliest weapon*.

The King boarded the pride of his personal navy, a ship newly built at Greenwich called the *Trinity Royal*, gay with banners and streamers. Being the vessel on which he slept, it was known as his chamber, while attendant ships were called his wardrobe, larder and kitchen (an indication of the comfort in which Henry, unlike his soldiery, campaigned). By the time the fleet sailed back into Dover in November, a vastly larger French army – cumbersome, over-confident and poorly led – had stumbled to annihilation in the muddy ditches of Agincourt, the densely packed ranks of French noblemen decimated by the ferocious hail of arrows.

By the time of his death, Henry V ruled a third of France, including Paris. His claim to the French throne had been cemented by marriage to a French princess, Catherine of Valois. However, the prospect of an English king ascending the throne of France was blighted by Henry's early death in 1422. Through his mother, Henry's son, Henry VI, inherited the strain of madness that also incapacitated the French king Charles VI.

*See Monmouth Castle, page 426

PORT LYMPNE *NEAR HYTHE, KENT*
Dazzling home of the aesthete, politician and airman Philip Sassoon

Philip Sassoon, with his sister Sibyl, later Marchioness of Cholmondeley and the chatelaine of Houghton (see page 274), was a glittering figure. Descended from Jews from Baghdad, he was most frequently referred to as 'oriental' – a term which applied to his riches, his spectacular hospitality, and his super-suave manner, which was generally thought to be an expression of homo-sexuality (although there is no documentation to confirm it, since his sister destroyed his intimate papers before her death). Sassoon came into his inheritance when he was twenty-three. His father had represented the Hythe constituency in Parliament, and Sassoon took on the seat at his death in 1912, becoming the youngest MP in the House of Commons.

It provoked him to commission a house from Herbert Baker, a rather stuffy choice, best known for his buildings in the Cape Dutch manner. A room was decorated by the Catalan artist José-María Sert with, as the Prime Minister Herbert Asquith put it, 'elephants in different attitudes'. 'Personally, I think it monstrous,' wrote Philip with studied nonchalance. Later, the murals were painted over and the gardens laid out by the more suitable Philip Tilden, in a style recalling the Hollywood film *Ben Hur*. The Roman theme evoked the nearby Roman fort of *Lemanis*.

Throughout the First World War, Sassoon served as Field-Marshal Douglas Haig's private secretary, which introduced him to many of the leading political figures in Europe. Afterwards, Sassoon made Port Lympne available to Lloyd George for post-war talks with the French government. His most important contribution to politics was as minister for the fledgling Royal Air Force. He learnt to fly, and invited crowds of airmen to mingle with the grand and influential guests at Port Lympne. It helped champion the young service. Eyebrows, however, were raised. Sassoon died in 1939. It would have pleased him that the airfields around Hythe helped save Britain from invasion during the Battle of Britain.

THE MARY ROSE

PORTSMOUTH, HAMPSHIRE

The perils of putting artillery on Tudor ships

The great development in Tudor warfare was artillery. This revolutionised the design of castles, such as St Mawes (see page 35); it also posed a question to Henry VIII's shipbuilders, who had to create vessels that would be floating platforms for guns. At fore and aft would be a raised superstructure called a castle, from which guns bristled in all directions. But the higher that ships were built and the more gun ports that were opened on the ships' sides down towards sea level, the less seaworthy they became. Many of them sank.

This was the fate of the *Mary Rose*. She had been commissioned shortly after Henry VIII became king in 1509. The young monarch, determined to prove himself on the European stage, spent heavily on upgrading his navy. The *Mary Rose* saw action against the French, was sent north to deter the Scots, and in 1520 escorted Henry VIII on his journey to the Field of the Cloth of Gold near Calais. After some years of inactivity, she sailed again into battle against a French invasion fleet off Portsmouth that had been mustered after the English capture of Boulogne. It was then, in July 1545, that she went down, possibly because the crew was too unruly to obey orders, possibly because water rushed in through the lowest level of gun ports, probably because of a combination of factors, of which the most fundamental was a flaw in design. She had been refitted and upgraded shortly before. It had made her top-heavy.

Nearly all the ship's company, from the officers with their shining pewter dishes to the crew with their wooden platters, were drowned. On the seabed, the ship settled on her starboard side, which quickly became filled with silt. The exposed timbers of the port side rotted away, and the site was sealed with a deposit of clay. This preserved not only the buried ship's timbers, but also thousands of artefacts, ranging from bronze cannons and iron shot to quill pens, an inlaid backgammon set and musical instruments. Boxes of longbows (made of yew; see page 426) and thousands of arrows (made of poplar, beech and ash) show that archers were still needed to support the cumbersome and wayward guns.

In 1982, the remains of the *Mary Rose* were raised in an astonishing rescue operation, and they are now preserved in a perpetual mist to prevent the timbers from crumbling away.

HMS VICTORY

PORTSMOUTH, HAMPSHIRE

The deck on which Nelson fell

Horatio Nelson and HMS *Victory* were born just one year apart, the admiral in 1758 at Burnham Thorpe in Norfolk, and the ship's keel being laid down at Chatham Dockyard* in 1759. When, aged twelve, he went to join his first ship at Chatham, he would have seen *Victory* floating at her moorings. She had been launched in 1765 but, without a war to provide money, she was not fitted out with the necessary 26 miles of rigging, 37 sails and 100-plus guns until 1778. Consequently, the hull timbers were unusually well seasoned, which may explain her longevity. She was one of the fastest 'first-rate' battleships, and was popular with a succession of admirals who raised their flag in her. Admiral Keppel was the first; later came Admirals Kempenfelt, Howe, Hood and Jervis, among others.

Fresh from her 'great repair', HMS *Victory* became Nelson's flagship in May 1803. By this date, Nelson was already a national hero, loved both by the crowds and Lady Hamilton. He would often say that a battle would win him either a tomb in Westminster Abbey (St Paul's Cathedral, as it turned out) or a peerage.

Once he had boarded the *Victory*, Nelson lived on her for two years. It was a monotonous period as he blockaded the French into the port of Toulon at the same time as trying to tempt them to put to sea so he could fight them. The effect of the blockades of Toulon and Brest was to prevent Napoleon from invading Britain. During this period, Nelson would invite his captains onto the *Victory*, explaining his ideas about warfare so that each was fully conversant with the planned strategy before battle was joined; thereafter, they had the confidence to act on their own judgement. The French slipped out of Toulon, were chased to the West Indies and back, and by the autumn of 1805 a combined French and Spanish fleet was blockaded into Cadiz. Napoleon, believing that his navy could perform the impossible, was as keen as Nelson to get the fleet onto open water. The result was the Battle of Trafalgar, fought on 21 October.

There were 821 men on board the *Victory* that day, their ages ranging from twelve to sixty-seven. Their faith in their admiral must have been tested as a light breeze carried the *Victory* at the head of one of the two columns at right angles to the enemy line. This allowed the French and Spanish ships to fire their broadsides at the approaching British, before the *Victory* could return a shot. The first of the *Victory*'s guns to fire was the carronade on the port side, loaded with 6½lb of powder, a cannon ball and 500 musket balls. This tore into the stern of the French flagship *Bucentaure*, raking it from end to end. Then came broadside after broadside from the 88 guns mounted on the three gun decks, sometimes only feet away from their opponents. By the end of the day, *Victory*'s gunners had used 7½ tons of gunpowder to fire 28 tons of shot.

Victory became locked in a deadly embrace with the French ship *Redoutable*, when their rigging became entangled. As fate would have it, Captain Lucas of the *Redoutable* had been one of the few captains to put the time that the French and Spanish had spent blockaded into Cadiz to good use, by training his men in musketry. It was a musket ball from a French sharpshooter in *Redoutable*'s mizzen-top that killed Nelson. A plate on the deck of the *Victory* marks the spot where he fell, but he died knowing that a great victory had been won.

*See Chatham Dockyard, page 62

THE GRANGE RAMSGATE, KENT
Pugin's moral crusade to revive Gothic architecture

Born in 1812, Augustus Welby Northmore Pugin was a one-man architectural revolution. Since the building of the Queen's House at Greenwich (see page 165), three centuries of English architecture can be explained as an attempt to re-create the glories of the ancient world through classicism. Pugin was proselytiser-in-chief for the Gothic revival. There had been an antiquarian interest in Gothic architecture before his time; in the late 18th century, Horace Walpole and others were captivated by its antiquity and associations. Pugin added the passion and self-conviction that came from his identification of the Gothic style with Christian belief. In his books, he referred to it simply as Christian architecture. Its propagation was, for Pugin, a moral crusade, associated with his vision of medieval England as a golden age of religion and social harmony, both of which were dispensed by a beneficent church. With some courage for an architect who aspired to build churches in 19th-century Britain, he converted to Roman Catholicism in 1835.

The son of the illustrator Auguste Charles Pugin, a French émigré, he had begun his career as an antique dealer, buying on the Continent and sailing home with his newly acquired stock. His moral and architectural ideals are embodied in the house and church that he built for his family in Ramsgate. He bought the land for it in 1840. By this date he had worked with Charles Barry on the Houses of Parliament*; built country houses at Alton Towers in Staffordshire and Scarisbrick Hall in Lancashire; finished his first church, St Mary's, Uttoxeter; and published *Contrasts*. That year he began St Giles,

Cheadle, and he continued the hectic pace of work that he had set himself, partly to pay for his building works, over the next decade. With money only available in fits and starts, it took ten years to build The Grange and the church of St Augustine; the architect had only two years to enjoy them before his death from syphilis at the age of forty.

Pugin had come to know Ramsgate through visiting an aunt. A seaside location suited his passion for sailing: he once remarked that 'There is nothing worth living for but Christian Architecture and a boat.' The Grange, as he called his house, was built with a look-out tower from which he would scan the Goodwin Sands for signs of ships in distress. Built of pale-coloured brick with stone dressings beneath a slate roof, the house is externally sombre, as is the church. It is easy to imagine Pugin obsessively working in his study, separated from the drawing room by a curtain so that he would not be disturbed by the sound of slamming doors. It is rather less easy to picture Pugin as an expansive host, with a succession of neighbours, priests, medievalists and the occasional noble client being welcomed to a household romping with eight children.

*See Palace of Westminster, page 197

RICHBOROUGH ROMAN FORT   NEAR SANDWICH, KENT
Rome's gateway to Britain

'Welcome to Britain. It is Roman now.' This was the implied message of a giant triumphal arch that stood in the centre of the Roman fort and seaport of *Rutupiae*, now Richborough. *Rutupiae* is likely to have been the place where Aulus Plautius landed with 40,000 troops in AD43, giving the arch, which was built some forty years later, additional significance. Rising to a height of over 80ft, it was the biggest structure that most of the natives had ever seen, and it must have been visible for miles across this marshy landscape. The faces of the arch were covered with white Carrara marble, brought from Italy, and adorned with inscriptions. All that remains of the arch itself are the foundations, extending to a depth of about 30ft. Above ground, visitors can see the footings for the piers of the arch and the base of the raised causeway, intersecting in the form of a cross, that went through it. This was the beginning of Watling Street, which runs via London to Wroxeter and Chester.

Julius Caesar* was long gone, following his invasion of Britain in 55BC, when Emperor Claudius, looking for a military triumph to put lustre on his rule, ordered the second Roman invasion. He arrived in person, after the fighting was over†. The fort at *Rutupiae* would then have consisted of two rows of deep ditches surrounding a timber palisade. The site was, at that time, practically an island, cut off from the mainland at high tide. This in turn stood in a wide channel that has since disappeared, dividing the Isle of Thanet from the rest of Kent. Military defences proved unnecessary, since the legions met little local opposition, but the fort became an important supply base for the march on East Anglia, and thereafter a port. Other stone buildings came to complement the triumphal arch – shops and a courtyard house that served as a rest house – and the whole site was enclosed by a wall made of flint inlaid with tile courses. Wine was brought in big earthenware jars, or *amphorae*, from the slopes of Mount Vesuvius. The Romans had indeed arrived.

*See Walmer Beach, page 97. †See Colchester, page 265

ROCHESTER CASTLE   KENT
The tallest Norman keep in England

Rochester Castle is the Norman keep of Norman keeps. The position was strategic: it was not only the place where the Roman road of Watling Street crossed the river Medway, but was in an area that was rich and productive. The town of Rochester had been important since Roman days, so in the years immediately after the Conquest a wooden motte and bailey castle was rushed up. The fortification that replaced it, probably on a different site, was one of the earliest to be built in stone. It is also, at 125ft, the highest Norman keep in England – an armoured Norman fist slammed down onto the Kentish countryside, to keep this valuable swathe of the new kingdom in its grasp.

Typically, the Normans made use of pre-existing Roman walls to help them build more quickly (they did the same at Pevensey, Portchester and the Tower of London*). Work began under the Conqueror's son, William Rufus. He commissioned Gundulf, Bishop of Rochester, to oversee the building of the curtain wall: Gundulf was regarded as an expert in stone construction and he seems also to have directed the building of the massive White Tower at the Tower of London.

In the next reign, Henry I granted the custody of Rochester Castle to the Archbishop of Canterbury and his successors in perpetuity. It was Archbishop William de Corbeuil who built the towering keep, which served both as a dramatic fortress and a luxurious residence. Although the keep has long been gutted internally, the arcade on the second, or principal, floor, with its fine round-headed Norman arches, survives as part of a grand apartment that was 27ft tall.

Politically, it was unwise to grant so important a castle to the Archbishops of Canterbury since an archbishop could easily combine with forces hostile to the king. King John greatly disliked Archbishop Stephen Langton, and had done what he could to block his appointment by the Pope. While the signing of Magna Carta in the spring of 1215 (see page 238) should have placated the rebellious barons, a party of them occupied Rochester in the summer of that year, with the intention of blocking John's route from Dover to their stronghold of London. It may be supposed that this was done with the Archbishop's tacit consent. John laid siege to the castle, undermining the walls and then burning the pit props using the fat of forty pigs which were slaughtered for the purpose. A number of the rebels had their hands and feet chopped off, although only one seems to have been hanged.

*See Pevensey Castle, page 82; Portchester Castle, page 84; The White Tower, page 189

LAMB HOUSE

RYE, EAST SUSSEX

Home of the master of the interminable sentence

Through his novels, Henry James created a platonic ideal of country-house life, as it could be lived – in theory – by cultivated, emotionally exquisite individuals in Europe and the United States. Born in America, he made England his home and eventually, during the First World War, he became a British subject. Although his social range was restricted to the rich and aesthetic, he defined a certain kind of Englishness, partly because he could contrast it so acutely with its equivalent across the Atlantic.

In the summer of 1896 James rented a cottage in Rye belonging to his friend, the architect Sir Reginald Blomfield. There he began what he thought would be a hopeless and unrequited passion for an early Georgian house that had been built by a mayor of Rye, James Lamb. A year later, the local ironmonger, to whom he had mentioned his love of the house, wrote to say that, unexpectedly, the owner had died; James finally acquired Lamb House, and revelled in the hunt for 'a sufficient quantity of ancient mahogany-and-brass odds and ends' with which to furnish it.

E. F. Benson, the creator of the Mapp and Lucia novels who was to later share Lamb House with his brother, A. C. Benson, after James's death, remembered the disembodied voice of the author dictating characteristically long and involved sentences to his patient secretary in the Garden Room (sadly hit by a stray bomb during the Second World War). The books written at Lamb House include *The Awkward Age*, *The Wings of the Dove*, *The Ambassadors* and *The Golden Bowl*.

THE WAKES

Gilbert White's painstaking record of Creation's daily wonders

Until the mid-19th century, Selborne in Hampshire was effectively isolated, being reached only by a narrow sunken lane, in places nearly 18ft below the level of the surrounding fields. In 1720, the naturalist Gilbert White was born in this village, where his grandfather was vicar. His family moved away, but came back when Gilbert was nine, occupying an old property called The Wakes on the other side of the road from the vicarage. White went up to Oxford: if he had chosen his grandfather's college, Magdalen, rather than Oriel, he might have become vicar of Selborne, which was in the gift of the college; as it was he became a fellow of Oriel, his modest funds being supplemented by the livings from two parishes, both inconveniently far from Selborne, to which he returned. From then on, he felt little need to leave his native village, becoming its curate: he was a home-loving, sometimes lonely bachelor, with a genius for observing the natural world around him.

During the 1750s, White improved The Wakes by creating a garden in the fashionable landscape taste, but on the homely scale that fitted his pocket. As well as laying out a path known as the zig-zag, digging a ha-ha and planting a quincunx of firs (four trees at each corner and one in the middle), he created a seat on a mound in the form of a half-barrel, which could be turned round, and a two-dimensional statue of Hercules, painted onto board. He began a 'Garden Kalendar', noting the progress of his vegetables. In 1767 he started a correspondence with the naturalist Thomas Pennant, whom he had probably met in his brother Benjamin's bookshop in London. Pennant encouraged him to keep a naturalist's journal, and in this he meticulously recorded trees as they came into leaf each spring, frogs as they developed, birds as they came and went, not to mention the weight of his pet tortoise Timothy, both before and after hibernation.

White's letters to Pennant and others, supplemented by historical research, formed the basis of his life's work *The Natural History and Antiquities of Selborne in the County of Southampton*, published in 1788. Its theme, as White wrote in the Advertisement, is 'the wonders of Creation, too frequently overlooked as common occurrences': the microcosm of an 18th-century clergyman, given new relevance as a yardstick by which Nature's response to climate change can be measured.

Dying in 1793, White was buried in Selborne churchyard.

SHOREHAM AIRPORT

Britain's oldest licensed airfield

The music hall artiste and painter Harold Piffard was also an aviator; he designed his own aircraft and flew it from what would become Shoreham airfield in 1910, only seven years after Orville Wright had made the first successful flight (lasting twelve seconds) at Kitty Hawk, North Carolina. An airfield was opened at Shoreham in 1911, in time for the Circuit of Europe and Circuit of Britain air races that took place later that year. Britain's first air cargo flight was made shortly afterwards, when a Valkyrie monoplane whined its way a few miles along the coast to Hove. Shoreham remains Britain's oldest licensed airfield*.

The terminal building is a perfect essay in the forward-looking International Style of the 1930s – boxy, bright, angular, with metal-framed windows folding around the corners. In the control tower, every side is a continuous line of windows, over which the roof seemingly hovers without visible support; from the inside, this gives unimpeded views in all directions. The tall booking hall leads into a restaurant, where it is still pleasant to watch the manoeuvres of light aircraft and helicopters only a few feet away. The architect, Stavers Hessel Tiltman, wanted his building, with its steel frame, to look as though it had been made out of concrete: in reality the concrete render is a skin covering walls of brick, but the message of the architecture was clear. By the time the terminal opened in 1936, flying had lost the pioneering, daredevil image of its Harold Piffard days; it was the way of the future.

*See Croydon Airport, page 64

SILCHESTER ROMAN TOWN

Best-preserved Roman walls in Britain

The Romans knew how to build. Some of the most impressive ruins that they have left behind, such as Hadrian's Wall and Caerleon*, were the work of the army, but civilian townspeople could also achieve remarkable feats of construction. In the late 3rd century, the civic authorities protected Silchester, then apparently called *Calleva Atrebatum*, with walls that were 1½ miles in circumference. A century earlier, earth ramparts had been deemed adequate to *Calleva*'s defensive needs; the new walls now stood on the ramparts and probably rose to a height of about 20ft, with a parapet on top. Although the highest point today, by the south gate, is only 14½ft, the line of the walls, enclosing an irregular polygon, remains complete: a testament to the determination of those who built them. They are nearly 10ft wide at the base, and are constructed mostly of flint dressed on the outside, with, as at Richborough (see page 89), bonding courses, in this case of stone. It has been estimated that over 100,000 wagonloads of flints, thought to have been hauled from 6 miles away, would have been needed; in addition, 45,000 wagonloads of stone slabs had to toil their way from near Bath, 50 miles away. Clearly the people of *Calleva*, like those of other towns around the western Empire, feared the growing unrest. Even so, life remained sufficiently safe during the next century for suburbs to continue outside the walls.

As its name suggests, *Calleva Atrebatum* was not just a Roman town. It had been founded before the invasion, by the Atrebates tribe, perhaps under a leader called Commius who had escaped from Gaul. The Atrebates traded with Rome, and therefore welcomed the invasion of AD43. Shortly before this, *Calleva* had been occupied by the Catuvellauni, a tribe centred round St Albans and similarly well disposed towards Rome. That early settlement had grown piecemeal but, with the arrival of the Romans, it was swept away and replaced by a typical Roman grid, complete with forum, amphitheatre, temples, public baths and inn. The streets are clearly visible in aerial photographs. Although only the walls are still standing, the 107-acre town that they enclosed is, to archaeologists, unusually intact. It was one of few important Roman centres not to develop into a modern town.

*See Hadrian's Wall, page 389, and Caerleon, page 411

STOKE D'ABERNON NEAR LEATHERHEAD, SURREY
The earliest example of an unusually British art form

The brass memorials in British churches provide the best portrait gallery of prosperous medieval society. There are some 3,000 altogether, situated above or near the place where the figures depicted are buried. While great nobles commissioned three-dimensional effigies, brass was for knights, merchants and priests, important figures in their communities but otherwise obscure. At one time, monumental brasses would have been equally common in Continental Europe, but religious upheaval, war and revolution have destroyed much of this visual record of the well-to-do. Only a handful of brasses survive in France, Italy and the Iberian peninsula; the greatest concentration is in the east of Germany and Poland.

Britain's oldest complete brass, dating from c.1320, commemorates Sir John d'Abernon the Elder, in the parish church of St Mary in Stoke d'Abernon. It portrays a sober, warlike figure in a painstakingly detailed suit of chain mail. He carries a lance with a pennon (a very rare detail), the end of the lance being chewed by a lion who just manages to keep out of the long spurs attached to Sir

John's feet. A remarkable feature of this effigy is that the blue field of Sir John's shield is made of enamel: no other example of this material on a brass is found before 1490. Next to Sir John lies the brass commemorating his son, also Sir John, who wears the more decorative plate armour that had developed by the time of his death fifty years later.

The d'Abernons were typical of the cadre for whom monumental brasses were made, very often ordered before their deaths. The family came over with the Norman Conquest but never rose above the gentry station into which they were first placed. Little is known about Sir John the Elder except for one episode that took place while he was sheriff of Surrey. An armed gang frightened him and his clerk into allowing ten barrels of woad to be removed out of his keeping in Guildford Castle, for which he was fined what must have been the enormous sum of £80. The exceptional event in his life was the decision to commission this beautiful and revolutionary memorial.

RAF TANGMERE   *NEAR CHICHESTER, WEST SUSSEX*
Airfield that helped win the Battle of Britain

In 1940, Tangmere outside Chichester became a familiar name on the cinema newsreels reporting the Battle of Britain; Biggin Hill to the east of Croydon and Hawkinge close to Folkestone on the Kent coast were others. Fighter Command was at Northolt to the west of London, but the best airfields were the ones closest to the south coast, where Spitfires and Hurricanes could be scrambled to intercept the enemy over the English Channel. A satellite airfield at Westhampnett, 1½ miles from Tangmere on the Goodwood estate, was the base from which the most famous pilot of the war, Douglas Bader, continued to fly, despite having lost both his legs.

The airfield at Tangmere was developed at the end of the First World War, after an airman returning from the Front made a chance landing there during fog. In the first months of the Second World War, three squadrons left Tangmere for new bases in France. When the British Expeditionary Force was pushed out of the country via Dunkirk, they were hurriedly recalled. During the Battle of Britain, Tangmere's squadrons – all Hurricanes – included a newly formed fighter unit that was equipped with radar fitted to the planes to help intercept German aircraft at night. The airfield itself was targeted by numerous German dive bombers, but the losses the Hurricanes inflicted meant that the Luftwaffe did not use them in such force against Britain again. Tangmere was damaged but remained operational. By the end of 1944, fighters flying from Tangmere could claim to have destroyed 866 enemy aircraft for certain, with a further 252 more 'probable kills', with 440 aircraft damaged.

A building on the edge of the airfield, Tangmere Cottage, housed the Special

Operations Executive and the Special Intelligence Service. Tangmere, being so close to France, was a natural base from which to fly Lysanders on secret missions into occupied territory, dropping agents at night-time rendezvous with the Resistance, and bringing home others.

THE VYNE
NEAR BASINGSTOKE, HAMPSHIRE

The first country house in Britain to be given a classical portico

The Englishman's home is his castle – or should that be his temple? There are more houses in Britain faced with columns than topped with battlements. The temple front has been adapted for Baroque palaces, such as John Vanbrugh's Blenheim (see page 206) in Oxfordshire, archaeologically correct exercises in the Greek revival, such as William Wilkins's The Grange in Hampshire, and grand terraces, such as Thomas Cubitt's Belgravia in London. Its continuing appeal is manifest wherever a speculative developer wants to endow a new housing estate with an air of pretension. Little or no thought may now be given to the origin of classical architecture in the ancient world, but the portico of columns still evokes, however faintly, a world of learning and tradition. In earlier times, when education was synonymous with Latin and Greek, temple architecture called to mind an ideal world, characterised by discipline, forti-tude, intellectual inquiry and universal values. Not for nothing are the different forms of the classical column (Doric, Ionic and Corinthian) called Orders. They are emblems of order: social, intellectual and artistic.

The first country house in England to be dignified by a portico is The Vyne. The house had begun life as a Tudor showplace, created out of an old monastery by William, 1st Lord Sandys, who was Henry VIII's Lord Chamberlain. Over the next century, the fortunes of the Sandys family declined before being wholly eclipsed by the Civil War, in which the Sandys supported the King.

In 1653, the estate was sold to the lawyer and MP Chaloner Chute, who was Speaker of the House of Commons. He employed John Webb to remodel the house, reducing it to a more practical size and adding a giant portico of Corinthian columns facing the lake. Webb's inspiration derived ultimately from a villa by Andrea Palladio, who had adapted the architecture of Ancient Rome to the domestic requirements of the Venetian aristocracy, spending summers on their farms beside the river Brenta. Palladio's work had been seen by Webb's mentor and uncle by marriage, Inigo Jones. Webb, like Jones, was a stout royalist and spent some time in prison when discovered taking money to Charles I at Beverley. How did he feel about a man such as Chute, who chaired the new Parliament? In these turbulent years, order was at a premium. Never was there a better time to dream of the Veneto.

WALMER BEACH

Julius Caesar lands in Kent

From Gaul, Julius Caesar could see the White Cliffs of Dover (see page 65) but knew little about the country that lay behind them; he was unable to elicit any information from traders that had crossed the Channel before him since they never ventured into the interior. On the edge of the world, Britain had attracted his attention because of the refuge it provided to rebellious Gauls, and the country was supposed to be rich in many desirable commodities: cattle, corn, gold, silver, tin and iron, not to mention freshwater pearls (Caesar had a passion for pearls).

In 55 BC, Caesar loaded the Seventh and Tenth legions into 80 ships and sailed from Boulogne across the English Channel to Dover to carry out the first Roman invasion of Britain. His own account tells the story of what happened next. Finding the White Cliffs lined with tribesmen, ready to hurl rocks and javelins down onto his troops, he ordered the flotilla to sail a few miles further up the coast to land between Walmer and Deal. This first visit was not a success; a storm damaged many of the Romans' boats and, seeing their difficulties, the Britons emerged from the cover of their forest and began to harry them. Caesar ordered a retreat to Boulogne.

The next summer Caesar returned. This time he was better prepared, with five legions and an astonishing 800 ships. They probably landed near Sandwich. In the face of this danger, the British tribes for once united under a single leader, Cassivellaunus – the first Briton whom we know by name. Caesar hoped to meet him in open battle, where the discipline of his legions was likely to overwhelm the tribal warriors. Instead, Cassivellaunus masterminded a hit-and-run campaign, during which the Britons galloped up in their war chariots, leapt down to fight, then as soon as reinforcements arrived, melted away again. Cassivellaunus gathered the tribes together the other side of the Thames: Caesar was only able to cross it by deploying his secret weapon, an elephant, which terrified the barbarous Britons.

Eventually, the tribes returned to old, bad habits and fell out among themselves, leaving Cassivellaunus no other option but to sue for peace. Caesar was probably more than relieved to grant it, exacting an annual tribute in return. As autumn set in, Caesar hurried back across the Channel, taking with him little more than some notoriously bolshie natives as slaves. He never returned.

See also Richborough Roman Fort, page 89, and Colchester, page 265

QUEBEC HOUSE

Telescope through which Wolfe viewed the Heights of Abraham

In September 1759, Major-General James Wolfe put the telescope that he had borrowed from a Colonel Williamson of the Royal Artillery to his eye, and studied the shoreline along the St Lawrence river, below Quebec. This was during the first global war in history – the Seven Years War, in which Britain joined Prussia against France and her allies, each side fighting the other in its colonies around the world, as well as in Europe.

Wolfe, aged thirty-two, had already taken part in the capture of Louisbourg at the mouth of the St Lawrence. He had now been sent back again to command the campaign to capture Quebec, which was the key to unlocking all the French-held territory in Canada and North America. So far, things had not gone well for him. His frontal assault had been a near-humiliation, only saved from total disaster by a providential thunderstorm that had soaked the French gunpowder. Always stick-thin, with a triangular profile formed by a pointed nose and receding chin, he had come down with a fever – a condition which added to the suffering caused by rheumatism and consumption. He asked his surgeon to 'make me up so that I may be without pain for a few days, and be able to do my duty; that is all I want.' As he looked through the telescope, his luck changed. He saw a path leading to some tents. It would be the route by which he would lead 4,500 men on a night march up the Heights of Abraham, appearing to the astonishment of the French general, the Marquis de Montcalm, on the plain west of Quebec.

The telescope is now in Quebec House in Westerham, where Wolfe spent the first eleven years of his life. Wolfe's brilliant coup, executed with the daring and personal bravery that would characterise his later admirer Horatio Nelson (see page 87), forced a quick response from the French, who hurried out to attack the British before they dug in. Wolfe's men were the better disciplined. With muskets charged with two bullets each, they waited until the French were near, and then unleashed a devastating volley. That volley decided the battle. Within a quarter of an hour, the French had been routed. Both generals had led their men from the front, Wolfe in his red coat and Montcalm in his white one. They were prominent targets. Wolfe, shot in the wrist and groin, fought on until he was hit in the chest and died on the field. Shot in the stomach, Montcalm was carried back into Quebec, where he also died.

Wolfe was not a perfect individual. He was apt to be extremely bad-tempered, perhaps due to his poor health. As an eighteen-year-old officer at Culloden (see page 447), he did not behave according to the standards of the 20th-century Geneva Convention. He was, however, an inspired and innovative soldier, possessed (again like Nelson) of more than usual aggression, amounting almost to a death wish. 'Mad is he?' exclaimed George II. 'Then I hope he will bite some other of my generals.'

WHITSTABLE

The shy charm of a bivalve

The native oyster has gone up in the world. In the 18th century, oysters were so common that Dr Johnson fed them to his cat. 'It's a wery remarkable circumstance,' said Sam Weller in Dickens's *Pickwick Papers*, 'that poverty and oysters always seem to go together.' A woman running an oyster stall in London told Henry Mayhew, author of *London Labour and the London Poor* (1851), how decayed gentlefolk would surreptitiously ask for 'two penn'orth', hoping not to be seen while they consumed what was probably their only dinner. Over the last century, pollution has destroyed so many of the native oysters' breeding grounds that they have become a luxury. The Roman historian Salus would have understood why bon viveurs are prepared to pay for them. Five years after Caesar's invasion of 55 BC, he wrote: 'The poor Britons, there is some good in them after all: they produce an oyster!' Oysters from the English coast were exported to the aristocratic dinner tables of Rome.

The history of Whitstable, with its mudflats, is interwoven with that of its oysters – glorified by the name Royal Natives. These could supposedly be identified by the exceptional whiteness of their shells. In the mid-19th century, Whitstable was an oyster town. The oyster beds were intensively managed, with oyster smacks or 'yawls' relentlessly dredging them – on some days to clean them and redistribute the immature oysters, on others to bring a harvest to market. Fraternities or Companies managed the beds, dividing them into squares of an acre; each acre required nine men to work it. The fortunes of the oyster fluctuated according to conditions: a boom in the 1860s followed exceptional discharges of 'spat', the seeds which emerge by the millions from the parent oyster.

With its clapboard cottages huddling along the steep shingle beach, and Victorian brick terraces from the boom days further inland, Whitstable still gives the appearance of being built on oysters. But the truth is that few, if any, of the native oyster beds have been commercially managed in Whitstable since the disastrously cold winter of 1963 wiped them out. Now, only a few native oysters are dredged for the town's pubs and restaurants. Long-shelled, faster-growing Pacific Oysters are farmed on a larger scale.

WINCHESTER CASTLE

Cult of King Arthur's round table

The round table that hangs on the wall of Winchester Castle is one of the icons of England. Nobody believes it is actually the round table that belonged to King Arthur and his knights (if they existed) in the 6th century, but it is nevertheless very old. The table was probably made in the late 13th century or early 14th century, showing that the myth of Arthur, a specifically English hero, inspired the medieval mind. Like medieval relics which may have started as innocent similes (nails like the ones with which Christ was hung upon the Cross) but were then assumed to be the originals, the table acquired something of a reputation of authenticity. The painted decoration, which was applied later, divides the table into a huge dartboard of dark green and buff segments, to each of which is attached the name of a knight. This illustrated what, in a society entirely structured around hierarchy, would have seemed the revolutionary principle on which Arthur organised his Court: no one knight could take precedence over another. Nevertheless, the King himself takes pride of place, being given a portrait that depicts him with robes, crown and regalia – every inch a King.

Who made the round table? It is unlikely to have been made at the same time as Henry III's Great Hall in which it hangs, because there is no suggestion that the King saw himself as *primus inter pares*, on the Arthurian model; the high table on the dais, which expressed his exalted status, would not have been round. A more convincing hypothesis associates it with the tournament that Edward I, freshly returned from three years' fighting in Gascony, held at Winchester in 1290. By this date, romance had begun to credit Winchester with a prominent place in the Arthurian legend, people believing that the castle had been begun by Arthur. In the next century, King Arthur and his knights were regarded as a pattern for the new age of chivalry. It has been suggested that Edward III, having founded the Order of the Garter as a fellowship of knights modelled on the Round Table (see page 249), may have paid tribute to the memory of Camelot by having the table painted. It may also have been Edward III who ordered the legs of the table to be taken off in 1348, in order to hang it on the east wall of the Great Hall – a complement to the Wheel of Fortune painted on the west wall.

By the time of Henry VIII, gunpowder had introduced an unpleasantly democratic note to warfare, and the age of chivalry was over. Henry may have commissioned the repainting of the portrait of Arthur since it bears a remarkable likeness to the King as a young man. The later repainting of the table by the Winchester artist William Cave in 1789 is unfortunate since it obscures the finer Tudor work; still, it demonstrates the extraordinary power of the Arthurian legend to reinvent itself for different ages, from the Gothick with a 'k' of 18th-century antiquarianism to the Gothic Revival that shaped the Victorian imagination.

WINCHESTER COLLEGE

William of Wykeham's educational ideal

In 1380, the Bishop of Winchester and Chancellor of England, William of Wykeham, established New College, Oxford*; to maintain an adequate supply of pupils who were well versed in Latin (apart from anything, so they might say prayers for his soul) he founded a school at Winchester. 'Our two colleges,' he wrote, 'though situated in different places, come from one root, and originally spring from one fountain.' In 1378, he had obtained papal permission to appropriate land in the diocese of Salisbury with which to endow his scholars; now he bought 5 acres of land outside the Winchester city walls. His foundation charter expounded a curriculum based on grammar, which 'is without doubt the foundation gateway and mainspring of all the liberal arts and without it arts of this kind cannot be known'. By grammar he meant the international lingua franca of Latin.

The school was opened in 1394. As the headmaster James Sabben-Clare wrote in his book *Winchester College* (1981): 'It is a quite remarkable thing that nearly six hundred years later most of the original buildings should still be standing, and within and around them the process of education should still be carried on by the same people as are named in the original statutes – albeit in different ways and in company with many others: a Warden and ten Fellows, two masters, seventy scholars, three chaplains, three lay-clerks, and sixteen quiristers or choirboys.' By tact, diplomacy and guile, successive wardens succeeded in dodging the blows aimed at them by the Dissolution of the Monasteries (see page 133) and the turbulence of the Civil War (during which the rest of Winchester was sacked). Indeed, Winchester College emerged from the Dissolution with its landholdings enhanced by the addition of the College of St Elizabeth, which lay next door.

With its ancient buildings, its spreading lawns, its arcadian surroundings, its traditions, its impenetrable tribal language, its studious calm and erudite ivory tower-ishness, Winchester is so profoundly English and unapproachably privileged, that it can inspire nostalgia even in visitors who never went there.

*See New College, page 228

WOLVESEY PALACE

Marriage of Mary Tudor to King Philip of Spain

On 25 July 1554, Queen Mary stayed at the Bishop of Winchester's Wolvesey Palace in Winchester. The next day she was married to King Philip II of Spain in Winchester Cathedral, and the east hall of Wolvesey formed the setting of the sumptuous wedding banquet. This illustrates not only the importance of Winchester and its Bishop, but of the Bishop's palace. It was built by Bishop Henry of Blois, a grandson of William the Conqueror and the brother of King Stephen, and enlarged and enhanced by his successors.

A medieval bishop played little role in his cathedral. Instead, he was a kind of grand supervisor of church affairs in his diocese, superintending the clergy, chastising those who erred, and administering his estates which, in case of the Bishops of Winchester, were vast. To perform these duties, a bishop was constantly on the move. The Bishop of Winchester had castles or houses all around the south of England: at Farnham and Esher in Surrey, at Taunton in Somerset, at Bishop's Waltham and Merdon in Hampshire, and at Downton in Wiltshire. These were in addition to the palace in London (see page 199), a necessity given the grand offices of state that Bishops of Winchester often held: for example, there were four treasurers and ten lord chancellors among their number.

Today, Wolvesey – which lies to the south-east of the cathedral – is a shell. The visit of Mary Tudor was the last to be made by a monarch, and soon afterwards the arrangements that had suited medieval prelates who, like other lords, maintained their standing by regularly showing themselves to their retinue in their halls, had come to seem inconvenient to an age that expected more comfort and privacy. Furthermore, the Bishop's estates had shrunk, Henry VIII having turned his greedy attention to the lands held by bishops after he had guzzled up those of the monasteries.

THE GURKHA MUSEUM
WINCHESTER, HAMPSHIRE

A record of outstanding valour

In 1855, the Secretary of State for War, Lord Panmure, sent an unusual order to the jeweller Hancock's of Bruton Street. It was for a new medal. The Crimean War was still being waged, and the public not only knew of acts of heroism – such as when the 93rd formed the 'thin red line' at Balaclava, or when the Light Brigade charged the Russian guns (see page 316) – but also the chaos and disease that dogged the campaign. Lord Panmure's predecessor, the Duke of Newcastle, had written to Prince Albert suggesting that a medal to commemorate the gallantry of ordinary soldiers would be a cheap way of bolstering morale: 'The value attached by soldiers to a little bit of ribbon is such as to render any danger insignificant and any privation light if it can be attained.' Such was the hierarchy of the armed forces – reflecting that of society as a whole – that there existed no medal to which all ranks would be equally eligible. Unlike the French, beside whom they were fighting, the British had no Légion d'Honneur or Médaille Militaire.

The Civil Service proposed that the new medal should be called the Military Order of Victoria; Prince Albert preferred the simpler Victoria Cross. The Queen herself amended the motto to read 'For Valour' instead of 'For the Brave': she did not want it to be thought that the only brave men on the battlefield were those who won the Cross. She also objected to the copper from which the prototype had been stamped, on the grounds that it would not look well against a red coat. Someone had the inspired idea that the bronze that was to be substituted should come from Russian guns captured in the Crimea. Two suitable cannons were identified at Woolwich Arsenal (see page 169); a long time passed before it was realised that these guns were actually Chinese and had been nowhere near the Crimea. The metal proved so hard that it could not be die-stamped but was cast instead. Queen Victoria, mounted on horseback, awarded the first 62 medals personally, at a parade in Hyde Park in 1856. With each VC went a less than fulsome pension of £10 a year. That is perhaps in the spirit of the VC, the honour of which outweighs everything else.

The next year saw the Indian Mutiny, in which Muslim and Hindu soldiers were provoked into rebellion against army insensitivity towards their religion (they were required to bite off the end of the new Enfield paper cartridge before loading, despite its being greased with animal fat). In 1858, Lieutenant J. A. Tytler, the son of a surgeon with the East India Company, was one of 500 men of the 66th or Goorkha Regiment of Native Infantry to come across 4–5,000 rebel infantry, along with 1,000 cavalry, at Charpura. On horseback, he dashed ahead of everyone else to take the enemy guns, where he was still fighting hand to hand – despite a shot in the arm, a spear wound in the chest and a bullet hole in his sleeve – when his comrades caught up with him. He was the first member of a Gurkha regiment to be awarded the VC.

Since then, the Gurkhas, who have been fighting in the British army since 1815, have won 26 VCs – an extraordinary tally, when it is considered that native Gurkhas were not eligible for the award until 1911. The first of those VCs for native Gurkhas was won by Rifleman Kulbir Thapa: he dragged a wounded British soldier and two fellow Gurkhas back from a German trench during the First World War, despite being already wounded himself. These and many of the other Gurkha VCs are displayed in the regimental museum in Winchester.

WOKING MOSQUE

SURREY

Britain's first mosque

Tucked away behind a retail park, next to the railway line, stands a little vision of the Mughal Empire: the Shah Jahan Mosque, Woking. A green dome rises above an immaculate garden, and a tall door opens into a dark square lit by stained-glass windows – invitingly cool on a hot summer's day. Built from

1889–94, on a site that had been taken over from the Royal Dramatic College, it was the first purpose-built mosque in Britain.

There have been Muslims living in Britain since the 17th century. Later, the East India Company employed them as sailors, and small communities developed around seaports. A mosque was opened in Cardiff in 1860, another in Liverpool in 1887. The Woking Mosque was founded by the Hungarian scholar Dr G. W. Leitner, who spoke forty languages and had previously worked as registrar of the university at Lahore. He hoped to establish a centre for oriental studies, and persuaded the ruler of Bhopal – Shah Jahan – to pay for it; W. I. Chambers was employed as architect. Leitner died in 1899, before more than the mosque and a house next to it had been finished, but the project was rescued by the Indian barrister Khwaja Kamal-ud-Din in 1913. He established a mission, the most prominent of whose converts was the Rt Hon Sir Rowland George Allanson-Winn, 5th Baron Headley, who exchanged the name of Lord Headley for Shaykh al-Farooq. (He said that he had been moved to convert by 'the intolerance of those professing the Christian religion'.)

It was Lord Headley/al-Farooq who first suggested that the British government should build a mosque in Regent's Park as a memorial to the Muslims who had 'died fighting for the Empire'. The Woking Mosque remained the focus of Islam in Britain until immigration from Pakistan in the 1960s shifted the centre of the Muslim population elsewhere.

London

THE GREATEST OF BRITISH cities is multi-faceted, and its landmarks reflect its teeming complexity. Kings died here – Charles I, outside the Banqueting House, part of the old Palace of Whitehall; Henry IV, praying to St Edward the Confessor, in the Jerusalem Chamber at Westminster Abbey; and William III, in a riding accident, when his horse shied at a molehill. While Buckingham Palace remains the ceremonial focus of Britain, other royal palaces have left a different legacy: the site of Greenwich Palace became the Royal Naval Hospital, and the Royal Observatory was built in its park. The Palace of Westminster became, and still is, the principal seat of government. A mile or so to the east, the financial genius of the City of London created institutions such as the Bank of England and Lloyd's of London. And so the capital grew rich, not just as the capital of Britain but of the British Empire. Museums and livery halls, law courts and hotels, religious institutions and public monuments, libraries and department stores – these are the public face of this confident, dogged, park-filled city beside the Thames.

Then there is the fabric of the place. Among those who lived here were politicians, poets, artists, composers, writers and scientists. Although Edward I expelled the Jews, Oliver Cromwell invited them back, and the first community to settle here rewarded London by building the delicious synagogue of Bevis Marks. Refugees came; Sigmund Freud was one of them. While charities were founded to look after unwanted children and abandoned dogs, the many-noosed gallows at Tyburn stood ready to receive other social rejects in an entirely different manner.

The sheer size of the city spawned engineering works, often on an epic scale. The elegant brick vaults of Bazalgette's Victorian sewers, seen at Abbey Mills Pumping Station, the 'cathedral of sewage', are still in use. So is the Thames Tunnel, the first under a navigable river anywhere in the world: how many of the passengers who rattle through it in their underground trains today know about the struggles the Brunels, father and son, had in engineering the tunnel, or that Isambard Kingdom had to struggle for his life when a roaring column of water broke through?

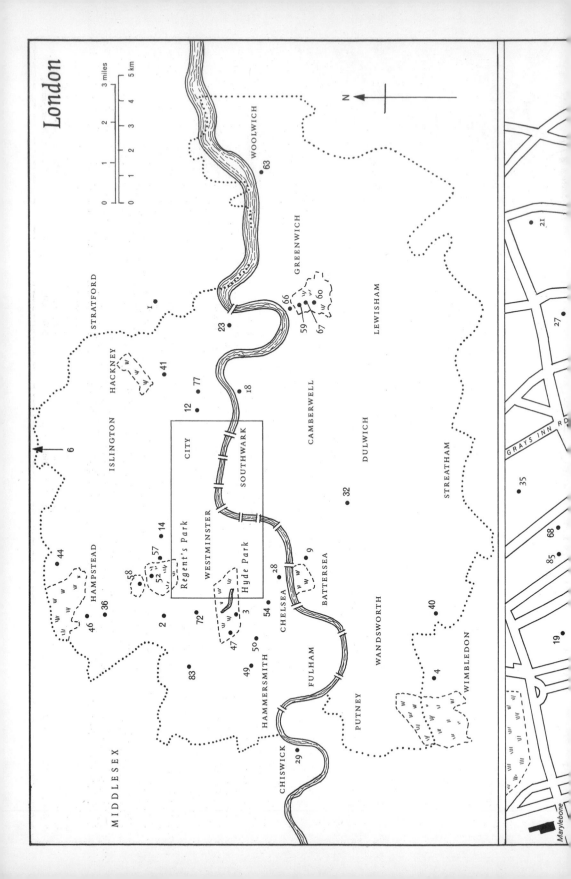

London

3 miles
5 km

N

MIDDLESEX

STRATFORD

WOOLWICH
• 63

GREENWICH
66 • w
59 • • 60
67 w
• 23

HACKNEY
w
w
• 41
• 1

ISLINGTON

• 12

• 77

• 18

CITY

WESTMINSTER

SOUTHWARK

CAMBERWELL

DULWICH

• 32

LEWISHAM

STREATHAM

• 6

HAMPSTEAD
• 44
w
w
• 36
w
46 •

Regent's Park

14 •
57 •
58 •
52 • w
w

Hyde Park
w

• 2
72 •
3
w
47 •
50 •
83 •
49 •

HAMMERSMITH

CHELSEA
54 •
28 •

BATTERSEA
• 9

FULHAM

PUTNEY

WANDSWORTH

WIMBLEDON
• 40
• 4
w
w
w
w
w
w

CHISWICK
29 •

GRAYS INN RD

• 21

• 27

• 35

• 68
• 85
• 19

Marylebone

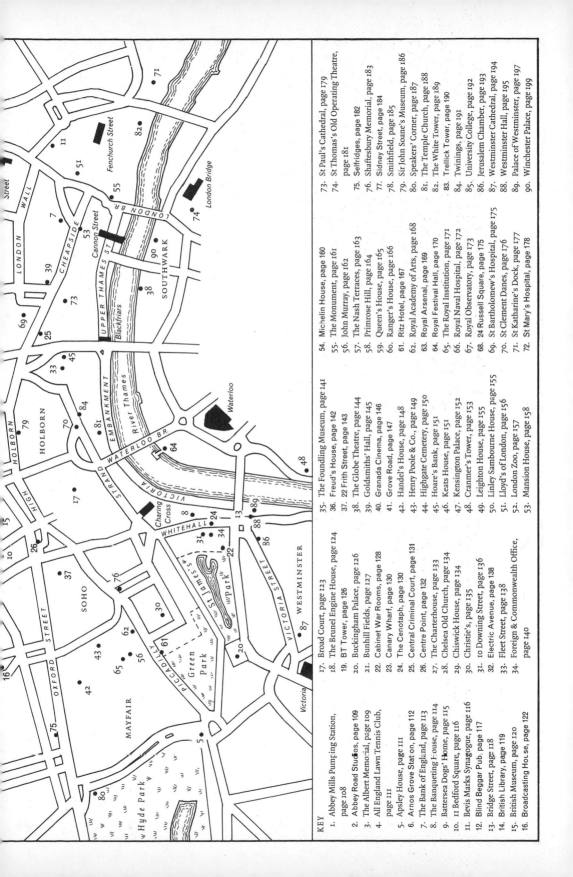

ABBEY MILLS PUMPING STATION STRATFORD, E15

The epic engineering achievement of London's sewers

In London, the summer of 1858 is remembered as the Great Stink, from the foul state of the sewage-infested river Thames*. The nation's parliamentarians, in session on the edge of the river at Westminster, suffered along with the rest of the population; their windows were hung with curtains soaked in disinfecting chloride of lime. The newly formed Metropolitan Board of Works was charged with finding a remedy.

They already knew what had to be done, since a number of Commissions had identified the problem of London's sewerage system, namely that much of it was discharged, untreated, into the Thames. Since the capital's drinking water was drawn from its river, cholera was a familiar evil, terrifying the rich as well as the poor. The degradation of the river was a relatively recent phenomenon. Fish had swum in the Thames until the 1820s. Until then, the conventional means of disposing of waste was by means of a cesspit dug under the house; this could be offensive to the occupants when it overflowed, and was hardly a joy to empty – although the contents had some value as manure. As the city grew, the price of manure necessarily fell, and the authorities allowed effluent to be drained into the streams and brooks that survived from the pre-urban landscape. These watercourses flowed into the Thames.

Joseph Bazalgette, the MBW's chief engineer, devised a new system, comprising around 83 miles of 'interceptory' sewers, running roughly parallel to the Thames, which would take sewage away to a safe distance to the east of the city. From the heights of Hampstead, the fall was sufficient to ensure a natural flow, but this was not the case in low-lying areas such as Westminster or along the south bank. Here the flow was maintained by four great pumping stations at Pimlico, Deptford, Crossness (where the great beam engines can still be seen, handsomely restored) and the 'cathedral of sewage', Abbey Mills. In addition, over a thousand miles of street sewers were constructed. All the sewers were built of brick, and a visit to Abbey Mills on one of Thames Water's open days shows that, after more than a century of service, they have survived in remarkable condition, complete with their original pointing.

Today the Thames is once again home to over a hundred species of fish, although on stormy days small quantities of raw sewage still reach the river: it is hoped that an overflow provision that was acceptable in Bazalgette's day will soon be replaced.

*See Kew Bridge Pumping Station, page 224

ABBEY ROAD STUDIOS 3 ABBEY ROAD, NW8
World's first purpose-built recording studio

On 29 November 1931 Edward Elgar (see page 331) conducted the London Symphony Orchestra in a recording session of 'Land of Hope and Glory'. It marked the opening of the world's first purpose-built recording studio at 3 Abbey Road.

EMI had bought the property two years earlier. It was simply a detached, stucco-fronted villa, planted among the prosperous, red-faced mansion blocks of St John's Wood. Despite the technological character of the business, EMI did not replace it with a work of Modernist architecture, but instead converted the existing structure, building additional studios in the garden. There were spaces to suit orchestral music, chamber works, solo instruments and singers. On the wax masters from which records, turning at seventy-eight revolutions per minute, were then cut, the child prodigy Yehudi Menuhin recorded Elgar's Violin Concerto. This was in 1932, the same year in which Noël Coward, fresh from Broadway, committed 'Mad Dogs and Englishmen' to disc. Indeed, the list of artists recording at Abbey Road during the 1930s – as later – reads like a house party of not always compatible musical geniuses, in which Sir Thomas Beecham and Artur Schnabel rubbed shoulders with the band-leader Joe Loss and the music hall performers, Flanagan and Allen. During the Second World War, they were joined by George Formby ('When I'm Cleaning Windows'), Glenn Miller (until his plane was lost over the English Channel), Sir John Barbirolli and Ministry of Information propagandists.

In 1950, the legendary producer George Martin arrived, working at first with comedians such as Peter Sellers (Martin made Sellers' recording of 'Goodness Gracious Me' with Sophia Loren in 1960). This was the age both of the long-playing record and the hit single. The release of Elvis Presley's 'Heartbreak Hotel' in America was quickly followed by recordings of Britain's own rock 'n' roll phenomenon, Cliff Richard and the Shadows. In 1962, Martin signed up The Beatles (see page 368), nearly all of whose records were made at Abbey Road, starting with the single 'Love Me Do'. Later, *Sgt. Pepper's Lonely Hearts Club Band* inspired a new method of recording in eight, rather than four, tracks – a system that would itself soon be superseded by multi-track. Appropriately, The Beatles' last recorded album, cut in 1969, was called *Abbey Road*.

THE ALBERT MEMORIAL KENSINGTON GARDENS, SW7
Shrine to Queen Victoria's beloved husband

The Albert Memorial was a defining moment in the Victorian age. Prince Albert, with his Germanic attitudes and tendency to interfere, was not universally popular while he was alive, but his death in 1861 at the age of forty-two elevated him to something close to sainthood. Like many other Victorians, he had been worn out by overwork. In a way that would be repeated when the monarchy was reinvented in the mid-20th century, he devoted himself tirelessly to good causes, from improved dwellings for the poor to the murals in the House of Lords. The Great Exhibition of 1851 was his idea. It is appropriate that his memorial should be erected within sight of the grand complex of museums and concert hall that was the permanent legacy of the Great Exhibition.

The conception of the Memorial, designed by Sir (George) Gilbert Scott, owes something to the heritage of medieval crosses around England; something also, presumably, to other memorials that had recently been erected – in Edinburgh to Sir Walter Scott and in Manchester to Prince Albert. Metalwork rather than architecture was another influence, since the Memorial is like a richly worked reliquary; every surface is ornamented with fine mosaics or sculpture. Medieval reliquaries were small; the Albert Memorial is over 172ft tall. There is a parallel with the medieval Eleanor Cross at Geddington (see page 323).

The seated figure of Albert that forms the centrepiece of the composition was sculpted by J. H. Foley, who showed the Prince contemplating the catalogue of the Great Exhibition. Bronze was favoured over marble because of its better resistance to the corrosive atmosphere of Victorian London. When finished, the bronze was gilded: its refulgence astonished Londoners when the Memorial was restored in 1996–8. Below Albert, a frieze depicts 175 poets, musicians, architects, sculptors and artists – the eternal greats, who appear to have come together to bless the state of the arts then prevailing in Britain. Freestanding sculptural groups representing Agriculture, Manufacture, Commerce and Engineering stand at the corners; below them, at the outer corners, four Continents. They were intended specifically to bring to mind 'the Great International Exhibitions which have done so much for art', although visitors may well have mistaken them for a satisfactory allusion to the reaches of the British Empire.

The upper sections of the Memorial are covered in a fanatical richness of decoration: there are bronze statues, a globe and a cross, while mosaic panels depict the arts, heraldic beasts and carved foliage. Much of this detail is too far from the viewer at ground level to be seen clearly, let alone interpreted, and visitors who climbed the scaffolding during the restoration were struck that even parts which could never have been seen were as elaborately finished as the rest. In this, the Memorial, which is as complete an interpretation of the Victorian view of the world as the Mappa Mundi was of the 13th-century one (see page 326), accorded with a prime tenet of the Gothic Revival, and indeed of Victorian moral life. Whatever the limitations of earthly sight, nothing is invisible to God.

ALL ENGLAND LAWN TENNIS CLUB

World's first tennis championship

Like football, cricket, rugby, boxing, polo, cross-country riding, mountaineering and some types of Alpine skiing, tennis was one of the many sporting pastimes that were either invented in England, or whose rules were codified by Englishmen. It emerged in the 1870s, as an outdoor development of real tennis (played by Henry VIII) and racquets.

Thanks to the invention of the lawn mower in the mid-19th century, grass could be cut shorter and more evenly than before, when scythes had been used. The vulcanisation of rubber, discovered by the American Charles Goodyear in 1844, allowed the making of balls that would bounce on this smooth sward. Tennis quickly became a vogue; it was a social game and allowed young people of both sexes to mingle decorously, and courts could be fitted into the large suburban gardens of the prosperous middle classes as much as in the acres surrounding country houses.

Croquet had preceded tennis in popularity. It was in the offices of *The Field* magazine that the All England Croquet Club was founded in 1868. The committee soon acquired 4 acres of lawn at the bottom of Wimbledon Hill. In 1875, some of the grass was turned over to tennis courts, and the words 'and Lawn Tennis' were added to the name of the Club. The world's first lawn tennis championship, using rubber balls covered in flannel, was held here in 1877. The Club moved to its present site, at the top of Wimbledon Hill, in 1922, when Centre Court was built to the designs of C. J. Pell & Partners. What would become the sacred turf was brought down from Cumberland, and tended by fifteen groundsmen.

Over the years, the original 'Who's for tennis?' atmosphere, epitomised by strawberries and cream, evolved into the multi-million-pound sporting fixture of today, with a staff of 1,500 dedicated to catering alone.

APSLEY HOUSE

No.1 London, the Duke of Wellington's town palace

Wellington bought Apsley House in 1817. He had spent the two previous years as Ambassador in Paris, and was now intent on following his military triumphs with glories on the political stage. His new house – known as No. 1 London from its position immediately inside one of the old toll gates – had originally been built for Lord Apsley (later 2nd Earl of Bathurst) in 1771–8 by Robert Adam. At this time, the house was two bays smaller and was faced in red brick. Wellington employed Benjamin Dean Wyatt to enlarge it, adding a giant portico and encasing the whole building in Bath stone. Inside, the new staircase swirled around a giant marble statue of Napoleon by Antonio Canova, while the first floor displayed the Duke's collection of Old Masters, many captured at the Battle of Vitoria in 1813, and presented to Wellington in gratitude by the King of Spain. The result was a town palace whose visitors could hardly to fail to regard the Duke as a natural leader of the country.

In 1828, Wellington became Prime Minister. After his government fell two years later, he led the opposition to the Reform Bill; this made him a hate figure for the rabble, which broke the windows of Apsley House on two occasions (they were thereafter reinforced with iron shutters). In 1848, the Duke organised the defence of London against the Chartist riots (see page 427). His rigid conservatism led to another period of unpopularity although, by the time of the Great Exhibition of 1851, in which he took a keen interest, he was mobbed by admiring crowds. The following year he died at Walmer Castle, a residence he used as Warden of the Cinque Ports.

ARNOS GROVE STATION ENFIELD, N11
Industrial patronage at its best on the world's first underground railway

Arnos Grove underground station, opened in 1932, was one of the beacons of the expanding London Underground, already the largest system of its kind in the world, as well as a pioneer of corporate image. The London Tube, as it had come to be generally known, had been running since the Metropolitan Railway opened its first line, between Paddington and Farringdon Street, in 1863 – the world's first underground railway. This sought to answer the problem of a city congested by the volume of traffic generated by the railway termini, which brought people and goods to the periphery of the city but then left them to battle their way across in a variety of horse-drawn conveyances. The traffic jams were horrendous*.

Despite the discomfort of smoke and smuts from the steam engines, the Metropolitan Railway was judged to be such a success that the first section of what is now the District Line opened in 1868. These lines were built just below the surface of London, by a method called cut and cover. Later, in order to push lines beneath London's densely built streets, the tunnelling system developed by Marc Brunel for the Thames Tunnel† was adopted, but only when it was possible to power trains by electricity; deep tunnels provided too little ventilation for steam trains. Another first came with the opening of an underground electric railway between the City and Stockwell in 1890.

By the 1930s, the appearance of the Underground had been systematised and enhanced by the enlightened patronage of Frank Pick, chief executive between 1913 and 1938. Art-minded contemporaries described Pick as an updated version of Lorenzo the Magnificent, as he commissioned typefaces from

Edward Johnston, posters from artists such as Laura Knight, Paul Nash and Graham Sutherland, and spotted the potential of the famous Tube map devised by an out-of-work signalling engineer, Harry Beck. The architect Charles Holden designed the new stations for the Piccadilly Line extension, and the great concourse of Piccadilly Circus's station was visited by Russian engineers who took it as an inspiration for the immense stations on the Moscow Metro. In the crisp style of the Modern Movement, the Piccadilly Line stations relied on simple shapes and exposed materials rather than applied ornament. Osterley, Southgate, Sudbury Town all brought the highest design ideals to bear on a mass transit system. Arnos Grove is in every sense a classic. The ticket office takes the form of a severe brick drum, with platform seats, lighting fixtures, ticket machine and clocks designed in keeping with it.

*See Bridge Street, page 118. †See The Brunel Engine House, page 124

THE BANK OF ENGLAND THREADNEEDLE STREET, EC2
The institution upon which Britain's credit is founded

'What remedy is there if we have too little money?' wrote the political economist Sir William Petty in 1682. Both the government and merchants had come to find the old banking system, based on goldsmiths' shops (see page 145), was now inadequate to their needs. When Charles II defaulted on some loans, financial chaos ensued. Economists could see that lack of public confidence in the banks, and the banks' lack of confidence in the public, limited the nation's trade. Petty knew the answer: 'We must erect a Bank, which well computed doth almost double the Effect of our coined Money; and we have in England Materials for a Bank which shall furnish Stock enough to drive the Trade of the whole Commercial World.'

When William III came to the throne in 1689, he brought with him a Dutch perspective on finance. In Holland, it had been found that trading based on credit helped to expand the economy. Besides, William had his own pressing concerns about money since he urgently needed to raise funds for his wars against France. Various means of doing so were mooted. The method favoured was that proposed by the Scotsman, William Paterson. In return for lending the Exchequer £1.2 million, Paterson was awarded a Royal Charter to establish a joint-stock bank; called the Bank of England, it opened in 1694. Investors were allowed limited liability, which was then rare; the bank could issue paper money which could be redeemed on demand in gold. There was no expectation, on the King's part, that this would become a national bank. He treated it solely as a convenient source of funds, and extracted further loans whenever the charter came up for renewal. The scale of the enterprise, however, together with the system of credit which it offered to merchants, proved irresistible. Almost a century after its foundation the Prime Minister Lord North could describe it as 'from long habit and usage of many years . . . a part of the constitution'.

In 1734, the Bank moved from the Grocers' Hall, its previous home, to the present location (on a much smaller site) in Threadneedle Street. The blind curtain wall, designed by Sir John Soane (see page 186) and enclosing the Bank's present 3½-acre site, was finished in 1827.

THE BANQUETING HOUSE WHITEHALL, SW1
Charles I is beheaded

On the morning of 30 January 1649, King Charles I was marched from St James's Palace to Whitehall, the King himself setting a cracking pace. He wore a long black cloak, his order of St George, a rich red-striped waistcoat and two linen shirts, in case the cold of the day made him shake and people imputed it to fear. He had told those that were with him that he did not fear death, and he appeared perfectly composed.

Whitehall was the palace that Charles would have rebuilt, if the financial chaos of his reign had not frustrated him: the Banqueting House, commissioned by his father from Inigo Jones in 1619, was all that had been accomplished. It is likely that Charles now walked the length of the Saloon, so often used for court masques, beneath the ceiling on which Rubens had painted the apotheosis of his father, James I. Where the present entrance to the Saloon now stands, an opening in what was then just a wall had been made. He went through this into the old building (since replaced) which contained the staircase; here another opening had been punched through the wall. It led onto a scaffolding, draped in black. On it stood an executioner and his assistant, grotesquely disguised in tight-fitting woollen suits, masks and wigs.

Charles made a short speech, declaring his 'innocency' and forgiving his enemies*. He then took his nightcap from the presiding bishop who, with the executioner, helped him tuck his hair under it. 'I go from a corruptible to an incorruptible crown, where no disturbance can be, no disturbance in the world,' the King observed. He then knelt at the block, and the executioner came forward again to adjust the hair. After some short prayers, the King thrust out his hands to signify he was ready. He was a small man and it took only one blow for the axe to do its job. The executioner picked up the bleeding head and held it up for the crowd, crying, 'Behold the head of the traitor!' The sight was greeted with a collective groan, interpreted by Puritan fanatics as 'a sober expression of great contentment' and by Royalist sympathisers as a 'groan of great sorrow'. The crowd was quickly dispersed by cavalry.

Historians of every persuasion agree that Charles I, whatever the failures of his reign or the obstinacy that led him to the scaffold, knew how to die like a king.

It is said that Inigo Jones – whose own war had ended ignominiously when he was secreted out of Basing House in Hampshire, then under siege by Cromwell – died 'through grief, as is well known, for the fatal calamity of his dread master'.

*See Battle of Naseby, page 332, and The Saracen's Head, page 342

BATTERSEA DOGS' HOME   BATTERSEA PARK ROAD, SW8
The Englishman's best friend is his dog

In the summer of 1860, a middle-aged widow called Mrs Major spotted a starving dog in a gutter. Horrified, she took it home to her house in Canonbury Square in Islington, where she showed it to a friend, Mary Tealby. This waif was soon joined by others, which Mrs Major and Mrs Tealby cared for. Indeed, Mrs Tealby went further, badgering her friends for subscriptions to provide a refuge for neglected dogs. A committee met that November in the Pall Mall offices of the Royal Society for the Prevention of Cruelty to Animals. (As the plain Society for the Prevention of Cruelty to Animals, it had been founded in 1824: it showed something about Victorian priorities that the National Society for the Prevention of Cruelty to Children was not founded until 1884.) The committee resolved to establish 'an institution . . . for the care of lost and starving dogs'.

This home for lost dogs had its first quarters in Holloway. By 1862, when Charles Dickens visited, at least a thousand dogs had been rescued from starvation and re-homed. 'It is the kind of institution which a very sensitive person who has suffered acutely from witnessing the misery of a starving animal would wish for,' he wrote, 'without imagining for a moment that it could ever seriously exist.'

In 1871, the Holloway arrangement ceased and new premises were found on the south side of Chelsea Bridge, where the Battersea Dogs' Home, as it would soon be known, has remained ever since.

In 1885, an approach was made to Queen Victoria, who had made a donation, to see if she would grant Battersea her patronage. 'Most certainly,' she wrote across the note passed to her by Sir Henry Ponsonby, her private secretary. 'No one *loves* Dogs more than The Queen or would wish to do more to promote their comfort and happiness. They are man's *truest* friends.' Informed by that sentiment, the Battersea Dogs' Home went on to become the most famous animal refuge in the world.

11 BEDFORD SQUARE BLOOMSBURY, WC1

Water recognised as H₂O

In 1903, the 11th Duke of Bedford erected a plaque to commemorate Henry Cavendish's occupancy of 11 Bedford Square on the Duke's London estate. Henry's father, Lord Charles Cavendish, had been a scientist, rather too hard-working, some thought, for a gentleman. Henry's mother died when he was two, leaving him chronically withdrawn but brilliant; it was perfectly natural for him to follow the paternal example. The Bedford Square house, conveniently close to the British Museum (see page 120) and the Royal Society (see page 179), became little more than a library, with virtually every room full of precious scientific books, which would be lent out to visiting scholars – Cavendish even wrote out a chit when he 'borrowed' one of his own books. Although he kept some instruments at Bedford Square, most of his experiments were conducted at the large but not aristocratic house (now demolished) that he rented on Clapham Common, which was equipped as a scientific institution. In the garden, a platform was built to enable him to get into one of the trees, from the top of which he made scientific measurements.

At his death in 1810, contemporaries compared his scientific contribution to that of Newton (see page 294). His rigorously methodical investigations extended from chemistry and physics to meteorology and to experiments to calculate the density of the earth. He is best known for the discovery, at some point before 1783, that water is not an element but composed of two gases.

In time, Cavendish became very rich through inheritance but, having been brought up parsimoniously, he retained his frugal habits, spending almost nothing on his personal comfort and forever wearing the faded violet coat and tricorn hat that had been the norm in his youth. He shunned most human and all female contact, living an anchorite's existence. Fashionable society may have been appalled by such determined asceticism, but fellow scientists regarded him as 'the wisest of the rich and the richest of the wise'.

BEVIS MARKS SYNAGOGUE BEVIS MARKS, EC3

The Jewish community is re-established

When it came to Roman Catholicism, Oliver Cromwell was a religious bigot. However, he was also the ruler who allowed the Jews back into England openly, for the first time since their expulsion in 1290*. He had noticed the contribution that they were making to the prosperity of England's greatest commercial rival, Holland. In 1655, Sephardim – Jews from the Iberian peninsula – who had been living covertly in the City of London, often after having fled the Inquisition, petitioned Cromwell to allow them freedom of worship, and the right to allow others of their faith to come from overseas. Their first synagogue was opened in a house (now demolished) in Creechurch Lane. By 1700, this community was rich enough to build a new temple, off Bevis Marks, a street running just inside the City walls. Their architect was a Quaker, Joseph Avis, who refused to take payment for the work. The future Queen Anne donated one of the main beams for the project.

The result was a building in the style of Christopher Wren's City churches (see page 180), which seems all the more remarkable today through having been hardly changed since its dedication in 1701. The Ark, containing the sacred scrolls, looks very much like the reredos from a contemporary church; for some years, churches had contained panels painted with the words of the Ten Commandments, as at Bevis Marks – although in the synagogue they are shown in Hebrew. The twisted balusters in front of the Ark could easily be altar rails. The gallery is another feature familiar from churches and chapels of this date; Christian visitors, however, might have been surprised to see that it was occupied only by women, the benches in the body of the synagogue being the preserve of the men. Naturally, Jewish worship dictated some conspicuous differences in form from Christian structures – notably the large Tebah or reading desk opposite the Ark. From the ceiling hang seven brass chandeliers from Amsterdam, which Nikolaus Pevsner goes so far as to call 'gorgeous'. Over the next century, the congregation gave silver ewers, scroll mounts, elaborate bells and other treasures.

While Cromwell tolerated the presence of Jews, it was not until 1858 that they obtained the right to enter Parliament, serve in the army or obtain degrees from Oxford and Cambridge.

*See The Jew's House, page 278, and Clifford's Tower, page 405

BLIND BEGGAR PUB   *337 WHITECHAPEL ROAD, E1*
Nemesis of the feared Ronnie Kray

On 9 March 1966, George Cornell, a South London gangster, glanced up from where he was standing at the bar of the Blind Beggar Pub. 'Well, look who's here,' he said. In the doorway stood Ronald Kray, the unstable half of the psychopathic Kray twins who had come to dominate the London underworld. Ronnie raised his Mauser semi-automatic pistol and shot Cornell three times in the head. Minders then hustled Kray out of the pub. When the police arrived, no one who saw the incident could remember quite what happened, let alone the identity of the murderer. They were too frightened of the Krays.

The Krays belonged to an East End world that was already vanishing, as slum terraces were cleared and immigration changed the ethnic mix. Born in 1933, their passionate attachment to their mother Violet, as well as to each other, made it difficult for them to form relationships with other people. At first, they operated protection rackets. When the 1960 Gaming Act made gambling legal, their 'services' were applied to the new gaming clubs that opened. They owned one of them, Esmeralda's Barn in Knightsbridge, themselves. This gave them access to the glamour that they craved. Wearing dinner jackets to lend an air of legitimacy, they became a feature of the Swinging Sixties, photographed with celebrities such as Judy Garland and Diana Dors.

A sadistic torturer, Ronnie was extremely sensitive about his image, fearing that his homosexuality might compromise his reputation as a hard man. Cornell had called him a 'fat poof', a remark that led to his murder. Three years later, as the Krays' expanding empire made them more enemies in gangland, someone at last talked and Ronnie was convicted. At the same time, Reggie was imprisoned for brutally killing Jack 'the Hat' McVitie. As their sentences wore on, and the East End became gentrified, their myth grew; it was remembered how they had been kind to old people and had loved their mum. Ronnie could never accept the justice of his sentence. Mad, violent and evil, he died in Broadmoor in 1995; in 2000, after serving more than the thirty-year recommended sentence, Reggie was released into an outside hospital where he died of cancer shortly afterwards.

BRIDGE STREET
WESTMINSTER, SW1

Site of the world's first traffic lights

During the 1860s, more than 1,000 people were killed annually on London's roads. It was the age of the railways, but horses were still used to pull the vehicles that took passengers, luggage and goods into or across the city. London was crowded with cabs, carts and omnibuses, slow moving and not very manoeuvrable, indeed often out of control.* In 1868, John Peake Knight proposed a new device to regulate the throng of vehicles: the traffic light.

Knight was an old railway hand. Born in Nottingham, he had left school at twelve to work in the parcel room of Derby Station. By the age of forty, he had advanced to be Traffic Manager for the London–Brighton line. He is credited with having introduced the communication cord, or alarm pull, for ladies. Knight's idea for a signalling system to control road traffic was borrowed from the railways. It took the form (at night) of a revolving gas lantern on a tall pole, showing simply red for stop and green for go. It was not automatic, and required a policeman to operate it by means of levers. The world's first traffic lights, situated outside the Houses of Parliament on Bridge Street, were inaugurated on 10 December 1868. Just a few weeks later, on 2 January, the gas container that supplied the lights exploded, nearly killing the policeman. Despite this setback, the lights continued in operation until 1872. They were not, however, replicated.

In fact, Knight's traffic lights were a false dawn in the history of road safety. It was not until 1920 that the first automatic lights with three colours – red, amber and green – were introduced in New York and Detroit. Nevertheless, Knight enjoyed some recognition during his lifetime. When he died in 1886, the Prince of Wales thought sufficiently highly of him to send a funeral wreath.

*See Arnos Grove Station, page 112, and The Brunel Engine House, page 124. See also St Helier, page 34, and Broad Court, page 123

BRITISH LIBRARY
The national shrine to the book

96 EUSTON ROAD, NW1

The British Library has claims to be the greatest in the world. Since 1999, it has been housed in a redbrick barracks of learning near St Pancras Station, but its soul still haunts the Round Reading Room in the British Museum (see page 120). Here, generations of scholars worked at blue leather desks beneath the ribs of an all-encompassing dome that seemed to magnify every noise – the bang of heavy catalogues, the whisper of inquiries at the counters of the raised central dais, the sudden sneeze. Marx, his feet resting on a heated rail and his body warmed by air emitted from a grille above the book, worked here daily for thirty years. A generation later, Lenin, Trotsky and other revolutionaries from Tsarist Russia received tickets made out for the aliases under which they were living. Political activists shared the heavy, leather-bound catalogues with literary and social rebels such as Algernon Swinburne and Oscar Wilde (see page 236). Thousands of other, less colourful readers would have agreed with the magisterial judgement which William Makepeace Thackeray confided to his diary: 'In the great circle of the library Time is looking into Space.' Beatrix Potter (see page 363) was less expansive, but equally observant, when she visited the library to consult an old book of rhymes, writing to a young admirer: 'There were not many people, but some of them were very funny.'

When the British Museum was formally named in 1759, it included not only the library assembled by Sir Hans Sloane, but the Cotton family's collection of ancient manuscripts. The latter, which included such treasures as the Lindisfarne Gospels (see page 395) and the manuscript of *Beowulf*, were bequeathed to the nation in 1700, but had not been housed in what would now be considered ideal museum conditions: the low point came when a fire broke out at the house where the collection was being kept in Little Dean's Yard,

Westminster, and half-charred books had to be thrown out of the window to safety. The collection of manuscripts belonging to the Harley family was also purchased and, in 1757, George II gave the Royal Library, founded by Henry VII, to the museum. At the same time, he granted the museum the privilege of 'copyright deposit', the right to require British publishers to give the library a copy of every book they publish, a right that continues today. This ensured that the library would expand indefinitely.

In 1823, George IV donated his father's library of 65,000 books and 800 volumes of unbound pamphlets, prompting the Trustees to commission Sir Robert Smirke to rebuild the museum. Even so, by the time the new building was finished in 1838, the space allocated to the library was full. This inspired the energetic, irascible librarian, Sir Anthony Panizzi – an Italian who could charm as well as infuriate – to campaign for a new library. This time, the commission fell to Smirke's brother, Sydney, who created the famous Round Reading Room in the centre of the square courtyard, the angles of which were filled with book-stacks. A soft light filtered down from round-headed windows and a glazed central oculus.

Technologically, the structure was innovative. In 1879, it was one of the first buildings to be lit by electricity (gas being considered too great a fire hazard) – its advent being greeted by, perhaps for the only time in the library's history, a murmur of spontaneous applause. A highly articulate campaign by the Reading Room's devotees was not enough to prevent the inevitable move to St Pancras: by the late 20th century, the library's collections were being stored in sites all over London. Happily, the nation's great temple to the book has been beautifully redisplayed as part of Foster and Partner's masterly reorganisation of the British Museum's central courtyard, designated one of Britain's Millennium projects.

BRITISH MUSEUM
The sum of human knowledge

BLOOMSBURY, WC1

In the 18th century, the readers of Diderot's encyclopaedia believed that all human knowledge could be gathered together in one place, arranged according to subject. This was the ambition followed by the creators of the British Museum. Founded in 1753, it was the first museum of its kind in the world.

The origin of the museum lies in the collection of the Irish doctor, Sir Hans Sloane, who formed one of the most successful medical practices in London. An early proponent of inoculation against smallpox, he numbered both Queen Anne and Samuel Pepys among his patients. Medicine gave him the money to pursue a gargantuan and omnivorous appetite for collecting. He amassed the beautiful and the curious, the useful and the bizarre, the natural and the artificial, the incredibly old, the new but exquisite, as well as (in Horace Walpole's words) 'hippopotamuses, sharks with one ear, and spiders as big as geese'. Plants, fossils, zoological specimens, anatomical oddities, antiquities, prints, drawings, coins, books and manuscripts all found their way into his house in Bloomsbury Place, coincidentally near the future site of the British Museum. In time, he was forced to move the vast assemblage to his country house in Chelsea, on land that would later be developed as Sloane Square, Sloane Avenue and Hans Place. By the time of his death, aged ninety-two, the collection comprised an amazing 80,000 or so objects. Its importance was recognised at the time; Frederick, Prince of Wales (son of George II, father of George III) honoured the old man with a visit, free of the usual court stiffness.

When Sloane died in 1753, Parliament voted to grant £20,000 to buy the collection. Montagu House in Bloomsbury, going cheap due to its poor repair, was bought to house the new institution. To Sloane's collection was added the contents of a number of eminent libraries* and, from 1759, the ever-growing collection in Montagu House was known as the British Museum.

After the Battle of the Nile of 1798 and the Treaty of Alexandria of 1801, the British Museum received the Egyptian antiquities that Napoleon had been preparing to take back to France. The arrival of these pieces, some of them massive, showed up the inadequacy of the Montagu House arrangements: big sculptures had to be kept in sheds. Money was found for a new building that would accommodate, among other collections, such products of the Grand Tour as the Townley marbles and the Hamilton vases. Sculpted friezes from the Temple of Apollo at Bassae, excavated by adventurers and bought by the Trustees at auction, arrived in 1815, along with a live scorpion in the packing cases. In 1816, the nation bought the Elgin Marbles, removed from the Parthenon in Athens, for £35,000. Seven years later, when George IV donated his father's massive library, the replacement of decaying Montagu House became imperative.

The new museum was designed by Robert Smirke, one of three architects attached to the Office of Works. Smirke was a product of the Greek Revival, the chaste neo-Classical style which drew upon the investigation of Greek temple sites, some of whose greatest monuments were now inside the British Museum. He was not its most exciting exponent (Pugin – see pages 88 and 197 – a dedicated Goth, complained of the 'New Square Style of Mr Smirke') but at the British Museum the combination of giant Ionic portico and colonnade was not only his personal masterpiece: it also provided the perfect image of a museum as his generation saw it to be, celebrating the continuity of culture with the classical world.

*See British Library, page 119

BROADCASTING HOUSE

High-minded home of 'Auntie'

In the 20th century, the BBC became Britain's face to the world: an ambassador of cultural values whose reach exceeded even that of the Foreign Office. Since the then British Broadcasting Company (as opposed to Corporation) was formed by a group of radio manufacturers in 1922, it has been financed not by a direct grant from government, nor by revenues from advertising, but by a licence fee, paid by every household that owns a television set – or, originally, a radio. For decades, the quality of its programmes seemed far better than that offered by commercial channels, whether in Britain or overseas, because budgets were not directly dependent on the size of the audience. Equally, its independence from government gave its news and current affairs programmes an impartiality that was envied around the world. This independence was sorely tested, particularly during early crises such as the 1926 General Strike. Since the first foreign language broadcast was made, in Arabic, in 1938, the measured tones of the BBC's World Service have seemed a touchstone of impartiality to foreign listeners whose own governments would often have preferred them to remain in ignorance of world events.

Looking like an ocean liner constructed from Portland stone, Broadcasting House, which opened in 1932, is in every sense the Corporation's flagship – retaining a symbolic authority, even though the television programmes are now broadcast from White City and numerous regional studios. It was designed by the otherwise little-known G. Val Myers, and seems as formal and conservative as the chimes of Big Ben, which preceded news bulletins, or the voice of King George V (first broadcast from the Wembley Empire Exhibition in 1924). The building reflects the dignified image of the BBC imposed on it by its first general manager, John Reith. To Reith, a Scottish engineer, the BBC had a mission to improve the taste and education of the nation, by bringing 'the best of everything to the greatest number of homes'.

Art, naturally, figured in the Reithian vision, and at Broadcasting House it was embodied in the very un-Reithian figure of Eric Gill, the sculptor and letter carver who had founded his own religious community. Gill, whose interpretation of divine love allowed him to commit incest with his daughters, caused a scandal through his relief of Prospero and Ariel above the entrance to Broadcasting House: the size of Ariel's manhood was a source of worry to the governors. Passers-by had already suffered exposure to Gill, working at the top of his ladder, clad only in the smock-like robe that he habitually wore, without – as they had occasion to realise – anything underneath.

BROAD COURT

The ubiquitous red kiosk that came to symbolise Britain

The Scotsman Alexander Graham Bell took out the first patent for a telephone in 1876, in America where he was then living. Whether he should be considered to be the inventor of the telephone is disputed, to the extent that in 2002 the House of Representatives in Washington controversially voted to accord that honour to the Italian immigrant Antonio Meucci who had been too poor to take out a patent for the 'teletrofono' that he had demonstrated in New York in 1860. In the event, Bell's patent was submitted just two hours before that of Elisha Gray, then regarded as his closest rival. By the time he was thirty, the soaring value of the Bell Telephone Company had made him a rich man.

The first use of the telephone in Britain was within the home. It was seen as a device which could save the legs of servants who previously would have been summoned up from the servants' quarters, often in the basement, by a bell to inquire what was needed, before returning downstairs to get it. By as early as 1884, however, its external applications were sufficiently recognised for the Postmaster General to authorise the first public telephones to be installed in wooden 'call offices', 'silence cabinets' or (after the Turkish) 'kiosks'. Some kiosks came with an attendant who would help callers cope with the new technology.

In 1912, the role of the competing telephone companies was absorbed by the Post Office, and nine years later an attempt was made to standardise the design of telephone boxes with Kiosk number 1 (K1), made of reinforced concrete. Its shortcomings were soon recognised, and in 1924 a limited competition was held for a K2 design; this was won by Sir Giles Gilbert Scott, grandson of Sir (George) Gilbert Scott. His kiosk was a masterpiece of industrial design: made of cast iron, which could be easily reproduced, it was a wholly new type of structure and yet handsomely Classical in spirit, with fluted corners, a domed top and glazing bars to the doors. With an embossed crown over the door, it was painted in the royal livery of red to match the post boxes. Variants of the K2, incorporating letter boxes and stamp machines, were not successful: the clunk of the machine as stamps were removed disturbed callers. About two hundred standard K2s survive in major cities.

By the mid-1930s, the network of public call boxes was being extended to every market town, village and island in Britain and a cheaper model was needed. The result was Scott's K6 or Jubilee Kiosk, introduced in the twenty-fifth year of George V's reign, 1936: this is the familiar red telephone box, which became a symbol of Britain. Smaller than the K2, it has horizontal glazing bars and something of the streamlined aesthetic associated with the Art Deco or Modern Movement. Thousands were made, a tribute to the era in which a public utility saw itself as having a public responsibility to maintain design standards on Britain's streets. The replacement design, K8, which was introduced in 1969, abandoned Scott's classicism without finding an equally pleasing Modern idiom: nevertheless, this version was still designed by an architect, Bruce Martin.

The nadir came after the privatisation of the telephone service in the 1980s, when British Telecom felt the need to update its corporate image by consigning the 'stuffy' red telephone boxes – sometimes poorly maintained – to the scrap heap. Thousands were torn out and replaced with cabins of Continental and American design. This campaign of corporate vandalism took place just as mobile phone technology was coming to make the old concept of the public pay phone obsolete. In 2001 British Telecom was given permission to reduce the number of public telephones on Britain's streets.

To make any one red telephone box, K2 or K6, a landmark in the sense of this book seems invidious, since – in the best classical tradition – its virtues were those of ubiquity not individuality. Aficionados, however, have a special affection for the row of six Scott boxes in Broad Court next to Bow Street police station in Covent Garden, the double pair of K2 and K6 boxes, symmetrically placed, outside the Law Courts in the Strand and the solitary K2 on the Embankment near Chelsea Bridge: in the background to the latter rise the four fluted columnar chimneys of the same architect's Battersea Power Station.

See also Marconi Wireless Station, page 27; St Helier, page 34; Bridge Street, page 118

THE BRUNEL ENGINE HOUSE   RAILWAY AVENUE, SE16
First tunnel under the Thames

By the early 19th century, London was the pre-eminent trading city in the world: ships were so tightly wedged into the river Thames around the docks that their masts looked like a forest. But the only means of crossing the river, except by ferry, was the bridge first built by the Romans: London Bridge. The carts taking cargoes to and from the ships suffered agonising delays*. Another bridge was unthinkable, given the number of tall-masted vessels that had to pass under it. The first attempt at building a tunnel was made in 1798, but soon petered out. A more determined effort was made in 1807 but flooded the next year. With the increase of trade at the end of the Napoleonic Wars in 1815, the problem became ever more urgent. The solution was provided by the engineer Marc Isambard Brunel: his Thames Tunnel, built from 1825–43, was the first to be built under a navigable river anywhere in the world.

Brunel was born near Rouen in 1769 but he fled from France during the

French Revolution, taking refuge in New York. Once he had accepted American citizenship (he was one of the few people ever to hold both American and British citizenship) he was appointed Chief Engineer for the city. In 1799, he returned to Europe, looking for the girl he had fallen in love with before leaving France. He found Sophia Kingdom in London, where he married and settled. His energy and enterprise should have made him a fortune – he patented several inventions and supplied the British army with boots – but instead he found himself imprisoned for debt. However, he was recognised to be a national asset, and the government settled his debts lest he went to Russia to work for the Tsar. It was while working on a bridge for the Tsar (never built) that he evolved the principle upon which the tunnel under the Thames was constructed. The difficulty of tunnelling under a river lay in the soft ground, which constantly needed to be shored up if it were not to collapse. To overcome this, Brunel invented a rectangular metal shield, the end of which was divided into compartments. In each of the compartments worked a miner, removing 4½ inches of soil at a time: slow work when one realises the tunnel was 1,200ft long. As each 4½-inch slice was removed, the shield was jacked forward. Behind the shield worked bricklayers who built the permanent structure of the tunnel.

To start the tunnel, it was necessary to sink the great iron shield into the ground. For this purpose, Brunel built a round tower whose walls, of two skins of brick with a yard of concrete and rubble in between, stood on a 25-ton iron hoop. As the soil beneath the iron hoop was removed, the tower sunk into the ground, to become a shaft. This was where the pumps were. The shaft still stands, next to the pretty church of St Mary, Rotherhithe. The engines were in time moved into an adjacent engine house which is now a museum.

In the course of digging the tunnel ten men lost their lives. Brunel's son, Isambard Kingdom, who had been working as 'resident engineer' for his father since the age of twenty, was nearly killed when a column of water burst in through the tunnel roof: as he was struggling to get out of the shaft a wave roared in and swept him all the way to the top. Young Brunel despaired of seeing the tunnel finished: he had become absorbed by his survey of the track for the Great Western Railway (see page 36). Despite an eight-year suspension of activity while new finance was secured, Marc Brunel persevered, the tunnel finally opening in 1843.

It was not, however, quite what had been hoped for at the outset. The backers were not prepared to spend the extra money that horse-driven lifts would have cost; it was not therefore possible for horses and carts to get down the shafts – originally there was another one on the Wapping side – that continued to provide the only access to the tunnel. As a result, the tunnel was only used by foot passengers, stallholders and dossers. However, the East London Railway Company bought the tunnel in 1865, extended it and it is still used by London Underground trains running between Whitechapel and Rotherhithe. It was not until 1908 that the Rotherhithe Tunnel fulfilled the original dream of a tunnel for carts and other road traffic.

*See Arnos Grove Station, page 112, and Bridge Street, page 118

BT TOWER

CLEVELAND STREET, W1

White heat of technology

When the Post Office Tower (as it was then and is still generally called) was opened by the Prime Minister Harold Wilson in 1965, it seemed to personify his vision of a Britain simmering with the 'white heat of technology'. At 620ft, this slender, futuristic minaret, silently calling the world from the apparatus clustered around its top, was then the tallest building in London. Its purpose was to transmit high frequency radio waves that expanded the telephone network without the vast cost of tunnelling under the capital to lay cables.

Because of the strategic importance of telecommunications, the Ministry of Public Building and Works designed the building so that it would withstand a nuclear attack on London. It was relatively unscathed by an IRA bomb that exploded in 1971. 'I made it to last, bombers or not,' said the chief architect, Eric Bedford. In the manner of the 1960s hero James Bond, the Post Office Tower combined glamour with technological wizardry: on the 34th floor, diners sipped champagne as they revolved above London in the Top of the Tower restaurant. A complete revolution took twenty-five minutes.

BUCKINGHAM PALACE

THE MALL, SW1

Public face of the British monarchy

Around the world, Buckingham Palace is the most famous residence of the British monarchy, and its position in the centre of London makes it a natural focus for national events and tourists. With the daily pageant of the Changing of the Guard unrolling before it, the building has subliminally conditioned the public's image of the monarchy. Unlike the Houses of Parliament, whose crockets and finials deliberately evoke a sense of hoary antiquity, the east front of Buckingham Palace – the façade it presents to the world – is dignified, reserved and proper.

How different this building seemed in late Georgian London. George IV was one of the few British monarchs to have a genuine passion for the visual arts. Unfortunately, it was a love that turned easily to lust. By 1825, John Nash, the creator of Regent's Park (see page 163) was an old man, too much a friend of the King to be firm with him, and the project of turning what had been Buckingham House into a palace became notorious for incompetence and waste. It is Nash that visitors have to thank for the monumental, unexciting Staterooms, awash with red and gold. The courtyard that he created facing St James's Park, with no fewer than three giant porticos as well as a triumphal arch, is no longer visible from outside the palace: Queen Victoria commissioned Edward Blore to block it off from view by building a range across the mouth of the courtyard. It was an insipid affair; in 1913, Blore's work disappeared from view behind a new façade added by Aston Webb.

In 1901, Webb, in conjunction with the sculptor Sir Thomas Brock, won a limited competition to design a memorial to Queen Victoria outside Buckingham Palace. The centrepiece of the scheme was a statue of the Queen Empress, sitting in front of a white marble pillar, topped by a gilded bronze figure of Victory. The whole of The Mall was turned into a processional way, landscaped to lead up to the Memorial and the Palace beyond it; the road surface is made of pink Tarmac as though it were an enormous red carpet unrolled in front of the monarch.

Enough money was left over from the Victoria Memorial to allow Buckingham Palace to be refaced in a severe style that suited the personality of George V. The work was achieved in just three months. Webb's scheme included the railings in front of the palace made by the Bromsgrove Guild, with elaborate locks. It is from these locks that notices of the royal family's health are hung, for an expectant public to read. Another feature of the scheme that would enter national life was added at this time – the balcony on the first floor; George V particularly wanted it to be prominent, allowing the royal family to show itself to the crowd. As a result, Webb had it carried forward on brackets. It is from this balcony that successive monarchs and their families have appeared at moments of national emotion: coronations, weddings, births, jubilees and the conclusion of wars.

BUNHILL FIELDS
BUNHILL ROW, EC1

Dissenters' burial ground

Shaded by tall plane trees, and surrounded by blocks of flats and the Honourable Artillery Company's parade ground, the old burial ground of Bunhill Fields on the edge of the City of London contains the graves of three of the greatest and most original figures from the history of English literature: John Bunyan, author of *The Pilgrim's Progress* (see page 205); Daniel Defoe, who, when not operating as a Whig spy and journalist, wrote *Robinson Crusoe*; and the poet, artist and visionary, William Blake. Later admirers put up conspicuous memorials, but their original graves lie somewhere below the forest of headstones that reflect the density with which this burial ground – like most others in 18th-century and early 19th-century towns – was used. All three writers were Dissenters, or Protestants who did not belong to the Church of England. Bunhill Fields was one of the few recognised burial places available to them.

Dissenters included Presbyterians, Baptists, Methodists, Independents, Congregationalists and Quakers. Like Roman Catholics, they suffered various disadvantages in the 17th and 18th centuries. They could not hold civil or military office, or take degrees from either Oxford or Cambridge universities. Discrimination pursued them even after death, since they could not be buried in ground consecrated by the Church of England. Until the development of cemeteries such as Highgate* in the 19th century, Anglican churchyards – overcrowded, unsanitary and offensive though they became – had something of a monopoly on the rites of death. Dissenting congregations were rarely rich enough to buy burial land next to their chapels.

The Corporation of London, perhaps because the City was inevitably more cosmopolitan than other areas, was the only civic authority to provide its own solution. During the Great Plague, which created an urgent need for sites where victims could be buried, it acquired Bunhill Fields. It had probably already been used for burials when, in 1549, the contents of the overflowing charnel house at St Paul's Cathedral were re-interred – hence the supposed original name of Bone Hill. The plague receded before Bunhill Fields was pressed into use, but the place remained available for burials, particularly, if not exclusively, for Nonconformists.

As well as writers and artists, Bunhill Fields contains the graves of pastors, doctors, soldiers, convicts and the representatives of many other callings – among them, some of the descendants of England's most conspicuous Dissenter, Oliver Cromwell (see page 275).

*See Highgate Cemetery, page 150

CABINET WAR ROOMS *KING CHARLES STREET, SW1*
Engine room of the Second World War

The nerve-centre of Britain's war effort during the Second World War was an overcrowded, smoke-filled, inadequately serviced basement under the New Government Offices off Whitehall. The war rooms had been hurriedly fitted out as a temporary measure, being finished just a week before war was declared in September 1939. Here, in a position conveniently near Downing Street and the House of Commons, the Prime Minister and his Cabinet could pursue their work sheltered, if not absolutely safe, beside the heads of the armed services. Since there is no reference to the underground war rooms in any German document, it seems that the enemy never knew of their existence. Perhaps they would not have believed in them, if they had.

Ever since the First World War, it had been obvious that London would be a prime target for enemy aircraft in times of war, and planners predicted massive destruction and casualties. The nation's top decision takers had to be protected, perhaps by removing them to deep tunnels dug in the suburbs. This proposal was rejected on the grounds that morale would suffer if Londoners thought their leaders were deserting them. Instead, it was decided to convert some old basement storerooms in Westminster, the traditional heart of government, into offices and sleeping quarters. The arrangement suited the temperament of Winston Churchill*, with his appetite for risk. Initially, he was reluctant to abandon 10 Downing Street† for the considerably less elegant underground war rooms but when he realised that Downing Street could well be flattened, he understood the sense of the arrangement. Whether the underground war rooms offered very much more protection to begin with is open to question. It was only in late 1940, after several Cabinet meetings had been held there, that a 3ft-thick concrete slab was laid over the top of the rooms.

Churchill's habit of working late into the night made it particularly necessary that he should have a bedroom. Given the shortage of space, it had to double as an office, which suited Churchill's routine (he invariably worked in bed, and would continue dictating from the bath). The underground map room, manned by officers who exuded nonchalance and glamour, was the heart of the complex. Here, the progress of the war – fighter scores during the Battle of Britain, the fate of convoys crossing the Atlantic, the advance of battlefronts across Europe, the toll on London taken by V-1 and V-2 rockets (see page 147) – was charted.

A bank of telephones, colour-coded, allowed updates to be quickly relayed. A small room – popularly supposed to contain the only lavatory – was equipped with a scrambler telephone that formed a hotline to the President of the United States; a predecessor of modern digital technology, the scrambler mechanism was so big that it could not be contained in the war rooms, but was outstationed in a basement under Selfridges in Oxford Street. By contrast, the conditions for typists, crammed into every available corner, were basic, although not so bad as the quarters, reached by a trap door, in which staff were expected to sleep. This was the spirit of stoic determination and make-do that won Britain the war.

*See Chartwell, page 61. †See 10 Downing Street, page 136

CANARY WHARF

Big Bang's soaring landmark

In 1986, the Big Bang of deregulation exploded the old clubby world of the City of London, and replaced it with trading floors, computer screens and global markets. The American property developer G. Ware Travelstead had already seen that financial institutions would need a new type of accommodation, which he proposed to provide in the form of 10 million sq ft of air-conditioned offices in twenty buildings above what had been the West India Dock*, now derelict, to the east of the City. Largely designed by American architects, they would include the tallest tower blocks in Britain. To the American mind, this was naturally a source of pride. To the Prince of Wales, agonised by the impact they would have on the view from Greenwich, it was an act of barbarism. Travelstead did not see through the development, however; he sold Canary Wharf to the Canadian company of Olympia & Yorke. Despite the princely revulsion, Prime Minister Margaret Thatcher laid the foundation stone in 1987. Canary Wharf began to rise at the astonishing rate of a floor a week.

Almost at once, Canary Wharf became a symbol. A symbol of the regeneration of Docklands, whose piecemeal, free-market development had until then lacked a sense of cohesion. A symbol of the re-orientation (literally) of the City of London, towards the East. A symbol of the new surroundings in which the financial services industry would operate: highly technological, glittering. A symbol of the workaholic culture and fabulous bonuses associated with the global trading that new technology made possible. Architecturally, the style was not innovative – more a throwback to 1930s New York – but the quality of the materials (granite, marble, York stone, cast iron, brass) was something that London had not seen very often since the Second World War.

Despite high-class shops, Canary Wharf is strictly a work zone: there are no houses, no children, no old people; nobody selling the *Big Issue*. The combined power of the financial institutions that occupy it is forcing London to reinvent itself, as a city where the East End offers more than poverty, crime and cheerful making-do.

*See St Katharine's Dock, page 177

THE CENOTAPH

'Their name liveth for evermore'

Eight and a half million soldiers were killed during the First World War; of these, about a million came from Britain and her Empire. Like the Black Death, the devastation caused by the war touched families of every social position, from all parts of the country. As the Allies prepared for their final Big Push, the nation – indeed the Empire – yearned for a means of expressing the grief that was now so deeply cut into its soul. Ultimately, that symbol was the Cenotaph in Whitehall, designed by the newly knighted Edwin Lutyens (see page 80).

The need for a memorial in Whitehall came to a head when a great military parade was planned to celebrate the peace in July 1919. A point was needed along the route at which the troops could honour the dead, and the Prime Minister Lloyd George asked Lutyens to design, very quickly, a catafalque. According to Lutyens's biographer Christopher Hussey, he had a flash of intuition: he thought of the poppies that bloom in shell holes and those that flower equally happily around a garden bench in Surrey, and from this he recalled a comment likening one rather massive bench to the Cenotaph of Sigismunda. A cenotaph, he remembered being told, is a monument to a dead person whose body is buried elsewhere. Lutyens had his design roughed out in a matter of hours. The temporary wooden structure, rushed up for the 1919 parade, was replaced, within eighteen months, by the Cenotaph as we see it today in Portland stone.

Inscribed simply with the words THE GLORIOUS DEAD, the Cenotaph takes the form of a tomb on top of a plinth. It is an almost completely abstract work of architecture. The millions of people who have paid their respects in front of it are probably unaware of the refinement of the calculations that Lutyens used to calibrate the very subtly curving surfaces. There was a call to place bronze figures of sentries at the corners but Lutyens firmly rejected it. Lutyens opposed the overtly Christian symbolism of the cross, on the grounds that the Fallen included Nonconformists, Jews, Hindus and atheists. While its subtle imagery and mathematical proportions were hardly typical, the Cenotaph became a national emblem for the many hundreds of memorials that were built on village greens, in churches and in public buildings after what optimists called the war to end wars.

CENTRAL CRIMINAL COURT   OLD BAILEY, EC4
England's premier criminal court

Blindfolded, a sword in one hand and a pair of scales in the other, the figure that F. W. Pomeroy sculpted to surmount the dome of the Old Bailey in London is the universal symbol of British justice. The Edwardian Baroque building above which she stands – as rotund as a barrister's peroration, as florid as a judge's face after luncheon – was designed by E. W. Mountford after a competition in 1900. Mountford was faced by a Herculean challenge, given that his building replaced one of the most formidable masterpieces of 18th-century architecture, George Dance the Younger's Newgate Gaol. Although hardly a cheerful building, Newgate was part of history, thanks to the number of villains and traitors who had met their ends there. Mountford also had the task of producing a design that would stand comparison with St Paul's Cathedral (see page 179), then soaring above the rooftops of the neighbouring streets. The result could have been worse.

There had been a court attached to the original Old Bailey since 1539. Here William Penn was tried for 'preaching to an unlawful assembly' in 1670. Rebuilt in 1774, it came to be England's most important criminal court, hearing not only the most sensational cases from around London, such as the trial of Oscar Wilde in 1895 (see page 236), but also those from other parts of England and Wales which are referred to it. Among the memorable trials which have taken place at the Old Bailey in the 20th century were those of Dr Crippen (1910), William Joyce, otherwise 'Lord Haw-Haw' (1945), the Kray twins (1969; see page 117) and Peter Sutcliffe, the 'Yorkshire Ripper' (1981). In the 21st century, the need for such courts shows no sign of abating.

CENTRE POINT

An unacceptable face of capitalism

103 NEW OXFORD STREET, WC1

Richard Seifert did more to shape the skyline of London than any architect since Sir Christopher Wren (see page 179). Of all the 600 tall buildings for which his firm, R. Seifert & Partners, was responsible, the 398ft-high Centre Point, at the junction with St Giles Circus, was the most famous. This was little to do with its architectural form, or its latticework of pre-cast concrete components that was likened to a gas fire. Instead, a generation whose sensitivity to the crisis of 'homelessness' had been heightened by the television play *Cathy Come Home* was outraged that this 34-storey building should stand empty for fifteen years, while its owner, the reclusive property tycoon Harry Hyams waited for rents to rise. Centre Point, the tallest building in London when it was completed in 1966, was invaded by students eight years later as a symbol of the 'rotten society'. In 1974, the Labour government considered nationalising it.

Centre Point embodies many of the architectural principles of the Modern Movement, derived from Le Corbusier. Rather than lining up with other buildings on a street, it breaks free of its surroundings, the sculptural quality of the exterior reflecting free-flowing spaces within. These ideas, in evolution since the 1920s, only caught on in Britain with the building boom after the Second World War. However, it was not Colonel Richard Seifert's artistic fancy that attracted his developer clients, so much as his genius for exploiting planning law and negotiating with local councils. That Centre Point is raised up on 'pilotis' (the pillars favoured by Le Corbusier to allow a more flexible use of space at ground level) is due to a deal struck with the London County Council: they allowed him more office space in return for being able to run a road below the building.

By the time of Seifert's death in 2001, Centre Point had become officially protected as 'a building of historic importance'. With his round spectacles, pipe and respectable air, his only indulgences being a Rolls-Royce and Havana cigars, the colonel was still widely regarded as a symbol of English architecture's lowest ebb – at least, by the thousands of Londoners doomed to work in his buildings.

THE CHARTERHOUSE CHARTERHOUSE SQUARE, EC1
Monks against monarch

On 4 May 1535, John Houghton, Prior of London's Charterhouse, and two of his monks were hanged, drawn and quartered at Tyburn (see page 187), their heads and limbs then being displayed on the gates of the City, and part of Houghton's body being nailed to the gate of the Charterhouse itself. Their crime had been to oppose Henry VIII's new authority as supreme head of the Church in England.

The Act of Supremacy, giving Henry the powers previously enjoyed by the Pope, was passed in 1534. The suppression of the smaller monasteries began under Thomas Cromwell following the Act of Dissolution passed in 1536. Some monks had already strayed from the ascetic ideal; Cromwell's agents collected any gossip or innuendo they could find with which to accuse monks of superstition, corruption and homosexuality. While it was not originally intended that the larger houses should also be closed, the taste of the land and riches seized from the smaller ones whetted the royal appetite, and following the 1539 Act of Suppression, these too fell into his greedy hands. Between 1536 and 1540, some 850 monasteries were surrendered. Most priors took the easy option, often encouraged by monetary bribes, and gave in peaceably, perhaps going on to occupy a position in the newly created Church of England. Some of the monks at the Charterhouse who witnessed Houghton's demise fared no better than their prior: another batch was executed the next year (they had been chained into a standing position for the thirteen days before they died), while ten monks who were imprisoned in Newgate Gaol were left to rot to death.

Under the will of Thomas Sutton, a civil servant who had enriched himself through coal mining and money-lending, the Charterhouse became a 'hospital' and a school. The hospital was to be home 'for such as had been servants to the King's Majesty; captains either at land or sea; soldiers maimed or impotent; men fallen into decay through shipwreck, casualty or fire'. It survives to this day. The school moved to Godalming, Surrey in 1872.

CHELSEA OLD CHURCH

CHELSEA EMBANKMENT, SW3

Sir Thomas More crosses the river to be tried

Sir Thomas More, lawyer, humanist and the author of *Utopia*, spent the night of 12/13 April 1534 in prayer. The day before, he had been handed a summons to go to Lambeth Palace, and More recognised this as the instrument by which Henry VIII would exact his revenge for resigning from the Lord Chancellorship two years earlier. The issue of his resignation had been the King's abrogation of powers previously exercised by the Pope. Now More was being required to swear an oath called the Act of Supremacy (see page 133), which annulled Henry's marriage to Catherine of Aragon and, more importantly for More, denied the Pope's authority.

More said farewell to his family in the garden of his manor house set in extensive grounds near All Saints church (now more usually known as Chelsea Old Church) beside the Thames; he did not want them to suffer the pain of parting at the side of the river. Only his son-in-law William Roper accompanied him on the short river crossing. At Lambeth, he appeared before Thomas Cromwell, the Lord Chancellor and architect of the Dissolution of the Monasteries, Thomas Cranmer, Archbishop of Canterbury (see pages 153 and 229), and other prelates. The cross-examination probably took place in the large Guard Hall, the interior of which is preserved within the carcass of the Victorian restoration. More refused to swear the oath. He was then sent out to reflect on his decision in 'the old burned chamber' – a room that had yet to be redecorated after a fire. As he did so, he saw a defiant Catholic being led off to the Tower. Taken back before Cromwell and the others, More refused to alter his position. Now it was his turn to go to the Tower.

It was a foregone conclusion that at his trial for treason he would be found guilty, and so he was: the King's one concession was to commute the sentence of disembowelling to beheading. On the scaffold on Tower Hill he kissed his executioner, saying: 'Thou wilt give me this day a greater benefit than ever any mortal man can be able to give me.' The axe severed his head at one blow. He was canonised in 1935, becoming England's first lay martyr and saint.

Although Chelsea Old Church was badly damaged by bombing during the Second World War, the chapel that More built there survived.

CHISWICK HOUSE

BURLINGTON LANE, W4

A mission to change taste – which succeeded

At Chiswick House, built from 1727–9, the 3rd Earl of Burlington reinvented the English architectural tradition. His new style looked back to Ancient Rome, through the eyes of the 16th-century Italian Andrea Palladio, the 17th-century

Englishman Inigo Jones and the experiences of 18th-century noblemen on the Grand Tour. Like the Queen's House at Greenwich (see page 165), Chiswick House was in every sense a novelty. It was designed by Burlington himself after his study of Palladio's buildings in their Veneto setting. It was originally no more than a pavilion, built primarily to display his ideas about architecture, and the art collection that he had amassed in Italy.

No artistic movement is created solely by one man. Before Burlington turned to architecture, Giacomo Leoni had translated Palladio's *Quattro libri dell'architettura* into English and Colen Campbell had published a compilation of recent classical architecture in Britain (mostly Baroque, but with an emphasis on Jones) called *Vitruvius Britannicus*. Nevertheless, it is not too much of an exaggeration to say that Chiswick House set the pattern of taste for a century. In it were combined a love of antiquity, a general respect for things Italian and a great collection of paintings and sculpture garnered on the Grand Tour.

It took the form of a new building type, the villa: it was not a self-sufficient country house but a place of recreation, on the outskirts of London. Around it was a garden, full of serpentine paths and evocative follies, designed by William Kent. Burlington had discovered Kent as a second-rate painter in Rome, and transformed him into a figure of incalculable influence on England's decorative style; he was the architect of Holkham Hall in Norfolk (see page 273) and Horse Guards Parade in Westminster, the designer of some opulently gilded furniture and the landscape genius who, in Horace Walpole's words, 'leaped the fence and saw that all Nature was a Garden'.

Although Lord Burlington owned a London palace, Burlington House, as well as vast estates in Yorkshire and elsewhere, it was increasingly to Chiswick House that he retreated. From here, consulted by everyone with aspirations to build grand houses themselves, he ruled contemporary society with a unique dictatorship of taste.

CHRISTIE'S
8 KING STREET, SW1
Focus of the London art market

Revolutions do wonders for the art market. After the English Civil War, Oliver Cromwell sold the greatest collection ever assembled by one individual in Britain, the works of art owned by Charles I. This released so many masterpieces onto the market that it was flooded for a century. By the mid-18th century, British aristocratic families had amassed enough wealth to go on Grand Tours and bring back the paintings and sculpture that often still adorn their country houses. It was the French Revolution, however, and the convulsions of Continental Europe that followed it which established the art market as we know it today, and in which London is still pre-eminent for Old Masters.

The firm established by James Christie in 1776 personifies the development of auctioneering, by which works of art achieve a value according to the free operation of the market. The commission that he took on sales ought to have made him 'immensely rich', but there was a rumour that some of the money went on gambling. He was credited with 'a very good head for scheming but wants education'. Since the diarist Joseph Faringdon's information came from a rival auctioneer, it is not a generous portrait. On the other hand, the world of the fine art auctioneer was not yet sanctified by art history or refined connoisseurship.

Early sales included artificial stone ornaments, coffins, barrel organs, farm implements, animals, silks woven in Spitalfields, and even hay. A clue as to the future direction of the firm is given by the sale of Sir Joshua Reynolds's collection after his death in 1792, the effects of the late Chevalier d'Eon (a diplomat friend of Christie who notoriously spent the last thirty years of his life in France dressed as a woman, and who died in 1810), the jewels of Madame Dubarry and Hogarth's *Marriage à la Mode*. Christie died in 1803, to be followed into the business by his Eton-educated eldest son, also James, whose charm and accomplishments are noted in succinct detail by Faringdon: 'very amiable – good scholar – music – languages – drawing'.

The younger Christie's scholarship created a more orderly market, and the dispersal of contents from aristocratic French houses swelled the collections of rich families in Britain, but there is little room for sentiment in an auction house: collections that grow inevitably feed on those that break up. The event that established Christie's at the pinnacle of its trade came in 1848 with the auction of the ruined Duke of Buckingham's art treasures from Stowe in Buckinghamshire. In quasi-Biblical fashion, the sale lasted forty days. The £75,562 4s 6d that it realised seems relatively modest, considering that the lots included a Rembrandt (now in the Wallace Collection) and the Chandos portrait of Shakespeare (now in the National Portrait Gallery). Auctioneering is a reflection of supply, demand, taste, opportunity and luck. Cézanne was still out of fashion when H. C. Marillier published his history of Christie's in 1926: today his paintings sit at the very top of the market. These dizzy changes in the perception of beauty help make a sale at Christie's (or its arch rival, Sotheby's) one of the best pieces of public theatre in London.

10 DOWNING STREET   WHITEHALL, SW1

Official residence of Prime Ministers

Ostensibly, 10 Downing Street is part of an 18th-century terrace of houses that would be unremarkable if it did not contain the official London residence of the Prime Minister. The architectural modesty of the façade, with its famous front door, could be thought to reflect British attitudes towards the constitution: the Prime Minister, although the most powerful person in the country, is not head of state, nor even the most highly paid member of the government. Appearances, in this case, are deceptive. No. 10 Downing Street is really two houses, the sober family house that overlooks the street being attached to a much bigger one overlooking Horse Guards Parade at the back. As a result, visitors who go under the curved lamp bracket and past the policeman into 10 Downing Street for the first time struggle to understand how it can contain so many handsome panelled and pillared interiors.

Downing Street was originally created on the edge of the old, sprawling Palace of Whitehall in the late 17th century. It takes its name from Sir George Downing, an American who was one of Harvard University's earliest graduates, coming to England in 1650 to run Oliver Cromwell's intelligence service. Having worked against the royalist exiles throughout the Commonwealth, he abruptly changed sides when it became clear that the Cromwellian legacy would not be maintained, and offered his services to Charles II instead. In the 1680s, he developed what had been the grounds of Hampden House; as might be expected of a shifty character such as Downing, the houses he built were not of the first quality, and gave constant trouble to those who later lived in them. The house overlooking Horse Guards Parade was an altogether more aristocratic structure.

The two houses were remodelled into one by William Kent in 1732–5. This was to make them ready for Sir Robert Walpole, regarded as Britain's first Prime Minister, who had been offered them as a gift by George II. Although Walpole was not generally shy of using his office to acquire personal riches, on this occasion he declined the offer, asking instead that 10 Downing Street (as it became) should be retained for the use of successive First Lords of the Treasury. It is as First Lord of the Treasury that the Prime Minister occupies it today.

For most of the 20th century, economy was the presiding genius at 10 Downing Street, and the interiors came to look tired and degraded. Remarkably, for a Prime Minister who was so associated with frugality, and by no means famous as a champion of the arts, Margaret Thatcher was responsible for elevating the architectural tone of 10 Downing Street, using the neo-Classicist Quinlan Terry. In 1989, gates were built at the end of Downing Street to protect ministers from attack by the IRA, sadly depriving London of a right of way that allowed voters a sense of proximity to the rulers whom they had elected.

ELECTRIC AVENUE
Epicentre of West Indian immigration

In 1948, the SS *Empire Windrush* docked at Tilbury, having arrived from the Caribbean with 492 West Indians on board. It was the start of the mass immigration from colonies and former colonies, which was to change Britain's self-image in the later 20th century. In the years after the Second World War, as the country struggled to rebuild itself, the government welcomed this extra source of labour, without which hospitals and railways would have ceased to function. People throughout the Empire held British passports and were, until 1972, allowed unfettered access.

Not that the conditions which awaited the young Jamaican men, walking down the gangplank of the *Windrush*, were especially enticing. Some of them had served in the Royal Air Force and had with them the address of a fellow pilot who lived in Brixton, a suburb of large Victorian terraced houses. He arranged for them to sleep, for the time being, in an air-raid shelter on Clapham Common. The nearest employment exchange was in Brixton, and once they had got work, it was understandable that the new arrivals should seek accommodation nearby. As the young men formed families, a Caribbean community developed, with Brixton as its natural focus. One of its streets is celebrated in Eddy Grant's 1983 reggae hit, 'Electric Avenue'.

Electric Avenue, a crescent of tall brick terraces, takes its name from the street lamps that used to hang from a glazed cast-iron canopy over the pavements on either side of the road. Opened in 1888, it was one of the first shopping streets in the country to be lit by electricity. Now it is home to Europe's largest Afro-Caribbean market, where yams and plantains are heaped beside stalls selling sunglasses, CDs, saucepans, brightly coloured clothes, bath towels, incense and exotic fish.

FLEET STREET
Metonym for the British newspaper industry

In 1476, the Kent-born merchant William Caxton arrived in London. He was fifty-four, and had spent the last thirty years in Bruges where he was governor of the Merchant Adventurers' Company. It is said that he learnt the art of printing in Cologne when he went there with his partner from Bruges. His *The Recuyell of the Historyes of Troye* was, in 1474 or 1475, the first book printed in English, albeit overseas. In London, he established a press in the precincts of Westminster Abbey, near the Palace of Westminster, where he hoped he might attract a courtly patronage. By the time of his death in 1491, he had published some hundred titles. He had also taken on an apprentice from Alsace called Wynkyn de Worde.

De Worde took over Caxton's press at Westminster, but in about 1500 moved to Fleet Street, the name coming from the river Fleet which would be covered over in the mid-18th century. Caxton, as a successful merchant, could afford to print luxurious books, and take the loss if they did not sell. De Worde had no such reserves: he needed to attract the London public who shopped among the booksellers around St Paul's Churchyard. He did not have the cultural resources of Caxton, who edited and, if necessary, translated the works he printed himself. But if de Worde was only a craftsman, he was shrewd enough to see that many more people were likely to buy cheap books than expensive ones. He was one of literature's first popularisers; at the sign of the Sun – the sign outside his house which denoted where he lived, there being no street numbers at that time – he was also the first printer to operate from Fleet Street, starting a tradition that lasted five hundred years.

Fleet Street is synonymous with the British newspaper industry. It would be too much to claim that the line from Wynkyn de Worde to the *Daily Express* building is unbroken, but it can be said that Britain's first daily newspaper, the *Daily Courant*, emerged from an office 'next to the King's Arms tavern by Fleet Bridge' in 1702. After a month, however, it moved to Ludgate Hill. For the next century, the association of Fleet Street with journalism remained sporadic. Founded in 1785, *The Times* thundered out from New Printing House Square, a little to the north.

In 1825, the *Morning Advertiser* moved to Fleet Street and from that year the link between newspapers and Fleet Street strengthened. By the mid-20th century, Fleet Street and its environs were home to most of the national newspapers. From their contrasting, purpose-built offices, the most conspicuous were those of the *Daily Express* which, in 1930, Lord Beaverbrook installed in a smooth-contoured, shiny black and plate-glass headquarters designed by Sir Owen Williams (see page 306). As the first of the Victorian penny daily newspapers, the *Daily Telegraph* was older (1855) than the *Daily Express*, and the Egyptian-style building that was built for it in 1928 was colourful, grandiose, but not Modern with a capital M. For the architecture of journalism, the palm goes to the grandly classical Reuters building designed by Lutyens in 1936; it was the last news office in Fleet Street, leaving in 2005.

By the 1980s, Fleet Street was not just a byword for newspapers, but for the restrictive practices that the print unions had imposed on weak managements. The printing of newspapers had become far more expensive than it needed to be, particularly now that the advent of computer technology was available to replace the old hot-metal method of setting type. In 1986, Eddie Shah challenged the dominance of Fleet Street, with a colour tabloid produced without union labour called *Today* (it lasted nearly ten years before folding).

His example was followed by Rupert Murdoch, whose News International acquired *The Times* in 1981. Murdoch covertly built and equipped a new printing plant at 'Fortress Wapping', and moved *The Times*, the *Sunday Times*, the *Sun* and the *News of the World* there in 1986. A new means of distribution, by road, was introduced, to prevent the rail unions refusing to deliver 'blacked' newspapers. Despite a long and bitter dispute, the print unions were unable to strangle the computers at birth, and one by one every other newspaper followed suit. For journalists, this entailed a painful move from the clubby, bibulous world of El Vino's and other famous watering holes, where professional rivalries were sunk in the camaraderie of the hack, to far away and disparate corners of the capital: Canary Wharf in the case of the *Daily Telegraph* (see page 130), Battersea for the *Guardian* and the *Observer*, Kensington for the *Daily Mail* and *Evening Standard*.

FOREIGN & COMMONWEALTH OFFICE WHITEHALL, SW1
Administering the Empire

The Foreign and Commonwealth Office grandly commemorates Britain's cultural schizophrenia in the Victorian age. Externally, the building results from the tussle between the architect Sir (George) Gilbert Scott and the Prime Minister Lord Palmerston, in which the latter compelled the former, a Gothic Revivalist, to build an Italianate classical design. 'Sir,' Palmerston told Parliament, 'the battle of the books, the battle of the Big and Little Endeans, and the battle of the Green Ribbands and the Blue Ribbands at Constantinople were all as nothing compared with this battle of the Gothic and Palladian styles. If I were called upon to give an impartial opinion as to the issue of the conflict, I should say that the Gothic has been entirely defeated.' He was wrong; he had not won the war for the classicists. However, work on Scott's wholly Italianate, if architecturally compromised Foreign and India Office, began in 1862.

Inside, the decorative focus rests on the India Office, as befits the bureaucracy that administered the Empire's richest prize. The India Office was established in 1858, after the Indian Mutiny had demonstrated that the East India Company was not competent to run the subcontinent by itself. At least in visual terms, the transition between the two organisations was seamless, since Matthew Digby Wyatt, who was the East India Company's official architect, was commissioned to decorate the new offices.

The legacy of the EIC survives in the furnishing of the India Office council chamber: the bottoms of government officials now descended onto the same chairs that had supported those of the EIC's directors since the early 18th century, their elbows rested on the same boardroom table. Of the same date, the overmantel above the fireplace by Michael Rysbrack depicts 'Britannia receiving the riches of the East Indies', with Asia and Africa personified as female figures, the former leading a camel, the latter accompanied by a lion. Little in this world view, in which England stood firmly at the centre, and foreign continents were treated as exotic, had changed by the mid-19th century when the spandrels of the Home and Colonial offices depicted Africa as a Hottentot with a hippopotamus and Asia as a woman with an elephant. The three-storey hall, known after the coronation of Edward VII as the Durbar Court, became the iconographic heart of the Empire.

THE FOUNDLING MUSEUM   BRUNSWICK SQUARE, WC1
Monument of humanity through art

When Samuel Pepys found the Duke of York (the future James II) and his little daughters – the future Queens Mary II and Anne – actually playing together towards the end of the 1660s, it was a matter for comment. Childhood, as a vital stage to the development of the individual, hardly existed before the late 18th century: until then, children were regarded essentially as miniature adults, whose work and suffering they often shared. The Foundling Hospital, established in London in 1739, is a monument in the development of a more humane approach.

Captain Thomas Coram, having made a fortune as sailor and shipbuilder in the New World, was horrified by the plight of unwanted children in London. Childless himself, he wanted to create a refuge for them and in 1739 did so with the help of his friend, the artist William Hogarth, another man without children. From this flowed one of the most remarkable artistic as well as charitable endeavours of the age: in order to raise money for the Hospital, Hogarth persuaded his artist friends to contribute their talents for nothing. They were joined by the composer Handel (see page 148), then at the zenith of his career, his 'Music for the Royal Fireworks' having recently had its first performance in Green Park. He gave the first of a series of benefit concerts for the Hospital in 1749, and became a governor, like Hogarth, the next year. This association with the arts made the Hospital a fashionable cause, which was a definite achievement in itself, given polite society's horror of the fallen women who were often the mothers of the unwanted babies. As a fund-raising technique, it is the ancestor of the sterling work of so many charitable ball committees today.

The Hospital was built on a site north of Lamb's Conduit Street from 1745–56 but when, in 1926, the children were moved to Hertfordshire (where the air was better), it was demolished. The Court Room, which had been created in 1746, was installed in 40 Brunswick Square. It is one of the most remarkable rooms in England, with Rococo plasterwork, a chimneypiece by Rysbrack and a series of paintings on the theme of charity and children masterminded by Hogarth, including his own *Moses brought before Pharaoh's Daughter*. He also painted Thomas Coram in a landmark of English portraiture (despite the grand Italian manner of the drapery, the figure is rough-hewn and un-wigged). Hogarth's third painting for the Hospital was *The March of the Guards to Finchley*, a satire lampooning the disreputable behaviour of His Majesty's troops. Perhaps not surprisingly, George II did not want it when it was offered to him; the work was then made the prize in a raffle, in which all but 157 of 2,000 tickets were sold. No one can have been very astonished to find that the winning ticket was one of the unsold ones, as a result of which the painting remained in the Hospital.

Some of the most moving objects in the Hospital's collection were not, however, works of art, but humble, everyday items such as buttons, locks, scraps of material and labels from bottles. They were left by mothers as a means of identifying their offspring, should they ever come back to reclaim them. Most of the boys grew up to become soldiers, while the girls went into service. The scale of the problem, however, meant that there were other mothers for whom the Hospital could not offer a solution. Babies were chosen by a kind of lottery, with each mother reaching into a leather bag containing three balls. If she lifted out a white ball, her baby was accepted; a red ball meant it would go on the waiting list; a black ball signified rejection.

FREUD'S HOUSE
20 MARESFIELD GARDENS, NW3

Last home of the founder of psychiatry

In the 1930s, 60,000 Jews fleeing from Nazi regimes in Germany, Austria, Czechoslovakia and Hungary found refuge in Britain. One of them was the founder of psychiatry, Sigmund Freud, who left his native Vienna in 1938. His personal fortune had already been confiscated, and a well-wisher had to pay the Nazis a ransom to allow Freud to leave. He was a sick man, having suffered from cancer of the mouth – he constantly smoked cigars, even after cancer was diagnosed – since the early 1920s. His son Ernst, who had been in England since 1933, found a house in Maresfield Gardens into which Freud and his wife, Martha, moved. It was a comfortable suburban house, built in the Queen Anne style in the 1920s and brought up to date by Ernst, who was an architect of the Modernist school. Freud moved in his library, collection of antiquities and famous psychiatrist's couch, covered in an opulently coloured rug and cushions, thereby re-creating something of the atmosphere of Old Vienna in Hampstead. He enjoyed objects from the ancient civilisations, and obsessively crowded his desk with little Greek and Egyptian figures. Freud owned hundreds of amulets (some phallic), primitive Greek pots, bodhisattvas and buddhas, jade carvings and turkey carpets.

He had visited England before, as a student, and found it congenial – despite his experience of fogs, conservatism and drunkenness. During his time at Maresfield Gardens, he was visited by H. G. Wells and had his portrait drawn by Salvador Dali. After Freud's death in November 1939, Martha kept the study as it had been arranged during his life. The shrine was preserved by his youngest child, Anna, who in turn practised psychiatry from 20 Maresfield Gardens, pioneering child analysis.

22 FRITH STREET *SOHO, W1*
'Seeing by wireless'

There are now over a billion television sets on the face of the planet, one for every five or so people who inhabit it. This proliferation is all the more remarkable in the case of an invention which has only been in existence for three-quarters of a century. The first television image of a living being – the head of an office boy who was paid half a crown for the privilege – was made in 1926, from John Logie Baird's attic laboratory in Soho.

In the late 19th century, it had been discovered that light could be converted into electricity. At about the same time, the invention of the cathode ray tube provided a means of translating electrical impulses into a picture on a glass screen. Baird managed to put these and other discoveries together, and convince a public that had until that point been highly sceptical of 'seeing by wireless'.

After studying at the Royal Technical College in Glasgow (at the same time as the future Lord Reith of the BBC, see page 122), Baird, the son of a Presbyterian minister, took a dispiriting factory job. The experience convinced him that life would be better as an entrepreneur, and he had a small success selling his own brand of medicated socks. Other ventures, including jam from Trinidad, Australian honey that he had bought cheap at the docks, an unserviceable soap known as Baird's Speedy Cleaner, and experiments with pneumatic shoes and razors made of glass, either prospered or failed, but even the promising starts were blighted by Baird's fragile health.

Baird was living in Hastings when he put together a television transmitter and receiver, crafted from biscuit tins, hat boxes, darning needles and four penny bull's-eye lenses. The contraption was held together with sealing wax and string. Nevertheless, it enabled him to transmit the flickering image of a back-lit Maltese cross over a distance of two or three yards. An explosion in the laboratory caused the owner to eject his tenant, and Baird moved to London. He found digs in Ealing and commuted to Frith Street. It was there that, on

27 January 1926, forty members of the Royal Institution (see page 171) arrived, in full evening dress, accompanied by a reporter from *The Times*, climbed three flights of stairs, and waited in a passage as groups of six were shown into the tiny laboratory for 'television' to be demonstrated. 'Baird has got it,' one of the audience was heard to remark. 'The rest is merely a matter of £ s. d.'

Like many British inventors, Baird never received the £ s. d. that his talents deserved. After five years, the Baird Television Company was overtaken by Marconi (see page 27), who had developed an electronic as opposed to mechanical system. Nevertheless, Baird went on inventing – colour television, stereoscopic television, big screen television – until his death in 1946.

THE GLOBE THEATRE

NEW GLOBE WALK, SE1

The great age of drama

In 1600, Southwark was a collection of medieval lanes and houses, mixed in with gardens and open ground: the very grand rubbed up against greater numbers of the very poor, some of whom fished for their suppers on the river Thames while others sold produce brought in from the nearby Surrey fields. In this unlikely setting, some of the greatest works of British theatre were born. Among the activities that were considered disreputable and not tolerated within the walled city of London, but flourished immediately outside (see page 199), were play houses. The first play house, named simply The Theatre, its name taken from Roman amphitheatres, had been built by James Burbage in fields at Finsbury to the north of London in 1576. Southwark followed with The Curtain the next year. Then came The Rose, The Swan and, in 1599, The Globe. The Globe was a replacement for The Theatre, which had been closed by its landlord. Timbers from it were surreptitiously carried across London to be used in The Globe.

Burbage's company was under the patronage of Henry Carey, 1st Baron Hunsdon, the Lord Chamberlain (who was responsible for all performances at Court), and was known as the Lord Chamberlain's Men, the most prominent among them helping to finance the building project. They included the actor/ playwright William Shakespeare*, who had just written *Much Ado About Nothing*, *Julius Caesar* and *As You Like It* and was about to complete *Hamlet*. All Shakespeare's subsequent plays, including *Twelfth Night*, *Measure for Measure*, *Macbeth*, *King Lear*, *Antony and Cleopatra* and *The Tempest*, had their first performances at The Globe in front of the demanding London audience. The Globe took the form of an open courtyard surrounded by galleries, the idea borrowed from the courtyards of inns where plays were first performed (and still were, when actors were on tour). A major difference from modern theatre was that performances took place in daylight, allowing actors to see the audience – making special effects (ghosts, devils, magic) in these action-packed dramas all the more difficult to achieve.

In 1613 when a cannon was fired during a performance of Shakespeare's last play, *Henry VIII*, a flaming wad set the thatched roof alight, burning The Globe to the ground. It was rebuilt with a tiled roof. This Globe was in turn demolished by the Puritans in 1644. Thanks to the lifelong passion of the American actor/director Sam Wanamaker for the Bard, the theatre was rebuilt as Shakespeare knew it, and opened in 1997.

*See Shakespeare's Birthplace, page 345

GOLDSMITHS' HALL   FOSTER LANE, EC2
Oldest medieval guild still to regulate its trade

The Worshipful Company of Goldsmiths was one of the dozen great livery companies in the Middle Ages to regulate trade in London: in order of seniority, these were the Mercers, Grocers, Drapers, Fishmongers, Goldsmiths, Merchant Taylors/Skinners, Haberdashers, Salters, Ironmongers, Vintners and Cloth-workers. These guilds were highly conscious of their antiquity, upon which their order of precedence was based. It was in 1515 that the Lord Mayor judged the Mercers to be the oldest. The Merchant Taylors and Skinners could not agree which was the older, and were compelled to alternate yearly between positions six and seven in the pecking order: they were literally 'at sixes and sevens', hence the expression. The livery, originally a grant of food and clothing, came to mean the robes they wore to distinguish them from other companies. They were 'worshipful' because, like any medieval association, they met together in Christian worship. The trades controlled by the livery companies naturally reflected the commerce of medieval London, some of it quite humble. They included Weavers, Butchers, Turners, Cooks, Coopers and Pepperers (the last becoming a branch of the Grocers' Company).

The Goldsmiths, proudly occupying fifth place, were granted their royal charter in 1327 although, like other companies, they were much older than that, having been in existence at least from the early 13th century. (There is evidence that some guilds or 'misteries' existed before 1066.) Because of the ever-useful nature of gold, the Goldsmiths' Company is the only one of the original twelve companies still to be directly involved in the regulation of the trade for which it was founded. It is the Goldsmiths who operate the London Assay Office, which is responsible for testing articles made from gold and silver to assess the quantity of precious metal they contain, and marking them with a stamp. Pure gold and silver are too soft to stand up to constant wear, and are therefore mixed with a hardening agent. Unscrupulous smiths used too much hardening agent in relation to the gold or silver. These tests, ordered by a statute of Edward I in 1300, represent by far the earliest examples of chemical analysis. Since the late 15th century, the stamp has been known as the hallmark, from the official requirement that gold and silver wares should be brought to the Goldsmiths' Hall to be tested and marked. It is the oldest continuously operating example of consumer protection in existence.

The very first hall occupied part of the site of the present building. However, it was probably no more than a merchant's house, which was rebuilt a couple of times before being gutted during the Great Fire of London. A new hall was built, but by the early 19th century it had fallen into such a poor state of repair that no dancing could take place in the Dancing Gallery for fear of collapse. From 1829–35, the company rebuilt the hall on a bigger scale and in an altogether more sumptuous style, with a façade of six giant Corinthian columns; the architect was Philip Hardwick, the Goldsmiths' Surveyor.

This hall still comes alive during feasts, when men in tail coats and white ties and women wearing long dresses file up the opulent, polychromatic staircase, beneath the eyes of marble children representing the Seasons. In the Livery Hall, flanked with yellow scagliola columns, the tables groan with rich vessels from the Company's collection, while prize pieces are displayed on a buffet at the end – much as they might have been in the Tudor period.

GRANADA CINEMA
MITCHAM ROAD, SW17
Cathedral of the motion picture

There were no cinemas in Britain before 1900. By the time of the Second World War, an estimated 5,500 had arrived – at least one in every town across the country. Architecturally, they were not always welcome visitors, their window-less bulk squatting awkwardly amid the older buildings in the high street. It was a time when the public was accustomed to taking its pleasures (watching football matches, going to the seaside) *en masse*; but in an era when only the rich had choice, life for most people was humdrum and monotonous. The great 'cathedrals of the motion picture', such as the Granada, Tooting, transported them to a make-believe world filled with romance, excitement and, in due course, colour. The atmosphere in the cinema itself heightened the mood of escapism.

There were two ways in which cinema-owners sought to provide their audience with the architectural and decorative glamour appropriate to the films they had come to see. Most films came from America and the medium was modern: transatlantic Art Deco provided the stylistic equivalent. This meant swooping concrete curves and jazzy lighting effects outside, geometric patterns and stylised figurative decoration within. The Odeon chain made this their house style. By contrast, the 'atmospheric' cinema sought to wrap its audience's imagination in a daydream of romance. Whatever the façade was like – Chinese, in the case of the Palace, Southall – the interior conjured up an Arabian Nights' vision of exotic places, in which audiences could lose themselves for the four hours they were likely to be there. This was a speciality of Sidney Bernstein's Granada cinemas, the inspiration being a visit that Bernstein had made in 1912 to the Roxy Cinema in New York.

The greatest of all the atmospherics is the Granada, Tooting, preserved as a Gala Bingo Hall. The street front (designed by Cecil Masey in 1931) takes the form of a classical tower, but this has little relevance to the interior. This is the masterpiece of the remarkable Theodore Komisarjevsky, a Russian who had studied at the Imperial Institute of Architecture in St Petersburg before becoming director of the Moscow State Theatre. Emigrating to England in 1919, he converted a small cinema into a theatre and ran a repertory company whose members included Edith Evans, Charles Laughton and the young John Gielgud. He was nearly fifty when he first worked for Bernstein. As befitted a chain called Granada, he perfected the Spanish-Moorish style, inspired by the Alhambra, but for the Granada, Tooting, he turned his sights to Venice. Beneath a roof that seemed to be partly open to the sky, an audience of 3,500 could sit as though on a gondola, surrounded by architectural effects (Gothic arcades, false windows, barley sugar columns) derived from the Doge's Palace and the palazzi on the Grand Canal.

Regaled by the full-time twenty-piece orchestra, or the strains of the Mighty Wurlitzer played by a maestro such as Reginald Dixon (all the children present were given a stick of rock on his birthday), they must have felt a world away from the gloom of the Depression that settled on Tooting, as everywhere else, in 1930s Britain. One aficionado remembered the cake that was commissioned from Hutchins the Bakers for the cinema's yearly anniversary and at Christmas. It weighed over a ton, so that each of the thousands of people who came to the three shows on the day could have a piece.

GROVE ROAD   *BOW, E3*

First V-1 terror weapon falls on London

Hitler was convinced that his *Vergeltungswaffen*, or Vengeance weapons, would win him the war. For London, already inured to years of bombing by conventional aircraft, they inaugurated a second Blitz, calculated to instil terror through the fearful randomness of the attack. The German air force had lost the Battle of Britain. On 6 June 1944, the D-Day landings began in Normandy. The first V-1 fell on a railway bridge in Grove Road, Bow, a week later.

The V-1, nicknamed 'doodlebug' by stoical Londoners, was a pilotless aeroplane whose engine made a noise like a motorbike without a silencer. A small propeller on the nose calculated the distance covered, and the engine was designed to cut out when the device had reached its target range. Doodlebugs could be relatively easily shot down, or sent off-course by RAF fighters that tipped their stubby wings. Up to half the 9,000 launched were brought down by these means. Nevertheless, the scale of the potential destruction from the ton of explosives that each V-1 carried caused, in the words of Herbert Morrison, Minister of Home Security, 'a state of anxiety'. Worse was to come. The first V-2 – a forerunner of the space rocket – arrived without warning three months later; flying at 3,500mph, greater than the speed of sound, the roar of its engine could only be heard once it had passed. And unlike the V-1, the V-2 could not be stopped. The Germans were unable to perfect the precision of the delivery, and less than a quarter of the 5,000 V-2s that were launched reached their target. Those that did killed 2,700 people and badly injured 6,000 more. Fortunately for London, the attacks stopped in March 1945, when the Allies overran the woods in Holland and northern France where the launch pads had been hidden.

The German rocket scientists, such as Walter Dornberger and Wernher von Braun, both of whom emigrated to the United States after 1945, went on to develop the technology that ultimately put men on the moon.

HANDEL'S HOUSE   25 BROOK STREET, W1
Where the Messiah *was written*

In 1711, the 26-year-old George Frideric Handel arrived in London from Hanover, an unofficial cultural ambassador paving the way for the Hanoverian dynasty that would ascend the British throne in 1714. Whatever his original expectations, he stayed and worked here for nearly half a century, until his death in 1759. The early years were dominated by his attempt to establish Italianate opera as a British taste – to which end he acted as impresario as well as composer. In this he ran up against Britain's growing artistic chauvinism, characterised by the paintings of his friend William Hogarth. As a result, he turned increasingly to English oratorios, building on the success that he had enjoyed in writing orchestral settings of church music.

Later that year he must have felt his finances were sufficiently secure to occupy a house in the newly built development of Brook Street. A portrait by Philip Mercier shows him at home, a red cap pushed to the back of his shaven head, one arm resting on his harpsichord, his other hand holding a quill, about to apply itself to the sheets of manuscript paper on the circular table in front of him. It was at Brook Street that he composed the *Messiah*. The bust by Roubillac, originally in

Vauxhall Gardens, now in the Victoria and Albert Museum, shows him in equally unbuttoned mood, again in dressing gown and cap, with one slipper off, although this time less realistically playing a lyre. This radiates the genial side of his character: he had a dry sense of wit, and could be very generous to causes such as the Foundling Hospital (see page 141).

London, the biggest city in one of the most go-ahead countries in Europe, provided a rich middle-class audience of music lovers, more attractive for an entrepreneurial musician than the patronage of continental princelings. Handel became a committed Londoner and was often seen as he made his way to the organ loft of St Paul's Cathedral.

HENRY POOLE & CO. 15 SAVILE ROW, W1
The English gentleman's suit

On 15 October 1666, Samuel Pepys noted that 'This day the King begins to put on his vest.' By vest he meant a garment 'being a long cassock of black cloth, and pinked with white silk under it, and a coat over it'. The English suit, in its essential elements of jacket, waistcoat and trousers, had been born. In Charles II's day, courtiers had their coats buttoned on the right, the more easily to whip out the swords that they wore on their left. Men's jackets button on the right to this day, as opposed to women's jackets which button on the left.

In the next century, the English gentleman's passion for the country caused the coat to change shape. They rode in coats of more aerodynamic cut, with separated tails (originally formed when the skirts of the frock coat were buttoned back). The silks and embroidery of another age were saved for Court appearances: country clothes found their way from the stable to the drawing room. The rough materials from which they were made were less showy than silk, but lent themselves to being tailored. Shooting and walking in the Victorian period led to the development of a coat without tails. Again, it leapt from country into the town, so that after the First World War, tails were retained only for formal dress at either end of the day. Standard dress for men became the lounge suit (its informality indicated by its name, a suit for lounging), supplemented by the blazer, as originally worn at Henley Regatta and other sporting events.

Given that Britain took the lead in these sartorial developments, it is hardly surprising that London came to be regarded as a centre of tailoring excellence. The epicentre is Savile Row, first patronised by Beau Brummell around the time of Trafalgar. Henry Poole & Co. has as good a claim as any other to being the oldest tailor on 'the Row': the firm's founder, James Poole, came to London from Shropshire in 1806, stitched his own tunics for the Volunteer Corps, and found his services in such demand that he could open a tailoring shop in 1822. His son, the eponymous Henry, did well out of the Victorian demand for hunting clothes and court dress. Poole's today continues to hold the royal livery warrant first granted by Queen Victoria.

HIGHGATE CEMETERY
Victorian city of the dead

Burial grounds are one of the services that cities are required to provide. By the Victorian era, those around London had become even more crowded than a modern Tube train: bones poked out of the ground, bodies were constantly being moved to make room for more burials and the smell was appalling. To provide more seemly resting places for a nation increasingly devoted to a cult of death, at a time when life expectancy was short, many new cemeteries were opened. In the early years of Victoria's reign, the suburbs of London were adorned with a ring of cemeteries known as the Magnificent Seven: Kensal Green (1832), West Norwood (1837), Highgate (1839), Abney Park, Brompton and Nunhead (1840) and Tower Hamlets (1841). Of these, Kensal Green and West Norwood probably contain the finest individual monuments, but Highgate, with its hilly topography and an 'Egyptian Avenue' that could have come straight from the set of Verdi's *Aida*, takes the palm. These days, the overmantling ivy and toppling monuments cast a pall of romantic gloom. This was not how the creators of the cemetery meant it. For the London Cemetery Company (founded in 1836), it was to be a place where families could walk along neatly manicured paths to commune with the deceased and contemplate the only certainty in life.

As they did so, they passed vistas of extravagant symbolism: broken columns, shrouded urns, weeping angels, pyramids, mournful dogs, sleeping lions, prayerful putti, obelisks. There are vast mausoleums for newspaper magnates and silk manufacturers, and simple crosses for foundling children. A couple of acres, unblessed by the Church of England, would be reserved for dissenters, such as the scientist Michael Faraday, a deeply devout member of the Sandemanian sect (see page 172).

The list of people buried here reads like a gazetteer of this thrusting, hard-headed yet death-obsessed age. They include Dr S. Birch, who translated the hieroglyphics on Cleopatra's Needle; J. Chubb, lock manufacturer; the novelist George Eliot and her unfortunate husband J. W. Cross; G. Green, balloonist; J. Lobb, of the St James's Street bootmakers; W. H. Monk, the professor of music who wrote 'Abide with Me'; C. H. Newton, founder of the artists' suppliers Winsor and Newton; Tom Sayers, bare-knuckle fighter; G. B. Sowerby, a conchologist; Sir Leslie Stephen, Virginia Woolf's father and the first editor of the *Dictionary of National Biography*; and G. Wombwell, of the famous touring menagerie. The best known of all the monuments is the least aesthetically pleasing: the memorial to Karl Marx. It is not Marx's fault

that he lies in the eastern extension of the cemetery, which has less architectural character than the West Cemetery. Nor can the form of the monument,
where his vast craggy head seems to burst angrily out of a tight-fitting granite
box, be blamed on him. At his death, Marx was too poor to afford more than a
simple slab. The overweening monument into which this slab is incorporated
was erected by the British Communist party in 1956.

HOARE'S BANK

37 FLEET STREET, EC4

Perhaps the oldest cheque in England

In 1665 Richard Hoare became an apprentice in the goldsmiths' trade, and set
up in business seven years later. He worked under the sign of the golden bottle
in Fleet Street. Samuel Pepys brought him a chocolate dish to mend and the
notorious Judge Jeffreys (see page 44) sent a gold snuff box to colour, but there
was another side to Hoare's business. It was natural for people to use
goldsmiths' shops, with their safes, as a place to deposit their precious items,
including gold. (They had once used the Tower of London, but this looked less
attractive after the deposits there were raided by Charles I.) The goldsmiths,
who had long been used to lending out their own gold, came to realise that
they could make use of the deposits confided to them by other people. They
could advance money against them.

The gold itself was inconvenient to handle, so they made their transactions
using pieces of paper inscribed with the relevant amounts. On 11 July 1676,
Hoare's friend William Hale wrote him a note which reads: 'Pray pay to the
bearer hereof Mr. Will Morgan fifty four pounds ten shillings and ten pence
and take his receipt for the same.' One assumes the note was honoured and the
said Mr Morgan benefited accordingly. Today this would be called a cheque,
and it was one of the first in England. The modern age of banking had arrived.

Mousey Abigail Masham, who had superseded the overbearing Duchess of
Marlborough as Queen Anne's favourite, brought the Queen's privy purse
account to Hoare's in 1710. The Hoares prospered. Henry Hoare II did well
from selling South Sea Company stock, while Henry Hoare III laid out the
landscape garden at Stourhead (see page 41).

KEATS HOUSE

KEATS GROVE, NW3

Where John met Fanny

In December 1818, John Keats moved into the house of his friend, Charles
Armitage Brown. At that time it was called Wentworth Place, and stood in what
was then still a countrified area on the edge of Hampstead Heath. Keats had

grown up in London, where his father had managed the stables of an inn at Moorfields. His parents were both dead by now, however, and of his two younger brothers, Tom had died (like his mother) of tuberculosis and George had emigrated to the United States, while his sister Frances lived out of London. Keats's arrangement with Brown, a companion on his long walking holidays, provided the warmth of a friendly home to a young man who found himself otherwise alone.

Wentworth Place, although it looks like a single Regency villa, was really two modest houses, of which Brown and Keats occupied only one. To the other came in May 1819 a widow, Mrs Brawne, and her three children, one of whom was Fanny. Keats fell head over heels in love with her, writing in July: 'I almost wish we were butterflies and liv'd but three summer days – three such days with you I could fill with more delight than 50 common years could ever contain.' Fanny, though less ardent, reciprocated to the point of forming an engagement, but Mrs Brawne was opposed to her daughter marrying an impecunious poet.

The next year, Keats coughed up a bright red spot of blood which, from his former training as a medical student, he recognised instantly as the first symptom of 'consumption', as tuberculosis was known, and his 'death warrant'. As Keats's health failed, and he lay on a day bed made up in Brown's drawing room, looking out of the window, it became increasingly urgent that he should consummate his union with Fanny before he died. He never did. Having gone to Rome in September 1820 in the hope that the warmth would help his condition, he died there the following February. He was twenty-five years old.

Keats's two years at Wentworth Place were the most intensely productive of his short life. Outside is a plum tree, planted on the site of the one under which, according to Brown, he wrote 'Ode to a Nightingale'. It was with Wentworth Place as a background to his life that Keats wrote, at a furious pace, many of his greatest works.

KENSINGTON PALACE KENSINGTON, W8
William III's favourite palace

In March 1702, William III – who was rarely in good health – died at his London home in Kensington after a fall from his horse. He was fifty-one. It was appropriate that he should have spent his last days here, since it was his favourite residence in England. It was built shortly after he and his wife Mary II assumed the throne in 1689* because Whitehall Palace was too damp for his health (he suffered from asthma), and Hampton Court was too far out of town (see page 74). In fact, even Kensington was regarded by his courtiers as off the beaten path, which made him seem more isolated than his accessible Stuart predecessors.

The King and Queen acquired a small Jacobean house belonging to the Earl of Nottingham in 1689 and to this Sir Christopher Wren added four pavilions: Queen Mary wanted the enlargements finished as soon as possible, and this was the quickest way to proceed. While William was fighting on the Continent the following year, Mary added another wing; it expressed the Queen's taste for domestic simplicity, acquired during the years she had lived with her husband in Holland. Both the King and Queen were in residence when the building burnt down just a year later: they personally helped carry out furniture in the middle of the night, laughing at the incongruous assemblage on the lawns. (William was particularly delighted to discover a cheese.) The building was remodelled, as it was again after Mary's death from smallpox in 1694 when she was only thirty-two. Unlike the English aristocracy, William was not much interested in literature or music, but he loved architecture, paintings, the decorative arts and gardens. His apartments were rich with tapestry hangings and festoons carved by Grinling Gibbons.

William had not been especially popular in England and even less so in Scotland and Ireland, but the successes of the new century partly rested on his achievements. During his reign, he created a constitutional monarchy, in which he and his wife occupied the throne at the invitation of Parliament rather than by right of conquest. He made judges independent and established the Bank of England. Famous regiments such as the King's Own Scottish Borderers, the Cameronians, the Inniskillings, the East Sussex, the Cheshires and the Green Howards all date from his reorganisation of the army. While he was not an entirely faithful husband to the Queen who secured him the English throne, he was so moved by her death that he fulfilled her wish to establish a hospital for seamen at Greenwich† – thereby instigating the greatest parade of Baroque architecture ever to be seen.

The home that William and Mary created at Kensington – it was not called Kensington Palace until after William's death – was occupied by each of the succeeding three monarchs: Queen Anne, George I (he employed William Kent to paint the ceilings of the royal apartments) and George II. In the next century, it was home to the Duke and Duchess of Kent, whose daughter, Queen Victoria, was born here in 1819.

*See Brixham Harbour, page 13. †See Royal Naval Hospital, page 172

CRANMER'S TOWER

LAMBETH PALACE, SE1

Writing the Book of Common Prayer

For four centuries, mainstream worship in the Church of England, with its rhythm of matins and evensong but little emphasis on Communion, was conterminous with the *Book of Common Prayer*. To many people, it would have been one of the few books that they ever held in their hands, and its plangent cadences shaped not only religious practice but also the common language of the country. The motive for its creation was Henry VIII's break with the Roman Catholic Church; the different drafts that it went through reflect the torment that Protestant divines, led by the Archbishop of Canterbury Thomas Cranmer, endured in their search for a new doctrinal orthodoxy – at a time when any political wrong turning could lead them to the stake.

It is not known exactly where Cranmer wrote his texts, or even who wrote which section, but much of the work must have been done either by Cranmer or under his control at his London residence, Lambeth Palace; a tower next to the chapel there is named in his honour. The principle upon which Cranmer proceeded is expressed in the preface: 'There was never anything by men so well devised or so surely established which in age and continuance of time has not been corrupted.'

This could have been a motto for the whole Protestant revolution; whereas previous authorities had placed greater faith in the customs and traditions of the Church, the likes of Cranmer sought a return to the Holy Scriptures. Until the death of Henry VIII, congregations in the new Church of England would have noticed little liturgical difference from the old services – albeit the churches in which they took place had now been whitewashed inside. It was only with Cranmer's first English Prayer Book, two years after Edward VI came to the throne, that services were held in English rather than Latin. However, this Prayer Book, introduced in 1549, retained the form of the old Catholic services.

In 1552, a second Prayer Book reflected the beliefs of more radical reformers. The act of transubstantiation (the literal conversion of Eucharistic bread and wine into Christ's body and blood) was denied; the Catholic altar was replaced by a Communion table; an emphasis on Calvinistic predestination replaced the Catholic doctrine of salvation through good works. On its first outing, this Prayer Book had a short life: Edward VI was succeeded by the staunchly Catholic Mary I who returned to the Latin Mass, and Cranmer was one of the Protestant theologians martyred at Oxford*. His language, however, continues to echo not only in churches and cathedrals, but also in phrases – 'dust to dust' and 'till death us do part', the latter being a 1662 version of Cranmer's 'till death us departe' – that are instinctively used at solemn moments, even by those who do not normally go to church.

*See Martyrs' Memorial, page 229. See also Llanrhaeadr-ym-Mochnant, page 420

LEIGHTON HOUSE 12 HOLLAND PARK ROAD, W14

Victorian England's answer to the Renaissance

Frederic Leighton was the pre-eminent artist of Victorian Britain. A dazzling figure who acquired his skill studying abroad, he effortlessly spoke five languages and seemed to re-embody the principles of the Italian Renaissance. He was equally successful a sculptor as painter. From 1878 he was President of the Royal Academy, and shortly before his death in 1896 he became the first artist to be made a peer.

From 1864, he began building a house-cum-studio in Holland Park, to the designs of his friend George Aitchison. The centrepiece was the Arab Hall, adorned with a collection of thousands of Islamic tiles from Damascus. The windows are covered with intricately worked screens, and a fountain plays on a sunken pool: all that is needed to complete the impression of languid Oriental voluptuousness is the searing heat of the Middle East, not always visited upon Holland Park. A studio was complemented by a gallery where his picture collection was displayed. His favourite model Dorothy Dene, a poor South London girl whom Leighton backed as an actress, is thought to have inspired George Bernard Shaw (see page 204) to create Eliza Doolittle in *Pygmalion*, Leighton's role being that of her egotistical mentor, Professor Higgins.

Leighton had discovered Holland Park through his friend, the seer-like George Frederick Watts, who in turn built a studio-house nearby. These streets became the centre of a community of successful Academicians. In this and other society, Leighton glittered, but few people felt that they really knew him. Apart from the servants' quarters, his house, which grew and grew, never had more than one bedroom. He had no need of overnight guests.

LINLEY SAMBOURNE HOUSE   18 STAFFORD TERRACE, W8

The most evocative Victorian interiors in London

Light seeps in through stained-glass windows, deep fringes hang off the plush curtains, walls are closely packed with framed prints and photographs hung over maroon-coloured lincrusta paper, and armies of knick-knacks – photograph frames, fans, figurines – bristle on every palm stand and bureau. Not a detail seems to have changed since the *Punch* illustrator Edward Linley Sambourne and his wife created these interiors in the 1870s, the house having been bought with the help of his wife's parents. The only significant change made since that date was the replacement of gas light by electricity in the late 19th century. The Sambournes saved everything and since, by happy chance, their son Roy had a weakness for actresses and did not marry, the house survived as an extraordinarily complete document of Victorian taste.

The house is testimony to the success of Punch's 'Second Cartoon', as Sambourne's job was described. Punch was established in 1841, on capital of £25. Although modelled on a French satirical daily called Charivari, and originally known as the London Charivari, Punch became so much part of the establishment that even today few country-house libraries are without a long row of its maroon-bound volumes. Furthermore, it was Punch that can claim to have invented the humorous drawing known as the cartoon. In early issues, the main wood engraving was known as Mr Punch's Pencillings (or, to insiders, the Big Cut). When the Houses of Parliament, rebuilt after the fire of 1834, were being decorated with murals, artists exhibited their proposals in the form of 'cartoons'– used in the Old Master sense of preparatory drawings. In response, Punch published its own 'cartoons' to lambaste the extravagance of Parliament's new home with the poverty elsewhere in the country. 'The poor ask for bread, and the philanthropy of the State accords – an exhibition.' The word cartoon stuck. Soon, the Punch cartoons were of two main types: topical quips about smart society and allegorical comments on political life. Sambourne specialised in the latter.

Originally apprenticed to a shipbuilder in Greenwich, Sambourne first worked for the magazine in 1867, having been introduced by the editor's son. Progress up the Punch hierarchy was slow because, once there, most illustrators stayed for life, and Sambourne was no exception. It was only in 1901 when Sir John Tenniel (the original illustrator of Alice's Adventures in Wonderland) retired, that he became the magazine's principal cartoonist. Often the subject was not finally decided until noon on Friday and the finished work, prized for its elaboration, would be completed by that evening's deadline.

Sambourne was not in the league of the great Academician, Frederic Leighton (see page 155). He did not have a studio as such, only an extension of the drawing room, which contained his easel. Next to the easel he kept a collection of reference photographs (said to be as many as 10,000), showing everything from a newborn baby to a youth wielding a sword. Perhaps the absence of a studio suited the image that Sambourne liked to cultivate – that of a portly, jovial, country squire, who had been so fond of riding his horse Blondin (named after a tightrope walker) that he had its hoof preserved in the drawing room.

LLOYD'S OF LONDON

The greatest insurance market in the world

In 1686, Edward Lloyd opened a coffee house in Tower Street, in the City of London. Earlier in the century, a 'drink of a soote colour dryed in a furnace and that they drink as hot as can be indured' had been introduced to England, and the coffee houses where this beverage could be enjoyed in company quickly became gathering places for merchants with interests in common. Both the

Stock Exchange and the Baltic Exchange grew out of coffee houses. Lloyd's coffee house was to give its name to the most famous insurance market in the world, Lloyd's of London. To this day, Lloyd's underwriters (who 'underwrite' or cover insurance risks) work from what are called 'boxes', a memory of the booths containing table and benches that would have been found in an old coffee house, while the staff are known as waiters.

Insurance had been offered on ships since the days of Samuel Pepys. The need for it grew as trade expanded during the 1720s and 1730s, when Britain was at peace. By 1740, when Britain was at war again, vital foreign news often arrived first at Lloyd's coffee house. In the 1690s, Edward Lloyd had published a news sheet called *Lloyd's News*; in 1734, the decade after his death, the first editions of what would become the maritime journal of record, *Lloyd's List*, appeared. Already Lloyd's was acquiring the reputation for god-like authority that it would enjoy for more than two centuries.

In 1769, the underwriters who provided insurance had become dissatisfied with the premises that Lloyd's then occupied. A group of them broke away, meeting in a new coffee house operated by one of the Lloyd's waiters but running their affairs themselves. Later they took rooms at the Royal Exchange. War increased the risks of insurance, but also the profits, and the growing power of the Royal Navy meant that, after the American Revolution, losses came in single ships rather than whole convoys. Insurance was entering a golden age, creating an industry that was not only peculiarly British but of immense value to the British economy.

In 1871, Parliament incorporated Lloyd's for the 'promotion of marine insurance and the diffusion of shipping intelligence'. During the next century its remit extended from shipping to everything else of value in the world: it was said that there was nothing which could not be insured at Lloyd's, from a pianist's hands to a film star's legs. Meanwhile, the search for the ideal working environment revived with the construction of what, for the City of London, was a daringly modern building by Richard Rogers Partnership. In what seemed to be the style of an oil refinery, it opened in 1986. The optimism it expresses is not always shared by the Lloyd's Names (private individuals who provide Lloyd's underwriters with unlimited backing) as they reel from the claims made as a result of crises such as asbestos poisoning, hurricanes and September 11.

LONDON ZOO REGENT'S PARK, NW1

The world's first zoological garden

In the 12th century Henry I kept a menagerie at his manor of Woodstock in Oxfordshire; Henry III transferred it to the Tower of London, when he was given three animals by his brother-in-law Frederick II, the Holy Roman

Emperor; it remained there until 1834. Presumably the animals were regarded as exotic marvels, with heraldic and symbolic overtones. In the 18th century, the age of scientific classification, menageries were objects of princely amusement, often associated with sport. It was not until the 19th century, however, that the idea of assembling collections of animals for the purpose of study took hold. The first such zoo – or zoological garden, as it was then known – was opened to the Fellows of the London Zoological Society which had been established in Regent's Park in 1828. The Society itself had been formed two years earlier.

Although the grounds of the zoo were elegantly laid out by Decimus Burton, there was no thought of admitting the public at the beginning. The doors only opened to them when it was necessary to raise money in 1847. Their presence seems not to have impeded the development of the zoo, if anything the reverse, to judge by the innovations made in the second half of the century: the world's first reptile house (1849), the first public aquarium (1853) and the first insect house (1881). In the 20th century, the zoo put itself in the architectural avant-garde: houses for animals seemed an appropriate forum for Modern Movement experiment, at a time when humans had yet to warm to the genre. Berthold Lubetkin's Penguin Pool, constructed in 1934, celebrates the new material of reinforced concrete, with white ribbon-like walkways intertwined above a blue pool.

Today, zoos are out of favour, and there has been intense discussion as to whether London Zoo should be relocated from Regent's Park into the country. However, it continues to house 650 species – reptiles, fish, invertebrates, birds and small mammals, as well as the famous lions, tigers, elephants and bears. Many of them are endangered in the wild. One modern purpose of the zoo is to support wild populations through breeding schemes, seen in the release of 100 sand gazelles into the Empty Quarter of Saudi Arabia in 1995 and the release of 4,000 rare British field crickets into southern England in 1998.

MANSION HOUSE
WALBROOK, EC4

The City of London shows off

By tradition, the Mansion House is a symbol of the City of London's wealth and independence, and so it remains today. It is impossible to visit the official residence of the Lord Mayor without being dazzled by the richness of the interiors and the quality of the paintings hanging within them – and this located in a square mile that is more associated with hard-nosed commerce than the ornaments of life.

From the late 12th century, the Mayor of London was head of the City's civic administration, supporting the king by organising loans, but also representing the interests of his electorate by maintaining their privileges. By the beginning of the 15th century the Mayor had transmogrified into a Lord Mayor. This reflected the growing prestige of the office, as the City itself became richer. The Lord Mayor was expected to entertain generously, give to charity and mark the beginning of his term with a pageant, surviving today as the annual Lord Mayor's Show.

During the Civil War the City, home to many rich men who saw no place for themselves in the old aristocratic order, supported Parliament. There was understandably a *froideur* between the City and King Charles II at the Restoration: he removed its privileges and made the Lord Mayor something of a puppet. It was at this time that the idea of a sumptuous house for the Lord Mayor was first mooted, as a means of bolstering the City's reputation. The Great Fire of 1666 (see page 161) brought the issue into focus when so many fine houses and livery halls were destroyed, thereby reducing the amount of appropriate space available for ceremonial events. Nothing, however, was done until 1728.

At last, a site was chosen where, before the Great Fire, St Mary Woolchurch and the old Stocks Market had stood. In 1735, following a limited competition – one of the first competitions in British architecture – the design of George Dance (the Elder) was chosen. There were other mansion houses, in Dublin, for example; but in London relatively few town houses, or palaces, were built on this scale, because aristocrats spent a considerable amount of their time on their country estates. The Mansion House required so many rooms for the Lord Mayor and his enormous staff that the site was hardly big enough to fit them all in.

The splendid portico of six giant Corinthian columns has more in common with contemporary country houses than town houses. Rising above it, however, were two attic storeys, which came to be irreverently known as Noah's Ark and the Mare's Nest. The attics were necessary to accommodate the upper parts of the Dancing Gallery (on the second floor) and the extremely tall Egyptian Hall (on the first floor). The Dancing Gallery again has overtones of the country house; it provided space like a long gallery that was well suited to the formal dances of the period. With its giant columns and Vitruvian proportions, the Egyptian Hall was a fashionable room, showing that the merchant princes of the City were fully equal to anything that could be offered by the royal family in the West End.

By 1795, however, the roof of the Egyptian Hall was suffering from dry rot and had to be rebuilt: in the process, the upper section of the room was replaced by a sumptuous barrel vault, taking in the space occupied by Noah's Ark; the Mare's Nest disappeared in 1842. This improved the profile from the outside and removed one source of contemporary criticism; disapproval of the cramped site and mean setting that had been provided for such a showy building remained. This drawback has never been entirely overcome, suggesting that, beneath all their finery, the City Fathers remain businessmen who know the value of money.

MICHELIN HOUSE
A celebration of motoring

Michelin House, designed by François Espinasse in 1911, is Britain's temple to the motor car. It originally served as a garage to sell tyres, and was built with gently sloping floors that allowed tyres to roll from one end of the building to the fitting bay at the front. The architecture and decoration of Michelin House is designed to make it one giant, jolly advertisement. Although advertising was still in its infancy, few companies have ever gone this far in expressing the identity of a brand through the physical presence of their building. This partly reflects the Michelin brothers' ferocious competition with Dunlop, whose British patent on tyres expired in 1904: this was the year that the first Michelin office opened in London.

The Michelin Man, or to give him his proper name Bibendum, shines out by night and day from the stained-glass windows over the entrance (the original was lit by mercury vapour, giving a ghostly bluish cast). Bibendum was called after the company's somewhat obscure motto: 'Nunc est bibendum' (now is the time for drinking). He first appeared on a French poster of 1898, showing how the Michelin pneumatic tyre *boit l'obstacle* (drinks obstacles).

At Michelin House, the first pre-cast concrete building in Britain, the central stained-glass panel shows Bibendum raising a glass charged with sharp objects, while below him are the tools of early tyre technology. In the second panel he is riding a bicycle, while round the corner he does a high kick to reveal the sole of a boot which is covered in road-hugging tread. On the skyline of the building stand glass cupolas shaped like stacks of tyres, replaced by Conran Roche when the building was carefully restored and converted in the mid-1980s. A series of tile pictures by Ernest Montaut tells the history of the pneumatic tyre through its greatest moments: from bicycling and motor-racing triumphs to Edward VII and the future George V riding in a Sedanca de Ville. Owners could pass the time while their tyres were being changed by inspecting the maps and guidebooks in Michelin's club-like Touring Office, the glass of whose windows was etched with maps.

What I Know, the memoirs of Edward VII's 'personal motor expert' C. W. Stamper (ghosted by Dornford Yates) demonstrates the crucial importance to early motorists of the tyre. They needed to be changed so frequently that George V would travel with a second car behind his own to avoid inevitable delays caused by punctures.

THE MONUMENT

1666: the world's biggest city destroyed by fire

With about 400,000 inhabitants in 1650, London was the biggest metropolis in the world. The Great Fire, which broke out in the early hours of the morning of 2 September 1666, destroyed much of the City. Samuel Pepys, who had gone to the Tower of London and seen the raging fire, took a boat to the Palace of Westminster to warn the King, Charles II. Charles instructed him to tell the Lord Mayor to pull down the houses that were in the path of the fire, in the hope of arresting it, but this was impossible. Flames spread because the houses, built largely of timber and sheltered by roofs of thatch, were jammed together in narrow streets.

The previous year, this hugger-mugger townscape had proved fertile ground for the Plague, which had killed 17,440 of the City's population of 93,000. The Great Fire incinerated the last of the plague bacilli, but may have claimed as few as half a dozen lives (one of the dead being the maid in the house of the King's baker, Thomas Farynor, in Pudding Lane where it is thought the fire started: she was too frightened to climb to safety over the roof). The devastation laid waste an area of 373 acres within the City and 63 outside the City walls. Eighty-five churches were destroyed, including St Paul's Cathedral. Tents and shacks for the people who had been made homeless stretched as far as Highgate.

The Monument, an enormous Doric column crowned by a flaming urn of gilded copper, was erected to commemorate the disaster. It was inevitable that the architect of this memorial would be Christopher Wren. Even before the ashes of the fire had stopped smouldering, he had come forward with a plan for a new City, complete with broad streets, unencumbered access to London Bridge and an open quay along the river. Not one of the old streets would have been kept. Wren's model plan was rejected: the King and his advisers wanted the City to be rebuilt quickly, which meant keeping the legal disputes over land ownership to a minimum, and the way to do that was to retain the old street plan.

Wren had to be content with rebuilding St Paul's* and with the ultimate responsibility for fifty-two City churches. Had it not been for the Fire it is possible that England's most famous architect would be better remembered for his brilliance as a scientist at Oxford than for his buildings.

*See St Paul's Cathedral, page 179

JOHN MURRAY

Britain's most distinguished publisher

One morning in 1819, the Piccadilly end of Albemarle Street was crowded with booksellers and their assistants, competing to collect the earliest copies of what they knew would be a literary sensation: the first cantos of Byron's *Don Juan*. This was a scene familiar to the publisher John Murray II who in 1812 had published Byron's *Childe Harold's Pilgrimage* from his previous premises at 32 Fleet Street. There he experienced such demand for copies that they had to be handed out through the windows to the impatient booksellers. Indeed, the profits from *Childe Harold*, combined with the mortgaging of his most precious copyrights, had enabled John Murray to move to Albemarle Street in 1812.

The publishing house of John Murray had been established in 1768 by Murray's father, John I, a retired marine who had come south from Edinburgh to set up as a bookseller and publisher. Although John Murray I published over a thousand titles, he did not have the same genius as his son for spotting talent.

It was from 32 Fleet Street in 1809 that John Murray II launched the *Quarterly Review* with the support of Walter Scott and George Canning, the Foreign Secretary. The *Quarterly* was to become the most influential periodical of the 19th century and brought to John Murray at 50 Albemarle Street many of the most important names of the period. The historic rooms became the meeting place of the famous (and not so famous) and it was here that John Murray II introduced Lord Byron to Walter Scott. This meeting is depicted in a water-colour that hangs in the rooms today.

Ever since, 50 Albemarle Street has retained its association with Byron*. As Caroline Lamb wrote to John Murray, 'Your room speaks of him in every part of it.' Other authors published by Murray at this time include Jane Austen, Robert Southey, Michael Faraday and Madame de Staël. Works of literature were complemented by books of travel, exploration and science as well as medical manuals and the Navy List. Mrs Rundell's *Domestic Cookery*, one of the first cookery books for housewives, had been a strong seller since its first appearance in 1806. (In 1813, Byron noted with amusement Murray's observation that '*Harold* and *Cookery* are much wanted'.)

After John Murray II's death in 1843, the famous publishing house continued in the safe hands of a succession of John Murrays, publishing such authors as Charles Darwin, Herman Melville, Arthur Conan Doyle, John Betjeman, Osbert Lancaster, Kenneth Clark, and Booker Prize winner Ruth Prawer Jhabvala. In 2002, after a record-breaking 234 years of independent publishing, John Murray VII sold the firm to Hodder Headline while retaining the famous building at 50 Albemarle Street for the Murray family.

*See Newstead Abbey, page 333

THE NASH TERRACES

An architectural vision for London

In developing Regent's Park, and the streets – Portland Place, Regent Street, Lower Regent Street and Waterloo Place – that lead to St James's Park, the Regency architect John Nash* achieved what no one else (except the Luftwaffe) has done before or since: redevelop a large area of London according to a single vision. The development was not a grand, formal exposition of geometrical principles, as it would have been in any other capital city of Europe. Nor was it an orderly succession of squares, crescents and circuses, in the manner of John Wood's Bath (see page 6) or the Adam brothers' Edinburgh New Town. Instead, John Nash devised a scheme that mixed Nature, variety and visual illusionism with the established repertoire of Georgian terraces and porticos.

Part of the manor of Marylebone had been enclosed as a deer park by Henry VIII. By the early 19th century it had become simply part of the countryside around London, although it was still owned by the Crown. As London grew, this holding presented the future George IV, then Prince Regent, with an opportunity for development, whose value was only limited by the difficulty of luring rich house buyers so far from the Houses of Parliament. Nash proposed to overcome this obstacle by building a new street that would connect Marylebone and Westminster, eliminating some of the slums that disfigured London along the way. The old deer park would once again become a park of a type: a densely planted landscape full of concealed villas. Each owner who looked out from his property would be unable to see the fifty or so other villa owners doing likewise; as a result, his imagination (and proprietorial instincts) would be satisfied by the illusion of owning the view.

In the event only eight of the villas, dotted about the park, were actually built. Around the perimeter of the park are a series of terraces, similar to hundreds of others in London, only these were designed to be seen, from the outside, as palaces, with richly allegorical pediments above and triumphal arches to the sides. Cumberland Terrace, of 1826, is the grandest of them. Originally, their stucco fronts were painted sand-colour and scored to look like stone. It had been intended, at first, that the Regent's Canal would form one of the features of the park, but it was judged that the appearance of bargees in the park would lower the tone.

The line of the new route took in Portland Place, already existing and fashionable, but then did a jink to avoid the aristocratic house at its base. This change of direction was concealed from the eye by building a church with a round portico, All Souls Langham Place. There was another slight wobble, artfully disguised by Oxford Circus; then, at the southern end, a fundamental change of direction was required so that the section below Piccadilly Circus (see page 183) could be aligned on the Prince Regent's palace of Carlton House (the site now occupied by Carlton House Terrace). Nash introduced a crescent, or Quadrant, to hide the join. This is the one strictly formal element of the design. Elsewhere, although Nash had originally envisaged a scheme as disciplined as the newly constructed Rue de Rivoli in Paris, from which he borrowed the idea of continuous arcades, he was forced to compromise. Individual developers had different priorities. Compromise brought out Nash's aesthetic best.

Little more than the public buildings – All Souls Langham Place, the Theatre Royal, Haymarket, the Athenaeum Club – survive from John Nash's original Regent Street project, but the line remains unaltered and, in one respect, the Picturesque content has been enhanced. Since the demolition of Carlton House, the metropolitan improvement that began in Regent's Park now ends in another park, St James's. This is part of the tangible legacy of the Picturesque, which strikes Londoners as nothing odd but is unique to their city.

*See Royal Pavilion, page 52, and Buckingham Palace, page 126

PRIMROSE HILL PRIMROSE HILL ROAD, NW3
Revival of Druidism

The more the Age of Enlightenment took hold of Georgian Britain, the more some people were drawn to its opposite – a world that was not modern or rational, but ancient and mysterious. The Lincolnshire doctor turned divine, William Stukeley, was one of the founders of the Society of Antiquaries (1718) and toured England looking for ruins, publishing an account of his findings in *Itinerarium Curiosum*. Following the crushing of the Jacobite rebellion at Culloden in 1746 (see page 447), literary London could risk lifting the Celtic fringe. It fell hook, line and sinker for the poems supposedly written by the Highland bard Ossian, but actually composed by their 'translator' James Macpherson in the 1760s. Before long, the visionary poet William Blake was conjuring up the shades of Druidism, somehow associated with the Jerusalem that he believed to have once existed near Primrose Hill.

By coincidence, it was on Primrose Hill that, in 1792, practising Druidism was reborn. A stonemason turned bookseller, poet and political radical called Edward Williams, writing under the name of Iolo Morgannwg, maintained that the Druids had never died out in his native Glamorgan, where their literary tradition stretched continuously back to the pre-Christian era. His powers of invention fuelled by opium, he set about devising an apparently ancient ceremony that he claimed to have discovered from a Welsh manuscript. He

Abbey Mills Pumping Station, page 108.
The building of the London sewers
was one of the great achievements of
Victorian civil engineering.

Arnos Grove Station, page 112. Modern yet classic, the architecture of the Piccadilly Line
summed up the corporate philosophy of the London Underground.

Above: The Banqueting House, page 114. In 1649, Charles I was executed outside the Banqueting House that had been built for his father, James I, by Inigo Jones.

Opposite: Kensington Palace, page 152. William III died at Kensington Palace in 1702 after a riding accident when his horse stumbled over a molehill; Jacobites celebrated, toasting the 'little gentleman in black velvet' who had caused the King's death.

Left: Royal Academy of Arts, page 168.
The Royal Academy was founded in 1768
to improve the 'Polite Arts' in Britain.

Right: Handel's House, page 148. George
Frideric Handel composed the *Messiah*
at 25 Brook Street, Mayfair, in 1742.

Below: Chiswick House, page 134.
The gardens at Chiswick House: Lord
Burlington set out to revolutionise taste,
and succeeded.

Above: Leighton House, page 155. The dazzling Victorian painter Frederic Leighton built this Arab Hall in his studio house in Holland Park.

Left: Sir John Soane's Museum, page 186. The architect Sir John Soane commissioned Joseph Gandy to record his flights of imagination.

London Zoo, page 157. The world's first zoo kept abreast of the Modern Movement with its famous Penguin Pool of 1934, constructed from the new material of reinforced concrete.

Michelin House, page 160. Bibendum,
a.k.a. the Michelin Man, demonstrates
the grip of the Michelin tyre.

Top: Smithfield, page 185. The Lord Mayor William Walworth kills Wat Tyler, leader of the Peasants' Revolt, in front of Richard II.

Above: Mansion House, page 158. The annual Lord Mayor's procession demonstrates the pride of the City of London.

Freud's House, page 142. The founder of psychiatry, Sigmund Freud, fled to London in 1938.

St Mary's Hospital, page 178. In 1928, Alexander Fleming discovered penicillin almost by accident in his laboratory at St Mary's Hospital, Paddington.

Above: Trellick Tower, page 190. Once reviled as the epitome of architectural arrogance, Ernö Goldfinger's tower block, completed in 1972, is being rediscovered.

Left: The Monument, page 161. The flaming urn crowning The Monument, which was designed by Christopher Wren, commemorates the Great Fire of London.

Sidney Street, page 184. Controversially, the Home Secretary Winston Churchill took personal control of the siege.

Westminster Hall, page 195. William II's hall, the largest of its age in Europe, was later crowned by the earliest and most magnificent hammerbeam roof.

Linley Sambourne House, page 155. The interiors created by the *Punch* illustrator Edward Linley Sambourne and his wife in the 1870s have hardly changed.

laid out a circle of pebbles on the grass inside which he and a group of London Welsh compatriots, including Blake's friend, the Welsh lexicographer William Pughe, performed his Gorsedd Beirdd Ynys Prydain, or Assembly of Bards of Britain, for the first time. The Gorsedd coincided with a movement to revive the eisteddfod* tradition around Wales, in an attempt to preserve Welshness in the face of the new Methodism. In 1819, Williams persuaded the organisers of the eisteddfod held at the Bush Inn, Carmarthen, to incorporate his Gorsedd, along with its three orders of bards dressed respectively in robes of white, blue and green. It remains part of the National Eisteddfod to this day.

The Gorsedd on Primrose Hill prefigured the Celtic Revival that entranced late Victorian and Edwardian Britain. The National Eisteddfod, held in Wales rather than London, has outgrown its bogus origins to become a cultural phenomenon, at which even the then future Archbishop of Canterbury, Rowan Williams, was inducted as an honorary white druid in 2002.

*See Cardigan Castle, page 414

QUEEN'S HOUSE PARK ROW, SE10
Jeu d'esprit *that became an icon of the Stuart dynasty*

In James I and Anne of Denmark, England was said to have a hunting King and a dancing Queen. Relations between them were more affectionate than one might have supposed from James's homosexual leanings. In 1614, James gave his Queen the palace of Greenwich.

The painter, masque designer, antiquarian, connoisseur and now architect Inigo Jones had been blazing his meteoric way through the Jacobean Court for a decade or so and since 1613 had been Surveyor to the King's Works. When finished, the Queen's House at Greenwich would be the inspiration for hundreds of sparsely decorated, rectilinear houses, so many that it is difficult to appreciate that Jones's contemporaries had seen nothing like it before. It has come to be considered the *fons et origo* of all neo-Classical architecture in Britain. Yet there remains something of the 'curious' about it, too. It was built some way from the rest of the palace, not merely beside the road from London to Dover but actually, by means of bridges, spanning it. There is a little, perhaps, of Raleigh's cloak about it: the building provided a permanent means of keeping the Queen's feet dry as she passed from the garden of the palace into the park.

Paintings suggest that, if the Queen's House had been completed by James I, it might not have been the architectural phenomenon that it became, but when Anne died in 1619, the King lost heart in the project and the Queen's House remained half-finished. Enthusiasm for it was rekindled in the next reign, however, when Charles I perhaps saw it as an essential distraction for his wife, Henrietta Maria, after the death of their first child. It seems that the design now changed dramatically. The new austere building was inspired by the works of such architects as Palladio, Scamozzi and Alberti that Jones had seen while travelling in Italy. However, he did not borrow a fashion, so much as use the principles he had studied to invent his own. As finished, the Queen's House is not only completely unlike anything that had previously been constructed in England, but has no real parallel anywhere else in Europe either.

A drawing from before 1640 shows the Queen's House as it has come down to us: a seven-bay façade of square-headed windows. Along the skyline runs a parapet, with two chimneys rising above it, as they do today. The drawing also shows two turrets; these would have been little banqueting rooms, following the Elizabethan practice. In the 16th century, there was a vogue among country-house builders for providing rooftop eyries to which guests could repair for the last course of a meal. Roofs were important: it was common practice to walk up and down on the leads. So it must have been at the Queen's House. Here, the roof would also have provided an observation point for the park, either to watch military parades or hunts. The drawing shows that the side of the building that faces the river may have been decorated with mural paintings. The Queen's House may therefore have served as a place to receive guests arriving by water, perhaps with theatre or poetry. Because of its position east of London, Greenwich was often the first stopping place for arriving ambassadors and other grand people.

The Queen's House was finished in 1639, leaving the royal couple just three years in which to enjoy it. On 10 February 1642, Henrietta and Charles spent a night at Greenwich for the last time. Seven years later, Charles stepped out of a window of another building by Inigo Jones – the Banqueting House, Whitehall – to be executed (see page 114). The Queen's House might easily have been swept away when the Royal Naval Hospital was planned in the 1690s (see page 172), had it not been for the strongly expressed wish of Charles I's granddaughter, Queen Mary, to keep it. It had become a Stuart icon.

RANGER'S HOUSE
CHESTERFIELD WALK, SE10

Where the arbiter of manners cultivated his garden

The 4th Earl of Chesterfield was one of the most glittering political and literary figures of 18th-century society and was regarded (not least by himself) as a trendsetter of manners. In Mayfair he owned a Palladian house built by Isaac Ware, but from 1748 he increasingly came to prefer the house at Blackheath, now called Ranger's House, which he inherited from his brother. It is typical of the villas that ringed London, providing a taste of the country for people who did not like to be too remote from the centre of affairs.

At first, Chesterfield found the Blackheath property something of a burden. For one thing, while Greenwich was adequately fashionable, it was not nearly grand enough for Lord Chesterfield, who prided himself on knowing all the most glittering people in Europe. He would much rather his newly acquired villa had been in Twickenham or Richmond, but within a few years he had fallen for the place. 'This,' he said, 'I find, is my proper place; and I know it, which people seldom do. I converse with my equals, my vegetables, which I found in a flourishing condition.' As this letter suggests, he took pleasure in cultivating his garden. By Chesterfield's standards, the house was not big. He made a joke of it to the Marquise de Monconseil, whose lodge in the Bois de Boulogne in Paris was known as Bagatelle, or trifle. His own 'very small house' five miles from London 'I would have called Bagatelle had not I felt such a respect for yours; so I call it Babiole' – meaning a bauble.

It was early in the next century that Chesterfield House became the Ranger's House, the official residence of the Ranger of the Park.

RITZ HOTEL *150 PICCADILLY, W1*
The first steel-framed building in London

Built in 1904–5, the Ritz Hotel in Piccadilly was the first steel-framed building of this scale in London. Steel-framed construction, in which the weight of the building is borne by the network of steel beams within it, is lighter than the traditional method of load-bearing walls. Pioneered in Chicago in the 1880s, it allows buildings to rise taller, as well as faster and therefore more cheaply. The Ritz could therefore be said to be the precursor of the skyscrapers built from the Second World War onwards in the City of London and Canary Wharf (see page 130). Where the Ritz led, the Gherkin followed.

The style of the Ritz does not imitate the aggressive modernity of Chicago: rather, it evokes the luxurious *douceur de vivre* of pre-Revolutionary France. This was the first such thoroughgoing essay in the Louis XVI Revival, which quickly became synonymous with sophistication. It was the perfect complement to the *entente cordiale* that blessed political relations between France and Britain in the Edwardian age; Edward VII, for whose tastes the Ritz could have been especially designed, was as familiar in Paris and the South of France as he was in his own kingdom. The Swiss-born hotelier César Ritz embodied the prevailing cosmopolitanism, with its assumption that life's most delectable pleasures came from France. He brought over the culinary immortal, Auguste Escoffier, to work first in the Savoy Hotel and then in the Carlton. Ritz deserves as much credit as anyone for the revolution in social behaviour which occurred when women of quality began to eat publicly in restaurants; before 1900 it was assumed that dinner was best eaten at home, not least because restaurants were a preserve of the *demi-monde*.

The architectural firm that built the Ritz, Mewès and Davis, also prefigured a trend that would become commonplace in the business if not architectural world. It was a kind of multinational company, with the Frenchman Charles Mewès employing different representatives in the different territories – France, Germany, Spain, South America – in which he worked. The *dix-huitième* neo-Classical style in which Mewès worked was equally transferable. In 1897–8, Mewès had built the Ritz Hotel in Paris, ingeniously shoehorned in behind a genuinely 18th-century façade in the Place Vendôme. Arthur Davis was an urbane young Englishman who had attended the École des Beaux-Arts in Paris.

A famous courtesan is supposed to have complimented Ritz by saying that he had 'reached the height of [his] profession – as I have of mine'. To which he replied: 'Alas, with far less pleasure and far more trouble than you have experienced, Mademoiselle.' Ritz's perfectionism in his *métier* came at the price of ceaseless overwork, as he raced between his different hotel enterprises across Europe. It led to a breakdown in 1902, said to have been precipitated by the shock of the postponement of Edward VII's coronation (towards which he had been working) due to the King's peritonitis. He never properly recovered. He died as the First World War drew to a close, without playing an active part in running the hotel in London that bore his name.

ROYAL ACADEMY OF ARTS PICCADILLY, W1
Raising the status of the fine arts

'An Academy, in which the Polite Arts may be regularly cultivated, is at last opened among us by Royal Munificence,' announced the painter Sir Joshua Reynolds to a celebrated artistic gathering on 2 January 1769. 'This must appear an event in the highest degree interesting, not only to the Artists, but to the whole Nation.'

The founding of the Royal Academy in 1768 was the culmination of a campaign to overcome Britain's sense of cultural inferiority in the visual arts. A century earlier, most artists working here had been foreign, the art market barely existed, the great collection amassed by Charles I had been dispersed and the artistic achievement of France and Italy was manifestly superior to our own. By the middle of the 18th century, the time was ripe for an artistic revival. Taste was cultivated as part of the new refinement of manners, connoisseurship was highly prized, and works of art were pouring into the country as a result of the Grand Tour, but native artists had yet to establish the same standing as their French and Italian counterparts. They were not only regarded as less skilful, but unable to scale the highest peak of their profession. By the time George III came to the throne in 1760, raising the artistic game in Britain had become a matter of national honour.

With Reynolds as President and the architect Sir William Chambers as Treasurer, the Royal Academy provided both a forum for art, with regular exhibitions, and a school to train young artists according to the best classical principles. The Academy was underwritten by the King himself, and education was free. By 1820, the Royal Academy, located at that time in Chambers's Somerset House, had trained 1,200 students, who went on to become, if not major artists, at least drawing masters and designers. In 1867, it moved to Burlington House, on the site of Lord Burlington's palace (see page 134), which it now shares with the Geological Society, the Royal Society of Chemistry, the Royal Astronomical Society, the Linnean Society and the Society of Antiquaries.

ROYAL ARSENAL *WOOLWICH, SE18*
Where the shells for the Western Front were made

The First World War was the first war in history in which artillery played the dominant role. As a result, the Royal Arsenal at Woolwich, where much of the ordnance was made, swelled to its greatest size. Over 80,000 people worked there, in furnaces and boring mills, at steam hammers, lathes and cranes, forging gun barrels and packing shells. Once in a while, a Zeppelin would pass overhead, disrupting production and, on one occasion, dropping a bomb that incredibly only destroyed a crane, a boring machine and one unfortunate worker. At this time, the Royal Arsenal occupied a compound three miles by one mile. Its decline came when the threat from the air made it prudent to distribute production among a number of sites.

In Tudor times, Woolwich was the dockyard where Henry VIII's *Henri Grace à Dieu* was built. Dockyards require supplies of stores, including ordnance, and in Elizabeth I's reign Woolwich was where Sir Francis Drake deposited the 'ordnance of brasse' that he had captured in the West Indies. A little down river from the dockyard was a property called the Warren, which was where, from 1665, ordnance was proofed. The proofing of the ordnance – accompanied by loud explosions as guns were tested – cannot have been particularly comfortable for the owner of the adjacent Tower House, Sir William Pritchard, who sold his estate to the government. This provided the space required for buildings in which munitions could be manufactured and repaired as well as stored. In 1716, an explosion at the foundry in the City of London, where previously all guns for government service had been cast, convinced the Board of Ordnance to create its own brass foundry at Woolwich. This was also the year in which the Royal Regiment of Artillery was founded, with its headquarters at Woolwich.

The years after the Jacobite rising of 1715 were a period of great expenditure on military projects, and Woolwich benefited from a brass foundry and other buildings to which the name of John Vanbrugh has been attached. When George III visited the foundry in 1773, the King commented that the name of Woolwich Warren hardly did the place justice; from henceforth it was known as the Royal Arsenal. In 1886, a group of workers from the Royal Arsenal formed a football team. Although the modern Arsenal Football Club has its ground in North London, it is still known familiarly as The Gunners.

ROYAL FESTIVAL HALL
BELVEDERE ROAD, SE1
Permanent legacy of the Festival of Britain

The Royal Festival Hall is the only substantial structure to survive from the Festival of Britain, the 'tonic to the nation' dispensed by the Labour government in 1951. Ostensibly, the Festival of Britain had been devised to commemorate the centenary of the Great Exhibition of 1851, although this did little to influence the content of the Festival, which was not an international trade fair so much as a celebration of renewal after the Second World War. The principal site itself, 27 acres on the south bank of the Thames, had been heavily bombed. Mounted at a time when Britain was under rationing, the Festival maintained a relentlessly cheery tone, the funfair created in Battersea Park being especially popular. Throughout, the focus was firmly on the new. London's blackened heritage of striped and decorated Victorian architecture had been made more dismal, to contemporary eyes, by the bombing.

The organisers of the Festival deliberately promoted a style that would be its antithesis: light, young (none of the fifty architects working on the project was over forty-five) and modern. Around 8.5 million people visited the Festival, taking away an image of furniture with canted legs, indoor plants, lily-of-the-valley splays of light bulbs, picture windows and flying staircases. These epitomised modernity, in a style that could be applied as easily to council houses and parades of little shops as it could to the new Coventry Cathedral designed in the same year (see page 314).

It was a style that owed something to the plate-glass and steel architecture of the Bauhaus, but rather more to the decorative charm of modern Swedish architecture. Yet the vision was also unmistakably British, with the exhibits including an embroidered relief mural called 'The Country Wife', made by, among others, members of the Women's Institute. In national terms, it was a partial vision, which left out most of the industrial Midlands and urban slums.

The Festival closed at the end of September and after the General Election on 26 October, when the Conservatives returned to power, most of the Festival architecture was cleared away. The project had been too closely associated with their opponents.

The Royal Festival Hall remained, however. It had been built to replace the Queen's Hall, a heavy Victorian building that had been bombed during the war. Designed in 1948 by Leslie Martin and Robert Matthew of the London County Council's Architects' Department, its auditorium took the form of an egg suspended within a box. The open-plan bars and foyers around the central egg provided an extra layer of soundproofing, desirable because of the proximity to the Hungerford railway bridge. Inside, the decorative scheme, with its Marion Dorn rugs, reflected the taste of the whole Festival and whose democratic nature was mirrored in the seating arrangements, in which differences were eliminated as far as possible, and even the private boxes did not imply more privileged status.

The Royal Festival Hall was the first major new public building erected in Britain after the Second World War. Architectural critics who sneered at the Festival's interpretation of the modern – sometimes felt to lack rigour – could take satisfaction in the other cultural buildings that came to join it on the South Bank complex. The New Brutalism style of the Hayward Gallery and the Queen Elizabeth Hall caused these to be regularly voted the ugliest buildings in Britain. The elegantly conceived National Theatre, which arrived in 1976, shared their use of the widely hated material of shuttered concrete. By contrast, the Royal Festival Hall continues to command admiration from passers-by and affection from the audiences who use it.

THE ROYAL INSTITUTION   21 ALBEMARLE STREET, W1
Where the principle of the electric motor was discovered

Michael Faraday, the 21-year-old son of a blacksmith, had a lucky break. From the age of fourteen he had been apprenticed to a bookbinder, George Riebau; one of Riebau's customers gave him tickets to the last four lectures that Sir Humphry Davy gave at the Royal Institution of Great Britain, which had been founded in 1799 to further scientific research. Faraday had already developed a passion for science, acquired from some of the books that he had bound. After listening to Davy, Faraday was emboldened to approach the scientist, and ask for a job. When the chemical assistant at the Royal Institution was sacked in 1813 after a fight, Davy got Faraday appointed. Davy, still in his thirties, had married an heiress, and thereafter did little more original science beyond inventing the miners' safety lamp that bears his name. It was to Faraday that the aged Italian nobleman Alessandro Volta gave one of his primitive electric batteries, a symbolic torch of learning passed from an old scientist to a young one. It remains in the Royal Institution.

The Royal Institution had some of the best-equipped laboratories in Europe. Faraday came to have his own basement laboratory there, as well as his own rooms in which to live. In this laboratory, in 1821, he discovered electro-magnetic rotation, the principle behind the electric motor. The next decade saw Faraday develop his reputation as a lecturer, and he became the first Secretary of the newly founded Athenaeum Club (a duty for which he cannot have been well fitted, since he was hardly gregarious). In the 1830s, he discovered how to make an electric transformer and an electric generator. Words such as electrode, electrolyte, anode, cathode and ion were coined by Faraday in the course of his research into electro-chemical action. Until this time, it had been believed that electricity was a fluid; Faraday demonstrated that it was a force. Faraday put his science to practical use, by improving the optics of lighthouses. In the mid-1840s, he proved that light was affected by magnetic force, and discovered that all matter was inherently magnetic. He developed the concept, so familiar today, that magnetism, like other kinds of force, operates in fields.

Throughout his life, Faraday belonged to the obscure Sandemanian sect, with its literal belief in the Bible. This was a source of anxiety to the Victorian establishment, who were concerned to see the most famous scientist of his day worshipping with artisans. True to his creed, Faraday is buried in the plot acquired by the Sandemanians in Highgate Cemetery (see page 150). Behind its screen of Corinthian columns, the Royal Institution, where Faraday had lived and worked for most of his life, continued to push forward the boundaries of science. Directors after Faraday include James Dewar, who liquefied hydrogen and invented the Thermos flask; William Bragg, the youngest ever Nobel Prize winner, who discovered the structure of lysozyme (the enzyme in egg whites and tears); and George (Lord) Porter, whose research into very fast, light-driven chemical reactions helped explain that process essential to life, photosynthesis in plants.

ROYAL NAVAL HOSPITAL   KING WILLIAM WALK, SE10
Queen Mary II's magnificent compassion for sailors

Before becoming King, James II had served his brother, Charles II, as Lord High Admiral, witnessing the appalling carnage that followed battles such as Sole Bay (see page 285). According to Samuel Pepys, it was he who first proposed founding a hospital to care for wounded seamen, although he did nothing to further it during the three years he occupied the throne. He was, however, indirectly responsible for promoting it during the next reign. After he had fled to

France in 1688, French ships that supported his return were routed by a combined Anglo-Dutch fleet off Cape Barfleur, near Cherbourg, a victory obtained at the usual dreadful human cost. With William III away fighting in the Low Countries, it was left to the tender-hearted Queen Mary, with whom he shared the throne*, to do what she could to relieve the suffering of the sailors who returned to Portsmouth, by sending surgeons and gifts. She had her Secretary of State, Lord Nottingham, bestir the Treasury 'to hasten . . . the grant of Greenwich as a hospital for Seamen, which is now depending before you'.

The Hospital at Greenwich was to be Queen Mary's memorial. When she died suddenly from smallpox in 1694, the King opened his heart towards what had been 'the darling object of her life'. The Charter to found a Hospital 'for the reliefe and support of Seamen serving on board the Shipps and Vessells belonging to the Navy Royall' was issued in the names of both William and Mary, and backdated to 25 October, before the Queen's death. With money, however, only fitfully available, the real hero of the story is the Hospital's first Treasurer, John Evelyn. The Hospital took fifty-five years to build.

Wren, the grand old man of English architecture (see page 179), first inspected the site in the autumn of 1694. Pepys, who accompanied him on that first visit, gives him the credit for elevating the notion of a hospital for the wounded sailors coming from recent wars into a great and permanent national memorial.

The day-to-day running of the project was delegated to Nicholas Hawksmoor. When Hawksmoor had the task, many years later, of justifying the long and costly construction to Parliament, he emphasised Queen Mary's desire for 'Magnificence'. Out of thrift, however, she had insisted on the retention of a range of buildings that was all that John Webb had succeeded in erecting towards Charles II's new Greenwich palace. She had been equally emphatic that the view to the river, which the Queen's House (see page 165) had enjoyed since the demolition of the Tudor palace, was preserved. By the mid-19th century, there were fewer wounded sailors to house, and most old sailors preferred family life to the regime offered by the Hospital, so it closed in 1869, to be replaced by the Royal Naval College in 1873. The building is now occupied by the University of Greenwich.

*See Brixham Harbour, page 13, and Kensington Palace, page 152

ROYAL OBSERVATORY   GREENWICH PARK, SE10
Charting the movement of the heavens

The reign of Charles II was a time of intense scientific excitement; the Royal Society was given its royal charter in 1662, and the King himself had a laboratory for chemical experiments. Of all the sciences, it was astronomy that seemed to offer most to contemporaries. Not only did the movement of the heavens seem to reflect the nature of God, but also understanding the stars provided sailors with a means of plotting their position on the seas; this would have had the very practical benefit of preventing costly shipwrecks. The King's mistress, the voluptuous Breton beauty Louise de Keroualle, badgered Charles II to support her countryman, Le Sieur de St Pierre, in discovering an astronomical method for finding longitude. But Le Sieur's scientific claims were bogus, and in his place the King appointed the 30-year-old John Flamsteed as his 'astronomical observator', being directed that he should devote his energies to rectifying 'the tables of the Motions of the Heavens and the places of the fixed Stars so as to find out the so-much-desired Longitude of Places'. Under the circumstances, this was a substantial job and the salary of £100 a year was hardly excessive.

Before Flamsteed's observations could begin, he needed an observatory. Sites in Hyde Park and Chelsea were rejected, perhaps because of the atmospheric pollution that already hung over London, obscuring the night skies. The idea of Greenwich came from Sir Christopher Wren, a scientist before he was an architect (see page 179). The fact that it was a royal park meant that the King could provide land for nothing. Economy was a consideration in the project, as can be seen from the decision to re-use the foundations of a tower that had previously stood on the site, on a bluff above the old palace and set back from the river. The money to fund the building work came from the sale of decayed gunpowder.

Wren needed to create an observation room with very tall windows and he did so in the form of a tower, appearing flat from the front but octagonal within, which gave the Observatory a faintly castle-like appearance. A glance at old engravings, depicting the 'Star Chamber' or Octagon Room in use, shows a room of great height. The only means by which the secrets of the heavens could be unlocked was the telescope. The longer the telescope, the more detail could be seen. A ladder and stand were necessary to support Flamsteed's telescope, which was 8½ft long. To know the precise time at which observations were made was critically important. Consequently, two clocks made by Thomas Tompion were fitted into the wall; they were regulated by 12ft pendulums that, unusually, were hung above rather than below the clock faces.

One of the garden pavilions added later by Wren formed a *domus obscurata*, or darkened house, for receiving sunspots and solar eclipses. There were outbuildings for large sextants, a great quadrant fixed to a wall aligned on the meridian, a 60ft telescope suspended from a mast and a telescope sunk in a well. Alas, none of this really made John Flamsteed a happy man; he refused to publish his observations until the restless scientific community dragged them out of him.

24 RUSSELL SQUARE

T. S. Eliot's spiritual home

Disjointed, allusive, detached, ironic, *The Waste Land* was arguably the most important poem of the 20th century, opening the door to distinctively modern ways of expressing thought and feeling. When it was published in 1922, T. S. Eliot was working for Lloyds Bank in Cornhill, in the City of London. Although he longed to pursue a life dedicated to literature, the routine of banking in some ways suited his American Puritan instincts. Its orderliness was a refuge from his chaotic marriage to a mentally unstable wife, Vivien. Before long, however, he was to find a spiritual home – and, ultimately, happiness – in the offices of the publishing company, Faber and Gwyer, 24 Russell Square.

Faber and Gwyer was founded by Geoffrey Faber in 1925; four years later it became Faber and Faber, although there was never more than one of them, the second Faber being added for effect. Eliot, having met Faber through a friend at All Souls, Oxford, joined as literary adviser the same year, his first season seeing the publication of his own *Poems 1909–25*. Other authors on the Faber list included Ezra Pound, Jean Cocteau, Herbert Read, Geoffrey Keynes and Vita Sackville-West. Siegfried Sassoon's *Memoirs of a Fox-hunting Man*, published (originally anonymously) in 1928, was the first of the firm's many commercial successes.

Born in St Louis, Missouri, Eliot had been brought up as a Unitarian. First coming to Britain on a travelling scholarship, he became a member of the Church of England before converting to Roman Catholicism; he became a naturalised British subject in 1927. Eliot's religion strongly coloured his later poetry ('Ash-Wednesday') and plays (*Murder in the Cathedral*). Generally severe in manner, he came to be known as the Pope of Russell Square.

It was at No. 24 that Eliot, aged sixty-eight, proposed to his thirty-year-old secretary Valerie Fletcher, embarking on a second marriage that was to prove an Indian summer.

ST BARTHOLOMEW'S HOSPITAL

William Harvey discovers the circulation of the blood

There has been an annual book fair in Frankfurt since the 15th century. In 1628, one of the books published in that literary city was William Harvey's *Exercitatio Anatomica de Motu Cordis et Sanguinis in Animalibus* (*An Anatomical Exercise on the Motion of the Heart and Blood in Animals*). The ideas of this book, the first account of how blood is pumped around the body by the heart, had already been shared with his audiences at the Lumleian lectures he had been giving at the College of Physicians in London since 1616. The purpose of this circulation was not as yet known – Harvey thought it might have been to warm the limbs – but his observations were the foundation of all future anatomy.

Harvey, however, was not only a theorist but also a practising physician. Having studied at Cambridge and Padua, in 1609 he became Physician to St Bartholomew's Hospital, which had been founded in the 12th century on what were then marshes outside the City of London. Since he was Physician to both James I and Charles I, he was often absent from the hospital. Nevertheless, he laid down some practical rules for administering medicine there, specifically ensuring that junior doctors could not exercise their skills without the approval of colleagues. Very short, swarthy, with a peppery temper, a doctor's typically execrable handwriting and an alarming tendency to fiddle with a small dagger that hung by his side, Harvey would personally see patients once a week. He sat at a table in the hall, surrounded by his apothecary, steward and matron.

Harvey was with King Charles at the battles of Edgehill (see page 319) and Naseby (see page 332). By the end of the Civil War he was in his late sixties and politically out of favour. The last years of his life, until his death in 1657, were devoted to building a library for the College of Physicians, to which he bequeathed his estate in Kent.

ST CLEMENT DANES STRAND, WC2
Viking legacy embedded in a name

'Oranges and lemons, say the bells of St Clement's.' The children who sing this nursery rhyme probably do not know that this refers to the church of St Clement Danes in the Strand, whose name, like other names embedded in common usage, reflects its origins as a Viking foundation.

From about 800, the Vikings had been raiding and settling in the east of England, an area that, during King Alfred's reign, came to be recognised as the Danelaw. Law itself is one of the many words which the Vikings gave the English language. From 1016–35, the King of England was a Dane – Cnut, sometimes known as Canute the Great. He was the son of the terrifying Danish King Swein 'Forkbeard', and was invited onto the throne by Anglo-Saxons who despaired of their ruler, Ethelred II, known as 'the Unready'. Perhaps reflecting their cultural ascendancy, Danes founded a number of churches during Cnut's reign, among them St Clement Danes. As the patron saint of sailors, St Clement had special appeal to the seafaring Vikings. He had been Pope at the end of the 1st century and died when the Emperor Trajan ordered him to be tied to an anchor and thrown into the sea.

Danes had settled the area between the City of London and Westminster known as the Ald wic, or old village ('wic' being the Saxon equivalent of the

Latin *vicus*, the smallest form of settlement recognised by the Romans); it remains today in Aldwych. They built St Clement Danes close by, perhaps replacing an earlier wooden church. The new church must have been roughly contemporary with the five churches in the City and one in Southwark dedicated to St Olaf (or Olave), the zealously Christian King Olaf II Haraldsson who died in battle in 1030, was soon after canonised and became the patron saint of Norway.

The St Clement Danes that we see today contains no outward sign of its Viking roots, having been completely rebuilt by Sir Christopher Wren* in 1680 – although, unlike the fifty-two churches for which he was responsible in the City, with an apse. The spire was raised by James Gibbs in 1719 and houses the famous bells. Two hundred years later the present carillon was made to ring out the tune of 'Oranges and Lemons' every hour – still charming any passer-by who can hear it above the traffic. The church was rebuilt after enemy bombing during the Second World War.

*See St Paul's Cathedral, page 179

ST KATHARINE'S DOCK ST KATHARINE'S WAY, E1
The only part of London Docks to survive partially intact

At the beginning of the 19th century, Britain was the richest country in the world and London was its main port. Trade had increased staggeringly in the last years of the previous century, two-thirds of it passing through London. The system for unloading and protecting the cargoes of the ships that were crowding the river Thames had not kept pace, however, with the traffic. Ships backed up in the river as they waited for a space at one of the quays. Congestion caused delays; it also increased the opportunity for smuggling. With precious barrels of rum, spices and sugar left lying unprotected on the quayside, pilfering was rife. In the age of sail, ships arrived unpredictably, none when the wind was adverse, many when it blew for home. The problem was compounded by the Napoleonic Wars, when merchant ships from the West Indies arrived in convoys, and all the vessels discharged their cargoes at once. London needed docks that could accommodate many vessels at the same time and store their cargoes in thief-resistant, fireproof warehouses.

When they were built, the Docks formed their own architectural world, made up of towering walls and broad expanses of water, sealed off from everyone except those who worked there. They were built by private companies, in fierce competition with each other. First came the West India Dock* on the Isle of Dogs, 1800-2, engineered by William Jessop who had constructed the Grand Union Canal. Hot on its heels followed London Dock, nearer the

City at Wapping, designed by Daniel Alexander with John Rennie supervising the work. The East India Dock, at Blackwall, opened a few years later, in 1806; this was to berth the ships of the vast East India Company. The Surrey Docks on the south side of the river were built in the commercially difficult years that followed the end of the Napoleonic Wars. Last in this phase of development was Thomas Telford's St Katharine's Dock, constructed from 1827–8. This was closest of all to the City; so close, in fact, that over 11,000 people had to be made homeless and the 12th-century Hospital of St Katharine pulled down to clear the site. St Katharine's is the only dock to have survived with water, ground plan and some buildings intact.

With the coming of steamships, which arrived to schedule, the new priority was to build docks close to railways. The Royal Victoria Dock, opened 1855, was followed by the Royal Albert Dock, both of which were in competition with Millwall Dock and ultimately Tilbury Dock. In 1889, dock workers went on strike for wages of 6d an hour – the 'docker's tanner'. They won it. It was the beginning of nearly a century of stormy industrial relations, which reached a nadir after the Second World War. During that war, the Docks were the most bombed civilian target in Britain. From the 1960s, goods started to arrive already packed in containers, which needed no warehousing; once out of the ship, they were moved on by road. The fork-lift truck replaced muscle power. By 1981, all the 19th-century docks except Tilbury were empty.

*See Canary Wharf, page 130

ST MARY'S HOSPITAL   PRAED STREET, W2

Where penicillin was discovered

Penicillin, discovered in 1928, has affected everyone's life, all but eliminating the fear of painful death from infection that haunted previous generations. Before the advent of penicillin, doctors had no means of treating many infections, and a quarter of all patients who underwent surgery died of gangrene. Penicillin conquered septicaemia, pneumonia, meningitis and the puerperal fever from which women could die after childbirth. It inspired all the modern antibiotic medicines that are now dispensed without a second thought, a freedom that is almost cavalier.

The effects of *Penicillium notatum*, a kind of mould, in destroying bacteria were first noticed by Alexander Fleming. He was one of eight sons of an Ayrshire hill farmer, and came to London at the age of sixteen to work as a clerk in a shipping office. He hated the job. Fortunately a small legacy from an uncle enabled him to train as a doctor. He hoped to work at St Mary's, Paddington, as a surgeon, but since there was no vacancy in surgery, he turned to bacteriology instead. Fleming had just been appointed professor of bacteriology when, in the autumn of 1928, he took a holiday, leaving behind on the mahogany workbench in his laboratory Petri dishes of the *Staphylococci* which he had been studying. It was cold for the time of year. On returning, Fleming noticed that one of the dishes had gone mouldy. He looked at it closely, and saw that microbes around the mould had been killed. He called the substance that had done the work 'mould juice'. It would soon be known as penicillin. Fleming published a paper on his discovery. However, being unable to stabilise and purify it, he could not develop it into a medicine.

Shortly before the Second World War, a research team at Oxford University, led by the Australian pathologist Howard Florey, began work on penicillin, and succeeded in producing enough for it to be tried on a patient. A 43-year-old policeman, Albert Alexander, was dying of *Staphylococci* and *Streptococci* infections, contracted through a scratch while gardening. He was treated with penicillin and began to improve. Alas, his recovery could not be sustained since the supply of penicillin was too small. Clearly, however, the penicillin had worked for a time and had to be produced in large quantities. This was hardly possible in Britain during the war, but a means of doing so was found in the United States. Penicillin saved the lives of many soldiers who had been wounded during the D-Day landings in Normandy; it cured others of venereal disease.

See also The Chantry, page 301

ST PAUL'S CATHEDRAL   ST PAUL'S CHURCHYARD, EC4

Reader, if you seek his monument, look around you

Sir Christopher Wren is acknowledged as one of the greatest Englishmen, and St Paul's Cathedral (1675–1710) is his masterpiece. Wren was fortunate to live at the time that he did. He had a ceaselessly inquiring mind, and the reign of Charles II was a time of boundless intellectual curiosity, in which the last superstitions of the Middle Ages were being dispelled and the foundations of modern science laid. In the tight-knit world of the Royal Society, that 'experimental philosophical clubbe' formed in 1662, gentlemen amateurs such as Samuel Pepys (who became its President) mixed with geniuses such as the mathematician Isaac Newton (see page 294) and the physicist Robert Boyle. An educated man could hope to master more than one branch of the new sciences. Wren, having taken a leading role in the formation of the Royal Society, became its President in 1680.

Wren's childhood, during the disturbances of the Civil War, had not been easy but he received part of his education at Westminster School, going up to

Oxford at the end of the war. There he became swept up in the new experimental approach to knowledge, studying anatomy among other subjects. Typically, given the practical cast of his mind, which delighted in three-dimensional problems, he made pasteboard models to demonstrate the working of muscles. At the age of twenty-five, he became Professor of Astronomy at Gresham College, London, and four years later returned to Oxford as Savilian Professor of Astronomy. Newton rated him as one of the three greatest geometers of his age.

Wren's thoughts seem to have turned to architecture after the Restoration. In 1663, without any architectural experience, he was asked to advise on the repair of old St Paul's Cathedral, parts of which dated from the late 11th century. His first built work – the chapel at Pembroke College, Cambridge – came the same year. This rather pedestrian debut was followed by the more spectacular D-shaped Sheldonian Theatre in Oxford, where his knowledge of geometry enabled him to formulate a novel form of construction for the roof. It was a sign of his growing fascination for architecture that he visited France, where he met Mansard and Bernini, and returned with an admiration for an architectural feature hitherto unknown in England: the dome. However, had it not been for the Great Fire of London in 1666*, Wren might have remained as nothing more than one of a number of amateurs who dabbled in architecture as occasion offered. After the Great Fire, he was given ultimate responsibility for the design of some fifty-two City churches (a priority in the rebuilding because of their role in civic organisation and communal life), as well as, above all, the new St Paul's.

The fire put an end to any thought of merely patching up the old cathedral; it was so far beyond rescuing that Wren, wisely, would have none of the old foundations for his new building. At an early stage, he hoped this would take the shape of a Greek cross, providing a central focus covered by a dome. This is the form embodied in the so-called Great Model – a large wooden representation of the proposed structure – of 1673. Wren is supposed to have wept when it was rejected at the insistence of the clergy, who wanted to stress continuity of worship rather than innovation, and to that end demanded a long nave. His revised design, known as the Warrant Design, was accepted in 1675. As built, St Paul's is still surmounted by a great dome, rising out of a circular drum of columns. The tall external profile bears little relation to the shape within, since the internal dome rises little higher than the base of that outside. This is only one example of Wren's illusionism: another is the parapet wall, giving the façades their rectilinear silhouette, which conceals the use of flying buttresses to distribute the thrust of dome and roof.

Wren's taste for masculine architecture, rich in detail but bold in mass, provided not only an appropriate expression for the first Anglican cathedral to be built in Britain, but for a seat of national life. The events that it has witnessed include Nelson's funeral in 1806, Wellington's funeral in 1852, Queen Victoria's Diamond Jubilee in 1897, Churchill's funeral in 1965, and the wedding of Prince Charles and Lady Diana Spencer in 1981.

During the Blitz in 1940, the cathedral symbolised London's endurance, miraculously evading the awful destruction suffered by many of the buildings around it.

Wren is buried in the crypt of St Paul's where a black marble slab bears the words: *Lector, si monumentum requiris, circumspice* – Reader, if you seek his monument, look around you.

*See The Monument, page 161, and St Clement Danes, page 177

ST THOMAS'S OLD OPERATING THEATRE

SOUTHWARK, SE1

Embodying the history of surgery

The attic over the church of St Thomas, once attached to St Thomas's Hospital in Southwark, illustrates several centuries of British medicine. St Thomas's Hospital was originally a monastic foundation. It was part of the Priory of St Mary Overie that, after the death and canonisation of Thomas à Becket (see page 57), was dedicated to him. The hospital closed when the priory was dissolved in 1540, but was restarted, under royal patronage, in the reign of Edward VI. It was then re-dedicated to St Thomas the Apostle – the King preferring not to glorify the memory of the martyred Becket.

When St Thomas's church was built from 1700–02, it formed part of one side of the hospital's courtyard. Since Sir Christopher Wren (see page 179) was a governor of the hospital, it is possible that he was involved in some way, but the master mason, Thomas Cartwright, who worked on three of Wren's churches, seems to have been principally responsible for all practical arrangements. In the roof of the church he inserted a large attic in which the apothecary's herbs were stored: herbs were the basis for most medicinal treatments, although a preparation for venereal disease included snails and earthworms. The herbs were either grown in the hospital garden or bought by the barrowload from the visiting herb woman.

In 1821, part of the Herb Garret was converted into an operating theatre. The need for strong daylight was met by constructing a skylight above. The furniture was built in much the same way as that for a contemporary kitchen, the centrepiece being a stout deal table. Beneath it, a box for sawdust could be kicked by the surgeon – working no doubt in his coat, without even sleeves rolled up – into whatever position was best suited to receive the small rivulets of blood that spilled off the oilcloth. Around the table an amphitheatre of 'standings' allowed the maximum number of students to watch the proceedings. It was an imperfect way of learning, but a way of doing so nevertheless. Before the introduction of anaesthetic, first used in the 1840s, part of the surgeon's skill was to work as quickly as possible, and the best could saw off a limb in less than a minute.

That medical care at St Thomas's was state of the art can be judged from the fact that Florence Nightingale (see page 212) chose to found her institution for the training of nurses here in 1860. Soon afterwards, most of the old hospital buildings were swept away when the railway from London Bridge Station to Charing Cross was constructed. It was on Florence Nightingale's advice that St Thomas's transferred to its present site at Lambeth. The Herb Garret was forgotten, not to be rediscovered until 1957.

SELFRIDGES
American retailing comes to London

398–454 OXFORD STREET, W1

Selfridges, which opened its bronze-and-plate glass doors in 1909, was built at the high-water mark of the department store. There had been department stores before – their pedigree goes back to the Regency – but Selfridges was the first on Oxford Street, and London had seen nothing like it. Harry Gordon Selfridge, a Wisconsin boy, had trained at Marshall Field's eponymous store in Chicago, then the most sophisticated emporium in the world. Field aimed to 'give the lady what she wants', and Selfridge followed his example. He made a study of ladies' clubs, in order to understand female tastes, and presented his new store as a blow struck for the emancipation of the sex. It was somewhere that women could meet, eat, read, post letters, book railway tickets, change foreign currency, be pampered. Architecturally, the place was something new, with a façade of giant Ionic columns striding out like a chorus line, the centre marked by an enormous clock incorporating an 11ft figure of the Queen of Time. The consulting architect was the American Daniel Burnham, a man who liked to think big, and who had previously designed Marshall Field's back in Chicago.

Selfridges was unusual in arriving in Oxford Street fully grown. Many department stores only achieved greatness – in size and recognition – in their second or third generation. Benjamin Harvey had a business in Knightsbridge in 1813; after his death, his daughter Elizabeth took a silk buyer called Colonel Nichols into partnership – hence Harvey Nichols. It was also in 1813 that William Debenham bought a partnership with a draper; Clement Freebody, previously one of Debenham's managers, was made a partner in the middle of the century, and the store became Debenham & Freebody. Dickins and Smith, the forerunner of Dickins and Jones, started even earlier, in 1790, moving to Regent Street in 1835. However, it was during the Edwardian age that the department store was at its most opulent. This was when that great cornucopia called the Harrods Food Hall opened to a public that, like the King himself, tended towards the portly. Harrods has always had an emphasis on food because of its origins as a grocery shop: Charles Henry Harrod from Essex opened his first shop in Stepney in 1835; twelve years later, he bought what was then a modest outlet in Knightsbridge.

After the First World War, advertising was one of the factors that encouraged stores to drop Edwardian abundance in favour of suave modernity. Peter Jones on Sloane Square, rebuilt in 1935–7, was the ideal. When the *Architect's Journal* asked a number of intellectuals and artists to name the best modern building in Britain in 1939, they put it first. It was elegant, functional, airy, rational – but in comparison to the exuberance of Selfridges in its prime, a little tame.

SHAFTESBURY MEMORIAL PICCADILLY CIRCUS, W1
Selfless love, too sensuous for some

The 7th Earl of Shaftesbury, born in 1801, devoted his life to the welfare of working children. In 1833, as Lord Ashley and a Member of Parliament, he led the campaign which resulted in the Factory Act of that year, limiting the hours that children were allowed to work and preventing mill owners from employing children under the age of nine. In 1840 he helped set up the Children's Employment Commission, whose report into mines and collieries, published two years later, revealed the extent to which women and children worked as miners. The shocked public reaction enabled Shaftesbury to pilot the Coal Mines Act through the House of Commons in 1842; this prohibited women and children from working underground. Meanwhile, the fight against child labour had yet to be won: a report published by Shaftesbury in 1863 showed that some mill owners were still using young children to work atrocious hours in their factories. Shaftesbury also carried the torch for working-class education, being the chairman of the Ragged Schools Union for more than forty years. His humanity, combined with personal rectitude, made him widely loved and admired, and after his death in 1885 money was raised to provide a prominent memorial to this admirable Victorian.

The commission to sculpt it went to Alfred Gilbert, a young exponent of what was known as the New Sculpture, inspired by a spirit of naturalism. Because of the difficulty of agreeing on a site – it had to be one in the public eye – Gilbert had many years to work up his idea, the result of which was unveiled in 1893. It was unlike anything attempted in British sculpture before. The god of selfless love (not, strictly speaking Eros, but his younger brother Anteros) alights on just the sole of one foot, as though he will only touch earth for a second before flying off again. The effect of weightlessness was helped by Gilbert's pioneering use of aluminum. The god's sensuous young body, modelled on that of a sixteen-year-old Italian boy, was too much for some late-Victorian critics, who felt that it hardly personified the values of the evangelical Earl. Shopkeepers lamented the statue's tendency to attract 'foreign ladies who promenade the streets and keep respectable people out of our shops'. However, the tittle-tattle did not prevent the Shaftesbury Memorial, popularly known as Eros, from quickly becoming a famous icon of London.

SIDNEY STREET *STEPNEY, E1*

Anarchy comes to London

The worst event in British police history occurred in December 1910, when officers called at a building in Houndsditch, in the City of London. Neighbours had heard sounds of banging. When PC Piper knocked on the door, he and his colleagues were ruthlessly shot down, leaving three of them dead and two wounded. They had disturbed a gang of Jewish Latvian refugees who were trying to tunnel their way into a jeweller's shop next door. Britain was the only country in Europe that offered Jews fleeing the pogroms in Tsarist Russia true political asylum. Those who arrived in Britain, however, were often highly political, and the 'Gardstein gang' wanted the money raised from their raid to fund revolutionary activity at home.

George Gardstein was badly wounded. His associates dragged him through Whitechapel to their lodgings, which were equipped as an armoury. They called a doctor to tend Gardstein but would not allow him to be taken to hospital; the doctor then raised the alarm. By the time the police came, Gardstein was dead and the rest had evaporated into the close East European community of the East End.

It was early January when the police tracked some of them to 100 Sidney Street, off the Whitechapel Road. The flat belonged to a woman called Betsy Gershon, whose skirt and shoes had been removed to prevent her going onto the street to get help. Again, the police were fired on, but this time a company of Scots Guards arrived from the Tower of London and took up positions on the surrounding rooftops. Winston Churchill, then Home Secretary, arrived (perhaps rashly) to take personal command. The soldiers steadily fired into the building and eventually it caught fire and collapsed. Two gang members were found dead. However, their mysterious leader, Peter Piatkow or Peter the Painter, was never caught.

SMITHFIELD

Where the Peasants' Revolt ended

The Peasants' Revolt of 1381 arose from the changes that overcame England after the Black Death had killed between a third and a half of the population in 1348–51 (see page 30). Economically, the shortage of labour had worked to the benefit of the peasant class. After the Black Death, wages shot up and the price of land fell. Peasants no longer felt obliged to endure the burden of villeinage, which tied them to the land of their feudal overlord and required them to work on it for nothing. Higher wages had an unsettling effect by causing expectations to rise. When an unsuccessful war in France drained the Exchequer, the imposition of the Poll Tax of 1379, requiring the same contribution from rich and poor alike, seemed bitterly unfair.

At Fobbing in Essex, peasants and fishermen turned on the tax collector who had come to extract the tax. They joined forces with the people of other villages and saw off the soldiers who came to restore order, beheading six of them. Their example was followed in Kent, where abbeys were attacked, tax papers burnt, Rochester Castle plundered and the city of Canterbury sacked. A leader emerged in the form of a rough labourer called Wat Tyler; his peasant army massed on Blackheath near London, and then marched on London itself. Sympathy for them was such that the City gates were opened. Tyler called for discipline, but the peasants degenerated into a drunken rabble.

Richard II had been only ten when he came to the throne in 1377, and was now fourteen. Although he has come down to us as a lover of the arts and courtly refinement rather than as a leader of men, he had no shortage of personal bravery. On 14 June, he met the rebels at Mile End and told them that he would remedy their grievances so long as they went home peacefully. Some did so, but others returned to the City where they dragged the Archbishop of Canterbury and the King's Treasurer out of the Tower of London and murdered them, along with any Flemish merchants they could find. The King spent the night in hiding. The next day, however, he met the rebels again at Smithfield, an open area outside the City walls that was used as a market for horses and farm animals. Wat Tyler brazenly rode up on his little horse, jumped off, and without much ceremony, took Richard by the arm, saying they could be friends. Then, with a crude oath, he demanded the end of villeinage. His boorish behaviour was too much for the King's retinue and a brawl broke out, in which Tyler was killed by the Lord Mayor, William Walworth. The militia was raised, and the rabble was corralled into St John's Fields at Clerkenwell 'like sheep in a pen'.

The King did not keep his word to the rebels, saying that his promises had been extracted under duress. The leaders were rounded up and hanged. The peasants were, for the time being, forced back into the old system of giving free labour to their lords, but over the next century economic pressures wrought the alteration in their lives that open revolt had failed to do. The demand for their labour meant that they achieved better conditions.

SIR JOHN SOANE'S MUSEUM
The most ingenious work of domestic architecture in Britain

12–14 LINCOLN'S INN FIELDS, WC2

Sir John Soane is not the best-known British architect but he had possibly the greatest imagination, in terms of form. His home in Lincoln's Inn Fields is his monument. This is as Soane intended, having made part of it into a museum and establishing a trust for it to be maintained exactly as he had created it after his death in 1837. Contained within the relatively cramped space provided by three London houses, the interiors represent surely the most ingenious work of domestic architecture in Britain.

The son of a bricklayer, Soane received a good education at the schools run by the Royal Academy (see page 168) where he absorbed all the latest currents in architectural and aesthetic thought and met many of the leading artistic figures of his day. His house, or houses, embodies many of the themes that characterise Regency taste, although refracted and enlarged through the lens of his individual genius. The many fragments and casts of antique buildings and sculpture reflect the prevailing obsession with ancient Rome, whose ruins had been measured and recorded by architects such as Soane. They are displayed in a claustrophobic, overwhelming manner – huge pieces of carved marble in small spaces – that would have delighted the Roman engraver Piranesi, whom Soane knew from his travels. Soane's own architectural style evolved out of his study of classical architecture. However, as his library and dining room show, he did away with conventional classical ornament in favour of an idiosyncratic interplay of form, with spatial effects being enhanced by strips of mirror. The world of the Gothic novel at its most gloomy is evoked in the Monk's Parlour.

With his obsessive nature, Soane was a natural collector, and he bought two of the great masterpieces of English painting of his time, Hogarth's series *A Rake's Progress* and *The Election*, which cannot have been the height of fashion in the early 19th century. Perhaps his greatest coup as a collector was the acquisition of the newly discovered sarcophagus of Seti I, offered first to the British Museum but rejected because the price of £2,000 was too high. To bring the sarcophagus into the Sepulchral Chamber required the demolition of a wall.

One of the most remarkable of all the spaces that Soane created was the Little Study, a narrow room that is little more than a corridor, decorated in deep cherry red and hung with fragments of classical architecture. Here, without any heating other than that supplied by the underfloor system (which did not work), Soane would pull out a little desk and draw the first ideas for his many great buildings.

SPEAKERS' CORNER MARBLE ARCH, W2
Crossroads where the gallows of Tyburn Tree once stood

Between the return of Charles II in 1660 and the death of George II a century later, Parliament increased the number of crimes that were punishable by death by 190. The most prominent mechanism by which the ultimate sentence was carried out stood at the north-east corner of Hyde Park, opposite what is now Marble Arch. This was the 18ft-high gallows known as Tyburn Tree. It was named after the Tyburn Brook, which now flows into the Serpentine in Hyde Park. Gallows often stood by crossroads, and this was where Watling Street (Edgware Road), London's most important road north, crossed Oxford Street, the most important route west. Hangings had taken place here since the 12th century, the first permanent gallows being raised in 1571. There were other places of public execution in London, such as Smithfield and Tower Hill, but Tyburn remained the most 'popular' until superseded by the gallows at Newgate Gaol in 1783. It was at Tyburn that the body of Oliver Cromwell, having been exhumed at the Restoration, was hung up and exhibited, his head being finally passed around as a curiosity.

Each of the three horizontal timbers of the gallows could accommodate eight nooses, theoretically allowing twenty-four people to be executed together. This multiple capacity was rarely, if ever, used to the maximum. Between 1703 and 1792, 1,232 people were hanged at Tyburn, an average of about fourteen a year. Nearly all the condemned were young men under the age of twenty-one; 92 were women. While five children under fourteen were hanged before 1800, those who were sentenced to death at the Old Bailey between 1801 and 1836 – 103 of them – were all reprieved.

The London public regarded hangings as a holiday, and would come in crowds of tens of thousands to watch the extremity of justice which, due to the inefficiencies of the method, could be protracted. The scene is engraved by William Hogarth in the *Idle 'Prentice Executed at Tyburn*, part of the series called *Industry and Idleness*; the hangman is shown casually smoking a pipe on top of the gallows, while the cart bringing the idle apprentice is followed by his coffin. When Arthur Thistlewood and the Cato Street conspirators were executed at Newgate in 1820, it was estimated that 100,000 people witnessed the spectacle.

From the 16th century, it became traditional for the condemned man to make a last speech to the crowd. For obvious reasons, the usual rules of censorship did not apply, and in the age of religious persecution martyrs dying for their faith would attempt to convert their audience to their beliefs. It was therefore appropriate that this area of London was chosen by Parliament as the place where British freedom of speech would be most famously exercised. This came through in the otherwise unexciting Royal Parks and Gardens Regulation Act of 1872, and followed a number of mass rallies opposed by the authorities. What would come to be called Speakers' Corner helped diffuse tension by demonstrating the right to free speech. It has been host to such orators as Lenin, Marx and Engels. In the early 20th century, suffragettes used it to promote their campaign for votes for women. Oratory of a type is still to be heard at Speakers' Corner, but the glory days are over.

THE TEMPLE CHURCH MIDDLE TEMPLE, EC4
Headquarters of the Knights Templar in England

In the late 11th century, the Turks swarmed westwards out of Central Asia, overrunning everything that stood in their way. In 1076, they captured Jerusalem, and ruled it with a new spirit of religious intolerance. It would have been difficult enough for an inhabitant of Norman England to make a pilgrimage to Jerusalem at the best of times, but now the Holy City was inaccessible to Christians. At the behest of the Pope, a ramshackle, virtually leaderless army was raised from the countries of Western Europe and – perhaps by a miracle – succeeded in taking Jerusalem, amid such scenes of slaughter that the streets of the city were said to run ankle-deep in blood. While Jerusalem was now safe for Christians, the path there was beset with dangers. The Knights Templar, an international order of warrior monks, was founded to safeguard pilgrims on their journey. The Templars were distinguished by their white robes and tunics, emblazoned with the red cross that was the symbol of the Crusades.

The Temple church off Fleet Street was consecrated in 1165 by the Patriarch of Jerusalem in the presence of Henry II. It was the headquarters of the Knights Templar in England and, like all Templar churches, it was round, in homage to the Church of the Holy Sepulchre in Jerusalem. By this date, they were already well established, the first Templar church in London having been at Holborn. One of the advantages of the new site was that there was more room for military training and the exercise of horses.

The Knights Templar enjoyed the patronage of successive kings, to the extent that Henry III let it be known that he wished to be buried here. To this end, the Templars added a long choir, lined with black marble columns, in 1240 – although, as it turned out, by the time of his death Henry III had decided to be buried in his rebuilt Westminster Abbey.

As the choir demonstrates, the austere and martial Templars had become rich and independent. In time, this made them distinctly unpopular with kings, who feared they would become too powerful. In 1312, the order was suppressed by the Pope, and in England Edward II took control of the London Temple, passing their properties in 1324 to the Knights of the Hospital of St John of Jerusalem, otherwise known as the Hospitallers. In due course, the Knights Hospitallers rented what had been the Templars' exercise yard to two colleges of lawyers, which came to be called the Middle Temple and the Inner Temple. Henry VIII grabbed the property at the time of the Dissolution of the Monasteries (see page 133), but James I confirmed the rights to two of London's inns of court, and in due course the Temple church was adopted as the lawyers' own.

THE WHITE TOWER

TOWER OF LONDON, EC3

William the Conqueror's naked display of power cows London

Having defeated Harold at the Battle of Hastings (see page 49), William the Conqueror imposed his authority on the rest of England by a combination of brutality, castle building and symbolism. The Tower of London – where the keep or White Tower survives much as it was known to the early Normans – demonstrates the last two parts of the technique; its construction was preceded by a harsh dose of the first.

After Hastings, London stood out against the invader. With his small force, William could not take it by storm; instead, he encouraged its leaders to submit by devastating the counties south of the Thames in a campaign of terror. The tactic was successful, and he entered the city without a fight. Even before he was crowned at the abbey founded by Edward the Confessor at Westminster – symbolically asserting his legitimacy as Edward's heir – he had begun building a castle on the eastern side of the city. A millennium earlier, the site had been occupied by a villa, perhaps built for a military governor. By contrast, the Tower that William built was no villa; it was intended partly as a stronghold, partly as an overawing display of power, partly as a palace where ceremonies could be enacted at a safe remove from the conquered native populace.

It is likely that William's first 'castle' was a hastily erected wooden affair. The stone replacement seems to have been begun in 1077, under the direction of Gundulf, Bishop of Rochester*. The Thames formed a defensive barrier to the south; to the east, William took advantage of the surviving Roman city walls. On the other sides, he ordered a deep moat to be dug, the earth thrown onto a mound in the centre of the site, above which the White Tower was constructed. There was no shortage of good building stone in England, but

William still ordered boatloads of marble-like limestone to be imported from Caen in Normandy to serve as dressings. Between them, the walls are built of rough Kentish rag, giving the exterior an appropriately rough and military appearance. For reasons of security, the only entrance was some 15ft from the ground, reached by an external stair. Inside, the space was divided into four floors, of three rooms each. In later centuries, the windowless ground floor (originally store rooms) was turned into a torture chamber: the constable in Henry VI's reign, the Duke of Exeter, is credited with having introduced the first rack used in England, known by the macabre pet name of 'the Duke of Exeter's daughter'.

An indication of the richness with which the other floors in the White Tower were finished can be gained from the Chapel of St John, an elegant space defined by two massive tiers of round-headed arcades and a tunnel-vaulted roof. If the comfort of the interior was at odds with the burly character of the outside, this was deliberate: externally, the object of the Tower was to express domination, and archaeologists have recently discovered that this was achieved by building the walls considerably higher than was really necessary. The famous silhouette, looking uncompromisingly four-square despite having just three towers, and even those of different designs, must have awed contemporary inhabitants of London, but was a sham. Marks on the stonework, discovered in 1996, show that the original two steeply pitched roofs came nowhere near the top of the parapet.

*See Rochester Castle, page 90

TRELLICK TOWER
GOLBORNE ROAD, W10

Failure of the Corbusian ideal

The Trellick Tower is a symbol of the Modernist dream. Thirty storeys tall, it is easily the most elegant and was for years the most loathed of all high-rise council blocks. From its position next to a motorway and a railway, it was one of the most conspicuous, too. It was also a last hurrah of the Modernist brigade, having been begun in 1968, the year that the tower block of Ronan Point collapsed after a gas explosion. By the time it was finished in 1972, public disenchantment with high-rise living had crystallised. Everything that was wrong with the system seemed to be exemplified by the Trellick Tower: lifts stank of urine, used condoms littered the public spaces, drug addicts huddled in dark corners, personal tragedies occurred – as they do when a very high building is involved.

The architect Ernö Goldfinger was undaunted. Born in Hungary in 1902, he had studied at the École des Beaux-Arts in Paris, becoming friendly with Le Corbusier and studying with the pioneer of reinforced concrete building,

Auguste Perret. In 1934, Goldfinger moved to London. Having married Ursula Blackwell, of the Crosse and Blackwell food company, he was now financially secure. His first project in London was, in 1937–9, to build a terrace of three houses in Willow Road, Hampstead, one of which became the Goldfingers' own home. To do this involved demolishing a row of cottages, which was bitterly opposed by local residents, including the creator of James Bond, Ian Fleming. Goldfinger was unstoppable – but Fleming got his own back by borrowing his name for one of the most famous villains of 20th-century fiction.

The Trellick Tower was a pure expression of the Corbusian ideal, with every apartment in the narrow tower having a plate glass window and balcony facing the south-west. It offered light and sunshine, albeit far from the street, in place of the dinginess of the decayed Victorian terraces it swept away. The lifts and other communal services were concentrated in a smaller, detached tower, connected to the main block by walkways at every third storey. The idea was that the tower would form a kind of vertical community, and to that end there were nurseries and games pitches at the bottom; however, when bored teenagers dropped objects onto a nursery's roof from upper floors it had to close.

Goldfinger always maintained that the tower's failures were the fault of the people who lived in it and of the authorities responsible for maintaining it. It was to have operated under the eye of a concierge, on the Continental model, but the council cut costs. Goldfinger died in 1987, embittered but defiant. By this time, Prince Charles had already told the Royal Institute of British Architects, on the occasion of its 150th anniversary in 1984, that planners and architects had 'consistently ignored the feelings and wishes of the mass of ordinary people in this country'. Families who had been forced out of terraced slums to live hundreds of feet up in the sky had at last found a champion, and the reputation of the Modern Movement collapsed.

The Trellick Tower has come to redeem itself, however. The council installed a uniformed concierge and security devices. The flats that come onto the open market are snapped up by young professionals, who respond to the light, the astonishing urban views and the clarity of the architectural idea. The Trellick Tower is no longer derided as a Brutalist carbuncle, but extolled by enthusiasts who enjoy finding a taste of Tribeca in Notting Hill.

TWININGS
216 STRAND, WC2

Oldest shop in Britain still to be selling the same product

Tea is generally considered to be Britain's national beverage, and yet the leaf from which it is made comes from far away. In this, it is a symbol of the country's status as a trading nation, whose culture is eclectic. Tea is first known to have been served in Britain at a coffee house called the Sultaness's

Head in 1658. Promotion of the drink was fiercely opposed by brewers who feared it would dent the sale of beer; they condemned it as an evil influence which ruined the health. The brewing lobby persuaded Parliament to tax it heavily, making it a luxury. At the end of the century, this did not deter Queen Mary II from serving it at Court, thereby encouraging a vogue that percolated down the social scale. In these early years, the leaves were considered so valuable that they would be locked in a caddy to which only the mistress of the house had the key.

In 1706, a dozen years after Queen Mary's death, Thomas Twining acquired a coffee house in Devereux Court off the Strand. By 1717, Twining had bought three little houses running up to the Strand, and as the great era of the coffee house drew to a close (to be superseded by the gentleman's club), he turned them into a shop selling tea and coffee. R. Twining & Co. Ltd (the R stands for Thomas's son Richard) has since become a multinational tea distributor, but the original shop survives, a long, thin slice of history squeezed between a bank and a building society. Employees claim that it is the oldest shop still selling the same product in Britain.

Throughout the 18th century, the very high price of tea continued to torment its growing band of devotees. In 1773, the tea monopoly given to the East India Company caused a group of colonials in Boston to protest; dressed as Mohawks, they boarded British ships in the harbour and threw chests of tea into the sea. It took William Pitt – eleven years after the Boston Tea Party, by which time Britain had lost America – to reduce the tax on tea. After this, the 'cup that cheers but not inebriates' (as Temperance campaigners had it) became so popular that Chinese seeds had to be planted in India to increase the supply. They did not take, but the discovery of native tea bushes in Assam in 1820 solved the problem.

UNIVERSITY COLLEGE
GOWER STREET, WC1

A philosopher's recipe for self-perpetuation

According to Jeremy Bentham (1748–1832), legal reformer and philosopher, human actions should be judged by utility or, as he later called it, the greatest happiness principle. He concluded that the political system mostly likely to promote happiness among the greatest number of people was democracy. In the early 19th century, when the advent of universal adult suffrage was a century away, that was still a radical concept; indeed, some of Bentham's proposals, such as the abolition of the second chamber of Parliament and the removal of all honours and titles, remain radical today.

Bentham was nothing if not tenacious in his thought. He applied the principle of utility even to the fate of his body after death. Scholars are uncertain as to the state of his religious belief, if he had any; certainly, however, he had no patience with the Church of England or social convention. He left his organs to be publicly dissected by his friend Southwood Smith. Bodies for dissection were in short supply, being limited to murderers who had been hanged. Afterwards, according to Bentham's detailed instructions, his head and skeleton formed the basis of what he termed an Auto-Icon. In a pamphlet on which he was working shortly before his death in 1832, Bentham believed Auto-Icons could replace sculpture as a means of portraying the dead; families would gradually acquire cupboards full of their relatives who had died, and yet remained present through their preservation in Auto-Icon form. Auto-Icons could be placed to advantage between the trees of an avenue leading to a gentleman's house.

Bentham's prescription was only partially successful. His head, dried out in the Maori fashion, became a grotesque object, its dark, leathery skin stretched tightly across the skull. It was replaced by a lifelike wax head, the original being displayed between Bentham's feet. The skeleton, underneath a padded body, dressed in Bentham's coat, breeches and slippers, eerily preserves the presence of the living man. Bentham instructed that the Auto-Icon should show him in the act of thought, as though in a pause in writing. However, there is no pen in his hand. Instead, the big straw hat above the wax head and the walking stick between his legs suggests that he has just sat down, somewhat uncomfortably, after a country walk.

Smith enclosed the whole in a glass case, and kept it in his consulting rooms. When he moved to smaller premises, he gave his strangely preserved friend to University College, London, where he was set, seer-like, on open view in the south cloister, the original ghoulish head still between his feet. This was too great a temptation for students, and it frequently went missing. Once it was run to ground in a left-luggage locker at Aberdeen station; on another occasion, it was apparently used as a football in the College's front quadrangle. After its final recovery in 1975, it was removed to the College vaults where it remains to this day.

JERUSALEM CHAMBER WESTMINSTER ABBEY, SW1
Henry IV dies in Jerusalem

In 1413, Henry IV was forty-six – not a vast age, even by medieval standards, but for some years he had been afflicted by a severe skin disease that some contemporaries, incorrectly, assumed to be leprosy. His body seemed to be rotting. From shortly after seizing the throne from Richard II in 1399, he suffered blackouts that were akin to epileptic fits. They might have been the result of kidney disease. Henry himself explained his condition in terms of divine punishment. He had almost certainly been instrumental in the death of his predecessor, an anointed king (see page 397). In addition, he had executed the Archbishop of York after the Battle of Shrewsbury (see page 341). These matters weighed on his conscience. He became depressed and slept fitfully. His relations with his son and heir, the future Henry V, were famously bad. It was in this condition, perhaps hoping that God would pardon him, that he decided to go on a pilgrimage to the Holy Land. Before doing so, he went to pray at the tomb of Edward the Confessor in Westminster Abbey.

Edward had founded the Church of St Peter, hurrying the work forward as his health declined; it was consecrated in 1065. He was just in time, since he died the following year, and was buried there. Edward was canonised in 1161; later he came to be particularly venerated by English kings, perhaps having had the merit of having been a king himself. Alarmed at the growing popularity of Thomas à Becket's shrine at Canterbury* which, for obvious reasons, could have been regarded as a rallying point for forces opposed to the King, Henry III had promoted the cult of St Edward, lavishing money on the rebuilding of Westminster Abbey from 1245 onwards. It was the tallest of all Gothic churches, and a fitting setting for royal ceremonials: since William the Conqueror, the only monarchs not to have been crowned in the Abbey are Edward V, who was murdered by Richard III before his coronation, and Edward VIII, who abdicated before he was crowned (see page 217).

While Henry IV was praying at St Edward's tomb, one of his fits came upon him. He was carried to the Jerusalem Chamber, a room that had been added to the abbot's lodgings in the late 14th century. (It was monastic practice to name rooms after holy sites.) When the King had recovered sufficiently to ask where he was, he was told 'Jerusalem'. He believed it was the fulfilment of a prophecy that he should die at Jerusalem.

Henry was not buried at Westminster. He had left instructions that he should be buried simply at Canterbury: perhaps he felt that Thomas à Becket's example in standing up to a reigning king justified his own action in deposing Richard II. His queen, Joan of Navarre, erected a splendid tomb there next to St Thomas's shrine.

*See Canterbury Cathedral, page 57

WESTMINSTER CATHEDRAL ASHLEY PLACE, SW1
After Roman Catholic emancipation, a new headquarters for the faith

After the Reformation, Roman Catholics in Britain were for centuries unable to vote, become Members of Parliament, serve in the army or take any other leading role in society. They were also forbidden from building churches.

From the late 18th century, their position began to improve. The Emancipation Act of 1829 gave them the vote, and in 1850 Pope Pius IX restored the Catholic hierarchy, dividing the country into a series of dioceses controlled by bishops. From now on, the Archbishop of Westminster was effectively the head of the Roman Catholic Church in the country, usually made a Cardinal by the Pope to strengthen the special relationship with Rome. But as yet the Archbishop had no Cathedral.

In 1882, Cardinal Manning identified a site. It was occupied by Tothill Fields Prison, built some fifty years earlier to house women and boys. It took until 1894 before Cardinal Manning's successor, Cardinal Vaughan, appointed an architect. This was the Catholic convert, John Francis Bentley, who had already designed a number of Roman Catholic churches in the Gothic style. Together, Vaughan and Bentley travelled to Italy, seeking inspiration. They found it in Ravenna and St Mark's Square, Venice: the Byzantine basilica, with its many domes, was the earliest form of Christian architecture, and the one that they would bring back to Victoria Street. It had the additional merit of being utterly different from the other great Christian building some half a mile to the south, Westminster Abbey.

There then arose one of the most extraordinary buildings in London, incorporating some Byzantine motifs but many others – such as the rugby shirt stripes of brick and stone – which had more to do with the Free Style that was Britain's answer to Art Nouveau. Externally, it is a triumph of subtly modulated brickwork, beautifully laid, its shallow ribs and niches companionable in a soft London sun. A slender, striped tower of almost absurd height soars up to the sky. Inside, visitors were awed by the great unadorned brick space, disappearing into a succession of only dimly visible domes. Over the years, the lower portion of the interior has been clad in marble, as Bentley always intended. Alas, Bentley did not live to see the first Mass celebrated in 1903, dying the year before.

WESTMINSTER HALL WESTMINSTER, SW1
An unrivalled hammerbeam roof

Westminster Hall is the oldest part of the Palace of Westminster, having escaped the disastrous fire of 1834 (see page 197). It is a monument to the continuity of Parliament, since councils have been held here since the Norman period. It is also a supreme work of Norman and 14th-century engineering, the Normans having determined the dimensions of the plan and Richard II's carpenters having built the hammerbeam roof – the earliest and greatest of its type.

It suited the Victorians to emphasise that Edward the Confessor had founded the Palace of Westminster. He was after all a saint and, as an Anglo-Saxon, more obviously English than the Norman kings. Westminster Hall, by contrast, owes its present dimensions to the altogether less saintly figure of William Rufus, William the Conqueror's second son and his successor. Building began in the last decade of the 11th century, and in 1099 William Rufus came over from France and held court in his new hall for the first time. It must have astonished contemporaries. It was 240ft long and 67½ft wide. This is the size of the present hall, whose outer walls, below the stringcourse, contain the original masonry behind later refacings. There was no other hall on this scale in England, and probably none in Europe, when it was built.

Although subsequent monarchs owned many royal manors and palaces, Westminster held pride of place until Henry VIII moved his court to the Palace of Whitehall, leaving Westminster to the administrators. Until then, every king had sought to do something to adorn this Palace that was at once a residence, a setting for state ceremony and the centre of civil administration; they came to hold their Councils more frequently at Westminster than elsewhere.

To some monarchs, state ceremony assumed a beauty of its own. Richard II was addicted to it. It was in keeping with his taste for ritual, as well as art, that he should have rebuilt Westminster Hall. Such was the scale and durability of William Rufus's achievement that his hall had remained virtually unaltered for 300 years. It had received various accretions, some to increase the king's privacy and comfort, and some to house departments such as the Exchequer, the Court of Common Pleas and the King's Bench. Now, at the end of the 14th century, the Hall itself was looking, to Richard II's sophisticated eye, distinctly old-fashioned, with its Romanesque detail and dark interior encumbered with columns.

His first contribution was to commission a series of stone statues of kings, showing all the monarchs from Edward the Confessor until himself. Made by Thomas Canon, a marbler from Dorset, and painted by Nicholas Tryer, they were intended to stand in the Hall, although for some reason only half a dozen were ever actually put in place. These larger-than-life figures, with glittering gold crowns and opulently painted robes of emerald green and crimson, must have seemed awesomely regal. Alas, their sumptuous pigmentation has long since disappeared.

The statues were but a prelude to the great work of rebuilding the roof. There is some reason to suppose that the weight of the old roof had finally come to push the walls outwards, making repairs necessary. The need for repair may have sown the idea of total replacement, but the new work went far, far beyond what was structurally necessary. It was English medieval carpentry's grand masterpiece, not only the largest hammerbeam roof in northern Europe but, as far as we can tell, the first. The master carpenter responsible was Hugh Herland. Spanning so great a width was a prodigious achievement. The glory of it, however, resides not just in the structural accomplishment but in the design: tiers of hammerbeams are combined with lateral arched braces, creating a grand and satisfying rhythm, a note of mystery being added by the half-light through which it is all seen. The timbers were shaped at a workshop near Farnham called The Frame, hundreds of oak trees being brought there from woods around London. Once the component parts of the roof had been carved, they were taken to the Thames by cart, and then to Westminster by river. The roof took two years to erect. The carved angels continue to look down on a hall that is still sometimes used for state occasions, just as they have done for 600 years.

PALACE OF WESTMINSTER
WESTMINSTER, SW1

Rebuilding the Houses of Parliament produces a national icon

The Houses of Parliament, overlooking the Thames, are a symbol of the British nation, instantly recognisable across the world. So intense is the atmosphere created by the architecture and design that it is difficult to imagine that the business of Parliament could be conducted in quite the same way anywhere else. (Which may be one reason why, in their House of Commons and House of Lords, British parliamentarians conduct themselves so differently from those of other countries.) Almost every inch of the Houses of Parliament was intended by its creators to project an image of the past onto the minds of those who are legislating for the future. Thus the building can be read as an illustrated history of Britain, laced with moral values, national identity and a sense of continuity. When built, however, it was also praised for its modernity: the first great Victorian building – first and greatest, according to some – designed before Queen Victoria's reign had even begun.

Together with Westminster Hall (see page 195), the Houses of Parliament are the constituent parts of a royal palace – the Palace of Westminster. Except for Westminster Hall, nearly everything in the old palace had been burnt in the spectacular fire of 1834. The old arrangements were not much mourned by those who had used them. The accommodation in the old building was a haphazard jumble of rooms that no architect had succeeded in rationalising. A competition was held. The Select Committee responsible for the rebuilding stipulated that the style should be Gothic or Elizabethan, quite avant-garde at this date but suggested by the associations of the old building. Advocates for it argued that these were national styles.

The competition was won by Charles Barry who, then in his early forties, had concentrated his energies on club houses, institutions and private houses, many of them very grand. His opulent Classical style appealed to clients who were tired of the austerity that had until then been the keynote of fashionable architecture. Gothic was not his forte: which is why he made the inspired choice of the 22-year-old A. W. N. Pugin as his draughtsman (see page 88). Pugin lacked any formal training in architecture, but was fanatically convinced of the moral, as well as architectural, rightness of Gothic architecture. He supplied many of the details.

The architectural challenges of the new building tended to pull in different directions. First, the site included an inordinately long river frontage, which only some degree of regularity was likely to order. Second, it was necessary to retain parts of the old architecture, notably Westminster Hall, which suggested a more Picturesque approach. Barry succeeded in reconciling these opposites, in a building of varied silhouette: this is thanks to two towers, a flèche and a forest of ventilation shafts, which appears symmetrical on the river front. The building composes differently from every angle that it is seen. Richness is given through the endless repetition of Pugin's ornament: coats of arms, niches and some two hundred statues of kings and queens (Queen Victoria recurs eight times).

Inside, the new structure had to incorporate all the facilities expected of the new Parliament. More was now expected of public buildings than in the 18th century; they had to accommodate not only public rooms but also provision for an expanding bureaucracy. At Westminster, Members of Parliament and peers demanded the same sort of facilities they could enjoy in their clubs, like dining rooms and smoking rooms. The volume of paper being produced in official reports required that each house had a library of four rooms, with an apartment for the librarian. Increasingly, interest from the press and the public called for galleries from which the proceedings of Parliament could be viewed. The Speaker of the House of Commons and other officials, although not at this stage the Lord Chancellor, were given apartments, befitting their status. In addition, the constitutional role of the monarch had to be acknowledged through the provision of a royal route, leading from the carriage entrance via a succession of richly ornamented rooms to the throne itself in the Lords' chamber. Since this was a royal palace, the sovereign's approval was critical. A Fine Arts Commission was established under the chairmanship of Prince Albert to plan the artistic decoration of the new palace.

Given the scale of the task, Barry's plan is a miracle of clarity, based around two dominant axes that intersect at the Central Lobby. The House of Lords occupies the southern half of the building, with a royal entrance provided by a porte-cochère (which allows a carriage to deliver its passengers beneath shelter) under the Victoria Tower. The hierarchy of Parliament is expressed in the decoration, with the Lords' side being much plusher than the Commons – an effect that became exaggerated when the House of Commons was rebuilt after being hit by an incendiary bomb during the Second World War. Naturally, given the place of the sovereign at the apex of the constitution, the grandest of all is the throne in the House of Lords chamber: a sunburst of gold that forms the decorative focus of the whole palace.

WINCHESTER PALACE

Prison whose name entered the language

From the 16th century onwards, 'clink' has been a slang word for prison. It derives from a prison that used to be part of the Bishop of Winchester's palace at Southwark, on the south side of the Thames in London. Originally the whole area used to be known as Clink, presumably from some local activity that made a clinking sound – nobody knows. The author of *London and its Environs* (1761) described the prison as 'a very dismal hole where debtors are sometimes confined'.

The land on which the Bishop of Winchester built his palace was given by Henry I in 1127. Medieval bishops often needed a residence near the Court at Westminster because of the offices of state they held (see page 102). Southwark, officially London's first suburb, was nearly all owned by the church and thirteen prelates had houses there. Little of Winchester Palace now survives beyond the wall containing the fine 14th-century rose window of the Great Hall. Most of the Palace burnt down in 1814, and the scant remains are now marooned in a street that is heavy with the atmosphere of Victorian docks and warehouses. In its day, however, it was grand enough to host James I's wedding breakfast. The prison may have dated from the 12th century.

Southwark's position just outside the City walls made it a centre for activities that were not acceptable within the strictly controlled City. These included bear pits, theatres (see page 144) and the prostitution with which theatres were often associated. Within the bishops of Winchester's private jurisdiction, greater latitude was allowed than elsewhere: a 15th-century bishop even tried to regulate the vice trade, insisting that any prostitute who took money from a customer should spend the whole night with him. The ladies who provided such entertainment were therefore sometimes known as Winchester geese. Carousers, visiting the stews, might find themselves ending up in the Clink if they broke the peace.

Prisons were another aspect of life that the crowded City was reluctant to accommodate; as well as the Clink, Southwark was home to four other gaols – the Compter, the King's Bench, the White Lion and the Marshalsea. At one time, the Marshalsea was second only in importance to the Tower of London as a national prison. In the 19th century, it had become a prison for debtors: Dickens's parents and all the Dickens children except for Charles and his sister Fanny were imprisoned here in 1824, and Dickens's character Little Dorrit was born at the Marshalsea. Today, only a wall of the Marshalsea survives, off Borough High Street.

Southwark, close to London but unprotected by the City walls, was the first port of call for rebellious mobs, and the Clink and the Marshalsea were stormed during the Peasants' Revolt in 1381 (see page 185) and Jack Cade's rebellion in 1450; the King's Bench was attacked in 1770, by supporters of the radical MP John Wilkes who was imprisoned there. Both the Marshalsea and the Clink prisons were burnt down during the Gordon Riots of 1780; the Marshalsea was quickly rebuilt but the Clink, already on the decline, ceased to function except as jargon.

The Home Counties

STRICTLY SPEAKING, the Home Counties are those that border London; the grouping of counties here is rather looser, but it preserves the quality of a countryside that in part rubs shoulders with the metropolis while never getting too chummy. Because of their proximity to London, the counties have always been popular with influential men and women in need of country air. Windsor Castle, its silhouette made even more chivalric for George IV, remains the Queen's most frequently used bolt-hole outside London. In 1963, Cliveden became famous for goings-on that caused a Cabinet minister to resign, yet would have seemed unremarkable to the rakes of the 18th-century Hell-Fire Club at West Wycombe. Would they have been puzzled to see Edward VIII signing papers of abdication at Fort Belvedere?

It was not only diversions that hid beneath the cloak of rural privacy, but dissent. William Penn, the founder of Pennsylvania, is buried at Jordans, the oldest Quaker meeting house in the country; John Bunyan, the tinsmith's son who wrote *The Pilgrim's Progress*, was baptised in the river at Bedford, while the blind John Milton finished writing *Paradise Lost* at Chalfont St Giles. They followed in the high-minded tradition of Britain's first saint, commemorated in St Albans Cathedral. In 1555, Oxford saw the Protestant martyrs, Ridley and Latimer, burn at the stake during Mary Tudor's persecutions, to be followed the next year by Archbishop Cranmer. A hundred years later, a group of Levellers from Cromwell's army made a brief stand for their principles of religious toleration and equality before being shot against the wall of Burford church.

As the gateway to London, the Home Counties were an important battle-ground during the Wars of the Roses. Blenheim Palace commemorates the great victory of the same name that the Duke of Marlborough won for Queen Anne in 1704. The Germans' Enigma code was cracked at Bletchley Park during the Second World War and, in 1981, American cruise missiles arrived at Greenham Common, sparking the most tenacious peace protests ever seen in Britain. I rather think that the gentle William Cowper, clergyman, poet and hymn writer from Olney, would have approved.

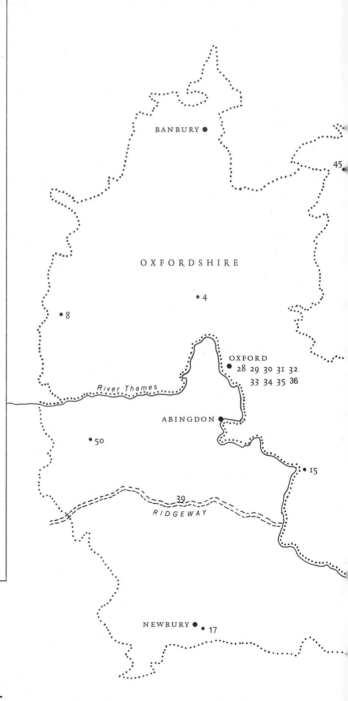

BANBURY ●

45 ●

OXFORDSHIRE

● 4

● 8

OXFORD
● 28 29 30 31 32
  33 34 35 36

River Thames

ABINGDON ●

● 50

● 15

39
RIDGEWAY

NEWBURY ● ● 17

The Home Counties

SHAW'S CORNER

Where GBS wrote his plays

It would have pleased George Bernard Shaw that his home at Ayot St Lawrence should have become a literary shrine; he had that end in mind for it, arranging for it to pass to the National Trust. For one of the ways in which the playwright, journalist, music critic, socialist, Jaeger-wearer, vegetarian, bicyclist, amateur photographer and blower-away-of-mental-cobwebs espoused modernity was in his mastery of public relations. He needed a home in the country to escape the attentions that he attracted as a media celebrity in London. Built as a vicarage, the house was not very comely. Shaw and his wife furnished it with a hint of Arts and Crafts austerity, in a style that could best be described as unpretentious. In the garden and wearing a Cornish tin miner's hat, Shaw would demonstrate his Tolstoyan principles by sawing logs.

Shaw cut a memorable figure in the village of Ayot St Lawrence where, as he wrote, 'the last thing of real importance that had happened was, perhaps, the Flood'. By the time he arrived there in 1906, he had achieved the celebrity status that he craved. Born in Dublin and speaking in a strong Irish brogue all his life, he came from a modest but complicated background – circumstances that he escaped by going to London. There he pursued a daunting regime of self-improvement. A torrent of trenchant, opinionated, Fabian journalism issued from his pen. The villagers of Ayot St Lawrence found that they had a successful playwright – author of *Man and Superman* and *Major Barbara* – in their midst. In 1913, he wrote *Pygmalion*. After the First World War, which he opposed, came *Heartbreak House*, *Back to Methuselah* and *Saint Joan*. Many of the later plays were written 'helter-skelter' in a revolving hut in the garden of the New Rectory, which the locals called Shaw's Corner. It was here that Shaw died at the age of ninety-four in 1950.

BATTLE OF BARNET

End of Warwick the Kingmaker

The Earl of Warwick* had stood beside the young King Edward IV as he battled his way to the throne, unseating half-witted Henry VI and putting his virago wife, Margaret of Anjou, to flight. Warwick had spent long years in the bitter work of mopping up Lancastrian resistance in the North. The fruits of this service turned to ashes, however, when Edward secretly married Elizabeth Woodville†. Eldest daughter of the Lancastrian Lord Rivers, Elizabeth was a widow whose husband had been killed at the Second Battle of St Albans‡. Presumably it was a love match, since for reasons of state Edward would have been expected to marry a foreign princess. Indeed, Warwick had been working towards just such a union, when he discovered that the King was no longer available. Matters were made worse by the flagrant self-promotion of the Woodville family – five brothers and seven unmarried sisters – once they had become in-laws of the King.

Warwick the Kingmaker, who was little less than a prince, could not brook these sleights. They drove him to perform a volte-face, and offer his services to the exiled Margaret of Anjou. He restored her husband Henry VI to the throne.

It was now Edward's turn to flee, leaving on Michaelmas Day 1470 for the Duke of Burgundy's court at Bruges. Soon enough, though, he was back, landing at Ravenspur, at the mouth of the Humber, with an absurdly small force of 2,000 soldiers, many of them Burgundians. After Edward had marched on York, however, his army swelled. The further south he got, the less ready people were to oppose him. He took London and recaptured King Henry. After some indecision, Warwick marched towards the capital, and the two armies met at Barnet, eleven miles up the Great North Road, on 14 April 1471.

Almost symbolically, given the confused politics and tangled loyalties which underlay the battle, it was fought in fog. Initially, the Earl of Oxford's men, fighting for Warwick in the centre, smashed the soldiers that they met and pursued them from the field. Returning to the battle, Oxford mistook the position and appeared unexpectedly. His banner of a star with streamers was mistaken for Edward's banner with blazing sun. When he was fired upon, he immediately suspected treachery, and retired from the fray. The battle was lost. Warwick, who had been fighting on foot, struggled to run, as best he could in heavy armour, towards a horse, but some of Edward's foot soldiers caught him, pulled up his visor and cut his throat. A month later, Henry VI was murdered in the Tower of London. An obelisk, erected in 1740, now commemorates the battle.

*See Battle of Tewkesbury, page 346. †See Queen's Oak, page 324. ‡See Second Battle of St Albans, page 241

BUNYAN'S BAPTISM POOL BEDFORD

Where John Bunyan found a new life

In 1653, John Bunyan joined the congregation of John Gifford, an independent minister practising in Bedford, and was baptised by him in a pool of the Great Ouse river; the pool lay on the opposite bank of the river from the Swan Hotel, between it and the weir. The baptism symbolised a rebirth for the tinsmith's son whose youth had been spent 'cursing, swearing, lying and blaspheming the holy name of God'. Joining the Parliamentarian army had enlarged Bunyan's horizons by introducing him to men who habitually argued about religion. All his life he had been haunted by nightmares in which he was tortured by devils; he was convinced he was destined for Hell.

As his masterpiece *The Pilgrim's Progress* shows, Bunyan knew the Bible intimately, and supplied references for the different images he used in his allegory in its margins. The mood of the Commonwealth favoured religious dissent, based on a close study of Biblical texts rather than on the rituals and teaching of the Church of England. It fell drastically out of favour after 1660, when the restoration of Charles II – who was himself blasé about religion – brought in a regime which was determined to restore the Church of England to its former pre-eminence. Bunyan was arrested for preaching without licence before 'unlawful assemblies'. Brought before a panel of five judges, all of whom had suffered for their religion under the previous regime, he refused to recant his opinions; exasperated, they threw him into gaol for three months. And then the authorities appeared to forget about him, only releasing him some twelve years later, when the King issued a Declaration of Indulgence.

During his time in gaol, Bunyan wrote many works, and began *The Pilgrim's Progress* during a further six months' imprisonment in 1677. It soon made Bunyan a hero of the Dissenting movement, and came to be read all round the world. In today's secular age it may be less accessible than in previous times, yet its imagery has entered the common language, even of people who have never opened its pages. It is to Bunyan that we owe phrases such as the Slough of Despond, the House Beautiful and Vanity Fair, the hymn 'To be a Pilgrim' and the words that follow Pilgrim's death: 'So he passed over, and all the Trumpets sounded for him on the other side.' When he died, he was buried in Bunhill Fields, the Dissenters' burial ground in London (see page 127).

BLENHEIM PALACE
WOODSTOCK, OXFORDSHIRE

Palace to monumentalise Marlborough's victories

The Duke of Wellington lost only one battle in the course of his military career; the Duke of Marlborough, however, lost none. Handsome as well as brilliant, though devious and tight-fisted, he crushed Monmouth's rebellion in 1685 for James II*. Four years later, he slunk away from James's camp to join William III. William did not quite trust him, but his hour came when myopic Queen Anne ascended the throne in 1702: his domineering wife, Sarah, had her in thrall. Marlborough became commander-in-chief of the army during the War of the Spanish Succession. The object was to prevent either France or Austria absorbing Spain into its direct sphere of influence, thus becoming too powerful in Europe.

In 1704, he marched 250 miles across Germany to defeat a larger French force, deployed behind marshes and streams, at Blenheim. It was such a resounding victory that Queen Anne gave her favourite the royal manor of Woodstock, which covered 15,000 acres; Parliament agreed to build a suitable house there at its expense. Parliament's generosity seemed to be justified since Marlborough went on to win further victories at Ramillies, Oudenarde and Malplaquet. With the Treaty of Utrecht, signed by Marlborough's enemies in government – the Tories – in 1713, Britain not only preserved the balance of power within Europe but also was enriched with a string of useful colonies, including Gibraltar.

Marlborough's duchess favoured the elderly Sir Christopher Wren as architect. Marlborough preferred Sir John Vanbrugh, the soldier turned play-wright who had recently launched his architectural career at Castle Howard in Yorkshire. It was an inspired choice, if the object was a commemoration of Marlborough's military victories. With his stage experience, Vanbrugh knew a thing or two about theatrical effects, and with its smoking grenades on the skyline and martial east gate, Blenheim is the architectural equivalent of a *marche militaire*. It was an effect which Marlborough did nothing to dispel, hanging captured standards in the Great Hall and displaying tapestries recording his triumphs throughout the Staterooms. As a house to live in, it was never going to be cosy, and for someone as careful about money as Marlborough – Prince Eugene of Savoy, when told that Marlborough was not in the habit of dotting his i's, thought that it might have been to save ink – Vanbrugh was definitely an indulgence. The business of cost control was left to Sarah, and she entered into it with relish. In expressing Queen Anne's desire to reward Marlborough, Parliament had, in 1705, referred to the future 'Castle at Blenheim'; it was soon known by the more appropriate designation of Palace.

*See Battle of Sedgemoor, page 38

BLETCHLEY PARK   NEAR MILTON KEYNES, BUCKINGHAMSHIRE
Where the world's first computer cracked the Enigma code

Like the space rocket, the computer is a legacy of wartime, which transformed everyday life. The world's first programmable electronic computer was built in a hut in the grounds of Bletchley Park, a singularly ugly Victorian house, in late 1943. Named Colossus, its purpose was to unravel the newly elaborated German Enigma ciphers and to try to get inside their secrets in the run-up to D-Day.

Bletchley Park had been home to the government's élite team of code-breakers since a party of unusually clever mathematicians and problem-solvers assembled there, under the guise of a house party, in August 1938; they included the Cambridge mathematicians Alan Turing and Gordon Welchman.

Facing them was the challenge of the German Enigma machine, originally pioneered in the early 1920s as a commercial service to companies who wanted to preserve their privacy. Its potential was quickly realised by the German military, who developed their own versions for army, navy and air force. An Enigma machine looked like a typewriter. But when a message was typed in, a series of notched wheels, or rotors, scrambled it into different letters of the alphabet. The Poles, with their close links to German industry, broke the cipher in 1933, having managed to construct their own Enigma machine. As the German invasion of Poland became imminent, they passed their information to the British, but the rate at which the Germans changed the sequence of rotors made it impossible to keep pace.

The Bletchley Park boffins made their first breakthrough in 1940. Initially, little use could be made of the information, not least because of the extreme secrecy which surrounded the code-breakers' success: not knowing the true origin of the information, military commanders were sometimes reluctant to act on it. However, real value was extracted from the Bletchley Park work during the Battle of the Atlantic when intercepts from the German navy made it possible for Allied convoys to avoid U-boat wolf packs. As a result, far fewer merchant ships were lost during 1943. During the North Africa Campaign, Enigma-derived intelligence helped chase Rommel out of Africa. More than 10,000 people worked at Bletchley Park at the time of D-Day, their decoded messages allowing Allied command to assess the extent to which its deceptions had succeeded in foxing the enemy.

The importance that Winston Churchill (see page 129) attached to Bletchley Park can be judged from a memo sent after he had been told that shortages were making it difficult for the code-breakers to keep up with new refinements added to German naval codes in October 1941. Headed 'Action This Day', it reads: 'Make sure they have all they want on extreme priority and report to me that this has been done.'

BRIDEGO BRIDGE *NEAR CHEDDINGTON, BUCKINGHAMSHIRE*
Scene of the Great Train Robbery

Just after 3am on the morning of 8 August 1963, a mail train drew up at what appeared to be a red signal outside Cheddington, a village near Tring. In reality, the red light came from a simple, battery-operated torch, while the green light was hidden by a glove. Some figures in blue overalls greeted the co-driver who climbed down from the diesel engine to investigate. They were not railway workers but members of a 20-strong gang that had been assembled to perform what rapidly became known as the Great Train Robbery.

As the trial judge Mr Justice Edmund Davies was to comment the following year, 'in its impudence and enormity' this crime was 'the first of its kind in this country'. The gang seemed to have left nothing to chance. The haul was particularly large because the previous Monday had been a Bank Holiday. Afterwards, holed up in an Oxfordshire farmhouse, they celebrated their fabulous £2.3m takings (made at a time when the most expensive footballer in the country was paid £100 a week) by playing Monopoly with real bank notes. However, they had not counted on passing, en route to the railway line, a hitchhiker who remembered seeing a convoy of what seemed to be military vehicles and reporting this to the police when news of the robbery broke the next day. Soon after they had left the farmhouse, the police located it. The fingerprints left on the Monopoly board were part of the evidence on which they were convicted. Seven of the gang, including the relatively inconsequential Ronnie Biggs, got thirty years' imprisonment each. During the robbery, the train driver, Jack Mills, had been repeatedly beaten over the head by an iron bar as he grappled with masked intruders on the footplate of his cab, and could never work again. This, and what seemed to be the shocking scale of the robbery, explains the unprecedented severity of the punishment.

The ringleader, Bruce Reynolds, fled to Mexico but returned penniless after three years. Biggs escaped from prison in 1965 and lived in Brazil, as hedonistically as circumstances permitted, until his health collapsed and he returned to England – and Belmarsh Prison – in 2001.

In the 1980s, the Great Train Robbery was eclipsed, in terms of monetary value, by robberies at a Brinks-Mat warehouse near Heathrow and a Knightsbridge safety deposit vault. Its place in British folklore, however, has been commemorated by Network Rail, who renamed the railway arch near where it took place Train Robbers' Bridge.

BROCKET HALL   NEAR WELWYN GARDEN CITY, HERTFORDSHIRE
Prime Minister who taught Queen Victoria her role

To the young Queen Victoria, her first Prime Minister, the 2nd Viscount Melbourne, was a hero. A girl of eighteen when she came to the throne, she hung on his every opinion – whether about politics, her mother, her taste in clothes, or his dislike of birdsong. As this 58-year-old man knelt to do homage during the Coronation, he became dewy-eyed. 'Oh! How different, how dreadfully different,' the Queen found her next Prime Minister, Sir Robert Peel, 'to that frank, open, natural and most kind warm manner of Lord Melbourne!' Peel resigned after Queen Victoria refused to follow custom and replace the Whig ladies-in-waiting, installed under Melbourne, with Tory ones.

It was Melbourne who, as Prime Minister under William IV, had given his name to the city in Australia. What fascinated Queen Victoria rather more, however, was the story of his wife, Lady Caroline Lamb. They had met when she came to Brocket Hall, the outwardly plain but internally sumptuous country house where he had grown up. Always volatile, she became increasingly unstable after childbirth (the one surviving son was retarded), and achieved notoriety after a tempestuous and very public love affair with Lord Byron*. Eventually, Melbourne separated from her; she continued to live at Brocket Hall, while he became chief-secretary to Ireland. She died, a prey to drugs, ten years before Victoria became Queen.

As Prime Minister, it fell to Melbourne to handle Chartist unrest (see page 427); his years in office coincided with unemployment and economic depression. He would have left office earlier, if he had not been persuaded to stay on by Victoria; when in 1841 his government fell, it is said that she was in floods of tears.

*See John Murray, page 162, and Newstead Abbey, page 333

ST JOHN'S CHURCH

BURFORD, OXFORDSHIRE

Cromwell crushes the Levellers

After the last battle of the Civil War near Stow-on-the-Wold in 1646*, the old Royalist general Sir Jacob Astley predicted that the Parliamentarian victors would 'fall out' among themselves. That falling out came soon enough. The Parliamentary army was composed of people naturally given to debate, pamphleteering and dissent. Extreme and radical ideas found adherents, particularly among soldiers who were discontented for want of pay. In May 1649, part of the army, camped at the Iron Age fort of Old Sarum in Wiltshire (see page 31), were given the choice of disbanding without arrears of pay or going to fight in Ireland. A group of a thousand 'Levellers' broke away, sacked their officers and appointed their own. They set off towards Oxford, hoping to hold Oliver Cromwell to a Solemn Engagement he had made at a meeting of the Commonwealth armies two years before on Newmarket Heath. The Engagement recognised demands such as religious toleration and the abolition of the House of Lords.

The Leveller force hoped to reach Banbury, where another mutiny had taken place, but finding their way blocked, settled for Burford instead. Exhausted by their march, they had not long been asleep when they were woken by the clatter of horses as Cromwell and 2,000 of his cavalry took over the town. Some 340 Levellers – complaining that Cromwell's troops treated them worse than the Cavaliers had – were herded into St John's church, where Cromwell preached to them. They were imprisoned there for three days (one prisoner, Anthony Smedley, spent the time carving his name into the lead of the font) before being marched onto the roof of the church to witness the execution of three ringleaders by firing squad.

It was the end of the Leveller insurrection. One of the Burford Levellers wrote a pamphlet entitled 'The Levellers' Vindication', lamenting the replacement of a despotic king with 'a Martiall Monarchie more cruell, Arbitrarie and Tyrannicall than England ever yet tasted of'. They were prophetic words. In 1653, Cromwell became Lord Protector – king by another name.

*See Stow-on-the-Wold, page 344

JOHN MILTON'S COTTAGE

CHALFONT ST GILES,
BUCKINGHAMSHIRE

Where Paradise Lost *was finished*

In 1665, the blind poet John Milton was one of the many Londoners threatened by the plague then raging in the capital. His pupil Thomas Ellwood found a cottage for him at Chalfont St Giles to which he retreated. Ellwood was a Quaker, then living with a Quaker family at Chalfont Grange, handy for the meeting house at Jordans (see page 224). There was a strong flavour of dissent in this corner of Buckinghamshire.

Milton had begun writing *Paradise Lost* – which describes the fall of man and hints at his redemption – in 1662, but had put it aside in favour of political work. His enforced absence from London gave him the time and solitude to take it up again. He rose early, composed long sections in his head, and by a phenomenal effort of will and memory would have them ready to dictate to a secretary by mid-morning. The image of Milton dictating to his daughters is false. Only one of the daughters could have spent much time with him at Chalfont St Giles. Ellwood was responsible for the idea that Milton should continue the theme, the result being *Paradise Regained*. It was begun at Chalfont St Giles but was finished when Milton returned to London on the retreat of the plague.

The cottage has been a museum for over a century. The trust that owns it was formed as part of Queen Victoria's Golden Jubilee celebrations in 1887; the Queen herself gave the first twenty pounds. Having therefore escaped the 20th century – when so many old houses in the Home Counties and beyond were modernised, often disastrously – without alteration, it is a pretty, well-preserved example of a late 16th-century village house: a comfortable enough dwelling but far from grand. Milton did not live here for long, but it is nevertheless the only one of his houses to survive.

CLAYDON HOUSE

Memories of Florence Nightingale

Feckless, naïve and a lavish patron, the 2nd Earl Verney's personality is reflected in the frothy Rococo interiors at Claydon House, which he built in the mid-18th century but was too financially embarrassed to occupy. His circumstances could hardly have been more different from his 19th-century successor, Sir Harry Verney, a model of Victorian piety and rectitude. In 1857, he married his second wife Parthenope Nightingale, whose sister Florence had recently returned from nursing British soldiers in the Crimea. The Verneys loved Claydon, and the unmarried Florence visited them often. Her bedroom, along with some artefacts associated with her, are preserved in her memory.

Florence, like her sister, took her name from the city of her birth – Parthenope being the Greek for Naples. They were educated at home in England by their father. In 1837, when Florence was seventeen, she felt that she had been called by God to do some kind of good work, although it was as yet undefined. Her parents initially opposed her interest in nursing, but relented when she was thirty, allowing her to study in Germany, and to travel elsewhere on the Continent.

After the Battle of the Alma in 1854, Florence arrived at the hospital in Scutari, a suburb of Constantinople, with 38 nurses. To begin with, their presence was not welcomed by the male doctors, but the arrival of more wounded soldiers from the Battle of Inkerman forced them to accept the nurses' help. Her influence was described by a war correspondent to *The Times* in February 1855: 'Wherever there is disease in its most dangerous form, and the hand of the spoiler distressingly nigh, there is that incomparable woman sure to be seen; her benignant presence is an influence for good comfort even amid the struggles of expiring nature. She is a ''ministering angel'' without any exaggeration in these hospitals, and, as her slender form glides quietly along each corridor, every fellow's face softens with gratitude at the sight of her.'

After the Crimean War, Nightingale established her institution for the training of nurses at St Thomas's Hospital* in London. Among other achievements, she was elected the first female fellow to the Statistical Society for the work involved in her campaign to improve the health of the soldiers in the British army and in British hospitals. Paradoxically, she herself spent many years as an invalid (possibly self-imposed), in need of the care and sympathy that she had in such measure shown to other people.

*See St Thomas's Old Operating Theatre, page 182

CLIVEDEN HOUSE

NEAR MAIDENHEAD, BUCKINGHAMSHIRE

Country-house setting for a national scandal

'There was no impropriety whatsoever in my acquaintanceship with Miss Keeler,' John Profumo, Secretary of State for War, told the House of Commons in March 1963. Ten weeks later, the urbane Harrow- and Oxford-educated Profumo reappeared before the Commons to admit that he had lied; he not only resigned from the Cabinet but left Parliament. Worse was to come when it emerged that Christine Keeler not only slept with Cabinet ministers, but also with Russian naval attachés. The scandal gripped the nation.

Profumo first met Miss Keeler at Cliveden, Lord Astor's luxurious country house set high above the Thames. She was swimming naked in the swimming pool at the time, as the guest of the society osteopath Stephen Ward at Spring Cottage on the estate. Not yet twenty, she was strikingly beautiful, and had already acquired a racy past. Ward used Keeler and other high-class call girls, like her friend Mandy Rice-Davies, as a lure to draw the rich and influential into his web. His flat in Wimpole Mews had two-way mirrors and other props for sex parties. Later, Miss Keeler claimed that Ward was a spy; at the time, despite a tempestuous, if platonic relationship with him, she was under his thrall. Once out of the swimming pool, Keeler and Profumo tried on some of Lord Astor's collection of armour, and a torrid affair began shortly thereafter.

The scandal hastened the end of Harold Macmillan's premiership: he resigned, on grounds of ill health, having made a humbling apology to the Queen. At the General Election the following year, the Tory government under Sir Alec Douglas-Home was chased from office. As for the principal players, Profumo devoted himself to charity work, Keeler was imprisoned for nine months on an unrelated charge of perjury and Ward, at the end of a trial for pimping, killed himself.

COOKHAM

BERKSHIRE

Idyll of a very English artist

Like many English artists, Stanley Spencer (1891–1959) was obsessed by place. Indeed, the intensity of his childhood response to his surroundings in the village of Cookham was the lodestone and driving force of his painting. His art was a means of recapturing those memories. Spencer, like William Blake, experienced heavenly visitations – it seems only in Cookham – and followed the example of early Renaissance painters in setting religious events amid locations familiar from everyday life. The dead rise from their graves in Cookham churchyard, chatting comfortably to each other as they re-enter the paradise that is Cookham. Christ, wearing a boater, is seen preaching to the holiday crowds who used to flock to this stretch of the Thames for the colourful Edwardian regatta: started in the 1880s, it had long ceased to take place by the time Spencer painted his regatta series in the 1950s.

To Spencer, marriage to his first wife Hilda was a sexual awakening, which threatened the purity of his Cookham vision; after the birth of their two children, he found her lethargic, given over to Christian Science and unwilling to listen to his endless expositions about his paintings, past history and ideas. It was of great significance to Spencer that he met the woman who was to be his second wife, Patricia, in Cookham. Unfortunately, since she was living there in a lesbian relationship, the marriage was a disaster, complicated by Spencer's insistence that he could maintain sexual relations with Hilda; Patricia saw Spencer as a means of support for herself and her lover, Dorothy. Cosy, redemptive Cookham was the only balm.

Despite the BMWs and burglar alarms that come with prosperity in commuterland, much of Spencer's Cookham survives: the Ferry Hotel, which features in the regatta paintings; the church of the Holy Trinity; the ceremony of swan-upping, when the Vintners' and Dyers' companies, who own the swans on the Thames, conduct their annual stocktake; the High Street, where Spencer's lumpy-figured St Francis preaches to the birds; and Cookham Moor, a scene of imagined free love. As a child, Spencer was taken to worship in the Methodist chapel that has been a museum of his art since 1962. It contains, as well as paintings, sketches, letters, documents and memorabilia, the pram used by Spencer to wheel his equipment around Cookham when painting landscapes.

DORNEY COURT BUCKINGHAMSHIRE
England's first home-grown pineapple

The first pineapple to be grown in England was presented to Charles II in 1661. The event was so remarkable that it was commemorated in a painting by Hendrik Danckerts. The monarch, wearing a broad-rimmed hat, long wig, garter star and tights, insouciantly receives the fruit from the royal gardener John Rose, kneeling amid the King's cavalier spaniels at his monarch's feet. Rose, who studied under Le Nôtre, was an expert on fruit trees; he wrote a book called The English Vinyard Vindicated, an apologia for viticulture in England. The glasshouse in which the pineapple was raised belonged to Dorney Court, owned by Sir Roger Palmer, who was married to the King's mistress, the beautiful, callous Barbara Villiers (otherwise Lady Castlemaine and Duchess of Cleveland).

It was an age of curiosity, not least in matters of diet. The potato was still a novelty, tea had only just been introduced. According to his diary, Samuel

Pepys lived mostly off robust native fare, such as chine of beef, brawn, venison pasties, oysters, herring, mackerel and eel. But occasionally he was able to taste lobster, caviar, melon and olives; in addition to these exotics, the picking of fruit in the King's garden is mentioned as a particular treat. The advent of the pineapple must have been a particularly exciting addition to the table, combining a strong fleshy hint of sweetness with (had anyone known it) the health-giving properties of vitamins A, C and potassium. Christopher Columbus had thought it looked like a pine cone – hence the name. Moreover, he found that the natives of Guadeloupe hung pineapples outside their huts as a symbol of hospitality, and the fruit retained this association when introduced to Britain. It quickly became a popular architectural emblem, seen notably on top of gate piers (the apotheosis of pineapple architecture is the summer-house in the form of one built at Dunmore House near Falkirk in 1761). A stone pineapple stands in the Great Hall of Dorney Court, commemorating its contribution to horticulture.

ETON COLLEGE BERKSHIRE
The most famous of English schools

When the boy king Henry VI assumed personal control of his realm at the age of sixteen, he wished to commemorate the event – and bring good fortune on his reign – by founding a great religious institution. This was focused on what had been the parish church of Eton, on the other side of the Thames from his birthplace at Windsor. He endowed what was intended to be a new minster not only with substantial estates but fragments of the True Cross and the Crown of Thorns. A school was also to be provided. Statutes were drawn up in 1440 and out of this vision grew Eton College.

It was typical of the pious, unmartial and sometimes mentally incapaci-tated Henry VI that he should have preferred founding a great church to mounting a military campaign. His vacillating temperament is shown in the way the undertaking developed. The scholarly dimension increased after the King had visited William of Wykeham's Winchester College*; like William, Henry also established a college – King's College, Cambridge – as part of a co-foundation. Henry, however, wanted his institution to outshine all others. To that end, after seven years' building work, he had most of what he had achieved pulled down, so that the church could be rebuilt on a bigger scale. Only the choir of the new church was ever constructed and this forms the present chapel. The domestic ranges proceeded more quickly, being built out of brick rather than stone (see page 216). The complement of seventy poor scholars and fifteen choristers arrived by 1447.

From these devout, yet megalomaniac beginnings, Eton grew in time to be the most famous school in the country. In the Elizabethan period, the regime was known to be rigorous: boys rose at five, chanted prayers while they dressed, were taught only in Latin, and went without food on Fridays. Later, Eton trained young aristocrats and bucks for a life that would be spent either running landed estates or in the army. Famously, Waterloo was won on the playing fields of Eton, and in the chapel the war memorials to the fallen of the Crimea and the First and Second World Wars evoke a world of chivalry and patriotism.

To one of its most famous old boys, George Orwell, writing in the *Observer* in 1948, Eton had become an anachronism long before 1939. However, even he felt that 'it also has one great virtue and that is a tolerant and civilised atmosphere which gives each boy a fair chance of developing his own individuality'. That virtue survives, despite the intense modern pressure for examination success.

*See Winchester College, page 101

GOD'S HOUSE
EWELME, OXFORDSHIRE

Playing the 'get out of Purgatory quick' card

There are few surviving landmarks associated with the first great poet to write in English, Geoffrey Chaucer. However, his granddaughter Alice Chaucer is remembered in the building of almshouses, school and church, the latter including one of the most beautiful tombs of the 15th century. Chaucer had been a familiar figure at the Court of Richard II; Alice became a great heiress when her first husband, the Earl of Salisbury, was killed by a cannonball while fighting in France. With her second husband, William de la Pole, Duke of Suffolk, she built what amounted to a palace at Ewelme.

Riches flowed to the Duke, who had such influence over the indecisive King Henry VI that he virtually ruled England in his stead. Nothing now survives of the building the Suffolks created for this world, but the arrangements they made for the next one have fared better. As the Middle Ages wore on, the doctrine of Purgatory took hold of the religious imagination. It was viewed as a kind of waiting room for the soul, before it was sent on its final journey towards Heaven or Hell. Since the length of time it spent there could be mitigated by prayer, rich people made sure that they left sufficient money to the Church for Masses to be said for them. The Suffolks rebuilt the parish church, and constructed a complex of almshouses and school known as God's House, in the newly revived material of brick. Knowledge of brick-making had lapsed since Roman times; God's House was begun in 1437, the very year that Henry VI imported a craftsman from Flanders to establish a brickworks to supply the new buildings at Eton College (see page 215) and Windsor.

Perhaps the luxurious Suffolks expected a long stay in Purgatory. Thirteen almsmen, living in the almshouses, were retained to pray for their souls, on an almost continuous schedule of devotion: their stipend was docked if they left the buildings for more than an hour at a time. The Duchess's alabaster tomb in the church, erected after her death in 1475, contains a reminder of the transience of the flesh, in the form of a carved cadaver which is set below the tomb – the only example of a female effigy to have such a *memento mori* in Britain. The Duke's effigy does not rest beside her. In 1450, the King was forced to commit him to exile after a disastrous treaty, followed by war, had lost England most of its possessions in France. However, his ship was intercepted, and his head was summarily hacked off with a rusty sword. His body was never recovered. *Sic transit gloria mundi.*

FORT BELVEDERE

NEAR WINDSOR, BERKSHIRE

A King chooses 'the help and support of the woman I love'

At the end of November 1936, Wallis Simpson fled London for Fort Belvedere, the toy castle overlooking Virginia Water – given its present form by Sir Jeffry Wyatville in the 1820s – where Edward VIII had made his home. Word about her relationship with the King – and the constitutional crisis it would provoke – was beginning to seep out. After she had gone, stones broke the windows of her London house; Fort Belvedere could only protect her for a few days. As the storm clouds gathered, she left (unlamented by the servants) for the South of France. Without her, Edward was distraught.

He was resolved to marry Mrs Simpson. She was, however, American, which hardly recommended her to a still insular British public. Far worse, she was a divorcee who, having already remarried, would have to be divorced again before becoming free for the King. Divorce was widely regarded as a stigma; the King's position as head of the Church of England made his choice of wife unthinkable to many people. The King decided that he too would have to leave the country. The first version of the speech he would deliver on the radio made it clear that he had hopes of returning.

Having been popular as the Prince of Wales, he thought the British public would forgive him. He waited anxiously at Fort Belvedere to hear the Prime Minister's verdict, but Stanley Baldwin was implacable. The King's supporters, such as Winston Churchill and the newspaper tycoon Max Beaverbrook, were dismayed to find that, faced with this hostility, the fight went out of him, but Edward's greatest anxiety was that Mrs Simpson might not be allowed her divorce.

On 10 December, the King's three brothers, including the Duke of York, who would imminently be King George VI, arrived at Fort Belvedere and the

Instrument of Abdication was signed. The next day, Edward astonished a largely unprepared nation by announcing his abdication in a radio broadcast made from Windsor Castle. Sir John Reith (see page 122), Director General of the BBC, announced it in person. He had been uncertain what to call the ex-King, suggesting Mr Edward Windsor. This was brushed aside by George VI, who made his brother a Royal Duke.

The Duke of Windsor left the country to join his beloved Wallis, rarely to return. He died in 1972, and was buried in the royal mausoleum at Frogmore near Windsor.

GREENHAM COMMON
Women against cruise missiles

American airmen first appeared at Greenham Common in 1943. Before long, furniture-makers who happened to work nearby were pressed into the production of 4,000 troop-carrying gliders – one of the makeshift solutions to the technical challenge of Operation Overlord's invasion of occupied Europe. After the Second World War, the base closed. It was reopened in 1951, as part of Nato's defence against the perceived threat from the Soviet Union. Village houses shuddered as noisy B-47 Stratojets roared overhead. Otherwise little was heard of the base, even after the first nuclear weapons arrived in 1953. From 1967, military activity was sporadic.

In 1979, however, newspaper reports suggested that something rather bigger was coming to Greenham than the annual air tattoo held in aid of the Royal Air Force Benevolent Fund. The Soviet Union had started to deploy SS20 nuclear missiles, which trundled around the countryside behind the Iron Curtain on huge transporters. Their range was such that they could hit Europe but not the United States. Despite not being directly under threat, the Americans moved their equivalent of the SS20 – the cruise missile – to Western Europe. One of the British sites chosen for its deployment was Greenham Common. In September 1981, three dozen women marched from their homes in South Wales to protest. In the feminist spirit of the times, they founded a women's peace camp on the perimeter of the base which lasted for nineteen years. Using a homely code ('black cardigan' stood for bolt cutters), they persistently broke into the base and obstructed missile convoys as they attempted to go out on manoeuvres.

In 1987, President Reagan and General Secretary Gorbachev signed a treaty to reduce 'intermediate' nuclear weapons, and Greenham's missiles were flown out four years later. It took another nine years for the peace camp to be dismantled. The last of the protesters left, banging drums and singing peace songs, in 2000.

SHAKESPEARE TEMPLE

David Garrick's tribute to Shakespeare

In March 1737, the young David Garrick set out from Lichfield for London, in the company of his teacher, the ungainly, pockmarked Samuel Johnson*, eight or so years his senior. They were both intent on making their reputations in the capital. Financially, Garrick's circumstances were no more buoyant than Johnson's. He was the son of a soldier, whose income had suffered from the absence of war. Appropriately, the first play that Garrick mounted as an actor-manager, at the age of twelve, was called *The Recruiting Officer*. In London, Garrick initially enrolled in the Bar, but as he soon wrote to his brother Peter, 'My mind (as you must know) has always been inclined to the Stage.' They were not words his parents wanted to hear, since acting was still regarded as a disreputable profession.

Garrick became the first great modern actor. Highly versatile, he grew to be the equivalent of a modern film star, using the fortune that he made to establish his position – and raise the status of the profession – by building a villa beside the Thames at Hampton, not far from Horace Walpole's Strawberry Hill (see page 243). His greatest contribution to the history of theatre (and of letters generally) was in rehabilitating Shakespeare† who, until then, had been performed in pale adaptations, if at all.

Garrick, who had first made his name playing Richard III, was one of the prime movers behind the Shakespeare monument in Westminster Abbey, erected in 1740. It was at the foot of this monument that he himself would be buried in 1779. Garrick was also behind the extraordinary Shakespeare Jubilee of 1769, which marks the beginning of Stratford-upon-Avon‡ as a national literary shrine.

Meanwhile, his personal tribute was an octagonal temple to the world's greatest dramatist, probably designed by Robert Adam and built on a lawn next to the Thames in 1756. This lay on the other side of the road from Garrick's villa (now demolished), and was reached by a tunnel in the form of a grotto, which included a bath house, presumably inspired by Alexander Pope's similar grotto at nearby Twickenham. Inside the temple was a statue of Shakespeare by Roubillac, the original of which is now in the Victoria and Albert Museum. Zoffany, who recorded Garrick in several of his leading roles, also painted a conversation piece of the actor and his wife elegantly relaxing on the steps of the temple, while their son runs through the portico and a servant brings tea.

*See Samuel Johnson's Birthplace, page 330. †See The Globe Theatre, page 144.
‡See Shakespeare's Birthplace, page 345

OLD PALACE, HATFIELD

Princess Elizabeth is told she is Queen

In November 1558, the then Princess Elizabeth was supposedly sitting under an oak tree at the old palace of Hatfield when a messenger galloped up to tell her that her half-sister, Mary, had at last died. Now she would be Queen. It was a reversal of fortune since, for the previous two and a half years, she had been under a form of house arrest at Hatfield, her childhood home.

For a child, the Hatfield years cannot have been easy. A brick mansion, then enclosing four sides of a courtyard, it had been built at the end of the 15th century by a Bishop of Ely. Henry VIII had confiscated it at the Dissolution of the Monasteries (see page 133), reserving it for the use of his children. Elizabeth, who had already bitterly disappointed her father by not being a boy, was first brought here at the age of three months. Even before her mother Anne Boleyn's disgrace two years later, her father had taken little interest in her, except as a potential dynastic alliance. At Hatfield she joined Mary who, through the declaration that her mother's marriage had been unlawful, had recently been rendered illegitimate. Mary was now expected to pay Elizabeth the respect that had previously been hers: it did not make for a happy relationship.

At Hatfield, this 'most christenly learned yonge lady' had a Latin secretary, an Italian tutor and a governor, Sir Thomas Pope, who had recently founded Trinity College, Oxford. When Mary thought herself pregnant by her husband, Philip II of Spain, the pressure on Elizabeth, as heir presumptive, eased. But the pregnancy proved false. At forty-two, Mary was already worn out by work and worry. Calais had been lost, and her husband, now that she was unlikely to bear an heir, had lost interest in her. When word got out that she was dying, the road to Hatfield was thronged with courtiers seeking to offer their services to Elizabeth.

Once Elizabeth left Hatfield, to be crowned in London, it appears that she never returned. Her successor, James I, did not care much for the place either; by the time he swapped it for Theobalds Manor, the old palace was in such poor condition that Robert Cecil pulled most of it down, retaining only the original hall as the stables for his new mansion.

See also Hatfield House, below

HATFIELD HOUSE

Architectural expression of a political gene

Hatfield stands as a monument to the political gene of the Cecil family. In the 16th century, Robert Cecil* inherited it from his father Lord Burghley, whom he followed as Queen Elizabeth's chief minister. It was Cecil who did more than anyone to negotiate, on Elizabeth's death, the succession of James VI of Scotland to the English throne as James I. James stopped at Cecil's house of Theobalds† on his stately journey south to claim the crown.

James had little affection for the old palace at Hatfield, which had been barely used since Queen Elizabeth had been confined there. On the other hand, as an addict of hunting he enjoyed his visits to Theobalds, some ten miles away, expressing his admiration by the backhanded means of proposing a swap. Having accepted the King's offer, Cecil – who had been created 1st Earl of Salisbury after the role he had played in uncovering the Gunpowder Plot (see page 317) – showed his disgust for the old building by demolishing three-quarters of it, and building the present house to the designs of Robert Lyminge. Help was enlisted from the Surveyor of the King's Works, Simon Basyll, and the great Inigo Jones – too late, presumably, for him to do more than sprinkle some Italianate stardust on the south front of an otherwise old-fashioned pile.

Two and a half centuries later, when the British Empire was at its zenith, Cecil's descendant, the 3rd Marquess, became Prime Minister no fewer than three times. In the Victorian age, owning a great country house was a political asset, thanks to the influence that could be exerted and the alliances formed during parties there. Once the railways arrived, Hatfield had the advantage of being convenient for London, and Salisbury – both scholarly and family-minded – managed to commute from it, even when running the Empire.

*See Burghley House, page 257. †See Old Palace, Hatfield, page 220

HESTON AERODROME
NEAR HOUNSLOW, MIDDLESEX
'Peace for our time'

On 30 September 1938 a Lockheed 14 plane landed on the grass of Heston Aerodrome and taxied to a halt, some way from where a crowd was standing. They watched the Prime Minister, Neville Chamberlain, emerge onto the steps. He waved a piece of paper. It had been signed by Adolf Hitler at his mountain retreat of Berchtesgaden the day before. In return for the Sudetenland in Czechoslovakia, Germany agreed to curb its territorial ambitions in Europe. The Czech prime minister, who had not even been at the meeting between Germany, Britain, France and Italy, protested in vain. At Downing Street, the Prime Minister declared: 'I believe it is peace for our time.'

Appeasement bought Britain, woefully under-prepared for war, twelve months in which to re-arm herself. While ordering the immediate stepping up of the armaments programme, Chamberlain did not, in fact, prevent Hitler's invasion of Czechoslovakia in March 1939. Later in the year, Germany invaded Poland, and Chamberlain gave Hitler an ultimatum to withdraw or force a war between Britain and Germany. Hitler scornfully dismissed the Munich Pact as just 'a scrap of paper' and on 3 September 1939, Britain and France declared war on Germany.

After the Second World War, Heston was superseded as an airport by nearby Heathrow*. What remains of the old airfield is now the Airlinks Golf Course. Being owned by the government, the rest was dedicated to the London–South Wales motorway (M4) and the adjacent Heston service station.

*See Croydon Airport, page 64

HOUNSLOW HEATH   MIDDLESEX
The beginnings of the Ordnance Survey

Hidden away behind the Three Magpies pub, on Heathrow Airport's busy Northern Perimeter Road (on what used to be Hounslow Heath), is a bollard made out of a cannon. There is another in a suburban road called Roy Grove in Hampton. They are exactly 3 miles apart. This distance, carefully measured in 1784, represents the Great Base from which the Ordnance Survey was made; the points at that time were identified by two buried cartwheels. (When the length of one side of a triangle and two of its angles are known, it is possible to calculate the length of the other two sides. Hence the importance of a baseline in 'triangulation', the method of surveying used until the advent of satellites.)

Major-General William Roy of the Royal Engineers, who created the Great Base, had been given the task of surveying the area between Greenwich and the south coast, as part of an attempt by the Royal Societies of London and Paris to measure the relative positions of their observatories – an important calculation for astronomers. Roy (after whom Roy Grove is named) died in 1790, but his work provided the starting point for a new project again related to the French. This time it was the prospect of invasion which provoked an urgent need for maps. Accurate knowledge of the country's terrain was vital for defence. (In a similar vein, the Highlands had been mapped after the 1745 Jacobite Rebellion.) The Board of Ordnance, the body responsible for fortifications, was charged with making the survey. By 1795, with Britain at war with France, it was decided that, unlike previous surveys, it should be comprehensive. It would also be published.

Most of southern England had been surveyed by 1815; most of the rest of the country by 1823. This was the beginning of a tradition that is often thought to have produced the best maps in the world. In recent years, an almost equally heroic task has been undertaken, with the digitising of the Ordnance Survey, with all the benefits of internet access which that has brought.

HUGHENDEN MANOR

Home of Queen Victoria's favourite prime minister

When Benjamin Disraeli died in 1881, Queen Victoria herself erected a memorial in the church at Hughenden, his country estate, to his 'dear and honoured memory'. Beneath it is inscribed a verse from Proverbs: 'Kings love him that speaketh right.' This is the only time in British history that a monarch has commemorated a subject in this way. The wall monument, although not an aesthetic marvel, stands as testimony to the spellbinding power of the dazzling, paradoxical Tory politician and novelist, who championed an idealistic image of government by aristocracy and the British Empire, while simultaneously addressing the rights of working people.

Disraeli was brought up amid books and trained at first to become a solicitor. Still in his twenties, he achieved some renown as a novelist, and even greater fame as a dandy. As a converted Jew, he was always something of an outsider. He entered the House of Commons in 1837 when, due to his florid clothes and foppish demeanour, his maiden speech was famously howled down. In 1839 he married a rich widow, Mrs Wyndham Lewis, whose fortune allowed him to buy Hughenden – an undistinguished house, which the Disraelis made uglier. Its saving grace was a beautiful park and estate of 750 acres which the Disraelis nearly doubled. Having known Burnham Beeches from childhood, he loved the Chilterns' beech woods. 'I am not surprised that the ancients worshipped Trees,' he wrote. He did not participate in the field sports that bound men of the ruling class together, preferring to walk in the woods; with him he carried a small hatchet, to cut down any ivy threatening the trees. He had become a squire, as was only right for someone for whom the landed estate was a metaphor for a properly ordered Britain: its rulers might enjoy the benefits of possession but also bore responsibility for their community and their successors. These were the ideals that underpinned his novels *Coningsby* (1844) and *Sybil* (1845) and found expression, politically, in the Young England Movement.

From Hughenden, Disraeli issued forth to become Lord Derby's Chancellor of the Exchequer in 1852 and 1858, and Leader of the House of Commons. He proposed the 1867 Reform Act, extending the male franchise and reorganising parliamentary constituencies. The following year he briefly became Prime Minister, departing at the General Election. His beloved Mary Anne did not live to see him win the next General Election in 1874, having died two years earlier. But now, Prime Minister again, he could at last put into effect the ideas he had formulated as leader of the Young England Movement, introducing a series of reforms on housing, public health, food, child labour, workers' protection and education. In 1876 Queen Victoria agreed to his suggestion that she should be called Empress of India. The same year Disraeli was elevated to the peerage as Lord Beaconsfield. He continued to serve as Prime Minister until his defeat in

1880. His hopes to spend his retirement writing novels at Hughenden were undone by his death the following year. Even so, Hughenden had already entered into a new phase in its owner's imagination: a museum to his distinguished life.

JORDANS MEETING HOUSE BUCKINGHAMSHIRE
Oldest Quaker meeting house

During the 1660s, the Quaker William Penn, founder of Pennsylvania, was continually being thrown into prison for his beliefs. Quakerism was one of the new styles of Christianity to evolve during the fundamentalist years of the Commonwealth. Its followers believed that God existed as a kind of inner light within everyone; services were held largely in silence, as Friends* (as Quakers called themselves) focused on their own spirituality. Their determination to act according to the dictates of their own consciences alarmed the authorities. In 1681, Penn obtained a grant of land in America for a colony for free-thinkers. The next year he made his famous treaty with the native Indians on the site of the future Philadelphia.

In 1684, Penn returned to England, and four years later the congregation or Meeting to which he belonged was able to take advantage of the new religious freedom brought in by James II (intended by the King to favour Catholics) to build a place of worship. This is the Meeting House at Jordans, a cottagey building reached, even today, through a cherry orchard. Until then, the Friends had been meeting in a farmhouse's kitchen. The contrast that Quakerism makes with the contemporary Church of England is immediately apparent inside the Meeting House, with its brick floor, tall casement windows and panelling of unpolished deal. There is no altar or pulpit, only simple benches arranged around a small table. A step, a rail and an upward sweep of panelling is all that marks the bench occupied by the presiding Elders. Fire ravaged the building in 2005; the roof was destroyed but the interior is recoverable.

Penn returned to America for two years, to give guidance to his colony, but it is in the simple graveyard at Jordans that he is buried.

*See Fox's Pulpit, page 360

KEW BRIDGE PUMPING STATION MIDDLESEX
The largest waterworks engine in the world

Without a supply of unpolluted water, no city can flourish. Unfortunately, viewed with a modern understanding of disease, the history of how water was supplied to British cities when they first became populous is grim. Take

London. Some people were fortunate enough to have wells sunk into the gravelly substratum to supply pure water (the gravel having acted as a natural filter); from the 17th century, others could buy the somewhat murkier product that had run along the New River Company's 39 miles of open channel to its reservoir in Clerkenwell. But until Victorian improvements, most Londoners took their water from the Thames*. From 1582, it was pumped to them by the London Bridge Waterworks Company, using waterwheels installed in the arches of London Bridge (where the current was fastest). Other water companies followed their example. Since the Thames came to absorb the city's discharge of sewage, it was a dire source of supply – bad enough for the West End, which was upstream, but far worse for the East End. Theirs was a rich brew indeed. The nadir was reached in the early 19th century when the rapid growth in population led to the general introduction of water-closets.

Kew Bridge Pumping Station represents the third attempt made by one company, the Grand Junction Water Works, to deal with the problem of unclean water. Supplying parts of west London, they had first built a pumping station in Paddington in 1811, taking water from the Grand Junction Canal (hence their name). Predictably, this proved less than ideal, so a new pumping station was constructed at Chelsea nine years later. But since this still drew polluted water from the Thames, they moved to Kew Bridge in 1837 where the water was cleaner. When the Metropolitan Water Board, which had absorbed the old company, ceased pumping in 1944, the building was kept, ultimately, as a museum. It still contains several of the old steam pumps, including one that was made by Boulton & Watt in 1820. James Watt, following his experiments with steam power in the 1760s, went into partnership with Matthew Boulton, a Birmingham factory owner, in 1774 (see page 303), and their engine was first used in the pumping station at Chelsea. The Grand Junction 90-inch Engine, built in 1846, was then the largest waterworks engine in the world.

*See Abbey Mills Pumping Station, page 108

LETCHWORTH GARDEN CITY HERTFORDSHIRE
The Garden City ideal

For much of the 20th century, intelligent people thought that the answer to Victorian industrialisation, which had blighted life in the big cities, was the new concept of the Garden City. Here, housing and community buildings stood next to architect-designed factories, in a setting that was more or less rural. The first was Letchworth Garden City, in Hertfordshire; located on a railway line to King's Cross, it was begun in 1904.

The Garden City Movement originated in a City clerk turned stenographer, Ebenezer Howard (1850–1928). As a young man, Howard had emigrated to Nebraska, intending to farm, but when this failed, he moved to Chicago. Here he saw at first hand the city being rebuilt after the great fire of 1871, which introduced him to the town planning ideas of landscape architect Frederick Law Olmsted. Returning to England, Howard incorporated them into his own vision, which he expressed in *Tomorrow: the Peaceful Path to Real Reform* (1898). A limited company was formed, capital raised, a landed estate purchased and an architectural competition held, the last being won by the firm of Parker & Unwin.

An intimation of the Parker & Unwin aesthetic can be gathered from their old office, now the Letchworth Museum. In this thatched building, austerity was mixed with self-conscious beauty and a dash of Socialism, a recipe prescribed by the Arts and Crafts tradition deriving from William Morris. George Bernard Shaw, the Socialist playwright (who lived nearby at Shaw's Corner, see page 204), and the suffragette leader Christabel Pankhurst, both spoke at the Mrs Howard Memorial Hall, which was Letchworth's first public building (named after Ebenezer Howard's wife, who had died of cancer in 1904). The pub, the Skittles Inn, famously sold no beer, since alcohol was banned from the precincts of Letchworth until 1958. Artists came. So did an American company that made ladies' corsets: the result was the light, airy and architecturally progressive Spirella corsets factory of 1912.

As soon as Letchworth was under way, Howard founded Welwyn Garden City nearer London. The example of these developments was followed in countries as far away as Australia and Japan. After the Second World War, Howard's ideas underpinned 'New Towns' such as Stevenage, built to rehouse the working classes who had previously lived in grimy industrial slums. Garden Cities fell out of favour, however, when it was seen that, in the motor car age, they led to Milton Keynes.

OLNEY
'Glorious Things of Thee are Spoken'

NEAR NEWPORT PAGNELL,
BUCKINGHAMSHIRE

The poet William Cowper lived at Orchard Side, Olney from 1768 until 1786. Today, he is most famous for having written 'John Gilpin', the poem telling the story of a hectic journey of a 'linen-draper bold' riding a bolting horse. It was published anonymously, and never seems to have been a work of which Cowper was particularly proud. (The tale had been suggested to him by a neighbour, Lady Austen, in an effort to rouse him from one of the fits of depression from which he suffered.) Weightier achievements include translating Homer into English verse and his long, proto-Romantic poem *The Task*, which elaborated upon events of his rather quiet domestic life. To an earlier generation, he was celebrated for having written the *Olney Hymns* with his friend, the Rev. John Newton, which include such classics of Anglican hymnody as 'Glorious Things of Thee are Spoken', 'How Sweet the Name of Jesus Sounds' and 'Amazing Grace'. It was to be near Newton that Cowper came to Orchard Side. Newton found him the house: a striking façade of c. 1700 looks out towards the marketplace, but behind lie two older cottages, one occupied by Cowper and his housekeeper-companion, Mary Unwin, the other by his servant, Dick Coleman, his wife, daughter and 'a thousand rats'. Cowper always entered the house from the back after one of his pet hares escaped through the front door.

Newton was a remarkable man. In his youth he worked on slave ships, was enslaved himself, escaped and became a captain. He believed that God had saved him from a violent storm and became deeply religious. First he preached, then he took holy orders, and put his knowledge of slavery at the service of William Wilberforce in the campaign to abolish it (see page 392). As the curate at Olney, his sermons drew people from miles around, many of whom he would entertain for supper afterwards; the suppers became so popular that he eventually had to issue tickets.

Cowper was tormented by his depression and tried to commit suicide three times. Gardening, however, gave him solace. His garden adjoined that of the vicarage and the two friends would often walk over to see each other. It is pleasant to think of them in the tiny brick summerhouse in Cowper's garden, enjoying the sunshine that came through the big sash window and writing hymns.

BALLIOL COLLEGE
BROAD STREET, OXFORD

The first English translation of the Bible

While at Oxford, John Wyclif and a group of friends were responsible for the first translation of the Bible into English. Wyclif was born near Richmond in Yorkshire around 1330, and seems to have embodied the Yorkshireman's characteristic stubbornness and plain speaking. In an England seeking supernatural explanations for the Black Death, he made himself an enemy of the Church establishment by preaching against its wealth and abuses; finally he alienated himself from it completely by denying the doctrine of transubstantiation. As a result, the Archbishop of Canterbury forced Wyclif to leave Oxford, where he had spent most of his adult life, being Master of Balliol College from 1361–82. His heresy was treated relatively leniently and he was allowed to retire to his living at Lutterworth.

It is not known how much of the Bible Wyclif himself translated: he was probably responsible for the Gospels, using the Latin Vulgate rather than the original Greek text, whose language he did not know. The Bible first appeared around 1382, with a second edition appearing in 1388, four years after Wyclif's death.

Hitherto, ordinary people had been discouraged from reading the Bible which, in any case, they could not have understood without knowing Latin. Wyclif, in the prologue to his translation, boldly asserted that 'no simple man of wit shoulde be aferde unmesurably to study in the text of holy Writ'. Even if they did not properly understand it, priests pretended they could. Salvation, he argued, would come from studying the Bible, rather than buying pardons from the Church. Laws should be obeyed only when they were grounded in Scripture. Wyclif's advocacy of such principles made him the leading English philosopher of the 14th century, and a forerunner of the Reformation in Europe. After his death in 1384, followers known as the Lollards (derived from a word meaning to mutter) continued his teaching.

See also Cranmer's Tower, page 153, and Llanrhaeadr-ym-Mochnant, page 420

NEW COLLEGE
NEW COLLEGE LANE, OXFORD

The college that gave new purpose to Oxford

The Black Death and following plagues took an exceptional toll on the clergy, exposed as they were to the bacillus when administering last rites. Whole monasteries were wiped out. This had an importance not just for religious life but civil administration, since most literate people were priests. William of Wykeham, Bishop of Winchester and Chancellor of England, set about replenishing the clergy's ranks by founding a college at Oxford to train them, and a school at Winchester* to provide students. New College had an effect even beyond that envisaged by its founder. It revitalised the university, which had been floundering, and set the pace for Oxford's later development as a seat of learning and an architectural showcase.

It is thought that Wykeham did not himself go to Oxford which was then, with Cambridge, one of only two universities in the country. His rise to power began through his love of architecture. Having been introduced to Court by one of his patrons, the then Bishop of Winchester, he oversaw some of Edward III's many building projects. His administrative genius made him indispensable. As the French chronicler Froissart wrote of his ascendancy: 'This William of Wykeham was so much in favour with the King of England, that everything was done by him, and nothing was done without him.'

Wykeham began gathering land for his college in 1369. The site lay just outside the city walls, which were incorporated into the college, on land that had been abandoned since the Black Death. By 1375 he had assembled his society of scholars. The following year, the last of Edward III's reign, Wykeham found himself overthrown by a faction wanting to dismantle recent reforms. He did not stay long in the political wilderness, being pardoned by Richard II, and in 1380 the foundation stone of New College was laid. The whole establishment, with hall, chapel, library and living quarters, was built as a piece. For the first time, fellows and students lived together in the college, rather than students being relegated to outside halls. There were exactly a hundred members, consisting of Warden, seventy fellows, chaplains, clerks and choirboys. With his superb administrative mind, Wykeham drew up statutes for both New College and Winchester College, setting out the regimes in detail, including the punishments that should be imposed for quarrelling. He died in 1404, leaving behind him many fine buildings, especially those of the Perpendicular style that he had helped establish.

*See Winchester College, page 101

MARTYRS' MEMORIAL
ST GILES' STREET, OXFORD

'We shall this day light such a candle'

On 16 October 1555, Thomas Cranmer, the first Protestant Archbishop of Canterbury, looked down from the roof of his prison near Oxford's North Gate to see two great pyres of wood. They had been prepared for the two divines who had been sharing the prison with him. After Roman Catholic Queen Mary had succeeded the fiercely Protestant boy-king Edward VI, she determined to rid herself of the most prominent churchmen of the previous reign. Dr Nicholas Ridley, the Bishop of London, walked out, wearing a bishop's black gown trimmed with fur. He was followed by seventy-year-old Hugh Latimer, once Anne Boleyn's chaplain and Bishop of Worcester, a sorrier sight in worn garments and a shroud. Ridley's pyre was lit first. Seeing the flaming brand, Latimer called out: 'Be of good comfort, Mr Ridley, and play the man; we shall this day light such a candle by God's grace in England as I trust never shall be put out.' Latimer died comparatively quickly. The green sticks of Ridley's fire, however, would not burn properly, and the agony of his death was only ended when he fell down and the flames reached a bag of gunpowder that had been tied around his neck.

It was not long before Cranmer shared their fate. He had been instrumental in forwarding the divorce of Catherine of Aragon, Mary's mother, from Henry VIII, and had officiated at his subsequent wedding to Anne Boleyn. After the Reformation, he introduced the *Book of Common Prayer**, providing a service book in English that everyone would use, and establishing a liturgy for the Church of England. He was not, however, a man of unimpeachable principle.

When, before the break with Rome, he first became Archbishop of Canterbury, he had been forced to hide the fact that he was married. During his imprisonment, he was persuaded to recant on his Protestant principles. When he realised that this would not save him from the stake, he resolved to thrust his right hand, with which he had signed the papers, into the flames first, to punish it. With that gesture he defeated Mary's hope of quashing the English Reformation. Although 'Bloody' Mary went on to burn another 400 heretics during her brief reign, the majestic language of the *Book of Common Prayer* became part of the shared heritage of worshippers for over four centuries.

In the Victorian period, a Martyrs' Memorial – modelled on the Eleanor Cross (see page 323) at Waltham in Essex which, ironically, had been erected during the great age of Catholic faith – was put up in St Giles'. The actual place of martyrdom lay outside the city walls, on what is now Broad Street. It is marked by a cross in the surface of the road.

*See Cranmer's Tower, page 153

OXFORD BOTANIC GARDEN HIGH STREET, OXFORD
Oldest physic garden in Britain

In 1621, Henry Danvers, Earl of Danby, gave the University of Oxford £5,000 to establish a physic garden, now the oldest in the country. This gift was in memory of his time at Christ Church. The purpose of a physic garden was to explore the medicinal properties of plants, for the 'glorification of God and the furtherance of learning'. It was an exciting time for botany. The age of the Tradescants, with their plant-hunting expeditions, was dawning. Unknown plants such as the potato were arriving from the American colonies and other newly mapped parts of the world.

Perhaps Danvers did not pay enough attention to his gift following the grand inauguration since very little was done, horticulturally anyway, during the next two decades. By 1633 the benefaction had been exhausted in building grand walls and gates. In 1642, a curator, Jacob Bobart, was appointed, but even then the University was not able to pay his salary. This was the first year of the Civil War, during which Oxford became the Royalist capital, and the University had other calls on its money. Bobart made a living from market gardening. Nevertheless, it says much for the quality of the man that by 1648 he was able to publish the garden's first catalogue of plants. Over three and a half centuries later, the walls that were built at such great expense are regarded as the perfect support for plants from every corner of the world.

ASHMOLEAN MUSEUM

BEAUMONT STREET, OXFORD

Britain's oldest museum

In 1626, John Tradescant the Elder assembled a museum, known as the Ark, in Lambeth on London's south bank. Tradescant had served a succession of grand masters, starting with Robert Cecil, 1st Earl of Salisbury at Hatfield House (see page 220) and ending with the royal favourite, George Villiers, 1st Duke of Buckingham, before Charles I made him Keeper of His Majesty's Gardens, Vines and Silkworms at Oatlands Palace in Surrey. These employments allowed him to scour Europe for rare plants. At the time of his death in 1638, his son, known as John Tradescant the Younger, was on a plant-hunting expedition in Virginia, but his interest was not only confined to flora and soon the Ark contained an extraordinary assortment of curiosities – armour, stuffed animals, shells, cups made of rhinoceros horn, Henry VIII's stirrups, the costume worn by Henrietta Maria's dwarf during court masks, and what was reputed to be a phoenix wing. Unlike an aristocratic cabinet of curiosities, it could be visited by the public for a fee.

In 1634, John the Elder published a *Catalogue of Plants*, listing those to be found growing in his Lambeth garden, and featuring many curiosities that he had obtained on his travels abroad. John the Younger extended this list in 1656, which he called *Musaeum Tradescantianum*, the publication of which was underwritten by Elias Ashmole. It is considered to be the earliest museum catalogue in Britain.

Ashmole, a fervent Royalist, was at that time under-employed. He trained as an attorney and obtained, in Civil War Oxford, a commission as one of Charles I's Gentlemen of the Ordnance, chosen perhaps because of his study of mathematics. At the Restoration, his loyalty was rewarded with the position of Comptroller of the Excise. One of the many curious branches of knowledge in which he excelled was heraldry and genealogy, resulting in his being appointed Windsor Herald. He not only financed the Tradescant catalogue but also helped compile it.

Tradescant the Younger was so grateful to Ashmole for his help with the catalogue that he gave the collection to him. Later, Tradescant had second thoughts about his largesse, and in his will, he attempted to bequeath the Ark to his wife instead. On her husband's death in 1662, she duly disputed the gift to Ashmole. After a legal battle, Ashmole retained the collection, which he donated to Oxford University. In 1678, a building in Broad Street (where the Museum of the History of Science is now) was commissioned to house it, and the Duke of York, later James II, opened it in 1683. The Ashmolean – although half a century younger than Tradescant's Ark – is the oldest surviving museum in the country. The collection was later rehoused in the present museum building in Beaumont Street, which was completed by C. R. Cockerell in 1845.

UNIVERSITY CHURCH OF ST MARY

Newman and the Oxford Movement

On 14 July 1833, the poet, scholar and priest John Keble mounted the pulpit of St Mary, the University Church in Oxford, and preached a sermon about the number of bishops in Ireland. He was outraged at government proposals to reduce them, which implied that the Church of England could be treated as a mere branch of the state. The whole country found itself in a condition of 'national apostasy'. According to the vicar of St Mary's, John Henry Newman, this sermon lit the rocket that was to soar heavenwards as the Oxford Movement. At a time of spiritual and social change, following the passing of the Catholic Emancipation and Reform Acts, the Oxford Movement sought to rescue the Church of England from doctrinal torpor, while enriching its liturgy and opposing state interference. It was to become the dominant spiritual influence of the Victorian period, surviving in the Anglo-Catholic wing of modern Anglicanism.

St Mary's had been party to some most significant moments in the Church of England's history including, in 1555, the trials of the Protestant martyrs, Latimer, Ridley and Cranmer* while, two centuries later in the 1740s, John Wesley, a fellow of Lincoln, had preached sermons that went perilously close to the bone of the university establishment. In 1827, the year before Newman's arrival, the pulpit had been renewed and a gallery built, thereby providing an ideal theatre for the brilliant and persuasive young churchman. Matthew Arnold later recalled 'the charm of that spiritual apparition, gliding in the dim afternoon light through the aisles of St Mary's, rising into the pulpit, and then, in the most entrancing of voices breaking the silence with words and thoughts which were a religious movement, subtle, sweet, mournful'. Although Keble had preached the 'Apostasy' sermon, it was Newman who became the Oxford Movement's prime mover, a role he felt called to perform after recovering from a desperate illness in Sicily: why else had he been spared death if not to perform a great task? The ideas of Newman and his circle were disseminated through a series of ninety 'Tracts for the Times' (hence the word Tractarian to describe Victorian High Churchmanship).

In 1845, Newman, then aged forty-four, shook Victorian society to its foundations by leaving the Church of England for the Church of Rome. Twenty years later, he wrote his poem *The Dream of Gerontius* whose words were later set to music by Edward Elgar (see page 331). Pope Leo XIII obviously approved of Newman since he made him a cardinal in 1879. Newman lived and worked in Birmingham for the rest of his life.

*See Martyrs' Memorial, page 229

MUSEUM OF NATURAL HISTORY PARKS ROAD, OXFORD

Bishop Wilberforce and Professor Huxley debate natural selection

One of the pivotal events of the Victorian era took place in the (then) Oxford Museum on 30 June 1860. The witty, conservative Bishop Samuel Wilberforce, supported by the clergy of the diocese, debated Charles Darwin's newly published *On the Origin of Species** with the scientist Professor Thomas Huxley. Whatever the practical consequences, this set-piece battle between the two dominant forces of Victorian Britain – religion and scientific discovery – appears, with hindsight, a turning point of the age.

The setting was appropriate. The just completed Oxford University Museum of Natural History (as it is now known) had been built to display the University's natural history collections (zoological, entomological, geological, palaeontological and mineralogical), assembled over two centuries. It was designed on a Ruskinian programme, in which the Gothic structure of the building was ornamented with motifs exactly copied from the natural world. John Ruskin (see page 356) was a friend of Sir Henry Acland, the professor who championed the museum. A contemporary recalled how the O'Shea brothers, red-bearded stone carvers, would come back from the Botanic Garden carrying plants that would 'reappear under their chisels in the rough-hewn capitals of the pillars'. The architect Benjamin Woodward, who won the competition for the design, produced a building that was thoroughly modern; it was lit by a magnificent glass roof supported on a forest of cast-iron columns.

Wilberforce flamboyantly ridiculed the thought that he or anyone else might have an ape in his family tree. Huxley retorted that he would rather have a grandparent who was an ape than an intellectually well-endowed prelate who dissembled the truth. With his phalanx of clergymen, all wearing their white clerical collars, lady supporters waving white handkerchiefs, and anti-intellectual undergraduates calling insults from the back, Wilberforce may not have been comprehensively demolished as some later accounts portrayed, but it was, of course, the Huxley camp which eventually won the campaign. Before long, even John Ruskin's religious faith had been shaken by the geologists' hammers, revealing the working of evolution through the fossil record.

*See Down House, page 67

CHRIST CHURCH

The inspiration for Alice

In February 1856, Henry Liddell, Dean of Christ Church, moved into the deanery of Oxford's grandest college. Christ Church had been founded by Cardinal Wolsey (see page 328), and although only partially completed at the time of his disgrace, the scale of his vision can be seen from the fact that Henry VIII subsequently ordered that his unfinished chapel should become the cathedral of the new diocese of Oxford. Even then, it was on a far smaller scale than Wolsey had intended. Later generations of fellows did their best to live up to their founder's ambitions, commissioning Christopher Wren to complete Tom Tower and assembling an incomparable picture collection. Liddell was an energetic Victorian, who took his duty of care towards the buildings seriously. Today, however, he is principally remembered for his daughters – Lorina, Alice and Edith – and their friendship with a bachelor mathematics don and amateur photographer, Charles Dodgson.

On sunny afternoons, they would take a boat on the river Cherwell, and Dodgson would invent stories for the children; he later published them, under the name of Lewis Carroll, as *Alice's Adventures in Wonderland* (1865) and *Through the Looking-Glass* (1872). Quite often, sights that they would all have known are transmuted through Carroll's imagination into the weird and haunting images that became famous around the world. They played croquet on the Liddells' lawn, beneath the gaze of their cat (in *Alice*, the game was played with flamingoes and the Cheshire Cat had a maddening habit of disappearing); they would have looked into the eel traps beside weirs (Father William, it will be remembered, balanced an eel on his nose); perhaps the elongated firedog in the Great Hall at Christ Church suggested the stalk-like extension of Alice's neck. The captivating Museum of Natural History (see page 233), with its stiffly organic architecture and natural history collections, was another favourite destination. The Dodo had a particular significance for the stuttering Do-do-Dodgson.

IFFLEY ROAD ATHLETICS TRACK

Breaking the four-minute mile

Three minutes 59.04 seconds: that was the time Roger Bannister took to run a mile at the Iffley Road Athletics Track in Oxford on 6 May 1954. No one before had run the mile in less than four minutes.

Like splitting the atom, breaking the sound barrier and landing on the moon, the four-minute mile became one of the totems of its age. Bannister stood on the cusp between the old-fashioned amateur tradition and today's world of professional super-athletes. He ran on behalf of the Amateur Athletic Association against his old university club, of which he had once been president. It was a gusty day. The crosswind was so bad that the attempt on the record was nearly called off.

Somewhat controversially, Bannister used what might have been termed pacemakers, in the form of Chris Brasher and Chris Chataway, to help him break the record. Initially, Brasher took the lead; when he began to tire, Chataway went ahead, with Bannister lengthening his stride and bursting forward in the last 200 yards. Pacemaking was strictly against the prevailing rules, but the ratifying authorities overlooked it, not least because it would have been impossible to prove. The record stood.

The crowd of 3,000 spectators did not wait to hear the time. They mobbed Bannister as soon as he had breasted the tape and collapsed exhausted into the arms of a clergyman friend. When it was realised that the record had officially been broken, pandemonium ensued and, as The Times report put it, 'What miserable spectators they would have been if they had not waved their programmes, shouted, even jumped in the air a little.'

Bannister was then a 25-year-old medical student who in time became a consultant neurologist. He returned to the track on 6 May 2004, to celebrate the fiftieth anniversary of the first four-minute mile: the world record then stood at three minutes 43.13 seconds.

THE HOOVER FACTORY　　　　　　　　*PERIVALE, MIDDLESEX*
Factory of the future

The Hoover factory is the best surviving example of a type of industrial building which, in the late 1920s and 1930s, was quite different from anything that had been built before. Hitherto, factories had been associated with smoke, grime and heavy physical labour. The Hoover factory was light, colourful, floodlit at night, set back behind lawns and rose gardens, placed prominently on one of the newly built arterial roads that sped motor traffic in and out of London. It was dedicated to the making of electrically powered, labour-saving machines, by a workforce that was largely female. It transformed a dreary workplace into a dreamland, in a style that could be readily appreciated by *habitués* of the new cinemas that brought mass entertainment to the suburbs. Like a cinema, the decorative content of Hoover and the handful of other similar new factories was confined to a few key areas; in the case of Hoover, the glamorous façade was but a sliver on one edge of a big industrial site. Travellers on the A40 (Western Avenue) are grateful for the bright white transatlantic smile that it brings to the otherwise drab face of Perivale.

Three events came together to produce the factories that, in addition to

Hoover (vacuum cleaners), were built for Gillette (razor-blades), Firestone (tyres) and Coty (cosmetics) all on the Great West Road, Wrigley (chewing gum) in Wembley, and other pillars of inter-war consumerism. The first was the formation of the architectural practice Wallis, Gilbert & Partners in 1916. To do this, Thomas Wallis (nothing is now known of Gilbert, if he existed) abandoned his previous *métier* as a hack architect of government buildings in order to represent the American company, Trussed Concrete Steel, in Britain. During the First World War, steel and timber were in short supply; concrete, however, was readily available, and when reinforced with steel rods provided a new building material that was particularly suited to large industrial sheds.

The second development was associated with the 1925 Exposition des Arts Décoratifs in Paris: the catalyst of the Art Deco style. Wallis had already evolved an Egyptian idiom for his factory architecture: in the late 1920s the veneer of ornament became vibrant, jazzy and modern. The third event was the Tariff Act of 1927, which imposed a tax of 33 per cent on goods manufactured outside the British Empire. This persuaded foreign companies to open manufacturing operations in the United Kingdom. Generally, these companies were American, and as such they brought with them transatlantic attitudes to efficiency and advertising. Factories such as Hoover became landmarks, whose architecture proclaimed not only the modernity of their products but the up-to-date working practices by which they were made.

It was already 1931, however, and late in the day for such quick-and-easy flamboyance: the gloom of the deepening recession joined with the architectural puritanism of the Modern Movement to kill it off. Official taste had not sufficiently caught up with the Firestone factory – Wallis, Gilbert's masterpiece – to prevent its outrageous demolition in 1980. Happily, that act of vandalism alerted the authorities and the Hoover factory, or at least its façade, was saved and survives as a vast supermarket – still, therefore, a temple of consumerism, although now on the demand as opposed to the supply side of the economy.

READING GAOL BERKSHIRE

Where Oscar Wilde was imprisoned for sodomy

On 21 November 1895, at about two o'clock in the afternoon, passengers at Clapham railway station saw the forlorn figure of a convict, waiting in handcuffs. A crowd formed to jeer at the prisoner. Six months earlier, an indignant judge had been sorry that the maximum sentence he was allowed to impose for the crime of sodomy was only two years' hard labour. The prisoner was Oscar Wilde, en route to Reading Gaol.

Wilde, the son of literary parents in Dublin, had fascinated London with his wit since moving there in 1878. Success came with *Lady Windermere's Fan*, only three years before his trial. But a few months before his arrest, *An Ideal Husband* and *The Importance of Being Earnest* had opened to audiences that included the Prime Minister and the Prince of Wales. Unfortunately, his appetite for fame got the better of his genius as a writer, and he precipitated his own downfall by suing the Marquis of Queensberry, father of his lover Lord Alfred Douglas, for libel; the loss of that action made criminal proceedings inevitable.

Redbrick, castellated and easily visible from passing railway trains, Reading Gaol, now Reading Young Offenders Centre, was a model prison, built on the panopticon principle (with radiating wings, so that the whole prison could theoretically be surveyed from a central observation point) in the 1840s. It offered a milder regime than Wandsworth Prison, where Wilde had served the first part of his sentence. There he had suffered from dysentery, been made bankrupt and had become severely depressed. However, talking to other prisoners was banned at Reading so the greatest wit of his age was stifled. A couple of months after his release from Reading in 1897, Wilde composed *The Ballad of Reading Gaol*. He wrote nothing else until his death three years later, penniless, in a Paris hotel, aged forty-six.

THE RIDGEWAY
FROM AVEBURY TO IVINGHOE BEACON
Possibly Europe's oldest road

It is said that the Ridgeway is Europe's oldest road. Unlike the younger Icknield Way, the meaning of whose name has been lost, it is exactly how you would think it to be: a track along a ridge. What is known today as The Ridgeway covers a distance of ninety miles. The thread is picked up near Avebury in Wiltshire; then, having crossed the Thames at Goring in Berkshire, it is lost again around Ivinghoe Beacon in Buckinghamshire. Originally the Ridgeway, with its web of connecting paths, would have given access to central England, starting from somewhere around Lyme Regis, and running for 250 miles to the Wash. The line taken – a broad line, for the path is at times over 100ft wide – runs along the crest of the chalk downs, a route chosen for safety more than convenience, since there is often no source of water for miles.

The people of the Old Stone Age walked this way before Britain had become an island. This was the road that later, about 4000BC, allowed Neolithic settlers from what had become the Continent, people who knew about growing crops and grazing animals, to penetrate England and replace the indigenous hunters. The track runs through a landscape crowded with the monuments left by their descendants: great standing stones (the vast circle of Avebury is not far away); immense earthworks such as Silbury Hill, also nearby; Neolithic burial chambers such as Wayland's Smithy; and those totemic lines etched into the chalk of the hillside that form the White Horse of Uffington (see page 247).

'It is not a farm track: you may walk for twenty miles along it over the hills: neither is it the King's highway,' wrote Richard Jefferies in 1879. 'Plough and harrow press hard on the ancient track, and yet dare not encroach upon it.' Since Jefferies' day, the demands of modern agriculture have become still more rigorous, and yet miraculously it has not been ploughed up. In recent years, the worst damage has been inflicted by off-road vehicles.

The Ridgeway was designated a National Trail by the Countryside Commission (now the Countryside Agency) in 1973.

See also The Fosse Way, page 321

RUNNYMEDE
King John signs Magna Carta

NEAR WINDSOR, BERKSHIRE

In spring 1215, King John* and his barons assembled on a broad meadow called Runnymede. It lay beside the Thames, midway between the King's stronghold of Windsor Castle and Staines, where the barons had gathered. The name, derived from the Saxon words for 'taking council' and 'meadow', implies that it must have been a traditional meeting place; while the ground was low-lying and apt to flood, it offered a broad plain on which tents could be erected and retinues could mill around. Here, John put his seal to a charter that was intended to end the civil war that had come to add itself to the many troubles of his reign.

John came to power on the death of his brother Richard I in 1199. John's nephew Arthur might have had a better claim, and when Arthur suggested it, John had him murdered – or even did the deed himself. He fell out with the Pope over the appointment of Stephen Langton as Archbishop of Canterbury, an argument which the Pope comprehensively won. While John was successful in subduing the Welsh, Scots and Irish, the province of Normandy – which had been part of the kingdom since the arrival of William the Conqueror – was disaffected, and with resources deployed around so many borders he was unable to prevent it from being seized by the King of France. At home, he did little to endear himself to his barons; he did not promote them to high offices at Court, and he was apt to be unsafe with their wives. They pressed him to restore the balance of the feudal society in which all parties operated: when he refused, they compelled him to do so. Magna Carta – the great charter – was the result.

King John's Magna Carta was very far from a bill of rights. Most of it concerns technicalities of feudal law, and there are no grand statements about constitutional liberty. However, it did establish that not even the King was above the law, and in a last-minute change in drafting, the charter was made to apply to any 'liber homo', as opposed to any baron. By extending its protection to every free man, it implied a new degree of equality under the law. Shortly afterwards, John persuaded the Pope – to whom he now paid tribute – to annul it, whereupon the barons rose against him, calling over the Dauphin from France to help them. When John died in 1216, his fortunes were at a low ebb. The struggle was inherited by his son, Henry III, then only nine. During his reign, a more comprehensive Magna Carta was sealed, and this is the one that has been so often quoted by lawyers.

*See Dover Castle, page 66, and Cross Keys Wash, page 267

ST ALBANS CATHEDRAL
HERTFORDSHIRE

The first British saint

In the middle of the 3rd century AD, a Christian called Amphibalus was attempting to flee from *Verulamium*, present-day St Albans. He was being persecuted for his faith, and had to hide from the authorities. A romanised Briton called Alban took him in. He wrapped him in his cloak, which would have been recognised and therefore unchallenged by the guards, and told him to slip out of the city. Before Amphibalus left, however, Alban, who had been impressed by the man's prayers and devotion, converted to Christianity himself. When the soldiers discovered that Amphibalus had gone, they arrested Alban instead. He was tried and sentenced to execution. On the hill where Alban died, a shrine was erected to him. The Saxon King Offa (see page 428), who ruled all England south of the river Humber, endowed a monastery on the site in 795, and persuaded the Pope to canonise Alban. He did so, giving St Alban the distinction of being the first British saint. In 1077, Paul of Caen began the work of rebuilding Offa's church, using the old Roman brick from the abandoned Roman city of *Verulamium*. His tower, transepts, presbytery and part of his nave survive in the present cathedral.

The cult of St Alban grew apace. A shrine was built to house his bones at the beginning of the 14th century. Pilgrims left so many rich tributes that, in about 1400, a watching loft, or timber gallery, was constructed beside it so that the monks could keep an eye on the treasure. The shrine was torn down and used as building stone after Henry VIII's Dissolution of the Monasteries (see page 133). In 1872, however, Sir (George) Gilbert Scott, who was responsible for restoring the cathedral, managed to reassemble it. Made of grey Purbeck marble, it is decorated with crockets, foliage, angels and scenes of the saint's martyrdom.

FIRST BATTLE OF ST ALBANS

Street fight that opened the Wars of the Roses

When Henry V died in 1422, his son, Henry VI, was only a few months old. Not only did a long minority stretch ahead, but he grew up to be simple, inheriting a strain of madness from his maternal grandfather, Charles VI (the Foolish) of France. There was a void at the heart of power, and the contending ambitions of powerful noblemen poured in to fill it. Struggling to push them out again was Henry VI's wife, Margaret of Anjou, determined to stand up for her husband's rights and her own position. She overthrew the regent, Duke Humphrey of Gloucester, who died of a stroke on what would probably have been the eve of his assassination in 1447.

In 1454, Henry VI suffered a bout of insanity, and Richard Plantagenet, Duke of York, backed by a large band of armed men, became Protector. He was a particular danger to the Queen, because he was descended from Lionel, Duke of Clarence, the second (surviving) son of Edward III, rather than, like Henry VI, John of Gaunt, Duke of Lancaster, who was Edward III's third (surviving) son. His claim to the throne was therefore stronger in law. Margaret nursed her husband back to health, and on his recovery her favourite, Edmund Beaufort, Duke of Somerset, assumed control of the government.

The following year, the King summoned a council of nobles in Leicester, from which the Duke of York and his supporters were excluded. In response, York rallied an army of 3,000 men, and came face to face with the King, Queen and Somerset at St Albans shortly after dawn on 22 April. With a force of about 2,000 men, the Court's party (Lancastrians) had dug ditches and embankments, and thrown barriers across the roads leading to the marketplace. What followed resembled a street brawl as much as a battle. In the middle of the morning, the Yorkists suddenly rushed the barriers, but were unable to get past them. Seeing this, the 26-year-old Earl of Warwick (for the Yorkists) led a detachment of 600 foot soldiers and archers to outflank the defenders. Under a hail of arrows, they stormed over the embankment, through the gardens and lanes; the fighting was over in half an hour. Although only 150 Lancastrians were killed, that figure included most of their principal commanders. For the time being, government was in the hands of the Yorkists, though they had not reckoned with Queen Margaret's strength of purpose. She and the Lancastrians fought back.

The Wars of the Roses*, as this struggle between exalted families came to be known, lasted another thirty years.

*See Battle of Wakefield, page 403; Second Battle of St Albans, page 241; Battle of Mortimer's Cross, page 332; Battle of Towton, page 402; Battle of Barnet, page 204; Battle of Tewkesbury, page 346; Battle of Bosworth, page 309

SECOND BATTLE OF ST ALBANS

Queen Margaret retrieves Henry VI from the Yorkists

King Henry VI has the reputation of being peace-loving and devout; he had none of the violent temperament needed to keep hold of the throne in the Middle Ages. Where he was weak, however, his Queen, Margaret of Anjou, was strong. In mid-February 1461 she led an army to recapture him from the Yorkists, who had seized him the previous July during the short Battle of Northampton, the third confrontation of the Wars of the Roses*.

Since Northampton, Parliament had been persuaded to appoint Richard, Duke of York, as his successor, passing over the King's son, Edward. The Queen would have none of this. She assembled an army, and York was killed at the Battle of Wakefield on 30 December 1460. This wild and ill-disciplined body of northerners, with the Queen at their head, then descended towards London. The Earl of Warwick, who had been left in charge of the capital for the Yorkists, set forth to meet them, doing so at St Albans. Six years earlier, St Albans had been the scene of a triumph for Warwick but in the rematch his leadership was less brilliant. He fortified the north-east of the town, but his scouts failed to spot the arrival of Margaret's forces; he was outflanked. Margaret recaptured the King. The way to London was now open.

Mystifyingly, she did not take it. Perhaps the presence of the King was a hindrance, causing indecision; perhaps she feared the political consequences of unleashing her unusually brutish army on the capital, which it would have sacked. Her wavering allowed Edward, Earl of March (son of Richard, Duke of York), who had won the Battle of Mortimer's Cross in Herefordshire a fortnight before, to enter London with Warwick at his side, and crown himself Edward IV. Queen Margaret hid Henry in Yorkshire until 1465, when he was captured in Ribblesdale. He spent the next five years aimlessly in the Tower of London, before Warwick, having changed sides, made a last throw of the dice on his behalf at the Battle of Barnet.

*See First Battle of St Albans, page 240; Battle of Wakefield, page 403; Battle of Mortimer's Cross, page 332; Battle of Towton, page 402; Battle of Barnet, page 204; Battle of Tewkesbury, page 346; Battle of Bosworth, page 309

SLOUGH TRADING ESTATE

Where the Mars bar came into the world

Outside the Masterfoods warehouse stand a dozen juggernauts, their sides brightly emblazoned with enormous pictures of confectionery – Bounty, Galaxy, M&Ms, Twix, Snickers, Skittles . . . These giants of the road will at any moment move off towards the nearby M4 motorway, on their mission to replenish supermarket distribution centres with sweets. There are not many other touches of colour to the Slough Trading Estate, where Masterfoods is based. Unlike the Cambridge Science Park, with its information technology and biotech industries, architecture has never been on the agenda at Slough. Established in 1920, it can, however, claim to be Britain's first industrial estate or business park, setting a trend that influenced the development of Britain's cities throughout much of the 20th century.

After the First World War, the area was simply known as The Dump, last home to 17,000 assorted vehicles for which the military had no more use. Lord Perry, who ran the British end of Ford, and Noel Mobbs bought the 600-acre site, along with the cars, trucks and motorcycles on it. The vehicles were repaired and sold to a public that was eager to get mobile: in due course, the workshops that had previously contained them became free. People wanted cheap space to rent near to London, and Perry and Mobbs quickly saw that this could form the basis of a longer-term business than that of fixing up army surplus vehicles.

Before the coming of the railway, Slough had been a coaching stop on the road between London and Bath. The best apple in the world, Cox's Orange Pippin, was raised at Colnbrook, just outside Slough's present borders, by the retired brewer Richard Cox; pursuing his hobby of horticulture in 1825, he crossed a Ribston Pippin with a Blenheim Orange. The railway arrived in 1849, and the market town was engulfed by Victorian terraces and grimy industry. By the Second World War, the poet John Betjeman had come to regard it as a synonym for everything that mass production and corporate greed had done to obliterate beauty and nature from daily life. He invoked the Luftwaffe with the famous lines: 'Come, friendly bombs, and fall on Slough! / It isn't fit for humans now.'

Ugly it may be, but the future Poet Laureate did not, perhaps, give sufficient credit to another form of sensory experience associated with Slough. The Slough Trading Estate is the birthplace of the Mars bar, invented by the American, Forrest Mars Sr, who had come to England after a quarrel with his father. An incredible three million Mars bars are now made at Masterfoods every day.

STOWE GARDENS BUCKINGHAMSHIRE
'As near an approach to Elysium as English soil and climate will permit'

When the German Prince Pückler-Muskau visited England in 1826, he told his wife that it would take her 'at least four hundred and twenty years to see all the parks of England, of which there are undoubtedly at least a hundred thousand, for they swarm in every direction'. The landscape garden, as the setting for a beautiful country house, was acknowledged to be an especially English art form – the French, for example, recognised *le jardin anglais* as an import. While Stourhead (see page 41), Rousham, Blenheim, Petworth and Castle Howard are all splendid, the most splendid of all – certainly the most important in terms of establishing the style – was Stowe. It is possible to find contemporary maps of England marked only with London, Bristol, Liverpool and Stowe.

Lord Cobham had been one of Marlborough's generals in the French wars. While Marlborough and his duchess were still urging Vanbrugh to complete Blenheim (see page 206), Cobham, coming from an immensely rich family, was able to enjoy the house built by his father in 1676–83, which he greatly enhanced. Bitter from the clash with the Prime Minister, Sir Robert Walpole, which ended his political career, he retired to his estates, to vent his frustration through gardening. Until now, fashionable gardens had been laid out in the French taste, with geometrical alleys, canals and clipped hedges. Lord Cobham was one of the first to do away with these artificialities and replace them with a sweep of open landscape dotted with clumps of trees and evocative follies: not exactly as Nature intended but more natural to look at. The inspiration behind this new style was the landscape artist turned architect, William Kent, who began to work here at some point during the 1730s; in the following decade, Stowe trained the 'Capability' of Lancelot Brown, who went on to transform dozens of gentlemen's parks around Britain.

To the poet Alexander Pope, Stowe was 'as near an approach to Elysium as English soil and climate will permit'. In due course, landowners from as far away as Russia and America were to follow Lord Cobham in their attempts to create heaven out of earth.

STRAWBERRY HILL
TWICKENHAM, MIDDLESEX

Showplace for Horace Walpole's avant-garde medievalism

Just as Lord Burlington set out to revolutionise English taste with his villa at Chiswick (see page 134), so Horace Walpole achieved – whether by accident or design – much the same effect by creating his 'little Gothick castle' at Strawberry Hill, a few miles further upstream on the Thames. Walpole was the youngest son of the Prime Minister Sir Robert Walpole, the latter a larger-than-life, corrupt, bullying country squire, who was nevertheless one of the greatest collectors of his age. Horace, effete and gossipy, was a marked contrast to his father, and Strawberry Hill, as it evolved from Walpole's purchase of an insignificant house by the Thames in 1747 until the 1790s, could hardly have been more different from Houghton Hall*. It became the foremost example of antiquarian taste, rejoicing in the quirks and curiosities of English history. As such, it was a reaction against the Italian grand masters and neo-Palladianism so beloved of his father. Rather than stun the senses with a blaze of opulence and order, Walpole wanted to intrigue the imagination with shadows, stained glass and worm-eaten wood. At Strawberry Hill, he created the first Georgian house to make a virtue of asymmetry, rather than classical balance.

To vet aesthetic progress on the house, Walpole formed a Committee of Taste, comprising the architect John Chute (who inherited The Vyne, see page 96) and Richard Bentley, son of a famous scholar. What he hoped to achieve above anything was to give visitors the creeps. As Walpole wrote in 1753: 'The armoury bespeaks the ancient chivalry of the lords of the castle and I have filled Mr Bentley's Gothic lanthorn [lantern] with painted glass which casts a most venerable gloom on the stairs that was ever seen since the days of Abelard.'

Although not remorselessly scholarly in his approach (medieval tombs, for example, were redesigned as chimneypieces), there is no doubting Walpole's thoroughness. He was obsessively fascinated by the medieval past. In its present forlorn state, the house gives no hint as to the richness and variety of Walpole's collections. Strawberry Hill was not the very earliest house to be built with pointed windows and battlements, but it quickly became the most famous (Walpole issued tickets to visitors and published guidebooks). Its influence was further disseminated through Walpole's vivacious, catty but immensely readable correspondence, filling forty-three volumes in the definitive edition.

Sadly, Walpole's 'little Gothick castle' became a considerably bigger one when the house passed to Lady Waldegrave in the mid-19th century, although at least her massive additions keep to the castellated style of the original.

*See Houghton Hall, page 274

SYON HOUSE
NEAR BRENTFORD, MIDDLESEX

The nine-day reign of Lady Jane Grey

Now a magnificent house on the bank of the Thames, Syon had once been an abbey – its name derives from Mount Zion – and at the Dissolution (see page 133) it was acquired by the Duke of Somerset who would become Lord Protector to the young Edward VI. Following Somerset's execution in 1552, the new owner of Syon was the man who replaced him in power, John Dudley, Duke of Northumberland. He was a person of overweening personal ambition, who hoped – wildly, as it turned out – that he could secure the throne for his own family. To that end, having himself failed to marry Princess Elizabeth (the future Elizabeth I, daughter of Anne Boleyn) – the obstacle being the small matter that he was already married – he arranged for his fourth son, Lord Guildford Dudley, to marry the sixteen-year-old Lady Jane Grey who, as a granddaughter of Henry VIII's sister, Mary, Duchess of Suffolk, seemed to provide another route to the throne. The marriage took place at Syon in May 1553.

A modest, well-educated girl, Lady Jane was apparently unaware that the boy king, Edward VI, dying and under pressure from the Lord Protector of England, had named her as his successor. It was feared that Mary Tudor, Henry VIII's daughter by Catherine of Aragon and nominated next in line to the throne after Edward in Henry's will, would undo the Protestant revolution, and forcibly return England to its old Roman Catholic ways. Edward VI died in early July. Northumberland has been accused of prolonging the suffering boy's life and then concealing his death in order to complete his arrangements. On 10 July, when she was told she was Queen, Lady Jane Grey was at Syon. The news came as a complete surprise to her, and she did what she could to refuse the honour. But her husband, father and father-in-law persuaded her otherwise, and a procession of barges set off for the Tower of London. It was there that she spent the rest of her nine-day reign.

Once Lady Jane knew she was Queen, or supposedly so, she played the role well. With her studious disposition, she refused attempts to have her husband made King Consort, and applied herself to the business of governing. She did not know that Mary had set out from Framlingham*, supported by the nobility and a substantial army. The band that Northumberland led out to meet Mary began to desert, as did the members of the Council as soon as they had the opportunity to leave the Tower. The end was swift and predictable. Mary, accompanied by her half-sister Elizabeth, made a joyful entry into London. Northumberland rapidly converted to Roman Catholicism but was beheaded all the same. Lord Guildford Dudley met the same fate. Lady Jane's life would have been spared, had it not been for the demonstrations that broke out a few months later when it was realised that Mary was going to marry the Roman Catholic King Philip II of Spain. She was beheaded on 12 February 1554 in the relative privacy of the Tower, on the lawn in front of the Chapel of St Peter ad Vincula.

*See Framlingham Castle, page 269

WADDESDON MANOR   NEAR AYLESBURY, BUCKINGHAMSHIRE
International finance and taste

In 19th-century Europe, the banking firm of N. M. Rothschild & Sons hovered between old-fashioned Jewish paternalism and progressive business internationalism. Of the founder's five sons – the five arrows represented in the family crest as clasped tightly in a fist – one went to London, one to Paris, one to Vienna and one to Naples (then Europe's third-largest city); the remaining brother stayed in Frankfurt, where the family originated. The London brother, Nathan, was able to organise, through his brothers on the Continent, shipments of gold to finance Wellington's army in the Peninsula; this and other transactions had to be carried out in absolute secrecy, which the family bond ensured. Nathan's eldest daughter, Evelina, married her cousin, Ferdinand, son of the Viennese Rothschild. They lived in Piccadilly, Ferdinand having no capital until he inherited after his father's death. Evelina died in childbirth, as did the baby; Ferdinand, an inconsolable, poorly, childless widower, went on to build Waddesdon Manor, in the style of a château on the Loire.

There were once forty Rothschild houses across Europe, furnished with a consistency that gave rise to the term le goût Rothschild. Waddesdon, begun in 1874, is one of the very few that remain intact. Like the others, it is rich in taste, luxurious, panelled with French boiseries and filled with wonderful objects. The dinner plates were Sèvres, the cabinets Boulle, the desk ornaments Meissen, the tapestries Gobelin, Baron Ferdinand's smoking room – the inner sanctum – was filled with princely Limoges enamels, engraved crystal cups and what he believed to be Renaissance jewels. As a family, the Rothschilds possessed what can only be described as a genetic urge to collect beautiful, usually French works of art, sometimes even bidding against each other for the same piece.

Waddesdon was created for Baron Ferdinand and his small circle of friends to enjoy. It was extremely comfortable, and the people who visited were very grand. However, the host who gave these Saturday-to-Mondays was, underneath, a lonely and far from merry individual. He had no interest in the family bank. Although he employed a superb French cook, he himself would only eat toast; he never touched wine. What he liked to call self-deprecatingly his gimcracks – the precious objects that had once been made for princes and kings – probably gave him more pleasure than anything else.

WEST WYCOMBE PARK
BUCKINGHAMSHIRE
Debauchery and dressing-up at the Hell-Fire Club

Improvement was a constant theme of the 18th century, when figures such as Dr Johnson and Lord Chesterfield wanted to reform manners, institutions, even the English language along rational, Christian lines. The occupant of West Wycombe Park, Sir Francis Dashwood, was the obverse of that trend. With fellow members of the Hell-Fire Club, otherwise known as the Friars of St Francis of Wycombe, he delighted in satanic rituals and ostentatious misbehaviour. Although Dashwood rose to become Chancellor of the Exchequer, among other posts, it is as though, having inherited West Wycombe when he was sixteen, he never properly grew up.

Like other rich young men, Sir Francis went on a Grand Tour, and it may have been in Venice that his interest in the black arts was aroused. On coming home in 1735, he employed Nicholas Revett, a pioneer of the Greek Revival, to refashion the house he had inherited. The Milanese painter Giuseppe Borgnis, whom Sir Francis had brought home along with a collection of Italian works of art, adorned the interior with some faintly indecorous frescoes. The garden was laid out in the form of a female body, with suggestively placed thickets, streams and mounds. Follies, statues and inscriptions enriched the conceit: later, they were cleansed of the worst excesses when Humphry Repton naturalised the landscape, although several of Dashwood's follies survive, and a Temple of Venus was built by Quinlan Terry in 1982.

From 1752, Dashwood rented Medmenham, the ruins of a Cistercian abbey on the Thames, as an appropriately venerable setting for the Friars' ceremonies. There had been other Hell-Fire Clubs earlier in the 18th century, as well as blasphemous rakes. None, however, took their sacrilege to the lengths of the Friars, who dressed in robes and performed elaborate anti-Christian rites, which ended in drunken orgies. The participants were men in middle age, some being prominent public figures. Dashwood himself was a man of culture and taste, whose prurient obsessions, although adolescent, prefigure the Romantic Movement. After a dozen years, public scandal drove the Friars from Medmenham to some underground caverns on his estate, once used by early man but enlarged when Sir Francis extracted chalk for road building.

Paradoxically, Sir Francis also rebuilt the medieval church for the village, turning it into an eye-catcher to be seen from the house. It was designed in a sumptuous Palladian style, and surmounted by a large golden ball. Inside the ball, 100ft above the ground, is a room with a bench: what Sir Francis did there can only be imagined.

THE WHITE HORSE

Oldest figure carved into England's chalk downland

The White Horse at Uffington is the oldest of the figures scoured into chalk hillsides in Britain. The purpose of these figures, which are special to the downland of southern England, is unknown: many of them, like the one at Uffington, are of horses, particularly mares. Recently, the Oxford Archaeology Unit found that the Uffington White Horse could be 3,000 years old. The ancient path known as The Ridgeway (see page 237) runs along the crest of the hill, and there is a Saxon hill fort nearby. A scoop-out of the downs is called the Manger, supposedly where the horse feeds.

It must have taken a Picasso to draw the horse, abstracting its flowing yet disjointed lines to the bare minimum. The result is a kind of hieroglyph. Like the horses to be seen around Lambourn a few miles away, it is shown as a racing Thoroughbred, although originally it may not have been quite so svelte: horses in the Bronze Age must have been stockier.

The lines are not etched directly onto the chalk, which could have been made simply by removing the turf: they are trenches that have then been filled with chalk. On a hot day in early summer, skylarks sing overhead and little blue butterflies dance over the sward; with the wide panorama of the Oxfordshire plain stretching below, man, horse and hillside seem in harmony. But to view the design of the horse – which is 374ft long, on a steep escarpment – there is little advantage in getting up close. Between Fernham and Longcot on the B4508 is as good a place from which to see it as any.

WINDSOR CASTLE BERKSHIRE
Chivalry and romance of England's greatest royal castle

Long before the building of the M4, which made the silhouette of Windsor Castle common currency to millions of passing motorists, the castle had been re-awoken from its post-medieval sleep by Charles II. His memory survives in the Long Walk, the grandest of Baroque avenues in Britain, stretching three miles across the parkland beyond the castle's walls. For a king who delighted in amorous intrigue, Windsor represented a welcome respite from the hugger-mugger Court at Whitehall. Here he could pursue his dalliances in a degree of seclusion – with the Duchess of Portsmouth in an apartment immediately below his own, and with Nell Gwyn occupying a house, with the royal bastards, at the bottom of the hill.

However, it took a very different monarch – the single-mindedly uxorious George III, with his string of daughters and an embarrassment of wayward sons – to turn it into a domestic centre. He renovated the Queen's Lodge, a now-demolished house such as any of his more prosperous subjects might have inhabited, and it was here, with the castle not far away, that he and the Queen lived when they were at Windsor. From the onset of his last period of so-called madness in 1811 until his death in 1820, he was confined to his apartments in Windsor Castle, alternately storming about or playing fragments of Handel on the harpsichord.

George IV loved the romance of chivalry. He employed Jeffry Wyatt, who changed his name to the more picturesque Wyatville, to reshape Windsor, making it even more the image of a castle than it was. Battlements were crenellated and machicolated, windows were Gothicised, bay and oriel windows made to project, the Norman Round Tower was built up by another 35ft. Following Waterloo, it became a symbol of national pride.

Inside, Wyatville remodelled St George's Hall (destroyed by fire in 1992 and rebuilt to a different design) as a setting for the Garter Feasts that had been reinstituted by George III during the Napoleonic Wars. With tall Gothic windows and a ceiling emblazoned with the shields of Garter Knights*, it was broadly medieval. The other reception rooms, opulently gilded, satisfied the King's taste for costly French decoration, full of marble, bronze, expensive craftsmanship and fine furniture.

George IV had only two years in which to enjoy them before he died. 'My dear boy, this is death,' he cried on 26 June 1830, his hand in that of his doctor. A few minutes later he had indeed died. The scene took place, appropriately, in the King's new apartments at Windsor Castle, the great icon of the British monarchy that he had done more than anyone since the medieval kings to shape.

Whatever Queen Victoria may have thought of her extravagant, gouty, risible but warmly human uncle, she became the monarch most closely associated – particularly in her long years of widowhood – with the castle he had remodelled, and which she hardly changed.

*See St George's Chapel, below

ST GEORGE'S CHAPEL · WINDSOR, BERKSHIRE
The ultimate in Christian chivalry

The Order of the Garter appears to have originated during Edward III's campaign in France, the high point of which was the Battle of Crécy. In 1348, the year after his return, he instituted the fellowship of twenty-five knights, all of whom had fought with him. The English battle cry, as it remained for hundreds of years, was 'St George', the patron saint of soldiers who was also adopted as the patron saint of England. St George features prominently in the iconography of the Order. The symbolism of the garter is more opaque. It is said to have been inspired by an episode while the King was dancing with Joan, Countess of Salisbury: when her garter slipped to the floor, the King fastened it to his own leg with the words of the Order's motto 'Honi soit qui mal y pense' (May disgrace come to anyone who thinks badly of it). This is probably a fable. Before he left for France, Edward promised his knights he would create a Round Table to emulate that of King Arthur, big enough to seat three hundred knights (see page 99). Can it be that the garter, similarly shaped, was conceived as a more intimate emblem of confraternity, as befitted the much smaller band of knights that finally evolved? Who knows? Like other aspects of chivalry, and indeed monarchy itself, the Order derives some of its hold over susceptibly disposed imaginations from the mystery that surrounds it.

The knights met at Windsor, where Edward III built a new chapter house for them. The existing chapel was altered for the services they shared. A new room was built for them to feast in, on the site of what is now St George's Hall. Windsor Castle* predated the Order of the Garter, but the prestige of the Order became such that it influenced both the architecture of the castle and its popularity as a residence for future monarchs. As the standing of the Order grew with time, so did the arrangements provided for its ceremonies. Edward IV began to rebuild St George's Chapel as the supreme expression of the late medieval Perpendicular style. Perhaps he was inspired to emulate the chapel at Eton College (see page 215), built by Henry VI whose throne he usurped, just on the other side of the Thames. The chapel, with its beautiful fan vaulting, was completed by Edward's son-in-law, Henry VII, with the knights contributing towards the cost. The coats of arms that the knights applied to their stalls constitute an outstanding collection of heraldry.

The vision of chivalry represented by the Garter has beguiled many later sovereigns. From the start, the order had a ceremonial uniform of dark blue robes, the design of which was sometimes revised and elaborated. Charles I introduced the garter star, which Nelson and others wore on their coats. George IV, always one for dressing up, was swept away by the chivalric dream, of which the Garter was part. Refashioning Windsor as an image of Camelot, he remodelled St George's Hall as a richly heraldic setting for the annual Garter feasts. Queen Victoria pictured her husband, Prince Albert, as the embodiment of knightly virtues, and it is as a knight that he is depicted in his effigy in St George's Chapel.

Each year, the Knights of the Garter assemble at Windsor on 23 April, St George's Day, processing down the hill from the royal apartments to St George's Chapel for the annual service, and back up again for luncheon in the Waterloo Chamber. They embody a unique institution, admission to which has been regarded as the country's highest honour for over six centuries.

*See Windsor Castle, page 248

Eastern England

THE EAST OF ENGLAND is another country. Perhaps the Pilgrim Fathers felt this when they began the journey that eventually led them from Boston in Lincolnshire to the New World. Many of them grew up around here, and the church tower known as Boston Stump would have been the last thing they saw of the region. This is flat land, where potatoes and celery grow in the black earth of the Fens, beneath CinemaScope skies and Metro-Goldwyn-Mayer sunsets. It is good farming soil, made more productive by Thomas Coke of Holkham towards the end of the 18th century. The silence is broken by the scream of a military jet: Frank Whittle's first jet-powered aeroplane took off from RAF Cranwell in May 1941.

The Fens have shrunk, literally, thanks to drainage; the soil level has dropped. Wicken Fen, where Charles Darwin collected beetles, became the nation's first official nature reserve. Ely is no longer an island, as it was when the shadowy Saxon Hereward the Wake resisted the Conqueror. Just over two hundred years later, the Bishop of Ely founded Peterhouse, the first of the Cambridge colleges. The East of England is a region of fine towns – as though the people who built them wanted to escape from the uneventful landscape – that seem to be on the way to nowhere. Remoteness has preserved them. Lincoln, which contains not only St Hugh's spectacular cathedral but also one of the oldest surviving houses in Britain, is a jewel.

The huge skies of East Anglia gave birth to remarkable painters, among them Gainsborough, who secretly preferred landscape to high society, and Constable, who loved scudding clouds and elm trees. The Poet Laureate, Alfred Tennyson, passed his gloomy childhood in the Lincolnshire Wolds; the composer Benjamin Britten often evoked the eerie, gaunt coastline of his native Suffolk in his music. As Britten felt the mystery of the place, so surely does the visitor to some of the region's most ancient landmarks: the pocks and hummocks of the evocatively misnamed Grimes Graves (not a graveyard at all, but a prehistoric flint factory), or Sutton Hoo, where a great Saxon ship was buried. Another country? It feels like that at Boston, almost like dropping off the edge of the world.

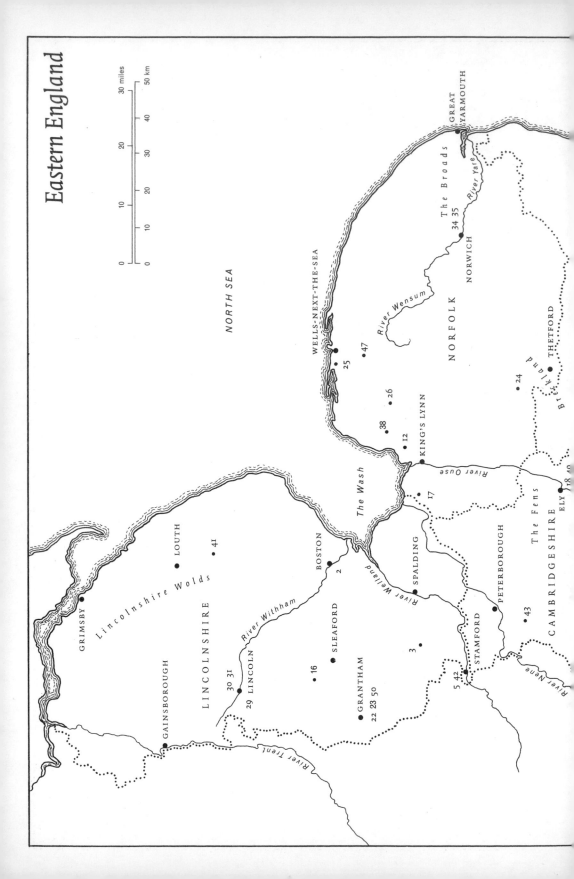

Eastern England

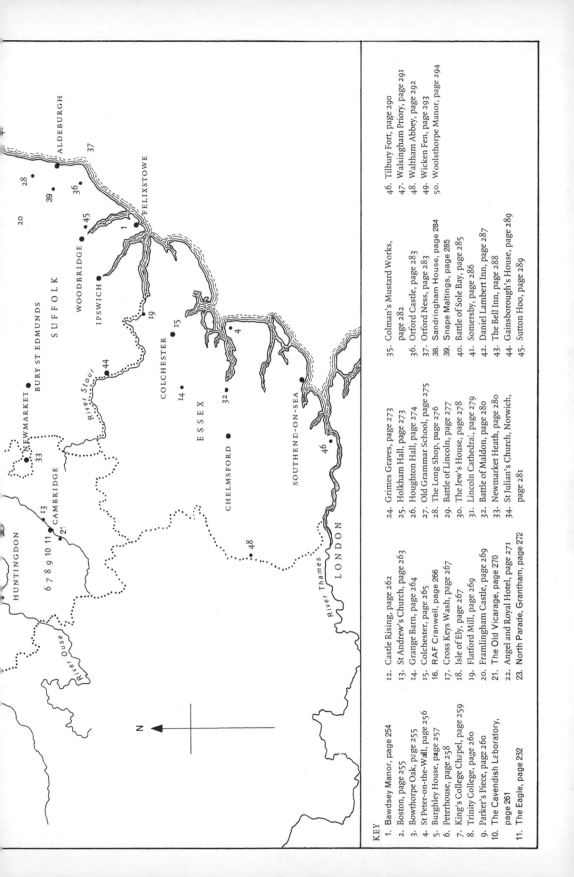

N

HUNTINGDON

NEWMARKET
CAMBRIDGE

BURY ST EDMUNDS

SUFFOLK

ALDEBURGH

WOODBRIDGE

FELIXSTOWE

IPSWICH

COLCHESTER

ESSEX

CHELMSFORD

SOUTHEND-ON-SEA

LONDON

River Ouse

River Thames

River Stour

KEY

BAWDSEY MANOR

Where radar was born

During the Blitz, the success of a certain night fighter pilot – who, it was claimed, was able to see in the dark, and who became known as 'Cats' Eyes' Cunningham – was officially attributed to eating carrots. The story was an attempt to distract enemy attention from the existence of RADAR (RAdio Detection And Ranging), developed at Bawdsey Manor in the late 1930s. Before the Second World War, the apparent invincibility of bombers was such that many people believed that London and other towns would be flattened if hostilities broke out.

In 1934, the Air Ministry seized on the idea that radio 'death rays' could be used to destroy incoming aircraft. The obvious scientist to consult was Robert Watson Watt, superintendent of the radio unit within the National Physics Laboratory. A descendant of James Watt, the pioneer of the steam engine, he had previously attempted to use radio to spot thunderstorms. Watson Watt suggested that, rather than annihilating aircraft, radio waves could be used to detect them. Beams, having bounced off the metal structure, could be picked up as they returned to earth. In February 1935, Watson Watt and his team successfully managed to demonstrate the principle in tests carried out at Daventry and Orford Ness (see page 283). Bawdsey Manor was bought to provide a base for further research.

By the start of the Battle of Britain, a chain of fifty-seven operational sites had been created along the south and east coasts. The early warning that radar provided was invaluable to the RAF, greatly outnumbered by the Luftwaffe; they were able to rest men and repair machines on the ground until an attack was imminent, rather than keeping them permanently in the skies. 'All the ascendancy of the Hurricanes and Spitfires would have been fruitless but for this system which had been devised and built before the war,' wrote Sir Winston Churchill in *The Second World War*.

Like jet aircraft and the space rocket, radar would become one of the bonuses that rapid development in wartime bestowed on post-war life. Without it, modern air travel would collapse. Magnetrons, invented by Watson-Watt in 1940 as part of an improved radar, are also the heat source in microwave cookers.

The last of the transmitter masts at Bawdsey came down in 2000, but associated structures – concrete transmitter blocks, receiver blocks and bunkers – are cared for by the Bawdsey Radar Group.

BOSTON

Gateway to the New World for the Puritans

In September 1620, a group of about 100 religious dissenters called the Pilgrim Fathers left Plymouth for the New World. Their journey had, however, begun thirteen years earlier, in Boston in eastern England. As persecuted Puritans from Gainsborough in Lincolnshire and Scrooby in Nottinghamshire, they tried to emigrate illegally to Holland in 1607. They were caught in the attempt and, for a time, some of them were imprisoned in Boston's Guildhall. They succeeded in leaving the following year. As they sailed across the North Sea, Boston Stump – as the exceptional tower of St Botolph's Church, the tallest in England, is popularly known – was the last sight that they would have had of the region where they grew up. Boston is thought to be a contraction of 'St Botolph's town', St Botolph having been a Saxon monk.

It was a name that was carried to the New World. Their spiritual leader there was John Cotton, who had been the vicar of St Botolph's. Cotton's time at the church is remembered by the pulpit – essential furniture for any Puritan divine whose services revolved around preaching rather than ritual – which he installed the year after his appointment there in 1612. Although he was greatly esteemed by his parishioners, Cotton found that by 1633 his criticism of the established church was no longer tolerated. He fled to America and joined his former parishioners – who had arrived from Plymouth in December 1620 – in Massachusetts. He is said to have landed at the settlement of Trimountain on the Charles river, which he rechristened Boston. Here he helped form the religious and civic institutions of the young colony.

BOWTHORPE OAK

Survivor of the trees that built the 'Wooden-walls'

Stupendously broad, hollow, the upper part of its trunk chained to prevent collapse, the enormous oak tree that stands on Bowthorpe Park Farm is a survivor of the millions of trees that have built Britain's houses and ships. When Henry VIII came to the throne – the Bowthorpe oak being already some 500 years old – about a third of England and Wales was covered by oak forest. Then wood was, after food, Britain's single most important resource, which all classes used for building and fuel. The mismanagement of the royal forests under the Stuarts, however, followed by the stripping of timber from landed estates under the Commonwealth, created something of a crisis for Charles II.

Ships were needed to pursue the trade wars with Holland, and nearly 4,000 trees – about 75 acres of woodland – went into every 74-gun ship-of-the-line.

The Commissioners of the Navy sought the advice of the newly formed Royal Society about the management of forests; their response was formulated by John Evelyn, who later published his opinions in *Sylva, or a Discourse on Forest Trees* (1664). According to Evelyn, nothing could more fatally threaten 'the strength of this famous and flourishing Nation, than the sensible and notorious decay of her Wooden-walls, when either through time, negligence, or other accident, the present Navy shall be worn out and impair'd'. Charles II, who had special reason to be grateful to the oak (see page 308), set about a replanting programme. Some of the trees planted then would, in due course, be harvested to build the ships that fought at Trafalgar. The shortage of oak continued to worry those most intimately concerned, however. Admiral Collingwood, Nelson's second-in-command at Trafalgar, would walk around his native Morpeth, in Northumberland, with his pockets full of acorns: by scattering them, he hoped to maintain the supply of oak for shipbuilding.

Today, the Bowthorpe Oak is a sight to stop you in your tracks. The extraordinary, gnarled girth of 42ft imbues it with a sense of mystery. It is a tree, but not as most living people have ever known one. It has been famous for centuries, and for centuries it has been decaying, hollow enough for a floor and benches to have been fitted inside in 1765. With wisps of green above, what could all too easily be taken for a cracked, carbuncular face, this venerable tree is not finished yet.

ST PETER-ON-THE-WALL BRADWELL-ON-SEA, ESSEX
The church's 'deepest living root'

In the middle of the 7th century, King Sigbert of the East Saxons was converted to Christianity by his friend King Oswy of Northumbria. Asking Oswy for missionaries to redeem his kingdom, he was sent Cedd, a monk from Lindisfarne who had recently been preaching in Mercia. Cedd came from a family of four brothers, all of whom were priests, two of them (Cedd and Chad) becoming bishops and saints. Cedd made his way by boat down the coast and landed at the old Roman fort of *Orthona* on the south side of the Blackwater estuary. This had been one of the 'Saxon Shore' forts (see page 82) which, after the Romans left, continued in use as a fishing village. Here he built a chapel and small monastery.

Originally the buildings would have been wooden, in the Celtic tradition to which Cedd belonged. However, with so much stone and Roman tiles at hand from the fort, it was soon decided to replace it with a masonry structure, large by Celtic standards, on the secure foundation provided by the gatehouse of the fort. This chapel still stands. As Britain's oldest ecclesiastical building of its size, it forms, as the guidebook evocatively describes it, 'the deepest living root of the church in this country'.

Although this is Essex, it is a remote spot, where skylarks sing overhead and waders pick their way across the saltmarsh and mudflats. Mysticism and an affinity with nature were characteristics of the Celtic church. This, however, was to lose ground to the Roman tradition, on which Canterbury was based, at the Synod of Whitby*. Cedd was present at Whitby, acting as an interpreter. By now, St Peter's was sufficiently independent for him to found another monastery in Yorkshire. It was here, at Lastingham, that Cedd died of plague, in the year of the Synod, 664. Thirty monks from St Peter's went to visit the sick man. They also caught the plague, and all but one of them died.

*See Whitby Abbey, page 404

BURGHLEY HOUSE NEAR STAMFORD, LINCOLNSHIRE
Prodigy house built by the ruthless Lord Burghley

William Cecil was indispensable. He was the son of a courtier, Richard Cyssell of Burghley, near Stamford, who rose to be Henry VIII's Groom of the Robes and Constable of Warwick Castle. In the portraits of his older years, William, dressed always in dark colours if not black, his head plated on a stiff ruff, hardly looks like a romantic; but as a young man he had married for love, rather than fortune. His father was infuriated – but since Mrs Cecil died almost immediately his prospects were unimpaired. He went to London, studied law and married again. His second wife was the daughter of the young King Edward VI's preceptor, or governor, and this connection introduced him to the innermost circle of power. He was taken up by the Lord Protector Somerset, nearly killed at the Battle of Pinkie Cleugh (at which the Scots army was routed near Edinburgh), and for three months found himself in the Tower when Somerset fell from grace.

However, he was too useful to stay in the wilderness for long. His administrative genius and his natural loyalty were a winning combination for each of the three children of Henry VIII. For nearly fifty years, he enjoyed an unrivalled position of power. When Elizabeth I came to the throne in 1558, she appointed Cecil as her secretary; and in 1572, he became her Lord High Treasurer of England.

By now he had been created Lord Burghley, declaring that he was the 'poorest peer in England'. Although he had inherited two fortunes, from his father and his father-in-law, as well as his mother's estate at Burghley, his greatest recreation was the expensive hobby of architecture. Work on the east range of Burghley House began in 1555 and continued for nine years. In 1563, Cecil bought Theobalds Manor* in Hertfordshire, creating a spectacular mansion; here and at his other house in Wimbledon he entertained the Queen on no fewer than twelve occasions, each visit costing a fabulous sum. (She went only once to Burghley, and on that occasion was prevented from staying in the house by an outbreak of smallpox.)

Lord Burghley's passion for building was such that he seems to have been his own architect. With its banks of fashionable windows, its alternately recessed and projecting elevations, its roofline of turrets and chimneystacks, the effect achieved was richness, set off by the essential Elizabethan quality of fantasy. Like Theobalds, Burghley was a declaration of pride, status and wealth – although Cecil was too worldly-wise to overstate his expenditure in public, modestly assuring guests that it was built using old foundations. Despite being ruthless in matters of state, Lord Burghley also loved music and books, was tender to children, and behaved affectionately to his family, including his dissolute eldest son Thomas (his genius for statesmanship was inherited by his second surviving son, Robert). He died, having outlived the rival courtiers of his early years, in 1598. Inevitably, given its length, his relationship with Queen Elizabeth had not been wholly untroubled: in particular, she chose to blame him for the execution of Mary Queen of Scots. But now, herself an old woman, she mourned the counsellor who had shaped her reign. It is said that in his last illness she fed him from her own hand.

*See Old Palace, Hatfield, page 220

PETERHOUSE
TRUMPINGTON STREET, CAMBRIDGE

Oldest Cambridge college

Cambridge, or a settlement thereabouts, grew up in pre-Roman times, at the point nearest the sea where the river Cam could be easily forded. Being forty miles from the Wash and on the edge of the Fens, it was a natural junction for communication, whether by water or road. By the early 13th century it was a reasonably prosperous inland port, with a smattering of religious houses. The first college, Peterhouse, was established in 1284 by Hugo de Balsham, a Benedictine monk and Bishop of Ely. He had introduced scholars into the Hospital of St John in 1280, but they moved to their present site, near the church of St Peter (now called St Mary the Less), in 1284. Two years later, when he died, he left enough money for more land to be acquired, and the hall to start being built.

The hall still exists, and is used in the same communal way as it was in the Middle Ages. Some carved mouldings and the rubble walls survive from the 13th century, although the restoration in 1870 by George Gilbert Scott – known as 'the younger' in order to differentiate him from his father, Sir (George) Gilbert Scott – with the exquisite stained glass by William Morris and the colourful stencilled decoration added in 1884, considerably heightens the aesthetic mood. The college's strongly Royalist tradition in the 17th century was expressed through the building of the Laudian chapel. It was begun before the Civil War, but its ornaments and images were destroyed as being 'popish' by the Puritans when the Master, Dr John Cosin – who was also the university's Vice Chancellor – was expelled on grounds which included his having sent the college plate to the King. He returned in triumph in 1660, to complete the chapel in what was by then an archaic Gothic style – a conscious assertion of continuity with the medieval past.

Although the earliest of Cambridge colleges, Peterhouse's innate conservatism prevented expansion, and it remains the smallest of them. Built outside the King's Ditch that formed the town boundary, it has the only deer park in Cambridge, although its inhabitants died before the Second World War, and were not replaced.

KING'S COLLEGE CHAPEL   KING'S PARADE, CAMBRIDGE
The largest fan vault in the world

Henry VII spent St George's Day, 1506 in Cambridge. His mother, Lady Margaret Beaufort, was busy refounding God's House as Christ's College, the site of God's House having been cleared as a part of Henry VI's ambitious plans for his own foundation of King's. When Henry VII celebrated the feast of St George at King's, the ceremony was held in a temporary wooden structure huddled under the soaring walls of the roofless chapel. He saw an opportunity for good works mixed with dynastic aggrandisement, and committed himself to completing the project his predecessor had started.

This involved building the largest fan vault in the world. The world, for this purpose, is England: the fan vault, an intricate lacework of stone which looks so light that it could blow away, as opposed to the structural geometry and sturdy ribs of the familiar lierne vault, was a purely English contribution to late Gothic architecture. Robert Hacumblen, the energetic Provost of King's, commissioned the master mason John Wastell to build it.

Worshippers were left in little doubt as to the patron. The antechapel is studded with Henry VII's heraldic devices: greyhounds and portcullises (Beaufort emblems), Tudor roses, dragons of Cadwallader (the Tudors were nominally Welsh), the royal coat of arms and fleurs-de-lys (English kings only formally renounced their claim to the French throne at the time of George III).

TRINITY COLLEGE TRINITY STREET, CAMBRIDGE

More Nobel Prizes than France

In 1546, King Henry VIII lay dying. Earlier in the year, he had founded a college that was intended both to exceed King's College at Cambridge and Cardinal Wolsey's Christ Church at Oxford. Cynics might say Trinity College was Henry's last attempt to reconcile himself with his conscience, before making the journey at the end of which all religious disputes are settled. More positively, it was a declaration that his reform of the Church was complete, with the creation of a centre of learning so splendid that it would vie with anything the Pope could offer. Here priests of the new Church of England could be trained.

The choice of Cambridge for his largesse was appropriate. It was to Cambridge scholars that the King had turned to provide learning that would justify his divorce with Catherine of Aragon. The influence of Erasmus, who had been Professor of Divinity, was still felt. Before the Dissolution of the Monasteries (see page 133), Cambridge had had a striking number of religious houses. Their suppression yielded land, some of which passed to Trinity, while their buildings provided stone and timber, materials that were difficult to obtain on the edge of the Fens.

Trinity was formed out of two earlier institutions, Michaelhouse and King's Hall, some of whose buildings were retained in the construction of Trinity's enormous Great Court. When completed – which was not until the reign of James I – this became the largest enclosed space in Europe. It will always be disputed whether Trinity is the most glorious of Cambridge colleges, but in time it certainly became the biggest.

PARKER'S PIECE CAMBRIDGE

Where the rules of Association Football were made

The game of football, whose origins lay in the Middle Ages when teams of any size kicked an inflated pig's bladder into their opponents' territory, desperately needed rules. Victorian England was a place of rules. Football became popular at public schools, but the tendency for each school to play a different version of the game led to difficulties when players met later at university. On Parker's Piece – the open ground where football was played at Cambridge – the confusion became too much for H. De Winton and J. C. Thring, two University footballers. In 1848, they met with representatives from the major public schools and, after an interminable meeting, drew up the first set of rules for Association Football.

Football is still played according to Cambridge Rules, although the original

Battle of Barnet, page 204. This picture of the 1471 battle at which Warwick the Kingmaker was killed does not show the fog in which it took place.

Si corp⁹ meū tradam igni caritatē autē non habeā nihil vtilitatis.&c.

Smith.

O Lord ſtrengtueachem,

Cranma

Father of heaue receiue my ſoule.

Latimer. Ridley. In man⁹ tuas domine.

M.Ridley I will re-member your ſuite.

L.Willia

Left: Martyrs' Memorial, page 229. The dourly Catholic Mary Tudor ordered the Reformers Hugh Latimer and Nicholas Ridley, and later Thomas Cranmer, to be burnt at the stake.

Right: Olney, page 226. The mentally fragile poet William Cowper, living at Olney, wrote many of the best-loved Anglican hymns.

Below: John Milton's Cottage, page 211. Milton, who finished *Paradise Lost* at the cottage in 1665, is shown being visited by fellow poet Andrew Marvell.

The Hoover Factory, page 235. Symbol of the new world of work, electrical appliances and American values that arrived in the late 1920s.

Heston Aerodrome, page 221. 30 September 1938: Prime Minister Neville Chamberlain declares that the newly signed Munich Agreement will mean 'peace for our time'.

Greenham Common, page 218. Cruise missiles arrived at the airbase in 1981, quickly followed by a camp of women peace campaigners.

Above: Cookham, page 213. *Swan Upping* by Sir Stanley Spencer shows Cookham, the village on the river Thames around which the artist's life revolved.

Left, top: Shakespeare Temple, page 219. The actor David Garrick, who restored Shakespeare to the fashionable theatre, erected this temple to the Bard's memory.

Left, below: Strawberry Hill, page 243. Horace Walpole opened his 'little Gothick castle' in Twickenham to the public, issuing tickets and providing guidebooks.

Above: Museum of Natural History, page 233. Part of Darwin's collection of crustacea. A famous debate took place here between Wilberforce and Huxley on Darwin's *On the Origin of Species*.

Opposite, above: Bowthorpe Oak, page 255. It is thought to have been 500 years old when Henry VIII came to the throne.

Opposite, below: The White Horse, page 247. It could be 3,000 years old. White horses carved into chalk are special to the downland of England.

The Old Vicarage, page 270. Rupert Brooke (seen here far right)
symbolised the golden promise of youth, killed in the First World War.

Above: Walsingham Priory, page 291. The tradition represented by this medieval pilgrim badge was revived in the late 19th century.

Left: Lincoln Cathedral, page 279. This window at Lincoln, whose cathedral was rebuilt after a supposed earthquake, shows St John the Baptist.

Left: St Andrew's Church, page 263. Olaudah Equiano's tragic story is told in his autobiography and on the tombstone of his little daughter at Chesterton.

Below: Holkham Hall, page 273. The great agriculturalist Thomas Coke inspects some of his Southdown sheep with the estate shepherds.

Flatford Mill, page 269. The Stour valley was the inspiration for one of the most English of artists, John Constable.

Burghley House, page 257. William Cecil, with a passion for architecture as well as politics, appears to have been his own architect for this house.

Tilbury Fort, page 290. In August 1588, Elizabeth I made her rallying Armada speech at the original fort; what is seen here is the 1670 replacement.

Cambridge Rules were somewhat different from their present form. It was then permissible to catch the ball, shoulder-barge opponents, and any member of the team could act as goalie when occasion demanded. These rules were revised in 1863, at a meeting which took place in the Freemasons' Tavern, Great Queen Street, London. The Football Association was born. Footballers who persisted in playing by different rules found that their game was then called rugby (see page 337).

For the time being, soccer retained some of its original gentlemanly overtones. The very word 'soccer' derives from assoc + -er (as in Association Football), following the public schoolboy's delight in diminutives such as brekker for breakfast. But a new era was dawning. The first issue of *Country Life*, published in 1897, contained an article asking whether football should go professional. In fact, professionals had been tolerated by the Football Association since 1885. In the course of the next hundred years, it became the most popular ball game in the world.

THE CAVENDISH LABORATORY
Where Rutherford split the atom

Before the Second World War, 'splitting the atom' caught the popular imagination in much the same way that supersonic flight and manned landings on the moon did after it. The feat was achieved at the Cavendish Laboratory, part of Cambridge University, in 1932 – the culmination of four decades of research by scientists, such as Ernest Rutherford, into radio waves, radiation and other phenomena that are invisible to the human eye. Rutherford and his colleagues were driven by a desire to understand how the smallest and most fundamental building blocks of life are composed. Their findings changed man's relationship with the natural world for ever.

Rutherford had first come to England from New Zealand in 1895. His work on radioactivity identified three different types of ray, which he branded with the Greek letters alpha, beta and gamma; the two former rays are made up of minute fragments of matter. By bombarding a sheet of gold foil with alpha particles, most of which passed through it, he showed that atoms do not form a solid wall; rather, they take the form of nuclei, around which electrons orbit through space in much the same way that planets do around the sun. For his work on the atom, Rutherford received the 1908 Nobel Prize for Chemistry – much to his amusement, given that he had always considered himself to be a physicist. Shortly before the First World War he was knighted, and in 1931 he was raised to the peerage.

It was under Lord Rutherford's directorship that the Cavendish Laboratory succeeded in breaking an atom into some of its constituent parts. The scientists fired alpha particles at atoms, sometimes making part of the nucleus (which Rutherford had shown to be made up of protons) split away; this was the first time that atoms had been made to disintegrate in a controlled way. By artificially turning one element into another, he unleashed the miraculous power of the atom, with all its potential to change our world for both good and ill. The laboratory moved from Free School Lane to a new site west of Cambridge in 1974.

THE EAGLE

BENET STREET, CAMBRIDGE

The structure of DNA is announced

On 28 February 1953, two young Cambridge scientists startled lunchtime drinkers at the Eagle pub by exuberantly declaring that they had discovered the 'secret of life'. They were Dr James Watson and Dr Francis Crick, who had that morning roughed out the structure of DNA (deoxyribonucleic acid) with the aid of pieces of cardboard. They published their discovery in a one-page article in the journal *Nature*. In the half-century since then, the understanding of DNA – the means by which hereditary characteristics are transmitted through the generations – has had vast implications for medicine (pinpointing the genetic component in many ailments), agriculture (with the genetic modification of food) and forensic science (thanks to DNA profiling). And yet, we know only a fraction of what there is to be discovered about DNA. It is safe to say that we are only at the beginning of a revolution that will affect human life in profound and incalculable ways.

The existence of DNA had been discovered in the Victorian period. Watson and Crick, working at the Cavendish Laboratory in Cambridge (see page 261), were able to use insights from others – notably Professor Maurice Wilkins and Dr Rosalind Franklin (who were unfortunately not on speaking terms) at King's College, London. There has been some controversy concerning the amount of credit to which Watson and Crick are entitled, stirred by the publication of Watson's book, *The Double Helix*. They and Wilkins won the Nobel Prize for 'physiology or medicine' in 1962. The cardboard model of the double helix can be seen at the Science Museum in London.

CASTLE RISING

NORFOLK

Where the 'She-Wolf of France' languished

After the horrible murder of Edward II* in 1327, his Queen, Isabella – known in later centuries as the 'She-Wolf of France' – ruled England with her lover, Roger de Mortimer, as regents during the minority of her son, Edward III. In due course, Edward III asserted his authority and had Mortimer killed, despite his mother's pleas. Her own life being spared, she withdrew to spend the rest of it far away from the centre of affairs, at Castle Rising in north Norfolk.

Castle Rising was on the way to nowhere. It controlled no river, no cross-roads, and it was not on the sea. The square Norman keep stands on the site of a Saxon hall, but there is still some mystery as to why, in 1140, William de Albini (who had married Henry I's widow, Adeliza) decided to build such a substantial castle – a smaller version of the castle at Norwich – in this seemingly unstrategic location. By the time Isabella arrived, it must have seemed hopelessly old-fashioned; she built a new set of lodgings, accessible by a stair tower, the footings of which can still be seen, and a new chapel. Brick was used in part of her new buildings, a material unheard of in other parts of the country but brought to Norfolk from Flanders.

This was not exactly a banishment. Isabella could come and go as she wished, and would visit her other castle at Pontefract in Yorkshire. Despite her liaison with Mortimer, who had probably contrived the late King's murder, Edward III did not sever relations with his mother, coming to visit her more than once. She died at Hertford in 1358.

*See Berkeley Castle, page 300, and Gloucester Cathedral, page 323

ST ANDREW'S CHURCH   CHESTERTON, CAMBRIDGESHIRE
The unhappy life of Olaudah Equiano, anti-slavery campaigner

In July 1797, a little half-caste girl – Anna Vassa, aged four – was buried in Chesterton churchyard. Black people were rarely seen anywhere in 18th-century England, and Anna would have been highly visible in her Cambridge-shire village. Mrs Vassa was a white woman from Ely, Susan Cullen, who had married the most famous African of his time, Olaudah Equiano.

Equiano also called himself Gustavus Vassa, an indication of his cultural uncertainty. As a native of the Benin coast, he had been captured and sold into slavery* at the age of ten. In 1789, he published an autobiography under the title *The Interesting Narrative of the Life of Olaudah Equiano, or Gustavus Vassa, the African, written by himself*. It told the extraordinary, sometimes heartbreaking story of his life in Barbados, in Virginia and on board different ships, as he attempted to win his freedom. Once he had succeeded in doing so, he became a seaman, before being employed to oversee stores for black settlers going to Sierra Leone. His stand against corruption earned him dismissal and vilifica-tion, although he was later vindicated. His book, almost hysterically pious at times, became a seminal text for the movement to abolish slavery. He died three months before little Anna.

Anna's story is told in the epitaph on her tombstone:

Should simple village rhymes attract thine eye,
Stranger, as thoughtfully thou passest by
Know that there lies beside this humble stone,
A child of colour haply not thine own.
Her father born of Afric's sun-burnt race,
Torn from his native fields, ah foul disgrace;
Through various toils, at length to Britain came
Espous'd, so Heaven ordain'd, an English dame.
And followed Christ: their hope two infants, dear,
But one, a hapless Orphan slumbers here.

It is possible that the other child, a son, became deputy librarian to Sir Joseph Banks at Kew (see page 76).

*See The Georgian House, page 11, and Wilberforce House, page 392

GRANGE BARN COGGESHALL, ESSEX
Timber monument to a great age of production

Medieval monastic orders were the equivalent of modern multinational corporations. From a worldly point of view, they specialised in amassing the most desirable commodity available in the Middle Ages: land. The scale of the production that this could yield is manifest in the great barns that they built, such as that at Coggeshall. The scale of this granary is as awe-inspiring as an ocean liner from the heyday of steam.

The Abbey of Coggeshall was founded in 1142 and Grange Barn, as it is known, is one of the oldest timber-framed barns in Europe. Tree-ring dating puts the earliest timbers of the barn to somewhere in the mid-13th century. Timber is not a very durable material to build with, and at some point in the later Middle Ages, around 1500, the barn was rebuilt, to take on its present form. This often happened to wooden structures, particularly utilitarian ones: two famous and very ancient barns at nearby Cressing Temple underwent the same fate. The Cressing Temple barns were erected by the Knights Templar, the order founded to protect travellers on pilgrimage (see page 188). Coggeshall Abbey was a Cistercian foundation, growing rich through the successful formula of having a body of worker monks, or lay brothers, who worked on the farms, supervised by choir monks, who were able to spare enough time from their religious duties to act as a board of directors.

The Cistercians were particularly associated with the new sheep economy that represented progressive agriculture after the Black Death. Coggeshall shows that they could be equally efficient cereal farmers. After the Dissolution of the Monasteries (see page 133), barns like Coggeshall were hardly exceeded in scale until the advent of the European Union's grain mountain, piled into vast intervention stores in the 1980s.

COLCHESTER   ESSEX
The Roman invaders' first capital

The Emperor Claudius ordered the second Roman invasion of Britain in AD43, arriving in person, with his elephants, once the fighting was all over*. It was he who led the army into what would be the capital of his new province, *Camulodunum*, present-day Colchester.

The town that he found was set on a gravelly rise overlooking the highest navigable point of the river Colne, and surrounded by earth defences. There had already been a settlement here for hundreds of years. The earthworks, some of which can still be seen, were necessary to protect the local Trinovantes from incursions made from the west. The Trinovantes, living in what is now Essex, became united with the tribes of Hertfordshire and Kent, forming a union of the south-east corner of the country. The tribe's capital was Colchester, presumably chosen because of its usefulness as a trading port, and it may have been Colchester's trade with Gaul that helped excite Roman interest in Britain. The squabbles between the tribes spilled over into Gaul, too, causing trouble there, and giving Claudius the excuse he needed to bolster his standing in Rome with a victory.

A Roman colony was established at *Camulodunum*, and settled with retired legionaries, which helped secure the region. Their first act was to raise a great temple to the deified Emperor Claudius on the hill later occupied by the Norman castle. It was perhaps an over-confident symbol of the new regime. The Iceni people of Norfolk and Suffolk had been outraged when, after the death of their king Prasutagus, the Romans flogged his widow Queen Boudicca and raped his daughters, before assuming his wealth and lands. They rebelled, the Trinovantes and other tribes joining in. While Colchester's commander was away fighting in Wales, they marched south, sacked St Albans and, in defiant mood, fell on Colchester. According to the Roman historian Tacitus, the inhabitants were totally unprepared. The town was destroyed, the inhabitants slaughtered, the temple pulled down and Claudius's capital left in smouldering ruins.

The Romans could not tolerate such a humiliation. Having repressed the Iceni with customary savagery, they rebuilt *Camulodunum*, this time with massive walls, parts of which still survive, and the imposing Balkerne Gate through which traffic passed on the three-track road for London. There were so many bricks that the Normans were later able to build their castle of nothing else. London had also been devastated by Boudicca; after the Romans rebuilt it, they designated it the country's capital. Colchester's greatest moment of Roman glory had lasted a mere seventeen years.

*See Richborough Roman Fort, page 89

RAF CRANWELL
NEAR SLEAFORD, LINCOLNSHIRE

First flight for the inventor of the jet engine

At 7.40pm on a May evening in 1941, the chief test pilot of the Gloster Aircraft Company taxied his aeroplane to the end of the runway at RAF Cranwell, opened up the engine with an unaccustomed roar and took off for a 17-minute flight. 'Frank, it flies!' gasped one of the few onlookers. 'That's what it was bloody well designed to do, wasn't it?' snapped back Frank Whittle, who had been working for fifteen hard years to fulfil his dream of an alternative to the propeller.

Whittle was born in 1907, the son of a Midlands engineer. He grew up to be so short that it was only on his third attempt, after an intensive feeding regime, that he succeeded in joining the RAF as a trainee officer and pilot, studying at RAF Cranwell. It was here that he wrote his thesis called 'Future Developments in Aircraft Design'. At a time when fighter planes could fly no faster than 150mph, with a ceiling of 10,000ft, Whittle predicted aircraft with speeds of 500mph flying at 60,000ft. He was now nineteen; he imagined that the engine which powered the new planes would be piston-driven. At the age of twenty-two, he had the inspiration which showed that the piston could become redundant. Air would be compressed and fuel ignited, but the expanding gas would not push against a piston but the casing of the engine. The working parts would be reduced from hundreds to a single turbine and compressor. Whittle was the first man to reach this conclusion.

The rest of the story, until 1939, was one of frustration, as the Air Ministry refused to see any potential in Whittle's idea. In Germany, the young Hans von Ohain, who arrived independently at a similar invention in 1933, had comparable struggles until his idea was adopted by Heinkel. A Heinkel jet got into the air in 1939 – one can only imagine what Whittle's feelings must have been. Both Germany and Britain produced jet fighters during the Second World War but afterwards leadership in technology passed to the United States. In 1976, embittered by lack of official encouragement at home, Whittle moved to the States to live. He returned to Britain to be given the Order of Merit in 1986, fifty-six years after his first patent.

CROSS KEYS WASH
NEAR SUTTON BRIDGE, LINCOLNSHIRE

Where King John lost the Crown Jewels

After signing the Magna Carta at Runnymede*, King John persuaded the Pope to annul it. This put him, once more, on bad terms with the barons, who invited the Dauphin of France to become king. John was busy marching against the King of Scotland, who saw advantage in supporting the rebellious barons, and in October 1216 he had reached Lincolnshire. He began to lead his army towards the south coast, where Dover Castle† was under siege. To do so, he rashly decided to cross the estuary of the river Nene at a point called the Cross Keys Wash. This meant negotiating a two-mile track across the sands, dry at low tide, running between the Wash House near Long Sutton and what is now the Cross Keys public house in Walpole St Andrew. It had always been treacherous. As the tide came in, it met the down-waters of the river and rose suddenly. John and his soldiers reached the other side safely, but the baggage train was sucked into the whirlpool. With it was lost the Crown Jewels.

According to the monk-chronicler Matthew Paris, the trauma of losing the jewels precipitated John's death, also brought on by the gluttonous eating of fruit – probably he suffered a burst ulcer (unless his enemies had succeeded in poisoning him). Unable to mount a horse, he was carried on a horse-litter to Newark Castle, where the Abbot of Crouton tended him. He died just after hearing that some of the disaffected barons were prepared to come onto his side. The jewels were never found. The oldest of the present Crown Jewels dates from Charles II's coronation in 1661, the previous regalia having either been pawned in Holland by Queen Henrietta Maria, on behalf of her husband Charles I, or smashed by Oliver Cromwell.

*See Runnymede, page 238. †See Dover Castle, page 66

ISLE OF ELY
CAMBRIDGESHIRE

The Saxons' last stand against Norman domination

Ely is only a dozen miles from the city of Cambridge, but even today, when the octagon of the cathedral is silhouetted against the blood-orange sunset of an immense fenland sky, it can seem isolated, spooky and remote. Until the Fens were drained by Dutch engineers in the 17th century, the slight prominence on which the city is built made it an island. Five hundred years before, this made it a refuge for one of the last Saxon leaders to stand out against William the Conqueror after 1066.

This man has come down to us as Hereward the Wake. Like the second half of Winnie-the-Pooh's name, nobody quite knows what 'the Wake' means; presumably it was intended to suggest that he was always on the qui vive against his enemies. He was, however, a real man, since his story appears in several chronicles, specifically that of John of Peterborough who applied the honorific to Hereward in the Middle Ages.

According to Charles Kingsley, who gathered together some of the legends in his novel *Hereward the Wake* (1866), Hereward was the son of a king's thane called Leofric, who held lands around Bourne in Lincolnshire; his mother apparently was Lady Godiva – or was this Kingsley's vivid imagination? Hereward was temporarily exiled from England when William invaded. He came home, about three years later, to find the family lands had been seized by Normans. His brother, having killed a couple of them who were abusing his sister, was himself slain, his severed head being stuck up over the gate of the house. Hereward entered the house in disguise, killed the remaining fourteen Normans with his own hands and put up their heads in place of his brother's. He then fled to Ely, sheltering in its abbey, which had been founded by St Etheldreda in 673. The Abbot, reckoning that he was about to be ousted by a Norman prelate, gave Hereward refuge. From here, Hereward led a raid on Peterborough Abbey to liberate its treasures before they could fall into Norman hands. They were used to pay for a Viking war band to act as mercenaries; William, however, formed an alliance with the Danish king, who recalled his men, and they sailed off with the treasure.

Hereward stayed on and, for a time, Ely became a centre of resistance. The Bishop of Durham and several hundred followers joined him there. When William sent an army against them in 1070, Hereward used his knowledge of the watery fens around the Isle of Eels to defeat them: he cunningly waited until the Norman troops were stationed on a pontoon of rafts and barges then crossed over the marsh to set fire to the pontoon, causing destruction and panic. In due course, one of the monks betrayed him, but Hereward was able to slip away – and out of the pages of history.

Even in the boggy marshes of the Fens, he was not able to delay the Norman expropriation of Saxon England by more than a couple of years. His supporters paid a heavy price. Ely, which had been the second richest abbey in the kingdom before the Conquest, was now compelled to melt down its crosses, shrines, dishes and chalices to pay the fine that the Conqueror imposed. Hereward, however, became an English folk hero.

FLATFORD MILL

Constable Country

John Constable, England's greatest painter of the domestic countryside, grew up in comfortable circumstances as the son of an East Anglian miller. The river and buildings around his father's Flatford Mill provided the subject matter for some of his best-known paintings, including *The Haywain*. The landscape that Constable knew in the early 19th century can still be recognised. The river Stour glides by the mill; the farmer Willy Lott may have left the house he spent only four nights away from in the whole of his life, but the building remains.

Constable found unending visual delight in the ordinary, worn, familiar details of the country scenes amid which he grew up. As he wrote: 'The sound of water escaping from Mill dams . . . Willows, Old rotten Banks, slimy posts, and brickwork. I love such things . . . As long as I do paint I shall never cease to paint such Places.' In today's neater, more prosperous world, the cottages of the Stour valley do not tumble down, and timber is replaced before it rots through, but by painting this pleasant, unspectacular scenery Constable made it famous, and because it is famous, it is preserved. On a summer day, under one of the perpetually changing skies that Constable studied so well, the charm of the place survives, too.

The Stour valley came to be known as Constable Country. Constable is the only British artist to have given his name to the area in which he painted; that may be because no other artist has such a broad appeal. The quiet rural scenes that he depicted represent for his countrymen an ideal of the world as it was and ought to be.

FRAMLINGHAM CASTLE

Mary Tudor regains the throne

Shortly before his death in 1553, the boy king Edward VI gave Framlingham Castle in Suffolk – a large castle, ringed by thirteen tall towers – to his half-sister Mary, then in her mid-thirties. Under the terms of their father's will, Mary was the next in line to the throne, but Edward, with all the ardour of adolescence, was a Protestant and was convinced that the obstinately Catholic Mary should not inherit the throne. In this belief he was encouraged by the Duke of Northumberland, who had seized power from other courtiers and wanted to promote his own family onto the throne, through the tenuous claims of poor Lady Jane Grey*.

In July 1553, Mary, who had been staying at Hunsdon in Hertfordshire, was summoned to the bedside of the dying Edward. Instead of complying, she fled through the night towards Framlingham where she had 'confidence in her friends'. It had the advantage of being near the coast, in case she had to escape the country altogether. It was not necessary. Noblemen and gentlemen were already making their way to her. They were joined by retainers and peasants in such numbers that before long 20,000 people were camped below the castle. The crews of seven ships that had been sent to guard the Norfolk coast came over to her side, hauling their cannons with them. Northumberland was forced to muster an army and set out for East Anglia. After he had left London, the governing Council declared for Queen Mary. Northumberland found his troops melting away, and in Cambridge he threw down his weapons.

Mary's accession was greeted with general rejoicing. By the time of her death five years later, after the loss of England's last remaining possessions in France and the religious persecution that earned her the sobriquet 'Bloody Mary', the mood had changed. Although buried in Westminster Abbey, she has no memorial.

*See Syon House, page 244

THE OLD VICARAGE
GRANTCHESTER, CAMBRIDGESHIRE
Poet who symbolised war's wastage of youth

The poet Rupert Brooke epitomises the flower of youth that was scythed down by the First World War. Born in 1887, he was so radiant in both looks and mind when he left Rugby School that Lytton Strachey pre-ordained him for membership of the secret Cambridge society of the intellectual élite known as The Apostles. In need of some quiet time in which to finish his postgraduate thesis on the Jacobean dramatist John Webster, he took rooms at The Orchard in Grantchester, a riverside cottage that was, then as now, a celebrated teashop. Solitude, if he had really sought it, was elusive, since Brooke's charisma drew constant visits from the group of friends whom the Bloomsbury Group called the neo-Pagans. One warm moonlit night, Virginia Woolf swam naked with him in Byron's Pool.

Returning from an extended visit to Munich, Brooke found new lodgings in 1910 at The Old Vicarage in Grantchester, a rambling house that had been rejected by a Victorian incumbent of the living as too small. This was to be recalled as a symbol of everything that he most loved about his homeland – open skies, unkempt hedgerows, river smells, lack of constraint – in one of the most famous poems in the English language, 'The Old Vicarage, Grantchester', composed during another visit to Germany in 1912. 'Ah God! to see the branches stir / Across the moon at Grantchester!'

His war sonnets, written in 1914, express the idealism that inspired many of his generation in the early months of the First World War; he did not live long enough to capture its true bleakness and horror, dying on a hospital ship off the Greek island of Skiros in 1915.

ANGEL AND ROYAL HOTEL   GRANTHAM, LINCOLNSHIRE
England's oldest inn?

Very few people travelled in medieval England: the perils to which a solitary individual was exposed on the lonely road were too great. Pilgrims, for whom visiting a shrine was a rare chance to see something of the country, banded together into groups, such as the one described by Chaucer in *The Canterbury Tales*. The Knights Templar, an order of warrior monks created to safeguard the passage to Jerusalem, provided a measure of protection (see page 188); the Knights Hospitallers, of which St John Ambulance is the descendant, existed to provide places of rest and care – the original 'hospitals'. These and other monastic foundations provided accommodation (free for two nights to the very poor) and owned inns.

The Angel and Royal Hotel at Grantham is one of a number of medieval inns still to offer hospitality to travellers. While the George, further south down the Great North Road (A1) at Stamford, claims to date from the 10th century, and has medieval vaulting in the cellars, the Angel, as it was originally called, is more securely documented, having entertained King John in 1209 and 1213. Originally it belonged to the Templars, then to the Hospitallers, who rebuilt it in the late 15th century. Outside, an angel supports the corbel beneath the central bay window which is set over the arch that originally led into the inn yard; there are other, larger bay windows to either side of the arch. Inside, these bay windows are handsomely vaulted in a variety of patterns, almost as though they were separate rooms. Of all Britain's medieval inns – the Falstaff at Canterbury, the Star at Alfriston, the New Inn at Gloucester, the George at Norton St Philip, the Pilgrim's Rest (now the George) at Battle and the Bell at Tewkesbury – only the George and Pilgrims Hotel at Glastonbury rivals the Angel and Royal inn for architecture.

In his polemic *Contrasts* (1836), the Roman Catholic architect A. W. N. Pugin (see page 88), with his romantic image of pre-Reformation life, chose the Angel Hotel as the epitome of monastic hospitality as opposed to the meanness of a modern railway hotel. The inn's greatest moment came when Richard III descended on it in 1483; it was here that he signed the death warrant for the Duke of Buckingham, who had raised a rebellion.

As travel increased in the Elizabethan period, the English became proud of their inns. 'The world affords not such inns as England hath,' wrote Fynes Morison in his *Itinerary*, 'either for good and cheap entertainment after the guests' own pleasure, or for humble attendance on passengers, yea, even in very poor villages.' By the early 19th century, inn- and tavern-keeping were the biggest single occupations in Grantham, thanks to the dozen stagecoaches that stopped there every day.

NORTH PARADE, GRANTHAM *LINCOLNSHIRE*
Cradle of Thatcherism

Nineteenth-century America had Abraham Lincoln's log cabin. To 20th-century Britain, the equivalent was Alderman Roberts' grocer's shop at 1–3 North Parade, Grantham, the childhood home of Margaret Thatcher. If you had shopped there in the 1930s, you might have found the young Margaret, who was born in 1925, weighing out the flour, or cashing up the till. Following the 1979 general election, when she became Prime Minister, the shop became part of the Thatcher mythology: a metaphor for the political virtues of thrift, self-reliance, business gumption and (considering the treacle, oranges, rice, dates and other goods from around the world that were sold there) free trade.

It may be that Mrs Thatcher's visceral loathing of public expenditure was inherited from her father, whose prime object in local politics was to reduce the rates. Her mother, baking an extra loaf for the less fortunate, gave a practical example of charity, so much to be preferred, in the Thatcher canon of values, to state aid. Shopkeeping allowed the family to work and live together, but left little time for themselves. Almost all Sunday was spent at the Methodist chapel. Although the older Margaret turned to the Church of England (once described as the Tory party at prayer), the Nonconformist background contributed to the Iron Lady's most famous quality: her inner strength. She was not only the country's first female Prime Minister*, but also the first leader whom the Conservative party elected after a contest (Edward Heath, whom she defeated, never forgave her).

Not everything in her premiership can be traced back to 1–3 North Parade. As a wartime teenager, Margaret Roberts escaped the narrowness of Grantham by going up to Oxford University. Alfred Roberts would not later have approved of the 'loadsamoney' ostentatiousness of some elements of the Tory party in the 1980s, still less of the Thatcherite assault on local govern-ment. But the grocer's daughter flaunted her origins in her battles with what she regarded as a wetly unprogressive House of Lords. The old order got its own back by suggesting that the blood of Harry Cust, the womanising aristocrat and MP whose family came from nearby Belton House, ran in her veins, following a supposed liaison with her grandmother.

*See Grand Hotel, Brighton, page 52

GRIMES GRAVES

Prehistoric flint factory

About the time that Stonehenge was begun, around 3000BC, miners began digging flint out of the Breckland near Thetford. The site came to be called Grimes Graves by the Saxons: Grimes after the god Woden, also known as Grim, and Graves because of the craters left by the old mine pits. The Stone Age workers used antlers to dig out the ground to a depth of anything up to 40ft. The nodules of flint were then hauled up to the surface, split and shaped – but not polished, since that was done elsewhere. Grimes Graves is thus one of Britain's earliest industrial monuments: not quite the oldest, because there were earlier, and larger, mines in Sussex, but here is the only flint mine that can be visited by the public.

Over 400 pits were quarried, across an area of nearly 34 acres. Short galleries gave off a pit's central shaft like the spokes of a wheel. Although flints can be found abundantly on the surface of fields, especial value was clearly attached to those brought up from the belly of the earth; not having been exposed to freeze and thaw, they were extremely hard. From the hearths that have been discovered, as well as carefully placed tools, it seems that the miners had rituals, probably intended to ensure a generous supply of flints or to keep them safe. Maybe it was for religious reasons that they put the spoil back into the pits after they had finished working them. The settling of the spoil has given the landscape a pockmarked appearance, as though the heath was once ravaged by a disfiguring disease.

Grimes Graves was in use for a thousand years. During that time habits changed, creating a demand for more piercing tools than cutting ones. Technological development, in the form of the arrival of metal tools, caused its demise, the last mines being dug as the great lintels were hauled onto the upright stones at Stonehenge.

HOLKHAM HALL

Championing new methods of farming

By the end of the 18th century, the Industrial Revolution had begun to transform the way goods were made, drawing many labourers away from their poor but self-sufficient cottages and installing them in factory towns. This system was far more productive than the old. Farming had yet to catch up. It was important that it should, since mill workers did not grow their own food. Furthermore, the French Revolution and Napoleonic Wars, which halted trade with the Continent, meant that Britain had to live off its own resources.

Thomas Coke of Norfolk (later 1st Earl of Leicester) championed many of the improved techniques that came to be known as the Agricultural Revolution. In 1776 he came into the vast Holkham estates on the north Norfolk coast, inheriting the palatial house that had been built by his uncle. Like his earlier neighbour, the 2nd Viscount Townshend (known as 'Turnip' Townshend) at East Raynham Hall, he advocated growing crops in a sequence that would increase yields. In this 'four-crop rotation' scheme, turnips or another root crop, which broke up the soil, were followed by barley, which produced malt for bread and beer. As the barley grew up, so too did an under-sowing of grass, including plenty of nitrogen-giving clover. The grass would be cut and dried as hay for animals – particularly the large number of horses used in farming – to eat during winter. The fourth crop was wheat, providing not only flour for bread-making but straw (both for animal bedding and thatch). Here, as elsewhere, common land – that was previously shared by the community – was 'enclosed' into privately owned fields, to be farmed more effectively.

As a landowner, Coke (pronounced Cook) was well aware that he relied on his tenants to increase the efficiency of his estate. To attract the best tenants, he built handsome farmhouses and up-to-the-minute farm buildings. He also granted them longer leases, between eight and twenty-one years, to encourage them to invest in their enterprise. Having replaced traditional Norfolk Horn with Southdown sheep, he instituted an annual July sheep-shearing fair to demonstrate his improvements to other agriculturalists; they were the forerunners of the modern agricultural show.

After Coke's death in 1842, a stone column in the park, its base decorated with bas-reliefs of his achievements, was raised by a subscription which, according to the plaque, originated 'with the Yeomanry and [was] supported by the Noblemen and Gentlemen of all parties'.

HOUGHTON HALL

NEAR KING'S LYNN, NORFOLK

Palace built by Britain's first Prime Minister

'I suppose this letter will find you at Houghton,' wrote Lady Burlington to her husband. 'I don't know the post town, but I conclude there is no occasion to be very particular in a direction to a place so well known.' Houghton Hall had been built by Sir Robert Walpole, a squire's son who rose, without many advantages, to become England's first and longest-serving Prime Minister.

Following James II's expulsion in 1688, there had followed a long period of uncertainty and wars – the Battle of the Boyne, the War of the Spanish Succession with Marlborough's victories (see page 206) – and Walpole's 21-year rule over politics, from 1721 until 1742, brought stability and peace. His job of political management was made easier by the disinterest shown by George I, newly arrived from Hanover. The King was bored by the House of Commons and was happy to delegate state affairs to Walpole, his premier minister. Inevitably, critics accused Walpole of corruption, and the evidence of Houghton suggests they may have had a point. It was built on the scale of a palace, reflecting Walpole's frank love of opulence and fine craftsmanship. Supposedly capable of accommodating a hundred guests at an hour's notice, it was a tool of political influence, as well as a hunting box and showcase of art.

Large, convivial, hard-drinking and coarse-grained, Walpole appeared to be a fox- and hare-hunting squire, after the pattern of countless other Norfolk gentlemen. But Houghton shows that he was much more sophisticated than his image suggested. As architect, he employed Colen Campbell, the pioneer neo-Palladian who publicised the movement through *Vitruvius Britannicus*. Walpole's art collection was truly princely in scope. When his extravagant great-grandson, lacking the income provided by a major public office to maintain Houghton, was forced to sell his inheritance, the collection was eagerly bought by Catherine the Great of Russia, and thus Walpole's Old Masters are now among the stars of the Hermitage Museum in St Petersburg.

See also Strawberry Hill, page 243

OLD GRAMMAR SCHOOL   HUNTINGDON, CAMBRIDGESHIRE
Educating Oliver Cromwell

What would have happened to Oliver Cromwell if there had been no Civil War? In the 1630s, the family was on the slide. At the end of Queen Elizabeth's reign, some thirty years earlier, it had been riding very high. The Cromwells, related to Henry VIII's chancellor, had been rewarded with grants of land for their help in dissolving the monasteries. They created Hinchingbrooke House out of a former nunnery, and built a summer house at Ramsey Abbey. Since Hinchingbrooke is close to the Great North Road, just to the west of Huntingdon, they were able to jockey for the honour of entertaining James I as he journeyed from Scotland to London on inheriting the throne in 1603. They fêted James, his retinue and everyone in the locality, with the sort of prodigal open-handedness that was designed to display both generosity and wealth. Their ploy succeeded only too well. James kept coming back. Despite heavy hints that the Cromwells could have done with some lucrative royal favours to keep the show on the road, James did not oblige. The extravagance broke Oliver Cromwell's uncle, who retreated to his house at Ramsey.

Born in 1599, Oliver was brought up in a household in Huntingdon, surrounded by women. The house no longer exists; however, a museum has been created out of the grammar school where he was educated. This is the last remaining fragment of the Norman Hospital of St John, built to assist travellers on the Great North Road. (Later, another great Englishman attended it, although of a quite different temperament and persuasion: Samuel Pepys.) It could be that the schoolmaster, Thomas Beard, helped shape Cromwell's religious leanings, although Beard was probably more anti-Roman Catholic than pro-Puritan. Aged seventeen, Cromwell went to Sidney Sussex College at nearby Cambridge, known for its Puritan disposition. He left after a year when his father died. To the responsibility that he assumed for his mother and six sisters, he now added that of a wife, by whom he had nine children.

Although he entered Parliament in 1628, his public career at home met a reverse. A dispute over the spending of a charitable bequest became so acrimonious that the burgesses of the town called upon the charter to be altered, in a way that excluded Oliver Cromwell, among others, from office. In London, Cromwell's angry denunciations of the proceedings, which had been sanctioned by the King, led to his being imprisoned for five days. Cromwell was so disgusted by the humiliation of his loss of office that he sold nearly all his land at Huntingdon and moved his family of many women and young children to a rented farm at St Ives. From being one of the leading gentry in Huntingdon, he declined to the status of yeoman farmer. For the time being.

THE LONG SHOP
LEISTON, SUFFOLK

Cathedral of agricultural machinery

In 1853, the Long Shop – known locally as the Cathedral – was opened in the Suffolk village of Leiston; it was possibly the first hall purpose-built for a production assembly line in the world. The factory was owned by Richard Garrett III. The weather-vane depicts the portable steam engine (on wheels but, unlike the later traction engine, without the ability to propel itself) on which the company's expansion was founded.

The first Richard Garrett worked in Leiston as a blacksmith; among other things, he made agricultural tools. His son, Richard Garrett II, married a daughter of John Balls, who pioneered the development of the threshing machine, and not long after that Garrett himself began to make the machines. By the time of the Great Exhibition in 1851, the firm over which Richard Garrett III presided was big enough to mount a stand at the Crystal Palace. So many orders were taken there that it became necessary to increase production. The example of the American arms manufacturer Samuel Colt, whom Garrett had met at the Great Exhibition, suggested the principles by which this could be done.

The Long Shop is nearly 85ft long. Vehicles would be assembled in the centre aisle, while component parts were manufactured to either side or in the galleries above. Gantry cranes ran overhead so that parts could be lowered onto the chassis. Vehicles progressed along the length of the building as they were built. Some 20,000 portable steam engines were manufactured here. Although fewer were manufactured, Garrett traction engines, introduced in the 1860s and literally driven along under their own steam, had an unrivalled reputation for their engineering. By the early 20th century, Garrett machines were being exported around the world, and the company employed over 1,000 people – not bad for rural Suffolk. Despite a continuing demand for Garrett steam wagons, trolley-buses and steam rollers, the company was unable to keep up with new forms of transport and went out of business in 1932.

BATTLE OF LINCOLN LINCOLN
King Stephen is clapped into irons

In 1141, England was six years into a devastating civil war that followed the death of Henry I. This dominating, sometimes cruel, ruler had coerced the barons into accepting his only surviving legitimate child, Matilda, as his successor, but since the age of eight she had lived in Germany, sent there to marry the emperor Henry V. After Henry I had died in 1135, Stephen of Blois, son of the Conqueror's daughter Adela, hurried to England, whereas Matilda, his cousin, stayed in Germany. The barons reneged on their enforced oath and swore loyalty to him as their new king.

As a young man, Stephen committed his share of atrocities, but as King he gained the reputation of being a soft touch, and the unruly barons tried to grab more castles and land. Stephen also alienated the Church by humbling a very rich dynasty of bishops, one of whom, Alexander, was Bishop of Lincoln. By 1139, Matilda was ready to invade. Just before Christmas 1140, one of her supporters, Ranulf, Earl of Chester, tricked his way into the castle of Lincoln, winning it for Matilda. Constantly on campaign, Stephen marched to expel him. When he appeared without warning, before the Christmas festival was over, he found the castle nearly deserted, but only because Ranulf had left to rendezvous with Robert of Gloucester, Matilda's illegitimate half-brother and principal supporter. Hearing that Ranulf and Robert were on their way back with an army, the King ordered his own army down from the high ground, between the castle and the cathedral, where they were camped, and drew it up on the plain to the west of the city. As soon as battle was joined, many of Stephen's barons deserted him. He was left fighting, with characteristic bravery, surrounded by a phalanx of diehards, until he was brought down by a stone and captured.

Matilda had him imprisoned in chains, which should have been the end of his reign. But it wasn't. Matilda's arrogance disaffected her supporters,

Stephen was released in a prisoner exchange, and the civil war dragged on. Peace was finally negotiated (after the death of Stephen's own son Eustace) when the King agreed with Matilda that her son, Henry, would inherit on his death. He did so, becoming Henry II in 1154.

THE JEW'S HOUSE
Early Jewish prosperity and persecution

In the late 12th century, Aaron of Lincoln was one of the richest men in England. As a Jew, he plied one of the few trades open to him, that of money-lender. Jews were prevented from joining craft guilds because of the Christian oaths that were sworn, while Christians were not supposed to lend money for profit. Aaron's activities helped finance the booming wool trade, which made Lincoln the fourth-richest city in the country, after London, York and Norwich. At the time of his death in 1186, a year after the collapse of Lincoln cathedral*, no fewer than nine Cistercian abbeys were in debt to him. During his career, he had even lent money to the King himself. In turn, Henry II imposed the medieval equivalent of a windfall tax, by confiscating Aaron's property when he died.

Aaron was the most prominent of a flourishing Jewish community in Lincoln, no doubt attracted by the prosperous trading conditions. Today, that community is commemorated in the name of the Jew's House, at the bottom of Steep Hill. Dated on stylistic grounds to the 1170s or 1180s, it has survived as one of the oldest houses in Britain, primarily because it was built out of stone, its first owner perhaps feeling that the then existing practice of constructing houses from timber was inadequate. There would have been shops at ground level, while a back stair would have led to the two upstairs rooms. The larger chamber had a built-in fireplace, at a time when many people could barely afford an open hearth. Consequently, it is expressed flamboyantly on the exterior of the building, the chimney emerging on corbels over a decorative arch above the front door. While the house was not large, it was opulent. We do not know the merchant, a contemporary of Aaron, for whom the Jew's House was built, but in the 1270s it is supposed to have been occupied by a Jewess called Bellesez, and it is known there was a synagogue next door.

By now, the position of the Jews in Lincoln, as elsewhere, was worsening. During the time of Aaron the money-lender, a century before, Bishop Hugh had been able to protect the Jews from harassment†, but in 1220 Moses of Lincoln was murdered. In 1255, Jews were accused of crucifying a small boy and throwing his body down a well, following which a number of them were hanged. Eleven years later, a gang of knights raided a synagogue and destroyed the records there, no doubt to erase the record of debts. At one point, the Archbishop of Canterbury attempted to prevent Christians from selling food to Jews. Those who still had houses probably had to take in impecunious fellow believers. Their circumstances continued to deteriorate until Edward I expelled the Jews from England in 1290, and they were not allowed back until the Commonwealth.

*See Lincoln Cathedral, below. †See Bevis Marks Synagogue, page 116, and Clifford's Tower, page 405

LINCOLN CATHEDRAL LINCOLN
Bishop Hugh begins Britain's most harmonious cathedral

In September 1186 – on the Feast of St Michael – a French Carthusian monk was enthroned as Bishop of Lincoln. His name was Hugh, and in due course he would become a saint. Lincoln was the biggest of all English dioceses, stretching from the Humber to the Thames, and taking in Stamford, Leicester, Huntingdon, Northampton, Bedford, Buckingham and Oxford on the way. Hugh's most immediate problem, however, lay close to home. The previous year, the cathedral had been rent from top to bottom in what was described as an earthquake. Hugh's first task was to set about rebuilding it. Fortunately, he had the backing of the King, Henry II, then recovering his reputation after the murder of Archbishop Thomas à Becket.

Lincoln was at this time at the height of its power as the wool capital of England. Even so, assembling enough money and materials to begin the work of rebuilding took six years. Hugh and his architect – perhaps Geoffrey de Noiers, perhaps Richard the Mason – established the model on which one of Britain's most harmonious and yet spectacular cathedrals would develop. He also began the rebuilding of the Bishop's Palace.

On the bishop's death in 1200, Lincoln's Jews – whom he had protected from harassment* – were among those who came out to mourn him. At the funeral, King John himself helped carry the coffin. Hugh was canonised in 1220. Half a century later, so many pilgrims were coming to pay homage that the east end of Hugh's cathedral had to be demolished; it was replaced by the Angel Choir. When it was finally finished in 1280, Edward I and Queen Eleanor, the Archbishop of Canterbury and eight bishops were on hand to observe St Hugh's shrine being moved to its new setting. The shrine no longer exists; St Hugh's monument, like Christopher Wren's, is his cathedral.

*See The Jew's House, page 278

BATTLE OF MALDON

ESSEX

Epic Saxon defeat, no reward for fair play

For a century after King Alfred defeated the Danes, England was spared Viking raids. But towards the end of the 10th century, the Norse longships began to return. One Viking raid took place in 991 when the fierce Olaf Tryggvason led a fleet of 93 ships, landing at Folkestone. Tryggvason then spent the next four months harrying Kent and East Anglia; one of his ploys was to bribe the inhabitants to give him money in return for his not attacking. The battle of Maldon, which took place during this campaign, was not more remarkable in itself than many other attempts by local people to repel the invaders, but it is remembered by the Anglo-Saxon poem, *The Battle of Maldon*, which records both the action and the values that inspired the defending warriors. It was written in Old English, and probably dates from the 10th century.

The band of Northmen or Vikings under Anlaf probably landed on the mudflats of Northey Island, in the river Blackwater. They were Tryggvason's men, but the poem does not relate whether Tryggvason himself was present. The local ealdorman Byrhtnoth summoned his house carls, or paid fighters, and the *fyrd*, or levy of farmers, to meet them. They lined up on the mainland, at one end of the narrow causeway leading to the island; the Vikings drew up at the other end. The causeway was easily defended and the invaders could not get across. One of their heralds shouted out the terms of the bribe they would need to go away without battle. Scornfully, Byrhtnoth rejected them, and then – impatient at waiting for the fight to begin – let the Vikings over the causeway. Later ages may think this was in the best traditions of fair play but it was nothing more than a fearful tactical mistake. Byrhtnoth, fighting at the head of his troop, was slain by the Vikings. The poem relates that while he was dying, he thanked God for the joys of life.

Some of his companions are scornfully described by the poet as fleeing; most, however, fought on until death. The poet writes of the men following their leader unswervingly, of their solidarity as 'hearth companions', and of the help that senior warriors extended to the youngsters. For all that – and although the end of the poem is missing some lines – there is no doubt about the outcome: the Anglo-Saxons lost, and presumably Maldon was sacked.

NEWMARKET HEATH

SUFFOLK

Charles II gives rules to racing

In 1664, Charles II founded the Town Plate, a horse race to be run on Newmarket Heath. It was not the first time that royalty had singled out Newmarket for favour. James I came here to hunt hares and bustards, and had built a small

palace right in the centre of the town (Inigo Jones's first architectural commission had been to construct outbuildings). Horse racing had already begun by his
time; the palm for the oldest race course still to occupy its original site goes to
Chester, the first meeting on the Roodee (a rood of land created from the silting
up of the Dee) having been held in 1539. As yet, however, it was an unregulated
sport: the Town Plate is thought to have been the first race with written rules.
These rules, or articles, now hang outside the Stewards' Room in the Jockey
Club. (In fact, a race at Kiplingcotes in east Yorkshire, run since 1555, was given
articles in 1619, but these were of local interest compared to the Town Plate.)
Charles's patronage of Newmarket, where he came to spend several weeks each
spring and autumn, established it as Britain's premier centre for racing.

At Newmarket, Charles employed the gentleman architect William Samwell
to replace his grandfather's palace, which had become uninhabitable during
the Commonwealth, and chose a site which was hugger-mugger with the
town, rather than regally detached from it. That drew criticism, but suited
Charles's temperament and love of human activity: when the court was at
Newmarket, the streets must have seethed with life, not all of it reputable, and
Charles had a ringside view from his palace windows.

Like his father, Charles II was a superb horseman, and he often rode his own
horses when they raced. He won the Town Plate in 1671. At other times he
adjudicated the disputes that inevitably arose, given the chaotic conditions
under which races were held. He felt comfortable in the company of jockeys
and he loved Newmarket. In 1683, a fire swept through part of the town, and
although it did not touch the palace, Charles packed up and left. This was as
well since the conspirators of the Rye House Plot had intended to seize him
and his brother, the future James II, on their way back to London, but the
unexpected change of plan foiled them. The palace was demolished after 1814,
except for the south-east pavilion, which was turned into Palace House.

ST JULIAN'S CHURCH NORWICH

First woman author in English

Born in the early 1340s, at about the same time as Chaucer, Julian of Norwich –
a woman – probably came from a family that was at least comfortably off, since
she had the time to reflect, if possibly not to read. (Most medieval women were
illiterate, and it is conceivable that Julian relied on others to read to her and
would then compose her thoughts which, again, others would write down for
her.) She became the first author in English whom we know for certain to have
been a woman. Passionately religious, she longed to identify herself with
Christ's suffering, yearning for an illness that would bring her to the point of
death, and praying that she would receive symbolic wounds. The illness was

granted to her: at the age of thirty she very nearly died. During it, she experienced sixteen visions, or revelations, which she endlessly teased over in her mind. These visions and their interpretation are the subject of her writings, now called XVI *Revelations of Divine Love*.

The last forty years of her long life were spent as an anchoress, walled up in a cell attached to a poor church near the docks. That church was St Julian's: it was presumably from the church that she took her name, her writings emphasising the little importance that should be attached to personal details. Her cell had a window through which she could talk to the people who came to her for advice, a window onto the church, to enable her to take part in services, and an opening to a room for a servant.

In 1942, a German bomb fell on St Julian's round flint tower, which collapsed onto the nave. Julian's cell had long ago disappeared during the Reformation. When the church was rebuilt, a room was constructed on its site, incorporating the few flints that survived from its foundations.

COLMAN'S MUSTARD WORKS NORWICH

The unique pungency of an English condiment

In the United States, it is sweet; in France, it lacks vim; in Italy, it hardly exists. Only in Britain does mustard take on the yellow hue and eye-watering strength of the 'English' variety, capable of delivering a heavyweight punch behind the nose. In the ancient world, mustard was known long before Jesus made the 'least of all the seeds' the subject of a parable about growth; archaeologists have found that it was used during the Stone Age. The form in which it is consumed today emerged after the development of mechanical milling techniques in the 19th century. Mustard, with its high oil content, requires sensitive milling, and the Colman family were unequalled in the art.

The Norwich miller Jeremiah Colman took over a mustard mill at Stoke Holy Cross in 1814. His business was inherited by his nephew James, and a London office was opened. In the 1850s, the firm transferred to its present site at Carrow in Norwich, growing into a Victorian megalith under the direction of Jeremiah James Colman, James's son, who took over at the age of twenty-four on his father's death. By 1880, some 950,000 casks and boxes were being dispatched each year. By the early 1930s, the volume of mustard leaving the works annually was enough to fill 9,700 railway wagons – the equivalent of thirty wagons a day, six days a week, throughout the whole year. All over Britain and the Empire, Colman's mustard was giving bite to a cuisine whose virtue was a plentiful supply of wholesome meat, but whose failing was insipidity and overcooking.

Parts of the Victorian factory still stand on the Colman's site, now owned by Unilever, and can be glimpsed from the Carrow Bridge, next to Norwich City's football ground. Not all the mustard bought can have been left on the side of the plate, although the company's profits must benefit greatly from the amount that does remain unused.

ORFORD CASTLE   SUFFOLK

Henry II protects East Anglia

Henry II inherited the throne of England in 1154 – indeed, an empire stretching from the borders of Scotland to southern France – after an 18-year civil war, during which his mother, Matilda, daughter of Henry I, had waged war on her cousin, Stephen of Blois*. The monarchy was at a low ebb. In East Anglia, only two inland castles – Eye and Haughley – were in the King's hands, and while he could temporarily confiscate those of his political opponents (giving them back in return for large fines), he needed to bolster his control of the region. A particular worry to Henry was that he had no base on the coast. The seriousness of the situation is reflected in the speed at which Orford Castle was built. It was completed in just eight years, at a cost of £1,415.

The design was innovative. Earlier Norman keeps had been more or less square, leaving their corners vulnerable to being undermined. Orford was constructed to a polygonal plan, to which were attached three towers and a gatehouse: this was a step towards the circular keeps that were stronger still.

Henry's wisdom in protecting the coast was soon proved. Following the murder of Thomas à Becket in 1170 (see page 57), Henry's elder son, Richard, took advantage of his father's unpopularity. Backed by his mother Queen Eleanor, from whom Henry had parted, he attempted to seize England, with the help of the powerful Earl Hugh Bigod of Framlingham Castle. Flemish mercenaries landed near Felixstowe, only to be ambushed by the King's forces.

*See Battle of Lincoln, page 277

ORFORD NESS   SUFFOLK

The coast changes shape

Being an island, Britain's history and character are permeated by the sea. Its tides have always been worrying away at the landmass, scooping out the base of chalky cliffs in one place, depositing silt and treacherous sandbanks in another. The process can be seen at work today, as sea levels rise and coastal defences are either strengthened, or abandoned in the name of 'managed retreat'. It has always been thus. Orford stands as an eloquent witness to Britain's shifting coastline, which ruined the prospects of what had been a flourishing sea port – on a par with Ipswich – in the Middle Ages.

Since the 12th century when Henry II built Orford Castle (see above), the mouth of the river Ore has moved five miles to the south-west; the castle and church are all that remain to recall the prosperity of the medieval port. The river Ore (by then the Alde) originally debouched into the sea five miles up the coast at Aldeburgh. Tides caused the water to deposit an attached spit of shingle bank parallel to the shore. This crept down to Orford, and then beyond it. In the Elizabethan period, Parliament itself determined to improve navigation, passing an Act for the Preservation of Orford Haven in 1584. This cannot have been very effective, however, for by the time John Norder surveyed the Sudbourne estate for its owner, Sir Michael Stanhope, in 1601, the river mouth had moved to more or less its present position. Orford's days of richness were over. It was washed up. At least its fate was not that of certain other significant ports, which disappeared entirely beneath the waves: for instance, there is now no trace of Ravenspur, on the mouth of the Humber, where Bolingbroke landed to claim the throne as Henry IV.

Shortly before the First World War, the Ness was taken over by the military for flying experiments. Later, the hardiness of Britain's earliest nuclear weapon – Blue Danube – was tested here. Personnel withdrew in 1971, leaving the tussocks of the saltmarsh to its population of lapwings, redshanks, meadow pipits and little terns.

SANDRINGHAM HOUSE

NEAR KING'S LYNN, NORFOLK

George V's domestic ideal

'Dear old Sandringham' was, to George V, 'the place I love better than anywhere else in the world.' It had been bought in 1862 by his father, the future Edward VII, when Prince of Wales, shortly before he married Princess Alexandra of Denmark. The attraction was not the house itself, which even after rebuilding was never beguiling, so much as the 8,000-acre estate. It had some of the best shooting in the country.

For the first fifteen years of his reign, until his mother's death in 1925, George V did not live in the big house at Sandringham, but at York Cottage (now the estate office), a house that was not much bigger than a suburban villa and was certainly cramped for a royal family with six children. But the informality suited his homely nature, and few other estates could rival the quality of the birds, 12,000 of which were released at Sandringham annually; George V was one of the best half-dozen shots in Britain.

Peppery, unimaginative, a stickler for decorations and devoted to his stamp collection, George V was ruled by a sense of duty that made him an admirable figurehead during the First World War. Afterwards, he personally refused permission for his cousin Tsar Nicholas II, of whom he was fond, to come to Britain, for fear of social unrest. Dying at Sandringham in 1936, it was said that he had an unshakeable faith 'in God, in the invincibility of the Royal Navy, and in the essential rightness of whatever was British'. Hurrah!

SNAPE MALTINGS
From derelict brewery to renowned concert hall

For a nation with such a rich musical life, Britain is rather short on major composers. However, Benjamin Britten is one of the greatest – his musical personality shot through with a peculiarly English sensibility, derived, in his case, from an acute sense of place. He was born in Lowestoft, on the Suffolk coast. Many of his works reflect the English countryside, if not – like *Peter Grimes*, *Billy Budd* and *Curlew River* – the haunting landscape of sea, pine trees and mud-flats around Snape and Aldeburgh. It was at Snape that he made his home, an old mill. With Eric Crozier, he helped convert a derelict industrial building – the Maltings – into the setting for the Aldeburgh Music Festival, which he had founded in 1948 and where his works often received their première.

The Maltings were begun in 1844 to malt barley for beer. It was an agriculturally based enterprise, appropriate to Suffolk, founded by a formidable Victorian businessman, Newson Garrett, two of whose daughters – Elizabeth Garrett Anderson and Millicent Garrett Fawcett – would become equally formidable as pioneering women, one the first female doctor, the other a leading suffragette (see page 70). By the 1960s, the labour-intensive, seasonal methods of the Victorian period had become uneconomic, and the marshy Snape works could not accommodate the machinery that would have been necessary to automate it. Snape Maltings Concert Hall opened in 1967, only to be devoured by fire two years later. It was rebuilt and reopened by the Queen in 1970.

Britten's genius as a composer was to look back to his hero Henry Purcell, interweave the inspiration he found there with modern developments in Europe, while infusing his music with the sense of Englishness that typifies Elgar (see page 331), Vaughan Williams and Holst. The arcadian, yet workaday setting provided by Snape formed the perfect backdrop; his neighbours around Aldeburgh assimilated him and his lifelong companion, the tenor Peter Pears, as national treasures.

BATTLE OF SOLE BAY
The future James II fights at sea

In 1670, Charles II signed the Treaty of Dover with Louis XIV, which contained a secret clause promising that he would become a Roman Catholic. As a result, England found herself in the unusual position of being an ally of France, and together they ganged up against the Dutch, hoping to divide the United Provinces between them.

In May 1672, the King's brother, James, Duke of York, went to Southwold, staying at Sutherland House in the High Street to oversee the preparation of the fleet that assembled in Sole Bay – a total of 98 ships and 30 fire ships, about a third of which were French. They were loading water and stores when a French frigate raced into the bay, firing its guns to warn that the Dutch fleet had been sighted. The last occasion that the English fleet had met the Dutch near Sole Bay had been the Battle of Lowestoft in 1665 when the English were triumphant, capturing or sinking seventeen ships; the Dutch admiral was blown up in his flagship.

This time, the Dutch admiral De Ruyter did not wait for the English to draw up into line, as his unfortunate predecessor had done. As a result, a ragged battle developed within earshot of the shore. The French squadron, perhaps as a result of a misunderstanding, sailed away from the main battle, towards the south, drawing some of the Dutch ships after them. James, Duke of York, however deficient he would prove as king, was a brave commander, whose example inspired his men. He moved his flag from one ship to another, as they were successively disabled.

The battle was typically bloody but inconclusive. The Duke of York pursued the Dutch back to Holland, but was forced to return without further action. By now, Charles thought it unwise to risk his brother and heir in a ship, and the passing of the Test Act in 1672 – Parliament's riposte to the unpopular Treaty of Dover – forbade Catholics from holding office. James, a Catholic, hauled down his flag, the last king of England – or, at least, heir apparent – to command his navy in battle in person.

In 1674, England made peace with Holland, after an inglorious campaign. France fought on in the Low Countries but without English support. After 1689, when William of Orange and Queen Mary came to the throne, normal hostilities with England's traditional enemy were resumed.

SOMERSBY
NEAR LOUTH, LINCOLNSHIRE

Tennyson's childhood home

By the law of primogeniture, the Tennyson family estates in Lincolnshire should have been inherited by George Tennyson. Instead, perhaps because of George's mild epilepsy, then considered to be a shameful condition, they went to his younger brother, Charles, who adopted the fanciful name of Tennyson D'Eyncourt and rebuilt the family home of Bayons Manor in castle-style. Dr Tennyson, as George became known, went into the Church, an embittered, violent-tempered man, holding the livings of Somersby, Bag Enderby and two other parishes. It was at Somersby Rectory that, in 1809, Alfred Tennyson was born, one of eleven children.

Somersby remained Alfred Tennyson's home until 1837. He was schooled there, grimly, by his father except for five years spent at the grammar school in Louth. At Louth, too, was the printing firm of J. & J. Jackson, who published Tennyson's first book of poetry, *Poems by Two Brothers*, written with his brother Charles. Cambridge provided something of an escape from the oppressive world of the rectory, and there he met Arthur Hallam. Hallam would often visit Somersby until his tragically young death in 1833. Three years later, at Charles Tennyson's wedding, Tennyson met the bride's sister, Emily Sellwood, a young woman from nearby Horncastle: Alfred was best man and Emily a bridesmaid. They were too poor to marry at first but did so seventeen years later, when Tennyson was forty-one and Emily thirty-seven.

In 1837, the Tennyson family moved away from Lincolnshire, and the poet never revisited his childhood home. Memories of the myopically-seen Wolds, its streams, willows and 'dewy-tassell'd' woods, would haunt Tennyson's poetry for ever.

DANIEL LAMBERT INN   STAMFORD, LINCOLNSHIRE
Britain's fattest man

On 20 June 1809, Daniel Lambert arrived at Stamford to go racing. Any journey undertaken by Lambert excited interest, because he weighed 52 stone 11lb. According to the *Dictionary of National Biography*, this made him 'the most corpulent man of whom authentic record exists' – the fattest man in British history. He travelled in an especially constructed carriage. At Stamford, he stayed at an inn called the Waggon and Horses, and on his second day there he died, presumably of a heart attack.

Quite what made Lambert so fat is a mystery. As a young man, he was strong and fit, much given to walking, riding and swimming. He was then a quite normal size. It was only in his twenties that he started to grow exceptionally heavy. Admittedly, he lived in an age when those who could afford to do so often ate voraciously. Jane Austen's family was not particularly well off, since her father was only a country parson; nevertheless, a dinner for ten people could include a dozen fried soles, a roast leg of mutton, a boiled ham and three chickens, followed by ducks and various tarts, olives and fruit. Wine would be consumed in equally heroic quantities. Lambert, however, drank only water and seems not to have eaten more than anyone else. Nevertheless, he became a phenomenon and – at a time when physical peculiarities were not politely overlooked – something to point and gawp at. At first he was understandably shy of exhibiting himself; then, perhaps because other forms of employment were impossible for him, he moved to London and started to charge people to make his acquaintance.

'When sitting,' wrote one observer, 'he appears to be a stupendous mass of flesh, for his thighs are so covered by his belly that nothing but his knees are to be seen, while the flesh of his legs, which resemble pillows, projects in such a manner as to nearly bury his feet.' To modern ears, the frankness of this account might sound cruel; perhaps, given the pride that landowners took in extraordinarily fat farm animals, it is possible to detect an undertow of admiration. Lambert was thirty-nine when he died. The epitaph on the tombstone erected by his friends in St Martin's churchyard in Stamford records that he had 'an exalted and convivial Mind, and in personal Greatness had no COMPETITOR', before detailing his gargantuan dimensions: 'three Feet one Inch round the LEG, nine Feet four Inches round the BODY'. His clothes were bought by the owner of Stamford's Ram Jam Inn, whose name was then changed to the Daniel Lambert, which is in St Leonard's Street. They are now in the Stamford Museum.

THE BELL INN
STILTON, CAMBRIDGESHIRE
The king of cheeses

Stilton was a coaching town: sitting astride the Great North Road (the Roman Ermine Street), it supported no fewer than fourteen inns. The town was already 'famous for its cheese' when Daniel Defoe wrote his *Tour through the Whole Island of Great Britain* in 1724–7. Rich and blue-veined, it was probably offered to travellers as a locally produced delicacy, although there was not actually enough good pasture nearby for this to have been possible. The Stilton story is a triumph of food marketing.

While blue-veined cheeses had probably been made for centuries, the version that we now know as Stilton is a product of the Agricultural Revolution. Until then, cows did not yield enough milk for cheese to be other than seasonal. In the first quarter of the 18th century, Frances Paulett, the house-keeper of Quenby Hall in Leicestershire, seems to have improved local recipes and begun production in sufficient quantity to supply the Bell in Stilton, the inn being kept by her brother-in-law, Cooper Thornhill, a successful Midlands corn trader. There it was stored in the cellars and served mature, in a state of unrivalled pungency and saltiness. Originally called Quenby cheese, it was now given the name of Stilton by the travellers who called in at the Bell and took a liking to it. In 1743 Thornhill also bought the Angel, which had stabling for as many as 300 horses. In 1745, he acquired fame for galloping 213 miles in a single day, going from Stilton to Shoreditch, back to Stilton and then to Shoreditch again, a feat that required eighteen changes of horse and won him a bet of 500 guineas. It was Thornhill who developed Stilton's national reputation, sending wagons loaded with cheese for sale in London.

As a town, Stilton's heyday ended abruptly in the 1840s, when the railways killed off the coaching trade overnight. By now, however, the cheese had taken on a life of its own. Today, Stilton cheese is protected by a 'designation of origin', meaning that it can only be made in the counties of Leicestershire, Nottinghamshire and Derbyshire. There are now six dairies making Stilton cheese, over a million of them each year. Colston Bassett & District Dairy, founded in 1913, still proudly resists the efforts of Whitehall's over-scrupulous food regulators to make the use of unpasteurised milk unviable.

GAINSBOROUGH'S HOUSE SUDBURY, SUFFOLK
Country boy who shows us the Georgians

Thomas Gainsborough helped create the image of Georgian England, his portraits radiating elegance, refinement, sensibility and wealth. Quite how he succeeded as an artist is a puzzle, since he freely admitted to being disorganised and lazy, and he much preferred painting landscapes to his profitable portraits – and was happier still when playing the cello with friends. There was nothing artistic in his immediate family. His father, John Gainsborough, was a weaver and dealer in cloth from Sudbury. He and his wife Mary lived in an old house – 14th-century in part – in what was then Sepulchre Street (now called Gainsborough Street), which they handsomely refronted. It was here that Gainsborough was born in 1727.

Sudbury is still, as it was then, a self-contained, prosperous market town. John Gainsborough, however, did not flourish in it: his business collapsed and he was only able to continue living in the family house through the generosity of a nephew. The young Gainsborough, educated at the Grammar School, tramped out into the East Anglian countryside to sketch, its woods and streams leaving an indelible impression. His first clients were local gentry, the men self-confident and shrewd, the wives thin and straight-backed. Before long, though, he had made his name in fashionable London and Bath, with portraits that combine the dashing swagger of Van Dyck with his own light and informal touch.

SUTTON HOO NEAR WOODBRIDGE, SUFFOLK
A spectacular Saxon treasure

Some 1,400 years ago, a king died. For his burial, a ship was taken from the river Deben, his body is thought to have been placed inside it, and around it were arranged some of the things that he had most valued in life: armour, weapons, cooking utensils, drinking horns, games and a beautiful silver bowl. The workmanship and materials were of the highest quality. The hilt of his sword was jewelled, his helmet took the form of a winged dragon, finely chased and with a thin line of garnets set above the eye-holes, and the gold buckles and shoulder clasps were masterpieces of design and craft. The king's people consigned all this treasure to the earth, along with, it is presumed, their lord's remains, under a great mound.

On the eve of the Second World War, the buried treasure was uncovered. It caused a sensation. Nothing else of this quality had been found from the Anglo-Saxon world. Generously, the landowner, Edith Pretty, gave it to the British Museum. As with many archaeological discoveries, it raised almost as many questions as it answered. Why was no trace of a body found with the treasure? Had it never been there, or had it disintegrated completely in the acid soil? Whose body was it? The astonishing quality of the objects surely indicates that it belonged to a warrior king or prince. Perhaps it was even that of Raedwald, King of East Anglia, who, having killed the King of Northumbria in battle, ruled over more of England than anyone previously. On the other hand, it is possible that the quality, however magnificent, was not as completely exceptional as it seems: we cannot know how many other hoards, if any, have disappeared or await to be discovered. The mostly frugal, battle-hardened, pre-Christian court that arranged the Sutton Hoo burial is little known to us. This site, which must have been mystical to the Anglo-Saxons, remains so to us.

TILBURY FORT
TILBURY, ESSEX

Scene of Elizabeth I's Armada speech

In Elizabethan England, military preparations were apt to be ad hoc. It was only when they had received word that the Armada had left Corunna in early July 1588 that an army was mustered, camped next to a fort that Henry VIII had built at Tilbury at the mouth of the Thames. Queen Elizabeth came to address her troops on 8 August. By then, the Armada had been beaten back by Sir Francis Drake but winds had forced them out of the English Channel and up the east coast of England towards Scotland (see page 33), from whence the remains of the Spanish fleet had limped home. Nevertheless, the fear of invasion remained, and the speech that Elizabeth, then aged fifty-five, delivered to rally her troops shows why she had star quality as a monarch, for her rough-hewn soldiers can hardly have failed to take inspiration from the bejewelled figure in their midst.

'Let tyrants fear,' she said, in terms calculated to woo her audience, 'I have always so behaved myself, that under God I have placed my chiefest strength and safeguard in the loyal hearts and goodwill of my subjects . . .' In what a later generation would think of as Churchillian mode, she was resolved to die, rather than surrender. But unlike Churchill she could play the card of gender, and it is this declaration that has come ringing down the ages: 'I know I have the body of a weak, feeble woman; but I have the heart and stomach of a king – and of a king of England too . . .' As it turned out, her army's 'virtues in the field' were never tested, and although she promised to be their personal 'rewarder' for the bravery she expected of them, the ordinary sailors in Sir Francis Drake's fleet were sent home with nothing more than their travel expenses. Elizabeth I was great; she was also frugal.

Of the fort at Tilbury as Elizabeth would have known it, nothing remains. In its place stands a major fortification, perfectly preserved with its geometrical earthworks, projecting bastions and complicated sequence of moats and ravelin (a fortified island in the inner moat, protecting the landward gateway).

The new fort was started in 1670 after the Dutch fleet had sailed into the Thames estuary and up the Medway three years before, destroying a large number of ships in the Chatham dockyard (see page 62). After the Great Fire of London in 1666, tax revenues were so low that the King was unable to pay his navy, and had therefore laid up most of the fleet. For the English, it was a miserable episode in a miserable war – the only positive outcome being the capture of a trading post on an island in a North American river, so inconsequential that the Dutch forgot to ask for it back in the Treaty of Breda in 1667. Their name for it was New Amsterdam. From now on it was known as New York.

WALSINGHAM PRIORY LITTLE WALSINGHAM, NORFOLK
Reviving the tradition of pilgrimage

Some time in the mid-11th century a youngish, widowed noblewoman, Richeldis de Faverches, had a vision. In it, the Virgin Mary instructed her to build a model of the house in Nazareth where the Annunciation had taken place. She did so, setting it near a holy well on her estates in north Norfolk. The little edifice was to prove immensely popular with later generations. Pilgrimage was medieval England's one opportunity to escape the bounds of a narrow local existence, and participate in a shared adventure. At the time of the Crusades, the Holy Land itself was too dangerous for many people to contemplate. England's Nazareth, at Walsingham, was altogether more manageable, and the figures of the Virgin and Child in the priory that grew up were loaded with jewels, rings and precious fabrics, left by the faithful. Walsingham was second only to Canterbury as a pilgrimage centre, and a little town developed as a result of the income generated by visitors.

The cult retained its hold until Henry VIII dissolved the monasteries. In an attempt to stop the King's men, a dozen Walsingham men planned an uprising.

It failed and eleven of the conspirators suffered the usual horrible deaths. The image of the Virgin was burnt. The priory was comprehensively dismantled, except for the east wall of the church, with its great 15th-century window.

Towards the end of the 19th century, both Roman Catholics and Anglo-Catholics revived the tradition of pilgrimage. The Anglo-Catholics built a new shrine, while the Roman Catholics acquired the little Slipper Chapel in the village of Houghton St Giles. Originally, there had been a series of chapels dotted along the main pilgrimage routes towards Walsingham. The Slipper Chapel was the last on the road from London; here pilgrims would take off their shoes in order to walk the last mile barefoot – hence the name.

WALTHAM ABBEY
ESSEX

Presumed burial place of King Harold

After the Battle of Hastings*, King Harold's mother, Gytha, offered the victorious Duke William the weight of Harold's body in gold if he would allow her to bury her son. William, believing Harold to be an oath-breaker, did not believe that he deserved a burial to befit his status, so he refused, giving the body to one of his countrymen who was told to bury it on the shore that Harold had been trying to defend. However, tradition has it that the body was later removed and taken quietly to Waltham Abbey in Essex.

Waltham was a Saxon foundation. Thirty years before the Battle of Hastings, one of King Canute's courtiers, Tovi the Proud, brought a miraculous stone crucifix here – hence the name that is sometimes used for the district, Waltham Holy Cross – and established a college of secular canons. The abbey was rebuilt, with all the magnificence that could be mustered, by the future King Harold and was rededicated in 1060. Nothing really survives of this building, although clearly the abbey retained its importance in the years after Hastings, since some of the windows and the great columns of the nave date from about 1100. In time, the abbey grew more magnificent still. In 1177, Henry II refounded it for the Augustinian order as part of his penance for the murder of Thomas à Becket (see page 57).

It was the last abbey to be disbanded during the Dissolution of the Monasteries (see page 133). Now, the church is only a fragment of its original size, being no more than the Norman nave; the 12th-century transepts and long choir, which more than doubled the length of the church, have gone. A simple stone stands beyond what became the east of the church when it was truncated. On it, an inscription says that it marks the site of the Saxon high altar, behind which it is thought Harold's body was buried.

*See Battle of Hastings, page 49

WICKEN FEN

NEAR ELY, CAMBRIDGESHIRE

Britain's first nature reserve

No part of England has changed more over the centuries than the Fens, the peaty expanse of low land between Cambridge and the Wash. Lower than sea level in places, it was once marshy and inaccessible. The Romans began to drain it. Their efforts were continued by the monasteries which, in the 13th century, cut the 14-mile drainage channel between Peterborough and Guyhirn known as Morton's Leam. It is still in use today. These sporadic works were eclipsed by the first systematic attempt at drainage, made by the Earl of Bedford in the 17th century, using the Dutch engineer Cornelius Vermuyden. Rivers were straightened, sluices built and artificial flood plains created. The prize lay in the rich black agricultural land that drainage uncovered. Bedford's scheme was only partially successful. As water ran away to the sea, the surrounding peaty land dried out and oxidised, thereby sinking further: as a result, windmills were needed to encourage the flow.

Only with the advent of steam-powered pumping engines in the Victorian period could the vision of modern agricultural efficiency be accomplished. Even that could not compare to what the 20th century was able to achieve. Peat digging (for fuel) and sedge cutting (for thatch) now represents only a fraction of one per cent of the original, traditional work in the Fen.

Part of it is Wicken Fen. In 1899, it became Britain's first nature reserve, when a 2-acre strip was bought for the National Trust (the Trust now owns 800 acres, including Adventurers' Fen). Always watery, liable to flood in spring, little disturbed by man, the old fenland landscape, with its tapestry of intertwining plants, hums with often invisible wildlife. Charles Darwin's interest in botany was quickened by collecting beetles on Wicken Fen in the 1820s. Later, so many lanterns for moth collecting, known as Eddystone Lighthouses, were set up on the Fen that their twinkling lights were said to resemble a small city. Over a thousand species of both moth and beetle have been recorded, and double that number of fly species. The biodiversity of the Fen has been likened to that of a tropical rain forest.

During the Second World War, Adventurers' Fen was requisitioned by the War Office, in order to be farmed as part of the 'Dig for Victory' campaign. Although it was handed back to the National Trust after the war, the original habitat was lost. Today, the success of Wicken Fen's conservation creates its own challenges: the water-soaked land has become higher than that of surrounding farmland, causing water to run away. Careful management is required to prevent the Fen drying out, while at the same time not allowing it to become so waterlogged that it is overrun with reeds and sedge. An old windmill still serves as a pump, but rather than draining the land, it now keeps up the water table.

WOOLSTHORPE MANOR

Sir Isaac Newton: the apple fell here

In the summer of 1665, Cambridge, like London, was victim to the plague. The University closed and, as a result, the 23-year-old Isaac Newton went home to his family's yeoman farmhouse, Woolsthorpe Manor. He stayed there for the next two years, which were the most productive of his life (or, as he put it, 'the prime of my age for invention'). He invented calculus, developed his Universal Law of Gravitation and used the wall of an upstairs room at Woolsthorpe to project the colours of the spectrum, proving that they were the constituents of light. This laid the groundwork for his great *Philosophiae Naturalis Principia Mathematica*, although it was not published until 1687.

It was at Woolsthorpe that Newton was born in 1642. His father died three months before his birth. When Isaac was three, his mother remarried and went to live with her new husband, leaving the young child to be brought up by his grandparents. At the age of twelve, he was sent to Grantham Grammar School, but did not shine. Nevertheless, his withdrawn personality, inventiveness and inability to master farming persuaded his mother to send him to Cambridge, where he developed his obsessive interest in mathematics and natural philosophy, including alchemy. Eventually, despite his distinct lack of social grace, he was elected to a fellowship at Trinity College and later became President of the Royal Society in London. He was knighted by Queen Anne in 1705.

What of the famous apple tree, without which (according to the legendary story, told by Newton himself to his friend, the antiquary William Stukeley) his theory of gravity might not have been formulated? An apple tree that had been alive in Newton's time – perhaps the very tree – blew down in 1820. Since it was so famous, locals cut up most of it for souvenirs and to make furniture, leaving the trunk in a field. In time, this trunk took root and a new tree grew out of it, at something of an angle. This cannot be said to be quite the original tree from which the apple fell, nor is it growing in exactly the same place, but it is genetically identical.

The Midlands

YOU COULD CALL the Midlands the English Shires but it would evoke a very different image. Midlands means industry. Its landmarks include numerous milestones of the Industrial Revolution: the Iron Bridge at Coalbrookdale, built to advertise the product of Abraham Darby's ironworks; Richard Arkwright's mills at Cromford, and the factories that established Josiah Wedgwood, Matthew Boulton and Jesse Boot. Canal barges, railway wagons, juggernauts – Midlands industrialists sent their manufactured products out around the country, sometimes around the world. One wonders what these men would have thought of the vast concrete legs of Britain's most famous motorway interchange, Spaghetti Junction, which plant themselves amid railway tracks and waterways.

There was a social cost to industry; life for a Redditch needlemaker was short, and death horrid. There was a cost, too, borne during the Second World War: Sir Basil Spence's new Coventry Cathedral expressed the rebirth of a city whose ancient centre was all but obliterated by German bombing. Apart from the peerless Shakespeare, born in Stratford-upon-Avon, the region produced Dr Samuel Johnson who, in 1755, published his remarkable dictionary, and out of an unremarkable town in the Nottinghamshire coalfields emerged a writer of genius, D. H. Lawrence.

The Shires are a landscape of great castles and houses – Berkeley and Kenilworth, Chatsworth and Hardwick Hall. The battles that decided the fate of England were often fought in this middle part of the country. The Wars of the Roses ended outside Market Bosworth. The next Civil War opened at Edgehill, turned at Naseby and closed at Stow-on-the-Wold. Charles II hid from the Parliamentary troops searching for him after the Battle of Worcester in an oak, at Boscobel.

The body relies on its heart, and the Shires are the heart of England, an echo – more than an echo – of whose beat can be heard in the music of Edward Elgar, the sonnets of Shakespeare and the legend of Robin Hood.

The Midlands

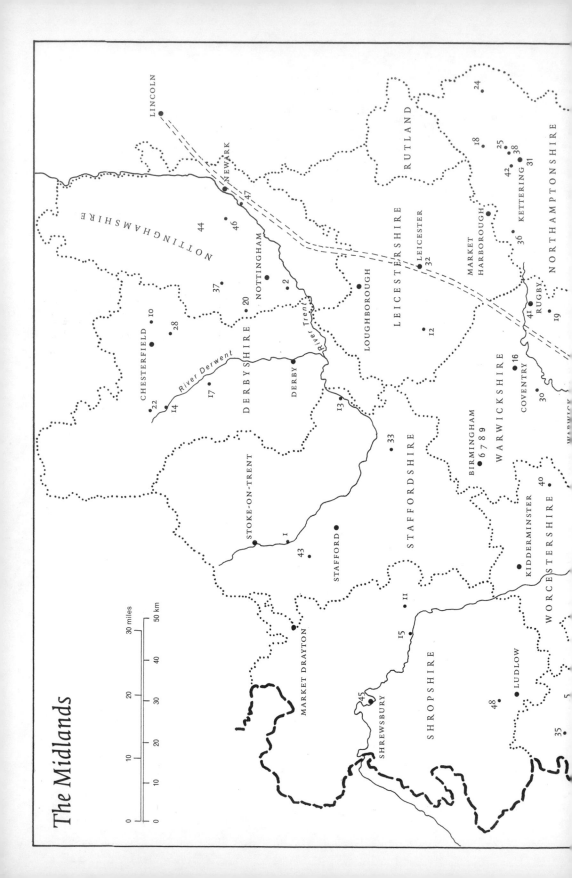

LINCOLN

NEWARK

NOTTINGHAMSHIRE

44
46
47

37
NOTTINGHAM
2

CHESTERFIELD
10
28
20
DERBYSHIRE
DERBY

River Derwent
22
14
17
River Trent
13

STOKE-ON-TRENT
33
STAFFORDSHIRE

1
43
STAFFORD

MARKET DRAYTON

11

15

SHREWSBURY
45

SHROPSHIRE

48
LUDLOW

35

5

RUTLAND
24

18
25
38
42
31
KETTERING
36
NORTHAMPTONSHIRE

LEICESTER
LEICESTERSHIRE
32

LEICESTER

LOUGHBOROUGH
12

MARKET HARBOROUGH

41
19
RUGBY

WARWICKSHIRE
16
COVENTRY
30

BIRMINGHAM
6 7 8 9

40

KIDDERMINSTER

WORCESTERSHIRE

WARWICK

30 miles
50 km

20

10

0

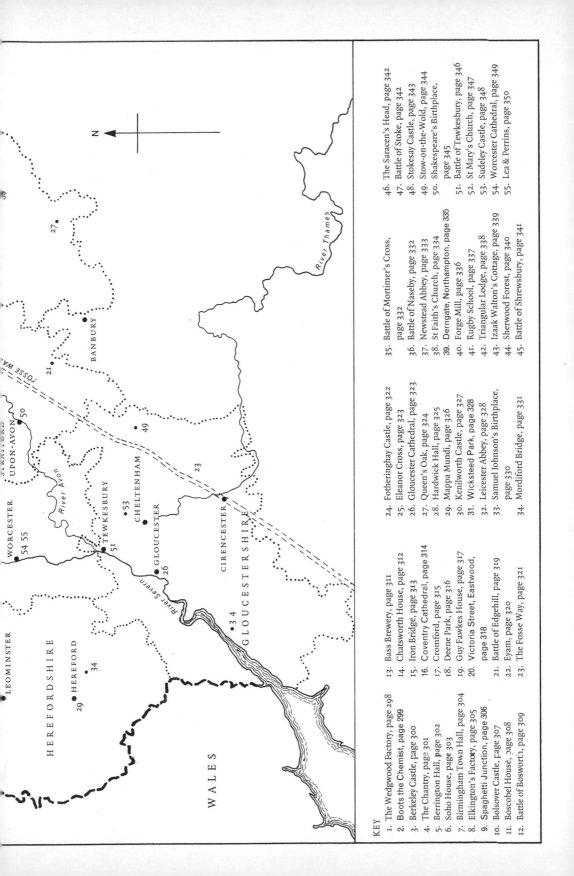

N

THE WEDGWOOD FACTORY

The genius of English pottery

Wedgwood's modern factory and showrooms at Barlaston give little hint of the company's beginnings as a cottage industry in Burslem – now one of what are called the Five Towns (actually six) that make up Stoke-on-Trent. By the time Josiah Wedgwood was born in 1730, his family had been potters for three generations, using clay dug from the nearby fields. Josiah not only transformed the standing of his family but the whole industry, putting English ware on dinner tables across Europe. He was the Renaissance man of 18th-century industry: a scientist and inventor as well as a craftsman, a pioneer of marketing and publicity, a promoter of canals and a campaigner against the slave trade. The destruction of most of his Etruria works (named after the Etruscans who were wrongly believed to have made the pottery that had recently been discovered at Herculaneum and Pompeii) ranks alongside the demolition of the great London palaces of the Georgian aristocracy as one of the more monstrous examples of architectural vandalism in the dark years of the 1960s.

Wedgwood's formal education ended at the age of nine, when the death of his father compelled him to join his brother in the family business. Wedgwood split from his brother in 1759 and opened his own manufactory, developing his famous cream ware, using a combination of clay, stone and flint. It was, as he wrote, 'quite new in its appearance', easy to manufacture and capable of 'bearing sudden alterations of heat and cold'. In 1765, he and his partner Thomas Bentley were delighted to receive an order for a tea service from Queen Charlotte. Wedgwood immediately saw the commercial advantage that royal patronage could give him, and rebranded his previously modest earthenware as Queensware. He took to calling himself Potter to the Queen. Throughout his career, he was not only alive to the aura that was conferred by fashionable clients, but particularly anxious to solicit female approval for his goods. Before introducing any new line, he sought the opinion of his wife.

It was also in 1765 that Wedgwood was pressed to apply his abilities to organising the construction of a canal planned to link the rivers Trent and Mersey. He became treasurer of the project and the 93-mile canal was opened twelve years later. In 1769, Wedgwood opened his famous factory at Hanley, called Etruria – which, not surprisingly, was only a matter of yards away from the planned canal. The canal reduced the cost of bringing in raw materials, and made it much easier to transport finished products, with fewer breakages, to the ports. At Etruria, his innovations continued apace.

He introduced black basalt, a style particularly suited to the austere lines of the new neo-Classical taste. In 1774, his efforts to create an earthenware that would imitate antique cameos met with success: the result was the famous Jasper ware, with figures in relief standing out against a background of what would become known as Wedgwood blue. His most spectacular commission was the Frog Service of 952 pieces that he made for Catherine the Great; destined for her palace of La Grenouillière, each piece was decorated with a frog. He produced more than 1,200 enamelled scenes of English country seats; these gave him the opportunity to flatter the noble families whose parks and houses were depicted. However, he came to realise that the making of 'uniques' for fashionable or royal clients was a profitable way of establishing an even more valuable trade, producing lines that could be made in quantity and sold to the middle classes. To this end, the Frog Service was exhibited in London, bringing 'an immense number of People of Fashion into our Rooms'. By such means, Wedgwood was able to maintain his prices even when trade was in the doldrums.

All that survives of Etruria is a domed roundhouse of uncertain purpose beside the Trent and Mersey Canal. His own house, Etruria Hall, can be seen in the distance, above a marina for canal barges.

BOOTS THE CHEMIST   *BEESTON, NOTTINGHAMSHIRE*
A revolution in everyday life

In 1933, Boots opened its famous D10 'Wets' factory, a structure whose walls seemed all of glass, designed by the progressive engineer, Sir Owen Williams (see page 306). Not only was it a monument of industrial architecture, which so improved the manufacture of medicines ('wets' as opposed to the tablets made in the D6 'Drys' factory next door) that working hours could be reduced for the same pay, but it marked the culmination of a revolution in everyday life that was begun by Jesse Boot.

Boot, from an ardently Methodist background, took over his father's herbalist shop in Goose Gate, Nottingham, in 1877. With his policy of buying and selling strictly for cash – at one time he called the company Boots Cash Chemists – Boot undercut more old-fashioned rivals, and opened other branches in Nottingham. With the railway network able to transport stock from his warehouse to other parts of the country, he opened a shop at Snig Hill in Sheffield in 1884. It was the start of an expansion, accompanied by brass bands and showmanship, which made Boots a familiar name in many high streets. The year in which D10 was inaugurated also saw the opening of the thousandth store.

Boot did not restrict himself to medicaments. Apart from the fancy goods department, the preserve of his wife Florence, there was another Florence inspiration: the Booklovers' Library. These were always carefully sited at the back of shops or upstairs to encourage subscribers to buy more goods en route. However, his achievement was rather more than a retail phenomenon: at a time when doctors made up their own prescriptions, Boot employed trained chemists to provide an alternative service at half the price. This brought medical drugs within the range of ordinary people. So the Boots empire was a commercial triumph with a hint of Methodist philanthropy about it.

After the First World War, Jesse Boot gave the philanthropy full rein by bestowing a New Park on Nottingham and creating a campus for Nottingham University. Although he sold the company to an American concern in 1920, his son John was able to buy back control, just as D10 was opening.

BERKELEY CASTLE GLOUCESTERSHIRE
The murder of Edward II

To his contemporaries, Edward II did not have a kingly temperament. He had no taste for warfare, or even the manly exercise of hunting, which improved the horsemanship that was vital on the battlefield. Every year, his father, Edward I, had done battle in Wales or had marched up to Scotland to subdue the Scots. Edward II, by contrast, neglected the northern border for half a generation, and when he did lead an army into Scotland, it was slaughtered at Bannockburn in 1314 (see page 444). Rather than the panoply of war, he liked such humble rural pursuits as hedging and ditching. He rowed, swam and bred horses, surrounding himself with male favourites, such as the exquisite Gascon, Piers Gaveston – assumed to be the King's lover. The favours that the King heaped on Gaveston made both men unpopular with the barons, and when Gaveston fell into the hands of Guy de Beauchamp, Earl of Warwick, he was brutally beheaded.

The cycle repeated itself with the Despensers, father and son, both named Hugh. The estates that they were given by the King, and the airs that they gave themselves, incensed other nobles, particularly the lords of the Welsh Marches. The Marcher lords went on the rampage against Despenser property. The King managed to regain enough power to punish them, hanging some and imprisoning Roger de Mortimer in the Tower of London. Mortimer escaped and fled to France. When Edward's neglected Queen, Isabella*, went to Paris on a diplomatic mission, she became Mortimer's lover. Together they led an invasion of England in September 1326. The King put up little resistance: the Despensers were butchered, Edward was forced to abdicate in favour of his young son, Edward III, and then imprisoned in Kenilworth Castle (see page 327). When Mortimer, notionally acting on behalf of the new young king, realised he would have to march north against the Scots, it was decided to move Edward II to a more secure gaol. Where better than remote Berkeley Castle, in the hands of Mortimer's son-in-law, Thomas, Lord Berkeley?

Incredibly, a rescue mission succeeded in getting Edward out of the formidable castle, and nearly to the Dorset coast; he was caught, however, and brought back to Berkeley, being confined in a small room. This attempt to free Edward illustrated the danger he posed to Mortimer and Isabella, and a party of knights came to Berkeley and murdered him. It is possible that they used the hideous technique of inserting red-hot irons into his bowels, through a horn placed on his rectum, perhaps chosen because it left no outward mark. While the only account of this appears in the *Polychronicon* written thirty years after the event by Ralph Higden, a Benedictine monk, it is significant that it was retained in the English translation made by John de Trevisa, who happened to be vicar of Berkeley and would therefore have been familiar with the folk memory of the event.

It was now September 1327. While the king's body lay in the castle chapel as preparations were made for its burial in Gloucester Cathedral†, Lord Berkeley concentrated, seemingly unconcerned, on his hunting and hawking. It was not long, however, before Mortimer overreached himself and was executed, in November 1330. The teenager Edward III hunted down some of his father's assassins but Lord Berkeley did not so much as flee the country. Arguing that he had been laid up sick at one of his other manors at the time of the murder, he was acquitted. His effigy, in full armour, lies beside that of his wife in Berkeley parish church.

*See Castle Rising, page 262. †See Gloucester Cathedral, page 323

THE CHANTRY
BERKELEY, GLOUCESTERSHIRE

Jenner discovers the principles of vaccination

In the late 1790s, the principles of vaccination were discovered by a country doctor, Edward Jenner. It was one of the greatest of all medical advances, leading to the worldwide eradication of smallpox, according to the World Health Organisation in 1979. Smallpox was an appalling disease, which either killed its victims within a fortnight or left them horribly disfigured from deep pockmarks caused by the pustules that covered face, body and limbs. Throughout most of the 18th century, it killed between 1,000 and 3,000 people in London every year. It had been realised that inoculation (by which a patient was infected with a hopefully mild dose of smallpox) provided protection, but the preventive dose sometimes killed, or left the patient blind.

Jenner, born in 1749, had been a distinguished pupil at St George's Hospital in London, but felt too attached to the countryside where he had grown up to leave it forever. In the West Country, dairymaids sometimes caught cowpox from the cows they milked, causing mild lesions on their hands. Jenner learnt that they would not then contract smallpox. He set out to prove that human beings could artificially be given cowpox, and that the cowpox could be kept alive if passed from one person to another. For the first part of the experiment, Jenner needed an individual who was known never to have had either cowpox or smallpox. As the village doctor, he knew the medical history of the young people in his care, and chose the eight-year-old son of his gardener, James Phipps. First, Jenner took some of the pus from a cowpox lesion and rubbed it into a nick on James's arm; cowpox developed satisfactorily. Then he repeated the procedure for smallpox. James survived, and Jenner went to London to find a body of people on whom he could test vaccination further.

His findings were published privately in 1798 as *An Inquiry into the Causes and Effects of the Variolæ Vaccinæ, a disease discovered in some of the Western Counties of England, particularly Gloucestershire, and known by the name of the Cow-Pox*. The idea of vaccination quickly spread around the world. In 1802, Parliament recognised Jenner's achievement by voting him £10,000; a further sum of £20,000 was granted in 1806. At The Chantry, a local vicar built a thatched Temple of Vaccinia, the door flanked with rustic tree trunks, and from here Jenner gave free vaccination to village people.

While Jenner's greatest legacy to mankind lies in medicine, he also made some remarkable observations in natural history, studying the hibernation of the hedgehog, closely observing the behaviour of cuckoos (it was for this work that he was elected to the Royal Society) and deducing the migration of birds.

See also St Mary's Hospital, page 178

BERRINGTON HALL   NEAR LEOMINSTER, HEREFORDSHIRE
Admiral Rodney saves the West Indies

If Admiral George Rodney had not been such an awkward character, whom contemporaries admired as a man of action but rarely liked, his reputation today might be almost as glorious as Nelson's. By his brilliant direction of the Battle of the Saints in 1782, he succeeded in saving Britain's colonies in the West Indies, then far more valuable to her than those that she was losing in North America. Before that, with the British navy fighting alone against the French, Spanish and Dutch, one island after another had been lost, and now the French admiral, the Comte de Grasse, was leading an invasion fleet towards Jamaica. Rodney caught de Grasse by the Îles des Saintes, between Dominica and Guadeloupe. Thanks to a change of wind, his fleet, capitalising on a piece of good luck, broke through the enemy line in three places; this flukish manoeuvre was later developed by Nelson into the strategy that won him Trafalgar.

The next year, 1783, the Treaty of Versailles confirmed the loss of America, but restored to Britain the islands of Antigua, St Lucia, St Kitts, Nevis and Grenada, among other West Indian possessions.

While the Battle of the Saints was being fought, Rodney's son, also called George, was finishing Berrington Hall, which had been begun to the designs of Henry Holland in 1778. George had married, much to his father's approval, Anne Harley, the daughter of a rich alderman Thomas Harley. Ironically, perhaps, the style of the architecture and decoration was in a neo-Classical style, much influenced by up-to-the-minute taste in France. The dining room contains four large battle pictures depicting Rodney's victories, including two showing the admiral breaking the French line and the French flagship surrendering.

SOHO HOUSE BIRMINGHAM
The manufacturing phenomenon of Birmingham

In 1759, Matthew Boulton inherited his father's business making metal ornaments – buckles, buttons, snuffboxes and other grown-up 'toys'. Two years later, he began to build a new factory in the Soho area of Handsworth, which would become a phenomenon; nowhere in the world could rival its scale or variety of production. It set Birmingham on the industrial course that it would follow for the next century and a half.

From decorative objects, now including cut-steel jewellery and sword hilts, Boulton progressed to Sheffield plate. With Sheffield plate, a layer of silver was fused onto copper sheets, out of which tableware could be made. It looked like silver but cost far less. Deducing that there would be a more affluent market for the same designs made out of silver itself, Boulton began a campaign to have an assay office opened in Birmingham, in order to avoid the expense and danger of transporting his pieces long distances to be hallmarked. It opened in 1773. Another product range was created from ormolu, a compound that produced a gilded effect.

By now, the Soho Manufactory employed hundreds of people, the many sheds in which they worked being concealed behind a domed façade. Power for the machinery came from a nearby brook. As a manufacturer, Boulton was alert to the potential of the steam engine, and when James Watt's early backer fell into financial difficulties, he took over the partnership. From 1774 Boulton & Watt steam engines powered the Industrial Revolution. In 1796 an especially dedicated foundry was built two miles away to make them. Already Boulton had found a new application for steam power: minting coins.

In its time, the Soho Manufactory was almost considered to be one of the wonders of the world, and yet in 1862–3, less than a hundred years after it was built, the factory was demolished. Nevertheless, the house in which Boulton lived, overlooking the works, remains. Acquired unfinished in 1761, it assumed its present form under the hands of the London architect Samuel Wyatt (with contributions, not well supervised, from his more fashionable brother, James) in 1799. At Soho House, Boulton would often entertain the group of enterprising, inquisitive amateur Midlands scientists and industrialists known as the Lunar Society.

BIRMINGHAM TOWN HALL BIRMINGHAM
'Noble edifice' that symbolises civic reform

Birmingham Town Hall is a symbol of the reform of civic institutions that many industrial towns badly needed by the 1830s. Certain Birmingham manufacturers opposed reform, on the grounds that freedom from regulation had helped them prosper, but the arrangements by which this town of over 100,000 people was governed had come to seem antiquated, if not quaint. A body of unelected Commissioners, who could raise and spend taxes with little public scrutiny, controlled the streets; otherwise the rights of the Lord of the Manor still held sway. All large meetings had had to take place in a building called Beardsworth's Repository.

Rising up like a Greek temple, in white Anglesey marble, over the ramshackle streets that originally surrounded it, the Town Hall provided altogether more dignified surroundings and soon came to represent a visible sign of the new order ushered in by the 1832 Reform Act. This act gave Birmingham, for the first time, representation in Parliament through two MPs. Local democracy came when Birmingham was finally incorporated as a municipal corporation in 1838.

As both architects and contractors, Hansom & Welch underestimated the cost of the work, which caused delays, but it was formally opened in 1834. The official Guide extolled the virtues of this 'noble edifice', which looked equally ravishing by moonlight as it did during the day. 'Good people of Birmingham,' exhorted the author, Mr Bates, 'let all strangers see the inside of your noble building . . . and the eye will sweep over a spectacle which is equalled by nothing but old Niagara – a spectacle at once awful, sublime, and heart-throbbing.'

If, however, the elders of Birmingham thought that the building of a Town Hall and the election of MPs on a limited franchise would satisfy industrial workers, who still had no vote, they were completely wrong. The Chartist leader Fergus O'Connor roused a meeting held in the Town Hall in 1838, with cries of 'physical force', and Chartists (see page 427) rioted in the Bull Ring the next year.

ELKINGTON'S FACTORY

Inventing the world's first plastic

At the International Exhibition of 1862 held in London, Alexander Parkes exhibited articles made of what is generally acknowledged as the world's first true plastic, which he called Parkesine. Today, plastic, in its many forms, is such a ubiquitous material that it is difficult to imagine a world without it. Whereas most raw materials, such as wood, stone, iron and steel, have been worked by man since time immemorial, plastics – synthetic substances that can be moulded to any shape – were the result of applied chemistry, developed during the Victorian age.

The impetus was the fortune which stood to be made from mass-producing everyday objects that had previously been shaped by craftsmen. The Industrial Revolution had already virtually eliminated the craft content in ironwork, textiles and pottery, all of which could be cheaply produced using machines, but the ornaments so beloved of the Victorians had to be hand-carved or moulded from expensive, naturally occurring materials such as horn, tortoise-shell and amber.

Parkes worked for the Birmingham firm of Elkington, Mason & Co. – set between Newhall Street and the Birmingham & Fazeley Canal – as manager of the casting department. Elkington's had already helped feed the insatiable Victorian appetite for apparently aristocratic trinkets and cutlery sold at middle-class prices by pioneering the electroplating of base metals with silver. It had been Parkes who discovered that adding cyanide to the silver solution would produce an even coating of silver. The resulting patent gave Elkington's a monopoly for several years.

Parkesine was an early form of celluloid. Parkes patented it in 1865 and established a company to produce it, in the form of knife handles and combs, at Hackney Wick outside London. In trying to drive down costs, however, he compromised on the materials he used, product quality was therefore unreliable, and the company failed. He sold his patents to Daniel Spill, who renamed his company Xylonite Ltd. In turn, Xylonite lost out to a company established in the United States by John Hyatt. Hyatt's early attempts to produce billiard balls using cellulose nitrate, rather than ivory, were hampered by their tendency to spark on contact, producing a sound like a percussion cap (in Colorado billiard saloons, men would pull guns when they heard it). He discovered that the answer was to add camphor as a plasticiser. He called the result celluloid. In the course of an epic legal battle over patents, waged between the Xylonite and Celluloid companies, it was recognised that Parkes had got there first.

SPAGHETTI JUNCTION *BIRMINGHAM*

Motorway madness

Finished in 1972, the Gravelly Hill interchange, a.k.a. Junction 6 on the M6, instantly became, for good or ill, a symbol of Britain's motorway system. Britain had been slow to meet the needs of the motor car. Germany, with its Volkswagen or 'people's car', was recognised as having stolen a march with its autobahns, the earliest stretch dating from before the First World War. In Britain, the Preston by-pass, a section of 8½ miles that eventually became part of the M6, opened in 1958 (the same year that parking meters were introduced). The first part of the M1, a 72-mile section from near Luton to near Crick, brought the idea of supposedly non-stop motorway driving over long distances to Britain the next year.

The engineer responsible for the M1 was Sir Owen Williams. Williams had been awarded his knighthood at the early age of thirty-four for his work on the British Empire Exhibition of 1924, whose permanent legacy was Wembley Stadium (the last fragments of which, the famous towers, were demolished in 2003). The M1 is not an elegant road. The line is straight, having been determined by existing railway and power lines, and the slab-like, standardised bridges lack grace. By the time Williams, helped by his son O. T. Williams, started work on the M6, it was a different matter. Having studied the roads engineered in the United States, Williams now contrived motorways that moved through the landscape in a series of subtly adjusted alignments, which would both be more interesting for the driver and more sympathetic to the countryside through which they passed. While they may not achieve the beauty of some Italian roads, in the right mood the M4, M5 and M6 can be appreciated for their aesthetic quality.

Spaghetti Junction, connecting the M6 with the A38(M) and various other roads leading into the centre of Birmingham, is the supreme expression of this approach. Seen from the air, the ribbons of curving carriageway seem to interlace with the pleasing intricacy of an Elizabethan knot garden. Seen from below, the knot is revealed as a three-dimensional wonder, with flyovers weaving in and out of each other at different levels. The 2½ miles of slip road are supported on a total of 559 concrete legs, which stalk confidently across the three canals and a railway line, recalling earlier periods of Midlands transportation.

The general public did not see the elegance of Spaghetti Junction as an engineering solution; instead, it immediately became a byword for the profligacy of the motor car, already accused of eating up too many green fields. Economy of land use seemed to have been a low priority when the whorls of road were created. The concrete of the construction did not charm the public eye. Motorways may have heralded what Prime Minister Margaret Thatcher, in the 1980s, called the 'great car economy', but unease was already being caused by their impact on both the rural and urban environments; the M6 tears its way through Birmingham with the ruthlessness associated with the Victorian railway promoters.

The Owen Williams company was called upon to respond to the criticism by designing the M54 (which runs west from the M6 to Telford in Shropshire) on environmental principles. Even this was not enough to satisfy the 'green' lobby. By the end of the 20th century, no government wanted to provide the new roads that would be needed if car ownership continued to grow at predicted rates. How to contain the car while allowing drivers the freedom to use it without traffic jams became a conundrum with which Britain continues to struggle. The M6 Toll Road, Britain's first toll-collecting motorway, opened in 2003, with the object of avoiding the dire congestion with which Spaghetti Junction and adjoining stretches of motorway have become associated.

BOLSOVER CASTLE
DERBYSHIRE

Temple to courtly horsemanship

William Cavendish, created Duke of Newcastle at the Restoration, was one of the most accomplished horsemen of his age. In particular, he excelled in the art of *haute école* or *manège*, by which horses could be disciplined to leap, prance and kick as the rider wished – in a style similar to that still practised at the Spanish Riding School in Vienna. It was regarded as a princely activity, since the apparently stylised paces of the horses could be useful on the battlefield. The greatest exponent in Britain, if not Europe, was Charles I. Cavendish was chosen as tutor to his eldest son: he regarded his greatest achievement as teaching the future king to ride. At his home, Bolsover Castle, Cavendish built a riding school in which he could pursue *haute école*.

Bolsover is the ultimate cavalier house. While it occupies the site of a medieval castle, Cavendish's father, Charles, the youngest son of that indefatigable builder, Bess of Hardwick (see page 325), had built a new 'Little Castle'. It was a castle of romance, with turrets and battlements but little practical use as fortification. All this was in the spirit of the Court entertainment known as the masque – an exquisite and costly fantasy, which used words, music, dance, elaborate costumes and spectacular stage effects to celebrate qualities of the King's rule – which were sometimes very far from reality. It was acted by courtiers, and Charles I and Queen Henrietta Maria would themselves descend (sometimes from the clouds) to lead the dance. When King Charles visited Bolsover in 1633, a masque called 'Love's Welcome', commissioned from Ben Jonson, was staged for him. The whole event, including an extravagant feast, cost the astonishing sum of £15,000.

Although he preferred *haute école* to soldiering, during the Civil War Cavendish raised, maintained and led Royalist troops in the northern counties. He was a cavalier to his manicured fingertips: a lover of the arts, poetry, swordsmanship, fine clothes and women, who spent his last years of exile during the Commonwealth living in the Antwerp house of the painter Peter Paul Rubens. These tastes did not fit easily with military life, particularly since his fastidious attention to his appearance meant that little could be done before midday.

BOSCOBEL HOUSE NEAR TELFORD, SHROPSHIRE
Where Charles II hid after the Battle of Worcester

Charles II was eighteen when his father Charles I was beheaded in 1649 (see page 114). Too young to participate in the Civil War, he had spent it in exile, but in 1650 he crossed from France to Scotland to take up what had become his own cause. Few recruits were gained, however, as he and his supporters moved south into England, and when Cromwell, with his disciplined and seasoned army, caught up with them at Worcester on 3 September 1651, they were crushed. At the end of the battle, Charles was forced to flee. But where? He seems to have had no plan of escape.

The immediate need was somewhere to hide for the night. One of his party knew of a place, about forty miles away, a hunting lodge hidden among the beautiful woods from which it took its name of Boscobel (originally Bosco Bello). The King's first night was spent at the neighbouring house of White-ladies, a mile from Boscobel: prudently, he only told a few of his party about Boscobel itself. At Whiteladies, whose owner was away, he was received by the servants, a family of brothers called Penderel. From here, he set out next morning dressed as a yokel; his hair had been cut short and soot rubbed into his face to dirty it. Hiding in a wood, he contemplated a return to Scotland, but finally made up his mind that the best course would be to cross into Wales, where he knew of several loyal families. After dark, he set off with Richard Penderel to walk to the river Severn. Finding that all the river crossings were guarded by Parliamentary troops, he returned, this time to Boscobel, with bleeding feet, at about three o'clock in the morning.

Boscobel began life as a timber-framed farmhouse, built about 1530 by Thomas Giffard. The brick hunting tower was added in the early 17th century, partly with the intention of holding services there for the Roman Catholic owners. For this reason, it was equipped with hiding places for priests. When Penderel approached the house, he found one of Charles's officers, with the splendid cavalier name of Charles Careless, already hiding there. At daybreak, Charles thought of hiding in the wood, but Careless persuaded him that it would be safer for them to climb into an oak that stood in open ground; its top had been lopped a few years earlier, so the crown was bushy. From his hiding place, he could see soldiers hunting for him through the wood. In the evening, the fugitives came down, and ravenously consumed a dish of chicken. The next day, Sunday, the King spent hiding under the floorboards at the top of Boscobel. Early on Monday morning he set off with the Penderel brothers to Moseley Hall in Staffordshire, the Giffards' main home. After two days, he was able to leave with Jane Lane, the sister of a royalist colonel, in search of a ship to France: she had a pass for herself and a servant. No ship could be found at Bristol, nor at Brighton. It was only when she and the King reached Shoreham that they found a ship to take them from England.

Having spent six weeks on the run, Charles now began nine years of exile in France. In 1660, he was invited back to the throne of England. With him on board the *Naseby* was Samuel Pepys, to whom he told the story of the oak tree. Thereafter, the King's birthday was celebrated as Oak Apple Day, and the Royal Oak is still seen on over 700 pub signs throughout England.

BATTLE OF BOSWORTH

Where Richard III would have given his kingdom for a horse

In 1485, Richard III was the last English king to lead a charge of knights in full armour. His example was not propitious. But whatever Richard's other faults, lack of bravery was not among them. He was a skilful commander, had assembled a more impressive force than his adversary and, at the moment he was killed, was risking all in a brilliant move that should have won him the battle. He lost. The rest is history, thickly veiled in Tudor propaganda.

For so calculating a man as Henry Tudor, Earl of Richmond, soon to be Henry VII, an invasion at the head of a largely French army of 2,000 men was a gamble. He landed at Milford Haven (see page 426) on 7 August, in the extreme south-west of Wales, and moved towards the Midlands, gathering strength. Within eight days, he had reached Shrewsbury and his force had doubled. His tenuous claim to the throne came through his mother, Margaret Beaufort, who was descended from Edward III through his fourth son John of Gaunt's union with his mistress Catherine Swynford. John of Gaunt's children, including Margaret Beaufort's grandfather John, were barred from succession since they had been born out of wedlock, although they were legitimised when the couple later married. It was Henry's mother's second husband, Thomas Stanley, later 1st Earl of Derby, who was supposed to supply a body of soldiers equal to his own. When Henry met him in Leicestershire, however, he found that his support was not assured. On the morning of Sunday, 21 August, his army deployed from their camp, and the sight of the

King's forces, more than twice as numerous as their own, formed up along the top of the commanding rise of Ambion Hill, must have been disquieting.

Richard had been on the throne for two years. Like his brother Edward IV, he cultivated the Renaissance taste for magnificence, and strove to quell the dissension that had bedevilled England for thirty years. However, having reputedly murdered the two nephews who were next in line to the crown, he had been unable to extend his northern power base to embrace the south. Like other kings, he ruled through fear. On hearing of Henry's landing, he summoned his forces with the bracing reminder that the noblemen who failed to appear in arms would lose everything. He had already taken the precaution of holding Lord Stanley's son, Lord Strange, as a hostage; although the father observed that he had other sons, it was an understandable deterrent. Stanley and his brother Sir William Stanley therefore formed a third force, stationed a little to the north of Bosworth Field, unwilling to commit themselves to either side. Stanley was a survivor.

While Henry's army was still manoeuvring around the marsh at the foot of the hill, the 1st Duke of Norfolk led a charge for King Richard down the slope that could have smashed them; the Duke died for his bravery. Formed into a wedge, they withstood the assault, but Henry knew that, faced by overwhelming odds, it was only a matter of time before they were overpowered. With a guard of eighty knights, his banner flying, he galloped towards Lord Stanley, to urge that they should combine forces. Richard saw his chance. Lowering his lance, he charged, followed by a thousand of his cavalry. It was ideal terrain, the slope, which was then unimpeded by hedges, allowing the horses to gather a crushing momentum. The King succeeded in killing Henry's standard-bearer, close to Henry himself, at which point Lord Stanley took advantage of Richard's exposed flank. He threw in his lot with Henry and ordered his front 4,000 troops into the fray. Richard III, unhorsed, was killed in a stream.

The coronet that Richard wore over his helmet was recovered from a thorn bush, and Stanley placed it on Henry's head. Richard's body was taken to Leicester and displayed for two days, before being buried at Greyfriars monastery. Henry VII went on to marry Elizabeth, daughter of Edward IV, and Richard's niece, an alliance that symbolically bound together the feuding dynasties of Lancaster and York and brought the Wars of the Roses* to an end. Richard's bones were not allowed to enjoy the fruits of the ensuing peace. When Henry's son, Henry VIII, dissolved the monasteries, his grave was dug up and his remains thrown into the river Soar.

*See First Battle of St Albans, page 240; Battle of Wakefield, page 403; Battle of Mortimer's Cross, page 332; Second Battle of St Albans, page 241; Battle of Towton, page 402; Battle of Barnet, page 204; Battle of Tewkesbury, page 346

BASS BREWERY

Slaking the thirst of an empire

Traditionally, the British drink beer rather than wine. The climate in the north was unsuitable, and the southern summers too unreliable to ensure good grape harvests; whereas barley, hops and yeast – the ingredients of beer – have been readily to hand for millennia. Beer was being drunk before the Romans invaded. Families brewed it for their own use. This remained the pattern for most of the next thousand years, larger production only becoming viable when organised by the monasteries.

It was an abbey that established Burton upon Trent's reputation for brewing. The brothers used water that had been sanctified by St Modwen, a 7th-century nun who lived as a hermit on a little island in the Trent. Water from the well there is supposed to have produced miracles. When used for brewing, it certainly had a benign effect: the high levels of calcium sulphate happened to suit the brewing process, making a beer of bright colour and bitter taste. After the Dissolution (see page 133), the monastic brew house passed into private hands, and local inns followed suit by establishing their own breweries; by 1604 there were no fewer than forty-six in the town.

With the passing of the Trent Navigation Act in 1712, brewers had the means to reach a wider market. Merchants took control of the trade. One of them was William Bass, a Leicestershire boy who had married the daughter of a pub landlord from London. He was a carrier by trade, but the couple set up home in a house in Burton's High Street, to which a small brewery was attached. By the 1780s, after the Trent and Mersey canal system had been opened (see page 298), Bass was sending his beer – dark and hoppy – to London, Manchester and Hull. They then began to export to the Baltic, North America and even Paris. In the next century, the lighter style of beer was exported in such volume to India that it acquired the name of IPA, standing for India Pale Ale.

If Burton water created a beautiful beer, the brewing industry did not repay the compliment by building a beautiful town. However, it provided employment not just for those directly involved in brewing, but coopers, blacksmiths, wheelwrights, engineers and others. Another by-product of the industry arose from the yeast waste that remained after brewing. In 1902, a disused malthouse in Burton upon Trent gave birth to the ambrosial or (depending on taste) tarry yeast extract spread, Marmite.

CHATSWORTH HOUSE

NEAR BAKEWELL, DERBYSHIRE

Country house of country houses

Chatsworth, begun in 1687, is the first Baroque palace – princely in style and magnificence – built for a subject rather than a monarch in England. While other houses are splendid in different ways, Chatsworth is now considered the most consummate example of a great English country house, where the visitor is awed not just by the scale and architecture of the building, but by the sumptuous decoration, rich furniture, numerous masterpieces, superb library, outstanding gardens, beautiful woodland and immaculate estate village.

The foundation of these glories was laid by William Cavendish, 4th Earl of Devonshire, one of the seven influential but not pre-eminent men who invited William of Orange to come to England in 1688, soon ousting his father-in-law James II (see page 13). As a reward for this service, he was created a Duke in 1694, and no doubt the financial advantages of his position at the new Court enabled him to raise his game in the decoration of Chatsworth. However, the project had begun in the last years of the previous reign. The then Lord Devonshire had inherited an Elizabethan courtyard house, built for the Suffolk gentleman Sir William Cavendish. Cavendish had been persuaded to sell up in Suffolk and move to Derbyshire by his formidable wife Bess of Hardwick, a Derbyshire girl. (Cavendish was the second of her four husbands; Chatsworth was the first of the three great houses that she built.) They employed the architect William Talman to rebuild first the sternly magnificent south front and then the east wing of the house; the authorship of the west wing, which was also eventually replaced, is in doubt.

Talman brought with him a team of craftsmen whose talents were otherwise employed in the royal palaces: the mural painters Louis Laguerre and Antonio Verrio, the sculptor Caius Gabriel Cibber, and the virtuoso metalworker Jean Tijou. They were complemented by the woodcarver Samuel Watson – not Grinling Gibbons, but capable of equally remarkable effects. The result is a sumptuous fusion of the arts. Behind the scenes, however, not all was harmony: in the State Dining Room, Verrio included a portrait of the bad-tempered housekeeper, Mrs Hackett, as one of the furies on the ceiling, cutting 'the thread of life'. Outside, the Cascade – a formal waterfall that takes advantage of the hilly site – survives from the Duke's Baroque garden, created amid what were then regarded as bleak and desolate moors.

Since the 1st Duke's day, Chatsworth has been altered and enlarged by those who came after him, notably the 6th Duke, for whom Jeffry Wyatville built the north wing. The contents of the house have been enriched by those from the Devonshires' London palace of Devonshire House, demolished in the 1920s, and Chiswick House (see page 134), which they also owned. The fact that it occupies its position as the country house that all other country houses aspire to be like is due to the energy and dedication of Andrew, the 11th Duke of Devonshire and his wife Deborah Mitford, who rescued it from the doldrums of death duties and use during the Second World War as a girls' school.

IRON BRIDGE
Advertisement for the Industrial Revolution

The Iron Bridge that the Quaker ironmaster Abraham Darby III built across the Severn gorge at Coalbrookdale was practically an advertisement for the Industrial Revolution. It showed that anything could be built from iron. The semicircle of the arch, reflecting in the river to make a full circle, must have seemed an emblem of perfection. Designed by Thomas Pritchard, otherwise an architect who built country houses for the Shropshire gentry, the Iron Bridge was an instant phenomenon. Even before its completion in 1779, Darby had publicised it through an engraving. Crowds of tourists came to marvel, other manufacturers to spy.

It was iron that had created the need for the bridge in the first place. Abraham Darby I, a Bristol brass founder, had arrived in the dale in 1708, buying up a derelict ironworks. His discovery that coke rather than wood could be used for smelting occurred the next year, although the invention was kept secret for nearly fifty years. Over the next three quarters of a century, the steep, wooded banks of the Severn – whose water powered the bellows of the blast furnaces – became the picturesque home to the fiery industry of iron making. The first iron wheels, for a colliery engine, were cast here in 1729; the first iron rails in 1767. Within a two-mile stretch, there were more furnaces than anywhere else in the world. Hundreds of boats plied the Severn between Gloucester and Welshpool, bringing raw materials and taking away finished goods, but the nearest fixed crossing was the medieval bridge at Buildwas, later washed away in a flood. Other crossings had to be made by ferries which were unreliable both in summer, when the river could be too shallow, and in winter, when the water invariably rushed down too strongly.

Abraham Darby III lived in comfort at Dale House, the tall, redbrick, typically Shropshire house built by Abraham I overlooking the gorge. Although the third generation in the company, he had no shortage of expansionist energy. He was only eighteen when he took over in 1768, his father Abraham II having died five years before. His wife wrote in mock horror of the amount of money Darby invested in industrial projects. The Iron Bridge, being the first of its kind, was necessarily an experiment. The constituent parts were cast in open sand moulds – as can be seen from their slightly rough surface. They were held together by carpentry-type joints, with dovetails and pegs, which is not surprising since Pritchard had begun life as a joiner. This construction provided enough give in the structure to help it withstand geological move-ment. In the early 19th century, the original stone abutments at either end of the bridge were replaced first by timber and then by iron to counteract ground movement that was cracking the bridge.

Structurally and symbolically, the bridge was a triumph, but it cost Darby far more than he could recoup through tolls, and when he died of scarlet fever at the age of thirty-nine, he was still in debt.

COVENTRY CATHEDRAL WARWICKSHIRE

Rebirth after the Blitz

On the night of 14 November 1940, the planes of the Luftwaffe obliterated medieval Coventry, killing 568 people. A generation of British men and women were appalled at the raid, not only because it was the first of its kind but because it left the cathedral in ruins. Until then, it had been one of the wonders of Perpendicular Gothic architecture. Now only a husk remained, although miraculously the beautiful spire survived. The decision to rebuild the cathedral was taken the next day. When work began fifteen years later, it became famous as a symbol of hope, of the new dawn, of Resurrection.

Basil Spence, chosen as architect after a competition and knighted for his achievement, saw the ruins as an emblem of sacrifice. It was his vision that they should be kept, with the new structure arising beside them. The latter was built at a right angle to the ruins, so that it faced north/south. It is clad in the red sandstone of the original fabric, to express continuity, and a great porch both invites visitors inside and provides a frame within which, once there, they can view the ruins. The whole of this side of the building – liturgically west – is a wall of glass, etched with figures of angels and saints. The openness and light – the very newness – evoke the Resurrection of Easter that follows the Good Friday of suffering. Even today, with its concrete walls, the new cathedral seems bold and modern. There are no columns, no screens, to interrupt the great, plain space. As you walk around the building, however, you realise that it is not as simple as it first seems. Looking back from the altar, stained glass shines in a series of tall strips, shaped like the gills of a fish. The plan is free but traditional, with what quite clearly are a nave and a chancel – here is none of the worship 'in the round' of Frederick Gibberd's Metropolitan Cathedral of Christ in Liverpool that was begun in 1962, the year Coventry was finished.

Furthermore, the cathedral stands squarely in the Arts and Crafts tradition by virtue of the exquisite works of art and applied art that were contributed by some of the leading artistic talents in Britain. Jacob Epstein sculpted the bronze figure of St Michael and Lucifer on the flank of the building (good stands triumphant, evil languishes in chains); Graham Sutherland designed the famous hanging, descending the entire height of the nave, of *Christ in Glory*; the Baptistery window, on the liturgical south side of the nave, was designed by John Piper, and the bronze eagle on the lectern is by Elisabeth Frink. Often, the small scale of the art contrasts with Spence's vast, unadorned envelope, creating a sense of intimacy and humanity. Unusually in post-Second World War Britain, Coventry Cathedral was a building in which even otherwise conventional people felt a sense of national pride.

CROMFORD
Birth of the factory system

Mill owner and inventor, Sir Richard Arkwright was one of the key figures of the Industrial Revolution, and did more than anyone to introduce the system of factory production using water power. By the time of his death in 1792, Cromford in Derbyshire, with what the visitor Viscount Torrington described as three 'magnificent' cotton mills, had become 'as crowded as a Chinese town', set amid water, rocks and woods. As well as the stern but titanic industrial complex, there were houses for vital workers, supplemented by a model village built by his son, Richard Arkwright II. Although Arkwright senior was not above using child labour and imposing a 13-hour day, he also took a pragmatic interest in the conditions in which his workers lived: Cromford was in the middle of the wild Derbyshire Peaks, and they needed to be tempted to move there.

Without formal education, Arkwright worked first as a barber and then moved into wig making. On his travels around the country to collect the necessary hair, he met people who were involved in what was then the cottage industry of spinning*, and realised that their job could be done more efficiently. Arkwright collaborated with John Kay, a clockmaker, to devise the first spinning frame: he was thirty-seven when it was patented in 1769. Success for Arkwright might have been slow in arriving, but when it did it was substantial. With other partners to provide capital, he opened his first mill in Nottingham, then the centre of the stocking trade, using horses to power the water frames. He soon transferred his operations to Cromford, where the fast-flowing streams provided a cheaper and more effective source of power. Within ten years he had become rich. From 'being a poor man not worth £5', commented a contemporary, he now kept a carriage and servants, and had become Lord of the Manor. In 1787, he was appointed High Sheriff of Derbyshire and was knighted.

Labour relations were not always easy. At one point Arkwright had to lay in a considerable armoury to protect his mills from a threatening mob. Nevertheless, he established a market for his workforce, offering stallholders prizes to encourage them to offer the best produce. The same principle was applied in the mills, where hard-working hands were allowed special clothes. Unlike Victorian paternalists, he did not build a church – that was left to his son. However, towards the end of his life he began Willersley Castle, a substantial neo-feudal pile directly overlooking the village.

*See Hall i' th' Wood, page 362, and Paradise Mill, page 369

DEENE PARK

'Half a league, half a league, half a league onward'

One of the survivors of the Charge of the Light Brigade, an engagement in October 1854 that personified the discipline, bravery, pride and sometimes bone-headedness of the Victorian army, stares gently out of a glass case under the main staircase of Deene Park. This is Ronald, the horse that carried the 7th Earl of Cardigan down the Valley of Death and back again. His tail is mounted on a plaque on the wall. The parts in between were every bit as beautiful, since Cardigan's mount was a thoroughbred, a fine, aristocratic horse for a vain aristocratic man, whose portraits show him to have taken an excessive amount of trouble over his beard and moustaches. Ronald had arrived from England shortly before the Charge, in bandbox condition. The horses ridden by the rest of the Light Brigade, who had been camped in the Crimea for weeks, may not have been on quite such good form, but Cardigan is said to have spent £10,000 of his own money to keep the 11th Hussars (or 'Cherry-Pickers' as they were known from the tight crimson trousers they wore) whom he commanded at the peak of smartness.

Ronald's handsome looks and condition reflected the prickly *amour propre* that characterised the officer cadre in the Crimea, causing the rivalries and hatreds that led to the infamous Charge. Lord Lucan, who was in overall command of the cavalry, let a personal quarrel with his brother-in-law, Lord Cardigan, commander of the Light Brigade, reach such a point that their respective staffs refused to cooperate. A young captain, Nolan, who held both men in contempt, galloped over to Cardigan with an order from the commanding officer, Lord Raglan, to stop guns captured by the Russians being carried away during their retreat. Cardigan could not see the guns and misunderstood the instructions as Nolan insolently gestured at the wrong valley. 'Here goes the last of the Brudenells,' murmured Cardigan as he set off at the head of his brigade; only a third of them returned in a condition to fight again.

Cardigan was not the last of the Brudenells. He returned to Deene Park, the house that his forebears had begun building in the early 16th century, and which Brudenells still occupy today. Cardigan may have been tried before the

House of Lords for duelling, and was known as a divisive, unreasonable commander, but his life at Deene seems to have been very happy. In 1868, his memorial was added to those of earlier Brudenells in the parish church: his marble eyes, above the moustaches, gaze towards heaven, while those of his wife are turned adoringly towards him. It is a touching image of Victorian marital values – commissioned by his second wife who was to survive her husband by forty-seven years. (Towards the end of her life, Lady Cardigan had her coffin set on trestles outside the ballroom, where she would invite friends to climb in and try it for comfort.)

Ronald lived until 1872. He was therefore on hand to lead the Earl's funeral procession. With his thoroughbred temperament, it was feared that he would be too skittish for the occasion, so he was given laudanum to calm him down. This worked only too well and he went into an impenetrable sleep from which the grooms were unable to rouse him. Finally someone brought a bugle and sounded a charge. Ronald woke up and was then able to escort his master on his last journey. This is the story told to me by one of the guides when I visited Deene Park. It would be nice to believe it was true.

GUY FAWKES HOUSE   DUNCHURCH, WARWICKSHIRE
End of the Gunpowder Plot

The Gunpowder Plot of 1605 was a Midlands affair. The Shire counties were remote from London and many of the big houses there held to the old religion. The plot – by which Catholics, disappointed at James I's failure to ease the penalties for recusancy, hoped to blow up the King and his family as they attended the opening of Parliament – is thought to have been hatched at Ashby St Ledgers in Northamptonshire, at a house owned by the ringleader Robert Catesby. While Guy Fawkes was hidden with his gunpowder in a cellar below the House of Lords, Everard Digby waited at the Red Lion Inn at Dunchurch. He had brought with him a hunting party of Catholic gentlemen who were not privy to the plot, but were expected to form the nucleus of the rising that was intended to follow the assassination of James I. It was Digby's task to seize James's daughter, Elizabeth, from Combe Abbey, with a view to making her a Catholic queen. The inn is believed to have been the timber-framed building that is now called Guy Fawkes House.

Parliament was due to open on 5 November. Ten days before, a Catholic peer, Lord Monteagle, received a letter warning him not to attend the ceremony. Monteagle, who was doing well under the new regime, handed the letter over to Robert Cecil, James I's Secretary of State. Fawkes was discovered during the night of 4 November. By this time, Catesby was already en route for Dunchurch. Hearing that the plot had failed, other conspirators, including Ambrose Rookwood, followed him. It was Rookwood, riding hard on a string of horses that he had already arranged to be ready for him along the road, who finally caught up with Catesby and told him the bad news. Even so, Catesby managed to persuade the plotters at Dunchurch that their plight was not hopeless: they could yet cause the Catholic Midlands to rise up. But the Midlands did not rise, and the conspirators were reduced to making a last stand at Holbeche House, four miles from Dudley in Staffordshire. By now, their own gunpowder had got soaked, but when they laid it in front of a fire to dry out, a spark ignited it, burning Catesby and blinding another conspirator.

The end came on 8 November when the Sheriff of Worcester led an assault, killing Catesby and three others. The wounded were captured; those who had escaped were soon rounded up. Eight plotters, including Digby, Rookwood and Fawkes, were hanged, drawn and quartered in the New Year.

VICTORIA STREET, EASTWOOD   *NOTTINGHAMSHIRE*
Birthplace of D. H. Lawrence

D. H. Lawrence was born at 8a Victoria Street, a terraced house in the redbrick mining village of Eastwood, in 1885. His father had begun work at the Brinsley Colliery at the age of seven, rising to the position of 'butty' or mining contractor. Reflecting this progress, the homes in which the Lawrence family lived became progressively more substantial. From Victoria Street, they moved to an end-of-terrace house in what is now Garden Road, with a more generous garden. Respectable from the front, it backed onto a squalid alley, which was Mrs Lawrence's *bête noire*. This occasioned another move, this time to Walker Street – 'a house on the brow of the hill, commanding a view of the valley, which spread out like a convex cockle-shell, or a clamp-shell, before it', as Lawrence described in *Sons and Lovers*. The final move took place when Lawrence was nineteen, and brought them to the gentility of a semi-detached house, 97 Lynncroft. Lawrence felt a quiet pride in the family achievement.

He left three years later, seldom to return, but the scenes that he knew during his childhood at Eastwood often recur in his novels, tense with the conflict between primeval emotion and civilised veneer. For a sensitive, bookish child, the narrow round of Eastwood, centred on church and colliery, was claustrophobic; just beyond it, though, lay 'an extremely beautiful country-side', with Matlock in Derbyshire sixteen miles away to the north-west and Sherwood Forest to the north. Jessie Chambers, who was fictionalised as Miriam Leivers in *Sons and Lovers*, lived at Haggs Farm, outside Eastwood, and it was there that Lawrence got his 'first incentive to write'. 'Whatever I forget,' wrote Lawrence to Jessie's brother, Professor J. D. Chambers, in 1928, 'I shall never forget the Haggs – I loved it so.'

Lawrence moved from Eastwood to Croydon in Surrey, where he took a teaching job and ran away with Frieda von Richthofen, the wife of his professor at Nottingham University. They travelled in Germany, Austria and Italy, returning to England on the outbreak of the First World War. In 1915, he published *The Rainbow*, an exploration of marriage, and was prosecuted for obscenity. In 1919 he left England again, living in the United States, Mexico and Australia; he died of tuberculosis in the South of France in 1930.

BATTLE OF EDGEHILL NEAR BANBURY, WARWICKSHIRE
The start of the English Civil War

In the 18th century, a tower overlooking the battlefield of Edgehill was built at the top of the steep escarpment by the landowner and architect Sanderson Mill. This was where the Royalist army drew up on the morning of 23 October 1642. They had been attempting to march on London but a Parliamentarian army, under the Earl of Essex, blocked their way. The Royalists were all the more eager for the fight, but could not tempt their enemy to attack them while they occupied the ridge. Eventually, they came down to face the Parliamentarians. The forces were evenly matched. Sir Jacob Astley, at the head of his regiment of infantry, offered up a soldier's prayer: 'O Lord! Thou knowest how busy I must be this day. If I forget Thee, do not Thou forget me.' Then, rising to his feet, he gave the order, 'March on, boys!' (If these were the first words of the Civil War*, he would also utter the last, at Stow-on-the-Wold.)

The first cannon shots were fired by the Parliamentarians, perhaps hoping to hit Charles I as he rode along the line of his troops. Prince Rupert of the Rhine, on the Royalist right, led a devastating cavalry charge, which captured the Roundheads' cannon but then careered off the field towards the village of Kineton to plunder the Parliamentary baggage train. Astley's 'hedgehogs' of pikemen and the other Royalist infantry, some armed only with cudgels and scythes, 'stood their ground with great courage . . . and took up the arms which their slaughtered neighbours left to them,' according to the Earl of Clarendon's later history. Sir William Balfour's Parliamentary cavalry forced a gap in the Royalist ranks, however; the Roundheads streamed through it, and Sir Edmund Verney was killed as he fought to keep hold of the Royal standard, with all its symbolism. For a few minutes it passed into Parliamentary hands, until Captain John Smith, who was making his way back from behind enemy lines, flung himself on the soldiers who were guarding it, and seized it back for the King; he was knighted the next day. The Royalists regrouped. The late appearance of a troop of Parliamentary horses under the captaincy of an MP from eastern England, Oliver Cromwell (see page 275), made little difference.

At nightfall, the two armies withdrew, and since the Roundhead Earl of

Essex eventually pulled back to Warwick Castle, the ultimate advantage lay more with the Royalists than with their enemy. The road to London lay open to them but they were dilatory in taking it. By the time Prince Rupert had advanced to Brentwood, the Earl of Essex had come down from Warwick to block his path. The King made his way to Oxford, which became his new capital for the duration of the Civil War.

*See Battle of Naseby, page 332; Stow-on-the-Wold, page 344; The Saracen's Head, page 342; The Banqueting House, page 114

EYAM
The heroism of a plague village

DERBYSHIRE

In the hot summer of 1665, an itinerant tailor called George Viccars lodged in the remote Derbyshire village of Eyam. Around it are the high Derbyshire peaks, which could only be crossed by rough, narrow tracks. Nevertheless, Eyam was not entirely without contact from the wider world. It is thought that, in September of that year, a bolt of cloth arrived from London for Viccars to make up. When he unrolled it, he would have been unaware that it hid an unwelcome stowaway, in the form of a flea. That flea carried the bacillus that caused some 100,000 deaths during the Great Plague throughout the country. Within a few days, Viccars himself was dead.

By the end of October, Eyam had suffered more deaths than it usually knew in a year; by April 1666, seventy-three people had died. The villagers must have hoped that the winter might have killed off the disease, and in May there was a lull. In June, however, the death toll rose again. The few who were able to leave had already done so, but most people had nowhere to go, and could not afford to leave their homes and possessions. Soon the sexton could not cope with digging any more graves in the churchyard, and victims were buried in their own orchards or fields.

The rector, William Mompesson, a new man in the village, took charge. He ordered that the church should be closed, to reduce close contact between his flock; henceforth services were held in the open air. The villagers who remained alive put themselves into quarantine. They no longer went to the market at Bakewell, a few miles away, but kept a brook between themselves and the traders, who threw their wares to the other side and waited for money to be tossed back in return. Isolated, the villagers waited stoically to see what would befall them. More than fifty died in July, nearly eighty in August. Mompesson called for a 'great burning' of possessions to eliminate the 'seeds' of the plague. To this end, he destroyed most of the contents of his rectory. He was one of the fortunate ones who survived; his children, whom he had sent to

Yorkshire at the beginning of the epidemic, also lived. But his wife Catherine, who had refused to go with them, was not so lucky: she is buried under a table tomb in Eyam churchyard. By Christmas 1666, somewhere between half and three-quarters of the village population had died.

But their self-sacrifice bore fruit. The plague stopped with them, and the rest of Derbyshire – perhaps the rest of the Midlands – was saved. They deserve to be remembered as heroes.

THE FOSSE WAY

FROM AXMINSTER TO LINCOLN

All roads lead to Rome

The Romans built roads. They were the best roads in Britain for over 1,500 years. In the 1st century AD, the Romans opened up the interior of their new province with roads, as straight as they could be made by using beacons and a surveying tool known as a *groma*. Among the best known are Ermine Street, joining London to Lincoln; Watling Street, from London to Chester; and the Fosse Way.

Following the line of an ancient track, the Fosse Way was initially a boundary as well as a road: it linked the line of forts built at the western extremity of the first Roman advance, just a few years after the invasion of AD43. Over 180 miles long, it cuts diagonally across the southern half of England, from Axminster in Devon, along the ridge of the Cotswold hills between Bath and Cirencester, then to Leicester and on to Lincoln. The line can still mostly be followed by car, generally along A-category roads such as the A358, A37, A367, A46 (in two sections), A433 and A429, but also along stretches of delectable B-category roads, the B4455 and B4114. The Fosse Way did not define the limit of Roman occupation for long. Within forty years of the invasion, they controlled as far northwards as the Clyde and the Firth of Forth, by which time they had built more than a thousand miles of road.

The roads were superbly engineered, with trenches to either side, a foundation of big stones, two layers of pebbles and broken tiles mixed with cement, and a top surface of paving stones. The Saxons who came after the Romans used the roads but were unable to maintain them. Metalled roads were not made again in Britain until the 17th century. For the whole of its length, the Fosse Way deviates little from the straight line that was the Roman road-maker's ideal.

See also The Ridgeway, page 237

FOTHERINGHAY CASTLE NORTHAMPTONSHIRE

Where Mary Queen of Scots was beheaded

By 1586, Mary Queen of Scots* had been imprisoned in England, in less and less comfort, for eighteen years. Despite being crippled with rheumatism and barely able to walk for lack of exercise, she had become an increasing liability in the eyes of Elizabeth I's chief advisers since Catholics – not recognising the marriage of Elizabeth's father, Henry VIII, to her mother Anne Boleyn – saw Mary as having a better claim to the English throne than the Queen. Spies were infiltrated into Mary's small household, and the temptation to treason was trailed before her in the form of the gossamer-thin Babington Plot. Mary's intercepted response appeared to show her acquiescing in a plot to kill Elizabeth, and she was taken to the grim fortress of Fotheringhay for trial.

Fotheringhay had already brought its share of grief into the world, having been the birthplace of Richard III. In the century that had elapsed since then, it had declined from being a Yorkist stronghold to the gloomy condition of being a state prison. On first seeing the castle from the curiously named Perryho Lane, Mary is supposed to have punned fatalistically: 'Perio! I perish.' There was never any doubt as to what the outcome of the trial would be. Mary was allowed no counsel to defend her, nor any access to her papers. She argued that she was a Queen, not a subject, and therefore should not be tried. She had only corresponded with Anthony Babington to secure her release from painful captivity, not to plot the death of Elizabeth. On the second day, many of the lords there to try her arrived already booted and spurred for departure, knowing that her trial would quickly be finished. They were soon on the road to London, to meet again in the Star Chamber to pass their inevitable verdict of guilty. The execution took place in the great hall of Fotheringhay on 8 February 1587. Witnesses were stunned when, raising the decapitated head, the executioner found that it parted company with its hair: Mary had been wearing an auburn wig.

The legend that Fotheringhay was razed to the ground for reasons of state – either to prevent relics of Mary being kept, or out of revenge when her son James VI of Scotland became James I of England – is far-fetched. The castle simply became derelict and crumbled. Now nothing remains but the castle mound and its earthworks, next to a farm by the river. Mary's lead-wrapped corpse lay in Fotheringhay church and then Peterborough Cathedral until James had the coffin transferred to Westminster Abbey.

*See Holyrood Palace, page 455, and Loch Leven Castle, page 473

ELEANOR CROSS
Elegant memorial to a beloved Queen

On 28 November 1290, Queen Eleanor of Castile died at Harby in Nottinghamshire, en route to join her husband in Scotland. She and Edward I enjoyed exceptionally good relations for a royal couple. She often went with him on his travels. On a crusade to the Holy Land in 1270, she is supposed to have sucked the venom from a wound that an assassin had made in his arm. Edward, having hurried back from his campaign against the Scots, was with her when she died. Afterwards he ordered that her body should be taken to Lincoln, embalmed and then carried to London. He himself led the procession as the chief mourner.

The progress made by the cortège was slow. It took nearly a fortnight to reach Westminster Abbey. The route was dictated by the royal houses and monasteries where the King could spend the night. Later, at each of these stopping places, Edward had erected an elaborate cross. The idea may have been inspired by the series of crosses between Paris and St Denis, erected to commemorate the last journey made by St Louis's mortal remains. There were twelve Eleanor Crosses altogether, the last being Charing (*chère reine*) Cross in London. Only three of the originals now survive, at Hardingstone on the edge of Northampton, at Waltham Cross in Hertfordshire and at Geddington. Of these, the first two have been heavily restored, but the Geddington cross stands just as the King's masons left it. Although the village in which it was built must have been humble, this is one of the most sophisticated pieces of architecture to survive from the Middle Ages, bearing a statue of the dead queen on each of its three faces. The sides of the cross are covered with a lattice of ornament in shallow relief, a highly unusual effect that makes the cross seem like a reliquary. Geddington was chosen because of the royal hunting lodge which once stood behind the church.

GLOUCESTER CATHEDRAL
Exquisite memorial for the murdered aesthete king

Edward II was murdered at Berkeley Castle* in September 1327. However, it was not until November that his body was moved to Gloucester, accompanied by a relatively small escort of monks and knights. By tradition, wherever the procession stopped to rest its horses, an oak tree was planted by local people. Then the body rested in a church until nearly Christmas, allowing Queen Isabella and her lover Roger de Mortimer, now *de facto* ruler of England, time to stage a funeral of hypocritical splendour. The tomb, surmounted by an elaborately pinnacled double canopy, is one of the most beautiful in England.

The alabaster effigy shows Edward as a figure of dignity, with long wavy hair and an elegantly curled beard. Angels weep at his head. His heart, in a silver vase, was sent to his wife. What she did with it is not known.

Mortimer's rule did not last long: he was executed as a traitor by Edward III, while Isabella was sent to live at Castle Rising† in remote Norfolk. Meanwhile, the royal tomb became an object of pilgrimage. The royal family came, but so too did crowds of ordinary people – so many that the sides of the pillars between which it stands had to be cut away to allow them to squeeze round. Edward's great-grandson Richard II, who was also deposed and murdered, visited the tomb, adding his badge of the white hart to the pillars. He tried hard to have Edward officially acknowledged as a saint. His efforts proved unsuccessful, but the cult of Edward continued almost until the Reformation, when the custom of pilgrimage and the reverence of local saints were abolished.

*See Berkeley Castle, page 300. †See Castle Rising, page 262

QUEEN'S OAK
GRAFTON REGIS, NORTHAMPTONSHIRE
Where Edward IV met his Queen

By tradition, the Queen's Oak at Grafton Regis marks one of the most romantic episodes of the Middle Ages. It was where Edward IV – who, as the young Duke of York, had elbowed Henry VI off the throne to take his place – met his future wife, the widow Elizabeth Woodville, in 1464. Here was a king who believed in the Renaissance principle of magnificence. He set out to dazzle his subjects into awed acquiescence, through the splendour of his possessions, the prodigality of his gifts and the display of his effulgent self to his people. In this he was helped by his superb physique: he was 6ft 4ins tall and the epitome of chivalry. It is difficult to think that Edward did not marry for love. Elizabeth Woodville was famous for her black-haired beauty but otherwise no great catch. The ceremony took place in secret. The Earl of Warwick, who had been planning a more conventional diplomatic marriage for the King whom he had helped to power, was furious. He was a dangerous enemy to make*.

It may have been that Edward hoped the union would help win over the Lancastrian faction to his rule. But Elizabeth Woodville was a minx, and her family, if anything, even worse. Eventually, after King Edward's sudden death, the Queen's unpopularity was a factor in allowing his brother, the Duke of York, to usurp the throne as Richard III. Her male children were the young princes murdered, on Richard III's orders, in the Tower of London; her daughter helped end the divisions caused by the Wars of the Roses by marrying Henry VII (see page 310).

None of this eventful history could have been foreseen when Edward IV met Elizabeth during a hunting party. The great palace that Henry VIII subsequently built here, bestowing the suffix of Regis on the village, has almost completely disappeared, having been demolished during the Civil War. The original Queen's Oak was badly mauled by souvenir hunters in the 18th century. Having suffered badly during the droughts of the 1990s, it finally expired in the scorching August of 1997. Cuttings from the last green bough failed to take. However, a DNA sample was taken from its leaves and a hunt is now on to find a related oak from whose acorns a replacement can be grown. What remains of the Queen's Oak lies behind Potterspury Lodge, not far from Grafton Regis.

*See Battle of Barnet, page 204

HARDWICK HALL

NEAR CHESTERFIELD, DERBYSHIRE

Haven for the philosopher Thomas Hobbes

The philosopher Thomas Hobbes looked after himself. Believing that the amount of air taken into the lungs tended to decline with age, he sang loudly, if not well, in bed. He gave up his pipe, drank moderately and exercised to work up a sweat, which he then paid servants to rub off. Man's life, according to his most famous saying, was apt to be 'solitary, poor, nasty, brutish, and short'. Having no discernible religion, he wanted his own life to be long, and it was: he died at the age of ninety-one at Hardwick Hall, his home for most of the previous seventy years.

Hardwick had been built by the formidable, much married and, at the end of her life, immensely rich Bess of Hardwick (see page 312), who died in 1608, the year that Hobbes first went there. On leaving Oxford, Hobbes, the son of a contumacious clergyman, became tutor to Bess's grandson, the future 2nd Earl of Devonshire, a lad who at eighteen was only two years younger than him. Quite what Hobbes imparted to his charge is not known, since Devonshire was a wastrel, and any teaching that Hobbes did must have taken place while they were hawking, hunting or riding to pay visits: Hobbes bought pocket editions of Roman authors to read while he was waiting for his young charge. Fortunately for the Devonshire finances, the 2nd Earl died only two years after inheriting. Hobbes then became tutor to his son, the 3rd Earl, who kept him as a paid member of his household until death.

When Civil War loomed, Hobbes left the country, and it was while abroad that he wrote his most famous work, *Leviathan*, published in 1651. It was the destructive effects of war that made human life 'nasty, brutish, and short'. *Leviathan* is an analysis of the conditions under which prosperity and civilisation can flourish. There should be one ruler, or sovereign, of the State, Hobbes believed; subjects should be prepared to give up some of their individual freedom and decision making, in return for the civic order that the monarch would guarantee. Religion was relegated to second place, and the Church – particularly the Roman Catholic Church – was censored for having adopted practices that originated in paganism. Although he was a supporter of the future Charles II, the book's radicalism made him unwelcome at the King's court in exile. He was not above trying to ingratiate himself with Cromwell since, in his sixties, he was anxious to come home.

MAPPA MUNDI
A medieval view of the world

HEREFORD CATHEDRAL, HEREFORD

The Mappa Mundi is the most elaborate map of the world to survive from the Middle Ages. It was made about 1290, using vellum from a single sheep's hide – hence the kite-like shape. To the medieval mind, a map was not only a record of geographical knowledge, but an index of many things that were known or believed about the world at that time, organised according to importance. It was a Christian world, therefore at the heart of the map stands Jerusalem. Nearby are such Biblical landmarks as the Garden of Eden, Noah's Ark and the Tower of Babel.

In the quarter of the map depicting Europe (the other continents are Asia and Africa), Rome is shown as the most spectacular city, closely followed by Paris. The kidney-shaped British Isles are squashed onto the edge of the world, with both Scotland and Cornwall severed from England by rivers. The map-maker drew some of the cathedral cities, as well as Conway and a very small Oxford; Ely is represented as being completely surrounded by water. Exceptional prominence is given to Lincoln, prompting the thought that this was the map-maker's home city. By contrast, Hereford appears to have been sketched in as an afterthought, presumably after the map came here; it was no doubt at this time that the local landmark of Clee Hill was added.

Spaces between the topographical features are enlivened by creatures of natural history and myth. The elephant and camel are surprisingly realistic, the rhinoceros rather less so. There is a pelican, plucking its breast to feed its young, as well as the Golden Fleece, the Minotaur, a salamander and a sphinx. Among the peoples of the world is a Norwegian, complete with bobble hat and skis; less instantly recognisable is the Sciapod from India, who shades himself from the scorching sun by raising his one enormous foot. The map would have been a valuable tool for teaching.

KENILWORTH CASTLE

Capital of Simon de Montfort's state within a state

The theme of Kenilworth is rivalry, and that of the most dangerous kind: with the Crown itself. By the time Simon de Montfort* was granted the castle by Henry III in 1253, it was already a formidable power base. In the middle was the massive Norman keep, its impregnably thick walls splaying out towards the ground as a defence against undermining. Around it, King John had not only thrown a curtain wall, protected by towers, but a big lake – the Great Mere – created by means of a fortified dam. De Montfort made Kenilworth the centre of his state within a state, from which, angry that he was unable to set up his family in the style that befitted a man who had married the King's sister, he led England's other magnates in opposition to Henry III.

The rivalry ended in disaster. Although de Montfort defeated Henry at the Battle of Lewes in 1264, and was subsequently one of those who presided over the Model Parliament, he did not have the political skills to prevent the King from forming a new coalition with his barons, who now had no use for a leader who was in danger of eclipsing them. In 1265, he and his small army were cornered at Evesham, in a loop of the river Avon. Escape was cut off by a detachment of royalist soldiers, who seized the only bridge. To begin with, it seemed that the army marching towards de Montfort from the east belonged to his son, also Simon; then the horror of the predicament dawned on them. Henry had achieved the deception by carrying the banners that he had captured from the younger Simon de Montfort, who had foolishly allowed his army – a large one – to enjoy the comforts that lay in Kenilworth town, rather than bringing it within the castle walls. They had been surprised as they slept. Simon de Montfort the elder was killed at Evesham and his body dismembered.

In 1266, the King moved against Kenilworth. The supporters of de Montfort who were still within replied to his reasonable surrender terms by cutting off the hand of his messenger. This outrage precipitated a siege, backed up by symbolism. The sword of state was brought to the tent in which the King was encamped. The Archbishop of Canterbury arrived to excommunicate the rebels; in return, they dressed up a barber in robes to perform a mock excommunication of the besiegers from the battlements. The castle withstood all the different means of attack – catapults, boats, tall-towers – that could be devised. Eventually, the defenders fell victim to plague and were forced to surrender. The siege had lasted nearly nine months. It was a testament to the elder de Montfort's defensive skills that Kenilworth stood out so long.

In the last years of the 14th century, John of Gaunt (named after his birthplace of Ghent), the third surviving son of Edward III, turned Kenilworth into a palace, adding a great hall and other domestic buildings. Robert Dudley, Earl of Leicester, made it still more magnificent, by building a new range and gatehouse. When

Elizabeth visited Kenilworth for nineteen days in 1575, he repaid his royal patron by transforming the castle into a fairy palace, where no extravagance was too lavish, no ingenuity too contrived, no symbolism too flagrant to enchant her eye. Sir Walter Scott wrote a fictional account of the visit in his novel *Kenilworth*. The castle was slighted, or rendered indefensible, by the Parliamentarian Colonel Hawkesworth during the Civil War. Since his eye was on buying the castle to live in the gatehouse, only one side of the keep was blown up – and the ghosts, which make the mighty ruin of Kenilworth so evocative today, did not flee.

*See Battle of Lewes, page 77

WICKSTEED PARK   KETTERING, NORTHAMPTONSHIRE
First theme park in Britain

Early 20th-century Kettering was a redbrick Midlands boot-making town, and Wicksteed Park, on the edge of it, has claims to be the first theme park in Britain. It was founded in 1916 by Charles Wicksteed, son of a Unitarian minister from Leeds, who made a fortune in Kettering from the late-Victorian/Edwardian transport revolution: first through Gaiety Cycles, then his patented gearbox for cars. Wicksteed's original plan was to create a model village on the site, but the First World War made that impossible; when hostilities were over, he used the land for a sort of high-minded funfair 'to give healthful recreation to the working classes'. It was run as a charity.

Like later theme parks, such as Alton Towers (established in the 1970s), Wicksteed Park occupies the grounds of a country house. The story goes that Charles Wicksteed needed water for his steam traction engine. He called at the house and asked permission to take some, but was refused. By an ironic stroke of fate, he went on to buy the house. Thereafter, the people of Kettering could – and still can – go fishing, swimming or boating on its 30-acre lake (spare clothes used to be kept for those who fell in). From the beginning, there were also formidable rides, some of the earliest of which are going today. It says something for the scope of Wicksteed's vision that his park still attracts more than half a million visitors a year.

LEICESTER ABBEY   LEICESTER
Death of Cardinal Wolsey

On 4 November 1530, the once all-powerful Cardinal Thomas Wolsey* was arrested near York. He had fallen from Henry VIII's favour the year before, but instead of retiring quietly he schemed to rebuild his position, planning a splendid ceremony to have himself re-installed as Archbishop of York – a position to which he had been appointed sixteen years before. Now, under guard, he was on his way south. By the time he reached Leicester Abbey, he was so sick that he could hardly sit on his mule. He prophesied that he would die before eight o'clock the following morning.

Fifty-five years earlier, Wolsey had been born in Ipswich, the son of a successful butcher. For someone so lowborn, the only path to greatness lay through the church. At the age of fifteen, he went to Oxford University where he would later found Cardinal College, the present Christ Church (see page 234). Having taken holy orders, he came to the notice of Henry VII, and became his chaplain and secretary. In 1509, a greater opportunity arose when Henry VII was succeeded by his eighteen-year-old son, Henry VIII, who was not inclined to bother himself much in the details of administration. Wolsey made the business of ruling easy for him. In return he was made Archbishop of York in 1514 and Lord Chancellor in 1515, the same year that Pope Leo X made him a cardinal. Wolsey persuaded Leo to make him his legate, or Papal representative, with plenipotentiary powers. This was an extraordinary appointment that made Wolsey more powerful than the Archbishop of Canterbury.

The Pope had yielded to Wolsey, in order to win his support in the struggle to free the papal state from foreign control. Later, Wolsey hoped to play Spain off against France, with the object of becoming Pope himself. It was to prove his undoing. Charles V of Spain, the Holy Roman Emperor, did not reward Wolsey as he expected; in return, Wolsey changed sides and gave English backing to the French king, Francis I. When Henry VIII, desperate for a male heir, found himself married to a queen, Catherine of Aragon, who had gone beyond child-bearing age, he expected the Cardinal to persuade Pope Clement VII to annul the marriage. But by this time, 1527, France had been disastrously defeated, and the Pope could not take the decision without deferring to the Emperor. Charles, however, had no inclination to help Wolsey; furthermore, Catherine was his aunt. Henry was not accustomed to having his wishes denied, and demanded that Wolsey should relinquish the vast palaces and riches he had amassed.

Whatever Wolsey said about Henry in his last moments was too spicy for anyone who heard it to repeat. His death did indeed come at eight o'clock. He was buried in Leicester Abbey, not far from the grave of Richard III in the monastery of Greyfriars (see page 310) – a coincidence noted by contemporaries. It is perhaps symbolic of the Cardinal's downfall that nothing now remains of the Abbey above its foundations.

*See Hampton Court, page 74

SAMUEL JOHNSON'S BIRTHPLACE

Provincial origin of a great Englishman

Samuel Johnson was one of the most extraordinary Englishmen who ever lived. A big, burly man, with poor eyesight and incurable scrofula, he acquired a formidable erudition, yet combined it with robust common sense. He translated Homer, wrote verse satires on London and the political world, spent nearly a decade compiling his famous *Dictionary of the English Language*, rushed out a biography of his unlikely friend, the dissolute poet Richard Savage, after he had died in Bristol Gaol, and went on to write a series of portraits of British poets. He also edited Shakespeare. Added to these amazing achievements in book writing was his titanic journalism, notably the two years that he spent editing and contributing moral essays to his own journal, *The Rambler*. His conversation was necessarily more ephemeral, but the sample recorded by his biographer, James Boswell, shows that it was itself one of the wonders of an age in which civilised talk was regarded as an important accomplishment.

Johnson was born in Lichfield, a cathedral city that was not much bigger than a market town, in 1709. The year before his father, Michael Johnson, had done sufficiently well as a bookbinder and small-scale publisher to complete a handsome town house in Breadmarket Street, the floors above the shop being supported on three fat columns. Thereafter, Johnson senior seems not to have prospered; he may have over-extended himself in buying Lord Derby's library of 3,000 volumes. Although the Johnson household was not a very happy one, it had books, and the young Samuel read them voraciously. Educated at a dame-school, then the grammar school, where he learnt Latin and Greek, Johnson went to Pembroke College, Oxford. There his relative poverty was a humiliation. He left before taking his degree; perhaps he was already dogged by the depression that he shared with his father. His father urged him to come into the book trade, but it was not for him.

He became a schoolmaster instead. Together with his wife Elizabeth, whom he called Tetty, a widow twice his age, he took Edial Hall, where one of the few pupils was the future actor David Garrick⋆. Later Garrick would regale his male friends with ribald accounts of what he claimed to have seen when peering through a hole in the door to the newlyweds' bedroom. The school failed. Johnson and his young friend and former pupil, Garrick, journeyed to London in 1737 in search of their different forms of glory.

Life was hard for the Johnsons – hence the prodigious scale of Samuel's output. Much of his income came from 'Grub Street', as journalism was called, initially writing reports for *The Gentleman's Magazine*. It was not until his *Dictionary* was published in 1755 that he won fame. Financial security was assured when George III, coming to the throne in 1760, awarded him a pension. This gave him the means to travel and he was able to return regularly to Lichfield and the other

Midland towns in which his school friends were living. The narrowness of the society did not enchant him. Nevertheless, he retained an affection for Lichfield. Johnson was – for all his colossal learning and weighty opinions – a touchingly human individual. It was part of his greatness.

*See Shakespeare Temple, page 219

MORDIFORD BRIDGE NEAR HEREFORD
Inspiration for a very English composer

Like so many English composers of the 19th and 20th centuries, Edward Elgar infused his music with evocations of the English countryside – in his case, that around the Malvern Hills. 'A country life I find absolutely essential to me,' he once told a writer; inspiration would come 'when I am walking, golfing, kite flying or cycling, or the ideas may come in the evening, and then I sit up until any hour in order to get them down.' He spent all but twenty of his seventy-six years in Worcestershire or Herefordshire, and late in his life confessed that he was 'still at heart the dreamy child who used to be found in the reeds by Severn side with a sheet of paper trying to fix the sounds'. Mordiford Bridge, where the river Lugg flows into the river Wye, was one of his favourite haunts, just a couple of miles by bicycle from his home in Hereford. Its name is inscribed on the score of *The Music Makers*.

Elgar was born in 1857 in a somewhat charmless brick cottage at Lower Broadheath, near Worcester, the son of a Roman Catholic piano tuner who also kept a music shop. This gave the composer, who came to embody the spirit of traditional England, a double sense of alienation: Catholicism was still regarded with suspicion, particularly in rural areas, and he felt keenly the stigma that attached to families engaged in trade. Shy and sometimes awkward, Elgar was acutely sensitive to these and other slights, and the feeling of grievance may have fuelled his craving for adulation.

Modest though it was, his background provided many opportunities for music making, resulting in masterpieces such as the 'Enigma' Variations, the 'Pomp and Circumstance' marches, *The Dream of Gerontius* (see page 232) and the Violin Concerto, all written in the 1890s and 1900s when he was living in Malvern and Hereford. He was heaped with honours, culminating in the Order of Merit. Despite the complexities of his personality, to the outward world Elgar was the iconic image of the bluff Englishman, his inner feelings hidden behind a luxuriant growth of moustache, and seemingly never happier than when watching cricket or going to the races at Worcester.

See also Abbey Road Studios, page 109

BATTLE OF MORTIMER'S CROSS

NEAR LEOMINSTER, HEREFORDSHIRE

Edward IV ousts Henry VI from the throne

At Christmas 1460, Richard, Duke of York, having made himself heir to the throne, was killed outside his castle of Wakefield in Yorkshire by a Lancastrian raid*. Two months later, his eldest son Edward, Earl of March – tall, good-looking, a natural prince – faced a Lancastrian army commanded by Jasper Tudor, Earl of Pembroke. The site was a crossroads near a bridge over the river Lugg in the Welsh Marches. Edward was on home territory, only ten miles from the Yorkist stronghold of Ludlow.

The fight did not last long. A hail of arrows from Edward's archers drove the Lancastrians back to the river, where many of them were slaughtered as they tried to escape. Pembroke got away, but his father Owen Tudor, grandfather of the future Henry VII, was one of several Welshmen captured during the battle. Afterwards he was beheaded at Hereford. Edward marched to London where he seized the crown from Henry VI, becoming Edward IV. Henry and his powerful Queen, Margaret of Anjou, fled to France. On Palm Sunday, the remaining Lancastrian support was crushed at the bloody Battle of Towton.

In 1799, a stone monument was erected to mark the site of the Battle of Mortimer's Cross, and stands in front of the Monument public house.

*See First Battle of St Albans, page 240; Battle of Wakefield, page 403; Second Battle of St Albans, page 241; Battle of Towton, page 402; Battle of Barnet, page 204; Battle of Tewkesbury, page 346; Battle of Bosworth, page 309

BATTLE OF NASEBY

NEAR MARKET HARBOROUGH, NORTHAMPTONSHIRE

Decisive battle of the English Civil War

There are two monuments to the Battle of Naseby, the decisive confrontation of the Civil War*. An obelisk just outside the village is nowhere near the heart of the battlefield. The other monument, a column with a stone ball on top, erected in 1936, lies on the road to Sibbertoft, and occupies roughly the position where the brave little Parliamentary vanguard standing in front of the main battle line – known as the 'forlorn hope' and intended to break up the Royalist advance – started the day. Opposite stands the appropriately named Dust Hill, where Charles I in person led the Royalist force on 14 June 1645.

Charles and his generals had been the ones to seek out the Puritan army, and pick the fight, even though they were heavily outnumbered. They made the mistake of laughing at what they called the New Noddle Army, re-formed by Oliver Cromwell, which was then on its first outing in the field. The King's nephew, Prince Rupert of the Rhine – testosterone in a plumed hat – planned the battle and should have commanded it. Instead, after nights of acrimony and indecision among the Royalist commanders, he worked off his frustrations by leading the cavalry on the Royalist right wing in a furious charge. He was famous for his furious cavalry charges, but at Naseby he overdid it. His cavalry smashed through one end of the enemy line, ignored the distraction provided by the Cromwellian Colonel Okey's dragoons, who had been concealed behind a hedge, and kept going until they came to the Puritan baggage train, which was drawn up outside the village. Foolishly, they stopped to pillage it. They found it was rather better defended than they had expected.

On the battlefield proper, the bristling 'hedgehogs' of the Royalist infantry – a square of men with their pikes sticking outwards – had stamped their way into the middle of the enemy line, but the numbers opposing them were too great for them to push any further. By the time Rupert found his way back to the main action, it was too late. In his absence, Charles himself had almost made a last throw. The little King, whatever his other qualities, was a brave man, and would have put himself at the head of the cavalry reserve – probably made up of the courtiers who surrounded him – for a last Royalist charge, except for a Scottish peer, Lord Carnworth, who seized the bridle of the King's horse and told him he would instantly be killed. The charge never happened, and Charles's fortunes began the inexorable decline that would end in his execution four years later.

Well into the 20th century, the place from which King Charles is supposed to have directed the battle was marked by the King's Oak. The landscape is now quite different from its 17th-century appearance. It had not been broken up into fields (which is why there was nothing to stop Rupert's charge). There were probably 25,000 men fighting at Naseby, 10,000 of them on horses. Therefore, the battle would have taken place over a wide area.

The construction of the modern A14, by-passing Naseby, was opposed by conservationists deploring the desecration of the battlefield. Rupert and his cavalry must have galloped over the line of the road, but not so much as a musket ball was found during the roadworks.

*See Battle of Edgehill, page 319; Stow-on-the-Wold, page 344; The Saracen's Head, page 342; The Banqueting House, page 114

NEWSTEAD ABBEY NOTTINGHAMSHIRE
Byron's bed – we draw a veil

During Lord Byron's time at Trinity College, Cambridge, he was famous for keeping a bear. To modern eyes, his bed was amazingly extravagant – a four-poster, surmounted by a domed canopy, the gilded tester bearing a baron's coronets; the hangings were of green chintz printed with yellow Chinese pagodas. When he left Cambridge in 1808, the bed was taken to Newstead Abbey. At the age of ten, he had inherited the house, along with his title, from a great-uncle whom he never met. Bed was important to the scandalously amorous young aristocrat. Newstead suited his taste rather less well, having fallen into a ruinous state of repair. Since his great-uncle's death it had been tenanted. Now, as he approached his coming-of-age, he borrowed enough money to refurbish two apartments, one for himself and one for his mother. He held a party for his friends to celebrate the completion of the work. Having stayed in bed until one o'clock, they passed the afternoon fencing, riding, sailing on the lake and playing cricket, before an evening spent dressed as monks.

In 1809, deeply in debt, he set out on the adventurous Grand Tour that would furnish the material for *Childe Harold's Pilgrimage**, which established his reputation. He returned two years later and became the favourite of London society, taking Lady Caroline Lamb as his lover (see page 210). In 1815 he married Annabella Milbanke, but the next year, under pressure of the scandal surrounding his supposed liaison with his half-sister Augusta Leigh, Byron left England for good.

Byron was that rare creature, a poet whose works were instant bestsellers. Why did he become such a legend that the adjective 'Byronic' characterises a certain type of person and attitude towards life? Because of what now seems to be an heroic craving for life, which made him a traveller, an advocate for unpopular causes (he was one of few Parliamentarians to speak up for the Luddites), a boxer, a fencer, a shot, a wit, a *bon viveur*, a famous lover, a man who could swim the Hellespont in spite of a club foot from a childhood bout of polio, a shamelessly irresponsible landowner who sold Newstead without a qualm in 1818; in short, a romantic icon. He died in 1824, fighting for Greek independence, at the age of thirty-six. His body was brought back to England, but was refused burial in Westminster Abbey. Let us draw the curtains of his bed; may his tumultuous spirit sleep in peace.

*See John Murray, page 162

ST FAITH'S CHURCH

Levellers versus enclosures: a first battle

NEWTON IN THE WILLOWS,
NORTHAMPTONSHIRE

In 1770, Oliver Goldsmith published his poem *The Deserted Village*, lamenting the depopulation of the countryside as old peasant ways of farming gave way to sheep. Under the old system, 'every rood of ground maintain'd its man', as Goldsmith put it. But landowners who farmed sheep required only a few shepherds to look after them, and now fenced off what had previously been common land to provide more land for grazing. In agricultural terms, it was efficient. In human terms, it led to rural poverty, a flight to the industrial cities, and emigration. The system to which Goldsmith objected proliferated as the century wore on, the process by which landlords could enclose common land being codified in the 1801 Enclosure Act. In 19th-century Scotland, 'improved' farming provoked the notorious Highland Clearances, in which landowners – often clan chiefs – turned crofters, already barely making a living, off their estates in order to run sheep on them.

However, the change in agricultural economics that caused this to happen emerged far earlier than the Highland Clearances, or even Oliver Goldsmith. In 1607, a pitched battle was fought at the Northamptonshire village of Newton in the Willows between poor families living (admittedly illegally) on land belonging to the Crown and a landowner determined to enclose it for sheep. The peasants had been living as squatters in this part of the ancient hunting forest of Rockingham for many years, perhaps generations, presumably because the Crown administration was not sufficiently rigorous to stop them.

When the local magnate, a member of the spreading Tresham family (see page 338), bought the land, he began felling trees, digging draining ditches and putting up fences for his sheep. The peasants responded by filling in the ditches and pulling down the fences. This gave them the name of Levellers, which would echo forty years later in Oliver Cromwell's army. They were led by a fiery character who called himself Captain Pouch, after the leather pouch on his belt that was supposed to contain a magic charm against the Levellers' enemies; his real name was Reynolds. There were supposed to be a thousand Levellers, armed with staves and bows. The militia that was formed to expel them from their encampment was better armed, and soon saw them off. Forty or fifty Levellers were killed.

Fulfilling what must have been the Levellers' worst fears, the village of Newton in the Willows became deserted, leaving only a delight of an ancient church, St Faith, by itself in the fields. Inside is a monument to one of the Treshams, but – perhaps by a quirk of historical justice – the Tresham house has disappeared as thoroughly as the village. The size of the dovecote (all that is now left) suggests that the owners had a prodigious appetite for pigeon.

DERNGATE, NORTHAMPTON NORTHAMPTONSHIRE
From Art Nouveau to Modern Movement

Between the two world wars, W. J. Bassett-Lowke won the gratitude of a generation of schoolboys for redirecting his grandfather's boiler-making business to produce model railway engines. On his marriage in 1917, his parents had given him a modest Georgian terraced house in Northampton,

78 Derngate, as a wedding present. Although Bassett-Lowke had left school at thirteen, he took a progressive interest in the arts, and now commissioned the fading flower of Scottish Art Nouveau, Charles Rennie Mackintosh (see page 463), to remodel it. Even Mackintosh could not disguise the fact that, while spatially ingenious, the house was small. By the mid-1920s, the Bassett-Lowkes had embarked on a new domestic project, which would provide the first sighting of the Modern Movement style in Britain.

Spurning local traditions, the Modern Movement presented itself as the aesthetic partner of the machine age. It was an architecture that was at home with cars, aeroplanes and mass production. Indeed, for half a century or more, followers of the Modern Movement, as it came to be called, claimed that it was not a style at all, but the only morally defensible way of building in a modern world. It opened a battle between the intellectual élite and the taste of the general public.

Like other architectural styles, the Modern Movement was pioneered by private individuals. In the suburbs of Northampton, the German architect Peter Behrens built the Bassett-Lowkes a square, white-painted house – New Ways, 508 Wellingborough Road – that proudly displayed the date 1926 on a kind of geometrical crest above the flat roof. Before the First World War, Behrens had won a reputation for efficient factory buildings, which frankly expressed their modern constructional techniques. New Ways, while not extravagant, gave the Bassett-Lowkes more room to pack in the labour-saving ideas that offered hope to a middle class without so many servants as before.

To employ any German architect, let alone a radically modern one, in England after the First World War took guts. Bassett-Lowke, described by the *Northampton Chronicle and Echo* in 1948 as a 'businessman, author, traveller, Repertory pioneer, photographer, and Fabian', had an international business outlook that made him 'as much at home in the lesser comforts of the transContinental wagon-lit' as in his Northampton home. As a friend of George Bernard Shaw, he no doubt took a sly delight in shocking more conventional neighbours.

FORGE MILL
The perilous trade of needle-making

REDDITCH, WORCESTERSHIRE

The needle is the unsung hero of civilisation: no needle, no clothes. For more than a century – an era during which formality in dress was, for all classes, a *sine qua non* of respectability – British needle production was focused on the town of Redditch, outside Birmingham. Without it, the impeccably correct British Empire, eating dinner on safari in evening dress, would have fallen apart at the seams.

In the City of London, the Worshipful Company of Needlemakers was incorporated in 1656. (The name of Threadneedle Street survives as a memory of the craft, although many needlemakers' workshops and the Needlemakers' Hall were destroyed in the Great Fire, see page 161.) The Worshipful Company's restrictions on trade drove some needlemakers to take their skills elsewhere. Redditch offered easy access to charcoal and iron, both needed for the industry, while nearby Worcester, with its many glovers, offered a market. By 1800, Redditch achieved needle-making pre-eminence; by 1900, it had a virtual monopoly of production in this country.

It was a perilous trade. Sharpening needles on grindstones threw up clouds of metal filings. The condition then known as Pointer's Rot is what we would call silicosis; few pointers lived beyond thirty – although, not surprisingly, the work paid well while they could do it. Altogether, some thirty operations were required to make the needles, from the stretching of wire to make it thin, to the scouring of the finished needles under rollers to polish them. The steel that went into the process was highly regarded: waste needles went to make gun barrels.

Forge Mill, now a museum of needle-making, was once, as its name implies, an iron forge. From 1730, it was used for scouring needles, with other processes being added over the years. In the early 20th century, under the name of the Salmon Fly Works, it specialised in making fish hooks. However, it was hardly quick to change. The 18th-century scouring beds were used all the way until 1958.

RUGBY SCHOOL

WARWICKSHIRE

Where the public school ethos was born

Uncompromising is the word to describe the architecture of Rugby School. William Butterfield produced a building that took the Gothic Revival principle of irregularity (the external form of the architecture expressing the plan) to an almost wilful extreme, made still more difficult to chew by the harsh striped brickwork in which it was cast. In doing so, he captured something of the Rugby spirit, as embodied by its most famous headmaster Dr Thomas Arnold. Having died in 1842, Arnold never saw Butterfield's streaky bacon New Quad and Chapel, begun in 1867 and 1872 respectively, but he might well have applauded its toughness; strength of purpose was written in every crevice of his face.

Thanks partly to Thomas Hughes' novel *Tom Brown's Schooldays*, Arnold became a figure of legend. It comes as something of a shock to discover that he was not, by modern standards, an especially benign educator, being capable of thrashing a boy to within an inch of his life, even when, as it transpired on at least one occasion, he himself was in the wrong. But he was determined to master the institution, and in doing so imposed his principles not only on Rugby but on the whole ethos of the Victorian public school. Although he was himself a formidable scholar, appointed to lecture as the Regius Professor of Modern History at Oxford, he saw the formation of moral character as being the ultimate goal of a school, not the mere instillation of learning. His priorities were summed up in the sentence: 'What we must look for here is, first, religious and moral principle, secondly, gentlemanly conduct, thirdly, intellectual ability.' Articulate speech, independent thought, informed taste – these characterised Arnold's pupils who, for all his severity, revered him.

Boys shivering on games fields cannot, however, blame Arnold for the obsession with team sports, typified by the game of rugby itself, which overtook the public school system. He saw exercise as complementary to brain work, but the cult of games developed after his time.

TRIANGULAR LODGE RUSHTON, NORTHAMPTONSHIRE
An Elizabethan meditates in stone

In 1580, the Jesuits sent two missionaries to reclaim England for the Roman Catholic faith. They were the inspired preacher Edmund Campion and his senior, Robert Parsons. In 1581, Campion was captured at a recusant house outside Oxford, and eventually put to death (and, having died for his faith, he was canonised in 1970). Sir Thomas Tresham, a Northamptonshire gentleman, was one of those accused of having consorted with him.

Tresham had indeed been converted to the Roman faith by Parsons in 1580. His portrait, now in Boughton House, presents him as one of those wonderfully show-off Elizabethans, holding an immense new-fangled pistol as a symbol of his modernity and wealth. He was not judged to be a threat to the Queen; even so, over the next dozen years he was imprisoned on and off and fined the colossal sum of £8,000. On his release in 1593, he turned to architecture to encrypt his faith, beginning the Triangular Lodge on his estate at Rushton the next year.

Three sides, three gables to each of them, trefoil windows with triangles of different patterns inside them – the three was principally that of the Trinity, although Tresham (from the first syllable of his name) also had a bit of three about him: his family crest was a trefoil. In addition, this little building is encrusted with carvings, lettering and numbers, the meaning of which was deliberately opaque, but can be decoded to reveal messages about his situation, the Mass for which he suffered and the universality of the Catholic faith. The more difficult the conceit was to puzzle out, the better. With its punning heraldry, obscure learning and ingenuity, the Lodge is a fascinating embodiment of the Elizabethan mind. Although it was built near a rabbit warren, it is unlikely that the lodge ever housed the warren keeper: it was probably used by Tresham – if use it had – as a small banqueting hall.

Tresham also began Lyveden New Bield nearby, but it was never roofed. Not surprisingly, in view of his fines, Tresham was unable to spend as much of his income as he would have liked on his building activities, despite their intricacy. While Tresham was prepared to suffer passively for his faith, his son Francis died in the Tower after implication in the Gunpowder Plot (see page 317).

IZAAK WALTON'S COTTAGE SHALLOWFORD, STAFFORDSHIRE
Gone fishing

After the Bible, the *Complete Works of Shakespeare* and Harry Potter, Izaak Walton's *The Compleat Angler* is said to be the most published book in the language, having had over three hundred impressions, and never having been out of print since it was first published in 1653. To Walton, a Royalist whose England had been overturned by the Commonwealth, fishing provided a sanctuary. He applied to the subject a mind that was both philosophical and inquiring, so that his book became a repository of piscine law that was revised five times during Walton's own lifetime. Despite the unfavourable times, he became a landowner, with investments that included Halfhead Farm at Shallowford – now known as Izaak Walton's Cottage – which he had bought in 1655 but never lived in. Presumably the income he received from rents gave him more time to go fishing.

The Compleat Angler was a remarkable achievement for a Staffordshire innkeeper's son whose first job in London was that of ironmonger. There, however, he broke into a literary circle by writing biographies; one of his subjects was the poet John Donne, whom he came to know well. Walton married a descendant of the martyred Archbishop Cranmer, but she died, exhausted, having given birth to ten children; none of them survived infancy.

He then married a second time, his wife Anne Ken being half-sister to the future Bishop of Bath and Wells. Walton himself was deeply religious. His son by Anne grew up to be a canon of Salisbury cathedral, and his daughter married a canon of Winchester cathedral. The best friend of his later years was George Morley, Bishop of Worcester and later of Winchester, whom he had hidden during the Civil War; after Anne's death, Walton lived with him in his bishop's palace. Perhaps surprisingly, he was also a good friend of the licentious, funny Charles Cotton, with whom he fished on the river Dove. He asked Cotton to contribute a section on trout fishing to the fifth edition of his work, published in 1676. As though to demonstrate the therapeutic qualities of fishing, Walton lived to the great age of ninety.

SHERWOOD FOREST

The legend of Robin Hood

It would be difficult to overestimate the importance of hunting to the English monarchy, at least from Norman to Stuart times. When William the Conqueror vanquished England, he set aside immense tracts as royal hunting preserves. His own son, William Rufus, would die while hunting in the New Forest (see page 80). These 'forests' were subject to their own laws and courts, capable of imposing horrific punishments on anyone found poaching the King's venison or game. Damaging the forest 'vert', which meant anything that bore green leaves, was regarded as almost equally heinous, although no doubt it was a severe temptation to peasants in need of firewood and building materials. It was known that hunting honed the skills in horsemanship that were invaluable on the battlefield. It was also an almost addictive pleasure, which to some monarchs (notably James I) became an obsession.

Sherwood Forest occupied some 100,000 acres of Nottinghamshire and Yorkshire. It was not a forest in the modern sense of being uniformly covered with trees: woods full of oak and birch trees stood next to swathes of grassland and heath, on which the King's deer could graze. Animals, of course, were not the only inhabitants of this forest. From at least the late 14th century, Sherwood was associated with the great hero of English folklore, Robin Hood.

William Langland, writing *The Vision of William concerning Piers the Plowman* at the end of the 1370s, refers to the story of Robin, which was evidently well known – presumably having been told by minstrels as they travelled around the country. Dressed in Lincoln green, Robin is supposed to have lived at the end of the 12th century, when the future King John was minding the realm while his brother, Richard the Lionheart, was on crusade. The Sheriff of Nottingham was the King's local representative, responsible, among other things, for enforcing the forest laws. Robin, unfairly dispossessed, became an outlaw – sharing the fate of other rebellious spirits who failed to answer the charge of poaching. He was joined by a large band of Merry Men, prominent among them being Little John, Will Scarlet and Friar Tuck, with love interest being supplied by Maid Marian.

The Great North Road, which passes through the Forest, provided a reliable stream of rich travellers whom the outlaws robbed, taking particular pleasure in outwitting the greedy and corrupt officials of the Church and State, redistributing their booty to the poor.

Was there a real Robin? We do not know, but some of the ancient, curiously shaped oaks in the forest – which may be more than eight hundred years old – hug the secret. From their contorted posture, it almost seems that they are trying to tell us.

BATTLE OF SHREWSBURY

Henry IV tightens his grip

Henry Bolingbroke had succeeded in deposing Richard II*, but as Henry IV he could not unite the country he had seized. Richard may have been temperamental, extravagant and injudicious, but he was the legitimate king; Henry was forever haunted by the way in which he was done away with. The fourteen years of his reign were dogged by rebellion, the most serious of which occurred in July 1403.

On the northern borders of England, the powerful Percy family felt that it had not been sufficiently rewarded for its support of Henry's usurpation. Sir Henry Percy – the dashing Hotspur (see page 382) – led an army to Cheshire, where support for the old king, Richard II, had been strong. With him were some Scottish lords – including his traditional enemy, the Earl Douglas – whom he had captured the previous year; they were to be set free without ransom if Henry were toppled. Hotspur's object was to capture the sixteen-year-old Prince of Wales, the future Henry V, at Shrewsbury and then wait for his Welsh allies, led by Owain Glyndwr, to join him there (see page 422). But Henry IV reacted with speed, and reached Shrewsbury before Hotspur. When Hotspur arrived, he camped on fields a couple of miles to the north of the town, protected by the river Severn. Diplomacy failed, since neither side trusted the other. Hotspur drew up his men at the top of a slight rise.

The fighting was long and bloody. Henry knew that the enemy's principal object would be to kill or capture him, so took the unchivalrous step of dressing some of his knights in his surcoat as a distraction. Despite his youth, the Prince of Wales led the left flank against Hotspur, who had once been his tutor. As he struggled up the sloping ground, he was wounded in the face by an arrow – ironically, the archers he faced at Shrewsbury would, some twelve years later, bring him victory at Agincourt. Later in the battle, he succeeded in taking his men around the back of the enemy and surprising them. At the end of the day, some of those on the battlefield were unsure who had won, and fell down in exhausted heaps. Hotspur, however, had been killed, while Henry lived. It was not the end of Henry's troubles, nor of Prince Hal's military efforts to put down disaffection; the Prince was put in charge of a long and wearisome campaign to subdue Glyndwr in Wales. But the kingship had been kept in family hands.

*See Pontefract Castle, page 397. See also Jerusalem Chamber, page 193

THE SARACEN'S HEAD

Surrender of Charles I

King Charles I spent his last hours of freedom, in 1646, at the Saracen's Head Inn at Southwell. He had been there before, four years earlier, en route to raising his standard at Nottingham to start the Civil War*. Now his cause had become desperate. Newark Castle – at the crossing of the Great North Road, the Fosse Way and the River Trent – remained indomitably loyal, despite having suffered two sieges. It was now on its third siege, but the new fortifications, probably designed by Sir Bernard de Gomme, served the defenders well. Sooner or later, however, it would have to succumb. The Parliamentarian troops were Scottish; the King, who had been confined to an Oxford that was surrounded by Parliamentarian forces, preferred to give himself up to the Scots, hoping that he would be taken to Scotland, rather than face his English subjects. The Scots' quarrel with the King was largely religious; if he could patch up those differences, it was possible that he could retain his throne north of the border.

In the early morning of 5 May, he and two others arrived at the Saracen's Head disguised as priests. Charles was escorted the short distance from the Saracen's Head (then called the King's Arms) to the Archbishop's Palace at Southwell, which Scottish troops had occupied: an armed troop then arrived to take him to Kelham Hall some ten miles away, which was General David Leslie's head-quarters for the siege of Newark. Leslie demanded the surrender of Newark, to which the King acceded – much to the anguish of the defenders, who were tempted to make a last brave stand, but finally agreed to march out of the castle with flags flying and bullets in their mouths. (They could not have stood out much longer. Such had been their privations that plague had broken out.)

The Scots, however, did not fall in with the King's plan. They could not decide what to do with their royal prisoner, and having taken him nearly to the Scottish border, finally decided to leave him, like a parcel, at Berwick, to be collected by the King's English enemies. The road south led, via Carisbrooke Castle on the Isle of Wight, to the executioner's block.

*See Battle of Edgehill, page 319; Battle of Naseby, page 332; Stow-on-the-Wold, page 344; The Banqueting House, page 114

BATTLE OF STOKE

The impostor, Lambert Simnel, gets his comeuppance

The Battle of Bosworth of 1485 (see page 309) may have ended the Wars of the Roses, but the death of Richard III did not quite signify the last gasp of the Yorkist cause. Two years later, a ten-year-old boy called Lambert Simnel, the son of an Oxford joiner, was put up to challenge the new king, Henry VII. Simnel had been trained to impersonate the Yorkist contender for the throne, Edward IV's nephew, Edward, Earl of Warwick. Edward was the son of Edward IV's brother, the Duke of Clarence, and was nominally next in line after his young cousin, Edward V, had been murdered in the Tower of London by his uncle, Richard III. Henry VII had imprisoned Warwick in the Tower, and there was a rumour that he had died (in fact, he survived until the appearance of another pretender, Perkin Warbeck, in 1499, when he was executed).

The rebellion began in Ireland, where Simnel was 'crowned' King as 'Edward VI'. From there, an invasion force made up of wild Irishmen and German mercenaries landed near Furness in Lancashire. King Henry, who was at Kenilworth Castle, called together an army and set off to meet them in Nottinghamshire. On 16 June, both sides drew up amid what are now broad fields near the village of East Stoke, south-west of Newark. In the featureless landscape, the battle was characterised by savage slaughter as each side tried to push the other back. The Irish, however, were poorly armed, and after three bitter hours the King succeeded in driving the rebels into a gully. There thousands were massacred, perhaps giving rise to the local field names of Dead Man's Field and, even more grisly, Red Gutter. A stone marks the spot where Henry placed his standard after the battle, as a sign of victory, at the top of Burnham Furlong to the south of East Stoke.

Little Simnel, whom Henry did not regard as a serious threat, was put in his place by being given a job in the royal kitchens.

STOKESAY CASTLE   NEAR LUDLOW, SHROPSHIRE
Wool magnate's 'castle' reflects prosperity and peace

Throughout the Middle Ages, wool was England's most valuable export, and the greatest magnate of the late 13th century to trade in wool was probably Lawrence of Ludlow. Wool grown in England was sold to textile makers in Flanders and Italy. Lawrence's business made him rich enough to lend money, including to the King, Edward I. It also provided the means to build the daringly innovative manor house of Stokesay Castle from 1270–80.

Despite its name and battlements, Stokesay is not a real castle: more a prosperous home that had sufficient fortification to withstand bands of marauders. A building of this type could not have been contemplated in the unruly Welsh Marches until Edward I's campaigns to subdue Wales began to bear fruit. Nor would a merchant such as Lawrence have thought of living in a true castle: merchants lived in town houses, leaving the gentry to run the rural areas. In building Stokesay, Lawrence provides an early example of city money setting itself up in the countryside; it may be that the licence to crenellate (add battlements) that he obtained from the King in 1291 was a bid for increased social status. (Battlements meant power, which is why permission had to be sought before building them.) The big windows, of which only the upper half would originally have been glazed, show that Lawrence was as much interested in convenience as withstanding military assault.

Life at Stokesay was centred on the hall, its roof supported on immense crucks that leave the floor space clear of aisles. Lawrence's timber staircase at the north end of the hall is another impressive example of carpentry. For greater comfort, the family would have withdrawn to rooms in the solar block, reached by means of an outside staircase. The absence of any door directly from the hall into the solar was a security precaution. At both ends of this range is a stout tower, and the whole site is surrounded by walls and a moat.

In 1294 Lawrence was leading a group of merchants whose objective was to raise money from wool for the King's wars in France when his ship was wrecked off the Suffolk coast and he was drowned. He was buried at Ludlow. In subsequent centuries, Stokesay fell down the social scale when used as a working farmhouse, which explains why it escaped later rebuilding.

STOW-ON-THE-WOLD
GLOUCESTERSHIRE
Last battle of the Civil War

Sir Jacob Astley provides the words with which the English Civil War* both opened and closed. Before the Battle of Edgehill, in 1642, he had composed the prayer: 'O Lord! Thou knowest how busy I must be this day. If I forget Thee, do not Thou forget me.' Four years later, he was commanding the last Royalist army to be left in the field, a body of 3,000 Welsh infantry, over half of them raw recruits. His task was to march from Worcestershire to Charles I's beleaguered headquarters at Oxford, in the hope that the reinforcements he provided would delay the King's surrender sufficiently for some new stratagem to save the day. The silver-haired general, aged sixty-seven, succeeded in crossing the river Avon but, having been harassed by the Parliamentarian garrison at Gloucester, was unable to escape Sir William Brereton's forces. He reached Stow-on-the-Wold on 20 March and the next day made the Royalists' last stand on the slope of a hill outside the town.

At first, to a battle cry of 'For Patrick and St George', Astley's men were successful in driving off the attackers as they charged uphill, but they were overwhelmed by the Parliamentary cavalry led by Brereton, who made a decisive attack on the right flank. The Royalist cavalry escaped but the foot soldiers were chased to Stow's market square where, after a fierce fight, Astley surrendered. Sitting on a drum, he addressed his captors: 'Gentlemen, ye may now sit and play, for you have done all your work, if you fall not out among yourselves.' These words were to prove only too prophetic, for fall out the Parliamentarians did (see page 210). For King Charles, however, the last hope of evading capture had gone. Six weeks later he surrendered to the Scots army at Newark.

*See Battle of Edgehill, page 319; Battle of Naseby, page 332; The Saracen's Head, page 342; The Banqueting House, page 114

SHAKESPEARE'S BIRTHPLACE
Britain's greatest literary shrine

Shakespeare's birthplace in Henley Street, Stratford-upon-Avon, is one of the icons of Britain. Pilgrims have been visiting the house since the 18th century. The actor David Garrick mounted the first Shakespeare festival at Stratford in 1769, and in the 19th century you could hardly claim to be a writer without worshipping at the shrine. John Keats (1817), Sir Walter Scott (1821), Alfred Tennyson (1840), Herman Melville (1857), Mark Twain (1873) and Thomas Hardy (1896) all inscribed their names in the visitors' book, while Charles Dickens (see page 72) helped organise the campaign that led to its being acquired for the public in 1847.

Now divorced from the buildings that abutted it at either end and marooned in a pedestrian precinct, it is as remote from its original function as a dwelling, as a saint's relict is from the living person of whom it was once part. There is not much in the house that Shakespeare would have known when he was growing up. On the other hand, the Birthplace gives a vivid impression of his family's standing in life. Stratford, having at that time just been reduced by plague, had a population of 1,200 people – little more than a village by today's standards, although then a reasonable size for a market town.

John Shakespeare, the playwright's father, was a glover. He took one bay of the present house about the time of his marriage (c. 1556), using the ground floor as a workshop and shop and the upper floor as living accommodation. As his prosperity and family grew, he added the next two houses. At the time of Shakespeare's infancy, he was a substantial citizen, who served for many years on the town council and in 1568, when William was four, rose to become its bailiff or mayor. Things did not go so well in the next decade, and the family sunk into debt as a result of illegal wool-dealing. This must have strengthened the boy's resolve not to follow in his father's footsteps as a glover. On John Shakespeare's death in 1601, William inherited the house; it is one of the few items personally associated with him to have come down to us. But by then he was living and working in the very different milieu of London*.

Genius is beyond the normal processes of human understanding. Certainly

Shakespeare's birthplace does not explain the child who grew up there. How did this son of a provincial glover acquire the knowledge displayed both in the action of the plays and the metaphors of the writing? The local grammar school, although training his memory and teaching him Latin, would hardly have trained him in Court etiquette, noble pastimes such as falconry, or have introduced him so thoroughly to the classics, not to mention English history or the Italy in which many plays are set. He must have sucked in knowledge of such subjects when he arrived in London in 1587, aged twenty-three.

By this date he was already married to Anne Hathaway, eight years his senior and already pregnant when the nuptials took place. Because what is now known as Anne Hathaway's cottage, outside Stratford where she and her family lived, remained in the Hathaway family for four hundred years, its structure is remarkably unaltered. Inevitably, one sees the interiors through the eyes of the 1890s, when it was acquired by the Shakespeare Birthplace Trust, rather than the frisky eighteen-year-old glover's son – as yet to become a playwright – who seduced the daughter of the house. A rather more sedate Shakespeare is represented above his tomb in Stratford's parish church, where Anne is also buried; it is believed that the likeness to the Bard is very close.

*See The Globe Theatre, page 144, and Shakespeare Temple, page 219

BATTLE OF TEWKESBURY
GLOUCESTERSHIRE
Death of the Lancastrian Prince of Wales

In the spring of 1471, Queen Margaret of Anjou, wife of Henry VI, landed at Weymouth, intent on recapturing the kingdom for her imprisoned husband and for her son, the seventeen-year-old Prince of Wales, who was with her. She had entered into an unlikely pact with the man who had until recently been one of the greatest enemies to her cause, the Earl of Warwick. To seal the alliance, Warwick's daughter, Anne Neville, was married to the Prince of Wales. Warwick was already in England: the year before he had forced King Edward IV to flee to the Duke of Burgundy in Bruges, although since then Edward had come back, landing in Yorkshire and raising an army as he marched south. The Queen was not leading an invasion force; her presence and that of her son were intended to reinforce a sense of dynastic stability once Henry VI was back on the throne. Her plan was to rendezvous with Warwick, but he did not keep it. On the very day that the Queen stepped off her ship at Weymouth, he was killed at the Battle of Barnet*.

Having got this far, the Queen did not wish to abandon her cause entirely by returning to France. Her principal commander, the Duke of Somerset, and other commanders had estates in the West Country. They moved through them, gathering an army, and were warmly welcomed by the people of Bristol. The object now was to unite with Jasper Tudor's Lancastrian army in Wales†. For this purpose they needed to cross the Severn, but by now King Edward IV knew of their arrival and, having dismissed his army after Barnet, hastily reassembled it. When Margaret arrived at the gates of Gloucester, they were shut to her. She had no time to lay siege to the city; instead, the army hurried on towards the next bridge at Upton upon Severn, its line straggling as it went. Exhausted, they stopped on the water meadows outside Tewkesbury. Edward had caught up with them, his own camp being only a couple of miles away.

The Lancastrians had the advantage of choosing the site of the battle, which, protected by streams and ditches, it was difficult to attack. The Duke of Somerset succeeded in leading a surprise attack on Edward's extreme left flank, commanded by his brother, the Duke of Gloucester. The need to reinforce this wing should have weakened Edward's centre, giving Lord Wenlock and the Prince of Wales, commanding the Lancastrian centre, the opportunity to advance. It is now impossible to know why they did not take it. Instead, the Duke of Somerset was beaten back. He decided to make good his escape, precipitating a rout of his army as troops scrambled over the ditch known as the Swilgate in order to clamber into Tewkesbury Abbey for sanctuary. The Prince of Wales died on the battlefield.

The Duke of Somerset was captured; with the other Lancastrian commanders who survived the battle, he was executed – Edward's only concession being that their bodies would not be mutilated and displayed. The Queen, who had left before battle was joined, was eventually found, and spent the next five years in prison: in due course, the King of France paid a ransom to free her.

A brass in Tewkesbury Abbey announces: 'Here lies Edward Prince of Wales, cruelly slain whilst but a youth, on May 4th 1471. Alas, the savagery of men! Thou art the sole light of thy mother and the last hope of thy race.' With the Prince of Wales dead, Edward IV had no political reason to keep his father, Henry VI, alive in prison, and he was quickly murdered. The Prince's widow, Anne, heiress to the vast Warwick estates, eventually did become Queen, since she then married the Duke of Gloucester, the future Richard III.

*See Battle of Barnet, page 204. †See Battle of Mortimer's Cross, page 332

ST MARY'S CHURCH

Sumptuous tomb of an English commander in France

The English commander who presided at Joan of Arc's trial and death was Richard Beauchamp, Earl of Warwick. His remains lie in a chapel next to the chancel of St Mary's church. At the astonishing cost of £2,481 4s 7d, the

Beauchamp Chapel took twenty-one years to build, and required the demolition of the deanery. In the centre of the chapel, a tomb of Purbeck marble, carved with figures of saints, supports his effigy, which shows him lying on his back, hands raised in prayer. It is a golden wonder, exquisitely made, with every buckle of his armour (even parts that cannot be seen) perfectly finished. The Earl's head, with its pudding basin haircut, rests on a helmet, bearing his crest of a swan's head on a coronet. A grille made of gilded hoops covers the whole figure. This is the only gilded bronze effigy of someone who was not royal to survive from the Middle Ages, but then in power, status and wealth, the Earl was almost on a par with royalty.

An inscription proclaims Warwick's status as Henry VI's 'Lieutenant General and Governer of the Roialme of France and of the Duchie of Normandie'. Joan of Arc's death took place while he was Captain of Calais, won for England the previous century. In 1429, this visionary girl, the fervently religious daughter of a poor farmer, succeeded in reversing a string of English victories by attacking the English army that was besieging Orléans and forcing it to withdraw. The next year, she was captured by the Burgundian army and sold to the English, who charged her with witchcraft and heresy. At Rouen, Warwick had the duty of supervising the ecclesiastical trial, which was followed by her being burnt at the stake in the market square. It was at Rouen that Warwick himself died in 1439.

SUDELEY CASTLE WINCHCOMBE, GLOUCESTERSHIRE
Where Henry VIII's last queen is buried

When Henry VIII died in 1547, his last and sixth wife Catherine Parr was still Queen, not having been divorced like Catherine of Aragon and Anne of Cleves, or beheaded like Anne Boleyn and Catherine Howard. Twice married to men who had died, she managed both to withstand the rages of the dying King, and also to get on well with her step-children, taking the young Princess Elizabeth into her household. But she was only to survive the King by eighteen months, dying in childbirth at Sudeley Castle, where she is buried in the pretty church.

In the interim, she found love. Indeed, she was so swept away by the man she was to marry, Sir Thomas Seymour, that they formed an engagement less than a month after she had become widowed. Seymour, the brother of the new Lord Protector, the Duke of Somerset, was an almost psychopathically ambitious individual, whose immense self-confidence and buccaneering charm were very attractive to women. It may have been the presence of Elizabeth that drew him to Catherine rather than her own considerable qualities, but the otherwise sensible Catherine, who had almost married Seymour before attracting the interest of the King, now threw common sense to the winds. The romance and marriage infuriated the Protector. Soon pregnant, Catherine withdrew to Sudeley, which Seymour had turned into a palace, and held what some regarded as a second Court. Catherine personally directed the decoration of the nursery, which was never to be used, her child dying a week after herself.

Seymour did not stay at Sudeley to attend the funeral. He had already gone to London to renew his pursuit of Elizabeth. He got his comeuppance in 1549, when he was beheaded for trying to marry her. 'The realme is well rid of him,' commented Bishop Latimer, echoing the general opinion.

WORCESTER CATHEDRAL WORCESTER
Death of Henry VIII's older brother

Henry VII, victor of Bosworth (see page 309) and the restorer of England's finances after the Wars of the Roses, was not given to flights of fancy. When he named his eldest son Arthur, recalling the greatest of royal heroes, he wanted to fuse the Tudor dynasty with English myth. In this he was following the example of Edward III, who established the Order of the Garter on Arthurian lines (see page 249) and probably created the round table hanging in the Great Hall of Winchester Castle (see page 99). It was no accident that Prince Arthur was christened at Winchester, which was then thought to have been the seat of King Arthur's Camelot.

The young Arthur grew into a tall, delicately-featured boy, with every quality to make him a good prince, including an exceptional fluency in the diplomatic language of Latin. He was showered with honours, being made a Knight of the Bath and of the Garter as a small child. He was also made Prince of Wales, a title that had particular resonance to the Tudors, who were themselves Welsh. By the age of fifteen, he was able to play his part in his father's European policy by marrying, by proxy, a Spanish princess – Catherine of Aragon. Catherine set out from the Alhambra palace in May 1501, but her ship was forced back by storms. She eventually landed at Plymouth on 2 October 1501. Henry VII was impatient to meet her, and pleased with what he saw. After the wedding at St Paul's Cathedral, the bride and bridegroom made for Ludlow which was, at that time, the administrative centre of Wales, and where the castle was virtually a palace. The young prince boasted to courtiers of having 'been this night in the midst of Spain', indicating, it might be thought, that the marriage had been consummated.

It was an important point in English history. Six months later, Arthur died of the sweating sickness. There followed a funeral of epic proportions, beginning in Ludlow and ending with a spectacular procession to Worcester Cathedral. There his body was interred in an elaborate chantry chapel. In time, his widow became the wife of the next King of England, Henry VIII. When she failed to bear him a male heir, Henry worried that he had incurred divine displeasure by breaching the injunction in Leviticus (20:21) against marrying a brother's wife ('they shall be childless', states the Biblical text). This became the pretext for the divorce that presaged the English reformation. It is poignant that among the many religious statues to be defaced in the iconoclasm that followed were some of those on Prince Arthur's tomb.

LEA & PERRINS

A uniquely British sauce, and taste of Empire

Like other sons of Empire, Lord Marcus Sandys' stint as Governor of Bengal left him with a taste for the strong spicy food that he ate there. He returned to England in the 1830s and asked two Worcestershire chemists, John Lea and William Perrins, to make up a recipe for a sauce he had brought back with him. When he came to collect the result, he pronounced it inedible and stalked out. Some months later, Messrs Lea and Perrins decided to sample the anchovy-based condiment they had been instructed to make, before throwing out the bottles. They found that, with fermentation, it had matured into a sauce that, if not obviously palatable in itself, would give a pungent fillip if added sparingly to other food. They bought the recipe from Lord Marcus, and Worcester Sauce – it was only later that the 'shire' was added – went into commercial production.

Lea and Perrins, both sons of farmers, were enterprising men, with shops in Kidderminster and Cheltenham as well as Worcester. They paid the stewards of liners to serve Worcestershire Sauce on the tables of ocean liners, to promote its use. In 1904 it acquired the first of the royal warrants that it has held ever since.

Since then Worcestershire Sauce has joined kedgeree, chutney and, more recently, chicken tikka masala (described by Foreign Secretary Robin Cook as 'Britain's true national dish' in 2001) as part of the Empire's legacy to Anglo-Saxon cuisine – part of the taste palette that must seem as curious to some foreigners as the habit of eating Welsh rabbit at the end of club dinners. However, international currency was achieved when it became an ingredient of the classic American Caesar salad. The small Victorian factory in Midland Street where Worcestershire Sauce is produced was rebuilt after a fire in 1897. Fragrant with spices, the air beguiles the gastronomic imagination with thoughts of the biggest Bloody Mary in the world.

North-West England

THE LANDMARKS OF the North-West reflect both the triumph of industry, in cities such as Manchester and Bolton, and the flight from it. In 1900, Lancashire was the cotton-spinning capital of the world. On the other hand, to readers of Wordsworth and Ruskin, not to mention Beatrix Potter, the Lake District represented a landscape alive with nature – formative, healing, wild. Another kind of escape from drudgery was offered by Blackpool, with its Pleasure Beach.

The world created by the Industrial Revolution may have been hugely profitable to the mill owners, but it was not necessarily happy for the workers. In 1819, an immense crowd in Manchester, demonstrating against low wages and high prices, was brutally charged by the Yeomanry Cavalry; the Peterloo Massacre became a rallying cry for reform. In Rochdale, just twenty-five years later, workers clubbed together to provide themselves with decent food and education; the Co-operative Movement seemed to promise much to a faltering society. Many of the poorest preferred to try their luck elsewhere, however, and travelled through Liverpool on the way to a new life in North America. In that same city, the most famous quartet of the twentieth century – the Fab Four – took on the world; John Lennon's 'Imagine' became an anthem for an idealistic generation.

Peace and love was not the universal instinct of the region, though. A small army of reivers – cross-border raiders – destroyed the bickering Scottish army at Solway Moss in 1542. Four centuries later, the Battle of the Atlantic was fought, to a large extent, from Liverpool, while much of Britain's submarine fleet was built at Barrow-in-Furness. The North-West entered the nuclear age early: Calder Hall, now part of Sellafield, was the world's first power station to produce electricity commercially. The bunker at Hack Green is a spooky reminder of the preparations that were taken as recently as the 1980s for civil administration to continue should Britain suffer a nuclear Armageddon. From death to birth: in 1978, the Royal Oldham Hospital triumphantly delivered the first baby to be produced by 'in vitro fertilisation'.

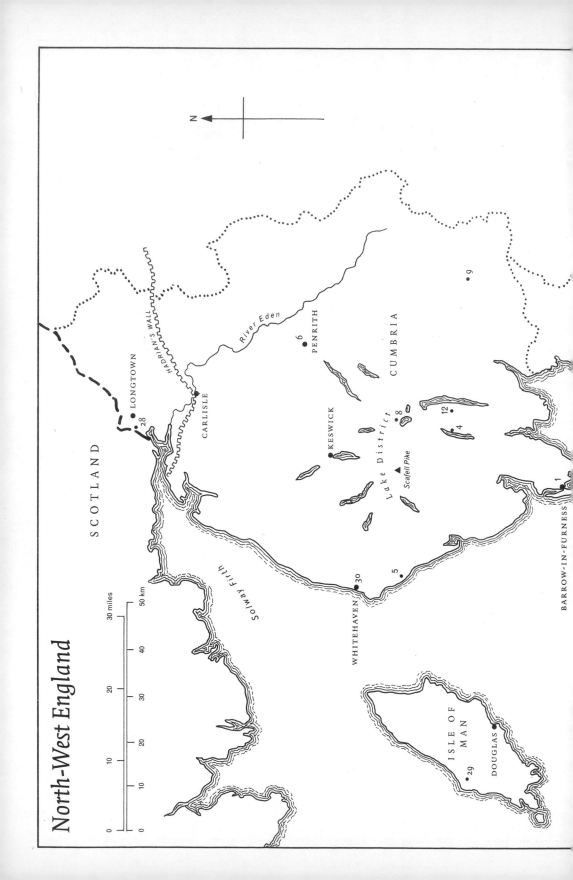

North-West England

N

SCOTLAND

Solway Firth

HADRIAN'S WALL

River Eden

● LONGTOWN
●28

● CARLISLE

● PENRITH
6 ●

CUMBRIA

● KESWICK

Lake District

▲ *Scafell Pike*

●8
12 ●
● 4

9 ●

● WHITEHAVEN
30 ●
● 5

BARROW-IN-FURNESS
1 ●

ISLE OF MAN

● DOUGLAS

29 ●

30 miles
0   10   20   30

50 km
0   10   20   30   40   50

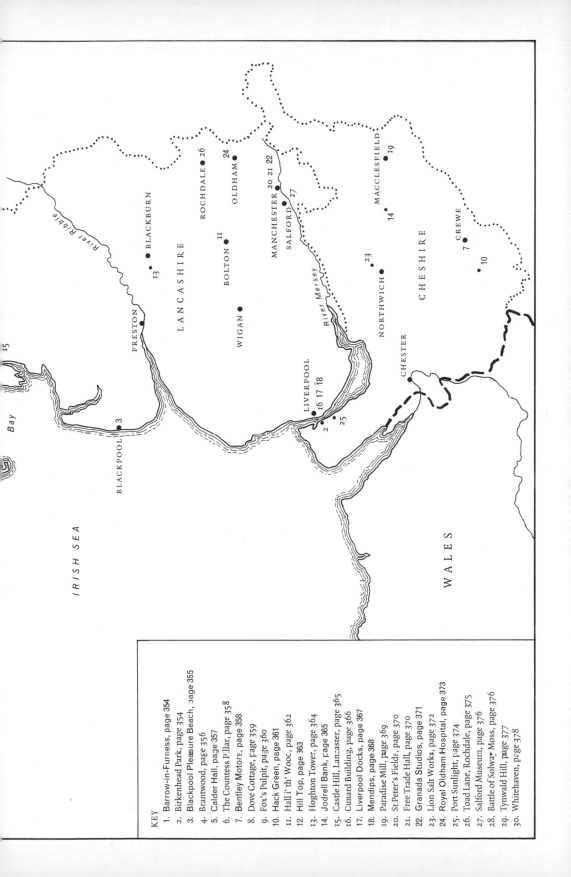

IRISH SEA

Bay

15

River Ribble

BLACKPOOL ● 3

PRESTON ●

LANCASHIRE

13 ● BLACKBURN

ROCHDALE ● 26

BOLTON ● 11

OLDHAM ● 24

WIGAN ●

MANCHESTER 20 21 22
SALFORD ● 27

LIVERPOOL
16 17 18

2 ●   ● 25

River Mersey

CHESTER ●

NORTHWICH ● 23

MACCLESFIELD ● 19

CHESHIRE

CREWE ● 7
● 10

● 14

WALES

BARROW-IN-FURNESS CUMBRIA

Where Britain's submarines are built

In nature, a torpedo is an electric ray, capable of administering a shock. The first submarine to fire the weapon to which the ray lent its name was originally built at the Vickers' shipyard at Barrow-in-Furness. That vessel was one of a pair of boats made for the Swedish industrialist Thorsten Nordenfelt in 1886, and was ultimately sold to Turkey.

While desperate Confederates had made underwater attacks during the American Civil War, it was only when around 1900 France developed a submarine capacity that the British authorities took serious notice. Suddenly the most powerful navy in the world looked vulnerable. To find an adequate defence, this method of warfare had to be understood. Destroyers provided part of the solution but, as the first Lord of the Admiralty, Lord Selborne, observed in a memo to the Cabinet in 1901: 'The true answer to the submarine is the submarine.' If other countries had them, so must Britain. Soon the view arose that submarines operating with destroyers could provide a more efficient means of deterring the invasion of home waters than costly battleships. The navy placed its first order for submarines in 1901. By 1914 it had acquired the most advanced submarine fleet in the world. Nearly all of it had been built at Barrow.

Although in the course of its history, starting from 1871, the Barrow shipyard has also built more than 500 surface ships, nothing can surpass its contribution to Britain's submarine fleet, including the four Vanguard-class ballistic nuclear submarines built in the 1990s to carry Britain's controversial Trident nuclear warheads. The Vanguards are on patrol somewhere under the water – their position top secret – around the clock, every day of the year. Within its enormous closed sheds, BAE Systems, Vickers' successors at Barrow, are currently building the first of the Astute-class nuclear attack submarines, which will operate without ever needing to be refuelled.

BIRKENHEAD PARK MERSEYSIDE

The municipal park is born

In 1843, the gardener Joseph Paxton started to lay out the world's first municipal park, in Birkenhead. At this time, Birkenhead was a small town, establishing itself as a salubrious residential area for families who found the booming port of Liverpool, just the other side of the Mersey, too rough. Paxton had just designed a park for Liverpool – Prince's Park, named after the birth of the Prince of Wales in 1841; it was a commercial development, financed, like London's earlier Regent's Park (see page 163), by the sale of houses. Birkenhead Park was acquired from town funds.

354 LANDMARKS OF BRITAIN

At this point Paxton, aged nearly forty, had already made a spectacular career out of gardening. The son of a farm labourer, his lucky break came when the 6th Duke of Devonshire spotted him as a young gardener, working in the Royal Horticultural Society's arboretum at Chiswick. Apparently on impulse, he appointed him head gardener at Chatsworth House (see page 312), where the park alone was eleven miles in circumference. Here he not only developed the gardens and park that had previously been landscaped by Capability Brown, but he designed and built glasshouses for the Duke's fine collection of exotic plants. This began for Paxton what became a successful parallel career. In time, he was responsible for the Crystal Palace, the immense, glittering iron-and-glass structure that housed the Great Exhibition of 1851.

The 185 acres at Birkenhead that formed the park were not naturally promising, being flat and marshy. An army of workers was employed to dig lakes and build mounds. Boathouses and bridges adorned the water, clumps of trees stood on the mounds, serpentine walks wound in and out, and a carriage drive with lodges ran around the perimeter. It became the model for Olmsted and Vaux's Central Park in New York.

BLACKPOOL PLEASURE BEACH   *LANCASHIRE*
World's tallest roller-coaster

In 1993 the Pepsi-Max Big One was opened at Blackpool Pleasure Beach. Rising to a dizzy 235ft above the ground, the steel skeleton of the world's tallest and fastest roller-coaster needed permission from the aviation authorities at nearby Blackpool Airport before it could be built. It now looms over the seafront like the outline of a small mountain range. Cars swooping down the steel valleys reach speeds of up to 85mph.

The Big One continues a tradition of mechanical innovation at the Pleasure Beach, which covers a 44-acre site. Among the scaffold towers on which the Big One is supported, the Flying Machines Whirligig, built in 1904, is still operating. It was designed by Sir Hiram Maxim, famous as the inventor of the Maxim gun. Among the other pioneering rides that still function are the River Caves (1904), the rocking Noah's Ark (1921), the Ghost Train (1931) and the Grand National (1935).

Blackpool began life as a seaside resort in the 1780s, but came into its own as a destination for holiday crowds from the mill towns of industrial Lancashire. The resort's zenith coincided with the arrival of electricity in 1879, which allowed the 7-mile seafront to be illuminated with strings of coloured lights, and 'fancy' trams to run between Blackpool and neighbouring Fleetwood: opened in 1885, the tramway was Britain's first. Holidaymakers still queue to go up the 520ft Blackpool Tower, built in 1894, to view the gaily lit promenade. Investment continued between the wars, attracting the throngs of visitors whose sheer cheek-by-jowl volume seemed to generate its own excitement in the age of mass transport and entertainment. Since then, Blackpool has changed remarkably little; it continues to attract tourists for whom donkeys on the beach, dancing in the Tower Ballroom and a turn on the Pepsi-Max Big One beats a cheap package holiday in Spain.

See also Margate Beach, page 78

BRANTWOOD
NEAR CONISTON, CUMBRIA
Ruskin's Lakeland home

John Ruskin commanded the aesthetic heights of Victorian England, influencing the way that painters painted, architects built and the public viewed. He was a passionate advocate of Turner and the Pre-Raphaelites, Gothic architecture and Venice, a society that worked with its hands, and utopian socialism. His touchstone was the wonderful individuality of God's creation, seen in wildflowers, rocks, rivers and mountains. It was a vision opposed to the ugly industrialism and joyless cities that were the money-generators of the age, producing not, in Ruskin's romantic view, true wealth but what he called ill-th. However, not even the prodigious tide of the great seer's prose was enough to purge capitalism of its aesthetic and social poisons, and in the end he went mad.

Ruskin's country home beside Coniston Water exemplifies many of his ideas. It was above all a house with a view. Ruskin knew the view but not the house when he bought it after his first serious bout of mental illness in 1871. The house itself, as he remembered in *Fors Clavigera*, 'a mere shed of rotten timber and loose stone', was previously occupied by the wood-engraver, printer and political radical W. J. Linton. Unlike the penniless Linton, Ruskin had inherited a fortune from his sherry merchant father, and began making improvements which included adding a turret to the house and building a lodge and a coach-house at the end of the steep drive – surprisingly modest, given his intense interest in architecture.

The house continued to grow piecemeal. While the most conspicuous legacy that Ruskin left to British cities resulted from his campaign on behalf of Venetian polychromy, there is little to recall the Serenissima at Brantwood. Rather it demonstrates his increasing commitment to local styles, prefiguring the Arts and Crafts movement. As Ruskin recalled, constant supervision was required to ensure that the local builder kept a degree of roughness. 'If I ever left him alone for a day, some corner stone was sure to be sent from Bath or

Triangular Lodge, page 338. Sir Thomas Tresham's architectural meditation on the Trinity expresses the intricacy of the Elizabethan mind.

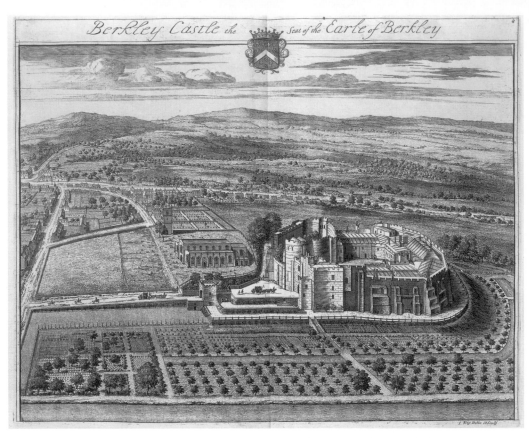

Berkeley Castle, page 300. Although Edward II managed to escape from Berkeley Castle, he was recaptured and murdered here in 1327.

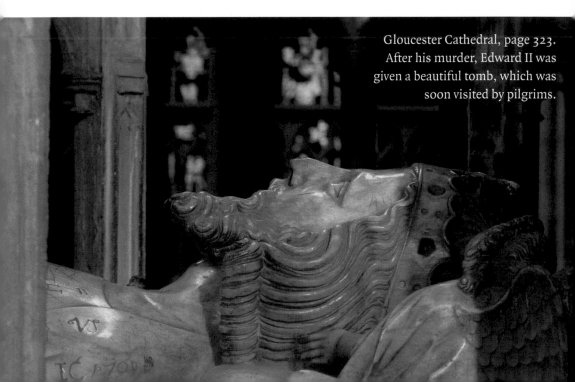

Gloucester Cathedral, page 323. After his murder, Edward II was given a beautiful tomb, which was soon visited by pilgrims.

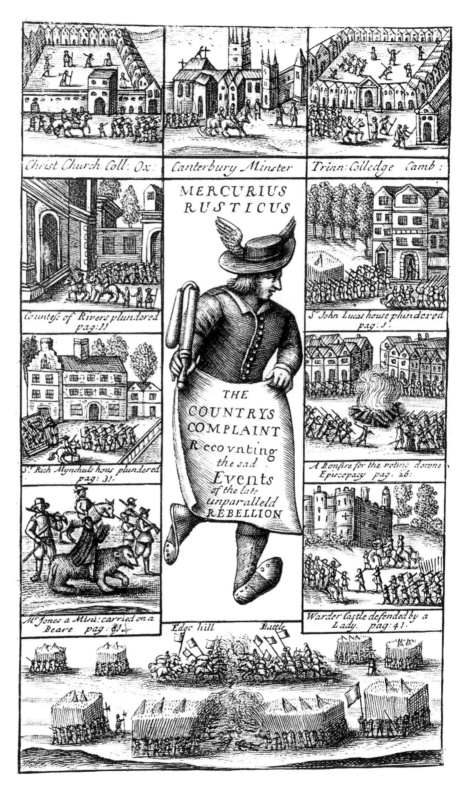

Edgehill, page 319. The first battle of the Civil War, with its 'hedgehog' formations of pikemen, is shown at the bottom of this sheet.

Above: Spaghetti Junction, page 306. Completed in 1972, the carriageways interlace with the intricacy of an Elizabethan knot garden.

Opposite: Coventry Cathedral, page 314. John Piper's Baptistery window contributes to a building that symbolised rebirth and hope after the Blitz.

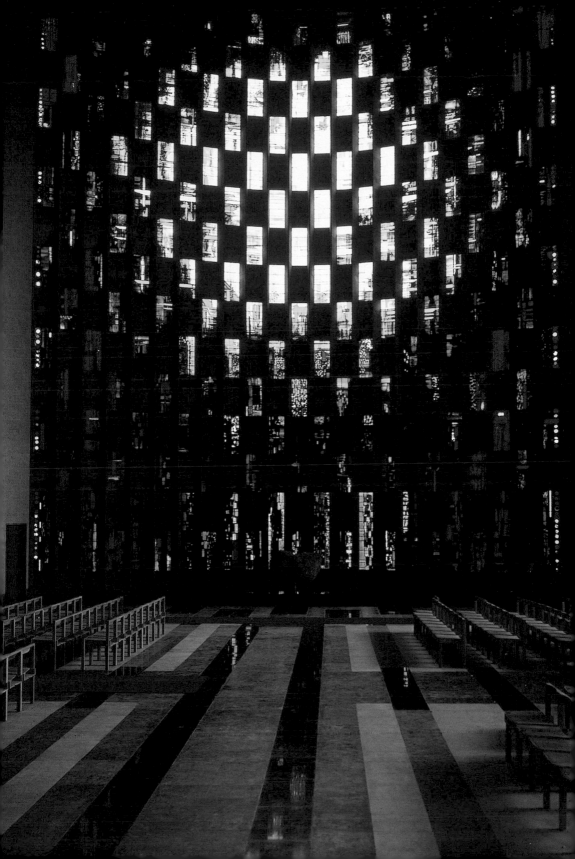

Top: Iron Bridge, page 313. Built in 1779 by the Quaker ironmaster Abraham Darby to advertise the possibilities of iron.

Above: Cromford, page 315. Richard Arkwright pioneered the factory system in his water-powered cotton mills, seen here by moonlight in a painting by Joseph Wright of Derby.

Right: Soho House, page 303. The great manufacturer Matthew Boulton, shown with his factory; the factory has gone but his house survives.

Below: Bass Brewery, page 311. Bottles of Bass are proudly displayed on the counter of the bar at the Folies-Bergère, painted by Manet.

Top: Chatsworth House, page 312. The country house that all other country houses want to be.

Above: The Chantry, page 301. The Temple of Vaccinia where Edward Jenner, who discovered the principle of vaccination in 1798, gave free treatment to local people.

Brantwood, page 356. John Ruskin's love of beauty can be seen both from his study (here, painted by his cousin Arthur Severn) and the scenery in which the house is set.

Dove Cottage, page 359. The poet William Wordsworth took inspiration from the landscape amid which he grew up and lived; the lake here is Grasmere.

Blackpool Pleasure Beach, page 355.
The shadow of the Blackpool Tower
falls on the sands of a resort famous
for its mechanical innovation.

Calder Hall, page 357. The world's first nuclear power station commercially producing electricity opened on the Cumbrian coast in 1956.

Jodrell Bank, page 365. Professor Bernard Lovell led the team that established the radio telescope at Jodrell Bank, completed in 1957.

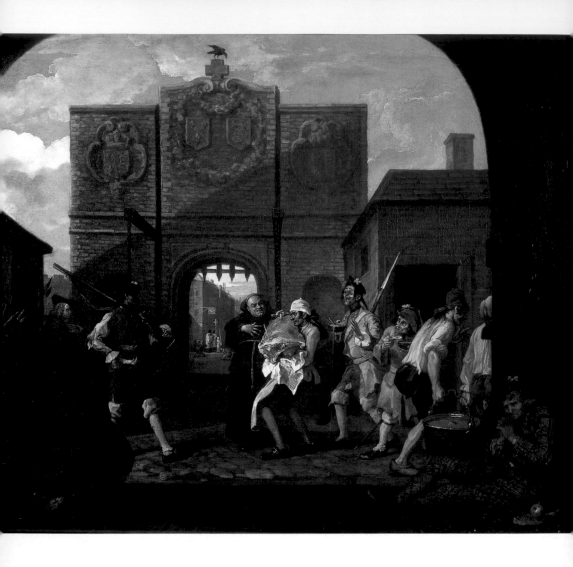

Above: Hoghton Tower, page 364. Hogarth's picture *O the Roast Beef of Old England*, painted in 1748, is a hymn of praise to the meat knighted by James I as Sir Loin.

Opposite, above: St Peter's Fields, page 370. The carnage that resulted from cavalry charging a crowd of political protesters in 1819 became known as the Peterloo Massacre.

Opposite, below: Free Trade Hall, page 370. The Band of Hope Workers Rally at the Free Trade Hall in 1908: continuing Manchester's tradition of radicalism.

MANCHESTER HEROES

Top left: Fountains Abbey, page 388. The cellarium of Fountains Abbey demonstrates the scale of the Cistercian foundation, despite the wildness of its setting.

Top right: Lindisfarne, page 395. The castle on Holy Island was built to take advantage of the remote location that, centuries earlier, had attracted both St Cuthbert and St Aidan.

Above: Clifford's Tower, page 405. In 1190, some 150 Jews who had barricaded themselves into the castle killed themselves rather than surrender to the mob.

Above: Alnwick Castle, page 382. Canaletto's view of the castle hardly suggests the rugged qualities that gave birth to the fiery Hotspur.

Right: Cragside, page 385. Built for the inventor and armaments manufacturer William Armstrong, Cragside was the first house to be lit by hydro-electricity.

Durham Cathedral, page 386.
Offsetting the austerity, the pillars
in the nave are simply but strikingly
decorated with carved zigzags,
spirals, grooves and diamonds.

Portland, and the ledges I had left to invite stonecrop and swallows, trimmed away in the advanced style of the railway station at Carnforth.' Ruskin planned the roof of the new dining room to shelter bees. In search of calmness of spirit, the idea of living in a cottage appealed to him. However, the art critic in Ruskin could not be kept entirely at bay: the wallpaper in the study was made especially to a design copied from the priest's embroidered sleeve in Marco Marziale's The Circumcision in the National Gallery.

Ruskin's most-loved paintings were hung in his bedroom. 'When I die,' he said of the Turners around his bed, 'I hope that they may be the last things my eyes will rest on in this world.' They were. Ruskin, increasingly troubled in mind but always rejoicing in the beauty of the Lakes, spent his last year at Brantwood, dying there in 1900. He is buried in Coniston churchyard.

CALDER HALL NEAR WHITEHAVEN, CUMBRIA
World's first commercial nuclear power station

In 1956, Calder Hall opened as the world's first nuclear power station commercially producing electricity. Nuclear fission had been achieved in the 1930s, and two atomic bombs were dropped on Japan in August 1945. In 1947, the British prime minister Clement Attlee ordered the construction of a plant at Windscale, next to Calder Hall, to produce plutonium for Britain's own atomic bomb. Construction of a power station for civilian purposes began in 1953. When it was opened three years later, the Queen commented that 'the new power, which has proved itself to be such a terrifying weapon of destruction, is harnessed for the first time for the common good of our community'. In his 'Buildings of England' volume for Cumberland, Sir Nikolaus Pevsner, always eager to embrace new architectural forms, comments that the 'noble shape of cooling towers can never fail to impress'.

The town of Workington, 15 miles up the coast, was the first to benefit from nuclear-generated electricity, which then flowed on around the country via the National Grid, reaching London four hours later. By the end of the century, nuclear power was generating a quarter of Britain's electricity, saving millions of tons of coal. By now, ten more reactors of the Calder Hall type – known as Magnox, from the magnesium alloy used to case the nuclear fuel – had been built, followed by fourteen advanced gas-cooled reactors. A pressurised-water reactor began operation at Sizewell in Suffolk in 1995; its construction, however, was preceded by the longest public inquiry in British history, and no more nuclear power stations have been ordered or built since then.

Calder Hall, now part of the Sellafield nuclear site, continued to produce electricity until 2003. Decommissioning the power station is expected to take a hundred years.

THE COUNTESS PILLAR

A strong-willed countess rebuilds her inheritance

Two miles east of Penrith on the A66 stands a stone pillar, topped by a sundial. It was erected by Lady Anne Clifford in 1656, to mark the spot where she last said goodbye to her mother, before the latter's death forty years earlier. To Lady Anne, history, particularly family history, was of consuming importance. Born in the Elizabethan age, she was the third and only surviving daughter of George Clifford, 3rd Earl of Cumberland. Cumberland's business was buccaneering; he ran a fleet of privateers that preyed on enemy shipping, but it left him heavily in debt. Perhaps as a result, he did not leave the family's estates in Westmorland and Cumberland to his daughter – she was only fifteen at the time of his death in 1605 – but to his brother, Francis. She regarded this as a great injustice, and she spent the next thirty-eight years seeking to overturn it.

She succeeded in 1643, inheriting the estates on the death of her first cousin. Because of the Civil War, she could not leave London and go north to control her estates in person until 1649. By now she was sixty. She had married twice – the Earl of Dorset, then the Earl of Pembroke – outliving both her husbands. The Civil War had overturned the rich, courtly world in which she had been brought up. Now her own woman and able to spend her fortune as she chose, she set about restoring that world through architecture. She rebuilt the family castles that were in ruin or decay – among them Appleby, Brough, Brougham, Skipton and Pendragon; she founded almshouses at Appleby; among the churches and chapels that she restored or built are St Wilfred's and St Ninian's (known locally as Ninekirks) at Brougham. A remarkable aspect of these projects was their architectural ultra-conservatism. With their buttresses and ogee arches, her churches are clearly Gothic in style – an affirmation of continuity with the past.

Dying in 1676, Lady Anne is buried in the church at Appleby beside her mother. A rafter in the Lady Chapel is inscribed 'Ann Countesse of Pembroke in Ano 1655 repaired all this building'.

BENTLEY MOTORS

Britain's motor-racing heritage

Britain's recent history as a major car producer has not been glorious. The country continues, however, to produce more than its fair share of world-class racing drivers, following the tradition established in the 1920s by the likes of Barney Barnato at Le Mans. The car that brought Barnato and others victory was the Bentley. Its dashing exploits were not confined to the race track. In

1930 Barnato, the first chairman of Bentley Motors, famously raced the Blue Train from the South of France, not only beating it to the Channel but also arriving at his London club before it reached Calais. (He won the bet that inspired the race – only to be fined a larger sum by the French authorities for racing on public roads.) In the intervening years, the Bentley marque has kept the memory of those victories alive, cherishing a particularly British reputation for big-engined super-performance combined with magnificent craftsmanship. Since the Second World War, the home of Bentley Motors – and its loyal workforce – has been Crewe.

This reflects a history which – for all the leather upholstery and cat-like smoothness associated with Bentleys – has not been without its share of turbulence. W. O. Bentley, born in 1888, began his working life as a railway engineer, exhilarated by the 'surge of acceleration' when a train left London and knowing 'nothing to compare with the sensation of rushing through the night'. In 1912, he and his brother took on the concession to import French DFP sports cars, which he tuned and raced at the Brooklands circuit in Surrey. During the First World War, Bentley worked as a designer of aero engines, and the first motor car to bear his name roared into existence in 1919. But the company was to have an independent life of only eleven years: the Wall Street stock market crash of 1929 left Bentley exposed to take-over by Rolls-Royce. It was not a happy outcome for Bentley, who found it impossible to work with Sir Henry Royce. The Crewe factory now occupied by Bentley Motors was originally constructed to produce the Rolls-Royce Merlin engines that powered the Spitfire and Hurricane fighter planes that won the Battle of Britain.

When divorce from Rolls-Royce came in 1998, it was Bentley that kept the house: Rolls-Royce, owned by BMW, decamped to a newly built factory on the Goodwood Estate in Sussex. That Bentley, in the old Merlin factory, should now also be in German ownership, as part of the Volkswagen group, may be something of an irony. If, however, computer-guided lasers are today used to cut the wafer-thin walnut and other veneers that finish the Bentley interiors, they are fitted by craftsmen who have, in some cases, worked for the company for forty-five years.

DOVE COTTAGE NEAR GRASMERE, CUMBRIA
Frugality and high-mindedness of the national poet

William Wordsworth could be regarded as England's national poet. But which Wordsworth? As a young man, after spending his loveless teenage years as an orphan, he travelled to France, attracted by the idealism of the Revolution. In the second half of his life he became Poet Laureate, a pillar of Victorian respectability from which position, it is generally thought, his poetry suffered.

The most productive years of his life – his late twenties and early thirties – were those he spent at Dove Cottage just outside the village of Grasmere, a modest 17th-century cottage, embowered in roses and jasmine, with runner beans scrambling up the back wall. He arrived, with his sister Dorothy, shortly before Christmas 1799. It perfectly suited their desire for frugality combined with high-mindedness.

Here Wordsworth wrote some of his greatest and most famous poems, including 'Daffodils', 'Resolution and Independence' and the self-analytical epic *The Prelude*. The unmarried Dorothy, who flouted convention by allowing her skin to become tanned by the sun, undertook much of the work of the house, but life at Dove Cottage did not conform to conventional stereotypes. Visitors such as Samuel Taylor Coleridge would arrive at all hours, sometimes bringing children. After Wordsworth's marriage, there was not only his wife Mary to accommodate but also her unmarried sister. 'We are crammed in our little nest edge-full,' wrote Dorothy to a friend in 1806.

Sunk into a hillside, the dark downstairs rooms were lit only by candles made out of lamb fat. The children's bedroom was papered with pages of newsprint. Sir Walter Scott so much objected to the constant diet of porridge that he climbed out of his bedroom window to eat at the local inn. For all its austerity, however, the Wordsworths were reluctant to leave the cottage for a bigger house in 1808. Growing affluence is reflected in their move a few years later to Rydal Mount, two miles nearer Ambleside.

FOX'S PULPIT

NEAR SEDBERGH, CUMBRIA

The birth of Quakerism

In 1652, the itinerant preacher George Fox felt moved by the Lord to climb Pendle Hill near Clitheroe. The son of a Leicestershire weaver, Fox had been wandering about the country for six years, following a divine revelation. He preached an extreme form of religious dissent, belonging to the Society of Friends of Truth, who had already come to be known, disrespectfully, as Quakers after Fox told a judge to 'quake at the word of the Lord'. According to Fox, organised religious ceremony of any kind should be rejected, because individuals should be guided by their personal relationship with God. Even reading the Bible, he believed, should take second place to the pursuit of the inner light that would be directly communicated by God. Although Fox's views were not far removed from those of other fundamentalists in the wake of the Civil War, they won him few friends among the Establishment.

Moved by the instructions of the Lord, Fox must sometimes have seemed deranged: once he had removed his shoes and run into the city of Lichfield, inveighing against the blood he imagined to be in the streets. Climbing Pendle

Hill would have seemed an eccentric act at the time; hills and mountains were not yet climbed for pleasure. On it, he received a vision commanding him to 'sound the day of the Lord'. This gave him renewed vigour to preach. A few days afterwards he addressed a crowd of a thousand people from a crag now known as Fox's Pulpit on remote Firbank Fell outside Sedbergh. 'The Kingdom of Heaven did gather us, and catch us all, as in a net,' remembered one of those present, the early Quaker missionary Francis Howgill.

The meeting on Firbank Fell gave Quakerism the impetus to become a movement. For Fox it had another consequence. Among the 'great multitude' there was Margaret Fell, then married to Judge Thomas Fell of Swarthmore Hall; eleven years after the Judge's death in 1658, she became Fox's wife. It was a domestic consolation in a life which, for Fox, was spent relentlessly sounding the day of the Lord, not only in Britain but in the West Indies, America, Holland and Germany. Often he and his followers, such as his friend William Penn*, were thrown into prison. However, after the Restoration of Charles II in 1660, Fox could not be accused of having taken up arms against the King: Quakers were among the first pacifists.

*See Jordans Meeting House, page 224

HACK GREEN NEAR NANTWICH, CHESHIRE
After Armageddon, civil servants

In 1984, the Cold War between the Soviet Union and the West was still on. In only another five years' time the Berlin Wall would fall and what President Ronald Reagan dubbed the 'Evil Empire', controlled from Moscow, would collapse under the weight of its own rust. But for now, plans for how Britain might survive in the event of a Soviet nuclear attack still had to be made. The North-West region, from Cheshire in the south to Cumbria in the north, would have been run from the bowels of a concrete bunker in a field near Nantwich that opened that year.

This was not the first military use for the site. During the early part of the Second World War, it had been laid out as a decoy to distract German pilots from bombing the railway centre at nearby Crewe. Then, as RAF Hack Green, it was developed as part of Britain's radar defences. In the 1950s, it was fortified against nuclear attack, and for the first half of the 1960s contributed to Britain's air-traffic control system, then shared between the military and civil authorities. By 1979, the first year of Margaret Thatcher's premiership, the site had been disused for thirteen years. It was then that it was chosen as a secret headquarters from which the region could be controlled in the event of a Third World War.

Under the Emergency Powers Act, a commissioner who was either a civil servant or a government minister would have governed his defence region, and perhaps neighbouring regions if their own administration had been destroyed. At his disposal was an updated version of Churchill's Cabinet War Rooms under Whitehall (see page 128), with better air-conditioning, Geiger counters, anti-contamination suits and banks of computers. From here, forty-two civil servants would have tried to run what was left of the region's infrastructure: hospitals, ports, power stations, food supplies, reservoirs and (importantly) burial facilities. Incoming attacks could be monitored and the extent of radioactive fallout mapped. By 1993, the threat of nuclear conflict had receded to the point that facilities such as Hack Green could be decommissioned – and the world breathed a sigh of relief.

HALL I' TH' WOOD
NEAR BOLTON, LANCASHIRE
Invention of Crompton's mule

Samuel Crompton stands in a proud tradition of British inventors who were unable to take financial advantage of their genius. From the age of five, his family had lived in three rented upper rooms of Hall i' th' Wood, a picturesque, partly half-timbered hall. His father, an unsuccessful farmer, had died soon after they moved there; his mother was left to support the family by spinning yarn on a wheel. Young Samuel watched her, and devised a machine that would make yarn of a higher quality, more quickly*. The result came to be known as the mule, supposedly because it combined elements of Hargreaves' spinning jenny and Arkwright's water frame: it was therefore a hybrid, like a mule. His first prototype was made in 1779.

The mule was able to satisfy the new demand for cotton yarn. Previous cotton yarns had only been suitable for wefts; the warps, having to be stronger, were made from flax which had longer fibres. The yarn that Crompton made was fine and strong. It therefore fetched a good price, and attracted the interest of other spinners, who tried to spy out his secret at Hall i' th' Wood. This was a period when hand-spinners, fearing that they would lose their livelihoods to mechanisation, were smashing machines in nearby Bolton and Chorley – a reaction that would develop into the Luddite unrest of the next century (see page 384). Crompton dismantled his mule and hid the pieces in the attic; the box that he is presumed to have used for the purpose is still there.

Crompton did not think he could take out a patent for his invention, since it might have conflicted with the many patents owned by the powerful Richard Arkwright. Instead, he sought to raise a subscription from manufacturers to whom he showed his machine. But he made little from it. He had hoped his invention would improve cottage production, thus helping people like his mother. The principles of the mule, once known, were quickly copied. The original was worked by hand but mill owners immediately saw that it could be powered by water – and steam soon followed. The number of bobbins on each machine could be increased from fifty to twelve hundred; then machine could be added to machine, with whole floors of them being driven by the same source.

Crompton, having petitioned Parliament, was awarded a grant of £5,000 in recognition of his contribution to the wealth of the country. It was badly invested. He died penniless in 1827.

*See Cromford, page 315, and Paradise Mill, page 369

HILL TOP

NEAR SAWREY, CUMBRIA

Home of Samuel Whiskers and Tom Kitten

You might think that the creator of Peter Rabbit, Mrs Tiggy-winkle and Jeremy Fisher was a countrywoman: her precisely observed characters seem so much at home in their rural settings. Instead, Beatrix Potter was born in west London in 1866, occasionally holidaying with her parents in the Lake District. The first six of her little books – *The Tale of Peter Rabbit, The Tale of Squirrel Nutkin, The Tailor of Gloucester, The Tale of Benjamin Bunny, The Tale of Two Bad Mice* and *The Tale of Mrs Tiggy-winkle* – were so successful that by 1905 she was able to buy into the world she had created. She acquired an old-fashioned farm on the west side of Windermere called Hill Top.

Miss Potter lived at Hill Top alone, her fiancé having died of anaemia shortly before she moved in. With no one else she had to consult, she was able to arrange the house just as she liked it, buying 17th- and 18th-century oak dressers and beds at local sales, before such things were generally the norm. The furniture features in many of the later stories, notably *The Roly Poly Pudding* (republished as *The Tale of Samuel Whiskers*), while the cottage garden appears in *The Tale of Tom Kitten*. When she eventually married, in her forties, she did not want to rearrange the house. Instead, she and her husband lived elsewhere in the village.

By now, Miss Potter – or Mrs Heelis, as she had become – was a landowner. As well as Hill Top, she owned another local farm, and after the First World War she bought Troutbeck Park Farm, north of Windermere. As a friend of Canon Rawnsley, one of the instigators of the National Trust, she was motivated as much by a desire to perpetuate the beauty and tradition of the Lake District as investment – although she turned out to be a committed and efficient farmer. She bought the Monk Coniston estate of 4,000 acres especially to leave to the Trust, along with her beloved Hill Top.

HOGHTON TOWER

Knighting Sir Loin

James Bond reckoned, munching lamb cutlets and peas with M, that English food, eaten in season, was the best in the world. His remark reflected a long tradition of culinary chauvinism, given pictorial form by William Hogarth in his painting *O the Roast Beef of Old England*, now in Tate Britain. This implicitly contrasts the robust diet of the Englishman with the unhappy lot of ordinary folk in pre-Revolutionary France, represented by a famished soldier who looks on ravenously as a side of beef is carried to a monastery kitchen beneath the gaze of a greedy monk. Even the French themselves tacitly recognised the quantity of meat eaten in England, by calling the English *les rosbifs*. In this respect, if no other, Britain was blessed by the weather; plentiful rainfall produces an abundance of sweet grass, which in turn translates into exceptionally good beef. Britain's slow-maturing, traditional breeds such as Aberdeen Angus, Hereford and Dexter are recognised for their excellence.

With such ingredients, it was not thought necessary to do much more than serve food plain. The English believed that other countries developed elaborate sauces only to disguise their inferior meat, which included parts of the animal that would not have been recognised in polite society. Admittedly French chefs, such as Auguste Escoffier, could turn this style of cooking into an art form, but in the days of the Empire, the place where they achieved their greatest acclaim was not Paris, but London.

The James Bond view of English food was strangely at odds with the prevailing reality and soon passed out of fashion. After the Second World War, food rationing was only slowly lifted. Years of shortage made Elizabeth David's *A Book of Mediterranean Food*, published in 1950, seem like a dream of gastronomic indulgence. The British developed a sense of cultural inadequacy about cooking, which they have only with difficulty started to shake off.

Another James – King James I – would, however, have sympathised with his namesake Bond. On a progress through Lancashire, ruinously expensive for his hosts, he is supposed to have paused for a while after a morning spent knighting the local business community (like Lloyd George, he raised revenue through honours). Seeing a succulent joint of meat on the table before him, he knighted it Sir Loin. Hoghton Tower once disputed the setting of the episode with Astley Hall in Chorley, which also has a Sirloin Chair; however, all reference to it has now been purged from the Astley Hall guidebook. If this event never actually happened, it should have.

JODRELL BANK

NEAR MACCLESFIELD, CHESHIRE

The only telescope in the West that could track the first Russian sputnik

Vast, unearthly, gazing forever towards the edges of the universe, the Lovell telescope at Jodrell Bank is an unnerving manifestation of the space age to encounter amid the flat fields of Cheshire. The telescope came into being at the dawn of the Space Race between the Soviet Union and the United States: as the only telescope in the West capable of tracking the first Russian sputnik in 1957 it assumed an immediate importance, and the payments made by the American government for this service helped pay off the debt incurred by the construction costs. In the 1960s, scientists using the Lovell telescope discovered the very distant, small, extremely intense light sources known as quasars. Research into quasars continues at Jodrell Bank. Scientists also confirmed the existence of gravitational lenses – the curving of light and radio rays emitted from a quasar, caused by the gravitational pull of a galaxy standing between it and Earth – as predicted by Einstein. In 1969, the telescope was given a new reflecting dish; this was again replaced in 1999.

The telescope owes its existence to Bernard Lovell, a scientist at Manchester University. During the Second World War, he had worked with radar, and on returning to the university wanted to use it for astronomical research. He set up some surplus army radar equipment outside his laboratory, but found that nearby trams interfered with its reception. His search for a site outside Manchester led him to some land at Jodrell Bank that was owned by the university's botany department. Using radar, Lovell was able to make observations about the dust trails left by comets as they circle the sun. In 1947, a 218ft radio telescope was built, using wire mesh and scaffolding poles. It was the biggest radio telescope in the world, but structurally flimsy; the present telescope is not only more robust, but also can be steered to point in any direction that the scientists require.

CASTLE HILL, LANCASTER

LANCASHIRE

The age of mahogany

In 1722, Robert Gillow arrived in Lancaster to begin his apprenticeship as a joiner. Although the town was a long way from fashionable London, it happened in one respect to serve the interests of an ambitious young furniture-maker very well. Then a thriving port, Lancaster had an expanding trade with the West Indies. By the middle of the 18th century, it sat beside Liverpool and Bristol as one of the principal ports of Britain's west coast. One of the imports from Jamaica, Cuba and Honduras was mahogany, then a new material for furniture; it was particularly welcome since the supply of French walnut had dried up. Gillow at once saw mahogany's potential. Some of the furniture that he made from it went back to the West Indies, in return for sugar and rum.

Robert Gillow died in 1772, but the business run from the workshop at 1a Castle Hill was continued by his sons, Richard and Robert. Robert went to London to solicit orders, and Richard ran the workshop. While the Gillows lacked the high tone of Thomas Chippendale, they seem to have been far more prolific – an impression encouraged by their care in marking their pieces. With a slightly less high-flown clientele, they were also more regularly paid. They did as much as anyone to establish solid brown furniture, elegant in line and not given to decorative excess, as a staple of English middle-class taste. Like other industrialists of their age, they were able to increase output by dividing labour, with different specialists responsible for carving, wood-turning and cabinet-making.

The Gillow name stayed in currency for longer than that of any other British furniture-maker. By the end of the 19th century, they had become one of the earliest interior decorators, capable of supplying all the furnishings for a home. Then, having overstretched themselves, Gillows was effectively absorbed by a Liverpool company to become Waring & Gillow. As such it survived until 1980, two and a half centuries after Robert Gillow established his workshop – although the last Gillow family member involved in the business, Richard's grandson, also Richard, retired in 1830.

CUNARD BUILDING LIVERPOOL
The ticket to a better life

The Pier Head at Liverpool is one of the most evocative architectural ensembles in the country. Flanked by the stylistically hysterical Royal Liver Building and the Edwardianly bombastic Liverpool Docks and Harbour Board Headquarters, the Cunard Building, opened during the First World War, stands like a well-tailored plutocrat, waving an opulent cigar. Nothing could better display the confidence and luxury appropriate to the headquarters of a great shipping company, in the heyday of the transatlantic liner.

The Cunard Steamship Company, which had begun its passenger service to the United States in 1840, did not just cater to the prosperous; like the other shipping lines (White Star, Harrison, Blue Funnel), it also served the needs of an altogether different class of traveller, the emigrant. By 1900, their conditions were spartan but not intolerable; in earlier periods, the overcrowding fostered disease on what were called 'fever ships'; on one occasion, 158 emigrants died during a single crossing to Quebec.

It has been estimated that in the century following 1830, 9 million emigrants passed through Liverpool. They did not all come from Britain. Large numbers arrived from Ireland, Scandinavia, Holland, Germany, Poland and Russia, their presence in the city, as they waited for their passage, feeding an industry of squalid lodging houses. Most were heading for the United States, Canada and Australia; in the case of the latter, the journey could last up to four months. Before they could enter their promised lands, they faced a limbo of seasickness and cramped conditions. Far above them on board, in the fashionably appointed saloons that were decorated to look as little like a ship as possible, first-class passengers were probably no more aware of their existence than they would have been of the small army of coal-blackened stokers who fed the boilers. In this, at least, life afloat differed little from life on shore.

LIVERPOOL DOCKS

The Battle of the Atlantic

On 3 September 1939 the passenger liner *Athenia*, owned by the Donaldson Atlantic line, was torpedoed without warning as it sailed between Liverpool and Montreal. It was only eight hours after the declaration of war against Germany, and the Battle of the Atlantic had begun.

Liverpool faces North America; this was why it prospered in the 18th century, as trade with America and the West Indies developed. By 1900, Liverpool is said to have owned a tenth of all the world's shipping by tonnage. This made its role in keeping open supply lines with North America critical to Britain's survival during the Second World War. The city itself became a target for the Luftwaffe, which sought to sink ships in the harbour and destroy the railway system. In what came to be known as 'May Week' 1941, Liverpool was blitzed on seven consecutive nights: the *Malakand*, a steamer of the Brocklebank line, blew up with a thousand tons of ammunition on board, hurling metal plates into the air, some of which landed two and a half miles away.

The convoys of ships which sailed to and from Liverpool were subject to another form of assault: that presented by the German U-boat wolf packs that roamed the Atlantic. To Winston Churchill, they represented the most worrying menace of the war. In 1939, the number of U-boats that could operate in the Atlantic at one time was no more than ten, but that number increased after the fall of France in June 1940, when they started using ports such as La Rochelle. In the autumn of that year, the United States loaned the Royal Navy fifty old but serviceable destroyers, which helped even the odds. The balance tipped in Britain's favour when the U-110 was hit, killing its commander. In their hurry to evacuate the vessel, the sailors failed to destroy their Enigma encoding machine, which was removed by a British boarding party; this enabled Britain to predict where the U-boat packs would lurk in the future (see page 207). The commander who died was the same man who had been responsible for sinking the *Athenia*.

MENDIPS
MENLOVE AVENUE, LIVERPOOL

Origins of the 20th century's most famous song-writing partnership

In the history of popular music, few places are more revered than Mendips, a semi-detached house on Menlove Avenue, Liverpool. It was here, behind the 1930s stained glass of the front porch, that John Lennon learnt to play what his aunt Mimi, who brought him up, called 'his silly guitar'. She feared that his passion for Elvis, Little Richard and girls would get in the way of his studies. And she was right: he failed all his O-levels.

Lennon was too undisciplined to take formal music lessons. But his mother (tragically killed in a road accident when he was seventeen) could play the banjo and taught him some chords, and he formed a skiffle group called the Quarry Men, named after the Quarry Bank High School that he attended. In July 1957, the Quarry Men were performing at a church fête at Woolton, when Lennon was introduced to Paul McCartney who, although two years his junior, had greater technique. Lennon did not like competition, but the challenge spurred him on. In 1960, the group, which McCartney had joined, became known as The Beatles.

Occasionally John and Paul were allowed to play music in the front room at Mendips, but were usually stopped before long for fear of disturbing the veterinary students who lodged in the house. The early songs were, in fact, written at Paul's house, 20 Forthlin Road in Allerton – a few minutes' bicycle ride away if, like John, you take the short cut across the golf course. This was a terraced house built as part of a council estate from 1949–51 – socially a rung or two down from Menlove Avenue. Paul's mother had died in 1956, leaving his father to bring up Paul and his brother Mike. It was a rather cramped house, not always spotlessly dusted, but crucially it was empty during the day, allowing the duo freedom to compose. Five years after the Beatles' first hit ('Love Me Do', 1962*), Lennon and McCartney paid tribute to the geography of their childhood with songs entitled 'Strawberry Fields' (named after a big Victorian house into whose grounds they sometimes broke) and 'Penny Lane'; the original street signs were promptly stolen.

*See Abbey Road Studios, page 109

PARADISE MILL

MACCLESFIELD, CHESHIRE

Last of Britain's silk industry

Silk is luxury. The development of Britain's silk industry in the 18th century reflected the rising number of people who could afford fashionable flowered waistcoats and enormous hooped dresses. This was the era evoked by Beatrix Potter in *The Tailor of Gloucester*, when stuffs had 'strange names' like lutestring and paduasoy. Silk weaving declined after 1850, confirming the impression that *objets de luxe* were more likely to be found in Paris than London. Leather goods came to seem characteristically British, not silk.

On the Continent, silk weaving was a speciality of French and Dutch Protestants, some of whom came to England following religious persecution in the late 16th century. By 1629, a company of silk 'throwsters' had been incorporated. The industry received a further boost from the French Huguenots who arrived after Louis XIV in 1685 revoked the Edict of Nantes, which had offered Protestants protection in designated towns. It was only in 1743 that a button merchant called Charles Roe established the first silk factory in Macclesfield: one of the uses of silk was as a cover for buttons. The industry thrived, not only in Macclesfield but the nearby towns of Manchester, Stockport, Congleton, Leek, Derby and Nottingham.

Since the British climate is too cold for silkworms, raw silk had to be imported from Italy, China, Japan and elsewhere. The cocoon that the silkworm makes for itself is formed from a single thread, which may be 300 yards long. This thread must be unravelled, wound, twisted, doubled and twisted again – the whole of the process being known as 'throwing'. Reductions in the duties charged on raw silk encouraged the industry in the north-west. Steam engines were brought in to power new looms. They not only reduced the hand-loom weavers to poverty but flooded the market with cheap silk, threatening their own viability*.

Leaders of the industry, however, did well. Silk continued to remain at the mercy of changes in duty, and a treaty of 1860 with France, which removed import duties from French silks coming into Britain while allowing France to charge thirty per cent on British silk going into France, proved disastrous. In Spitalfields in East London and in Norwich, the silk industry had already collapsed; now it contracted in the north-west, leaving only Macclesfield to struggle on by itself. An indication of the reduced circumstances of the trade can be gathered from the number of silk winders, turners, weavers, piecers and fancy trimmers listed as inmates of the Macclesfield Workhouse in the 1881 census. Crêpes, bandanas, handkerchiefs and ties were still being made in Macclesfield in the 1930s, but the industry was on its last legs. It now only continues on a very small scale; on all sides, however, memories survive in buildings such as the Paradise Mill.

*See Cromford, page 315, and Hall i' th' Wood, page 362

ST PETER'S FIELDS
Site of the Peterloo Massacre

Estimates of the size of the crowd that gathered on St Peter's Fields, Manchester, on 16 August 1819 vary. The Manchester *Observer* put it at 153,000, although the figure of 60,000 was more generally accepted. Even at the lower figure, it was probably the largest meeting ever to have assembled in Britain. The Lancashire and Cheshire magistrates, looking out of the windows of the Star Inn, could see waving banners carrying such slogans as 'Let us DIE like men and not be SOLD like slaves'. Since the end of the Napoleonic Wars in 1815, wages had gone down and prices had gone up. Both spinners and weavers were driven to strike. They associated their grievances with a corrupt political culture, in which a town the size of Manchester could have no MP, no elected local government and working people had no vote. Some of the men who were present at St Peter's Fields had fought at Waterloo, and thought they deserved better.

In the face of such an enormous gathering, the magistrates became nervous. They instructed the Manchester Yeomanry Cavalry to arrest the Radical speakers who had begun addressing the crowd. The Yeomanry was an unfortunate choice. They had been drinking since their arrival early that morning. Their way to the hustings was blocked by a densely packed crowd so they decided to hack their way through it. Women and even special constables were sabred. People were trampled as the crowd recoiled. Once a path had been cleared, the Yeomanry started to break up the hustings. Since their actions were obscured by a cloud of dust, the magistrates, from their distant vantage point, thought they had been beset by the mob. 'Good God, Sir, don't you see they are attacking the Yeomanry,' said magistrate Hulton to the commanding officer that day, Lieutenant-Colonel Guy L'Estrange. 'Disperse them.' L'Estrange ordered the 15th Hussars to charge the assembly.

A quarter of an hour later the Fields were empty of everyone except groups of cavalry, the wounded and nineteen dead bodies. Both the magistrates and the government were roundly condemned. Although Radicalism declined after 1819, the Peterloo Massacre became a rallying cry for reform.

The area around St Peter's Square in the modern centre of the city is where St Peter's Fields lay.

FREE TRADE HALL
Monument to Manchester liberalism

'If ever a town endowed its main contribution to political thought with a fine building, Manchester has done so here,' wrote the Professor of Architecture, C. H. Reilly. He was referring to the Free Trade Hall, built from 1853–6.

Free trade had been the rallying cry of the Anti-Corn Law League, founded to campaign for cheaper food. Its target was the infamous Corn Law, introduced in 1815. This law artificially supported the price of grain, in order to perpetuate the golden age that British farmers had known during the Napoleonic Wars when they experienced no competition from imports. Manchester was at the centre of the campaign against the legislation. The owners of the Lancashire mills, whose priority was feeding factory workers rather than protecting agriculture, were the prime agitators. The political battle raged until the Conservative prime minister Sir Robert Peel persuaded Parliament to repeal the Corn Laws in 1846, splitting his supposedly protectionist party as he did so. It was a resounding triumph for the manufacturing interest and a blow to the landed aristocracy.

A wooden Free Trade Hall had been erected in Manchester in 1840. Two years later this was replaced by a brick structure, its hall being bigger than any other in the country except Westminster Hall (see page 195). By the 1850s, even this no longer seemed adequate, and a public subscription, supposedly non-partisan, was launched to provide a hall appropriate for the town's literary, religious and musical gatherings. The result was a Renaissance palazzo rising up above an arcade, with a *piano nobile* of coupled pilasters and arches and a richly swagged cornice, the masterpiece of the architect Edward Walters. With sheaves of corn to one side and ships' rigging behind her, the figure of Free Trade epitomised the Manchester liberal point of view.

This handsome building, having been burnt out after being bombed in the Second World War, has now been converted to a hotel: whatever would the proponents of the free market who paid for its original construction have made of that?

GRANADA STUDIOS   *WATER STREET, MANCHESTER*
The longest-running soap opera ever

Seven o'clock in the evening of 9 December 1960 was, in all senses, an epic moment for British television. It was then that the first episode of what has become the world's longest-running television soap opera was broadcast. *Coronation Street*, whose first writer was the 23-year-old Tony Warren, capitalised on the vogue for kitchen-sink dramas set in northern towns that had emerged towards the end of the 1950s, launched by John Osborne's *Look Back in Anger*. For television, it was nevertheless a bold move to create a series so far removed from the Reithian concept of high culture, purveyed through clipped, southern voices, which still permeated the BBC (see page 122).

The lugubrious signature tune, introducing a world of cobbled streets, railway viaducts and factory chimneys, grated on many television critics, including that of the *Daily Mirror*, whose point of view perhaps reflected the media's already London-centric bias. However, characters such as the indomitable Ena Sharples and vampish Elsie Tanner became so familiar that viewers felt they actually knew them. In time, real-life politicians took to dropping into the Rover's Return, the pub where much of the action is set, as a sure means of establishing their image on the retina of the gullible voting public.

The term soap opera derives from 1930s America, where detergent manufacturers were among the first commercial sponsors of radio drama. In Britain, Radio 4 still broadcasts *The Archers* – a soap of even greater antiquity than 'Corrie', the first episode being aired in 1951. Both *The Archers* and *Coronation Street* have managed to retain their popularity long after the close-knit communities that inspired them disappeared. Visitors to Salford, where *Coronation Street* is notionally set, will no longer find a townscape of terraced houses, in which everyone knows their neighbours and spends time gossiping with them. Inhabitants of the fractured urbanism that has replaced the old back-to-backs do not have garden walls to chat over; besides, they are probably indoors, watching the likes of *Coronation Street*.

LION SALT WORKS
The very salt of the earth

MARSTON, CHESHIRE

Cheshire was an inland sea 250 million years ago. Water that was lost from evaporation was constantly replenished from the outlying ocean, which meant that the water became saltier and saltier. Eventually the salt crystallised and fell to the bottom. Over thousands of years, deep beds of rock salt were formed. From the late 17th century, these salt deposits were being mined, in much the same manner as coal. Salt is not only an essential component of the human diet; it has many industrial applications, being used in glass making, the glazing of pottery and the tanning of leather. These days, ever increasing amounts are sprayed from gritter lorries onto winter roads, and this is the destination for most of the mountains of grubby white salt that are still seen outside the modern works from where salt is extracted.

Instead of mining it, the Lion Salt Works at Marston, outside Northwich, used a different and much older technique of salt extraction. This method evaporates vast pans containing brine until only salt is left. Brine bubbles naturally to the surface in springs whose water has run through underground deposits of salt. The Romans are known to have extracted salt from Cheshire springs soon after their arrival here in the 1st century AD. Brine can also be created by pumping water through the underground salt and channelling it to the pans to evaporate. This is what happened at the late 19th-century Lion Salt Works, named after the nearby Red Lion Inn. The salt that was panned here was loaded onto canal barges or railway trucks and shipped to places as far away as the United States, South America and Africa.

The works did not create an attractive or safe working environment: smoke billowed from the furnaces that kept the brine at boiling point, and the job of de-scaling the wooden pans was carried out by 'wallers' walking through the steaming brine, standing with each leg in a half barrel. Victorian campaigners were equally concerned about the morality of bare-chested men working next to women in petticoats.

Another hazard caused by the salt industry was subsidence. This would sometimes occur naturally, as underground streams wore away at beds of salt; industrial salt extraction caused it to happen more frequently and to some-times spectacular effect, as the façades of houses lurched forwards at crazy angles and long, thin lakes known as flashes opened up in the pastoral Cheshire landscape. As a result, there are few old buildings in Northwich, but many timber-framed ones of Victorian date: the latter were easier to jack up than earlier brick structures that they often replaced.

ROYAL OLDHAM HOSPITAL *OLDHAM, LANCASHIRE*
World's first 'in vitro' baby

To Mr and Mrs John Brown, a girl, Louise, five pounds twelve ounces. She was delivered by Caesarean section at the then District General Hospital at Oldham (now the Royal Oldham Hospital) on 25 July 1978, the first 'test-tube baby' in the world.

In comparison with later attempts to manipulate nature, Louise Brown's conception, using an egg fertilised outside the womb, was not radical. The popular term test-tube baby (rather than the correct term 'in vitro fertilisa-tion') is inaccurate: test tubes are not involved, since the process happens on a glass dish (hence the 'in vitro'), and the sperm happily sets about penetrating the egg, which then divides, in a perfectly straightforward manner. The difficult part comes when the fertilised egg is placed into the womb. Before that happy night in 1978, the medical pioneers, Cambridge research physiologist Robert Edwards and consultant gynaecologist Patrick Steptoe, had spent eight long years trying to overcome the problems that this presented.

Some Church figures regarded the successful birth with deep misgivings. To Mr Brown, anxiously waiting at the hospital, the news of little Louise's arrival caused a paroxysm of joy, in which he banged his fist against the wall, wept copiously and kissed everyone in sight. Since then, more than a million couples have had their hopes realised through IVF. In 1978, the medical achievement was almost equalled by that of the *Daily Mail* in protecting their 'buy-up' of the Browns' story, rumoured to be the largest example of cheque-book journalism that Fleet Street had ever seen.

On Louise's twenty-fifth birthday it was reported that she was working as a postwoman in Bristol and was planning to marry.

PORT SUNLIGHT
MERSEYSIDE

Lord Leverhulme's model village for soap workers

Victorian industrialism had a conscience. Often it was Nonconformist in religion, and posed itself the question of how industrial methods of produc-tion could co-exist with a decent standard of life for the workforce. In 1851, the mill owner Titus Salt had moved his operation from Bradford to the country-side, building a model factory and village at Saltaire, to which he gave a Congregational church, Sunday school, club, infirmary, park and other amenities. In the same spirit, the Quaker chocolate-making Cadbury brothers took their business from Birmingham to rural Bournville, with recreation ground, swimming pool, dining rooms and semi-detached houses; Bournville flourished, and the Cadburys bought surrounding farmland to protect it from encroachment by Birmingham. So when in 1890 William Hesketh Lever, the future Lord Leverhulme, created a new soap works and model village beside the Mersey, Port Sunlight, he may not have been the first to believe that happy workers were productive workers, but he added a new ingredient to the mix, in the form of art.

Lever, the son of a grocer, had left school at sixteen to join his father's business. If he had been able to pursue his studies, he would have liked to become an architect. Instead, he showed a genius for organisation, coupled with dynamic business methods, which eagerly embraced the potential of advertising – then a novelty – to expand demand. His Sunlight soap would, it was claimed, wash clothes by itself, and keep housewives looking young at the same time. Sir John Millais was not unduly put out when his painting *Bubbles* was used to promote Pears soap, but W. P. Frith caused a controversy by objecting to his Royal Academy painting *The New Frock*, in which a girl holds up a white pinafore, appearing under the title 'So Clean' in another Lever advertisement.

By the beginning of the 20th century, Lever's business was flourishing and provided the means to allow him to satisfy his artistic enthusiasms by becoming a compulsive architectural patron. Having bought a pair of Derby figures as a young man, his collection of porcelain, tapestries, Pre-Raphaelite paintings and English and French furniture filled an ever-expanding country house, Thornton Manor in the Wirral. In March 1914, King George V laid the foundation stone of the Lady Lever Art Gallery, where much of it was put on public display for the benefit of his workers.

TOAD LANE, ROCHDALE   LANCASHIRE
Birthplace of the Co-operative Movement

In 1844, a group of twenty-eight men, mostly weavers, teamed together to open a shop at 31 Toad Lane in Rochdale, each contributing a pound towards the capital needed to stock it. This was the first successful co-operative society in the world, and the written principles that they established – including democratic control and the need for education – were to underpin what became a global movement.

Like other mill towns, Rochdale had been forged on the anvil of the Industrial Revolution. Until the late 18th century, it had been a remote market town, but then in 1791 the first factory chimney appeared. In the next fifty years, the population more than quadrupled. Steam engines put the old hand-loom weavers out of work. There were bread riots, and the first meeting for political reform held in England took place outside Rochdale on Cronkeyshaw Common. Conditions worsened in the 'Hungry Forties'. Workers were at the mercy of mill owners, who insisted that they spent part of their modest wages in company shops, where produce was often adulterated. A particularly bad year for industry in Rochdale was 1844, and a reduction of wages by mill owners was followed by a bitter strike.

Co-operative ideas were in the air, thanks to the example of Robert Owen (see page 476) and the influence of Chartism (see page 427). The Rochdale Society of Equitable Pioneers, which opened the shop at 31 Toad Lane, was by no means the first such association: hundreds of co-operative societies had been formed in the previous two decades but, unlike them, it flourished. Idealism was backed by common sense. The collapse of the Rochdale Savings Bank in 1849 brought a flood of new members. In the 1850s, the Pioneers made the leap from merely retailing food to manufacturing it when they acquired a corn mill. The success of this enterprise was the undoing of some of the idealism that had been their first inspiration; as the business grew, they raised finance from shareholders who sometimes had little interest in Co-operative principles. The Pioneers' aim of establishing a co-operative community with its own schools and government receded. Nevertheless, their example in providing cheap, unadulterated goods was followed by dozens of other co-operative societies around Britain.

After 1900, improved living standards overtook the co-operative ideal, but

Rochdale is still said to lend its name to a co-operatively made wine in France, an electricity co-operative in the United States and a fleet of taxis in Mexico.

SALFORD MUSEUM
LANCASHIRE

First free public library in Britain

In 1849, Britain's first unconditionally free public library opened at Salford near Manchester. It occupied Lark Hill, a mansion house originally built in the 1790s by James Ackers, 'father of the Manchester silk trade'.

Provision of local public libraries had been a concern of enlightened Victorians for some time*. They saw them as a means for the industrial poor to better their position, and as an alternative to the evils of the pub. The first Parliamentary attempt to introduce public libraries came in 1835 with the Public Institutions Bill, introduced by the temperance campaigner and Sheffield MP James Buckingham. This linked libraries to other forms of urban improvement, such as open spaces. As the Salford MP Joseph Botherton told the House of Commons, 'anything that tends to promote the comfort and improve the morals of the lower classes deserves the most favourable consideration'. The Bill failed, and for the time being readers who could not afford the charges made by commercial circulating libraries had to rely on Chartist reading rooms and mechanics' institutes which offered adult education to artisans and cheap access to books. The first Public Libraries (England) Act was passed the year after the Salford library opened, in 1850.

At Salford, the Royal Museum and Public Library, as it was then called, was built by public subscription, which also financed the purchase of two parks in Manchester. Only a couple of years after it was opened, a new wing was built. This was followed by further enlargements until, in the 1930s, the decayed Lark Hill itself was demolished and replaced by a new structure. There is still a local history library on the site.

*See Moodie Street, Dunfermline, page 451

BATTLE OF SOLWAY MOSS
CUMBRIA

Destruction of James V's army precedes his death

The Scottish king, James V, was Henry VIII of England's nephew. Despite the relationship, he was friendlier towards France than England. In 1542, Henry was feeling less than usually avuncular following an escalation of the tit-for-tat raiding that was an established feature of life on the Scottish borders. When some English noblemen, on their way back from burning Scottish farms around Jedburgh, were captured, Henry ordered the 3rd Duke of Norfolk to raise an army. James's efforts to negotiate a peaceful conclusion to their differences foundered on an inability to agree on a place to meet Henry.

The army that Norfolk assembled was not able to do much beyond burning some villages, since it quickly ran out of the beer without which the men would not operate. On 24 November, a much larger Scottish force – some 18,000 men – crossed the border near Gretna. They were led by King James's favourite, Oliver Sinclair, who was detested by the other nobles. With the leadership in disarray, they were attacked in the bogs known as Solway Moss near Longtown. Although the English force was negligible – perhaps as few as 800 reivers (as the Border raiders were known) – the Scots were hemmed in by the bogs and, anyway, in no mood to fight. They ran away, abandoning their arms. The shame, compounded with the birth of a daughter rather than a son, is supposed to have sapped James's will to live (see page 461).

Twenty Scots noblemen were imprisoned in the Tower of London, but released when it was secretly agreed that James's baby girl, Mary – now Queen of Scots – would marry Henry's son Edward. The tug of France was too strong, however, and she eventually married the son of the French King (see page 455).

TYNWALD HILL ST JOHN'S, ISLE OF MAN
Survival of Viking parliaments

By the time Magnus Barefoot, King of Norway, landed on the Isle of Man in 1068, the island had been settled by Vikings for two and a half centuries or more. They met in an open-air Parliament called the Tynwald, which has operated continuously for at least a millennium, perhaps considerably more. It may be the oldest parliament in the world. Certainly it is the most ancient in Britain, far older than Westminster.

Every 5 July, the Manx National Day, the Tynwald, which normally sits in Douglas, perpetuates the tradition of meeting in the open air. They do this on Tynwald Hill, an ancient mound made up of different terraces, which stands next to the chapel of St John the Baptist at St John's. The original meeting place may have been a field in the middle of the island. On the top tier of the artificial mound stands the Queen, or her representative the Lieutenant-Governor, acting as President of the Tynwald; sharing it are the Bishop of Sodor and Mann, the Surgeon to the Household, the Sword Bearer and the members of the legislative council. The next tier is occupied by Members of the House of Keys (the Manx equivalent of MPs). On the third tier are other dignitaries, such as the chief registrar and the chief constable. Two 'Deemsters' proclaim the island's new laws in Manx Gaelic and English.

One of the Viking features of the Tynwald is the right of individuals to proclaim their grievances and seek redress. It has not always been without risk. At the Tynwald of 1237, a pitched battle broke out between Lauchlan, the island's custodian, and some local petitioners, three of whom were killed. Today, Tynwald Days may be quieter but remain an unbroken link with the Viking past.

WHITEHAVEN CUMBRIA
The American War of Independence comes to England

None of the battles in America's war of independence – or revolution, as the British preferred to call it – took place on British soil. Nevertheless, an incident in April 1778 gave George III's subjects at home a scare. The captain of the American warship *Ranger*, John Paul Jones, broke off from a cruise spent capturing smaller prizes in the Irish Sea to raid the town of Whitehaven. At that time, Whitehaven was still an important coal port, with a prosperous Atlantic trade. Jones, the son of a Scottish gardener and born at Kirkbean on the north coast of the Solway Firth, knew Whitehaven well: he had served his apprenticeship on the *Friendship of Whitehaven*. Later, after an adventurous career around the West Indies, he acquired a commission in the infant American navy that gave him carte blanche as a privateer. In the Whitehaven raid, his object was to seize a prominent individual who could be traded for American sympathisers (such as captured seamen) in prison. Since they could not find anyone worth kidnapping, they burnt a few colliers in the harbour instead, and returned to their ship.

The raid had no practical consequence, but property owners were to have further palpitations when they learnt that Jones's men had overpowered the Earl of Selkirk's house on St Mary's Isle, on the north side of the Solway Firth, with the Countess inside it. They stole the silver, down to the teapot that still contained the warm tea leaves from the Countess's breakfast. (The Countess behaved with such dignity that Jones himself bought the silver back and presented it to her after the war.)

In 1779 Jones became a hero – or villain – of international repute when his ships, the *Bonhomme Richard* and *Pallas*, took on two British warships off Flamborough Head: he succeeded in capturing both of them, although his own, the *Bonhomme Richard*, sank. To the British, he was nothing but a pirate; in the United States he is revered as the father of the American navy. In 1905 his body was dug up from its grave in Paris and re-interred in a marble sarcophagus in the Naval Academy in Annapolis, Maryland.

North-East England

A FURIOUS AND OFTEN dramatic story is told by the landmarks of the North-East. In 866 York fell to the Vikings under Ivar the Boneless; just over 1,100 years later, remains of the invaders' houses were excavated in the city. The Vikings may have settled peaceably in the end, but the monks on the island of Lindisfarne were not prepared to take any chances; they had been raided far too often already. They left the island in 875, taking their most valuable possessions with them – the body of their beloved St Cuthbert and the Lindisfarne Gospels. The saint's remains eventually came to rest at Durham, where the magnificent cathedral was later built.

At Stamford Bridge, King Harold took Saxon revenge on the Norsemen, killing William the Conqueror's ally, Harald Hardrada, before hurrying his men south towards Hastings. It was at Norham that Edward I cunningly settled the question of the Scottish succession in such a way that he became overlord to the new king of Scotland. The result was many years of bitter campaigning as Edward and his successors asserted their presumed rights. Berwick-upon-Tweed is the ultimate border town, changing hands between Scotland and England more than a dozen times during the Middle Ages.

The deposed Richard II met his end in Pontefract Castle. From the Percy stronghold of Alnwick, Richard's enemy, Harry Hotspur, blazed across the medieval sky like a meteor. During the Wars of the Roses, the bloodiest battle ever fought on British soil took place at Towton in Yorkshire, while in 1513 King James IV of Scotland, along with the flower of the Scottish nobility, died in the slaughter of Flodden Field.

All this bloodshed is apt to overshadow the North-East's more peaceable character. It is the birthplace of Captain Cook, and the three remarkable and short-lived Brontë sisters. At St Paul's monastery in Jarrow, on the then edge of the known world, the 7th-century monk Bede edited the Bible, established the concept of recording time from the date of Christ's birth, as is universally used today, and wrote a five-volume history without which our knowledge of early British history would be a virtual blank.

North-East England

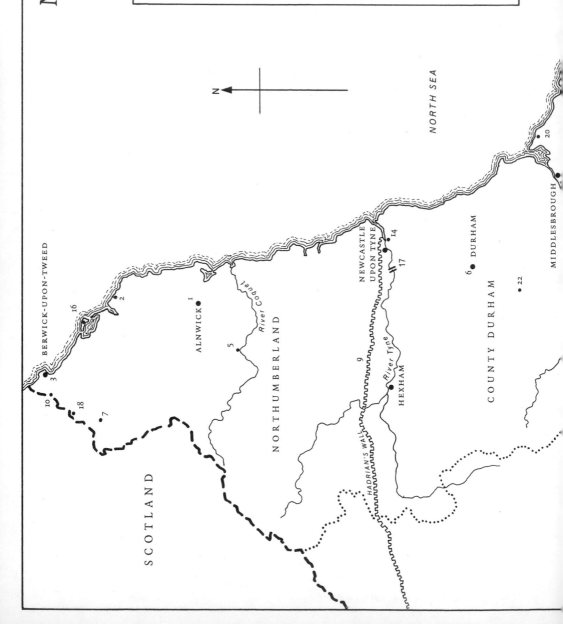

N

NORTH SEA

SCOTLAND

BERWICK-UPON-TWEED

NORTHUMBERLAND

ALNWICK

River Coquet

River Tyne

HADRIAN'S WALL

HEXHAM

NEWCASTLE UPON TYNE

DURHAM

COUNTY DURHAM

MIDDLESBROUGH

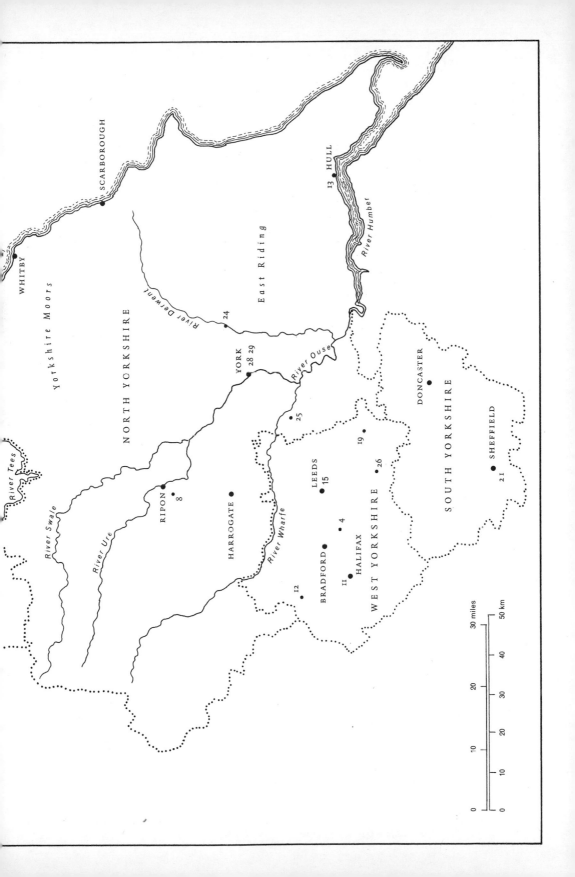

WHITBY

Yorkshire Moors

SCARBOROUGH

NORTH YORKSHIRE

River Tees

River Swale

River Ure

River Derwent

River Ouse

River Wharfe

River Humber

HULL · 13

East Riding

YORK · 28 29

24 ·

RIPON ●
8 ·

HARROGATE ●

· 25

19 ·

LEEDS ●
15 ·

DONCASTER ●

· 26

4 ·

BRADFORD ●
11 ·
HALIFAX ●

SHEFFIELD ●
21 ·

12 ·

WEST YORKSHIRE

SOUTH YORKSHIRE

0   10   20   30 miles

0   10   20   30   40   50 km

ALNWICK CASTLE
Border fortress that bred Hotspur

Harry Hotspur blazed across the north-east of England in the late 14th century, glamorising (if only in retrospect) the interminable territorial disputes that characterised Border life for centuries. Hotspur, or Sir Henry Percy as he should be more formally known, was born at Alnwick Castle in 1364. Alnwick had been the home of his family since 1309, and it had by now assumed more or less the appearance it has today, a massive and impregnable fortress poised on a bluff over the river Aln, surrounded by a curtain wall studded with strong towers and gatehouses. From Alnwick, the Percys ran what was virtually a private kingdom, issuing forth with armies of 10,000 men to fight, if needs be, the King of Scotland himself. It was on one such raid on Berwick* in 1378 that Hotspur, a lad of only fourteen, acquired his nickname from the eagerness with which he rode into battle.

Ten years later, the Scots, led by the Earl Douglas, took on the English once more at the Battle of Otterburn – celebrated in Border ballads as the Battle of Chevy Chase. After a fight outside Newcastle, the raiders had retreated to Otterburn, with Hotspur, his brother Ralph and a force of 8,000 infantry and 600 knights at their heels. Hotspur, now in his twenties, insisted on a night attack. His men were exhausted by their 32-mile march, and the moonlit battle was a disaster, mitigated only by the death of Douglas; Hotspur was held capture for ransom. Four years later he got his own back, defeating the new Earl Douglas and his massive army on Humbleton Hill to the west of the town of Wooler. By now, Hotspur had been given Warkworth Castle – one of the most elegant of 14th-century fortifications – to live in. It is there that Shakespeare's *Henry IV, Part II* opens with news of the battle.

In 1399, the Percys precipitated the fall of Richard II: having refused to appear before the King to answer a charge of treason, they and other nobles rebelled, as a result of which he was deposed and Henry IV took the throne†. They fell out with Henry over ransoms and other money they had hoped to receive. This led to the Rising of the Percys in 1403, when they joined forces with the Welsh prince Owain Glyndwr (see page 422). Hotspur was killed, brave and tempestuous to the last, at the Battle of Shrewsbury in 1403‡. His father surrendered at York, but although he was pardoned, he never gave up the cause of rebellion: in a desperate last throw, he led a band of retainers from Scotland, where he had been forced to take refuge, and was killed at the Battle of Bramham Moor in 1408.

The Percy family recovered from this defeat and by the 19th century, when the great rooms at Alnwick were decorated in a sumptuous Italian Renaissance style, they owned land all over the country. Among their seats was North-umberland Park, on the rough grass of Tottenham Marshes in North London.

Hotspur was chosen first as the name of the local cricket club in the area and then – in August 1882 – as the name of Hotspur Football Club. This later became Tottenham Hotspur FC.

*See Berwick-upon-Tweed, below. †See Pontefract Castle, page 397. ‡See Battle of Shrewsbury, page 341

BAMBURGH CASTLE NORTHUMBERLAND
First castle to fall to artillery

For more than three and a half centuries after it was begun by the Normans, Bamburgh Castle, opposite the Farne Islands on the Northumbrian coast, remained impregnable. In June 1464, however, the Earl of Warwick, on behalf of Edward IV, arrived to besiege it as one of the last bastions of Lancastrian resistance in the North. Inside was Sir Ralph Grey, a veteran of the confused border warfare that accompanied the Wars of the Roses. He had survived other sieges, and may have thought that Bamburgh would resist this one. Until now, digging under walls to make them collapse was about the only quick way to reduce a castle, but this was impossible at Bamburgh because of the basalt outcrop on which it stood. The enormous wooden siege engines known as trebuchets, capable of hurling 2-ton lumps of stone, were slow and laborious. Warwick, however, drew up weapons that would bring the invincibility of even the proudest castles to an end. These were cannons from the King's arsenal: two of his 'great guns', called London and Newcastle, and a brass cannon, called Dijon. As a contemporary chronicle described it, they 'so belaboured the place that stones of the walls flew into the sea'.

Bamburgh was the first British castle to fall to gunpowder. Sir Ralph was badly wounded, Dijon, it was claimed, having 'smote through' his chamber 'many times'. Sir John Neville, who took over command from the injured Grey, negotiated a settlement but it did neither man any good, both being executed in due course.

BERWICK-UPON-TWEED NORTHUMBERLAND
Border town which changed hands thirteen times

Berwick-upon-Tweed spent the Middle Ages in a kind of no-man's-land, being endlessly besieged by either the English or the Scots. In the three centuries until 1482, the town changed hands thirteen times. In 1296, Edward I, furious that the Scots refused to swear allegiance to him, stormed the wooden palisade that was the castle. Although the garrison, held by Sir William Douglas, surrendered, Edward's army showed no mercy and it is said that nearly 20,000 inhabitants of the town were slaughtered 'so that the mills could be turned round by the flow of their blood'.

The town became an essential base for English operations whenever an army was sent into Scotland. In 1306, the Countess of Buchan, who had crowned Robert the Bruce, was imprisoned in a cage shaped like a crown, suspended from the castle walls. Until James VI of Scotland became James I of England in 1603 – all the guns of the castle were fired, for the last time, as he passed through on his way to London – the inhabitants of Berwick must have found life confusing and precarious.

The architectural result of Berwick's many crises was the greatest system of fortifications in England. Until the Tudor period, Berwick had been protected by tall, thick walls. After a short period of Scottish rule, ending in 1482, the walls were lowered and backed by earth ramparts, providing a better defence against artillery. The appearance of French troops in Scotland in the 1520s, following the disaster of Flodden (see page 387), caused another bout of activity. Bulwarks were constructed, and in 1530 Henry VIII's Master of Ordnance began work on Lord's Mount – a massive, two-tier artillery fortification, protecting a weak point in the walls. In the 1540s, the 'rough wooing' intended to precipitate a marriage between the infant Mary Queen of Scots and the future Edward VI re-emphasised Berwick's importance.

The greatest period of building activity, however, followed Mary I's loss of Calais in 1558, when France egged Scotland on to attack England. It had become impractical to retain the full 2-mile length of the old walls; instead the town withdrew behind a massive series of ramparts, earthworks and bastions, their complex, clean-edged geometry being carefully calculated to provide a clear range of fire for guns shooting from any angle. They ruthlessly built across the citadel that had been constructed for Edward VI, just as the railway crossing the river Tweed on Robert Stephenson's Royal Border Bridge would later run through the middle of what had been Berwick Castle.

CLECKHEATON WEST YORKSHIRE
Attack and defeat of the Luddites

The Industrial Revolution replaced people with machines. Big textile mills, clattering with the noise of water-driven spinning frames and weaving looms, could produce cloth more cheaply than the old cottage system*. But the machines were resented. Opposition appeared to be led by a shadowy and perhaps fictional figure called General Ned Ludd: the name was apparently that of a simple farm labourer who destroyed some stocking frames in a fit of temper. In 1811, his 'followers', known as Luddites, started to attack factories in Nottingham, a centre for the manufacture of stockings. From Nottingham, the unrest spread to Derbyshire, Leicestershire, Lancashire and Yorkshire. The poet Lord Byron spoke up for the Luddites, but most of the ruling class ran scared. The Prime Minister Spencer Perceval introduced the death penalty for machine-breaking. After two decades of war with France, with the price of bread rising due to successive bad harvests, Britain seemed on the point of violence, if not revolution.

The worst Luddite event took place in Cleckheaton. Lying in the Spen valley, Cleckheaton was a centre of blanket-making whose villages were to mushroom into mill towns during the 19th century. In 1812, a new shearing frame had recently been introduced to the area, alarming the skilled cloth finishers, known as croppers, who feared that they would no longer have work. In April, 200 of them attacked Rawfolds Mill, but the owner, suspecting trouble, was ready for them and two of the croppers were shot dead by his guards. A week later, William Horsfall, a mill owner who had promised to be 'up to his saddle girths in Luddite blood', was killed. The authorities reacted by arresting a hundred people, seventeen of whom were convicted and hanged: three for murdering the mill owner, the rest for the attack on Rawfolds Mill.

It was not the end for the Luddites. With further increases in the price of bread, this time due to the Napoleonic Wars, they became increasingly desperate. There were more attacks, particularly around Manchester, followed by more hangings. But the cause was hopeless, and before long the movement died out.

*See Cromford, page 315; Hall i' th' Wood, page 362; Paradise Mill, page 369

CRAGSIDE

Where the King of Siam talked guns

In 1884, the architect Richard Norman Shaw made what would be his last addition to Cragside, the house that he had built incrementally for the inventor and then armaments manufacturer Sir William Armstrong (later 1st Baron Armstrong of Cragside). For some years, Armstrong had withdrawn from the running of his businesses on Tyneside. There he had entertained important guests in his house of Jesmond Dene, near his Newcastle manufacturing base. But since he had given Jesmond Dene to the City Corporation as a park, he now needed a suite of grand rooms in which hospitality could be shown to the visiting heads of state who came to buy arms; this is what Shaw built for him. The richly decorated drawing room was modelled on Haddon Hall in Derby-shire. Among the potentates whom he welcomed to Cragside were the King of Siam, the Shah of Persia and the Crown Prince of Afghanistan.

No doubt they did talk about the heavy artillery that Armstrong had developed, but they would also have been astonished by a house which embodied the passion for the innovative engineering that was the foundation of Armstrong's success as a businessman. A lift ran on the hydraulic power that he had perfected for cranes in the Newcastle docks, and there were other hydraulic devices, such as spits in the kitchen. A man of Armstrong's inventive frame of mind was naturally attracted by the new power source of electricity, and Cragside boasted the world's first hydro-electric power station, albeit on a domestic scale. The arc lights that this powered may have proved unsatisfactory, but not so the 'incandescent lamps' or light bulbs brought to perfection by Armstrong's friend, Joseph Swan. In 1880, what Swan called 'the first proper installation' of them was made at Cragside and improvements to the power supply continued until Armstrong's death in 1900.

DURHAM CATHEDRAL   CO. DURHAM
The cult of St Cuthbert

Eleven years after St Cuthbert's death in 687 on the island of Inner Farne, the monks of Lindisfarne wanted to elevate his bones by placing them in a reliquary. When they opened the coffin, they were astonished to find that the saint's body had not decomposed. They therefore made another coffin, using planks from an oak tree. Its lid and cover were incised with figures of the Evangelists, the Apostles and the Virgin and Child (the earliest depiction in English art). Now in the Treasury of Durham Cathedral, the coffin is a unique survival of Anglo-Saxon wood carving – its preservation, if not of quite the same order of miracles as those performed by the saint himself, showing the importance attached to his cult, which made Durham Cathedral the longest-lived pilgrimage site in Britain.

A native Anglo-Saxon, Cuthbert had trained as a monk at Melrose. When the abbot there transferred to Lindisfarne, Cuthbert went with him, retiring still further into the spiritual life by becoming a hermit on the little island of Inner Farne. He became prior of Lindisfarne in 664, nineteen years later being persuaded to forsake his solitude, temporarily, to become bishop, with its many pastoral duties.

By 875 the monks of Lindisfarne had had enough of the Vikings, who had not only been raiding the monastery on and off for the past eighty years but were now becoming a permanent presence. They therefore left, taking with them their most precious possessions, including Cuthbert's body and the Lindisfarne Gospels*. Their wanderings took them to Chester-le-Street and Ripon, before divine intervention through Cuthbert himself directed them to a wooded crag over the river Wear. Here, in 995, they built a monastery. It was completely effaced by the present stupendous cathedral, started in 1093, but the Normans continued to revere St Cuthbert. As soon as the apse was finished, his coffin was brought to a position behind the high altar. When the apse was replaced in the 13th century, a shrine reached by steps was created, with room enough for the many pilgrims who now flocked there to venerate the saint.

*See Lindisfarne, page 395

FLODDEN FIELD
Death of King James IV of Scotland

In 1513, King James IV of Scotland died at the Battle of Flodden Field. He had been one of the better Scottish kings, improving administration and developing trade. His marriage to the sister of Henry VIII should have inspired greater harmony between Scotland and England, and for a time it did, but in 1512 he revived the Auld Alliance with France. When Henry VIII invaded France the following year, King James was obliged to attack England.

The army that assembled outside Edinburgh that summer was the most impressive the Scots had yet mustered. It included twenty earls, fifteen barons, numerous bishops and archbishops, and countless knights. On 22 August, it crossed the Tweed at Coldstream, and set about burning the English castles. However, the Scots' appearance was not entirely unexpected. The force that Henry took to France had come largely from the southern half of England: this left the northern counties to be raised by the seventy-year-old Earl of Surrey. He called on his son, Thomas Howard, the Lord Admiral, to help him. They assembled an army of some 26,000 men, a few thousand smaller than that of the Scots. By 3 September, it had reached Alnwick.

After a fortnight on the English side of the Border, the Scottish army had only advanced four miles, and was now, on 9 September, encamped on the high ground of Flodden Hill. James declined Surrey's challenge to fight on Milfield Plain, so Surrey took his army on a long march round the flank, successfully getting men and artillery over the river Till, and appearing behind the Scots. The Scots were unprepared for this manoeuvre, which threatened to cut their supply lines back to Scotland. They hurried to occupy Branxton Hill to the north-west. Atrocious weather helped the English deception: because of the low visibility, their vanguard, under the Lord Admiral, almost ran into the whole Scottish army, now drawn up facing northwards. Fortunately for them, the Scots lost the moment to attack.

The English marched over a ridge opposite the one occupied by the Scots. Initially, the battle went well for James: the soldiers of the Earls of Home and Huntly rushed down the hill and set about devastating the English right wing until Lord Dacre, commanding the only cavalry on the English side, rode in with his Prickers. Unfortunately for James, this early good fortune then inspired him to lead a similar downhill charge; he jumped from his horse, seized a pike and led his men down. Here, though, the ground was steeper, the rain had made it slippery and the slope ended in a bog. The long pikes with which the French had equipped them proved cumbersome in close combat. They floundered, and were devastated. Next day, it was almost impossible to identify the King's body, which had been stripped bare and lay with a gaping wound around the neck. The body was taken to London and buried in an unmarked grave at St Michael's Cornhill. The flower of the Scottish nobility, including nine earls, had perished with him.

FOUNTAINS ABBEY

Legacy of the businesslike Cistercians

NEAR RIPON, NORTH YORKSHIRE

In the early 12th century, the Cistercian Order was founded by monks who sought a more austere way of life than that available to them under the rule of St Benedict (Benedictine Order), which had lost something of its original zeal. Originating in France, the Cistercians came to England in 1128, founding Waverley Abbey in Surrey, then Tintern Abbey in Monmouthshire (see page 434) and Rievaulx and Fountains Abbeys in Yorkshire, the latter being started in 1133. Despite the vast scale of the later buildings at Fountains, it is easy to imagine the tough conditions that the early monks found beside the river Skell. They were forbidden underwear, their habits were made of coarse, undyed sheep's wool (hence the Cistercians' name of White Monks) and they ate sparingly. For long spells they were silent, communicating only by sign language. Their days were made up of worship and prayer.

All Cistercian houses – there came to be eighty-six in Britain – are laid out to the same pattern. They tended to grow large because each site effectively incorporated two monasteries in one, with one set of buildings for the monks and another for the lay brothers. While the monks – usually a few dozen – dedicated themselves to their devotions, the business of running the ever-expanding estates fell to an army of illiterate lay brothers, who tilled the land and cared for the sheep flocks. It was more like a business over which the monks presided in the manner of a board of directors. They were in the happy position of being able to control an unpaid workforce, free of feudal obligations. As a result, the Order became so rich that, after the Black Death decimated the lay workforce, the original system began to disintegrate under its own weight. The monks now owned far more than they could control themselves, so let out their granges to tenants, living on the rents.

However, the ideals of the Order survived in the architecture. Despite its size, Fountains is unadorned. The gaunt tower, built in the early reign of

Henry VIII, stands witness to Abbot Huby's efforts to reform the Order, in line with the spartan intentions of its founders. They were not enough to prevent the Abbey from being dissolved in 1539.

HADRIAN'S WALL

FROM BOWNESS-ON-SOLWAY TO WALLSEND

The limit of the Roman Empire

Hadrian's Wall was perhaps the most impressive fortification ever undertaken by the Roman Empire. It was, indeed, meant to impress. A 73-mile collar across the throat of Britain, the wall is an extravagant, almost theatrical construction, far stronger, taller and more elaborate than it needed to be to separate conquered England from the wild tribes north of the Border. When it was built in AD122, the Roman Empire covered most of the known world, stretching from what is today Iraq to the North of England. The wall would seem to be an emphatic declaration that here the Empire had stopped its expansion; this was the final northern boundary. The Roman army was now required to consolidate the territory it had conquered, and Hadrian's Wall is surely an imperious symbol of its success.

Hadrian became Emperor in 117 and while there is no evidence that he had seen the terrain that the wall would cross, it must have been described to him. The wall he planned was immensely thick – about 9ft – and nearly 15ft high; where the terrain permitted, landscape features such as crags gave even greater height. There was a steep ditch, some 30ft deep, on the northern side. On the southern side of the wall was the massive banked *vallum*, 20ft wide, and then a military road. At mile intervals there were gates, protected by guardposts, known as milecastles. Between each milecastle were a couple of observation turrets. Sixteen forts were built at intervals that could be marched in a day, and from these garrisons the border could be controlled.

The forts – of which the best preserved today are Chesters, Corbridge and Housesteads – were either sheltered by the wall or, more often, lay astride it, projecting into the hostile northern side. They always took the form of squares, with gates in each of the four sides. These gates provided the only means of crossing from one side to another. The forts contained barracks, granaries that were raised above the ground, and bath houses set outside the forts; the one at Chesters is in good condition.

The wall was built by the soldiers of three legions, probably assisted by local people. The legionnaires did not come from the Mediterranean but from regiments raised in northern Europe. They were therefore better able to withstand the bitter winters of the high open moorland across which the wall strides. The stone was quarried from sites nearby. Since neither the soldiers nor the materials cost the Empire more than it would have paid in controlling the Border piecemeal if it had not been built, the wall was not a vastly expensive undertaking. It was mostly completed in six years, although modifications were still being made at the time of Hadrian's death in 138. His wall continued to be manned until around 400. When the soldiers in the garrisons found that their pay was no longer arriving, they must have sought other occupations to sustain themselves, becoming either farmers or brigands.

See also Offa's Dyke, page 428

HALIDON HILL   NEAR BERWICK-UPON-TWEED, NORTHUMBERLAND

Edward III saves Berwick for the English

Throughout the Middle Ages, the frontier town of Berwick-upon-Tweed* repeatedly changed hands between Scotland and England. In 1333, it was in Scottish hands. That year, in the longest and most fiercely fought assault on the town, the young Edward III laid siege to it. He had come to the support of the new Scottish king, Edward Balliol, who had been forced to flee across the border half naked after losing the Battle of Annan to rebels.

Edward III's army arrived in May and besieged the town for two months. A Scottish force finally arrived, and on 19 July the two armies formed up opposite each other on nearby Halidon Hill.

Before battle commenced, a hand-to-hand combat was held between a champion from each side. The Scotsman, William Turnbull, was well over 6ft tall and had the advantage of an extra weapon – his huge bull mastiff dog. Although much smaller, his English opponent, Sir Robert Benhale, managed to kill both the Scotsman and the dog. The terrain was similar to Bannockburn (see page 444), only now the English had the advantage, the Scots being forced to negotiate a bog before attacking uphill. When they were met by a hail of English arrows from above, the Scots broke ranks and fled. The Berwick garrison surrendered the next day, and from then on the town remained more English than Scots.

*See Berwick-upon-Tweed, page 383

THE PIECE HALL   HALIFAX, WEST YORKSHIRE

Britain's greatest monument to cottage industry

Weaving was one of the first industries to be transformed by the Industrial Revolution, concentrating manufacture in factories. Before that, it had been an activity which weaving families had pursued at home, using hand-looms*; they wove cloth in 'pieces' of 30yds or so, and sold them through markets. The area around Halifax in Yorkshire – Calderdale – was propitious to weaving, having an abundance of water and a landscape that suited sheep farming, but little else. Weaving had taken place here since the Middle Ages. In the 1770s, the weavers decided to make better provision to market their cloth. The result was the Piece Hall at Halifax which, according to the inscription over the North Gate, was opened on 1 January 1779.

A vast courtyard of 10,000 sq ft is enclosed by stone arcades, surmounted by galleries. Because of the sloping site, one side has only two tiers while the others have three. Apparently designed by John Hope of Liverpool, the effect is rough but, from scale alone, imposing. Around the courtyard, 315 rooms provided weavers with shop space. To ensure fair competition, no merchant could enter the Piece Hall or buy cloth before ten o'clock, and business closed at noon.

The impressive size of the Piece Hall must have helped Halifax make up the ground it had lost to other West Riding towns, such as Leeds, Huddersfield, Bradford and Wakefield. They had already built themselves Cloth Halls; in the case of Leeds, two. Within a decade after the Piece Hall was built, however, Edmund Cartwright had invented his power loom, making the hall's purpose redundant. It was financially unattractive for merchants to buy small lengths from numerous hand-loom weavers when they could buy more cheaply in bulk from one or two factories. By the early 19th century, the Piece Hall was in decline. It became a fish, fruit and vegetable market in the 1870s.

*See Cromford, page 315, and Hall i' th' Wood, page 362

BRONTË PARSONAGE HAWORTH, WEST YORKSHIRE
Where the Brontë sisters nursed their genius

In 1847 the novel *Jane Eyre*, supposedly by Currer Bell, was published, followed by *Wuthering Heights* by Ellis Bell and *Agnes Grey* by Acton Bell. They were in fact the work of the Brontë sisters, Charlotte, Emily and Anne. The next year Emily died of tuberculosis after nursing her brother Branwell (addicted to opium and alcohol), to be followed by Anne the next year. For any family to produce three novelists of such calibre is extremely rare: added to this, the literary reputation of the trio rests heavily on first novels. Not surprisingly, the place where the novels were written – their father Patrick's parsonage at Haworth, in Yorkshire – has long been a literary shrine.

Victorian Haworth had little of the charm that this village, built around a precipitous high street, has today. It was industrial and unsanitary, and the graveyard that lay next to the parsonage was – like many others before reform – dangerously overcrowded. The Brontës would, therefore, take their exercise on the moors, whose presence haunts their work. Their father, an Irishman who changed his name from Prunty to the more evocative Brontë (perhaps inspired by the Sicilian dukedom awarded to Nelson), had no income beyond his stipend. Therefore, his daughters prepared themselves for careers in teaching – one of the few professions open to middle-class Victorian women. Charlotte and Emily studied in Brussels, in the hope of opening a school at the parsonage (it failed to attract pupils); Anne worked as a governess for five years. Since their mother had died when they were young children, the parsonage was run by their aunt, Elizabeth Branwell. Her death simultaneously brought a small legacy, which saved them from teaching, while providing a reason for them to stay at Haworth, keeping house for their father. In 1854 at the age of thirty-eight, Charlotte married Arthur Bell Nicholls, her father's curate, dying in the early stages of pregnancy the next year.

As Victorian rectories went, the Haworth parsonage was not large: a Georgian box built, like the rest of the village, out of the dark-coloured local stone known as millstone grit. Here, Mr Brontë had a study to which he would retire for some meals, pleading ill health, but the children had no work room of their own; instead they wrote in the dining room. In the evenings they would walk round the table, discussing their literary projects.

WILBERFORCE HOUSE   HULL
Champion of emancipation

In 18th-century Britain, sugar made many families rich. It was extracted from the sugar cane grown on plantations on British-owned islands in the West Indies. With the heat, humidity and tropical diseases, Europeans could rarely stand working in the fields for long. As a result, black slaves from Africa were used instead. Slavery* had its origins in Africa itself, where tribesmen and women were captured and sold into slavery by members of opposing tribes. Once the slaves had reached the coast, however, British ships – protected by the powerful British navy – played a prominent role in transporting them to the southern states of North America or the Caribbean, in such filthy, cramped conditions that many died en route. By the end of that century, the slave trade had come to seem an abomination to most educated Britons who cared to think about it, and the courts declared that it was contrary to common law (meaning that slavery never existed on mainland Britain). The evangelical Christian William Wilberforce led the parliamentary campaign that finally caused slavery to be abolished in the British West Indies, decades before his example was followed by other slave-owning societies, such as the United States.

Wilberforce was born in Hull in 1759. From the age of seven, he went to the

Hull Grammar School, and later the town was to become the constituency that he first represented in the House of Commons. On the death of his father in 1768, he went to live with an uncle in Wimbledon. He went up to St John's, Cambridge, where he led an idle and convivial existence, forming a close friendship with the future Prime Minister William Pitt.

Wilberforce, a tiny man who enjoyed the pleasures of fashionable society, was a moving orator. When a society for the suppression of the slave trade was formed in 1787, he was recruited as its parliamentary spokesman. The anti-slavery movement became central to his life and, after years of frustration, he succeeded in getting a Bill to prohibit the slave trade through Parliament in 1807. This made it illegal to transport slaves in British ships, although the institution of slavery still continued in the British colonies. On 26 July 1833, while on his deathbed, Wilberforce heard that the Bill to free all slaves in the colonies had passed its second reading in the Commons. 'Thank God that I should have witnessed a day in which England is willing to give 20 millions sterling for the Abolition of Slavery,' he exclaimed.

*See The Georgian House, page 11, and St Andrew's Church, page 263

MONASTERY OF ST PAUL

JARROW, CO. DURHAM

Where Bede established the use of Anno Domini

Had it not been for a 7th-century monk called Bede, we might not be living in the 21st century AD. Bede did not invent our system of numbering years from the birth of Christ but, writes H. P. R. Finberg in The Formation of England, 'his reasoning and example led to its rapid adoption throughout Christendom'. This alone would qualify Bede for a position of influence in Western culture, but he is also the conduit through which much of our knowledge of the Dark Ages has been transmitted. Bede wrote the remarkable five-volume history of the Church and the Anglo-Saxon kings, Historia Ecclesiastica Gentis Anglorum, which are the principal sources for our understanding of the period up to 731, when he completed the work. Even so, the achievement of which Bede himself was probably most proud was his editing of the Bible; an illustrated version of the result was sent to Rome and remained in use until 1963. Later ecclesiastics went so far as to give him the honorific of 'Venerable'. If that sounds strange to our ears, it is still possible to recapture some of the piety and austerity amid which he lived by visiting the site of his monastery of St Paul at Jarrow.

Jarrow Priory, founded in 681, was the twin of the slightly earlier St Peter's at Monkwearmouth (674), both of which had been established by Benedict Biscop. Biscop came from a noble family attached to King Oswy of

Northumbria. When he was twenty-five he travelled to Rome, and then became a monk. He was to make five further visits to Rome in the course of his life, and the monastic order that he established at Monkwearmouth and Jarrow was based on a composite of Continental practice. This meant living communally, rather than in hermit's cells, as St Cuthbert did on Inner Farne (see page 386). He seems also to have brought stonemasons back from the Continent. With their vine-scroll carving and turned columns (made on lathes), his monasteries had a high artistic content. Archaeological finds include the earliest known Anglo-Saxon glass.

Bede entered the monastery at Monkwearmouth when he was seven, transferring to the new foundation at Jarrow a couple of years later. He then lived at Jarrow until his death aged about sixty-three. The library enabled him to acquire a reputation for learning that was recognised throughout Christendom. Bede was buried at Jarrow but his remains were taken to Durham Cathedral in about 1022.

KIRKGATE MARKET
LEEDS, WEST YORKSHIRE

Small beginnings of a legend in knickers

With its 800 stalls selling meat, blankets, knickers, carpets and every other staple of life, Kirkgate Market in Leeds is one of the biggest markets in Europe. In 1884, it was rather less rumbustious externally than it became after its refacing in the Edwardian period, in the flamboyant style of a gin palace or music hall; but the scale of the cast-iron interior must have been daunting to the young Michael Marks, who had arrived from Poland two years before. He had to do something to get himself noticed. His catchphrase became, 'Don't ask the price; it's a penny.' Six years later he had expanded beyond Leeds to neighbouring towns with a chain of five Penny Bazaars. Soon the point had been reached when this inspired market trader needed the help of an accountant to keep a track of the takings and further his expansionist ambitions. He found one in Thomas Spencer, a cashier for a wholesale company. The firm of Marks and Spencer was born.

By the time Spencer died in 1905, no fewer than seventy bazaars had been opened. The company owned a warehouse and head office in Manchester, as well as a shop in the Cross Arcade, Leeds. It began to evolve out of market trading into shopkeeping. Two years after Spencer's death, Marks followed him to the great emporium in the sky, and a new generation came into the business. Between the wars, the business that Marks founded went public, his own first name being commemorated in the St Michael trademark – ironically Christian, given the store's strongly Jewish association, it was calculated to appeal to a generation brought up to know their saints (this one clothed a beggar).

In 1930 the famous Marble Arch store was opened in London; a food department was introduced the next year, and in 1934 a scientific research laboratory was established for textiles – the first, it is claimed, of any British retailer. A programme of staff benefits offered subsidised health and dental services, hairdressing, holidays and pensions. If the object was to inspire long service, it certainly worked in one case: Michael Marks's son Simon retired in 1964, after fifty-six years with the company. By now, Marks and Spencer was a national phenomenon, its fundamentally decent, made-in-Britain values symbolised by its most famous product: reliable underwear.

LINDISFARNE
The writing of the Lindisfarne Gospels

In monasteries such as Lindisfarne – also known as Holy Island – off the Northumberland coast, the lamp of civilisation (languages, books, artistic tradition) was kept alive in the dark centuries after the Romans had left Britain. The most beautiful product of this time was the Lindisfarne Gospels. St Aidan, coming from Iona, had founded the monastery in the early 7th century, and the Gospels were created between 715 and 720 by a monk called Eadfrith, who was at that time Lindisfarne's bishop. He seems to have undertaken them in honour of St Cuthbert*, who had died in his cell on the island of Inner Farne, off Lindisfarne, in 687.

Eadfrith's script is strong and confident. The opening of each Gospel is decorated with a picture of the Evangelist, wearing a toga with folds drawn in the Roman style. They are not stiff or lifeless figures, while the accompanying beasts, such as St Mark's lion, are particularly lively. Equally remarkable are the panels of geometric or 'carpet' decoration, in which lines of ornament interweave to form complex patterns. These elaborate linear mazes, drawn to fascinate the eye, are a tribute of the love shown for St Cuthbert.

The Gospels were a lavish artefact. Over 100 calf hides went to make the vellum on which they are written, and the finished result was encased in covers richly studded with jewels. Their survival is almost as much of a miracle as the cures performed by St Cuthbert. When Viking raids made life at Lindisfarne impossible, the Gospels were taken on the monks' travels, with the saint's body, which ended up in Durham Cathedral 120 years later. Nothing now survives of the monastery in which they were made. However, the cult of St Cuthbert grew to such an extent that a new priory was raised towards the end of the 11th century, around the place where the cenotaph or support for his coffin had originally stood.

*See Durham Cathedral, page 386

MILLENNIUM BRIDGE
Reinventing the North-East

The expression 'taking coals to Newcastle' means offering an item of which there is already an abundant supply. The North-East was where coal came from. It was also where ships came from, and clothing. It was where glass, soap, salt and paper came from. But few of those things come from either Newcastle upon Tyne, or Gateshead on the south bank of the river, any more. The shipbuilding and repair yards shrivelled to a husk of their former selves during the 1980s. At the beginning of that decade, thirty per cent of the male work force used to work in traditional heavy manufacturing industries. Fifteen years later, just one per cent did. The streets onto which thousands of shipyard workers used to stream at the end of a shift are now empty.

Then, in the late 1990s, the North-East reinvented itself. One symbol of the renaissance is Antony Gormley's sculpture *The Angel of the North*, a 65ft tall figure made of metal, its enormous wings stretching out of the industrial landscape of Gateshead. This vast, primitive, yet hope-inspiring figure is intended to personify the transition from the age of coal mining to that of information technology. Another landmark is the Millennium Bridge in Newcastle itself – one of many projects in Britain that revived national prestige around the year 2000, thanks to the enthusiasm with which the public played the new national lottery. It symbolised the transformation that had overtaken Newcastle, from a place of decaying heavy industry to a city now famous for its cultural buildings and youth culture.

The old dockyards have been replaced by town-house developments, based around marinas; Victorian warehouses have been turned into Manhattan-style lofts; a city where Saturday night would once have been spent in the pub is now packed with young people, some from the popular and sociable university, going from club to club. In Gateshead, the Baltic Flour Mill has become a fashionable arts centre, while Foster & Partners have created the Sage music centre in the form of a giant, shiny caterpillar – a bravura display of the North-East's new cultural self-confidence.

The elegant curve of the Millennium Bridge complements these developments. Shaped like a giant eyelid, it serves to connect Newcastle's thriving quayside, with its markets and restaurants, with the flourishing arts buildings on the Gateshead side. When the bridge needs to be raised for tall ships, the eyelid blinks – that is to say, the curving walkway tilts upwards to meet the arch above. Yet to describe the bridge in terms of an ultra-modern crossing for pedestrians and cyclists misses its real meaning for the North-East. The bridge became an instant icon for a city whose 21st-century eye is wide open to its new future, inspiring other stagnating post-industrial towns to ask: could we do the same?

NORHAM NEAR BERWICK-UPON-TWEED, NORTHUMBERLAND

Edward I judges claimants to the Scottish crown

In the summer of 1291, Edward I, King of England, arrived at Norham on the banks of the Tweed, which forms the border there with Scotland. He had come to adjudicate between the many different claimants to the Scottish throne. The succession had been thrown into crisis by the death, first, of Alexander III, galloping through a stormy night to be with his new French bride, and then of little Margaret, the Maid of Norway, who expired in Orkney*. At Norham, Edward lodged in the Bishop of Durham's castle, built on a steep bluff above the river. The legal proceedings took place in the parish church of St Cuthbert (whose body had rested there on its way to Durham, see page 386), a stout Norman structure, now much battered by centuries of Border raids. Later, the litigation came to be known as the Great Cause: the root of the Scottish Wars of Independence.

Before Edward gave judgement, he persuaded the two principal claimants, Robert Bruce and John Balliol, to recognise him as feudal overlord. In November 1292, he found in favour of Balliol. Balliol swore fealty to Edward in Norham church, and was proclaimed King of the Scots at nearby Berwick-upon-Tweed. Unfortunately, he did not have the force of character to withstand Edward, who was soon interfering in legal suits, raising taxes and demanding that Scotland contribute troops to his army in France. Before long, even Balliol turned against his supposed patron, forming an alliance with France. This was tantamount to a declaration of war. In 1296, Edward returned to Scotland. Balliol was captured and ritually humiliated, having the heraldic insignia stripped from his tabard, which led to his nickname of Toom (or empty) Tabard (see page 482).

Bullying Balliol, however, was a different matter from conquering the Scots. For many years, Edward annually led his army on a Scottish campaign. He died in 1307, bequeathing an unresolved conflict with the Scots, now led by Robert Bruce, grandson of the original claimant, to his son, the ill-starred Edward II.

*See Battle of Largs, page 472

PONTEFRACT CASTLE WEST YORKSHIRE

Death of Richard II

In June 1399, while Richard II was campaigning in Ireland, the banished Henry Bolingbroke, Duke of Lancaster, sailed from France. His ship seems to have put into different ports along the eastern seaboard, to test the mood of the country, before landing at Ravenspur at the mouth of the Humber – a town that has since disappeared beneath the sea without trace (see page 283).

Bolingbroke's father, John of Gaunt, had died the previous February, and Richard had used the cover of Bolingbroke's banishment to confiscate Gaunt's vast estates, whose owner was likely to be financially better placed than the King. This violation of property rights shocked other landowners, making them feel insecure. Bolingbroke's landing place was near some of his own castles, such as Pontefract, and not far from his Percy allies in Northumberland (see page 382). He swore that he had only come to reclaim his rightful inheritance. He was prepared to swear practically anything to garner support – it was an oath that had later consequences*.

Richard hurried back, leaving his army in Ireland, but was dismayed to find that the army he was expecting to find waiting for him in Cheshire had evaporated. He delivered himself – whether willingly or as a result of subterfuge – into Bolingbroke's hands, and Bolingbroke forced him to abdicate. He was taken to London, and the King, whose Court had radiated art and beauty, rode to Westminster on a miserable nag, dressed only in black. Bolingbroke's usurpation had taken barely five weeks.

Richard's abdication was ratified by a Parliament which never heard his defence. A deposed king was, to the medieval mind, something that should not exist. Sir Richard of Bordeaux, as King Richard was now known, was disguised as a forester and spirited away to Pontefract Castle. At Christmas, a plot by Richard's supporters forced Henry IV (as Bolingbroke was now known) to flee for his life; although the conspiracy was easily quashed, it sealed Richard's fate. Exactly how he ended his days at Pontefract – perhaps in the now ruined Gascoigne Tower – is not known; he may have been starved to death or murdered. What is certain is that he never emerged from Pontefract alive: he was dead by the middle of February 1400.

*See Battle of Shrewsbury, page 341

THE OLD LIFEBOAT STATION REDCAR, CLEVELAND
Oldest surviving lifeboat in the world

The oldest surviving lifeboat in the world is the Zetland, housed on the seafront at Redcar. She was built by the South Shields boat builder, Henry Greathead, in 1802, the eleventh of what would be thirty-one especially created lifeboats; they had a layer of cork around the gunwales for buoyancy. The Zetland – 30ft long, with a beam of 10ft – was designed to face either way: to reverse their course, the crew simply turned round to row in the opposite direction. There were ten oars, those on one side painted blue and those on the other white. This enabled the coxswain, steering the boat, to shout 'pull on the blues' or 'back on the whites', to avoid confusion.

Redcar was nothing more than a fishing village when the *Zetland* was ordered. Lord Dundas and the Rev. Y. Williamson helped the fishermen and villagers raise the necessary £200. Wrecks were commonplace, at a time when fifty ships might be seen on the horizon together. Not all coasters were seaworthy, and the waters off Redcar were made treacherous by the fingers of rock, or scars, that stretch out from the land. On 6 December 1802, eight weeks after the boat's arrival in Redcar, she went into action, rescuing fifteen sailors from two brigs, the *Mary* and the *Friendship*. The lifeboat crew were all fishermen, roused by the beating of an alarm drum. Local farmers also helped, since the boat had to be hauled by carthorses to a position opposite the distressed ship.

In 1857, the *Zetland* became part of the Royal National Lifeboat Institution. Her last rescue took place in 1880. During her 78-year career, she had saved over 500 lives. She is now housed in the old lifeboat station, a couple of hundred yards along the Esplanade from its 1970s replacement.

KELHAM ISLAND MUSEUM   SHEFFIELD, SOUTH YORKSHIRE
Steel to build the Empire

Guns, ships and railways: in 1855 Henry Bessemer invented a process by which these fundamentals of the Victorian age could be made cheaply out of steel. Until then, steel had been made on an artisan scale, a couple of pounds at a time, for blades and tools. It was high quality but expensive. Bessemer's 'converter' could produce thirty tons of medium-quality steel in half an hour. Molten pig iron was poured into the mouth of a pear-shaped vessel, looking somewhat like a large concrete mixer; air was then blasted through the bottom of it, burning off excess oxygen in the iron in a spectacular spout of flame. Sometimes carbon was also added, before the newly made steel was tipped into a ladle and finally cast into ingots.

The Bessemer Works were in Sheffield, already a steel town famed for its cutlery. Soon his process was adopted by other steelyards, including John Brown & Co. and Wilson Cammel & Co., both of which went on to acquire shipyards that would provide an end destination for their product. Within twenty years, 10,000 tons of Bessemer steel were being made each week in Sheffield. By 1900, the world output of steel had multiplied a thousandfold. However, nothing except a single office block in Carlisle Street, built seven years after Bessemer's death in 1898, now survives from the Bessemer Works. The only remaining example of a Bessemer converter, 30ft tall, is outside the Kelham Island Museum; it was in use until 1975.

SHILDON STATION

World's first public railway

The world's first public railway, the Stockton and Darlington Railway, began to operate on 27 September 1825. The inaugural journey took a train of coal wagons and a coach for the company's directors from the Brusselton incline, near Shildon, to the river Tees at Stockton. The engine that pulled it, Locomotion Number One, had been delivered from the Stephenson works at Newcastle eleven days earlier. George Stephenson himself stood on the footplate. A horseman carrying a flag preceded the train, whose progress, at a rate of five miles per hour, was watched by thousands of excited spectators.

There had been steam-driven trains before the Stockton and Darlington, but they were generally used by mines for hauling coal and ore (see page 425). Indeed, the main purpose of the new railway was to transport coal from the west Durham pits to barges on the Tees. Unlike previous railways, however, the Stockton and Darlington was open to anyone, and it took passengers.

The original proposal had been for a canal to be constructed, but for reasons of topography the directors came to prefer a railway: some still had misgivings when the Bill to develop it went before Parliament in 1822. The western terminus was not, as the name of the railway implied, at Darlington, but fifteen miles beyond it, at Witton Park. This made an overall length of 26 miles. By reducing the cost of transport, the price of west Durham coal was halved, providing an economic stimulus to the area.

The first passengers to use the railway had to board the train from the top floor of a warehouse near Shildon. As their numbers grew, Shildon station was built for them in 1833, to be replaced with the present building nine years later. Locomotion Number One can be seen in the Darlington Railway Centre. The oldest engine at Shildon's museum is the Sans Pareil, built in 1829.

STAITHES

James Cook is called by the sea

The explorer Captain James Cook was the son of a farm worker, born at Marton-in-Cleveland in 1728. Aged sixteen, he went to work as an apprentice to a haberdasher in the fishing village of Staithes. In his spare time, he tasted life at sea with the fishermen. Since smuggling was rife, it is possible that it was here that he acquired his skill in sailing soundlessly through the dark, put to good use later when he surveyed the St Lawrence river under the noses of, and sometimes hotly pursued by, the French, before General Wolfe's landing at Quebec (see page 98). Shopkeeping was not to his taste, the call of the sea being irresistible. The haberdasher's shop was swept away in a storm but a plaque on the replacement building acknowledges Cook's association with this little village crouched at the foot of steep cliffs. He moved ten miles south along the coast to the busy coaling port of Whitby. It was Whitby that in every sense equipped him to explore the South Seas and circumnavigate the world.

Cook was apprenticed to a Quaker, John Walker, who lived at 17 Grape Lane. The Quaker principles of integrity and plain living chimed with Cook's own taciturn temperament. Throughout the summer months, Cook helped to sail Walker's small fleet of sturdy coalers, known as 'cats', along the coast. In the winter months, he applied himself to studying seamanship in the Walkers' home. By the spring of 1755, Whitby and coaling voyages had come to seem too narrow a canvas for the adventurous Cook, then twenty-six. With war against France imminent, he joined the Royal Navy. Thereafter, for the short periods of time he spent ashore, his home was in the East End of London. After nine years he had risen to command a schooner, charged with surveying the shores of Newfoundland. This supremely qualified Cook to captain the vessel that the Royal Navy put at the disposal of the Royal Society to observe the Transit of Venus from Tahiti.

The ship which Cook chose for this mission was none other than a Whitby 'cat', previously known as the *Earl of Pembroke* but transformed into the *Endeavour*. It was strong, and it could sail in shallow waters. Whitby built all of Cook's four ships, including the *Resolution* of his ill-starred third voyage, during which the now ill and perhaps reckless Cook landed on Hawaii in 1779, only to be clubbed to death.

STAMFORD BRIDGE   NEAR YORK, NORTH YORKSHIRE
King Harold's last triumph

All through the spring and summer of 1066, King Harold II waited for William, Duke of Normandy, to invade the south coast. By August, the *fyrd* – or militia composed of farmers – had served their time and were desperate to harvest their crops. Harold let them go. Towards the end of September, however, he heard that Harald Hardrada of Norway had sailed a war fleet into the Humber and seized York. With him was Harold's disaffected half-brother, Tostig, who had been banished by Edward the Confessor for his ruthless greed. Harold raised an army, made up mostly of his own house carls and thegns, and marched north at incredible speed, covering nearly 200 miles in four days.

He entered York, learnt that an important exchange of hostages was about to take place at Stamford Bridge, a few miles away, and posted sentries to make sure that the news of his appearance did not reach the enemy. He rested his army, and then led them to a place just out of sight of Stamford Bridge. When all the Vikings had assembled, he attacked. They were taken completely by surprise – so much so that they were not wearing their protective leather jerkins sewn with iron rings. Legend has it that one ferocious Viking held the bridge single-handed until an English soldier, using a barrel, managed to manoeuvre into position under the bridge and stab him from beneath. If so, the English attack cannot have been held back for long, because the slaughter was immense. Both Harald Hardrada and Earl Tostig were killed, and when Hardrada's son, Olaf, having sworn to behave, was allowed to sail back to Norway, he took only twenty-five of the original three hundred ships.

Stamford Bridge shows that King Harold was a fine general. During his victory feast at York, however, news arrived that Duke William had at last landed in Sussex. Harold's next battle would be at Hastings*.

*See Battle of Hastings, page 49

BATTLE OF TOWTON NEAR TADCASTER, NORTH YORKSHIRE
Bloodiest battle ever fought on British soil

After the Battle of Mortimer's Cross, one of the major confrontations of the Wars of the Roses*, Edward IV proceeded immediately to London, where he wrested the crown from Henry VI. The Lancastrian army that had won the second Battle of St Albans and were loyal to Henry VI, however, was still in the field. Edward, gathering the different elements of his forces together, pursued the Lancastrians northwards, reaching the castle of Pontefract. From its battlements he could see his enemy encamped about halfway to York. He crossed the river Aire at Castleford, the bridge at Ferrybridge having been put out of action. The two armies faced each other on broad, slightly undulating countryside to the east of the Cock Beck, south of the village of Towton. It was Palm Sunday, 1461.

A medieval battle would open with an exchange of arrows and cannonballs. Then the opposing lines of foot soldiers would advance and become locked in brutal hand-to-hand combat. They would set about each other with heavy swords, maces and billhooks, those who wore armour only being able to see through a narrow slit in their helmets. To preserve the loyalty of their troops, it was common for commanders to fight in the midst of their men: this Edward did at Towton. The battle usually ended with a charge of heavily armoured knights, exploiting whatever weakness had been opened up in the enemy lines. At Towton, this final stage was never reached. The battle front chosen by the Lancastrians was too narrow for manoeuvring. Furthermore, the fight took place in a blinding blizzard – the cavalry could not see where to charge.

Once locked together, the two sides stood their ground, hacking each other to pieces. The end finally came when Edward's reserves arrived, having finally been able to cross over the repaired bridge at Ferrybridge. The Lancastrians broke rank, many of them drowning in the beck as they struggled across it in armour. It was estimated that 28,000 soldiers were killed during that single battle. Among them were most of the remaining Lancastrian leaders. Edward could now be crowned king. Once the last of the Lancastrian castles had been taken, the country was able to enjoy a period of domestic peace – until the Battle of Barnet some ten years later.

*See First Battle of St Albans, page 240; Battle of Wakefield, below; Second Battle of St Albans, page 241; Battle of Mortimer's Cross, page 332; Battle of Barnet, page 204; Battle of Tewkesbury, page 346; Battle of Bosworth, page 309

BATTLE OF WAKEFIELD WEST YORKSHIRE
Turning point in the Wars of the Roses

In October 1460, Richard, Duke of York persuaded Parliament to disinherit Henry VI's son in favour of his own line. It was a crucial turning point in the Wars of the Roses*, a power struggle fought between contending magnates who supported different branches of the Plantagenet family – the Houses of York and Lancaster – for the throne.

After the first Battle of St Albans, York had himself declared as heir to the throne on Henry VI's death, in place of the Prince of Wales. This was not to be brooked by the Queen, Margaret of Anjou. Urged on by her, a Lancastrian army assembled in the north, and York set off to meet them. Over Christmas, he established himself at Sandal Castle near Wakefield, an impressive stronghold only nine miles away from the Lancastrian fortress at Pontefract.

On 30 December, a foraging party from Sandal was surprised by the Lancastrians. For some reason that has never been explained, York decided to leave his hilltop castle and go down to the plain to help them. He had about 5,000 men with him and they were overwhelmed by a force of 17,000 Lancastrians. York was killed somewhere near the memorial in Manygates Lane in Sandal, which was erected in 1897. The Duke's young son, Edmund, Earl of Rutland, sought to escape with his tutor but was captured and brutally killed as he knelt before Lord 'Butcher' or 'Bloodsupper' Clifford, in revenge for Clifford's father's death at St Albans.

The feud between the Lancastrians and Yorkists continued until York's fourth son, Richard, Duke of Gloucester, who became Richard III after the murder of his nephews, was killed at Bosworth Field in 1485.

*See First Battle of St Albans, page 240; Second Battle of St Albans, page 241; Battle of Mortimer's Cross, page 332; Battle of Towton, page 402; Battle of Barnet, page 204; Battle of Tewkesbury, page 346; Battle of Bosworth, page 309

WHITBY ABBEY

Synod to decide the direction of Christianity in England

In 655, Oswy, brother to the dead King Oswald of Northumbria, led a small army into battle. His enemy was Penda, slayer of Oswald, who had now fought his way to the crowns of both Mercia and Northumbria. Oswy's forces were greatly outnumbered. He promised God that if his cause were successful, he would build a monastery and offer up his daughter as a nun. Against the odds, Penda and many of his followers were slain, and Oswy's daughter, Aelfled, duly entered a monastery at Hartlepool. The abbess there was Hilda, and in 657 he persuaded her to run his new foundation at Whitby. In centuries to come, Whitby would become a centre for pilgrimage, with a church so big and richly furnished that it crippled the abbey with debt. To begin with, however, the buildings were as austere as the setting – on a dramatic, rain-lashed headland above what is now the port of Whitby. The monastery was a community for both men and women in the manner of Gallic monasteries, while spiritually the example was probably that of Iona, the monastery established by St Columba off the west coast of Scotland in 563 (see page 469).

The Celtic church, of which Whitby was also part, had developed different traditions from those of the Roman church, established by St Augustine in Canterbury (see page 56). These differences were a source of acute distress to early churchmen. The three most vexed areas of disagreement concerned the method by which the date of Easter was calculated, the correct way to consecrate a bishop, and the style of the tonsure adopted by monks: the Roman church favoured a shaved circle on top of the head, whereas the Celts shaved the whole front half of the scalp, leaving the hair to grow long behind.

It was at Whitby in 664, just seven years after Hilda had established her monastery, that King Oswy called together a Synod to resolve matters. An influential monk called Wilfrid successfully argued that the authority of St Peter, as followed by the Church of Rome and practised by all Christians elsewhere, was superior to the Celtic ritual founded by St Columba of Iona; King Oswy, presiding, found in his favour. By standardising the customs of the church, he paved the way to England eventually becoming a single country.

COPPERGATE

The Viking capture of York

In 866, a great Viking army landed in East Anglia. Viking longships had been raiding the eastern coast of England in terrifying surprise raids for seventy years, but this time the intention of King Ivar the Boneless and his brother Halfdan was different. They meant to stay and settled in for the winter. Then they marched north and seized York without trouble, since a civil war in Northumbria had diverted local attention. In the spring of 867 the Northumbrian forces, having sunk their differences, were demolished by the Danes. After the battle, one of the Northumbrian leaders, Aella, was spatchcocked like a bird – a method of punishment known as blood-eagle. According to the sagas, this was in revenge for the death of Ivar and Halfdan's father at the hands of the Northumbrians.

For fourteen years, the Vikings' Great Army moved around England. By the 880s they had conquered the eastern half of England, which became subject to the Viking legal system known as the Danelaw. Like other societies, the Vikings bred craftsmen who worked leather, turned wooden bowls, hammered utensils out of iron and shaped horn into tools; in time their maritime skills were used for trade rather than pillage. Their ships transported wool, tin, silver and soapstone carvings, bringing back swords and wine from France and slaves from Ireland. The houses in the Coppergate area of York, where some of them settled, were built of wooden timbers, the spaces between which were filled with woven wicker daubed with mud (wattle and daub). In the damp soil near the river they survived, hidden beneath later streets, and were excavated in remarkably good condition in 1976.

After 1066 the Viking influence in England was supplanted by the comprehensive Normanisation. Ironically, William's ally that year had been Harald Hardrada; leading the last serious Viking attack on England, he was defeated at Stamford Bridge (see page 401).

CLIFFORD'S TOWER

YORK

English history's worst episode of anti-Semitism

For much of English history, Jews were not subject to the same degree of persecution as beset them in most other European countries, with the exception of Holland. They were useful to medieval kings, who endlessly borrowed money from them for wars and crusades, and who (while not condoning usury) mercilessly taxed the profits that they made from lending money to other people*. However, at a time when any foreigner was regarded as exotic, the presence of a small number of rich Jews living near the general population of less prosperous – sometimes indebted – Gentiles inspired envy and suspicion. The Crusades, by emphasising the purity of the Christian religion over Islam, had the effect of inflaming anti-Semitism: members of the race that had put Christ to death were an easier target when they lived in England than the Mohammedans occupying the sacred sites of the Holy Land.

In 1189, the coronation of the Crusader-King Richard I itself provoked an anti-Jewish riot. Jews who had come with gifts for the King were barred from the ceremony, and a false rumour that the King had ordered a pogrom caused an assault on Jews in the City of London. The King showed his displeasure by hanging three of the ringleaders, but as soon as Richard had set off on crusade in 1190, rioting broke out again. In York, the house of Benedict of York, a Jew who had died as a result of wounds suffered in London, was sacked. Numerous other Jews from the city took shelter in the castle, at that time a wooden tower on top of the motte that still exists in heightened form. The constable, who had originally let them in, was himself shut out, in case he betrayed them. Thereupon the castle was besieged by the mob, assisted by the sheriff Richard Malebisse, who happened to owe the Jews a great deal of money. As bad luck would have it, a monk who had been exhorting the mob to fury was killed beneath the battlements by a falling stone, further inciting the attackers. The Jews, with few provisions, were unable to hold out for long, and around 150 preferred to kill themselves, setting fire to the castle, rather than suffer a worse fate – including compulsory baptism – at the hands of the mob. Those who did not die by their own hands were butchered.

Afterwards, Malebisse and his companions rushed to the cathedral to burn the records in which their debts were enumerated. King Richard, who had no desire for the Crown to lose the revenue that came from mulcting the Jews, instituted a system of registering debts twice. A century later, in 1290, the Jews were expelled from England under Edward I, but returned during the Commonwealth†.

*See The Jew's House, Lincoln, page 278. †See Bevis Marks Synagogue, page 116

Wales

THE ALLURE OF WALES is her castles. The affable though warlike Lord Rhys held the first eisteddfod, with contests for music and poetry, to mark the completion of his castle at Cardigan; a forlorn tower on a bluff is all that survives of Llywelyn the Great's stronghold of Dolbadarn. These were some of the achievements of native Welsh princes, for whose triumphs you must look to history, legend and the spirits that haunt the mountains. The English invaders, on the other hand, hammered down castles around the coast like nails to keep their conquest from blowing away. Chepstow is the oldest; Beaumaris on the Isle of Anglesey the most beautiful; Caerphilly the most gaunt; Caernarfon – built on an already mythical site, in a manner that was intended to evoke the walls of Constantinople – the most magnificent.

South Wales was once a landscape of coalfields and ironworks; now most of the slag heaps and pitheads have been swept away, leaving Big Pit at Blaenavon as a conserved relic of coal mining, upon which a whole way of life was dependent until the mines closed in the late 20th century. The natural land-scape, thank heavens, shows fewer changes. The beauties of the Wye Valley were celebrated by Picturesque tourists, for whom Tintern Abbey embodied everything that an evocative ruin should. Although born in Swansea, Dylan Thomas, the poet whose genius for the music of words seemed to epitomise Wales in the 20th century, wrote *Under Milk Wood* beside the estuary at Laugharne. Legislators protected the wild habitat of the Gower Peninsula, near Swansea, by making it the first Area of Outstanding Natural Beauty in 1956.

Pura Wallia is what the Normans and Plantagenets called 'Pure Wales', to distinguish it from the anglicised legislative region of the Marches. But apart from a profusion of castles, it is hard to pin down Pure Wales. Is it to be found in St David's on the ravishing Pembrokeshire coast, at Owain Glyndwr's power base of Machynlleth, in the unpronounceable wilds of Llanrhaeadr-ym-Mochnant, where William Morgan translated the Bible into Welsh, or architect Clough Williams-Ellis's simple grave for David Lloyd George, set above the river at Llanystumdwy? It is to be found in all of them.

Wales

N

HOLYHEAD

ANGLESEY

1

26 19

4

Snowdon ▲

Caenarfon Bay

CONWY

9

RHYL

FLINT

12

CLWYD

River Dee

WREXHAM

LLANGOLLEN

GWYNEDD

15

Mountains

17

DOLGELLAU

16

Cardigan Bay

OFFA'S DYKE

WELSHPOOL

27

MONTGOMERY

24

POWYS

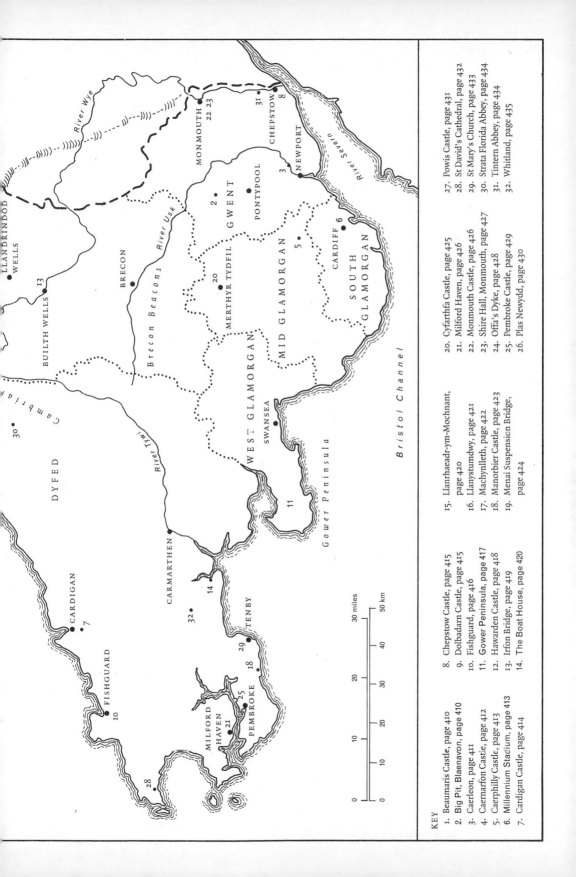

Bristol Channel

KEY

1. Beaumaris Castle, page 410
2. Big Pit, Blaenavon, page 410
3. Caerleon, page 411
4. Caernarfon Castle, page 412
5. Caerphilly Castle, page 413
6. Millennium Stadium, page 413
7. Cardigan Castle, page 414
8. Chepstow Castle, page 415
9. Dolbadarn Castle, page 415
10. Fishguard, page 416
11. Gower Peninsula, page 417
12. Hawarden Castle, page 418
13. Irfon Bridge, page 419
14. The Boat House, page 420
15. Llanrhaeadr-ym-Mochnant, page 420
16. Llanystumdwy, page 421
17. Machynlleth, page 422
18. Manorbier Castle, page 423
19. Menai Suspension Bridge, page 424
20. Cyfarthfa Castle, page 425
21. Milford Haven, page 426
22. Monmouth Castle, page 426
23. Shire Hall, Monmouth, page 427
24. Offa's Dyke, page 428
25. Pembroke Castle, page 429
26. Plas Newydd, page 430
27. Powis Castle, page 431
28. St David's Cathedral, page 432
29. St Mary's Church, page 433
30. Strata Florida Abbey, page 434
31. Tintern Abbey, page 434
32. Whitland, page 435

BEAUMARIS CASTLE

Architecturally most perfect of Edward I's Welsh castles

With the death in 1282 of Llywelyn ap Gruffydd (see page 419), Edward I completed the conquest of Wales, which he secured by building a chain of powerful castles. They included Builth, in the centre, not far from where Llywelyn met his end, but were otherwise placed around the northern coast, from Aberystwyth to Flint. A castle was planned for Anglesey – one of the new shires that were now being organised – but work did not proceed immediately, due to the enormous effort of erecting the mainland castles.

In 1294, however, Magod ap Llywelyn led a revolt, during which the Sheriff of Anglesey, Roger de Pulesdon, was hanged. Edward's response was typically draconian. Among other measures, it involved driving all the Welsh inhabitants out of the town of Llanfaes and immediately beginning Beaumaris Castle. The name Beaumaris means 'beautiful marsh', and the flat site allowed Master James of St George, master of the King's works in Wales, to create the most architecturally perfect of all Edward's great fortifications. Nearly symmetrical, it takes the form of a large inner ward, guarded by powerful double-towered gatehouses and six round towers. Around this was thrown a curtain wall, with a further twelve towers and two gates. The whole castle was surrounded by a moat that was flushed by the tide. A dock enabled ships to unload supplies directly into the outer ward.

Between 1295 and 1298, over 2,500 skilled workers and labourers were involved in the building of Beaumaris Castle, but they were unable to complete it according to the original vision. Even after another thirty-year campaign at the beginning of the next century, the towers of the inner ward were left without their upper storeys and turrets. They were never needed; history largely passed Beaumaris by and, having held out for Charles I until the end of the Civil War, it was merely surrendered in 1646. A rebellion two years later led to a fine rather than the dismantling of the castle; after the Restoration, Beaumaris was abandoned – left to watch peacefully over the Menai Strait in much the same condition as it did in the 14th century.

BIG PIT, BLAENAVON

Eloquently named relic of the coalfields

In 1789 an ironworks was established at Blaenavon, which is today the best-preserved industrial relic of its kind. There was ironstone to hand, as well as limestone. The ironworks also needed coal; this was so plentiful that it appeared in outcrops on the surface of the mountainside from which it had been dug since the 14th century. Now pits were sunk, with names like

Old Coal Pit, Cinder Pit and Dick Kear's Slope. They came, went and changed function, as coal seams were exhausted. The one that, from its sinking in 1860, remained a constant throughout the colliery's subsequent history, was the eloquently named Big Pit. Down in the valley, wagons waited on fans of railway sidings for a constant supply of coal trucks, run down to them from the mine on the tramway, which still survives. At its busiest, before the First World War, Big Pit employed 1,300 men. The face of the mountain was blackened with new mountains of waste, but old photographs show even then that sheep would wander within yards of the pithead as they grazed: a reminder that this was still a remote location.

Big Pit survives as an emblem of an industry that once typified the Welsh valleys but has now almost disappeared. New forms of energy – nuclear power, North Sea gas – came to challenge coal, and the Welsh miners could not dig coal as cheaply as their counterparts overseas. In the early 1980s, Mrs Thatcher provoked a bitter dispute with the National Union of Mineworkers as she withdrew government subsidy, shrank the nationalised industry and then sold it as part of her privatisation programme. By the end of the decade, what the mining communities regarded as a way of life was almost over. Big Pit did not live through these painful transformations. The coal had already run out, and the last of the workforce had left in 1980. By then, however, the decision to preserve the workings as a museum of coal mining had been taken. The shanty town of headframe, engine houses, fitting shops, blacksmith's shop and 1930s pithead baths was not swept away, therefore, and the winding gear still clanks the lift cages (full of visitors, not miners) down to the tunnels underground.

CAERLEON

NEAR NEWPORT, GWENT

Home of the Second Augustan Legion

Nineteen hundred years ago, a Roman legionary accidentally trod on a terracotta tile that was being made, and to this day the print of his hobnailed sandal remains visible on the rim of the Roman swimming baths at Caerleon. Caerleon was a fortress: a series of permanent stone structures, stronger than the temporary wooden forts that the Roman army built on campaign. Although the Romans reached Wales shortly after the invasion of AD43, it was not until thirty years later that they began Caerleon, or *Isca* as they called it. The legion stationed there was the Second Augustan, named after its founder, Augustus. Their logo – LEG II AUG – appears in other tiles.

The baths, built on the scale of a medieval cathedral, provided a recreation complex for the 5,000 soldiers serving in this remote and inhospitable location. It provided a kind of sports centre-cum-gentleman's club, where soldiers could play games, gamble, eat and drink, as well as enjoy different temperatures of bath. Some of them wore engraved gemstones set in rings, which worked loose in the steamy atmosphere and were recovered – eighty-eight of them – when the drain to the baths was sieved by archaeologists in 1979.

The baths seem to have been built when the fort was laid out, and occupy a place within the walls. Ten or so years later, about AD80, the threat from the local Silures tribe had reduced sufficiently for the legion to build an amphitheatre outside the walls. This would not have been possible if the Romans had feared serious attack, since it obscured sight-lines from the fortress. Today, this is the only complete Roman amphitheatre left in Britain. When it was working, it would have resembled a provincial Spanish bullring, with tiers of wooden seats above a ground storey of stone. A fragment of Roman painted glass recovered at Caerleon shows a gladiator.

CAERNARFON CASTLE
GWYNEDD
Edward I gives Wales a new Prince

On 25 April 1284, Edward I's queen gave birth to a second son, named Edward like his father. The happy event took place within the precincts of Caernarfon Castle, the building of which had begun only the previous year. Only four months later, little Edward's elder brother Alfonso died, so that he now became the heir to the throne. Tradition has it that the King showed him to the Welsh nobility, giving the newly vanquished country a prince 'that was borne in Wales and could speake never a word of English'. Edward of Caernarfon – as the future Edward II, in the medieval manner, was known after his birthplace – was officially confirmed (or created) Prince of Wales in 1301.

That the birth should have happened at Caernarfon was propitious. The place already possessed mythical associations for the Welsh, having been the site of what must have been, on that remote frontier, an impressive Roman fort, the ruins of which were still standing. Edward I built on this reputation. Not only were the works on a scale never seen before in Wales, but also the silhouette created by his architect, Master James of St George, was intended to evoke the walls of Constantinople. The castle was burnt down during an uprising of 1294 (see page 410), but Edward quickly regained his lost territory, put down the rebellion with devastating efficiency and rebuilt the castle, finished, as far as it ever would be, in 1330. Edward intended that Caernarfon should be both the capital of his new dominion and a royal palace (hence the size); his successors, however, rarely used it as he envisaged.

The present Prince of Wales, whose investiture took place at Caernarfon in 1969, followed the example of his great-uncle, Edward VIII, in having this ceremony take place in Wales. Many of his forebears had their investiture (if they were invested at all) in front of Parliament in London.

CAERPHILLY CASTLE

Gilbert de Clare's fortress against the last Welsh Prince of Wales

Caerphilly Castle is a monument both to the volcanic Norman lord Gilbert de Clare and to his opponent in south Wales, Llywelyn ap Gruffydd*. The latter's stronghold was in Snowdonia, but by skilful political manoeuvring, at a time when the English crown was weak, he managed to extend his dominion almost to Wales's southern coast.

In 1268 Gilbert de Clare began building Caerphilly Castle. Clearly it was intended to counter the threat from Llywelyn, who had begun raiding his lands. In 1270 Llywelyn burnt what had been constructed at Caerphilly, so that Gilbert had to begin again the next year. Henry III sent a delegation of bishops to separate the two sides; they took charge of the castle and imposed a truce. However, after a trick, Gilbert's men seized the castle again, and building work continued at a hectic pace. It is astonishing to think that nearly all of this massive fortification – said to be second only to Windsor in size – was erected in less than a handful of years.

Gilbert had been present at the siege of Kenilworth (see page 327), and this must have shown how effective water could be as a defence (since it made undermining impossible). Two broad lakes surround Caerphilly. With its perimeter wall enclosing an inner ward, reached by vast inner gatehouses, the plan foreshadows that of the concentric castles built later in the century by Edward I. Once completed, Caerphilly was never taken by Llywelyn or, it seems, anyone else. The threat from Llywelyn proved short-lived, and after his death at Irfon Bridge, Caerphilly, for all its bulk, became militarily redundant. The ruin of a tower leans at a famously rakish angle, the result of slighting after the Civil War combined, probably, with subsidence.

*See Irfon Bridge, page 419

MILLENNIUM STADIUM

Home of Welsh rugby

In 1787 a house on the outskirts of Cardiff, then a market town, was converted into a coaching inn, known as the Cardiff Arms. Behind it was an area of damp moorland running down to the river Taff; in due course, this became a park. When the 2nd Marquess of Bute straightened the river, improving navigation, the park became dry enough to use for sporting events, and it was until 1966 the home ground of the Glamorgan Cricket Club. However, it is as the cathedral of Welsh rugby that Cardiff Arms Park echoes most loudly in the Welsh soul.

Romantics speak of a time when the roar from a Cardiff Arms Park crowd was so deafening that you could not have heard yourself scream. In the land of the male voice choir, hymns were sung with fervour. 'The passions, the sense of communion, the oneness of the team and the people were simply, utterly electrifying,' remembered a sports journalist when the old national stadium was demolished in 1997. There were times of great emotion during the days of illustrious players like Cliff Morgan, Barry John, Gareth Edwards and J. P. R. Williams – legends all.

The site is now occupied by the shining spaceship of the Millennium Stadium which, at a cost of £129m, opened on time for the Rugby World Cup in 1999 – a woeful contrast to the halting redevelopment of the sacred home of English soccer, Wembley Stadium.

CARDIGAN CASTLE
The first eisteddfod

On Christmas Day 1176, Rhys ap Gruffydd, generally known as the Lord Rhys, celebrated the completion of his new castle at Cardigan (Ceredigion) with a house-warming party. The event was significant in two ways. First, it symbolised the power that Rhys exercised over his kingdom of Deheubarth in the south, facing off the Norman Marcher lords who wanted to seize it. The old castle had been a Norman construction that Rhys had captured after a siege. This he had pulled down, starting work on the present structure in 1171. It was the first stone castle built by a native Welsh prince. Rhys was now the most powerful prince in Wales, and recognised as such by Henry II. Although he had rebelled against Henry many times, the English King had appointed him his justice in Wales – a move necessary to provide a counterpoise to Richard de Clare, nicknamed Strongbow (see page 430), who had made himself King of Leinster in Ireland.

Secondly, the celebrations of 1176 included the first known eisteddfod*, with separate contests for music and poetry. A local boy, the son of Eilion, the crowder (or fiddler) from Rhys's own court, won the competition for harpists, while the best bard came from the northern kingdom of Gwynedd. It was a sign of Rhys's appreciation of the role that culture could play in establishing his prestige. Although warlike, Rhys was also genial and cultivated; as well as patronising the arts, he gave generously to the church. Alas, by the time of his death in 1197, his sons were already falling out with each other. While several of Rhys's descendants – including his eldest son Gruffydd and a younger son, Maelgwyn – are buried in Strata Florida Abbey, the 'Welsh Westminster Abbey' (see page 434), the squabbling of his progeny quickly dissipated their inheritance. Maelgwyn sold Cardigan Castle to King John in 1200.

*See Primrose Hill, page 164

CHEPSTOW CASTLE

Perhaps Britain's oldest castle

When William of Normandy conquered England, he divided the old Saxon earldoms up among a close band of supporters, with those who had done most to further the invasion doing best. Foremost among the latter was William fitz Osbern, son of William's steward and his childhood companion. To him went the earldom of Hereford, with lands that stretched as far as Chepstow. His job was to keep the Welsh out of England. The grant of Chepstow, which formed part of a buffer zone known as the Marches, extinguished the 700-year-old kingdom of Gwent.

The castle at Chepstow may be the oldest in the country. Begun in 1067, it was of such strategic importance that it was built of stone – assuming the present Great Tower to belong to that period. Chepstow controlled the crossing of the river Wye that formed the gateway to Wales. The site of the castle, on cliffs above the river, was formidable: any weakness on the landward side was addressed by the architect of the Great Tower by building a windowless wall. From the windows overlooking the river, fitz Osbern could have enjoyed – had the mood taken him – one of the finest views in the new Norman realm.

There is now some doubt that the Great Tower really does date from 1067, since its form and style suggest a period later in the 11th century. It remains, however, an extraordinary expression of Norman military triumphalism, and even in its roofless state, it is easy to imagine the Norman lords feasting in the hall that occupied the whole of the first floor – a vast structure for its day. William fitz Osbern was not to enjoy his English possessions for long: he was killed fighting in Flanders in 1071. His son foolishly sought to depose the King and forfeited his estates.

DOLBADARN CASTLE

Stronghold of Llywelyn the Great

Visitors to Caernarfon Castle (see page 412), on the Menai Strait, see a grand demonstration of Edward I's power, with much of the structure that was put up during the late 13th century still intact. Only a few miles away, overlooking a lake beside the Llanberis Pass in Snowdonia, stands a very different monument, in the form of one decayed tower on a lonely rock. Historically, this is a site that deserves almost as much attention as the castles of Edward I's conquest, having been the power base of Llywelyn ap Iorwerth, or Llywelyn the Great, who built the castle in the 1220s.

Having defeated his uncle Dafydd, Llywelyn became the undisputed prince of Gwynedd after 1200. The next year he swore allegiance to King John, and before long married his illegitimate daughter, Joan. If, however, John thought this would leave him free to fight his barons, he was wrong. Llywelyn took advantage of his father-in-law's troubles to extend his rule to most of Wales, all the territory to the west of the Marches. John reacted by invading Gwynedd, defeating Llywelyn beside the Menai Strait. Many of Llywelyn's lesser supporters deserted him, preferring to give their allegiance to a king who was sufficiently far away, they thought, not to interfere with their affairs. But that was not John's style. He built a castle at Aberystwyth, and the Welsh revolted. In 1215, Llywelyn captured Shrewsbury, an event which helped convince John that it would be worth making peace with his barons by signing Magna Carta (see page 238). Magna Carta declared that *Pura Wallia* (the wholly Welsh part of Wales) should be governed by Welsh laws, whereas Marcher laws should rule the Welsh Marches. Two years after John's death, when England was ruled by the child Henry III, Llywelyn's position as the Welsh overlord was consolidated by the Treaty of Worcester of 1218.

Wales prospered under Llywelyn. Trade grew, and new settlements were established. He maintained his power by establishing a feudal system similar to the one that existed in England. The feudal system was expressed, architecturally, in castles, and so the tower at Dolbadarn stands as a forlorn memory of this vision. Llywelyn's dominion did not long outlast his death in 1240. By now Henry III was a man intent on smashing the allegiances that Llywelyn had created. It would be left to his grandson, Llywelyn ap Gruffydd, the last Welsh Prince of Wales, to build them up again (see page 419).

FISHGUARD   PEMBROKESHIRE
Welsh heroine defeats French invasion

The last invasion of the British mainland took place in February 1797, when four French frigates anchored off Carregwastad Point, north of Fishguard, and landed 1,400 troops on the Strumble Peninsula. This was dramatic news for Lieutenant-Colonel Thomas Knox, commander of the Fishguard Fencibles, the local volunteer defence force, members of which rapidly left their fields and fishing boats and assembled in Fishguard Fort. Uncertain of the scale of the enemy landing, this small body waited until the following day when they united with the Yeomanry Cavalry under Lord Cawdor.

The French expedition was the last remaining element of what was intended as a full-scale assault on Ireland. Its leader, William Tate, a seventy-year-old veteran of the American Revolution with a pathological hatred of the English, had assured the Directoire (as the French legislature was then known) that the oppressed Welsh would rise up and join his army in attacking their rich lords and masters. The Paris authorities must have thought it was worth a try. The troops they gave him, however, were of the lowest quality, many of them convicts. It was strategically significant that a Portuguese merchantman had recently been wrecked off the Pembrokeshire coast. As a result, the cellars of the local houses were liberally stocked with port, which the invading thugs had no will to resist. Often drunk, they were beyond the control of their officers. After three days it was all over: French officers presented themselves at Lord Cawdor's headquarters, the house that is now the Royal Oak pub, and surrendered.

In the surrender negotiations, Cawdor managed to convince the French that they were heavily outnumbered. Legend has it that the French troops mistook the local Welsh women, with their black hats and red shawls, for guardsmen. If this is true, it would have strengthened Cawdor's hand. Certainly, there were some redoubtable women in the story: Jemima Nicholas became, in the words on her tombstone, 'the Welsh Heroine who boldly marched out to meet the French Invaders' and, apparently, captured twelve of them single-handed.

The name of the Royal Oak may have been taken from that of the prison hulk on which Tate was confined in Portsmouth harbour for a year, before being exchanged and sent back to France.

GOWER PENINSULA
First Area of Outstanding Natural Beauty

WEST GLAMORGAN

In 1956, the wonderful Gower Peninsula, a jigsaw of woodland and pine forest, sand dunes, rock pools and estuary, was designated as Britain's first Area of Outstanding Natural Beauty (AONB).

Pressure to protect Britain's most remarkable landscapes had been growing for half a century. The origins of the movement that caused it lay in the late 18th-century cult of the Picturesque, which attributed an aesthetic dimension to landscape, followed by the poetry of Wordsworth, whose inner being was shaped by the scenery of the Lake District. To the followers of Ruskin and William Morris, the rural landscape took on the prelapsarian quality of a world as yet unsullied by industrialisation. As life in the northern mill towns and mining villages became ever grittier, the desire to visit soul-refreshing country- side that was often visible beyond the chimneystacks of the factories became increasingly urgent.

This yearning was frustrated by landowners who wished to preserve their estates, especially their grouse moors, from outsiders. In the south, the advent of the motor car was accompanied by an uncontrolled orgy of development, with ribbons of semi-detached houses along the new arterial roads stretching out of London and the sort of unregulated development that was typified by Peacehaven in Sussex. The Ramblers' Association campaigned vociferously for access, and the Council for the Protection of Rural England for protection.

The National Parks and Access to the Countryside Act of 1949 was born as part of the Labour government's attempt to build a new world after the Second World War. As its name implies, the Act's purpose was partly to enable the public to visit beautiful areas by creating National Parks – ten of them originally, led by the Peak District, Lake District, Snowdonia and Dartmoor. Preservation was the second object. As well as National Parks, the act enabled the designation of smaller patches of exceptional landscape, where the emphasis would be more on habitat than recreation. There are now forty Areas of Outstanding Natural Beauty in England and Wales. Gower was presumably chosen to be the first of them because of the threat posed by its proximity to Swansea. While protection has paradoxically generated its own threat in the shape of tourism, the home of the Great Green Bush Cricket, the Bloody-Nosed Beetle and the Gorse Spider Mite, all of which live in the AONB, is secure.

HAWARDEN CASTLE
NEAR BUCKLEY, FLINTSHIRE

Bookish home of the Grand Old Man

On 19 May 1898, William Ewart Gladstone, four times Prime Minister, died at Hawarden Castle. It had been the seat of his wife Catherine's family, the Glynnes, and the Gladstones made it home for themselves and their eight children. According to a contemporary account, 'The villagers regard Mr Gladstone almost in the light of a patron saint, and speak proudly of his prowess as a woodchopper.' When not chopping wood, Gladstone would spend much of his time in the study that he called his 'temple of peace', located in a specially built tower. Of its three tables, one was assigned to his political work, one to his literary work and one was for his wife, who constantly helped him. This room alone contained 15,000 volumes. In 1889 Gladstone founded St Deiniol's Library in Hawarden, giving it 30,000 books for scholars to study.

Gladstone was a fully rounded British politician: an Englishman by birth with a Scottish constituency (in the election of 1880, he was returned as MP for Midlothian) and a Welsh home. With Disraeli (see page 223), Gladstone was one of the twin pillars of Victorian public life. He was a strong Chancellor of the Exchequer, holding that office four times; he saw finances as 'the stomach of the country, from which all other organs take their tone'. Unfortunately, he was less able with foreign affairs. He believed devolution was the best way to keep Ireland within the United Kingdom; however, his plans for that country, including a Land Purchase Bill that aimed to buy out the Anglo-Irish landowners, were deemed too radical.

Gladstone lost the General Election of 1888 but was returned to power for the fourth time in 1892. Aged eighty-five, he resigned in 1894 and retired to his beloved Hawarden.

IRFON BRIDGE BUILTH WELLS, POWYS

Death of the last Welsh Prince of Wales

On 11 December 1282 the last Welsh Prince of Wales, Llywelyn ap Gruffydd, grandson of Llywelyn the Great, died at the hand of an English soldier, and Edward I's conquest of Wales was complete. The early part of Llywelyn's career had been a success. He was a sufficiently formidable element in Henry III's war against Simon de Montfort for the King to recognise him as the Prince of Wales, although in return he demanded feudal homage and the payment of dues. For a period of some twenty years, Wales seemed about to become a united, independent nation. But Henry III's son, Edward I, discovered that Llywelyn had never presented himself to pay the required homage and the money never materialised. Increasingly frustrated, he led an army close to Llywelyn's power base of Snowdonia (see page 415) in 1277, where Llywelyn was forced to submit. This time he honoured the terms of the treaty.

But Llywelyn continued to harbour grievances. There were unresolved legal disputes, and he suffered what he considered to be a series of humiliations. At Easter 1282, his youngest brother Dafydd, who had supported Edward five years before, was expected as a guest at Roger Clifford's castle of Hawarden: instead he appeared on Palm Sunday and murdered his would-be host. Presumably Llywelyn knew of the uprising in advance; at all events, he felt compelled to support it. Edward, whose reign was spent on almost constant campaign on one or other of his kingdom's borders, quickly assembled a force to crush the insurrection. Initially, the Welsh won a striking victory in Anglesey, destroying an English detachment as it apparently retreated across a bridge of boats. They were also heartened by the demise of the powerful Marcher lord, Roger Mortimer.

Seeking to make the most of this opportunity, Llywelyn left his fastness of Snowdonia, not wanting to risk being trapped there as he had been in 1277, and began raiding English castles in Cardiganshire. As the year drew to an end, he marched for Builth Wells to forestall the English force that had been sent to deter him. While waiting for the castle at Builth to fall to his local supporters, he incautiously went without armour to inspect the bridge. He did not know that the castle had already been unsuccessfully attacked: now the English, having obtained intelligence from a captive they had taken, had secretly crossed the swollen Wye at a ford upstream, and were ready to surprise Llywelyn's army. Realising this, Llywelyn hurried after them, but was swept off his horse as it crossed the river. An English knight, seeing a lone figure without armour running from the bank, ran him through, without realising who it was he had killed. After the battle, if battle it can be called, Llywelyn's head was cut off.

THE BOAT HOUSE

'Down to the sloe black, slow, black, crow black fishing boat-bobbing sea'

In the spring of 1949, the poet Dylan Thomas and his wife Caitlin moved into a new home. It was called the Boat House, and overlooked the estuary of the river Taf at Laugharne; it was paid for by an admirer of Thomas's poetry. The financial arrangement, providing the Thomases with a secure base, suited the poet. He personified the dishevelled, chaotic genius, who liked to give the impression that he was permanently without money, whether or not this was strictly the case. Laugharne more than anywhere provided the setting for Thomas's most lasting work, the radio (later stage) play 'for voices' *Under Milk Wood*, originally called *Quite Early One Morning*.

Thomas was born in Swansea in 1914, the son of a schoolmaster. Brought up to love words, he had a poetic gift for the sound of language, using assonance, alliteration, onomatopoeia and other devices with an exuberance that seemed expressively Welsh. They were deployed to their full in one of the first poems that he wrote at Laugharne, 'Over Sir John's Hill'. It was, in part, the small-town Welshness of the place that appealed to him; he had known the village well before moving there. In breaks from writing, Thomas would lean out of the window of the Boat House, throwing bread to the waders on the estuary's shoreline below.

Thomas was too self-destructive a personality for the idyll to last. Caitlin resented his absences, while he was lionised in London and New York. After she left him, Thomas became even more vulnerable to the drinking that had always been part and parcel of his bohemianism. Before the age of forty he had drunk himself to death, dying in New York – after what may have been a carelessly administered dose of morphine – in 1953.

LLANRHAEADR-YM-MOCHNANT

William Morgan translates the Bible into Welsh

With his long white beard and penetrating eyes, William Morgan was the image of an Elizabethan divine. He was born in about 1540 in a stone farmhouse called Tŷ Mawr Wybrnant, in the wild Wybrnant valley near Betws-y-Coed. Morgan's parents were lesser gentry of good lineage, tenants of the Wynns of Gwydir. It was at Gwydir that he received his schooling from the local chaplain, who did a sufficiently good job to get him to Cambridge. Here he studied, among other subjects, ancient languages. Having been ordained, he acquired a number of Welsh livings, becoming vicar of Llanrhaeadr-ym-Mochnant.

It was while he was here, in the remote village set against the backdrop of the Berwyn mountains, and far from the libraries of Oxford and Cambridge, that he translated the Bible from the original Greek and Hebrew into Welsh. For Wales, Morgan's translation was as important as the later Authorised Version in England. While the Tudor dynasty, Welsh in origin, had brought Wales into the national fold by making the Welsh people full and equal subjects, the Acts of Union sought to cement unification by banning the use of Welsh for legal and official purposes. Not only did Morgan's Bible make the text comprehensible at a time when many Welsh people did not speak English, but it helped perpetuate the Welsh language in the face of governmental attempts at suppression. It was published in 1588 and superseded the Welsh New Testament translated by William Salesbury in 1567.

In 1595, William Morgan became Bishop of Llandaff, and later Bishop of St Asaph, now the smallest of the British cathedral cities. He died in 1604, and his body lies somewhere beneath the bishop's throne in St Asaph Cathedral. Outside the cathedral, established in the 6th century, its medieval architecture much restored by Sir (George) Gilbert Scott, stands a memorial to Morgan, Salesbury and other translators.

See also Cranmer's Tower, page 153

LLANYSTUMDWY
NEAR CRICCIETH, GWYNEDD

Village that shaped the Welsh wizard

In 1863, David Lloyd George – 'the most brilliant and picturesque Welshman since Glendower', according to an early biographer – was born in Manchester, where his father was teaching. On the death of his father the following year, the family – mother, David, sister and an as yet unborn brother – went to live at Highgate, the small terraced cottage rented by David's uncle, Richard Lloyd, at Llanystumdwy. Richard Lloyd was the village bootmaker: he was a high-minded, pensive man, who belonged to an extreme Baptist sect that did not believe in paid clergy, and therefore looked to the congregation itself for preachers. David's famous oratory first flowered in chapel.

Llanystumdwy, on the banks of the river Dwyfor and a couple of miles from the sea, is set among hills. David used to roam there as a boy, acquiring an abiding hatred of the landed class through what he took to be the repressive laws against poaching. At the age of seventeen, he left to join a solicitor's firm in Portmadoc. Politics quickly attracted him. In 1890 he was elected Liberal MP for Caernarfon Boroughs, and he soon established a reputation as a fearless speaker. As Chancellor of the Exchequer his 1910 budget, proposing to tax land to pay for social reforms and naval expansion, provoked a furious stand-off with the House of Lords (famously described by Lloyd George as 'a body of five hundred men chosen at random from amongst the unemployed'), whose powers to frustrate legislation were curbed by the Parliament Act the next year. From 1916 he was the coalition Prime Minister, popularly acclaimed after the Armistice for winning the First World War. He was re-elected at the head of another coalition government, but Irish independence, industrial unrest and the sale of honours tarnished his reputation.

At the end of his life, Lloyd George lived in a pretty farmhouse called Tŷ Newydd in Llanystumdwy; he died here in 1945. His body rests beneath a boulder at a favourite spot overlooking the river, in a setting designed by another 'Welsh wizard', the architect Clough Williams-Ellis. Williams-Ellis also designed the Lloyd George Museum, which was opened in 1960.

MACHYNLLETH   POWYS
Owain Glyndwr's parliament

'I can call spirits from the vasty deep,' announces Owen Glendower in Shakespeare's *Henry IV, Part I*. Whether or not Glyndwr possessed supernatural powers, he undoubtedly had a mysterious and charmed life.

Self-styled Prince of Wales, Glyndwr, like the Shakespearian character, was well educated, coming from a wealthy landowning family of princely descent and having studied law at Westminster. He was provoked to revolt in 1400 by his rival Lord Grey of Ruthin, who failed to summon him, as he should have done, to join Henry IV who was fighting in Scotland, and then called him a traitor for staying at home. With racial tensions high, and widespread economic grievance against the English crown and nobles, who were perceived to be exploiting their Welsh estates too harshly, conditions were in any case ripe for rebellion. Henry's expeditions to crush Glyndwr were defeated by heavy rain and the Welsh guerrilla tactics.

Before the Battle of Shrewsbury in 1403 (see page 341), Glyndwr had hoped to join forces with the Percys (see page 382), but a defeat at Carmarthen prevented him and the battle was lost. This did nothing to dent Glyndwr's power in Wales, though, and 1404 saw him at his zenith. The Machynlleth parliament of that year, not being a Welsh tradition, must have been inspired by the parliament at Westminster. (It cannot have taken place in the interesting town house called Owain Glyndwr's Parliament House, since that building dates from later in the 15th century.) Glyndwr captured the great castles of

Harlech and Aberystwyth, giving him unfettered control of central Wales. An alliance was formed with France, and an independent Wales seemed on the point of being born.

It was not to be. Glyndwr's star began to wane, and Henry of Monmouth (the future Henry V) won back Aberystwyth in 1408 and Harlech in 1409. Glyndwr returned to the role of guerrilla leader and finally disappeared from the stage altogether, in what might have been a puff of smoke. English writers said he starved in the mountains; alternatively, he may have lived out his old age with his daughters in Herefordshire. Or perhaps, as Welsh legend has it, he only vanished and, one day, will join battle once again.

MANORBIER CASTLE PEMBROKESHIRE
Early medieval Wales's Renaissance man

Of all Wales, wrote the 12th-century cleric Gerald of Wales in his *Itinerarium Cambriae*, the province of Demetia (south Wales and also known as Deheubarth) was the most beautiful; Penbroch was the finest part of Demetia, and the area surrounding Manorbier Castle the most beautiful corner of Penbroch. It is evident, therefore, that Manorbier is 'the sweetest spot in Wales'. Having followed Archbishop Baldwin of Canterbury through Wales on a preaching tour in 1188, raising money for the Third Crusade, he was in a better position than most other people of his age to know. Understandably, however, he was partial: Manorbier Castle, a little west of Tenby, was his birthplace.

Despite his epithet, Gerald of Wales – also known as Giraldus Cambrensis or Giraldus de Barri – was not exactly Welsh. The Marcher family into which he was born, in about 1146, was Norman. According to his own account, while his brothers made sand castles on the beach, he built sand cathedrals. It was easy to enter the church, since his uncle was Bishop of St David's. He studied in Paris, then the premier university in Europe. Thereafter he rose rapidly through the church hierarchy but never achieved the pinnacle of public life, ending his career as Archdeacon rather than Bishop. He was too original to be regarded as a comfortable appointment by the king: he was twice nominated to the see of St David's (1176 and 1198), but on both occasions was rejected on the grounds that he was Welsh, and might seek to separate the Church of Wales from Canterbury. Instead, he wrote prolifically*, leaving a remarkable legacy of manuscript books.

Gerald's *Itinerarium* and later *Descriptio Cambriae* provide us with a vivid picture of the country and its people, with their sparing meals and unusually good teeth (cleaned with green hazel and polished with pieces of woollen cloth). Interspersed with ecclesiastical subjects are Gerald's own observations of natural history, along with rumour, superstition and gossip. Personal opinions are never far from the surface.

Giraldus Cambrensis died in about 1223, and was buried in St David's Cathedral, in his beloved Pembrokeshire, just along the coast from where he was born.

*See Strata Florida Abbey, page 434

MENAI SUSPENSION BRIDGE ANGLESEY
Last link in Telford's great road

On 26 April 1826, crowds packed both sides of the Menai Strait, whose waters were crowded with boats. From the Caernarfon side, a raft carrying a massive 450ft-long chain was swung into the centre of the Strait, and positioned between two enormous towers. A fife band started to play; gangs of men strained at capstans; the spectators cheered as the chain slowly lifted free of the raft and swung into the air. A couple of hours later it hung between the towers. This operation was repeated another fifteen times over the coming weeks. The Menai Suspension Bridge was on its way to completion.

The Menai bridge was the last, essential link in the road between London and Holyhead in Anglesey, engineered by Thomas Telford. A packet boat was running from the new harbour at Holyhead to Howth in Ireland, providing an improved mail service between Ireland and mainland Britain. The state of British roads became a matter of concern in the stagecoach era. On the route to Holyhead, the road between London and Shrewsbury was controlled by no fewer than seventeen Turnpike Trusts, which earned enough from tolls to keep it in reasonable condition, but it deteriorated drastically once traffic fell away in sparsely populated Wales. Telford, 'the Colossus of Roads', as the poet Robert Southey called him, built his new carriageway on Roman principles – far stronger than the lighter, more flexible surfaces created cheaply by fellow Scot, John McAdam. It was a road for the age, since the scenery through which it passed was among the most ravishingly picturesque in Britain.

Thomas Telford (1757–1834), the son of an Eskdale shepherd, came to engineering through architecture, having started work as a journeyman mason at Somerset House. In time he would build a thousand bridges, culminating in the Menai Suspension Bridge and its sister at Conwy. Famous for his canals as well as roads, Telford was eventually derided for not seeing the potential of the railway. Instead, the engineer predicted that steam carriages, running on his roads, would be more successful. In 19th-century terms he was wrong; now, to judge from the traffic thundering along the A5, it seems he was more or less right.

CYFARTHFA CASTLE

The first railway engine

Outside Cyfarthfa Castle, once the home of an ironmaster, stands a replica of the first steam engine to haul a load on rails. The towering Cornish engineer Richard Trevithick – a giant of a man, who could fling a heavy sledgehammer over the roof of his engine house when he wanted to – designed the original for Samuel Homfray of the Penydarren Ironworks. Trevithick described the first run, which took place on 21 February 1804, in a letter to the Royal Society: 'We carried 10 tons of iron, five wagons, and seventy men riding on them the whole journey. It is above nine miles, which we performed in four hours and five minutes. We had to cut down some trees and remove some large rocks out of the road. The engine, while working, went nearly five miles per hour; no water was put into the boiler from the time we started until we arrived at our journey's end . . . We shall continue to work on the road, and shall take 40 tons the next journey.' The object was to take the iron to the Glamorganshire Canal via which it was shipped to Cardiff.

In his *Rural Rides* William Cobbett praised Merthyr Tydfil, then a rural parish, for its 'fairytale loveliness'. Now it was a boom town, well on the way to becoming the 'Vision of Hell' that Thomas Carlyle found it. There were four principal ironworks, employing a workforce of newcomers who, in miserable conditions, sometimes rioted (the Merthyr Rising of 1831 has been called the 'Welsh Peterloo'). By the Second World War, the industry had collapsed, and nothing remains of the Penydarren Ironworks. Enthusiasts, however, may still walk along the route of Trevithick's tramroad.

Cyfarthfa Castle was built, after Trevithick's day, by the Crawshays, whose Cyfarthfa Ironworks was the biggest in Merthyr Tydfil. Richard Crawshay doubted that Trevithick's invention would work, but nevertheless played a role in stimulating it: it was his domination of the local section of the Glamorganshire Canal that brought the rival tramroad into being. Trevithick did not grow rich from his inventions. As he wrote at the end of his life: 'I shall be satisfied by the great secret pleasure and laudable pride that I feel in my own breast from having been the instrument of bringing forward and maturing new principles and new arrangements of boundless value to my country.' Just as well. He was buried in a pauper's grave.

See also Shildon Station, page 400

MILFORD HAVEN

Landing place of Henry Tudor in search of a crown

On 7 August 1485, a handful of ships, 500 Englishmen, a French rabble about three times that size and Henry Tudor, Earl of Richmond landed at Mill Bay, on the north-west corner of Milford Haven. Today, as you look out from St Ann's Head, the promontory behind which the bay snuggles, the most conspicuous features on the opposite shore of the haven are the flaming towers of the oil refinery. Henry Tudor would have been conscious of Pembroke Castle, not far away; it was the seat of his uncle Jasper, Earl of Pembroke, and Henry is thought to have been born in one of its towers. The landing was not only unopposed but probably unseen by Richard III's forces, even though the King – who had marched north, to place himself strategically in the centre of the country, at Nottingham – must have had good warning that an invasion was imminent.

For the previous fourteen years, Henry had been sheltering in Brittany. It was largely thanks to his mother, Margaret Beaufort, a descendant of Edward III, and to Elizabeth Woodville, Edward IV's widow, that he came to be seen as an alternative monarch to Richard III. Elizabeth's support depended on Henry marrying her daughter, also Elizabeth, but the death of Richard III's queen, Anne Neville, in March 1485 raised the dreadful prospect of his marrying her instead. Henry acted decisively and, despite only modest French support, he assembled an invasion force. As Henry marched up the Welsh coast and then inland towards Shrewsbury, it was touch and go whether his support and numbers would swell. But they did. Rhys ap Thomas joined him at Newport, and in Leicestershire he received the ambiguous, although in the end crucial, support of the Stanleys.

Two weeks and a day after landing at Milford Haven, Henry defeated Richard III on Bosworth Field*; Richard's crown, rescued from the battlefield, was placed on Henry's head and he was proclaimed Henry VII.

*See Battle of Bosworth, page 309

MONMOUTH CASTLE

Birthplace of Henry V

It was appropriate that the future Henry V should, in 1387, have been born at Monmouth Castle. Although the town was not otherwise destined to play much part in his life, the archers who would bring him victory at Agincourt in 1415 came from this region, just as they had done for his great-grandfather, Edward III, at Crécy in 1346. The archers had learnt to draw the strings of their longbows back to their ear, a feat made possible, surely, by the suppleness of the Gwent yews or wild elms from which they were made. The longbows – with a shaft 5ft long – could shoot as far as 600ft and a proficient archer could fire ten flights a minute. The prowess of the Welsh bowmen had been famous as early as the 12th century. Richard II so admired them he had a bodyguard of Welsh archers. In all Wales, Gwent archers were the crack force of their time, and they dominated the battlefields for two hundred years from 1300.

Monmouth Castle was only one of many possessions belonging to Henry's grandfather John of Gaunt, Duke of Lancaster: his vast estates were mostly those of Simon de Montfort, which had been confiscated after the Battle of Evesham (see page 327) and bestowed on an ancestor of Gaunt's wife. Gaunt and his son, Henry Bolingbroke, Henry V's father, would always have been on the move between their castles. It may have been that Bolingbroke came to Monmouth to hunt in the Forest of Dean, bringing his seventeen-year-old wife, pretty Mary de Bohun, with him. It is known that he was not present when his son was born; there was an invasion scare, and he was away organising the forces to meet it on behalf of Richard II. The baby Henry was an important heir, but no one expected him to become king. It was only when Bolingbroke seized the throne as Henry IV in 1399, having deposed Richard II*, that he became Prince of Wales. Then Harry of Monmouth, as he was known, found that his birthplace had special resonance. Wales accepted him as one of its own.

Little of the old castle now survives, beyond the ruins of the tower and the great hall; most of it was swept away by the 3rd Marquess of Worcester (later 1st Duke of Beaufort) when he built his splendid Great Castle House in 1673 using some of the castle's old stones.

*See Pontefract Castle, page 397

SHIRE HALL, MONMOUTH MONMOUTHSHIRE
Scene of the biggest Chartist trial

In December 1839, Monmouth was appointed as the place of trial for the 125 Chartists who were arrested during the Newport rising earlier that year. Chartism – the demand for a People's Charter – was the crystallisation of working-class discontent, grounded for the most part in the industrial cities. It was a response to gruelling factory conditions, the high cost of food following the agricultural protectionism of the Corn Laws, and indirect taxation that bore most heavily on the poor. Somewhat naïvely, supporters believed that their woes would be remedied if all men had the vote. To quote the radical Chartist George Harney, speaking at Derby in 1839: 'We demand Universal Suffrage, because we believe the universal suffrage will bring universal happiness.' He looked back to a time when a musket hung in every English cottage, and beside it a flitch of bacon. No musket, no bacon, was his conclusion. But to the middle classes, 'Universal Suffrage in reality means nothing else but universal pillage,' was how the lawyer Archibald Alison expressed it in *Blackwood's Magazine*.

Life for the coal miners and foundry workers of the Welsh valleys was particularly harsh. They were therefore natural converts to Chartism. When one of their number, Henry Vincent, was arrested for making inflammatory speeches, between 3,000 and 5,000 people marched on Newport in protest. According to contemporary accounts, the majority of them were armed with homemade pikes, spears, guns, pickaxes, scythes and crowbars, and any law-abiding gentry whom they encountered were handled roughly.

Not unnaturally, the magistrates of Newport were alarmed and summoned all available police and special constables to them at the Westgate Hotel. When it was found that some of the specials were notorious Chartists themselves, they were arrested and held in the hotel; when the marchers arrived they shouted for their release. In the ensuing mêlée, twenty-four of them were killed. While the outcome of the battle had never been in doubt, there were nasty moments for some prominent Newport citizens, and the government feared that the example of these Physical Force Chartists (as opposed to Moral Force Chartists) would be copied elsewhere.

Inside Monmouth's 18th-century Shire Hall, faced with its clumsy statue of Henry V, the courtroom where the Chartist trial was held is little altered. Defendants were marched up a precipitous staircase from the cells, through a trap door and into the narrow box pew that served as the dock. There, three of them – John Frost, Zephaniah Williams and William Jones – were convicted of high treason and sentenced to be hanged, drawn and quartered. The medieval punishments reflected the funk of the governing class. On the recommendation of the Lord Chief Justice, the sentences were commuted to transportation for life. It was not, however, the end of Chartism, the first mass movement of the working class, which continued to frighten the ruling class with the spectre of revolution until 1850, although the repeal of the Corn Laws and other reforms drew its sting.

OFFA'S DYKE
FROM CHEPSTOW TO PRESTATYN

Legacy of the first King of the English

When the Romans left Britain in 410, England fell apart. Pagan invaders from Germany – the Angles, Saxons, Jutes and Frisians – pushed the indigenous Celtic population into remote and mountainous regions, such as Wales, and established a number of smaller kingdoms that continually bickered among themselves. In the 8th century, the most powerful of these kingdoms was Mercia in the Midlands. For over four decades – from 757 to 796 – it was ruled by King Offa. Brought to the throne by civil war, Offa went on fighting until he had dominated his neighbours, marrying daughters to the kings of Wessex and Northumbria on the way. As a result, he controlled all England south of the Humber and was the first Anglo-Saxon to be called 'King of the English'. On the new silver pennies which he introduced – a unit of currency that was to be standard for six hundred years – his head is shown with a diadem in his hair, in the manner of a Roman emperor. Offa aspired to rival the great Charlemagne, Holy Roman Emperor and King of the Franks. A marriage between their children was discussed. However, it came to nothing, and Offa went out of his way to ensure that later issues of his penny were a different size from Charlemagne's *denier*, and strictly forbade the use of the latter in his realm.

The scale on which Offa operated can be judged from his most substantial legacy, Offa's Dyke. At times, this earthwork is as much as 26ft high; with the ditch alongside it, it can be 65ft wide. It created an impressive demarcation line between Offa's kingdom and the land of the Welsh princes, running from the Severn Estuary near Chepstow in the south to the river Dee near Prestatyn on the north Welsh coast. Natural boundaries were used where they could be, but this still left a length of about 80 miles of dyke to construct. There are no written records associated with the dyke to tell how it was constructed or even what it was used for (whether simply for defence or, as now seems more likely, to mark the western boundary of the kingdom), but it is clear that Offa could mobilise an awesome number of men to build it.

Today, the line of the dyke can be followed by walking the Offa's Dyke Path, a national trail; the most impressive parts of the earthwork survive near Montgomery in Powys.

See also Hadrian's Wall, page 389

PEMBROKE CASTLE

The largest round keep in Britain

William Marshal achieved fame – and royal gratitude – as a knight errant. While leading the military household of Henry II's son, Prince Henry, 'the Young King', he not only acquired a dazzling reputation but also met most of the key magnates in France and England. On the death of the Prince in 1183, Marshal went on crusade with the Knights Templar (his effigy lies in the Temple Church, London, see page 188). Returning, he fought for Henry II against his rebellious children: they included the future Richard I, although Marshal was too valuable a figure against whom to harbour a grudge when

Richard became king in 1189. That same year, Marshal, the embodiment of medieval chivalry, married Isabel de Clare. He was forty-three, she was seventeen. The union had been arranged for him by Richard I in reward for loyalty to the Plantagenets. With Isabel, who was the heir to Richard de Clare, otherwise Strongbow, came the immense estates that were appropriate to a knight of Marshal's calibre but which, as a landless fourth son, he had always lacked. To defend them, he built Pembroke Castle.

After Richard I's death in 1199, the new king, John, created Marshal the Earl of Pembroke. However, John turned against him after Marshal paid homage to the French king in order to protect his lands in Normandy, rather than campaigning on behalf of John's cause. Royal disfavour fixed Marshal's thoughts on distant Pembrokeshire. He needed to keep the rising Welsh princes, such as the Lord Rhys (see page 414), in check. Rhys disrupted Marshal's first attempt to erect the castle by burning the building site. Marshal persevered, creating the area that now forms the inner ward; this includes the largest round keep in Britain, a strengthened gatehouse and a watergate to the vast natural cavern beneath the castle, known as the Wogan. Pembroke Castle was Marshal's launch pad for a personal invasion of Ireland, where he wished to secure the county of Leinster as part of his wife's inheritance. Marshal was eventually reconciled with King John. When John died in 1216, he was made Regent for the young Henry III.

PLAS NEWYDD   ANGLESEY
The charge of the Scots Greys at Waterloo

Preserved at Plas Newydd, on the shore of the Menai Strait, is the trouser leg cut from Lord Uxbridge, soon afterwards 1st Marquess of Anglesey, at the Battle of Waterloo and one of the articulated wooden legs that he wore thereafter. He is famous for leading perhaps the most devastating cavalry charge in British military history.

Coming from the Château de Hougoumont onto the ridge behind which most of the Allied forces were disposed at Waterloo, Uxbridge saw a mass of French infantry, supported by cavalry, march through the tall standing corn and sweep a Dutch brigade from the field. They seemed to be on the point of breaking the British centre and winning the battle. Already the British artillery gunners were abandoning their posts. He instantly launched a charge of 2,000 cavalry from the Household and Union Brigades, including the magnificent Scots Greys (see page 468). The effect was spectacular.

Previously hidden from view, the nineteen squadrons turned the French advance into chaos and in a few minutes seemed to have cleared the plain. Now it was the British who thought, mistakenly, the battle was won, but the inevitable happened: the heady exhilaration of the charge made it unstoppable, and when the exhausted horses turned to make their way back to their own lines, they were cut to pieces by Napoleon's Polish lancers.

Later in the battle, Lord Uxbridge urged on the remaining cavalry units to repulse the continuous waves of Marshal Ney's *cuirassiers* as they attempted to break the squares of British infantry. Eight of nine horses were shot from under him. As Wellington's second-in-command, as well as Allied cavalry commander, he had been anxious as to what might happen if Wellington were killed or disabled, since he had little idea about his leader's plans. In the event, it was Anglesey who, in the closing phase of the battle, was struck. Grapeshot shattered his right knee.

Wellington, to whom he had been talking, supported him, to stop him falling from the saddle. According to a popular account, Uxbridge is supposed to have cried: 'By God, sir, I've lost my leg!' To which Wellington, momentarily removing his spy-glass from his eye, replied, 'By God, sir, so you have!' Observers were awed by his sang-froid during the amputation. 'I have had a pretty long run,' he joked. 'I have been a beau these forty-seven years and it would not be fair to cut the young men out any longer.'

When the Prince Regent made the hero a Marquess, he took his title from the island on which Plas Newydd is set. He was rarely there, however, preferring to use Beaudesert in Staffordshire as his country house: he either let or shut up Plas Newydd in an attempt to recover from his father's financial imprudence. Nevertheless, the people of Anglesey and Caernarfonshire claimed him as their own, erecting a handsome stone column 'in grateful commemoration of the distinguished military achievements of their country-man' in 1817. It was surmounted by a statue in 1860.

POWIS CASTLE
NEAR WELSHPOOL, POWYS

The legacy of Robert Clive

The military genius of Robert Clive established British rule in India, driving out the French and subduing local rulers. After the Battle of Plassey in 1757, the new nawab whom he installed in Bengal gave him £260,000 and a pension of £27,000 a year. These were fabulous sums. As a souvenir of the battle, Clive kept the palanquin (a litter carried on the shoulders) of the old nawab and sent it home to England, where it can now be seen, along with other Indian artefacts that he collected, at Powis Castle. A painting by Benjamin West depicts, somewhat fancifully, Clive receiving the grant of the *diwani* (or right to collect taxes) from the Great Mogul – the coup that provided the British with their main source of revenue in India. Needless to say, it made him richer still.

Clive had grown up in Shropshire. He joined the East India Company as a clerk at the age of seventeen, but soon transferred into its army. On returning from India, he bought land in Shropshire, as well as building a country house and garden, Claremont House at Esher in Surrey. With the governor of the East India Company, Warren Hastings, he was savagely criticised in parliament for the wealth he had amassed in India – to which he replied that, in comparison to the treasures that had been laid at his feet after Plassey, his self-enrichment had been moderate. However, the censure seems to have exacerbated a tendency to depression, perhaps made worse by the climate of India. In 1774, when only forty-nine, Clive is assumed to have committed suicide by taking an overdose of laudanum at his home in Berkeley Square.

The Clives' son Edward married Henrietta Herbert, the Earl of Powis's daughter who became, on the death of her brother, his heir. Thus Edward Clive, who in time assumed the earldom of Powis, acquired the social position that his 'nabob' father never achieved, along with one of Britain's most magnificent castles.

ST DAVID'S CATHEDRAL PEMBROKESHIRE
Inspiration of Christianity in Wales

St David, patron saint of Wales, was an ascetic monk in the Celtic tradition. He would stand for hours in cold water in order to mortify the flesh; probably for this reason he became known as David the Waterman. At the end of the 6th century, he founded a monastery in a wild Pembrokeshire valley near his birthplace. The monks lived meagrely on bread and herbs. However, this distant tip of Pembrokeshire was not as remote then as it might seem today. Water, not roads, provided the best means of transport, and ships would pass the peninsula on their way to Ireland. As a result, visitors started flocking here, attracted by St David's reputation for holiness. In time, pilgrims, venerating his remains, replaced them. The present St David's Cathedral grew up where the monastic church had been.

Nothing survives from St David's time; the cathedral was rebuilt by the Normans, then remodelled by the energetic 14th-century Bishop Henry de Gower. He also built the sumptuous Bishop's Palace, with dual sets of apartments for domestic and ceremonial use – the days of the self-denying rigours of St David were long gone. Since the community lived under constant fear of attack, a protective wall was built around the cathedral and palace; this could only be entered via four strong gateways. Nevertheless, as visitors coming from the town emerge through the fortified gateway that is roughly at the level of the cathedral roof, and see the whole complex set below them, rather as though they had temporarily been transformed into birds, they can hardly fail to be moved by the spirit of the place. 'Brothers and sisters,' St David is supposed to have said as he died, 'be joyful and keep the faith and do the little things which you heard and saw with me.'

ST MARY'S CHURCH TENBY, PEMBROKESHIRE
Inventor of the equals sign

Robert Recorde was born in Tenby about 1510; some 400 years later, a bust of him was erected in the church there – the only memorial to a man who would have a daily influence on the lives of all children and many adults. It was Recorde who invented the equals sign in mathematics. In *The Whetstone of Witte*, published in 1557, he explained his thinking: 'To avoide the tediouse repetition of these woordes: is equalle to: I will settle as I doe often in woorke use, a paire of paralleles, or Gemowe [twin] lines of one lengthe, thus: $=\!=\!=$ bicause noe .2. thynges, can be moare equalle.'

Recorde was anxious to make mathematics as comprehensible to his compatriots as possible. *The Whetstone of Witte* is one of several textbooks that he wrote in plain English, rather than Latin or Greek. (Even so, he embedded a Latin pun in its title, since cos, a contemporary term for algebra, is the Latin word for whetstone.)

Recorde left Tenby to study at both Oxford and Cambridge, after which he practised medicine in London. He was known at Court, and was appointed controller of the Bristol Mint. In this role he fell out with Sir William Herbert, soon to be created Earl of Pembroke, who sought money from the mint to be channelled to his army in the West Country, where he was suppressing rebels. Recorde was confined to Court for sixty days, but climbed back into favour, being given what turned out to be a thankless commission to oversee Edward VI's silver mines in Ireland.

In Queen Mary's reign he made the spectacular misjudgement of suing his old enemy, the Earl of Pembroke, for misconduct. By now, however, Pembroke was leading Mary's army against the Protestants, and crushed Recorde with a counter suit for libel, the damages for which cost Recorde £1,000. Unable to pay this great sum, he died in a debtor's prison in 1558.

It may have been that Recorde the man lacked the understanding of human psychology that would have steered him through the whirlpools and rapids of Tudor politics, but as a scholar he established the teaching of mathematics in England, as well as introducing algebra.

STRATA FLORIDA ABBEY

The 'Welsh Westminster Abbey'

Strata Florida Abbey, set in the hilly green dampness of remote west central Wales, has been called, a little extravagantly, the 'Welsh Westminster Abbey' since here lie the remains of no fewer than nine princes of the southern Welsh kingdom of Deheubarth. The Abbey, which was founded in 1164 by Robert fitz Stephen, belonged to the Cistercian Order, which was usually associated with the Anglo-Norman enemies of the native Welsh. However, the following year, the Lord Rhys (see page 414) seized fitz Stephen's estates, and took over the patronage of Strata Florida. This abbey dates from 1184 when it moved to its present position. The Lord Rhys, with his warm nature and cultivated disposition, was a generous benefactor to the Church; he founded Talley Abbey not far away in Carmarthenshire.

Strata Florida became a centre of Welsh culture. Here it was that the scholar and traveller Gerald of Wales, Giraldus Cambrensis, established his library (see page 423), that *Brut y Tywysogion*, the national annals of Wales, were written, and that monks copied the chronicles and poetry that were the foundation of Welsh literature. It was also the reputed burial place of the 14th-century poet Dafydd ap Gwilym. Henry IV expelled the monks during Owain Glyndwr's rebellion (see page 422) and billeted his soldiers there instead. Henry VIII dissolved the monastery in 1539, and its stone was pillaged by the locals for their own farms and houses.

Little now survives of the abbey buildings beyond the west doorway, composed of six rolls of masonry joined together by bands. This stylistic oddity has been associated with the masons of the Deheubarth court.

TINTERN ABBEY

The most celebrated of Picturesque ruins

To the 18th-century sensibility, the Wye Valley was the home-grown equivalent of the romantic landscapes of Italy, experienced by noblemen on the Grand Tour. Artists, writers and tourists took the boat from Ross-on-Wye to Chepstow, and seemed to see a succession of pictures unfold before them. This was not how prehistoric man, secure in his hill forts, or the castle-builders of the Middle Ages, would have valued the landscape. To them, the high cliffs and panoramic views were seen in terms of defence. The change was heralded around 1700, when John Kyrle created his Prospect Gardens in Ross-on-Wye, simply to take in the sight of the Wye winding across the plain. In 1770, the Rev. William Gilpin made a sketching tour that later formed the basis of his *Observations on the River Wye*. Here he wrote that 'the whole is such a display of picturesque scenery it is beyond any commendation'. Of all the ruins and vantages points that Gilpin and his followers admired, Tintern Abbey was the most celebrated.

Close by the river, Tintern was a Cistercian monastery, founded by Walter de Clare in 1131 and rebuilt in the seventy or so years following 1269. It was the richest abbey in Wales at the time of the Dissolution in 1536 (see page 133). Today, the ruin is remarkable for its completeness, especially the window tracery. It was rather too complete for Gilpin, who thought it would, from a Picturesque point of view, have benefited from greater dilapidation. That did not deter J. M. W. Turner and many other artists from making it a subject; there are sixteen views by Turner in Tate Britain alone. In 1798, William Wordsworth (see page 359) offered his own perspective on the Picturesque with his poem 'Lines composed a few miles above Tintern Abbey'.

Such responses encouraged a cult of visiting the Wye Valley. Like other tourists, Picturesque travellers saw only what they wanted to see: they generally ignored the commercial boat traffic on the Wye, along with the abject condition of the labourers' cottages around the abbey. Tintern retained its appeal into the romantic era. One night in 1883, about 600 people came from Gloucester and Cheltenham to see it in the moonlight.

WHITLAND
NEAR ST CLEARS, CARMARTHENSHIRE

Hywel the Good gives laws to Wales

Whitland is not the most obviously historic of Pembrokeshire villages; little remains of the Cistercian abbey, which lies some miles to the north. Few other places, however, are as resonant in Welsh history, for it was here in about 930 that the great ruler Hywel Dda (Hywel the Good) called together an assembly of learned men, to give Wales its first written laws. Not only did they serve as the foundation of the Welsh legal system, remaining extant for several centuries, but provided a unifying force to a land often fought over by local rulers. They did more than anything to promote a sense of Welsh identity as a nation in the Middle Ages.

After inheriting the small western kingdom of Seisyllwg around 900, Hywel had himself united most of Wales. He did so by the traditional means of strength and guile, perhaps murdering his brother-in-law in order to annex Dyfed. Successful 10th-century rulers were necessarily ruthless. Nevertheless, Hywel was also well travelled, having made a pilgrimage to Rome, and may have been inspired by Alfred the Great's example in law-making. In any case, now that he ruled several historically separate kingdoms, some legal stan- dardisation was needed. Hywel's laws were really the codification of existing practices. Unlike the English system, his laws were concerned less with the punishment of crime than the promotion of good relations between tribal groups. They also acknowledged, to some extent, the rights of women and children, and accommodated various types of union between men and women other than marriage blessed by the church. Illegitimate sons needed only their father's acknowledgement to inherit.

Hywel avoided conflict with England by accepting Athelstan, grandson of Alfred the Great, as feudal overlord. After Hywel's death in 950, however, his kingdom broke down into its constituent parts. These smaller kingdoms were larger units than had once been the case, but they were once more at each other's throats until the appearance of Llywelyn the Great (see page 415).

Scotland

SCOTLAND IS ALL LANDMARKS. It is other things, too – lochs and glens, tower houses and classical terraces, stags and golden eagles, to name a few. But above all these is Scotland's sense of history, which at times has become so deeply embedded in myth that it is almost impossible to disinter. Mary Queen of Scots and Bonnie Prince Charlie dazzle. Bannockburn, fought nearly seven hundred years ago, continues to resonate in Scottish breasts, as do the Highland Clearances of the 19th century. The 'Butcher of Culloden', otherwise the Duke of Cumberland, is reviled as a Hanoverian ogre. Robert Burns's birthplace is a shrine. When Sir Walter Scott – the writer who did more than anyone to shape Scotland's self-image – rediscovered the Scottish crown jewels, or Honours of Scotland, in Edinburgh Castle, this exercise in self-publicity quickly became a legend.

Dunfermline Abbey became the royal shrine of Scottish kings, although Robert the Bruce's heart rests in Melrose Abbey. From the scriptorium of Arbroath Abbey emerged Scotland's Declaration of Independence. John Knox thundered from the pulpit of St Giles's Cathedral in Edinburgh. At the House of the Binns are a pair of boots in which, it is said, water would boil if poured into them; they were worn by 'Bluidy' Tam Dalziel, the scourge of the Covenanters. Even Scotland's more peaceable landmarks take on a vivid hue. The life journey that Andrew Carnegie made from his birthplace in Dunfermline to Skibo Castle, dispensing libraries and philanthropy on the way, still inspires wonder. Charles Rennie Mackintosh's Glasgow School of Art has a worldwide following; even the café where J. K. Rowling invented Harry Potter has become a required stop on Edinburgh's tourist trail.

On one of Scotland's watery extremities is Skara Brae on Orkney, the oldest village in Britain, and nearby the mysterious Neolithic chamber of Maes Howe, whose walls were later marked with Viking graffiti. From St Ninian in his fastness at Whithorn to St Columba's Iona, from the shadowy Picts to the towering North Sea oil rigs queuing for repair in the Cromarty Firth, from malt whisky to Peter Pan, Scotland's landmarks radiate national pride.

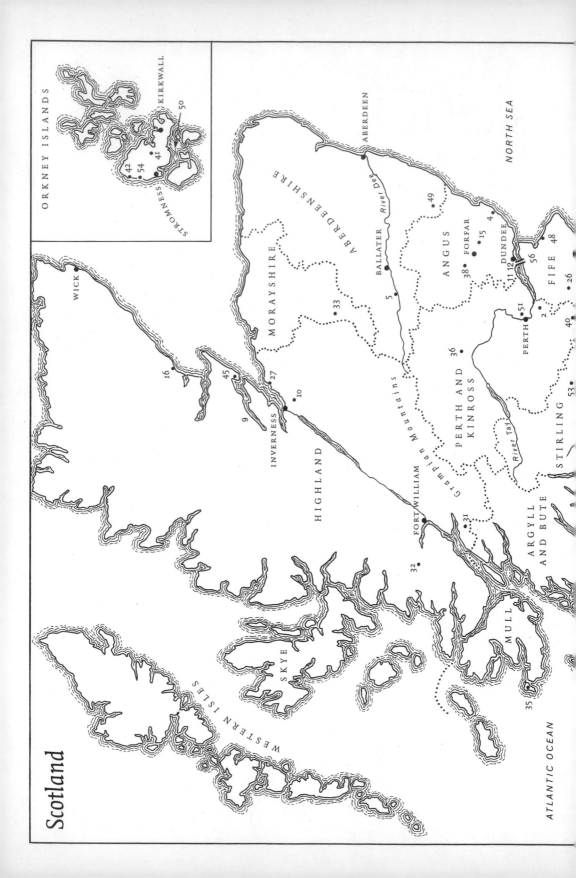

Scotland

ORKNEY ISLANDS

KIRKWALL
50
41
42 54
STROMNESS

WICK

NORTH SEA

ABERDEEN

ABERDEENSHIRE

River Dee

BALLATER

MORAYSHIRE

33

5

49

ANGUS

FORFAR
15
4
38
DUNDEE
11 12
56
48
FIFE
26

51
PERTH
2
40

16

45

27

10

INVERNESS

9

HIGHLAND

Grampian Mountains

PERTH AND
KINROSS

36

River Tay

STIRLING

53

FORT WILLIAM

31

32

MULL

SKYE

ARGYLL
AND BUTE

WESTERN ISLES

35

ATLANTIC OCEAN

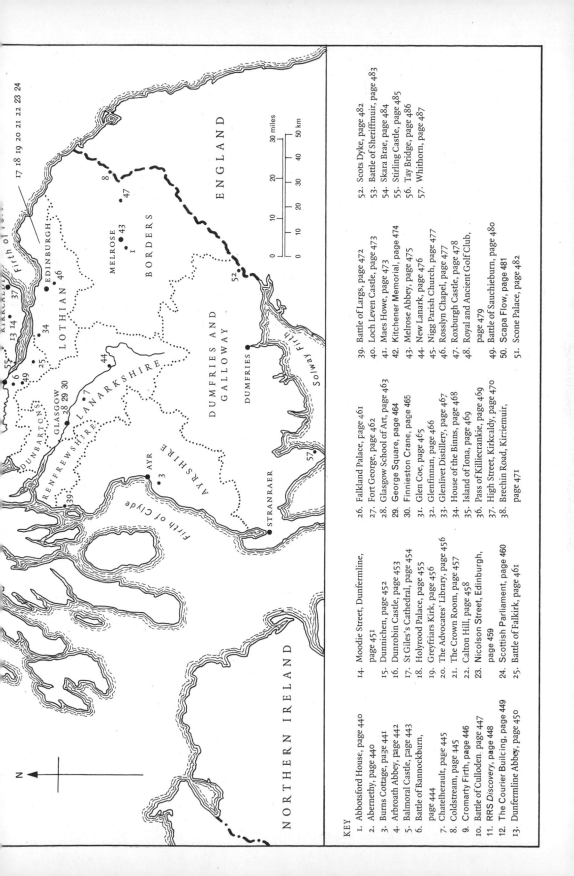

N

NORTHERN IRELAND

ENGLAND

BORDERS

DUMFRIES AND GALLOWAY

AYRSHIRE

LANARKSHIRE

RENFREWSHIRE

DUNBARTONS

GLASGOW

LOTHIAN

MELROSE

Firth of Clyde

Solway Firth

Firth of Forth

EDINBURGH

DUMFRIES

AYR

STRANRAER

17 18 19 20 21 22 23 24

13 14

37

25 34

6

19

28 29 30

7

44

3

39

1

43

46

8

47

52

57

0   10   20   30 miles

0   10   20   30   40   50 km

ABBOTSFORD HOUSE

Where the 'Waverley' novels were written

In 1814 Sir Walter Scott published his first novel, *Waverley*. Two years before, he and his family had moved into Abbotsford, then merely a farmhouse but now on the way to becoming one of the first Baronial Revival mansions of the 19th century. Scott, the son of an Edinburgh lawyer, had already published the poems *The Lay of the Last Minstrel* and *The Lady of the Lake*. The money brought in by the phenomenally successful 'Waverley' novels would enable him to create the three-dimensional equivalent of the world of his fiction.

The interior of the house breathes romance. Like Horace Walpole at Strawberry Hill (see page 243), Scott surrounded himself with objects that told stories. As well as 9,000 rare books, the Library contains a lock of Bonnie Prince Charlie's hair, Robert Burns's tumbler (Scott met him once; the glass has verses scratched on it) and Rob Roy's purse. Elsewhere can be seen James VI's hunting bottle and Bonnie Dundee's pistol (see page 470). Swords and breastplates speak of the courage that brought men to battle long ago; stained glass enriches the mood of antiquity. Scott also enjoyed objects that evoked the history of the Borders countryside in which Abbotsford is set, and which he explored constantly.

In Scott's novels, readers became engaged in the lives of both ordinary and great figures similarly affected by the grand workings of history. His personal history was itself dramatic. In 1825, a time of economic recession, his publisher Archibald Constable, the publishing business John Ballantyne & Co., which Scott himself established, and James Ballantyne's printing business, in which Scott was partner and principal shareholder, all went bankrupt. Scott was ruined. Nobly he strove to pay off his creditors, but wrecked his health in the process. He died at Abbotsford in 1832.

ABERNETHY

The Norman Conquest remains an English affair

The round tower at Abernethy looks something like a factory chimney, being very tall and thin. To the local population, particularly the Celtic missionaries who brought Christianity to southern Scotland, it could have served various uses – bell tower, look-out post and refuge. While there are over seventy such towers in Ireland, Abernethy is one of only two to survive in Scotland, the other being at Brechin. Nobody quite knows when it was built, but it was probably in existence by the time that William the Conqueror visited the town – now little more than a village – in 1072. If so, it could well have been the site of the meeting that William held at Abernethy with King Malcolm III, called Canmore, of Scotland.

William, at the head of a large army, crossed the Border after a series of raids that Malcolm had made into the north of England – a sport which he manifestly enjoyed. Although it was Malcolm who, *pace* Shakespeare, took the throne from Macbeth (not such a bad king as he was painted), he was a wild heathen by Saxon, let alone Norman standards. Nevertheless, he had married the pretender to the English throne Edgar the Atheling's sister Margaret, and the union made Malcolm doubly dangerous to William.

A few miles south of the river Tay, before it widens into the Firth of Tay, Abernethy marked the ultimate northern limit of William's military campaign, and symbolised the extent of his conquest. Malcolm, rather than fight an overwhelmingly more powerful enemy, agreed to be William's man so that, in theory at least, Scotland as well as England came under the Norman's control. The Treaty of Abernethy, while not defining the border between England and Scotland, ensured a degree of quiet on the northern front.

BURNS COTTAGE
ALLOWAY, AYRSHIRE

Birthplace of Rantin', Rovin' Robin

Robert Burns's birthplace is Scotland's greatest literary shrine. The poet's father, William, built it out of rammed earth in 1757. He was a gardener who had come to the area from Kincardineshire and married a local girl. Robert was born in 1759, in the cottage's one room, which served for cooking, eating, reading, spinning, cheese making and sleeping. Next door, as in any 'but and ben' cottage, lived the animals, whose presence contributed to the heating. The young children slept first in a pull-out cot and, when they were older, on a platform above the parental bed.

Although his market garden failed and he was forever in financial difficulties, William Burns was a literate man, who read the Bible to his children and paid great attention to their education. From his scant income, he contributed to the cost of hiring a young schoolmaster, John Murdoch, and later sent Robert to board briefly with Murdoch at the grammar school in nearby Ayr. Another influence was an elderly cousin who came to help out in the house: Betty Davidson was a superstitious woman with a limitless number of tales about 'devils, ghosts, fairies, brownies, witches, warlocks, spunkies, kelpies, elf candles, dead-lights, wraiths, apparitions, cantraips, giants, in-chanted towers, dragons and other trumpery'.

Shortly after Robert's birth, a gable end of the 'auld clay biggin' collapsed. This dramatic moment in the family story is recalled in the poem written for his own birthday, 'Rantin' Rovin' Robin'. Local landmarks, such as Alloway's haunted kirk and the bridge over the river Doon, often feature in the poems, which were written in Ayrshire dialect. Burns grew up in a rural world, with its round of manual work, religion, lasses, drinking and friendship: it was one he never left. His earliest impressions, formed at the cottage of his birth, would have been reinforced by those at nearby Mount Oliphant, to which the family moved when he was eight. The intellectual conversation in which Burns could participate as a young man is vividly evoked in the Bachelors' Club at Tarbolton, an alehouse where Burns and his friends would meet once a month to debate knotty questions.

ARBROATH ABBEY
ANGUS

Rallying cry of Scottish nationhood

In 1320, Abbot Bernard de Linton settled himself in the scriptorium of Arbroath Abbey and drafted what would become the most famous document in Scottish history, the Declaration of Arbroath, or Declaration of Independence. Like other grand statements of belief – for example, the American Declaration of Independence – it was drawn up to meet a specific historical emergency, but the need provoked thought that would have an application long after the exigencies which caused it had passed.

Abbot Bernard, who was also Chancellor of Scotland, had taken it upon himself to argue the Scottish cause with Pope John XXII. Although King Robert I, known as Robert the Bruce, had comprehensively defeated Edward II at Bannockburn*, he remained in excommunication, having come to power by murdering John Comyn in a kirk. As a result, the Pope sided with England. Writing on behalf of all the Scottish nobles, Abbot Bernard set out the case for Scotland being considered an independent nation, declaring (in Latin): 'It is in truth not for glory, nor riches, nor honours that we are fighting, but for freedom – for that alone, which no honest man gives up but with life itself.' Noble sentiments indeed. Cynics have suggested that they may have been produced to justify a continuing war with a neighbour, when all Christian countries were supposed to be focused on the Crusades.

Constitutional historians have been intrigued by the Abbot's corollary. If Robert the Bruce were to betray the cause and submit to the English king, the nobles would feel no compunction in replacing him with someone else. In practice, the likelihood of this happening may have been remote, but it appears to have promoted a new idea – namely that a monarch only governs by consent.

It took a while, but eventually the Pope recognised Robert the Bruce as King of an independent Scotland. Whether or not it was Abbot Bernard's eloquence that won him over, the stirring words of the Declaration have proved as robust as the red sandstone abbey in which they were written, still sturdily resisting the ravages of the sea wind.

*See Battle of Bannockburn, page 444

BALMORAL CASTLE

Royal example creates the myth of the Highlands

When Queen Victoria first came to the Highlands in 1842, nearly a century had passed since the Jacobite rising of 1745. Six years later, she and Prince Albert leased the Balmoral estate, sight unseen, having heard good reports of it from her doctor, Sir James Clark. Four years later, Prince Albert bought it outright. The royal association with Deeside fuelled a new myth, based on the good-heartedness of the tough, down-to-earth people who lived in this sublimely rugged landscape. There was a little of Marie Antoinette playing at milkmaids about it. Here the royal couple could pretend that they were like other comfortably-off families, living, as the diarist Charles Greville wrote, 'not merely like private gentlefolks, but like very small gentlefolks, small house, small rooms, small establishment'. The Queen would come and go as she pleased, rejoicing in four-hour walks in the pure air. Prince Albert would shoot or stalk at every opportunity, then join his wife or busy himself about some project of building or estate improvement. They loved it.

As children multiplied, smallness came to seem less of a virtue. They decided to build a new castle, keeping the old one for their annual visits until the work was finished. The architect, William Smith of Aberdeen, could never be accused of having designed an over-pretty building, but it became an icon of the Highland revival, and despite the unyielding grey granite, looks more delicate in the flesh than in photographs.

After Prince Albert's death in 1861, the Queen spent increasingly more of her year here, breaking previous habits by returning in the spring after Albert's death to supervise the construction of the model dairy that he had begun. Devoted to the cult of her dead husband, she wreathed herself with the happy memories the castle perpetuated – in contrast to the hated associations of Windsor (see page 248), where he had died. Her increasing preference for the solitude of Balmoral over her other homes was the despair of her Prime Ministers, the 'airs of Deeside' being, in the well-chosen words of the guidebook, 'keener than those of the Thames Valley'.

The ritual of an annual Highland retreat remains a fixed point in the royal calendar. It is not thought that modern Prime Ministers view the place any more warmly.

See also Osborne House, page 81

BATTLE OF BANNOCKBURN
The English are driven out of Scotland

In 1306 Robert the Bruce became King of Scotland* after murdering a rival, John 'the Red' Comyn; to make it worse, the crime was committed in front of the high altar of a kirk. His reign began in civil war and disorganisation. Despite these unpromising beginnings, he proved himself to be a great guerrilla fighter. Eventually this secured his position, and at Bannockburn – which he would probably have preferred not to fight as a pitched battle – he achieved one of the most dramatic victories ever won on British soil.

Edward I regarded the Scottish king as his feudal vassal (see page 397). At the Battle of Falkirk (see page 461), he defeated William Wallace's attempt to assert independence, and in 1307 he was on his way north to confront the new threat from Robert the Bruce when he died at Carlisle. His son did not inherit his father's martial spirit, having no taste for yearly campaigns. By 1313, few Scottish strongholds were left in English hands, but the mighty, near-impregnable castle of Stirling was one of them. It, too, was under siege, the Scottish forces being led by Robert the Bruce's brother, Sir Edward Bruce. Sir Edward struck a chivalrous bargain with the keeper of the castle, Sir Philip Moubray, who agreed to surrender if the siege had not been raised by Midsummer's Day the next year. The prospect of losing Stirling was too much even for Edward II, and he raised an army of 20,000 men which assembled near Berwick-upon-Tweed on 10 June 1314. This great mass of men marched towards Stirling on 23 June – the day before Midsummer's Day. The King himself was the nominal commander. He no doubt expected the Scots force to be overawed.

Robert the Bruce's army was only a quarter the size of King Edward's. He had no knights in armour (the equivalent of modern tanks) and few archers. He had plenty of warning, however, that the English were coming and had chosen a position behind the Bannock stream from which to fight. Surrounding bogs and an unusually high spring tide on the Forth made the position more treacherous than it would have appeared to the approaching English army. In addition, Robert's men had buried spikes in the bogs to lame the English cavalry. Robert succeeded in driving the English van, undoubtedly troubled by the spikes, back across the burn; a force of some 500 English knights was also defeated by a Scottish schiltron or shield wall, a circle of men whose 12ft spears stuck out like the bristles of a hedgehog. These reverses must have demoralised the English, even though they had technically relieved the siege.

That night, the main body of the English army crossed the Bannock Burn to occupy a plain that was hemmed in with streams and ditches. They were unable to manoeuvre effectively: the knights had no room to charge. When

Robert the Bruce attacked, the battlefield was so crowded that the English archers could not fire without hitting their own side in the back. Edward II fled. Most of his soldiers were unable to get away, either dying in the burn that had been swollen by the tide or being cut down by the Scots.

Fourteen years later, when England was in confusion after Edward II's deposition and murder (see page 300), Robert the Bruce attacked England, forcing the government of Edward III to grant Scotland independence in the Treaty of Northampton. However, the death of Robert, leaving his infant son David II to be King, reopened the matter of the succession.

*See Arbroath Abbey, page 442

CHATELHERAULT NEAR HAMILTON, LANARKSHIRE
The grandest dog kennel in Britain

Chatelherault, built by the 5th Duke of Hamilton in the 1730s, survives as an opulent architectural witness to the aristocratic love of stag hunting and dogs. It takes the form of a grand gateway, stretched out along the crest of a hill: it provides not so much an entrance to the park as an heroic exit from the hunting field. Here the Duke had a banqueting hall decorated with a Rococo stuccowork ceiling depicting Bacchus and Ariadne, as well as stags' heads and other hunting trophies. The huntsman also had an apartment here, although it was understandably less elaborate. The hounds were quartered at the back. When William Adam, the architect, prepared a plate of the building for publication in *Vitruvius Scotius*, he labelled it, perhaps with a degree of humorous false modesty, as the Dogg Kennell.

Set on its ridge, its flamboyant skyline of finials and balls made a grand view-stopper from Hamilton Palace on the other side of the park. Hamilton Palace, as its name suggests, was one of the most splendid houses ever raised in Britain, filled as much with treasures as the Dukes were with family pride. The Palace was so comprehensively demolished in the 1920s following mining subsidence (coal having contributed to the Hamiltons' Victorian wealth) that not a stone now stands above ground, leaving only Chatelherault to recall its glories.

COLDSTREAM BERWICKSHIRE
The Restoration started here

On 1 January 1660 General George Monck led 7,000 troops out of the Border town of Coldstream, and headed for London. The son of an impecunious Devon squire, he had always been a soldier. During the Civil War, he had fought first for the King, then, after two years in the Tower of London, changed sides. In 1650, he helped Cromwell defeat the Scots, who supported Charles II, at the Battle of Dunbar. Three years later he applied his military skills to the sea, successfully fighting in a trade war against the Dutch as a naval commander. In the murky political waters that followed the Lord Protector's death in 1658, he manoeuvred himself into the position of commanding the army in Scotland, immediately arresting the many ultra-Protestant officers who were likely to oppose him. Having secured Edinburgh, he marched through the Borders and made his headquarters in what was then a thatched cottage at 12 Market Square, Coldstream. With him was the regiment that he had raised ten years earlier as 'Monck's Regiment of Foot'.

As Monck and his small army marched south, they gathered support. In London, Monck organised a new Parliament, which voted for the restoration of Charles II. Not a drop of blood had been spilt. For his services, Charles II created Monck Duke of Albemarle and head of the forces. Neither Monck nor his men forgot their none too comfortable days in Coldstream. From the many tales that they told of their considerable privations, they came to be known as Coldstreamers. They did not object to it. After Monck's death in 1670, his regiment formally acquired its name, worn with pride ever since, of the Coldstream Guards.

CROMARTY FIRTH HIGHLAND

Heroic adventure of North Sea oil

Dawn brought a bright morning over the North Sea on 17 September 1965. Forty-two miles out from Grimsby, the men on the drilling barge *Sea Gem*, used to all conditions, had been working throughout the night. Their drill bit had reached a depth of 8,500ft beneath the seabed. For twenty-one months, oil companies had been probing the geology below the North Sea, without result. But today something was different about the sludge disgorging from the top of the drill shaft. It was bubbling. The froth came from natural gas, similar to that from the huge reservoirs that had been found in the Dutch province of Groningen in 1959. Householders would soon begin the process of converting their cooking appliances to the new power source. In 1969, an even more valuable find was made: oil.

Until the 1960s, prospecting beneath the North Sea had been discouraged by uncertainty as to which countries owned the mineral rights. This was resolved by the United Nations Continental Shelf Convention. Furthermore, it was only when oil prices elsewhere in the world rose that the enormous investment in the technology needed to extract oil and gas in waters that can be more than 5,000ft deep came to seem viable. The rigs that were developed to achieve this feat have become a familiar, if still eerie sight in Cromarty Firth: they are as big as castles, and their immense rusty towers serve as legs, rather than look-outs. Out to sea, others can be glimpsed from the Caithness shore, shimmering like miniature Camelots when the sun catches them. The perils of working on the oil rigs was exposed when the Piper Alpha platform caught fire and exploded in 1988, killing 167 people.

Receipts from North Sea oil helped finance the restructuring of British industry during the 1980s. Aberdeen boomed. All good things come to an end, however: rigs are no longer built at Invergordon and Nigg, as the known, big oil fields start to run dry.

BATTLE OF CULLODEN NEAR INVERNESS, HIGHLAND
Savage end of Bonnie Prince Charlie's rebellion

For the Jacobites, the Battle of Culloden in 1746 was hopeless from the start, and reflected what had become the brave shambles of their cause. Its aftermath ended the Stuart dream of recapturing the British throne forever, and inflicted a generation of misery on the Highlands of Scotland. Yet the indomitability of Bonnie Prince Charlie*, hunted by the Hanoverian army over five months, became him better than his leadership during the battle, or the dissoluteness into which he sank during the exile in which he passed the remaining four decades of his life.

The previous autumn, his impromptu Highland army had seemed unstoppable; the capture of Derby caused panic in London, where the Bank of England was reduced to paying out in sixpences to prevent a run on its money. But the Prince had failed to attract new adherents as he marched south, and his commander, Lord George Murray, insisted on a retreat back to Scotland. Prince Charles hotly argued the case for striking at London, but found himself out-voted by his advisers, and reluctantly agreed to this prudent course. The clansmen were not prepared for a long campaign away from home. By the time the Jacobite army reached Glasgow, where the Prince had commandeered 6,000 blue bonnets, he found he had only two-thirds of his troops left to wear them. In February 1746, they took Inverness, previously occupied by the Prince's adversary, the Duke of Cumberland, third son of George II.

Cumberland, who had spent the winter drilling his troops in a manoeuvre that he believed would defeat the famous Highland charge, advanced on Inverness from Nairn. Bonnie Prince Charlie, determined to prove the military prowess that would help support his claim to the crown, took command of his army himself, rejecting Lord George Murray's suggested site. His choice, Drumossie Moor near Culloden House, was the sort of bare, open space that suited Cumberland's artillery and cavalry, but provided no downhill impetus for the Highland charge. In addition, the Prince's troops were poorly fed and tired: they had marched through the night, hoping to surprise Cumberland's men at Nairn, where they had been drinking the Duke's health on his 25th birthday, but delays meant that they did not arrive until dawn, and then had to trudge back to the Moor.

Cumberland's army, half as big again as the Highlanders, marched out in two disciplined lines, wheeling into position in a manoeuvre that took only ten minutes. They were supported by cavalry, and had field guns and mortars positioned in front of their line. As the Highlanders waited in the sleet, their ranks were cut to pieces by well-aimed shot. Cumberland also placed a detachment at right angles to the expected charge, providing a withering crossfire. Within half an hour, the battle was over. The Prince fled, telling his brave followers that each man should save himself as best he could.

The battle was followed by the disgraceful revenge that earned Cumberland his sobriquet of 'Butcher'. His men had been led, falsely, to believe that Bonnie Prince Charlie had ordered the Highlanders to give no quarter to government troops should they defeat them. Consequently, they set about slaughtering the wounded on the battlefield and even mutilating their bodies. The dragoons hacked down everyone that they came across, including women and babies. In the ensuing weeks, the remaining Scottish soldiers were hunted down with a brutality that would now be called genocide. In their plaids and bonnets, the Highlanders seemed a race apart from the soldiers pursuing them; from now until the romantic revivalism of Sir Walter Scott's novels (see page 440), their culture would be, as far as possible, extinguished. Bagpipes were declared instruments of war, and people could be hanged for playing them.

Culloden was the last battle fought on British soil.

*See Glenfinnan, page 466

RRS *DISCOVERY*

DUNDEE, ANGUS

Ship that took Scott to the Antarctic

They needed a wooden ship, and it had to have sails. In 1899, this was exceptional, because the age of wooden-walled sailing ships was over. But the National Antarctic Expedition, exploring the South Pole, would be taking magnetic records, which might be distorted by a metal hull, and the expected length of the expedition meant that the ship would not be able carry enough coal to fuel the steam boilers for more than auxiliary power. Captain Robert Falcon Scott, aged thirty-one, was put in charge of the expedition, leading ten officers and thirty-six other ranks. The Royal Research Ship, *Discovery*, specially constructed by the Dundee Shipbuilders Co., left England for New

Zealand in August 1901; on Christmas Eve, she left New Zealand for the ice floes around the Antarctic Circle.

As yet, no man had set foot on the South Pole. The purpose of the expedition was to collect scientific data, including information about wildlife and geology: a balloon named Eva was sent up so that photographs could be taken from altitude. From the ship, Scott launched two gruelling expeditions to conquer the South Pole, the first with dogs, who died in the exhausting conditions, the second with sledges pulled only by men. Neither succeeded. Meanwhile, the Discovery, which had become icebound, was forced to spend two dark winters in the Antarctic. Fortunately her reinforced hull proved strong enough to resist the pressure of the expanding ice. It was only in February 1904, as the prospect of a third winter drew near and it seemed that Discovery would have to be abandoned where it lay, that the ice broke up and Scott and his team were able to sail home to a hero's welcome.

In 1910, Scott set off again for the South Pole, this time aboard the whaling ship Terra Nova which had helped rescue Discovery. The team of five reached the Pole, only to discover that the Norwegian Roald Amundsen had preceded them by a month. Scott and his companions died on the return trek, their bodies being left to become entombed in accumulating snow and ice. They were recovered by a search party eight months later.

After an active life, Discovery fell into decay, but returned to Dundee in 1986, where she has been restored. She is now displayed as she would have appeared in 1925, undertaking another Antarctic expedition to research whales.

THE COURIER BUILDING

DUNDEE, ANGUS

Home of Dennis the Menace

Who would believe that the Edwardian façade of the Courier Building in Dundee – city of jute, jam and journalism – could be a front for such mayhem? The newspaper and magazine publishers D. C. Thomson was founded in 1905. While some of its journalists laboured to produce the Dundee Courier and Sunday Post newspapers and The People's Friend magazine, others on the staff were dedicated to creating the anarchic worlds of Korky the Cat, Desperate Dan and Minnie the Minx. These are just some of the characters from the Dandy and the Beano, which first appeared in 1937 and 1938 respectively; they are Britain's oldest comics still to be published.

The comic has its origin in illustrated stories published in the 19th century. Dickens remembered frightening himself with The Terrific Register, whose content, accompanied by a single, grisly picture, was designed to make the flesh creep. The first weekly magazine composed of light-hearted pictures, jokes and notes was Funny Folk (1874), but as yet the readership was adult. The genre began its descent down the age range, as well as down the social scale, with *Comic Cuts* in 1890. *Puck* (1904) and the *Rainbow* (1914) followed, comics aimed principally at children. They built on the success of *The Boy's Own Paper*, a high-minded magazine produced by the Religious Tract Society, whose readers devoured such writers as Jules Verne, Conan Doyle and G. A. Henty.

High-minded is not a term that could be applied to the David Couper Thomson stable of comics. Rather than just printing blocks of text below pictures in an attempt to encourage children to read, the *Dandy* and the *Beano*, smaller-sized than previous comics, began telling stories mainly through illustration. Where words were not necessary to the plot, they were left out. Children quickly saw the outlandish, catastrophe-prone world of the comic strip as an extension of their own lives. While Lord Snooty, in his Eton collar, left what had become a more egalitarian stage in 1990, Roger the Dodger and Dennis the Menace appear well-nigh immortal.

DUNFERMLINE ABBEY FIFE
Burial place of Scottish kings

David I was the third of his brothers to inherit the crown. Although brought up in England, he successfully exploited the civil war between Stephen and Matilda to seize a large part of the kingdom. Despite losing the Battle of the Standard to King Stephen in 1138, he succeeded in absorbing Northumbria into Scotland, pushing the Scottish border further south than it had ever been before or would be since. Perhaps to bolster his hold on the sparsely populated border country, he established Jedburgh and Melrose Abbeys (see page 475) on the southern verge of his kingdom – a location that was to prove perilous to later generations of monks, exposed to continuous cross-border raids by the English.

By contrast, Dunfermline, which David rebuilt on the north bank of the Forth, was safely within his own realm; there was nothing else like it in Scotland. The original Culdee or Celtic church had not only been the burial place of his parents, King Malcolm III Canmore (see page 440) and Queen Margaret, but they had also been married there.

Born in Hungary, Margaret was a granddaughter of Edmund Ironside, son of King Ethelred II, the Unready. When the Norman Conquest swept aside her brother Edgar's claim to the English throne, they both fled to Scotland, where she married Malcolm. The Scottish King and his Court spoke Gaelic. Queen Margaret regarded it as a barbarous language and never mastered it. Instead, she sought to bring some of the elegance and decorum associated with the Norman Court into the northern kingdom, introducing as she did a degree of somewhat unsaintly luxury in the shape of rich materials, tapestries and spiced meat. She inspired her husband to reform the church, banning Gaelic from use in services and attacking the lax ways of the clergy. She imported English monks to run the small priory she founded in Dunfermline in about 1072.

Margaret, however, did not care for this royal city in Fife, preferring Lothian, south of the Forth. Here she came to spend the last years of her life, in a royal hall on top of the steep rock called Dun-eideann. It was to form the site of Edinburgh Castle. Margaret died in Edinburgh in 1093, a few months after Malcolm was killed at Alnwick, leading yet another raid on Northumberland. She was canonised by Pope Innocent IV in 1251. With her refinement and propriety, she prefigured the tone that would be peculiarly associated with Edinburgh in later centuries.

King David I set about making the priory – later promoted to an abbey – into a shrine to the royal house. The first abbot, Geoffrey, came to Dunfermline from Canterbury in 1128, the year in which Bishop Flambard died at Durham. With building work at Durham Cathedral in abeyance, David seems to have been able to poach its masons: the round piers of the abbey church at Dunfermline, with their incised geometrical decoration, are similar to those at Durham. Not only was David himself buried here, but so also was his young grandson Malcolm IV who succeeded him (so chaste that he was known as the Maiden), and Robert the Bruce (reputedly without his heart, which was interred at Melrose Abbey). Altogether, Dunfermline Abbey became the burial place for eight Scottish kings, four queens, five princes and two princesses.

MOODIE STREET, DUNFERMLINE FIFE
Humble beginnings of a plutocrat turned philanthropist

The cottage in which the American steel boss Andrew Carnegie was born in 1835 should be seen in conjunction with Skibo Castle at Dornoch in Sutherland, the immense country house that he built in 1901, and now a hotel. No man in Britain has left such a vivid architectural picture of his life's journey.

Andrew was born in the little weaver's cottage in Moodie Street where the Carnegie family struggled to make ends meet during the early years of the boy's childhood. Living conditions were cramped: both downstairs rooms were occupied by looms, leaving only one small room for parents and two surviving children to live and sleep in. A hole in the floor allowed Andrew's mother to drop the bobbins she had wound down to her husband below.

Unfortunately for the family, weaving was changing. First came the Jacquard loom which, with patterns encoded on strips of punched card, did away with the need for master weavers who had until then kept patterns in their head. Next, the factory system did away with hand-looms* altogether. The new water- or steam-driven looms needed only a boy or a woman to supervise them. In 1848, the Carnegies decided to emigrate to the United States. But life proved little easier for them in Allegheny, Pennsylvania than in Dunfermline, particularly after Mr Carnegie's early death.

Andrew Carnegie rose by ability and ambition from his first job as a bobbin winder to being a telegraph operator. That set him on the path to becoming a railway magnate and finally the Steel King of America. He sold his Carnegie Steel Company in 1901 for $400 million, which made him one of the richest men in the world. He then began a career of philanthropy in which most of his fortune was given away. By the time of his death in 1919, over 2,500 towns throughout the English-speaking world had received a library endowed by Andrew Carnegie, and known as Carnegie Libraries. There were 660 in Britain and Ireland, and Dunfermline was – naturally – the first.

*See Cromford, page 315, and Hall i' th' Wood, page 362. See also Salford Museum, page 376

DUNNICHEN
NEAR FORFAR, ANGUS

The Picts keep Scotland for themselves

The Picts* were a mysterious people, and almost nothing is known of their history in the 7th century. However, one shining event penetrates this darkness: a battle that contemporaries in England and Ireland regarded as sufficiently important to record – as well they might have done, since it shaped the future of Scotland. It took place in 685 near the village of Dunnichen. For thirty years the aggressive, land-hungry Northumbrians had occupied the Lowlands that formed the southern half of the Pictish kingdom. King Ecgfrith of Northumbria now wanted to conquer the rest of Pictland, that which lay north of the river Tay. He had been advised against it by no less a figure than St Cuthbert. Nevertheless, he led the army himself, and crossed the Forth without opposition. He must have laughed at the saint's caution when, encountering the Pictish army in Angus, he saw it immediately retreating.

The Pictish King Bridei was setting a trap, however. The Northumbrians plunged on into what Bede called 'inaccessible mountains'. The Picts turned at a place called Duin Nechtain, or Nechtan's Mere, identified as present-day Dunnichen, where they were joined by reinforcements. Presumably the mere, or boggy lake, which was drained in the 19th century, played an important part in the strategy which, for the Picts, was triumphant. In the battle, Ecgfrith and most of his followers were slaughtered. The disaster that St Cuthbert feared, as he waited with Ecgfrith's queen at Carlisle, was complete. Never again did the Northumbrians occupy land north of the Forth. The territory that would become Scotland had been defined.

Top: The Old Lifeboat Station, page 398. The *Zetland*, the world's oldest surviving lifeboat, saved over 500 lives in her 78-year career.

Above: Kelham Island Museum, page 399. The Bessemer process was invented by Henry Bessemer in 1855; by 1900 the global output of steel had multiplied a thousandfold.

Wilberforce House, page 392. *The Kneeling Slave:* painted to further the abolition of slavery, a cause championed by William Wilberforce.

Shildon Station, page 400. The opening of the world's first public railway, the Stockton and Darlington, in 1825.

Hawarden Castle,
page 418. The Prime
Minister William
Ewart Gladstone at the
home in North Wales
that he loved so much.

Caerleon, page 411. Built outside the walls of the Roman fortress, this amphitheatre was where the legionaries were entertained.

Beaumaris Castle, page 410. Edward I built this magnificent castle after Magod ap Llywelyn had led a revolt in Anglesey during which the sheriff was hanged.

Manorbier Castle, page 423. This was 'the sweetest spot in Wales', according to Gerald of Wales, who was born here in the mid-12th century.

Gower Peninsula, page 417. Rhossili Bay, near Swansea, forms part of Britain's first Area of Outstanding Natural Beauty, designated in 1956.

St David's Cathedral, page 432. This holy building stands on the site where the 6th-century ascetic St David founded his monastery.

The Boat House, page 420. Overlooking the estuary of the river Taf at Laugharne, Dylan Thomas's home provided inspiration and imagery for his poetry.

Top: Menai Suspension Bridge, page 424. The last, essential link in the road between London and Holyhead in Anglesey, opened in 1826.

Above: Powis Castle, page 431. This painting by Benjamin West shows the Mogul Emperor granting Robert Clive the lucrative *diwani*, or right to collect taxes.

Top: Battle of Culloden, page 447. An elegant depiction of the Battle of Culloden that ended Jacobite hopes – in reality, a sordid slaughter.

Above: Abbotsford House, page 440. Sir Walter Scott, the novelist, expressed his love of Border history through his home.

Right: Burns Cottage, page 441. Robert Burns was born in 1759 in the humble cottage that has become Scotland's greatest literary shrine.

Below: Balmoral Castle, page 443. Especially after Prince Albert's death, Queen Victoria loved the solitude of Balmoral; she is shown here with the enigmatic John Brown.

St Giles's Cathedral, page 454. John Knox, the most influential churchman of his age, is shown preaching with customary vigour.

Calton Hill, page 458. The Greek Revival monuments on Calton Hill complemented Edinburgh's reputation as the Athens of the North.

Glasgow School of Art, page 463.
Charles Rennie Mackintosh's
masterpiece, with its attenuated lines
and simple use of wood, contrasts
with the rest of imperial Glasgow.

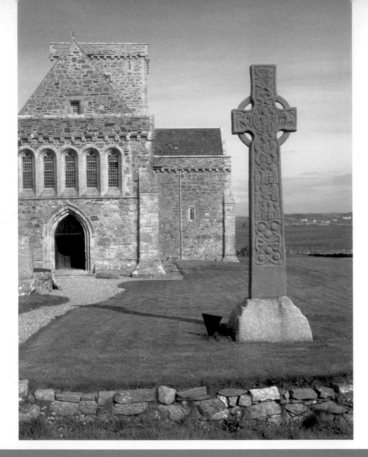

Island of Iona, page 469.
The inspiration of St Columba
produced an artistic tradition,
the pinnacle of which was the
8th-century Book of Kells.

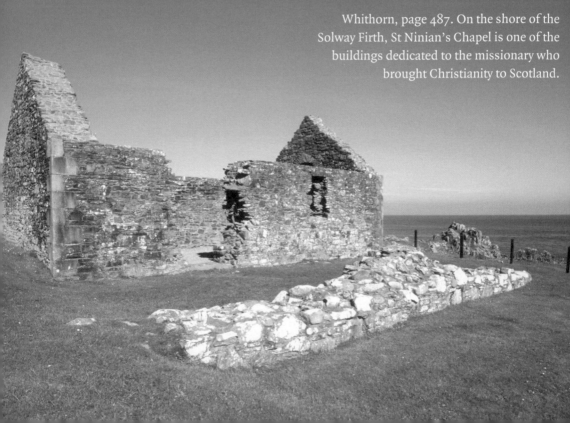

Whithorn, page 487. On the shore of the
Solway Firth, St Ninian's Chapel is one of the
buildings dedicated to the missionary who
brought Christianity to Scotland.

Glen Coe, page 465. The bleak landscape has changed little since the Campbells attempted to massacre the MacDonalds in 1692.

Above: Maes Howe, page 473. Vikings carved runes into the walls of this Neolithic burial chamber that they occupied in the 12th century.

Right: Abernethy, page 440. It is possible that William the Conqueror met Malcolm III of Scotland in this Pictish round tower.

Royal and Ancient Golf Club, page 479. The Royal and Ancient, founded in 1754, has become the most sacred of golf's institutions.

Tay Bridge, page 486. This model from a film set illustrates the disaster that overcame the Tay Bridge in 1879, which remains Britain's worst railway accident.

Kitchener Memorial, page 474. Lord Kitchener, the face on this famous recruiting poster, died when his ship struck a mine in Scapa Flow in 1916.

"YOUR COUNTRY NEEDS "YOU"

Scapa Flow, page 481. In June 1919, the German navy scuttled 52 of its ships interned in Scapa Flow, erroneously thinking that hostilities were about to recommence.

Scottish Parliament, page 460. The architectural embodiment of Devolution, with no expense spared.

A modern monument to the battle, erected on the 1300th anniversary, stands outside the church, along with a copy of an 8th-century Pictish stone that had been found locally.

*See Nigg Parish Church, page 477

DUNROBIN CASTLE
Infamous for its part in the Highland Clearances

On some days, Dunrobin looks like an enchanted fairy castle perched next to the sea, but when the mist comes in, enshrouding this coastline while the rest of Britain is bathed in sunshine, its towers and turrets can take on a demoniacal quality – and this is how many people metaphorically envisage it. Dunrobin was a show-off country house, engulfing a much more modest earlier castle and extended by the 2nd Duke of Sutherland to the designs of Charles Barry between 1835 and 1850. It is the architectural emblem of the Highland Clearances.

The Clearances are part of Scottish mythology. They resulted from the landowners' desire to 'improve' Highland agriculture which, until then, had been based on an unprofitable peasant system. To free up the land and replace people with sheep was more efficient. The Countess of Sutherland (only daughter of the 18th Earl of Sutherland who, after the Scottish custom, was able to inherit the title) made an advantageous marriage to George Granville, Lord Gower who was to become the richest man in Britain on the death of his father, the Marquis of Stafford, and his uncle, the Duke of Bridgwater. After inheriting from his father in 1803 (he was created Duke of Sutherland in his own right in 1833), he allowed her to pour money into her impoverished Highland estate, which ran to nearly a million acres. It was the practical, even philanthropic thing to do. She was moved by the destitution of the High-landers, who suffered frequently from famine, as well as a business-like desire to put the estate on a firm financial footing. The money was just in time since, not long before, her family had contemplated selling the estate.

Unfortunately, her schemes for the bettering the lot of her tenants – implemented after the leases fell in – did not take into account her tenants' resistance to being improved. She wanted them to move to specially built fishing villages on the coast; they wanted to stay where they had always lived, inland. She had thought they would move voluntarily, with gratitude; in the end, they had to be coerced, with the houses they had vacated being deliberately damaged to prevent them moving back in. The destitution that had existed in the old communities was simply relocated to the coast. Eventually many of the Countess's clansmen solved her problem by emigrating to America. Although the poor Countess was by no means perfect (tenants who did not join her regiment during the Napoleonic Wars felt the consequences), she did her best to rescue her crofters from the miserable conditions in which they lived. However, the Sutherlands have never been forgiven.

ST GILES'S CATHEDRAL
Echoes of the preaching of Knox

When John Knox preached in St Giles's Cathedral, it was as though he were about to 'ding that pulpit in blads' (break the pulpit into pieces) and fly out of it. He was the most influential churchman of his age, and perhaps of any age in Britain; he shaped the character of Scotland in ways that can still be felt today. Politically, he roused the populace against Mary Queen of Scots and her Frenchified, Roman Catholic and often scandalous behaviour, contributing to the pressures that forced her to flee to England (see page 473), leaving her own supporters and those who had taken possession of her infant son, James VI, to civil war.

By the time that Knox became minister at St Giles in 1559, he had lived through danger and exile for his extreme Protestant faith. Born about 1513, he had originally been ordained as a Roman Catholic priest, but his doubts about the Church took him to St Andrews University, where he came under the influence of the Protestant reformer George Wishart, who, according to Knox, 'excelled in all human science'. Wishart died at the stake for his beliefs. Knox was to endure persecution when James V's widow, Mary of Guise, then Regent of Scotland, condemned him to serve in the French galleys. The intervention of the English boy king Edward VI, himself a severe Protestant, won his release, and he became one of the chaplains at the English Court.

When Edward died at the age of sixteen, he was succeeded by the Catholic Mary Tudor, and Knox fled to the Continent where he met and worked with John Calvin in Geneva. In 1559, the year in which he returned to Edinburgh, under the protection of the pro-reform nobles known as the Lords of the Congregation, he published his *First Blast of the Trumpet Against the Monstrous Regiment of Women*. This was an attack on female rulers, and although it was aimed at Mary I and Mary of Guise, it was taken personally by Elizabeth I, who had become Queen of England the previous year.

The *frisson* of gloom that still affects visitors to St Giles, with its forest of grey stone columns, evokes Knox's lingering presence. He preached there until his death in 1572. After he died, the church was divided in four, to serve the different quarters into which the parish of Edinburgh had been divided. Among the objects that came to be stored there was the burgh's guillotine, known with gallows humour as the Maiden.

HOLYROOD PALACE

Mary Queen of Scots and the murder of Darnley

On 29 July 1565, Mary Queen of Scots* married her cousin Henry Stuart, Lord Darnley, at Holyrood Palace. Holyrood was Mary's favourite residence. Her father, James V of Scotland, had died a few days after her birth, muttering inauspicious prophecies about the ability of a woman to rule Scotland. Engaged to marry the Dauphin of France, the future Francis II, Mary had been brought up at the French Court amid luxury and refinement. Her marriage was short-lived, because the Dauphin, briefly King, died at the age of sixteen. This left Mary free to return in 1561, after negotiation, to the country of which she was Queen. It was primitive in comparison with the world she had known, and the joyless preacher John Knox (see page 454) seemed bent on eradicating any further pleasure she might take in it. She could have lived at Edinburgh Castle on the top of the hill; instead, she chose Holyrood, formerly a monastery (Holy Rood meaning Holy Cross), at the bottom of it. It had been modernised by her father, who had used French masons; it was the nearest thing to France she could find.

Her marriage to Darnley was the turning point of her career. The nobles had pressed her to make a marriage that would further the interests of Scotland; in England, Queen Elizabeth, realising that this granddaughter of Henry VIII's sister was a valid claimant to the English throne, hoped that her choice of husband would be equally advantageous to England. Mary satisfied no one, however – not even, very shortly, herself – by making a love match with Darnley. She found out soon enough that he was vain and ambitious as well as charming. He became jealous of her friendship with her secretary David Rizzio, with whom she used to play cards, admittedly late into the night. A year after their marriage, when Mary was pregnant with the future James VI, Darnley and his friends burst into her room at Holyrood, dragged the screaming Rizzio onto the staircase and murdered him. Mary was traumatised. She turned for consolation to the Earl of Bothwell. However, she continued to live at Holyrood until her child was born.

When, in February 1567, Darnley's house was blown up and Darnley himself was found, half naked and strangled, in its garden, the finger pointed at Bothwell. He stood trial, but the presence of 4,000 armed supporters ensured a verdict of innocence. Very soon, Mary and Bothwell were married. This was more than the Scottish Court, however brutalised to the effects of political bloodletting, could bear. The nobles rose up; the army that Mary and Bothwell could muster was pathetic and, in June 1567, was roundly beaten at Carberry Hill outside Edinburgh. Bothwell fled and Mary was imprisoned in Loch Leven Castle where she was forced to abdicate in favour of her young son.

*See Fotheringhay Castle, page 322, and Loch Leven Castle, page 473

GREYFRIARS KIRK

The signing of the National Covenant

Greyfriars Kirk in Edinburgh's Old Town – the first church to have been built in the city since the Reformation – is a barn of a building. Its broad, unadorned nave formed a fine meeting place, and on 28 February 1638 a group of nobles and barons assembled there to hear the National Covenant read out. In the words of Archibald Johnston of Warriston, the Edinburgh advocate who co-drafted it, the date would be remembered as 'that glorious marriage day of the Kingdom with God'.

The Covenant defended the form of Christian worship that had developed in Scotland. Presbyterian services had little formal structure; the men and women who went to them relied on divine inspiration of the moment to give them shape. The wily James VI of Scotland, also James I of England, had temporised with the Presbyterians, but then he had been brought up in the tortuous world of Scottish politics, and knew when to hedge. His son, Charles I, knew little of Scotland. To him, politics were seen through the glittering prism of a detached and self-absorbed court. Taking advice from the High Churchman, Archbishop Laud, he sought to impose a version of the new *Book of Common Prayer* – the Scottish Prayer Book – on Scotland, along with a panoply of ritual that smelled strongly of the 'Roman Antichrist'. Protestant opinion was scandalised. The day after the Covenant was signed in front of the pulpit in Greyfriars, it was taken to the Tailors' Hall in Cowgate to be signed by the ministers and burgesses.

The Covenant gave the crisis of Charles I's reign a different dimension in Scotland than it had in England. The Covenanters differed with the King over religion, but otherwise supported him. When Charles I was beheaded in 1649 (see page 114), the Scots immediately recognised his son as monarch, and he was crowned Charles II at Scone in 1651 (see page 482). At this point, he agreed to uphold the Covenant. However, at the Restoration in 1660, after spending the intervening years in exile, Charles reneged on his promise. There followed several decades of persecution, culminating in the 'Killing Times' of the 1680s (see page 468). In 1690, in order to win Scottish support, William III recognised Presbyterianism as the national religion.

THE ADVOCATES' LIBRARY

Workplace of the Scottish Enlightenment's great philosopher

David Hume, the philosopher, worked as keeper of the Advocates' Library from 1752 until 1757. The library had been established in 1689. Lying off the hall of the old Scottish Parliament House, its 30,000 books served as a resource for the advocates, who would sweep straight from the library into court; it still bustles with figures in wigs and gowns, completing last-minute researches before arguing their cases. However, the library contained a general collection as well as legal texts; during Hume's time many works of English history were purchased, an essential aid for his own six-volume *The History of England* that appeared between 1754 and 1761. Indeed, it was to have easier access to the library's books that he took the job, which he described as 'a genteel office, though of small revenue'. This major work established Hume's reputation as a historian and remained the standard work until the publication of Thomas Macaulay's *History of England* a century later.

Hume, one of the most brilliant figures of the Scottish Enlightenment, had himself studied law, entering Edinburgh University at the age of twelve, but other interests distracted him. Although his early philosophical works did not receive the attention he had hoped, his pantheism was sufficiently well known for his appointment as librarian to be opposed. ' 'Twas vulgarly given out,' he wrote to a friend, 'that the contest was betwixt Deists and Christians; and when the news of my success came to the play-house, the whisper ran that the Christians were defeated. Are you not surprised that we could keep our popularity, notwithstanding this imputation, which my friends could not deny to be well founded?' Convivial, witty and kind, he had many friends. In Paris, where he served as Secretary to the British Embassy in the 1760s, he was acquainted with all the great thinkers of the day to whom he was known as 'le bon David'.

In 1776, Hume, then living in Edinburgh, faced death with, in the words of his friend, the economist Adam Smith (see page 470), 'the utmost cheerfulness, and the most perfect complacency and resign'. He is now often regarded as the most important philosopher to write in English.

THE CROWN ROOM EDINBURGH
Romance of the Scottish crown jewels

In 1818 the novelist Sir Walter Scott obtained George IV's permission to break into a room in Edinburgh Castle. He hoped to pull off the coup of finding the regalia of the Kings of Scotland, which had been locked away since the Act of Union made them redundant in 1707. As he described the scene, perhaps heightening the tension for journalistic effect, no one knew what would lie at the bottom of a chest when it was opened. But lo and behold, there they were, just as they had been left more than a century before: the crown, the sceptre and the sword of state.

The regalia, known as the Honours of Scotland, are remarkable objects. With the exception of three swords and the Coronation Spoon, all the English

Crown Jewels were melted down or sold following the execution of Charles I. After the Scottish coronation of Charles II in 1651, however, the Honours were taken to Dunnottar Castle on the coast of Kincardineshire. When the castle came under siege from the Parliamentarians, the Honours were lowered out of a window onto the seashore where a serving woman who was pretending to collect seaweed gathered them up. They were then concealed under the floor of Kinneff church by the minister; he and his wife would dig them up every three months at night to clean them. Thus they survived until Charles II's restoration in 1660, when they were returned to him. In 1707, they were locked up in a chest in the Crown Room of Edinburgh Castle, where they remained until Scott 'discovered' them.

Having survived Oliver Cromwell, they are therefore older than most of the Crown Jewels* in the Tower of London. The Sword of State was presented to James IV by Michelangelo's patron, Pope Julius II, in 1507; at some point the blade broke, probably when the Honours were being hidden in the 1650s. The sceptre, in its original form, was also the gift of a Pope, this time Julius II's predecessor Alexander VI, although it was remodelled in 1536. The crown took its present form in 1540. Their rediscovery by Scott, who told the tale to such effect, caused a sensation. Exhibited in the castle, the Honours became a tourist attraction, contributing to the mist of romantic nationalism in which, three-quarters of a century after the '45 uprising, it was now acceptable to envelop Scottish history.

*See Cross Keys Wash, page 267

CALTON HILL   EDINBURGH
The Athens of the North

Buzzing with intellectual activity, awash with clever lawyers and determined to make itself as architecturally sophisticated as anywhere in the kingdom, Georgian Edinburgh acquired the title (originally ironic) of the Athens of the North. In the years of prosperity that followed Waterloo, the city played up to the compliment that was being paid to it.

Already the New Town, developed to plans drawn by the 22-year-old James Craig in 1766, made it one of the most handsome classically planned cities in Europe. Now it embraced the austere Greek Revival style, inspired by the archaeological digs in Greece and the books of engravings which published the treasures that the excavations produced. Prophetically, the very first of such books, James 'Athenian' Stuart and Nicholas Revett's *Antiquities of Athens*, 1762, compared Edinburgh's topography to that of the Greek capital; both are built on hills by the sea.

When the architect C. R. Cockerell was asked to design a Scottish Valhalla or National Monument on Calton Hill, at the east end of the New Town, he conceived it as a variation on the Parthenon itself. It was intended as a church that would commemorate the fallen of the Napoleonic Wars and serve as a resting place for national heroes. The money for what would have been a vast edifice ran out before more than fourteen columns were built. Although Cockerell would no doubt have preferred to have seen his building completed, the columns in their unfinished state are perhaps more poignant in their symbolism. Certainly Cockerell's difficulties did not deter other architects on Calton Hill from archaeologising. The National Monument was soon joined by clusters of other memorials and monuments recalling Ancient Greece, specifically Thomas Hamilton's Burns Monument and William Playfair's Dugald Stewart Monument, both of 1830.

The stylistic consistency is all the more remarkable because they were built piecemeal, to no predetermined plan, and this inevitably introduces a note of the Picturesque, which is typically British. For this reason, the one conspicuously un-Classical structure – the monument to Lord Nelson, pushing up like a 90ft castellated telescope, complete with rigging which is dressed with flags on the Admiral's birthday – does not look as out of place as one would expect of such an oddity. It also demonstrates that Edinburgh could be more up-to-the-minute than London. While Trafalgar Square had to wait until 1843 for the completion of Nelson's column, the hero's Calton Hill monument went up in 1807, a mere two years after the admiral's death.

NICOLSON STREET EDINBURGH

Café where Harry Potter came into being

They said that children had stopped reading books. Then Joanne Kathleen Rowling wrote the Harry Potter stories, which have sold over a hundred million copies. The tales have been translated into forty-two languages. Parents around the world have acclaimed her. She has introduced a new generation to the joy of turning pages to get to the end of a wonderful yarn.

Her own life is something of a fairy story. Having read French and Classics at Exeter University, she went to Portugal, taught English, married and had a daughter. Shortly after the birth she parted from her husband, and found herself penniless in Edinburgh. Suffering from depression, she sketched out the background for *Harry Potter and the Philosopher's Stone* in a first-floor café at 6a Nicolson Street, while her baby slept. The wand waved. Within a decade, she had become richer than she could ever have imagined – richer, it was said, than the Queen.

The café to which children and Warner Bros. owe so much ought to have been preserved as one of the literary landmarks of Edinburgh. Instead it has become Buffet King, a Chinese restaurant. But that's magic for you. As any reader of Harry Potter will know, it doesn't always turn out as expected.

SCOTTISH PARLIAMENT *EDINBURGH*
Scotland is devolved

In a referendum on 11 September 1997, the people of Scotland voted in favour of a Scottish Parliament, which would take control of most of the powers until then exercised from Westminster, except foreign affairs and defence. Pressure for devolution had been growing since the Thatcher years, which saw the wholesale closure of heavy industry in Scotland followed by the intensely unpopular 'poll tax' experiment in which a policy, which was finally to prove unworkable in the United Kingdom as a whole, was pioneered north of the Border. Big Tory majorities in Westminster during the Thatcher reign were not reflected in Scotland, where the number of Conservative MPs dwindled to a handful and then, after the 1997 election, none. At the same time, the Labour Party had its own reasons for supporting devolution, as a means of drawing the sting of their own principal opponents in their Caledonian heartlands, the Scottish Nationalist Party. The referendum took place the year that Tony Blair came to power, and the first Scottish Parliament since 1707 was inaugurated in 1999.

Any new Parliament needs an appropriately symbolic building to house it. In Edinburgh, a site occupied by an old brewery was found next to Holyrood Palace, at the foot of the steep, green Salisbury Crags that lead up to Arthur's Seat. Enric Miralles, the avant-garde Catalan architect who won the competition to design the new Parliament building, devised a series of white hulls, intended to evoke the upturned boats that he had seen around Scotland's coastline. He died in 2000, before the building's official opening.

The project quickly became a *cause célèbre*, not because of the architectural daring so much as the financial imbroglio that saw costs rising to a figure forty times higher than the original £10m budget. The problem was that the architects were asked to design a building before the ultimate client, the Scottish Parliament, had come into existence. The MSPs rejected the seating arrangement proposed for the Chamber, which was supposed to reflect a less adversarial style of politics than Westminster. They demanded bigger entrance areas, more rooms for civil servants and more space for their researchers and assistants. The roof had to be strengthened to prevent a terrorist bomb being lobbed onto it from the Salisbury Crags. Rather than an elegant sequence of hulls, the building came to resemble a vast albino lobster, scavenging at the deep end of the Royal Mile, hoovering up any ingredient for scandal that it could find. That impression may pass in time.

BATTLE OF FALKIRK

Defeat of Sir William Wallace

By the third week of July 1298, Edward I's army was tired, hungry and quarrelsome. While the Bishop of Durham had succeeded in devastating three Border castles, the main body had not managed to bring the Scots to battle. With their powerful cavalry, they should have been the stronger force, but the fabian tactics of the Scottish leader, Sir William Wallace, coupled with the failure of supply ships to arrive, had sapped their morale. At last, however, Edward's scouts made contact with them.

For his part, Wallace could not procrastinate indefinitely: his volunteer troops would not have lasted out a long campaign. The place that he chose to defend was a hill at Falkirk, in a district now called Wallacestone. His foot soldiers were massed in tight clumps called schiltrons, which acted rather as the infantry squares did at Waterloo: two ranks of men, the foremost kneeling, pointed their 12ft long spears outwards, to repel cavalry attacks. Wallace had reason to feel confident. 'I have brought you to the ring,' he cried to his troops, 'dance the best you can.' Two divisions of Edward's knights charged uphill; Wallace's cavalry fled but the schiltrons held firm. Then Edward himself led the English infantry into battle. The arrows of the longbowmen cut into the schiltrons enough for the cavalry to get among them. Stirling Bridge, at which the English had been defeated the previous year, was avenged. The slaughter of the fleeing Scots that followed the Battle of Falkirk ended a period of rising Scottish hope.

Wallace managed to escape, but his prestige as a leader was fatally weakened. Little is known of his movements until he was captured by Edward in 1305, brought to London, tried in Westminster Hall and executed. A crudely lettered stone commemorating Wallace's presence at the Battle of Falkirk was erected in 1810.

FALKLAND PALACE

James V dies, but not the Stuarts

In 1542, James V of Scotland lay dying at Falkland Palace, a building that had featured prominently in his life. As a boy, he had been confined there by his stepfather Archibald Douglas, Earl of Angus, who ruled in his name. In 1528, at the age of sixteen, he managed to escape, dressed as a groom, and took back his throne. Eight years later he began transforming Falkland Palace, turning it into the most architecturally sophisticated residence in the British Isles. Attached columns and classical portrait medallions announce its Renaissance credentials.

This work was finished in 1541, but the King had little enough time to enjoy it before his last illness. By now he was a disappointed and embittered man. Both his sons were dead, and when the news arrived that his army had been annihilated at Solway Moss (see page 376), he is said to have turned his face to the wall. The birth of a daughter, rather than the son he longed for, was greeted with gloomy foreboding. 'The de'il gang with it,' he said. 'It will end as it began. It cam' wi' a lass, and will gang wi' a lass.' The throne of Scotland had come to the Stuarts through Robert the Bruce's daughter Marjorie, who married Walter the Steward (he took Stewart as his surname; their son was Robert II); now James predicted that it would leave through his own daughter.

And so he died, aged only thirty. His forecast, however, was wrong. The daughter was Mary Queen of Scots (see page 455), whose son James VI became also James I of England. The Stuart dynasty had some way to run.

FORT GEORGE

MORAY FIRTH, HIGHLAND

Keeping the Highlands under control

The Jacobite rising of 1745–6, which saw a Highland army marching as far south as Derby, had been an uncomfortable experience for the Hanoverian government. After the Battle of Culloden (see page 447), it quickly constructed a series of roads and fortifications that would quell further unrest. The greatest expression of this policy is Fort George, which even now seems awesome in its scale and planning. It stands on a promontory on the south bank of the Moray Firth, midway between Inverness and Nairn: a previous fort nearer the former had been easily taken and blown up by the Jacobites. The new Fort George was protected by broad ditches overlooked by rampart bastions, the approaches to which – cleared of trees and bushes – could be raked by artillery fire. Three sides are surrounded by sea, and the fourth side was provided with additional fortification in the form of a ravelin, a spear-shaped rampart and ditch projecting beyond the main fort, which would have provided a first line of defence in case of attack.

Until the development of longer-range guns, which could have bombarded the fort from the hills a mile or so away, Fort George must have seemed impregnable. To Lieutenant-Colonel James Wolfe, who was stationed there in 1751, eight years before his heroics at Quebec (see page 98), it was 'the most considerable fortress and the best situated in Britain'.

In the event, however, Fort George was never put to the test. Begun in 1748, it had become unnecessary by the time it was completed twenty years later. By now the Jacobite threat had evaporated, and the garrison buildings – capable of holding 1,600 men – became a recruiting base for the Highland regiments that were so important to maintaining the British Empire.

GLASGOW SCHOOL OF ART RENFREW STREET, GLASGOW

An architectural antidote to the industrial city

Nineteenth-century Glasgow was the powerhouse of the British Empire. It also produced a flowering of the visual arts that reflected the internationalism of the City's trade, while rejecting the industrial grimness on which it was built. The school of painters known as the Glasgow Boys – the Scottish answer to Impressionism – emerged in the 1880s. In 1897, the city received the first intimation of the building that would prove the most lasting symbol of Glasgow's aesthetic yearnings, the Glasgow School of Art.

Like the leading members of the Glasgow Boys, the architect Charles Rennie Mackintosh had studied at the Glasgow School of Art, where he had shown as much aptitude for delicate, stylised watercolour painting as for architecture. He was therefore well placed to interpret the brief for the school's new building, both practically and aesthetically. Money, however, was extremely short: this meant that it had to be built in two phases. Moreover, the site that had been bought sloped steeply, presenting a structural challenge. Of necessity, Mackintosh could not allow himself the use of expensive materials or elaborate ornament, but the simplicity of the result is touched with genius.

For the exterior, Mackintosh drew on a number of influences, some historical, to create an effect of startling modernity. His love of Scottish castle architecture is evident in the stretched side elevations, with their tall, rough stone walls (an effect of the slope) in which sparse window and door openings appear seemingly at random. There is perhaps a whiff of the Orient in the banks of windows on the entrance front: Mackintosh, like every aesthete of his generation, owned Japanese prints. Japanese influence can certainly be detected in some of the cast-iron ornament. This, however, also embodies the ideas of the contemporary Arts and Crafts theorist W. R. Lethaby (in fact, much better than Lethaby managed to do in any of his own buildings): Lethaby believed that the best architecture is a web of sometimes mysterious symbolism. He followed Ruskin in his tenet that ornament should be part and parcel of structure. Thus, in the Glasgow School of Art, Mackintosh's intriguing rosebuds, scarabs and ladybirds are confined to metalwork railings and balconies. In the second phase, the west half, completed in 1907, these Art Nouveau touches disappear, to be replaced by spare mouldings in anticipation of the Modern Movement of the inter-war years.

Passers-by could hardly have been unaware of the artiness of the building, which was only appropriate, considering its function, but the most magical effects are reserved for the students who work there. The interior is almost completely of wood, and its dark tone gives a richness even to studios that are flooded with light, either from the side or above. Yet the structure seems so delicate as to be almost weightless, with light fittings hovering in the air at the ends of slender wires. It is, for all its simplicity, a sensuous building, in which long passages lined with Classical casts alternate with airy studios and contrast with the more opulently finished library, of double height and galleried. It is a joy to walk around; it must be an even greater joy to work in.

When it was finished, the Glasgow School of Art rose serenely above what was then still an industrial city, the hammering of whose shipyards could sometimes be heard in the distance. It was the masterpiece of an architect who was too sensitive an individual to build very much. Its influence on the modernist architecture that came after the First World War is disputed, but there is no doubting the acclaim that is now accorded to it by architects from around the world: it is a rare day when a Japanese student is not seen in Renfrew Street with his camera.

GEORGE SQUARE GLASGOW
Tanks on the streets of Britain

The only time that tanks have been ordered onto the streets of mainland Britain, against the public, occurred on 1 February 1919. The day before, 'Bloody Friday', 60,000 striking workers from the shipbuilding and engineering industries marched into George Square, the heart of Victorian Glasgow, demanding a forty-hour week. During the First World War, the concentration of huge numbers of workers in munitions factories had encouraged trades unionism. Soldiers returning to Glasgow after the war did not find a land fit for heroes, but extensive unemployment and bad housing. The forty-hour week was supposed to generate more jobs. In London, the government feared that the example of the Russian Revolution could be followed in Britain.

While the strikers' leaders were meeting the Lord Provost in City Chambers, mounted police charged the crowd, but the ex-servicemen who were present seized iron railings and bottles, and fought back. The police had to retreat, and fighting continued around the centre of Glasgow for several hours. That night, trains brought some 10,000 English soldiers into the city. Although the Maryhill Barracks contained a battalion of Scottish soldiers, the authorities feared that the sympathies of local troops might all too easily be with the strikers. Tanks, which had been used for the first time in the Battle of the Somme less than three years before, rolled into George Square. The red flags that had been seen on Bloody Friday no longer flew. Glasgow had the appearance of an occupied city.

Although the strike, which had spread to the coalfields, quickly collapsed, the strikers won a concession; their week would be reduced from fifty-seven hours, not to forty hours but to forty-seven hours. For the rest of the 20th century, the Glasgow workforce would be known as Red Clydeside, reflecting the turbulence of its industrial relations – a tradition that lasted until most of the remaining mines and shipyards closed during the 1980s.

FINNIESTON CRANE
Symbol of a great shipbuilding past

Around 1900, Glasgow was at its zenith as the workshop of the British Empire. The development of heavy industry went hand in hand with that of the docks, from where machinery that had been made in Glasgow could be shipped to the rest of the world. From 1768, a succession of engineers – including Thomas Telford and John Rennie – had dredged and embanked the previously shallow river Clyde, to allow big ships to reach the docks. By the early 20th century, Glasgow shipyards were building a fifth of all the world's ships, while its locomotive works were producing a quarter of Britain's railway engines.

The Finnieston Crane, on Stobcross Quay, was built in 1932 to load boilers into the ships being built (they included the original *Queen Mary* and *Queen Elizabeth*) and heavy machines onto freighters. Nearly 200ft high, the crane is capable of lifting weights of 175 tons. It still fulfils its original function, although the collapse of shipbuilding and other forms of Scottish heavy industry after the 1980s means that its services are now only required occasionally.

GLEN COE
HIGHLAND
Brutal Highland massacre

In the bitter February of 1692, an attempt was made to exterminate the MacDonalds who lived among the inhospitable mountains of Glen Coe. For centuries, clans had been feuding with and raiding each other, prompted by inequalities of wealth. Next to Glen Coe, the Campbells who farmed the fertile lowlands round Blair Atholl had become more prosperous than the MacDonalds, and threatened to encroach on their land. To the Glen Coe MacDonalds, cattle rustling seemed eminently justifiable. In 1685, they took advantage of the Campbells' weakness after two of their leaders were executed in Edinburgh, and pillaged their territory. To the government in Edinburgh and London, they looked beyond control.

The splendid old brigand who led the Glen Coe MacDonalds was a few days late in swearing allegiance to King William III*. This was made an excuse to root out not only the chief and his family but also all his followers. Two detachments of government soldiers, 128 men, were sent to Glen Coe, under the command of a Campbell – John Campbell of Glen Lyon. For ten days, the soldiers lived in the homes of the MacDonalds, but then came the order that the Highlanders were to be massacred. The work was done early in the morning. About forty MacDonalds were butchered, including the chief, Ian, and others who had run for the hills perished in the cold. The number of MacDonalds killed was, in fact, relatively small, leading one to think that perhaps the soldiers were unwilling to take part in such a disgraceful affair. It was not long before the brutality of the massacre, against all laws of hospitality as well as humanity, made it a national scandal.

*See Pass of Killiecrankie, page 469

GLENFINNAN
NEAR FORT WILLIAM, HIGHLAND
Bonnie Prince Charlie's standard is raised

On 19 August 1745, a rowing boat made its way up Loch Shiel; one of the small party on board was the pale, brave young man whom history would know as Bonnie Prince Charlie, the grandson of the deposed monarch James VII of Scotland and II of England. A month or so earlier he had landed on the island of Eriskay, to a less than encouraging welcome from the likes of Alexander Macdonald of Boisdale, who urged him to go home. 'I am come home, sir,' the Prince replied.

By now, Charles had discarded the clerical dress that he had been wearing, to disguise himself as a divinity student in the French town of Nantes, where he had been living since the collapse of a well-funded invasion attempt the previous year. This time, the money, all borrowed, was scant. The second of the two ships with which he arrived had been forced back to France, taking most of the expedition's stock of arms with her. Charles realised he would have to rely on the loyalty of the Highland chiefs to raise an army. Climbing out of the rowing boat at Glenfinnan, he went to a barn and waited. A party of Clanranald Macdonalds arrived; then the pipes of the Camerons from Achnacarry were heard coming over the mountain – a body of 700 men. On top of a small hill, the royal standard, a large flag of red silk with a white spot in the middle, was unfurled.

Within a month, Charles was in Edinburgh, where his father was proclaimed King James VIII. On 1 November, the Highland army set out for London, but four months later, the Jacobite cause was lost for ever at Culloden*. After months of perilous hiding, Charles Stuart managed to slip away and return to France; he left from Loch nan Uamh, about 12 miles from Glenfinnan. Terrible retribution followed in the Highlands, but by 1815 the rising seemed sufficiently distant for Alexander Macdonald of Glenaladale to erect a column, placed to superb effect at Glenfinnan at the head of Loch Shiel.

Surmounted by a lone figure of a Highlander, a nobly worded inscription explains its purpose: 'To commemorate the generous zeal, the undaunted bravery and the inviolable fidelity of his forefathers and the rest of those who fought and bled in that arduous and unfortunate enterprise.'

*See Battle of Culloden, page 447

GLENLIVET DISTILLERY MORAYSHIRE
Is this the classic whisky?

When George IV asked for a taste of 'Highland whisky' on a visit to Edinburgh in 1822, the Lord Chamberlain immediately began a hunt for some whisky from the Livet valley. Glenlivet was not at that time a single distillery, not even a village, but a remote Speyside glen, which was all but impenetrable to the excisemen charged with collecting duty and destroying illicit stills. Whisky-making at that date was mostly a cottage industry. An exception was the Ferintosh whisky produced by the Forbes family, who had negotiated what was virtually a tax-free arrangement. When this concession ended, however, so did the production of Ferintosh, its demise being eloquently lamented by the poet Robert Burns (see page 441). There were over 200 illicit distilleries in the glen. Smugglers travelled in armed bands that could be several dozen strong. After delivering their supplies, they would ride home beating the empty barrels with their cudgels. It was not difficult to find a dram for the King.

In 1823, the government sought to regularise the situation. It introduced an Act reducing duty on whisky produced from small stills, in an effort to encourage the inhabitants of Glenlivet and elsewhere to go legitimate. Someone who did so was George Smith, from Upper Drumin in Glenlivet, whose family were experienced contraband whisky-makers. It did not make him popular with his neighbours. Illicit distillers feared not only the competition but also the attention that could be attracted to the glen from the excisemen. Legal distilleries were attacked. Smith had to take strong measures to protect his business, and the brace of pistols that he owned is now on display at the distillery. It is claimed that he was forced to use them twice. Eventually the glen was tamed, the illegal stills disappeared and George Smith was left with the only distillery in the glen; it could justifiably be called The Glenlivet.

Whisky-drinkers who regard some of the other forty-four Speyside malts as yet more ambrosial, or who prefer an offering from Mull, Islay, Jura, Skye or the Highlands, will have landmarks of their own.

HOUSE OF THE BINNS

NEAR LINLITHGOW, WEST LOTHIAN

'Bluidy' General Tam Dalziel and his boots

Two 17th-century Russian leather riding boots decorate a wall of the dining room of The House of the Binns. They belonged to Sir Thomas, otherwise known as 'Bluidy' Tam Dalziel (or Dalyell), and were used to such terrifying effect as the general hunted down Covenanters that water was said to boil if poured into them.

General Tam was the son of the Edinburgh butter merchant who built The House of the Binns. A fervent royalist, he not only fought for the King during the Civil War but also, after Charles I's execution, vowed never to cut his hair or beard until the monarchy was restored; eventually the beard grew to his waist. Following the Battle of Worcester, he was imprisoned in the Tower of London, becoming one of the few people who ever managed to escape. During the Commonwealth, he served as a soldier of fortune in Russia fighting for Tsar Alexei Mikhailovich, the father of Peter the Great. In snowy Poland, he noticed the camouflage effect of the grey uniforms of the troops; after his return to Scotland following the Restoration, he adopted the colour when founding what would become, in 1681, the Royal Scots Greys (see page 430).

Charles II appointed General Tam as his commander-in-chief in Scotland. As such, his duties included suppressing the unrest of the Covenanters, extreme Protestants who believed that worship should be spontaneous and rejected the church hierarchy being imposed by the government (see page 456). In 1666, General Tam was at the head of a force which met 1,000 Covenanters, armed with farm implements, at Rullion Green, south of Edinburgh; fifty of the Covenanters were slaughtered. It was one of the most notorious of the many episodes of anti-Covenanting persecution that continued into the 'Killing Times' of the 1680s, ending only with the expulsion of James II in 1688 (see page 14).

Superstitious contemporaries thought that this fearsome soldier, with his diabolical looks, had something of the night about him. The new towers he built at the Binns were supposedly needed to stop the devil blowing the house down. The Scottish word for devil, de'il, sounds remarkably like his family name, pronounced DL. He may not, however, have been as pitiless as his reputation had it. Distressed by the slaughter of women and children at Rullion Green, against his orders, he resigned his commission. Despite that, he was given a spectacular funeral by Charles II on his death in 1685.

ISLAND OF IONA

St Columba's mission to Scotland

Iona is a tiny island, three miles long, lying off the island of Mull. The monastery there is closely associated with – and may actually have produced, or at least started – the illuminated manuscript now known as the Book of Kells, one of the greatest masterpieces of Early Christian art. This lovingly ornamented book of Gospels was probably scripted in the 8th century. Theory has it that when the Viking raids on Iona became intolerable – in 806 the Norsemen killed sixty-eight of the monks – it was taken, as a precious possession, to Ireland, hence its name. In the 12th century the Benedictines arrived and built an elaborate new abbey, the most sumptuous in the west Highlands.

These projects testify to the lasting inspiration of St Columba. Until he was forty-two, Columba had spent his life in Ireland and is credited with founding numerous churches. In 563, he gathered twelve followers – to match Christ's disciples – and set sail in a coracle towards the Western Isles of Scotland. The sea was narrow at this point; it is said that he chose Iona for his monastery because, from here, it was not possible to see his beloved native land. The monks built themselves individual beehive-shaped cells, and dug a ditch around their encampment. The rule was unusually severe, monks being expected to work and pray until the tears flowed. Not only women but also cows were banished from the island, together, apparently, with snakes and frogs.

Columba, who was the grandson of an Irish king, had the diplomatic skills to befriend both Scottish and Pictish rulers, carrying the Christian message to their tribes. His achievement was magnified by a hagiography written in the century after his death in 597, and this established his cult. In the Dark Ages, the flame of Christianity and civilisation had to be passed carefully from hand to hand, or it could have been all too easily extinguished. The tradition founded by St Columba established Iona as a centre of learning with a great library, from which missionaries travelled as far as France, Italy and Switzerland. Iona became the burial place of kings, including the much-maligned Macbeth. A memory of this era, in which Iona kept the light of civilisation burning through the darkness, survives in the elaborately patterned stone crosses, some of which still stand on the sites for which they were made.

PASS OF KILLIECRANKIE

The Highlands reject William III

When William III ousted James II in the supposedly bloodless revolution of 1688 (see page 13), it took the Highlands of Scotland some time to adjust to the new reality. For reasons of religion and Scottishness, they remained Jacobite (adherents of *Jacobus*, the Latin name for James), viewing James II as James VII of Scotland. Opposition was co-ordinated by the striking figure of Sir Ewen Cameron of Lochiel, whose fierce looks, flaring moustaches and war-like armour made him seem to Highland contemporaries the personification of Mars, god of war.

In July 1689, General Mackay was given the unenviable job of subduing the rising. He set out from Stirling to Perth with 3,000 men, heading towards the strategic stronghold of Blair Atholl. In order to reach it, he had to traverse the alarming defile known as the Pass of Killiecrankie. Word reached him that the Highlanders, under their inspiring commander, John Graham of Claverhouse but known as Bonnie Dundee, were on the point of taking it. Cautiously, he led his men through. They are unlikely to have appreciated what now seems a spectacularly beautiful landscape. The freshly raised government troops must have found the narrow defile, with its many hiding places for an ambush, extremely spooky. Nevertheless, perhaps wanting to lure Mackay's men on before the government dragoons, a definite threat to the Highlanders, had arrived, Dundee did not attack them in the Pass.

Emerging from it, Mackay saw Dundee's army assembling on the ridge of a hill. The two sides manoeuvred until late afternoon. It was early evening when the Highlanders cast off their plaids and, crouching behind their shields, made their descent. Having suffered a few musket rounds, they charged before the government troops had time to screw on their bayonets. Their cries alone were blood-curdling. At one point, General Mackay rode forward, hoping to extricate his cavalry. He found himself alone on the battlefield. Not only had his cavalry not followed him, but also the whole of his army had fallen back. Mackay managed to get back to Stirling, marching through the night, with a force of just 400 men. The rest of his army lay horribly slaughtered around the Pass.

Although it was one of the greatest Highland victories, it was to little avail. Despite wearing armour, Dundee had been shot in the side, and died later of the wound. Without his brilliant leadership, the Jacobites lost heart, and the army dissolved.

HIGH STREET, KIRKCALDY
FIFE

Where the great theory of the free market was completed

The economist Adam Smith was born in Kirkcaldy in 1723 and died there in 1790. Neither of the houses in which these events took place survives. His mother's house at 220 High Street, where he completed, arduously, his *Wealth of Nations*, was replaced with a larger building in 1834, although a plaque commemorates its famous occupant, offering a diagrammatic sketch of the earlier one. Diagonally opposite is a branch of McDonald's. Kirkcaldy has not always been aesthetically improved by its commerce-driven development since Smith's time, but the changes he would encounter, should his ghost ever return here, would no doubt seem perfectly in order to this great apostle of the free market.

When Smith was growing up, Kirkcaldy, across the Firth of Forth from Edinburgh, was a prosperous seaport, trading in coal and salt. His father, also Adam, who died before he was born, had been Comptroller of Customs, leaving his widow relatively well off. Kirkcaldy's schools served young Adam well and he went on to study at Glasgow and Oxford Universities, before becoming tutor to Henry, the future 3rd Duke of Buccleuch. Smith, with his harsh, slightly stammering voice and protruding teeth, had the job of escorting the rich young nobleman around France; it says much for his personal qualities that Buccleuch would later describe him as 'a friend whom I loved and respected, not only for his great talents, but for every private virtue'. During his travels he met Voltaire and other eminent philosophers.

An Inquiry into the Nature and Causes of the Wealth of Nations was published in 1776, just as Britain's economic relations with her American colonies had provoked Revolution. It analysed human motivation in relation to trade, which is promoted by the universal desire of individuals to better themselves. The second part of the book attacks the monopolies and restrictions that were intended to foster the British economy, but in reality fettered it. To a later age, the collapse of the centrally controlled Soviet Empire turned Smith's theories into a mantra for Tory Chancellors of the Exchequer.

BRECHIN ROAD, KIRRIEMUIR ANGUS
The childhood that shaped Peter Pan

J. M. Barrie, the author of *Peter Pan*, was born at 9 Brechin Road in the little town of Kirriemuir in 1860. Kirriemuir – which Barrie later fictionalised as Thrums, a weaving term meaning 'the ends of the threads' – made its living from linen. Barrie's father, a hand-loom weaver, was sufficiently prosperous to call himself a 'linen manufacturer', which probably meant that he employed an assistant. But as Andrew Carnegie's father would also find (see page 451), hand-loom weaving was soon to be undercut by steam-powered factories*. When Barrie was growing up, the family moved to Forfar, where his father found a new job as a book-keeper. They moved back a couple of years later, to a different part of town.

One of ten children, Barrie rarely mentioned his father, but adored his mother, Margaret. Together, they talked interminably about her youth when, like Wendy in *Peter Pan*, she was forced to take responsibility for her little brother, their mother having died when she was eight. Death also marked

Barrie's childhood. His brother David, greatly loved by his mother, died aged thirteen. In his biography of his mother, *Margaret Ogilvy*, Barrie describes David's coffin being laid on the kitchen table. Barrie could never quite replace David in his mother's life, not least because, as Barrie grew up, David remained a child. Perhaps he became immortal as Peter Pan.

When, in *Peter Pan*, the Lost Boys build a little house for Wendy in Never-Never Land, it was – according to Barrie's dedication in the front of the book – the wash house at Brechin Road that he had in mind; it had been here that, aged seven, he had put on his first play.

*See Cromford, page 315, and Hall i' th' Wood, page 362

BATTLE OF LARGS

AYRSHIRE

Last of the Viking raids

In 1263, King Haakon of Norway assembled the greatest fleet that had ever been seen off Scotland, perhaps as many as two hundred vessels. He led it himself, in his ship with the gilded dragon's head. The previous year, when King Alexander III of Scotland turned twenty-one, an attempt had been made to buy back the Hebrides from Norway; when that failed, the Scots made a bloody assault on Skye. Now Haakon was out to seize Arran and Bute, which he did, before sailing next to Great and Little Cumbrae.

But as sometimes happens in Scotland, the weather was against him. Fierce storms battered his ships so badly that he was forced to put his men ashore on the Scottish mainland, at what is now the holiday town of Largs. Alexander, who had been watching the progress of the Vikings from Ayr, rushed his men down to the shore, and engaged the Vikings in a running battle which lasted three days. Haakon never established a bridgehead. Retreating to his ships, he was compelled to limp back to Orkney. Thus ended the last Viking raid on the Scottish mainland, and the Western Isles became part of Scotland.

The feud between Norway and Scotland was ended by the marriage of Haakon's grandson, Erik II, to Alexander's daughter, Margaret. Margaret was to die in childbirth. With her two brothers also dead, this left her infant daughter, also Margaret, heir to the throne of Scotland. Alexander married again, but there were no further children. It was to be one of Scotland's greatest tragedies: in 1286, when galloping through a tempestuous night to see his new wife, Queen Yolande, Alexander was thrown from his horse over a cliff. At the age of three, Margaret, 'the Maid of Norway', became Queen. She remained in Norway until she was eight, but then she too died during the crossing to Scotland in 1290. This gave rise to another feud, this time between Scotland and England, providing Edward I with the excuse to intervene in the succession (see page 397): the so-called Great Cause which was only settled (in Scotland's favour) with Robert the Bruce's Treaty of Northampton in 1328 (see page 445).

LOCH LEVEN CASTLE PERTHSHIRE
Prison from which Mary Queen of Scots escaped

June 1567 saw the Earl of Bothwell's supporters trounced at the battle of Carberry Hill, at which point Mary Queen of Scots*, who had made the error of marrying him only a month earlier, just three months after the death of Darnley, gave herself up to her enemies. They forced her to ride, without so much as a change of clothes, to the castle set in the middle of Loch Leven. It was a damp, cramped tower-house whose curtain walls entirely embraced what was then a tiny island, perfectly suited to its new role as prison. Mary had visited the castle several times before, in happier circumstances. She went there to hawk and dine, and on one occasion she debated the treatment of Roman Catholics with the Protestant cleric John Knox (see page 454). Now her enforced, tragic stay would last eleven months.

When Mary arrived, she was pregnant with twins. Not surprisingly perhaps, they miscarried. The response of her host, Sir William Douglas, was to move the Queen from a tower in the curtain wall to more secure quarters in the main castle. A month after arriving, she was forced to abdicate in favour of her infant son, James VI of Scotland (who would become James I of England). To add to her distress, Sir William fired the castle's guns and lit a bonfire in the courtyard to celebrate. There followed long months during which she could do little except sew and walk in the small courtyard. During her time at Loch Leven, she succeeded in captivating Sir William's brother, George (he hoped eventually to marry Mary), and a young orphan, Willy Douglas. With their help, she achieved the impossible and escaped.

Alas, the army she mustered was easily defeated, and she fled to England, on a course that led eventually to the executioner's block at Fotheringhay Castle.

*See Fotheringhay Castle, page 322, and Holyrood Palace, page 455

MAES HOWE NEAR STROMNESS, ORKNEY
Orkney's answer to the pyramids?

Five thousand years ago, a community living on the smoothly contoured, windswept island of Orkney hauled some standing stones into the upright position. These were the Stones of Stenness, and the operation was followed some centuries later by the Ring of Brogar. Nearby was built a series of burial chambers known as Maes Howe; these stone rooms are one of the greatest examples of Stone Age architecture in Europe. Since they lie beneath a great earth mound, rising like an enormous molehill out of the flat landscape, their existence was not suspected – in modern times, anyway – until the 1860s.

Why was it built? Whose bodies lie in the tombs? In relation to the size of the population, the effort of constructing Maes Howe must have been vast. Was it the Orcadian equivalent of the pyramids, to be occupied by princes? Or was it a last resting place for the community as a whole? These were farming people, growing little fields of wheat and barley. They lived in settlements like Skara Brae (see page 484), of which there were many on Orkney. The entrance passage was arranged so that the sun shines into it around the shortest day of the year. For these Neolithic people, whose lives were so dependent on the seasons, the winter solstice – the moment at which the darkness threatening to embrace their world receded each year – must have been of great importance. Maes Howe seems to commemorate it. Perhaps the chambers were used for worship as well as burial.

Several millennia later, in the 12th century AD, the Vikings arrived. They broke into the chamber and added their runic inscriptions to the jerky sort of drawing (a series of triangles) engraved into the rock in the Stone Age. Salacious, boastful, fabulous – speaking of women and treasure, or just leaving the name of the carver – they are the Viking equivalent of graffiti. They seem to telescope the centuries and bring those Norsemen close to us. The original builders of Maes Howe left no such intimate clues as to their lives, but they can be half glimpsed through the mysteries of this extraordinary monument.

KITCHENER MEMORIAL
MARWICK HEAD, ORKNEY

'Your Country Needs You'

In the early years of the First World War, Field-Marshal Lord Kitchener was literally the face of the British war effort. His were the virile moustaches and jabbing finger which, in the famous recruiting poster, stood above the legend, 'Your Country Needs You'. As Secretary of State for War, he raised immense new 'Kitchener's armies' to serve in the trenches, before general conscription was deemed politically practicable.

Herbert Kitchener was a product of Victorian imperialism. He took his title, Kitchener of Khartoum, from the city he occupied after crushing the force of the Mahdi – attempting to prise the Sudan from British rule – at the Battle of Omdurman in 1898. After Omdurman, his administration of the Sudan was humane; but not so the methods he employed to crush Boer resistance in

South Africa at the end of the Boer War; then Boer farms were burnt and their occupants herded into the world's first concentration camps, whose conditions rapidly degenerated as numbers grew. Nevertheless, being adventurous, experienced and successful, he was loved by the British public, even if by 1916 the Cabinet was finding him a difficult colleague, too used to running his own show.

In June that year, Kitchener set off on a mission to Russia, intended to persuade the Tsar to stay in the war. He reached Thurso on a stormy night, and sailed to Scapa Flow where the Grand Fleet was anchored. This lagoon had been protected against German submarines by the sinking of blockships. Kitchener dined with Admiral Jellicoe on his flagship, then boarded HMS *Hampshire*. The anti-submarine precautions had not been completely successful. As the *Hampshire* steamed out of Scapa Flow, it struck a mine off Birsay and sank within minutes, with the loss of all but a few dozen crew. After the war, a stout tower was erected to Kitchener's memory on Marwick Head. At the time, the potential blow to British morale was so great that islanders who knew about the disaster were ordered never to mention it.

MELROSE ABBEY BORDERS
Burial place of Robert the Bruce's heart?

In 1136, King David I built an abbey on the banks of the river Tweed, near the site of an earlier monastery founded by monks who had come from Iona. He had pushed the boundaries of his kingdom far into what is now England, so Melrose Abbey became vulnerable when the Border settled back to its old position, an easy target for raids. It suffered repeatedly. One of the worst depredations was inflicted by Edward II, whose army sacked it in 1322. Robert the Bruce helped with the rebuilding, and formed such an attachment to the place that, dying apparently of leprosy, he ordered his heart should be buried there. The rest of his body joined the other Scottish kings in Dunfermline Abbey (see page 450).

In the Middle Ages, it was not uncommon for the heart, as the traditional organ of emotion, to be removed after death and buried separately, if not otherwise preserved. John Balliol's widow, Lady Devorgilla, mother of the John Balliol who became King of the Scots for a short time, had his heart placed in an ivory casket which she kept always with her, as a 'sweet silent companion'. Sweetheart Abbey in Dumfriesshire, which she founded in his memory, took its name from this practice. Chroniclers have it that Robert the Bruce, who had always wanted to go on pilgrimage to the Holy Land, instructed that his heart should do the journey for him. His friend Sir James Douglas was begged to carry it against the enemies of Christ, which he did in Spain, fighting the

Moors. A human heart, encased in a lead casket, was found at the Abbey in 1921; whether this belonged to Robert the Bruce is not known. Having been examined, the heart in its casket was re-interred.

The present form of the Abbey, famous for its beauty, dates from another rebuilding, this time after Melrose had been burnt down by Richard II's army in 1385.

NEW LANARK
LANARKSHIRE

Robert Owen's social experiment

The son of a Welsh saddler, Robert Owen had become the manager of a Manchester cotton mill by the age of nineteen. Eight years later, in 1799, he married Caroline Dale, daughter of the Scottish mill owner David Dale. Briefly in partnership with Richard Arkwright, Dale had built a textile factory at New Lanark, harnessing the power of a fast-flowing stretch of the river Clyde for water-driven spinning jennys housed in four new mills. When the time came for Dale to retire, Owen, although only twenty-seven, raised the £60,000 required to buy the factory. In this first age of the Industrial Revolution, when factory employees were driven harshly by the mill owners, New Lanark was to become famous for its humane principles, co-existing with profit.

Owen's arrival was not at first greeted with warmth by the workforce. Dale had been a model employer by the standards of the time. However, although Owen was beholden to his backers to provide a return on their money, he kept the workers on full pay in 1806 while work halted due to an American embargo on cotton. When he fell out with his original partners in 1810, over plans to create a school, he found new ones, and this second partnership was replaced by a third in 1813 when at last he had sympathetic investors. Education was a central priority for Owen, who relied heavily on child labour. He published his ideas for social and educational reform in a number of tracts such as *A New View of Society* (1813).

Owen improved the hours of his young workforce. Grecian tunics were the uniform for his Institute for the Formation of Character, opened in 1816, where much time was spent dancing and singing. A village shop, stocked by Owen, offered goods at trade prices. He toured the country, promoting the values of the 'new moral world' he had created. However, his ideas – particularly in education – proved too much for his more conventional partners and Owen sold New Lanark in 1828. He devoted the last thirty years of his life to helping groups with a remit for social reform, championing shorter factory hours, an extension of the franchise and trades unionism.

NIGG PARISH CHURCH

Who were the Picts?

In the 6th century, St Columba (see page 469) set out to convert the Picts* to Christianity, taming the bad-tempered, mythical sea horse in Loch Ness along the way. His effort was to be supported by other holy men, among them St Boniface who founded a monastery at Rosemarkie in Pictish Easter Ross, St Ninian from Whithorn (see page 487), St Maelruba from Applecross, and St Donnan from Eigg. By about 700, the job was done. Having learned the art of stone-dressing from the Northumbrians, the Picts began making the carved stone slabs which are a three-dimensional equivalent of the Lindisfarne Gospels. The central motif was generally a cross.

We do not even know what the Picts called themselves. The name – meaning 'painted people', probably deriving from the local custom of body tattooing – may have been an all-purpose term of abuse applied by Roman legionnaires to anyone living beyond the rule of the Empire. These cross slabs, or symbolically carved stones, provide a vital source of information about a race that is otherwise mysterious. Symbols found on the slabs include 'Z rods', the 'crescent-and-V rod' and the comic 'spectacles'. It is thought that slabs showing only a cross date from the end of the Picts' independence. It is from these carvings that we know that lords – perhaps even ladies – rode into battle with their men. At Portmahomack, stones that may have come from a monastery there show that some of the Picts knew Latin.

My favourite cross slab is at Nigg, now housed in the pleasing 17th-century parish church. As well as a central cross surrounded by interlaced designs, it shows St Anthony and St Paul being fed with bread in the desert, a meditation on the Eucharist; the bird that delivers the bread is a homely crow. On the other side, King David is shown forcing the jaws of a lion to stay open in order to prevent the beast from devouring his sheep: any shepherd would hope to do the same. Huntsmen on horses and with spears pursue deer, while a figure seems to be clashing symbols to flush out game. Rural life in Easter Ross stays pretty much the same.

*See Dunnichen, page 452

ROSSLYN CHAPEL

An event in architecture

The building of this extraordinary structure, carved with the intricacy of a coral reef, must surely count as an historic event in itself. A first impression of Rosslyn Chapel is that it must have been influenced by Spain or Portugal, but its starting date – 1446 – makes it earlier than the exuberant late Gothic of those countries. There is nothing else like it in the kingdom.

This stylistic mystery embraces a number of further enigmas. The chapel belonged to a castle owned by the St Clair family, who had come over from Normandy with William the Conqueror. The builder of Rosslyn Chapel was Sir William St Clair (or Sinclair), who drew designs on timber boards to guide the carvers in their work. Not surprisingly the chapel, which was originally conceived on a bigger scale, took forty years to build, its completion being left to Sir William's son, Sir Oliver St Clair.

Nobody quite understands the iconography of the virtuoso carving, with its plethora of flowers, angels, figures and inscriptions. There are associations with the Knights Templar, since Sir William St Clair was a descendant of the last Scottish Grand Master of the order. After abolition in England and excommunication by the Pope (see page 189), the Templars were able to survive in Scotland, where Robert the Bruce had been outlawed by the Church. (William de St Clair is supposed to have been one of the knights who took the dead Robert the Bruce's heart into battle against the Moors, see page 475.) It has been claimed that Rosslyn was built on the plan of Herod's temple in Jerusalem to house Templar relics that were brought back from the Holy Land. Certainly a sealed vault in the Chapel has, at different times, been thought to contain wondrous objects, such as the Holy Grail and the Ark of the Covenant. The strange carvings have even been used to argue that Freemasonry was established in Scotland 250 years before its advent in England.

It is safer to say that Rosslyn, so fantastic and intriguing, has long been a destination for tourists. 'To go to Roslin and eat Strawberries is one of the proper things to be achieved by an inhabitant of Edinburgh,' wrote a Victorian guidebook to 'Tartan-land'.

ROXBURGH CASTLE   NEAR KELSO, BORDERS
James II is killed by an exploding cannon

James II of Scotland had the misfortune to be the first monarch killed by gunpowder. His death took place at the siege of Roxburgh Castle, sandwiched between the rivers Tweed and Teviot, in 1460. James, 'mair curieous nor becam him or the maiestie of ane King', was standing too near to a cannon, the Lion, when it exploded, severing his leg. It was the end of a reign characterised by violence and aggression.

James came to the throne when he was six, his father having been murdered at Perth. During the course of his minority, the 'Black' Earls Douglas established themselves in a position of dangerous power. In 1452, James invited the 8th Earl Douglas to Stirling Castle but stabbed him in the throat after the Earl had refused to swear loyalty. Douglas's brother, now the 9th Earl and Bishop of Aberdeen, burnt Stirling in revenge. Later he raised an army of 40,000 against James, but it was defeated at the Battle of Arkinholm in 1455. After a sustained campaign, James 'of the Fiery Face', as he was known from a birthmark, succeeded in crushing the Douglases; he was now free to turn his attention to a foreign enemy – England – which still had a toehold in Scotland.

Roxburgh Castle, only the stump of which now remains, was an important Border stronghold in the Middle Ages. It was first captured for the English by Edward I in 1296, then retaken for the Scots in a famously daring night raid by Sir James Douglas in 1313. Since 1334, it had been in English possession. A flare-up in the Wars of the Roses, which diverted attention away from the Border, gave James the opportunity to attempt to win back the castle for Scotland. 'Ane gret ost' was assembled for the siege, and the castle fell just after the King's death. According to one account, the Lion was being fired to celebrate the arrival of James's Queen, Mary of Gueldres, when it blew up.

ROYAL AND ANCIENT GOLF CLUB   ST ANDREWS, FIFE
The Mecca of golf

Golf, originally a Scottish game, boomed across late-Victorian Britain as the expanding middle class saw the charm of a pursuit that could be played without horses or teams. As a result, the rules, which until then differed between clubs, had to be standardised. In 1897, a rules committee was established at the Royal and Ancient Golf Club at St Andrews, to which all other golfing institutions in the country were to defer.

Golf had been played at St Andrews, as elsewhere in Scotland, since the 15th century. The game is first mentioned in a decree of 1457, when James II of Scotland banned it in order to encourage archery practice. In the next century, Mary Queen of Scots was censured for playing golf too soon after the murder of her husband, Lord Darnley: she thus became the first named woman golfer. In the 18th century, the Royal and Ancient, founded in 1754 as the Society of St Andrews Golfers and run under the rules formulated in 1744 by the Honourable Company of Edinburgh Golfers, was only one of a number of clubs formed by Scottish gentlemen, who often played in quasi-military uniforms. In 1834, William IV granted permission to St Andrews to call itself the Royal and Ancient.

The famous Royal and Ancient Club House was built in 1854. Three years later, a Grand National Tournament, between teams from different clubs, was inaugurated at St Andrews, but the contest for which it is most famous, the Open Championship, did not arrive until 1873. It had first been played at

Prestwick in 1860, and for many years rotated among leading Scottish and English clubs. In 1920, the Royal and Ancient was asked to take responsibility for its management, along with the Amateur Championship. The Open is now so big that few clubs can accommodate the event; it has been most frequently held at St Andrews.

Today, the most sacred of golf's institutions, the Royal and Ancient, remains a private club, while the authority for the rules of British golf (indeed, of golf everywhere in the world, except the United States) and the organisation of international championships has been devolved to a group of companies called the R&A.

BATTLE OF SAUCHIEBURN NEAR STIRLING
Death of James III

James III of Scotland was an unpopular monarch and an unpleasant man. Having debased the coinage with his infamous copper 'blak pennyis', he became a hoarder of gold, which he was reluctant to spend either on dispensing justice or beautifying his realm. He left behind no great work of building. He did not show himself to his people, only leaving Edinburgh to hunt at Falkland; however, it is from his time that Edinburgh began to assume its importance as the country's principal seat of government. He also sought to cut a figure on the European stage, although Scotland was not, at that time, equal to it.

In one respect, James was far-sighted: despite persistent rebuffs, he wooed England, seeking English marriages for his children. It came to nothing. The pro-English policy only made him more disliked by his nobles. Matters came to a head in October 1488. James's eldest son, the fifteen-year-old Duke of Rothesay (the future James IV), was so alarmed by his father's obvious favouritism towards his younger brother, which must have made him fear for his future or even his life, that he was persuaded to join disaffected nobles in a rebellion. Their army met James's just south of Bannockburn. What happened during the fight is not well recorded, but since some of the King's closest supporters chose to defect in the months before battle was joined, the outcome was a predictable rout. Legend has it that James was stabbed to death by one of the enemy disguised as a priest. This is probably fanciful. It seems that he was fleeing when some common soldiers killed him.

For the rest of his days James IV, horrified at his part in his father's death, wore an iron chain round his waist in atonement for his part in it.

SCAPA FLOW
The German battle fleet is scuttled

Before the First World War, it had seemed that the coming conflict would be as much about battleships as trench warfare. Since the launch of HMS *Dreadnought* by Britain in 1906, Britain and Germany had been engaged in an arms race to outbuild the other in this new class of battleship. Britain's navy, protecting the Empire, was the most powerful in the world. If it could be outgunned, argued the German strategists, Britain would not risk conflict, leaving Germany free to pursue its belligerent ambitions in Europe. In fact, their aggressive policy had the reverse effect, forcing Britain to defend its control of the seas.

During the war, sea power was put to the test less often than might have been predicted from the building programme before 1914. In 1916, both sides claimed to have won the Battle of Jutland, the only time that the two fleets met for a set-piece battle. The advantage was with the British, however, since the Kaiser's fleet stayed in port thereafter. After the Armistice, German officers did not feel that they had been defeated. They were outraged at Britain's insistence that, pending the outcome of treaty negotiations, their High Seas Fleet should sail to Scapa Flow, a lagoon enclosed by the islands of Orkney, South Ronaldsay and Hoy. During the talks that preceded the Treaty of Versailles, which formally ended the war, the commander of the interned fleet at Scapa Flow, Rear Admiral von Reuter, incorrectly formed the impression that hostilities might be about to restart. As a result, he ordered the entire fleet of seventy-four ships to be scuttled.

The event occurred on Midsummer's Day, 1919. The English ships that had been guarding the German fleet had temporarily left on manoeuvres. As a result, the principal witnesses to this extraordinary event were a party of schoolchildren who were being taken to view the ships when quite suddenly they listed, upended themselves and sank. 'Out of the vents rushed steam and oil and air with a dreadful roaring hiss,' recalled one of the youngsters, many years later. 'And as we watched, awestruck and silent, the sea became littered for miles round with boats and hammocks, lifebelts and chests . . . and among it all hundreds of men struggling for their lives.' Altogether fifty-two German ships went to the bottom, including eleven great battleships, like the *Konig*, *Kronprinz Wilhelm* and *Markgraf*, which turned turtle.

With 400,000 tons of steel sinking under the waves, it was the worst loss of shipping experienced on a single day in the history of the world. The German sailors got safely into lifeboats and the only fatalities – the last recorded in a dreadful war – were a handful of Germans who were shot during the confusion as the British personnel attempted to thwart the ships being scuttled.

SCONE PALACE

Where Scotland crowned its kings

In April 1296, John Balliol, Edward I's placeman on the throne of Scotland, renounced his fealty to the English monarch. Edward promptly marched north, defeated the Scots at the Battle of Dunbar, stripped Balliol's surcoat of its heraldic devices*, imprisoned him and, on the return journey, seized the Stone of Destiny from Scone.

Even since the 8th century the Picts, the 'painted people' who lived north of the Forth (see page 477), and their successors had enthroned their kings on a mound just north of Perth. From at least 906 they had sat on a roughly shaped block of red sandstone, which acquired great symbolic importance. Perhaps it was Jacob's pillow, carried from the Holy Land; perhaps it was a Roman altar; perhaps it was an ancient heirloom of the Picts – the mystery only adds to its aura of sanctity. Edward carried it south, and for seven centuries it rested in Westminster Abbey, under a specially made coronation chair, where it became an essential icon in the ceremony of crowning English monarchs.

The mound in Perthshire continued to serve its ceremonial purpose, without its Stone. In 1249, Alexander III (see page 397), then seven years old, was the first king to be crowned there, and the tradition continued until the coronation of James IV (see page 387) in 1488. This was not, of course, the last time a Scottish king sat on the Stone of Destiny: in 1603 James VI of Scotland was crowned also James I of England, in Westminster Abbey, uniting the two kingdoms under one monarch. The mound at Scone came out of retirement when Charles II was crowned there in 1651 (see page 456); with England lost to the Royalist cause and Cromwell in the south of Scotland, the choice was expedient as well as appropriate.

In 1996 the Stone of Destiny was returned to Scotland, now being housed in Edinburgh Castle, although it will come south again for coronations.

*See Norham, page 397

SCOTS DYKE

A national border is dug across the Debatable Land

In the early 16th century, much of England was unknown to its King, Henry VIII. His annual progresses rarely took him to the North, and never to the disputed border with Scotland. On both sides, this was still a lawless territory, where the better off sheltered in pele towers or fortified farmsteads to protect themselves from the depredations of any unruly neighbours. Families like the Armstrongs, Irvines, Nixons and Maxwells made careers out of marauding and extortion, activities known locally as 'reiving'. As occasion offered, they would join the armies that their kings (English or Scottish) sent across the border, giving legitimacy to their raids. Ownership of a strip of some thirty square miles, between Gretna and Langholm, was so insecure that it was known as the Debatable Land. With the exception of Canonbie Priory, it was a wasteland.

On the English side, open season was declared when Henry made annoying the 'King of Scottis' an object of the 'Rough Wooing' intended to bring about a marriage between his son, the future Edward VI, and the infant Mary Queen of Scots. Canonbie Priory was destroyed in 1542. Afterwards, the lawless West March – as this half of the border was called – became a haunt of thieves and murderers, whose talents complemented those of the native inhabitants. An attempt was made to burn all the dwellings in Debatable Land, in order to facilitate an agreement over the border. After French efforts at mediation, there followed a period of anarchy.

Eventually, in 1552, the obvious solution was accepted, and it was agreed to divide the area in two. Since no natural boundary existed across the peaty 'moss', a ditch was dug. Hardly on the scale of Hadrian's Wall (see page 389), it was nevertheless quite an operation, nearly four miles in length. Although the pointed stones that originally marked the beginning and end have disappeared, the dyke and some cut stones along the way survive. The Scots Dyke can best be seen from the A7, two miles south of Canonbie.

BATTLE OF SHERIFFMUIR   NEAR DUNBLANE, STIRLINGSHIRE
The Old Pretender is driven back to France

In 1714 Queen Anne died, to be succeeded by the Elector of Hanover, George I. This gave James II's son, James, called the Old Pretender, the chance to regain the thrones of England and Scotland for his family, which they had previously occupied for (in the case of Scotland) three and a half centuries.

James's proposed revolution was based around an uprising in the south-west of England, supported by another in Scotland. But the dubious characters attracted to his court in exile gave the game away, and the government quashed the south-western revolt before it had even begun. In Scotland, the Earl of Mar (who had been snubbed by George I) energetically roused the Highlands. By November 1715 his army of 9,000 men had reached Kinbuck, north of Stirling. From Stirling, however, the 2nd Duke of Argyll marched out with an English force a third that size, anxious to prevent the Jacobites from reaching the Forth. They met on a freezing morning on the open ground of Sheriffmuir. Argyll's troops, on the high ground, were still forming into position when the Highlanders crested the hill. The left wing was devastated by one of the fearsome Highland charges that would strike terror into government troops thirty years later. On the right wing, however, the Highlanders were driven back by repeated cavalry charges. Some drowned trying to escape across the Allan Water.

Hearing of the disaster on his left, Argyll halted his remaining men – a thousand of them – and drew them up behind some mud walls. As light faded, they stared at Mar's force which was four times the greater, but Mar lost the initiative, and night fell without his attacking. It was not a glorious victory for Argyll – in fact, hardly a victory at all – but enough to take the steam out of the Jacobite engine. It was the last battle of the rebellion.

What of the Old Pretender? He did not arrive until the second half of December. Gloomy, cold and taciturn, he did little to inspire his followers, particularly since he arrived without the eagerly anticipated support of French troops. His army melted away. Six weeks later, he was back in France.

SKARA BRAE

NEAR STROMNESS, ORKNEY

Uncovering Britain's oldest village

In 1850, a great storm swept across Orkney. Among other damage, it tore a layer of soil and sand off a site beside the Bay of Skaill, revealing dry-stone walls that had been buried there. They were the remains of a Stone Age village which, when excavated, was found to be the most complete in northern Europe.

The first houses at Skara Brae were built about 3000BC, which makes them older than the Pyramids of Egypt. They were built into midden – a sort of compost made of household waste and animal dung, strengthened with pebbles, bones and shells. A pile of midden must have been assembled over a long period, then heaped up into a mound on the site of a proposed house; what then became the living spaces were hollowed out of it, the interiors being lined with stone. The midden dried to form a strong material, like a weak kind of concrete. It is because of the buttressing effect of the midden that Skara Brae has survived for so long. The shoulder of midden gave the villagers a degree of weather-proofing and protection against Orcadian winds.

The enveloping sand not only preserved the walls of the houses, but the furniture as well. Orkney is a bald island, devoid of trees. As a result, furniture was made not out of wood – although some driftwood must have been washed up on the beach – but sheets of the easily worked local Caithness stone. Dressers, beds and hearths are all stone. Everything stands just as it did, as though the original inhabitants are about to come back.

This was a peaceable farming community, who seem to have had no use for weapons and little obvious hierarchy within the group, since all the houses are the same size. One detail suggests an unexpected degree of sophistication: from the position of drains, it seems that the houses had indoor lavatories several millennia before they became commonplace.

STIRLING CASTLE

Scene of James VI's coronation and early adventures

In December 1566, the future James VI of Scotland and James I of England was christened at Stirling Castle. It was a comfortable base for his mother, Mary Queen of Scots*, having been modernised by her father, James V. On its dramatic hill, it remained a formidable fortress, which was a considerable attraction given the bitterness and feuding of Scottish politics in the second half of the 16th century. The chapel had escaped the Reformation, enabling Mary to give her son a christening of maximum Roman Catholic elaboration. From England, Queen Elizabeth sent a solid gold font in which the ceremony could take place. The person conspicuous by his absence was James's father, Lord Darnley: he had shut himself up in his chamber so as to avoid the embarrassment of being treated as a nobleman, rather than King, by the visiting ambassadors.

Stirling was also the scene of James's coronation in July 1567; his mother, by now incarcerated in Loch Leven Castle, had been forced to abdicate in his favour. Without her presence at the coronation, the ritual was Protestant. The castle was to remain James's principal home for most of his childhood. Here he received a rigorous education in religion and the Classics from the elderly humanist scholar George Buchanan (who missed no opportunity of bad-mouthing his mother). Access to the young King was strictly controlled and he lived under a constant threat of abduction by the different noble factions who wished to rule in his name.

Nonetheless, in 1582, when James was fifteen, he was successfully kid-napped while out hunting by a group of noblemen led by William Ruthven, 1st Earl of Gowrie, an extreme Protestant. The object of the Ruthven Raid, as it became known, was to separate the King from a handsome pro-French, pro-Catholic cousin, Esmé Stuart, 1st Duke of Lennox, for whom James had formed an infatuation. Stirling was one of the places where he was held. James escaped after ten months; within two years Gowrie had been executed.

Just as Stirling had been the setting for the celebrations surrounding James's own arrival in the world, so it also saw those for the birth of James's first son by Anne of Denmark, Henry, Prince of Wales, in 1594. Guests at the banquet gasped as a fully rigged ship, laden with fish, was dragged into the hall. Nevertheless, given James's bleak Stirling childhood and the constant danger he was in, his delight at swapping his dour, bickering Court in Edinburgh for the comparative richness and cosmopolitanism of London, which he was able to do on Elizabeth I's death in 1603, is understandable. Once he had crossed the Border going south, it was fourteen years before he returned.

*See Fotheringhay Castle, page 322, and Holyrood Palace, page 455

TAY BRIDGE

Britain's worst structural engineering failure

At 7.14pm, on Sunday, 28 December 1879, the mail train from Edinburgh slowly passed the last signal box before the Tay Bridge, checking that the way was clear. The driver then gathered speed, and the signalman was left watching the red lights on the guard's van as the train pushed ahead, into what had become a ferocious westerly gale. Sparks could be seen spraying from the wheels of the train, and there was a flash of fire. The red lights disappeared into the darkness.

In Dundee, on the other side of the Firth of Tay, the stationmaster anxiously tried to contact the signal box by telegraph, but the line was dead. He and the locomotive superintendent struggled onto the bridge. Ominously, they encountered a broken pipe spouting water. As they struggled forward into the gale, sometimes crawling on hands and knees, they saw that the whole of the central section of the bridge, known as the High Girders, was missing, along with the train. The latter had plunged into the river, killing seventy-five people. The incident remains Britain's worst structural railway engineering disaster.

Exactly what caused the catastrophe remains open to debate. Only two years before, the bridge, nearly two miles long, had been opened to public acclaim as one of the wonders of the age. By bridging the Firth of Tay and, it was planned, the Firth of Forth, the Edinburgh and Northern Railway, spurred on by its recently knighted engineer Sir Thomas Bouch, would make Dundee and Aberdeen far more accessible. Weak design, faults in the cast iron, unnoticed deterioration, disregard of safety procedures – it may have been that a combination of all these factors was to blame. When dawn broke on 29 December, distraught spectators could see that a dozen piers were completely missing, their position marked only by the stumps of their platforms poking out of the water.

'Oh! ill-fated Bridge of the Silv'ry Tay,' exclaimed the local poet William McGonagall, in a famous metrical garnish, if only the central girders had been supported by buttresses . . .

> For the Stronger we our houses do build,
> The less chance we have of being killed.

Other engineers rebuilt the bridge, with improvements, but Bouch never saw it; his career ruined, he died less than a year after the accident.

By contrast, two famous political theorists who had intended to travel on the doomed train had a narrow escape. At the last moment, Karl Marx and Friedrich Engels decided to stay one more night in Edinburgh with the friends with whom they had been spending Christmas. How different the 20th century might have been if *Das Kapital* had never been finished.

WHITHORN

DUMFRIES & GALLOWAY

Origins of Christianity in Scotland

Whithorn is the cradle of Christianity in Scotland. Today, tucked away in a landscape of stone walls, gorse bushes and cattle, it lies in one of the most out-of-the-way corners of Britain; on the north side of the Solway Firth, it would have seemed more accessible in an age of sea travel, but still isolated enough to St Ninian. He is supposed to have arrived here in 397AD, before the Roman soldiers had left England. Ninian began his journey in Rome. A Briton, he had trained there and been ordained a bishop before being sent back as a missionary to his homeland. On his way, he seems to have stopped at the monastery at Tours, ruled by St Martin, who apparently befriended him and assisted him in his mission. It is said that masons from Tours helped him build his church. Being built of stone, it was – in a land of wooden houses – a striking edifice, known as the *Candida Casa*, or white house. Whithorn derives from this name.

Beyond this, St Ninian is a shadowy figure; we first hear of him from Bede (see page 393), writing in about 730. In time, a great monastery arose, which became a centre of pilgrimage. It drew kings, such as Robert the Bruce and James III, James IV and James V. The shell of the priory church-cum-cathedral, with its Norman doorway, still stands, surrounded by handsome 19th-century tombstones built to remember mariners and farmers: it was the parish church until a new one was built next to it in 1822.

However, the pilgrims sought not only the ecclesiastical splendour of a national shrine, but the simple St Ninian's Cave, about three miles to the south-east, where it is said that the saint withdrew to reflect and pray. It is easy to imagine him scrunching over the pebbly beach. Walking there – and you have to walk – on a bright spring morning, whose sky seems to be reflected in the aconites and bluebells sparkling on the lush woodland floor, is itself a spiritual experience.

Gazetteer

THE PURPOSE OF this section of the book is to help you plan your tour of the landmarks. For each site, I have provided a telephone number if possible, and a website if relevant. Where one or more of these has not been available, or to aid navigation to some of the more remote landmarks, I have given an Ordnance Survey grid reference.

Sometimes I have noted where booking in advance is definitely necessary, or where visits are by guided tour only, but these observations are by no means exhaustive and I would strongly advise ringing in advance to check opening hours. A handful of the landmarks are, regrettably, not open to the public, or have very limited opening hours. Telephone numbers and website addresses are correct at the time of compilation, but inevitably a few will have changed by the time you read this. The publisher will be more than happy to correct them in any reprints.

South-West England

Abbotsbury, near Weymouth, Dorset
01305 871858
www.abbotsbury-tourism.co.uk

Roman Baths, Bath, Somerset
01225 477785
www.romanbaths.co.uk

Bath Abbey, Somerset
01225 422462
www.bathabbey.org

Queen Square, Bath, Somerset
www.visitbath.co.uk

Lansdown Tower, Bath
01225 422212
www.bath-preservation-trust.org.uk

Bovington Tank Museum, near
Wareham, Dorset
01929 405096
www.tankmuseum.co.uk

Bowood House, near Chippenham,
Wiltshire
01249 812102
www.bowood-house.co.uk

St Mary Redcliffe, Bristol
0117 929 1487
www.stmaryredcliffe.co.uk

The New Room, Horsefair, Bristol
0117 926 4740
www.newroombristol.org.uk

The Georgian House, Bristol
0117 921 1362
www.bristol-city.gov.uk/museums

SS Great Britain, Bristol
0117 926 0680
www.ss-great-britain.com

Brixham Harbour, Devon
01803 851854 (Brixham Harbour
Master's Office)
www.torbay.gov.uk/brixhamharbour

Brownsea Island, Dorset
01202 707744
www.brownsea-island.org.uk
www.nationaltrust.org.uk

Buckland Abbey, near Yelverton,
Devon
01822 853607
www.nationaltrust.org.uk

Cadbury Castle, near Wincanton,
Somerset
01935 845946 (tourist information
centre)
OS grid reference ST 624250

Gough's Cave, Cheddar Gorge,
Somerset
01934 742343
www.cheddarcaves.co.uk

Christchurch Priory, Dorset
01202 488645
www.christchurchpriory.org

Chysauster Ancient Village, near
Penzance, Cornwall
07831 757934
www.english-heritage.org.uk/chysauster
OS grid reference SW 473350

Clouds Hill, near Wareham, Dorset
01929 405616
www.nationaltrust.org.uk

Delabole Wind Farm, near
Camelford, Cornwall
www.bwea.com
OS grid reference SX 086854

Eddystone Lighthouse, Plymouth Hoe,
Devon
01752 603300
www.plymouthdome.info

Exeter Cathedral, Devon
01392 285983
www.exeter-cathedral.org.uk

Geevor Tin Mine, near Penzance,
Cornwall
01736 788662
www.geevor.com

Glastonbury Abbey, Somerset
01458 832267
www.glastonburyabbey.com

Lacock Abbey, near Chippenham,
Wiltshire
01249 730459
www.nationaltrust.org.uk/places/lacock

Marconi Wireless Station,
The Lizard, Cornwall
01326 290384
www.lizardwireless.org
www.nationaltrust.org.uk

Longleat House, near Warminster,
Wiltshire
01985 844400
www.longleat.co.uk

Maiden Castle, near Dorchester,
Dorset
www.english-heritage.org.uk
OS grid reference SY 670885

Meare Fish House, near Glastonbury,
Somerset
www.english-heritage.org.uk
OS grid reference ST 458418

Melcombe Regis, near Weymouth,
Dorset
01305 785747 (tourist information
centre)
OS grid reference SY 682802

Old Sarum, near Salisbury, Wiltshire
01722 335398
www.english-heritage.org.uk/oldsarum

Plymouth Hoe, Devon
01752 304849 (tourist information
centre)
OS grid reference SX 477538

Isle of Portland, Dorset
01305 785747 (tourist information
centre)
OS grid reference SY 696709 (Church
Ope Cove)

St Mawes Castle, near Falmouth,
Cornwall
01326 270526
www.english-heritage.org.uk/stmawes

Salisbury Cathedral, Wiltshire
01722 555120
www.salisburycathedral.org.uk

Royal Albert Bridge, Saltash,
Cornwall
www.royal-albert-bridge.co.uk
OS grid reference SX 434587

Battle of Sedgemoor, near
Bridgwater, Somerset
www.battlefieldstrust.com/resource-centre
OS grid reference ST 351356

Sherborne Castle, Dorset
01935 813182
www.sherbornecastle.com

Stonehenge, Salisbury Plain, Wiltshire
01980 624715
www.english-heritage.org.uk/stonehenge

Stourhead, near Warminster,
Wiltshire
01747 841152
www.nationaltrust.org.uk

Tolpuddle, near Dorchester, Dorset
01305 848237 (Tolpuddle Martyrs
Museum)
www.tolpuddlemartyrs.org.uk

Market Place, Wells, Somerset
01749 672552 (tourist information
centre)

South-East England

The Clergy House, Alfriston,
East Sussex
01323 870001
www.nationaltrust.org.uk/places/alfriston

Arundel Castle, West Sussex
01903 882173
www.arundelcastle.org

Battle of Hastings, Battle, East Sussex
01424 773792 (Battle Abbey)
www.english-heritage.org.uk/battleabbey

Red House, Bexleyheath, Kent
01494 755588 (guided tours only;
booking essential)
www.nationaltrust.org.uk

Royal Pavilion, Brighton, East Sussex
01273 290900
www.royalpavilion.org.uk

Grand Hotel, Brighton, East Sussex
01273 224300
www.grandbrighton.co.uk

Broadlands, near Romsey, Hampshire
01794 505010
www.broadlands.net

Buckler's Hard, The Solent,
Hampshire
01590 612345
www.bucklershard.co.uk

Bateman's, Burwash, East Sussex
01435 882302
www.nationaltrust.org.uk/places/batemans

St Augustine's Abbey, Canterbury,
Kent
01227 767345
www.english-heritage.org.uk

Canterbury Cathedral, Kent
01227 762862
www.canterbury-cathedral.org

Charleston Farmhouse, near Lewes,
East Sussex
01323 811265
www.charleston.org.uk

Fox Hall, Charlton, West Sussex
01628 825925 (open for holiday lets
only)
www.landmarktrust.org.uk

Chartwell, near Westerham, Kent
01732 868381
www.nationaltrust.org.uk/places/chartwell

Chatham Dockyard, Kent
01634 823807
www.chdt.org.uk

Jane Austen's House, Chawton,
Hampshire
01420 83262
www.jane-austens-house-museum.org.uk

Croydon Airport, Surrey
020 8669 1196
www.imperial-airways.com

White Cliffs of Dover, Kent
01304 202756
www.nationaltrust.org.uk/places/whitecliffs

Dover Castle, Kent
01304 211067
www.english-heritage.org.uk/dovercastle

Down House, near Orpington, Kent
01689 859119
www.english-heritage.org.uk/downhouse

The Redoubt, Eastbourne,
East Sussex
01323 410300
www.eastbournemuseums.co.uk/redoubt

Emsworth, Hampshire
01243 373780
www.emsworthmuseum.org.uk

Epsom Racecourse, Surrey
01372 726311
www.epsomderby.co.uk

Fishbourne Roman Palace, near
Chichester, West Sussex
01243 785859
www.sussexpast.co.uk

Gad's Hill, near Rochester, Kent
Now a school, not generally open to
the public; visible from the road.
01474 822366
www.gadshill.org

Broadhalfpenny Down, Hambledon,
Hampshire
01730 825711
www.broadhalfpennydown.com

Hampton Court, Surrey
0870 752 7777
www.hampton-court-palace.org.uk

Hever Castle, near Edenbridge, Kent
01732 865224
www.hevercastle.co.uk

Royal Botanic Gardens, Kew, Surrey
020 8332 5655
www.rbgkew.org.uk

Battle of Lewes, East Sussex
01273 483448 (tourist information
centre)
OS grid reference TQ 395112

Margate Beach, Kent
01843 583334 (tourist information
centre)
OS grid reference TR 349707

Munstead Wood, near Godalming,
Surrey
01483 417867 (garden open
under National Garden Scheme
and by private appointment)
www.ngs.org.uk

Rufus Stone, New Forest, Hampshire
023 8028 2269 (tourist information
centre)
OS grid reference SU 270124

Osborne House, near Cowes,
Isle of Wight
01983 200022
www.english-heritage.org.uk/osbornehouse

Pevensey Castle, East Sussex
01323 762604
www.english-heritage.org.uk/pevenseycastle

Polesden Lacey, near Dorking, Surrey
01372 452048
www.nationaltrust.org.uk/places/
polesdenlacey

Pooh Bridge, near Hartfield,
East Sussex
www.pooh-corner.org
OS grid reference TQ 470337

Portchester Castle, Hampshire
023 9237 8291
www.english-heritage.org.uk/portchester

Port Lympne, near Hythe, Kent
01303 264647
www.totallywild.net/portlympne

The Mary Rose, Portsmouth,
Hampshire
023 9283 9766
www.maryrose.org

HMS Victory, Portsmouth, Hampshire
023 9286 1533
www.hms-victory.com

The Grange, Ramsgate, Kent
01628 825925 (open for holiday lets
from 2006)
www.landmarktrust.org.uk

Richborough Roman Fort, near
Sandwich, Kent
01304 612013
www.english-heritage.org.uk/richborough

Rochester Castle, Kent
01634 402276
www.english-heritage.org.uk

Lamb House, Rye, East Sussex
01797 229542
www.nationaltrust.org.uk

The Wakes, Selborne, Hampshire
01420 511275
www.selborne.parish.hants.gov.uk

Shoreham Airport, West Sussex
01273 296900
www.shorehamairport.co.uk

Silchester Roman Town, Hampshire
01483 252000
www.english-heritage.org.uk

St Mary's Church, Stoke d'Abernon,
near Leatherhead, Surrey
01932 869922
www.cofeguildford.org.uk/parishes/
leatherhead/stoke-d.shtml

RAF Tangmere, near Chichester,
West Sussex
01243 775223
www.tangmere-museum.org.uk

The Vyne, near Basingstoke,
Hampshire
01256 883858
www.nationaltrust.org.uk/places/thevyne

Walmer Beach, near Deal, Kent
www.walmerweb.co.uk
OS grid reference TR 377501

Quebec House, Westerham, Kent
01732 868381
www.nationaltrust.org.uk

Winchester Castle, Hampshire
01962 846476
www.hants.gov.uk/discover

Winchester College, Hampshire
01962 621227 (guided tours only)
www.winchestercollege.org

Wolvesey Palace, Winchester,
Hampshire
01962 854766
www.english-heritage.org.uk

The Gurkha Museum, Winchester,
Hampshire
01962 842832
www.thegurkhamuseum.co.uk

Woking Mosque, Surrey
01483 760679
www.wokingmosque.org.uk

London

Abbey Mills Pumping Station,
Stratford E15
0118 9642803 (booking essential;
guided tours only)
OS grid reference TQ 386832

Abbey Road Studios, 3 Abbey
Road, NW8
020 7266 7000
www.abbeyroad.co.uk

The Albert Memorial, Kensington
Gardens, SW7
020 7495 0916
www.english-heritage.org.uk

All England Lawn Tennis & Croquet
Club, Church Walk, SW19
020 8946 2244
www.wimbledon.org

Apsley House, Hyde Park Corner, W1
020 7499 5676
www.english-heritage.org.uk/apsleyhouse

Arnos Grove Underground Station,
Enfield, N11
www.tfl.gov.uk/tube
OS grid reference TQ 293924

The Bank of England, Threadneedle
Street, EC2
020 7601 5491
www.bankofengland.co.uk/museum

The Banqueting House,
Whitehall, SW1
0870 751 5178
www.banqueting-house.org.uk

Battersea Dogs' Home, Battersea Park
Road, SW8
020 7622 3626
www.dogshome.org

11 Bedford Square, Bloomsbury, WC1
Not open to the public.
OS grid reference TQ 298817

Bevis Marks Synagogue, Bevis
Marks, EC3
020 7626 1274
www.sandp.org

Blind Beggar Pub, 337 Whitechapel
Road, E1
020 7247 6195
OS grid reference TQ 349818

Bridge Street, Westminster, SW1
OS grid reference TQ 302796

British Library, 96 Euston Road, NW1
020 7412 7332
www.bl.uk

British Museum, Bloomsbury, WC1
020 7323 8299
www.thebritishmuseum.ac.uk

Broadcasting House, Portland
Place, W1
Not open to the public.
OS grid reference TQ 288816

Broad Court, Covent Garden, WC2
OS grid reference TQ 304811

The Brunel Engine House, Railway
Avenue, SE16
020 7231 3840
www.brunelenginehouse.org.uk

BT Tower, Cleveland Street, W1
Not open to the public.
OS grid reference TQ 292818

Buckingham Palace, The Mall, SW1
020 7766 7300
www.royal.gov.uk

Bunhill Fields, Bunhill Row, EC1
020 7374 4127
www.cityoflondon.gov.uk

Cabinet War Rooms, King Charles
Street, SW1
020 7930 6961
cwr.iwm.org.uk

Canary Wharf, Docklands, E14
020 7418 2000
www.canarywharf.com

The Cenotaph, Whitehall, SW1
www.britishlegion.org.uk
OS grid reference TQ 301799

Central Criminal Court,
Old Bailey, EC4
020 7248 3277
www.cityoflondon.gov.uk

Centre Point, 103 New Oxford
Street, WC1
Not open to the public.
OS grid reference TQ 298813

The Charterhouse, Charterhouse
Square, EC1
020 7253 9503 (booking essential)
OS grid reference TQ 319819

Chelsea Old Church, Chelsea
Embankment, SW3
020 7795 1019
www.chelseaoldchurch.org.uk

Chiswick House, Burlington Lane, W4
020 8995 0508
www.english-heritage.org.uk/chiswickhouse

Christie's, 8 King Street, SW1
020 7839 9060
www.christies.co.uk

10 Downing Street, Whitehall, SW1
www.number-10.gov.uk
OS grid reference TQ 300799

Electric Avenue, Brixton, SW9
OS grid reference TQ 311753

Fleet Street, Holborn, EC4
OS grid reference TQ 314811

Foreign & Commonwealth Office,
Whitehall, SW1
020 7008 1500 (open days and by
special arrangement)
www.fco.gov.uk

The Foundling Museum, Brunswick
Square, WC1
020 7841 3600
www.coram.org.uk

Freud's House, 20 Maresfield
Gardens, NW3
020 7435 2002
www.freud.org.uk

22 Frith Street, Soho, W1
Not open to the public.
OS grid reference TQ 297810

The Globe Theatre, New Globe
Walk, SE1
020 7902 1400
www.shakespeares-globe.org

Goldsmiths' Hall, Foster Lane, EC2
020 7606 7010
www.thegoldsmiths.co.uk/hall

Granada Cinema, Mitcham
Road, SW17
020 8672 5717 (now Gala Bingo)
OS grid reference TQ 275713

Grove Road, Bow, E3
OS grid reference TQ 362828

Handel's House, 25 Brook Street, W1
020 7495 1685
www.handelhouse.org

Henry Poole & Co., 15 Savile Row, W1
020 7734 5985
www.henrypoole.co.uk

Highgate Cemetery, Swain's Lane, N6
020 8340 1834
www.highgate-cemetery.org

Hoare's Bank, 37 Fleet Street, EC4
020 7353 4522
www.hoaresbank.co.uk

Keats House, Keats Grove, NW3
020 7435 2062
www.cityoflondon.gov.uk

Kensington Palace, Kensington, W8
0870 751 5170
www.kensington-palace.org.uk

Cranmer's Tower, Lambeth
Palace, SE1
020 7898 1200 (tours by special
arrangement)
www.archbishopofcanterbury.org/palace

Leighton House, 12 Holland Park
Road, W14
020 7602 3316
www.rbkc.gov.uk/leightonhousemuseum

Linley Sambourne House, 18 Stafford
Terrace, w8
020 7602 3316, ext 305 (limited
opening times)
www.rbkc.gov.uk/linleysambournehouse

Lloyd's of London, Lime Street, EC3
01245 609425 (not generally open to
the public; tours by special
arrangement only)
www.lloyds.com

London Zoo, Regent's Park, NW1
020 7722 3333
www.zsl.org/london-zoo

Mansion House, Walbrook, EC4
Group visits only, by written request
to the Principal Assistant, Mansion
House, London EC4N 8BH.
www.cityoflondon.gov.uk

Michelin House, 81 Fulham
Road, SW3
020 7581 5817 (Bibendum restaurant
and oyster bar)
www.bibendum.co.uk

The Monument, Fish Street Hill, EC3
020 7626 2717
www.cityoflondon.gov.uk

John Murray, 50 Albemarle Street, W1
Not open to the public.
OS grid reference TQ 291804

The Nash Terraces, Regent's
Park, NW1
www.royalparks.gov.uk
OS grid reference TQ 287830

Primrose Hill, Primrose Hill
Road, NW3
OS grid reference TQ 276838

Queen's House, Park Row, SE10
020 8858 4422
www.nmm.ac.uk

Ranger's House, Chesterfield
Walk, SE10
020 8853 0035
www.english-heritage.org.uk/rangershouse

Ritz Hotel, 150 Piccadilly, W1
020 7493 8181
www.theritzlondon.com

Royal Academy of Arts, Piccadilly, W1
020 7300 8000
www.royalacademy.org.uk

Royal Arsenal, Woolwich, SE18
020 8855 7755
www.firepower.org.uk

Royal Festival Hall, Belvedere
Road, SE1
0870 380 4300
www.rfh.org.uk

The Royal Institution, 21 Albemarle
Street, W1
020 7409 2992 (tours by special
arrangement)
www.rigb.org

Royal Naval Hospital, King William
Walk, SE10
020 8269 4747
www.greenwichfoundation.org.uk

Royal Observatory, Greenwich
Park, SE10
020 8858 4422
www.nmm.ac.uk

24 Russell Square, Bloomsbury, WC1
Not open to the public.
OS grid reference TQ 301818

St Bartholomew's Hospital,
Smithfield, EC1
020 7837 0546
www.brlcf.org.uk

St Clement Danes, Strand, WC2
020 7242 2380
www.st-clement-danes.co.uk

St Katharine's Dock, St Katharine's
Way, E1
020 7264 5312
www.skdocks.co.uk

St Mary's Hospital, Praed Street, W2
020 7886 6528 (Alexander Fleming
Laboratory Museum)
www.st-marys.nhs.uk

St Paul's Cathedral, St Paul's
Churchyard, EC4
020 7236 4128
www.stpauls.co.uk

St Thomas's Old Operating Theatre,
Southwark, SE1
020 7188 2679
www.thegarret.org.uk

Selfridges, 398–454 Oxford Street, W1
08708 377377
www.selfridges.co.uk

Shaftesbury Memorial, Piccadilly
Circus, W1
OS grid reference TQ 295806

Sidney Street, Stepney, E1
OS grid reference TQ 350816

Smithfield, EC1
0870 444 3852 (Museum of London)
www.museumoflondon.org.uk
OS grid reference TQ 317816

Sir John Soane's Museum, 12–14
Lincoln's Inn Fields, WC2
020 7405 2107
www.soane.org

Speakers' Corner, Marble Arch, W2
www.speakerscorner.net
OS grid reference TQ 277808

The Temple Church, Middle
Temple, EC4
020 7353 3470
www.templechurch.com

The White Tower, Tower of
London, EC3
0870 756 6060
www.tower-of-london.org.uk

Trellick Tower, Golborne Road, W10
Not generally open to the public,
except through the annual Open
House London event.
www.londonopenhouse.org
OS grid reference TQ 246820

Twinings, 216 Strand, WC2
020 7353 3511
www.twinings.com

University College, Gower Street, WC1
020 7679 2000
www.ucl.ac.uk

Jerusalem Chamber, Westminster
Abbey, SW1
020 7654 4900
www.westminster-abbey.org

Westminster Cathedral, Ashley
Place, SW1
020 7798 9055
www.westminstercathedral.org.uk

Westminster Hall, Westminster, SW1
020 7219 3000
www.parliament.uk

Palace of Westminster,
Westminster, SW1
020 7219 3000
www.parliament.uk

Winchester Palace, Southwark, SE1
020 7973 3468
www.english-heritage.org.uk

The Home Counties

Shaw's Corner, Ayot St Lawrence,
Hertfordshire
01438 820307
www.nationaltrust.org.uk/places/
shawscorner

Battle of Barnet, Hertfordshire
www.warsoftheroses.com
OS grid reference TQ 248976

Bunyan's Baptism Pool, Bedford
01234 213722 (Bunyan Museum)
www.bedfordmuseum.org/
johnbunyanmuseum

Blenheim Palace, Woodstock,
Oxfordshire
01993 811091
www.blenheimpalace.com

Bletchley Park, near Milton Keynes,
Buckinghamshire
01908 640404
www.bletchleypark.org.uk

Bridego Bridge, near Cheddington,
Buckinghamshire
OS grid reference SP 917209

Brocket Hall, near Welwyn Garden
City, Hertfordshire
01707 335241
www.brocket-hall.co.uk

St John's Church, Burford,
Oxfordshire
01993 823788
OS grid reference SP 252123

John Milton's Cottage, Chalfont St
Giles, Buckinghamshire
01494 872313
www.miltonscottage.org

Claydon House, near Winslow,
Buckinghamshire
01296 730349
www.nationaltrust.org.uk

Cliveden House, near Maidenhead,
Buckinghamshire
01628 605069
www.nationaltrust.org.uk

Cookham, Berkshire
01628 471885 (The Stanley Spencer
Gallery)
www.stanleyspencer.org.uk

Dorney Court, Buckinghamshire
01628 604638
www.dorneycourt.co.uk

Eton College, Berkshire
01753 671177
www.etoncollege.com

God's House, Ewelme, Oxfordshire
www.ewelme.info
OS grid reference SU 647912

Fort Belvedere, near Windsor,
Berkshire
Not open to the public.
OS grid reference SU 968679

Greenham Common, near Newbury,
Berkshire
01635 30511
www.greenham-common.org.uk

Shakespeare Temple, Hampton,
Middlesex
020 8831 6000
www.garrickstemple.org.uk

Old Palace, Hatfield, Hertfordshire
01707 262055
www.theoldpalace.co.uk

Hatfield House, Hertfordshire
01707 287010
www.hatfield-house.co.uk

Heston Aerodrome, near Hounslow, Middlesex
OS grid reference TQ 117782

Hounslow Heath, Middlesex
OS grid references TQ 076769 and TQ 137709

Hughenden Manor, near High Wycombe, Buckinghamshire
01494 755573
www.nationaltrust.org.uk

Jordans Meeting House, Buckinghamshire
Not currently open to the public due to the 2005 fire.
OS grid reference SU 975909

Kew Bridge Pumping Station, Middlesex
020 8568 4757
www.kbsm.org

Letchworth Garden City, Hertfordshire
01462 487868 (tourist information centre)
www.letchworth.org

Olney, near Newport Pagnell, Buckinghamshire
01234 711516 (Cowper and Newton Museum)
www.cowperandnewtonmuseum.org.uk

Balliol College, Broad Street, Oxford
01865 277777
www.balliol.ox.ac.uk

New College, New College Lane, Oxford
01865 279555
www.new.ox.ac.uk

Martyrs' Memorial, St Giles' Street, Oxford
01865 726871 (tourist information centre)

Oxford Botanic Garden, High Street, Oxford
01865 286690
www.botanic-garden.ox.ac.uk

Ashmolean Museum, Beaumont Street, Oxford
01865 278000
www.ashmol.ox.ac.uk

University Church of St Mary, High Street, Oxford
01865 279111
www.university-church.ox.ac.uk

Museum of Natural History, Parks Road, Oxford
01865 272950
www.oum.ox.ac.uk

Christ Church, St Aldgate's Street, Oxford
01865 276150
www.chch.ox.ac.uk

Iffley Road Athletics Track, Oxford
01865 240476
www.sport.ox.ac.uk/facilities

The Hoover Factory, Perivale, Middlesex
OS grid reference TQ 166829

Reading Gaol, Berkshire
Not open to the public.
OS grid reference SU 720736

The Ridgeway, from Avebury to Ivinghoe Beacon
01865 810224
www.nationaltrail.co.uk

Runnymede, near Windsor, Berkshire
01784 432891
www.nationaltrust.org.uk/places/runnymede

St Albans Cathedral, Hertfordshire
01727 860780
www.stalbanscathedral.org.uk

Slough Trading Estate, Berkshire
OS grid reference SU 950816

Stowe Gardens, Buckinghamshire
01494 755568
www.nationaltrust.org.uk/places/
stowegardens

Strawberry Hill, Twickenham,
Middlesex
020 8240 4224
www.friendsofstrawberryhill.org

Syon House, Brentford, Middlesex
020 8560 0881
www.syonpark.co.uk

Waddesdon Manor, near Aylesbury,
Buckinghamshire
01296 653203
www.waddesdon.org.uk
www.nationaltrust.org.uk

West Wycombe Park,
Buckinghamshire
01494 755573
www.nationaltrust.org.uk

The White Horse, near Uffington,
Oxfordshire
www.english-heritage.org.uk/uffington
OS grid reference SU 301866

Windsor Castle, Berkshire
020 7766 7304
www.royal.gov.uk

St George's Chapel, Windsor,
Berkshire
020 7766 7304
www.royal.gov.uk

Eastern England

Bawdsey Manor, near Felixstowe,
Suffolk
01394 277669
www.bawdseyradargroup.co.uk

Bowthorpe Oak, near Bourne,
Lincolnshire
01778 590269
www.bourneonline.co.uk

St Peter-on-the-Wall, Bradwell-on-
Sea, Essex
www.bradwellchapel.org
OS grid reference TM 030081

Burghley House, near Stamford,
Lincolnshire
01780 752451
www.burghley.co.uk

Peterhouse, Trumpington Street,
Cambridge
01223 338200
www.pet.cam.ac.uk

King's College Chapel, King's Parade,
Cambridge
01223 331212
www.kings.cam.ac.uk

Trinity College, Trinity Street,
Cambridge
01223 338400
www.trin.cam.ac.uk

Parker's Piece, Cambridge
www.cuafc.org/history
OS grid reference TL 455580

The Cavendish Laboratory, Free
School Lane, Cambridge
Not open to the public.
www.phy.cam.ac.uk

The Eagle, Benet Street, Cambridge
01223 505020

Castle Rising, Norfolk
01553 631330
www.english-heritage.org.uk

St Andrew's Church, Chesterton,
Cambridgeshire
www.ely.anglican.org/parishes/chesandr
OS grid reference TL 463595

Grange Barn, Coggeshall, Essex
01376 562226
www.nationaltrust.org.uk

RAF Cranwell, near Sleaford,
Lincolnshire
www.cranwell.raf.mod.uk
OS grid reference TF 002495

Cross Keys Wash, near Sutton Bridge,
Lincolnshire
OS grid reference TF 519199

Flatford Mill, near Colchester, Essex
01206 298283 (the Field Studies
Council runs courses here and can
organise group visits)
www.field-studies-council.org/flatfordmill
01206 298260 (Bridge Cottage,
Flatford, National Trust)
www.nationaltrust.org.uk

Framlingham Castle, Suffolk
01728 724189
www.english-heritage.org.uk/
framlinghamcastle

The Old Vicarage, Grantchester,
Cambridgeshire
Not open to the public, but there
is a Rupert Brooke museum at
The Orchard tea garden.
01223 845788 (The Orchard tea
garden)
www.orchard-grantchester.com

Angel and Royal Hotel, Grantham,
Lincolnshire
01476 565816
www.angelandroyal.com

1–3 North Parade, Grantham,
Lincolnshire
01476 406166 (tourist information
centre)
OS grid reference SK 910364

Grimes Graves, near Thetford,
Norfolk
01842 810656
www.english-heritage.org.uk/grimesgraves

Holkham Hall, near Wells-next-the-
Sea, Norfolk
01328 713104
www.holkham.co.uk

Houghton Hall, near King's Lynn,
Norfolk
01485 528569
www.houghtonhall.com

Old Grammar School, Huntingdon,
Cambridgeshire
01480 375830 (Cromwell Museum)
www.olivercromwell.org

The Long Shop, Leiston, Suffolk
01728 832189
www.longshop.care4free.net

The Jew's House, Steep Hill, Lincoln
01522 524851 (now a restaurant)

Lincoln Cathedral, Lincoln
01522 544544
www.lincolncathedral.com

Battle of Maldon, Essex
www.battleofmaldon.org.uk
OS grid reference TL 865054

Newmarket Heath, Suffolk
01638 667200 (tourist information
centre)
www.newmarketracecourses.co.uk

St Julian's Church, Norwich
01603 727627 (tourist information
centre)
OS grid reference TG 235081

Colman's Mustard Works, Norwich
Not open to the public.
01603 627889 (The Mustard Shop
Museum)
OS grid reference TG 238077

Orford Castle, Suffolk
01394 450472
www.english-heritage.org.uk/orfordcastle

Orford Ness, Suffolk
01394 450900
www.nationaltrust.org.uk/orfordness

Sandringham House, near King's
Lynn, Norfolk
01553 612908
www.sandringhamestate.co.uk

Snape Maltings, near Aldeburgh,
Suffolk
01728 688303
www.snapemaltings.co.uk

Battle of Sole Bay, near Southwold,
Suffolk
01502 726097 (Southwold Museum)
www.southwoldmuseum.org

Daniel Lambert Inn, Stamford,
Lincolnshire
01780 755991 (Daniel Lambert Inn)
01780 766317 (Stamford Museum)
www.stamford.co.uk

The Bell Inn, Stilton, Cambridgeshire
01733 241066
www.thebellstilton.co.uk

Gainsborough's House, Sudbury,
Suffolk
01787 372958
www.gainsborough.org

Sutton Hoo, near Woodbridge,
Suffolk
01394 389714
www.nationaltrust.org.uk/places/suttonhoo

Tilbury Fort, Tilbury, Essex
01375 858489
www.english-heritage.org.uk/tilburyfort

Walsingham Priory, Little
Walsingham, Norfolk
01328 820255 (Anglican shrine)
01328 820217 (Roman Catholic
shrine)
www.walsingham.org.uk

Waltham Abbey, Essex
01992 702200
www.english-heritage.org.uk

Wicken Fen, near Ely,
Cambridgeshire
01353 720274
www.wicken.org.uk

Woolsthorpe Manor, near Grantham,
Lincolnshire
01476 860338
www.nationaltrust.org.uk

The Midlands

The Wedgwood Factory, Barlaston,
Staffordshire
01782 282818 (Wedgwood Museum)
www.wedgwoodmuseum.org

Boots the Chemist, Beeston,
Nottinghamshire
Not open to the public.
OS grid reference SK 544366

Berkeley Castle, Gloucestershire
01453 810332
www.berkeley-castle.com

The Chantry, Berkeley,
Gloucestershire
01453 810631
www.jennermuseum.com

Berrington Hall, near Leominster,
Herefordshire
01568 615721
www.nationaltrust.org.uk/berrington

Soho House, Birmingham
0121 554 9122
www.bmag.org.uk

Birmingham Town Hall, Birmingham
www.birmingham.gov.uk/townhall
(closed for renovation until 2007)

Elkington's Factory, Birmingham
OS grid reference SP 065872

Spaghetti Junction, Birmingham
OS grid reference SP 092903

Bolsover Castle, Derbyshire
01246 822844
www.english-heritage.org.uk/bolsovercastle

Boscobel House, near Telford,
Shropshire
01902 850244
www.english-heritage.org.uk/boscobelhouse

Battle of Bosworth, near Market
Bosworth, Leicestershire
01455 290429
www.leics.gov.uk/country_parks_bosworth

Bass Brewery, Burton upon Trent,
Staffordshire
0845 6000 598
www.bass-museum.com

Chatsworth House, near Bakewell,
Derbyshire
01246 582204
www.chatsworth.org

Iron Bridge, Coalbrookdale,
Shropshire
01952 884391 (Ironbridge Gorge
Museums)
www.ironbridge.org.uk

Coventry Cathedral, Warwickshire
024 7652 1200
www.coventrycathedral.org.uk

Cromford, near Matlock, Derbyshire
01629 823256
www.cromfordmill.co.uk

Deene Park, near Corby,
Northamptonshire
01780 450278
www.deenepark.com

Guy Fawkes House, Dunchurch,
Warwickshire
Not open to the public.
www.dunchurch.org.uk

8a Victoria Street, Eastwood,
Nottinghamshire
01773 763312
OS grid reference SK 466470

Battle of Edgehill, near Banbury,
Warwickshire
www.battlefieldstrust.com/resource-centre
OS grid reference SP 353490

Eyam, Derbyshire
01433 631371 (Eyam Museum)
www.eyam.org.uk

Fotheringhay Castle,
Northamptonshire
01832 274333
OS grid reference TL 061929

Eleanor Cross, Geddington,
Northamptonshire
01604 735400
www.english-heritage.org.uk/eleanorcross

Gloucester Cathedral, Gloucester
01452 528095
www.gloucestercathedral.org.uk

Hardwick Hall, near Chesterfield,
Derbyshire
01246 850430
www.nationaltrust.org.uk

Mappa Mundi, Hereford Cathedral,
Hereford
01432 374200
www.herefordcathedral.org

Kenilworth Castle, Warwickshire
01926 852078
www.english-heritage.org.uk/
kenilworthcastle

Wicksteed Park, Kettering,
Northamptonshire
08700 621193
www.wicksteedpark.co.uk

Leicester Abbey, Leicester
0116 2998888 (tourist information
centre)
OS grid reference SK 586056

Samuel Johnson's Birthplace,
Lichfield, Staffordshire
01543 264972
www.lichfield.gov.uk/sjmuseum

Mordiford Bridge, near Hereford
01905 333224 (Elgar Birthplace
Museum)
www.elgarfoundation.org
OS grid reference SO 568374
(Mordiford Bridge)

Battle of Mortimer's Cross, near
Leominster, Herefordshire
www.battlefieldstrust.com/resource-centre
OS grid reference SO 427627

Battle of Naseby, near Market
Harborough, Northamptonshire
www.battlefieldstrust.com/resource-centre
OS grid reference SP 684799

Newstead Abbey, Nottinghamshire
01623 455900
www.newsteadabbey.org.uk

St Faith's Church, Newton in the
Willows, Northamptonshire
OS grid reference SP 885833

78 Derngate, Northampton
01604 603407 (admission by pre-
booked timed entry)
www.78derngate.org.uk

Forge Mill, Redditch, Worcestershire
01527 62509 (Needle Museum)

Rugby School, Warwickshire
01788 556109 (Rugby School
Museum)
www.rugbyschool.net

Triangular Lodge, Rushton,
Northamptonshire
01536 710761
www.english-heritage.org.uk/rushton

Izaak Walton's Cottage, Shallowford,
Staffordshire
01785 760278
OS grid reference SJ 876289

Sherwood Forest, Nottinghamshire
01623 824490 or 01623 824545
www.sherwoodforest.org.uk

Battle of Shrewsbury, Shropshire
OS grid reference SJ 512173

The Saracen's Head, Southwell,
Nottinghamshire
01636 812701
www.thesaracenshead-hotel.co.uk

Battle of Stoke, East Stoke,
Nottinghamshire
www.battlefieldstrust.com/resource-centre
OS grid reference SK 740490

Stokesay Castle, near Ludlow,
Shropshire
01588 672544
www.english-heritage.org.uk/stokesaycastle

Stow-on-the-Wold, Gloucestershire
www.battlefieldstrust.com/resource-centre
OS grid reference SP 191272

Shakespeare's Birthplace, Stratford-
upon-Avon, Warwickshire
01789 204016
www.shakespeare.org.uk

Battle of Tewkesbury, Gloucestershire
www.warsoftheroses.com
OS grid reference SO 888311

St Mary's Church, Warwick
01926 403940
www.stmaryswarwick.org.uk

Sudeley Castle, Winchcombe,
Gloucestershire
01242 602308
www.sudeleycastle.co.uk

Worcester Cathedral, Worcester
01905 28854
www.cofe-worcester.org.uk/cathedral

Lea & Perrins, Worcester
Not open to the public.
www.leaperrins.com

North-West England

Barrow-in-Furness, Cumbria
01229 820993 (Submarine Heritage
Centre)
www.submarineheritage.com

Birkenhead Park, Merseyside
0151 652 5197
www.wirral.gov.uk/er

Blackpool Pleasure Beach,
Lancashire
0870 444 5566
www.blackpoolpleasurebeach.co.uk

Brantwood, near Coniston, Cumbria
015394 41396
www.brantwood.org.uk
www.ruskinmuseum.com

Calder Hall, near Whitehaven,
Cumbria
01946 727027 (Sellafield Visitor's
Centre)
www.sellafield.com

The Countess Pillar, near Penrith,
Cumbria
01768 862488 (Brougham Castle)
www.english-heritage.org.uk/countesspillar
OS grid reference NY 546289

Bentley Motors, Pyms Lane, Crewe,
Cheshire
Not open to the public.
www.bentleymotors.com
OS grid reference SJ 684566

Dove Cottage, near Grasmere,
Cumbria
015394 35544
www.wordsworth.org.uk

Fox's Pulpit, near Sedbergh, Cumbria
OS grid reference SD 618936

Hack Green, near Nantwich,
Cheshire
01270 629219
www.hackgreen.co.uk

Hall i' th' Wood, near Bolton,
Lancashire
01204 332211
www.boltonmuseums.org.uk

Hill Top, near Sawrey, Cumbria
015394 36269
www.nationaltrust.org.uk

Hoghton Tower, near Blackburn,
Lancashire
01254 852986
www.hoghtontower.co.uk

Jodrell Bank, near Macclesfield,
Cheshire
01477 571339
www.jb.man.ac.uk/viscen

1a Castle Hill, Lancaster
01524 32808 (Judges' Lodgings
Museum, Church Street, Lancaster,
including collection of Gillow
furniture)

Cunard Building, Liverpool
Not generally open to the public.
0151 236 6407
www.cunard-building.co.uk

Liverpool Docks, Liverpool
0151 478 4499 (Merseyside Maritime
Museum)
www.liverpoolmuseums.org.uk/maritime

Mendips, Menlove Avenue, Liverpool
0870 900 0256
www.nationaltrust.org.uk/places/
mendipsforthlinroad

Paradise Mill, Macclesfield, Cheshire
01625 612045
www.silk-macclesfield.org

St Peter's Fields, Manchester
0161 234 3157 (tourist information
centre)
OS grid reference SJ 839979

Free Trade Hall, Manchester
0161 835 9929 (Radisson Edwardian
Hotel, on the site of the Free Trade
Hall)
www.radissonedwardian.com/manchester

Granada Studios, Water Street,
Manchester
Not generally open to the public.
OS grid reference SJ 829979

Lion Salt Works, Marston, Cheshire
01606 41823
www.lionsaltworkstrust.co.uk

Royal Oldham Hospital, Oldham,
Lancashire
Not open to the public except on
hospital business.
OS grid reference SD 920062

Port Sunlight, Merseyside
0151 644 6466
www.portsunlight.org.uk
www.ladyleverartgallery.org.uk

31 Toad Lane, Rochdale, Lancashire
01706 524920
OS grid reference SD 895137

Salford Museum, Lancashire
0161 736 2649
www.salford.gov.uk/salfordmuseum

Battle of Solway Moss, Cumbria
OS grid reference NY 380674

Tynwald Hill, St John's, Isle of Man
01624 685500
www.tynwald.org.im
OS grid reference SC 276818

North-East England

Alnwick Castle, Northumberland
01665 510777
www.alnwickcastle.com

Bamburgh Castle, Northumberland
01668 214515
www.bamburghcastle.com

Cragside, near Rothbury,
Northumberland
01669 620333
www.nationaltrust.org.uk

Durham Cathedral, Co. Durham
0191 386 4266
www.durhamcathedral.co.uk

Flodden Field, near Branxton,
Northumberland
OS grid reference NT 890370
www.flodden.net

Fountains Abbey, near Ripon,
North Yorkshire
01765 608888
www.fountainsabbey.org.uk

Hadrian's Wall, from Bowness-on-
Solway to Wallsend
01434 344363 (Housesteads Fort)
www.nationaltrust.org.uk

Halidon Hill, near Berwick-upon-
Tweed, Northumberland
OS grid reference NT 969548

The Piece Hall, Halifax,
West Yorkshire
01422 368725 (tourist information
centre)
www.piecehall.info

Brontë Parsonage, Haworth,
West Yorkshire
01535 642323
www.bronte.info

Wilberforce House, Hull
01482 613902
www.hullcc.gov.uk/wilberforce

Monastery of St Paul, Jarrow,
Co. Durham
0191 489 7052
www.english-heritage.org.uk/stpaul

Kirkgate Market, Leeds,
West Yorkshire
0113 242 5242 (tourist information
centre)
www.leedsmarket.com

Lindisfarne, Northumberland
01289 389244 (Lindisfarne Castle,
National Trust)
www.nationaltrust.org.uk
01289 389200 (Lindisfarne Priory,
English Heritage)
www.english-heritage.org.uk

Millennium Bridge, Newcastle
upon Tyne
0191 433 8420 (Gateshead tourist
information)
0191 277 8000 (Newcastle tourist
information)
www.gateshead.gov.uk/bridge

Norham, near Berwick-upon-Tweed,
Northumberland
01289 382329
www.english-heritage.org.uk/norhamcastle

Pontefract Castle, West Yorkshire
01977 723440
OS grid reference SE 460223

The Old Lifeboat Station, Redcar,
Cleveland
01642 494311 (Zetland Lifeboat
Museum)
www.redcarlifeboat.org.uk

Kelham Island Museum, Sheffield,
South Yorkshire
0114 2722106
www.simt.co.uk

Shildon Station, Co. Durham
01388 777999 (The National Railway
Museum at Shildon)
www.nrm.org.uk
01325 460532 (Darlington Railway
Centre & Museum)
www.drcm.org.uk

Staithes, near Whitby, North
Yorkshire
01947 841454 (Captain Cook and
Staithes Heritage Centre)
www.captcook-ne.co.uk

Stamford Bridge, near York, North
Yorkshire
www.battlefieldstrust.com/resource-centre
OS grid reference SE 720551

Battle of Towton, near Tadcaster,
North Yorkshire
www.towton.org.uk
OS grid reference SE 479377

Battle of Wakefield, West Yorkshire
www.warsoftheroses.com
OS grid reference SE 334181

Whitby Abbey, North Yorkshire
01947 603568
www.english-heritage.org.uk/whitbyabbey

Coppergate, York
01904 543403 (York Archaeological
Trust)
www.jorvik-viking-centre.co.uk

Clifford's Tower, York
01904 646940
www.english-heritage.org.uk/cliffordstower

Wales

Beaumaris Castle, Anglesey
01248 810361
www.cadw.wales.gov.uk

Big Pit, Blaenavon, Gwent
01495 790311 (National Mining
Museum of Wales)
www.nmgw.ac.uk/www.php/bigpit

Caerleon, near Newport, Gwent
01633 422518
www.cadw.wales.gov.uk

Caernarfon Castle, Gwynedd
01286 677617
www.cadw.wales.gov.uk

Caerphilly Castle, Mid Glamorgan
02920 883143
www.cadw.wales.gov.uk

Millennium Stadium, Cardiff
0870 013 8600
www.millenniumstadium.co.uk

Cardigan Castle, Dyfed
Not open to the public.
OS grid reference SN 178459

Chepstow Castle, Monmouthshire
01291 624065
www.cadw.wales.gov.uk

Dolbadarn Castle, Llanberis,
Gwynedd
01443 33 6000 (Cadw headquarters)
www.cadw.wales.gov.uk

Gower Peninsula, West Glamorgan
01792 361302 (tourist information
centre)
www.swansea.gov.uk/aonb

Hawarden Castle, near Buckley,
Flintshire
Not open to the public.
OS grid reference SJ 322653

Irfon Bridge, Builth Wells, Powys
www.builth-wells.co.uk
OS grid reference SO 042511

The Boat House, Laugharne,
Carmarthenshire
01994 427420
www.dylanthomasboathouse.com

Llanrhaeadr-ym-Mochnant, near
Welshpool, Powys
01690 760213 (Tŷ Mawr Wybrnant,
National Trust)
www.nationaltrust.org.uk

Llanystumdwy, near Criccieth,
Gwynedd
01766 522071 (Lloyd George
Museum)
www.gwynedd.gov.uk/museums

Manorbier Castle, Pembrokeshire
01834 871394 (open Easter to
September)
www.manorbiercastle.co.uk

Menai Suspension Bridge, Anglesey
OS grid reference SH 556714

Cyfarthfa Castle, Merthyr Tydfil,
Glamorgan
01685 723112
OS grid reference SO 040072

Monmouth Castle, Monmouth
01600 772175
www.monmouthcastlemuseum.org.uk

Shire Hall, Monmouth
01600 713899
www.monmouth.org.uk/Shirehall

Offa's Dyke, from Chepstow to
Prestatyn
01547 528753
www.offasdyke.demon.co.uk

Pembroke Castle, Pembroke
01646 681510
www.pembrokecastle.co.uk

Plas Newydd, Anglesey
01248 714795
www.nationaltrust.org.uk

Powis Castle, near Welshpool, Powys
01938 551929
www.nationaltrust.org.uk

St David's Cathedral, Pembrokeshire
01437 720691
www.stdavidscathedral.org.uk

St Mary's Church, Tenby,
Pembrokeshire
01834 842402 (tourist information
centre)
OS grid reference SN 133004

Strata Florida Abbey, Dyfed
01974 831261
www.cadw.wales.gov.uk

Tintern Abbey, Monmouthshire
01291 689251
www.cadw.wales.gov.uk

Scotland

Abbotsford House, near Melrose,
Borders
01896 752043
www.scottsabbotsford.co.uk

Abernethy, near Perth
01738 850889 (Museum of Abernethy)
OS grid reference NO 189164

Burns Cottage, Alloway, Ayrshire
01292 443700
www.burnsheritagepark.com

Arbroath Abbey, Angus
01241 878756
www.historic-scotland.gov.uk

Balmoral Castle, Ballater,
Aberdeenshire
013397 42534
www.balmoralcastle.com

Battle of Bannockburn, near Stirling
01786 812664
www.nts.org.uk
OS grid reference NS 797905

Chatelherault, near Hamilton,
Lanarkshire
01698 426213
OS grid reference NS 739532

Coldstream, Berwickshire
01890 882630 (Coldstream Museum)
www.holy-island.info/coldstream-museum

Battle of Culloden, near Inverness,
Highland
01463 790607
www.nts.org.uk
OS grid reference NH 745450

RRS *Discovery*, Dundee, Angus
01382 201245
www.rrsdiscovery.com

The Courier Building, Dundee,
Angus
Not open to the public.
OS grid reference NO 402304

Dunfermline Abbey, Fife
01383 724586
www.dunfermlineabbey.co.uk

Moodie Street, Dunfermline, Fife
01383 723638
www.carnegiebirthplace.com

Dunrobin Castle, near Golspie,
Highland
01408 633177
OS grid reference NC 850010

St Giles's Cathedral, Edinburgh
0131 225 9442
www.stgilescathedral.org.uk

Holyrood Palace, Edinburgh
0131 556 5100
www.royal.gov.uk

Greyfriars Kirk, Edinburgh
0131 226 5429
www.greyfriarskirk.com

The Advocates' Library, Edinburgh
0131 226 4531 (National Library of
Scotland; The Advocates' Library can
be visited by appointment only)
www.nls.uk

The Crown Room, Edinburgh
0131 225 9846
www.historic-scotland.gov.uk

Calton Hill, Edinburgh
0845 2255121 (tourist information
centre)
OS grid reference NT 263742

6a Nicolson Street, Edinburgh
0131 557 4567 (Buffet King Chinese
restaurant)
www.buffetkingedinburgh.com
www.jkrowling.com

Scottish Parliament, Edinburgh
0131 348 5200
www.scottish.parliament.uk

Battle of Falkirk, Stirlingshire
OS grid reference NS 872790
www.britishbattles.com

Falkland Palace, near Glenrothes, Fife
01337 857397
www.nts.org.uk

Fort George, Moray Firth, Highland
01667 460232
www.historic-scotland.gov.uk

Glasgow School of Art, Renfrew
Street, Glasgow
0141 353 4500
www.gsa.ac.uk

George Square, Glasgow
0141 204 4400 (tourist information
centre)
OS grid reference NS 592653

Finnieston Crane, Stobcross Quay,
Glasgow
0141 204 4400 (tourist information
centre)
OS grid reference NS 570651

Glenfinnan, near Fort William,
Highland
01397 722250
www.nts.org.uk

Glenlivet Distillery, Morayshire
01340 832157
www.theglenlivet.com

House of the Binns, near Linlithgow,
West Lothian
01506 834255
www.nts.org.uk

Island of Iona, Argyllshire
01681 700512
www.historic-scotland.gov.uk

Pass of Killiecrankie, near Pitlochry,
Perthshire
01796 473233
www.nts.org.uk

220 High Street, Kirkcaldy, Fife
Not open to the public.
www.adamsmith.org

9 Brechin Road, Kirriemuir, Angus
01575 572646
www.nts.org.uk

Loch Leven Castle, Perthshire
07778 040483 (mobile)
www.historic-scotland.gov.uk

Maes Howe, near Stromness, Orkney
01856 761606
www.historic-scotland.gov.uk

Kitchener Memorial, Marwick Head,
Orkney
OS grid reference HY 225251
www.kitchenerscholars.org

Melrose Abbey, Borders
01896 822562
www.historic-scotland.gov.uk

New Lanark, Lanarkshire
01555 661345
www.newlanark.org

Nigg Parish Church, Easter Ross,
Highland
www.niggoldtrust.org.uk
OS grid reference NH 804717

Rosslyn Chapel, near Loanhead,
Midlothian
www.rosslynchapel.org.uk
OS grid reference NT 274630

Roxburgh Castle, near Kelso, Borders
0870 6080404 (tourist information
centre)
OS grid reference NT 712337

Royal and Ancient Golf Club,
St Andrews, Fife
01334 460000
www.theroyalandancientgolfclub.org

Battle of Sauchieburn, near Stirling
0870 7200620 (tourist information
centre)
OS grid reference NO 664696

Scapa Flow, Orkney
01856 791300 (Visitor's Centre)
www.scapaflow.co.uk

Scone Palace, Perthshire
01738 552300
www.scone-palace.net

Scots Dyke, near Canonbie, Dumfries
& Galloway
01461 337834 (tourist information
centre)
OS grid reference NY 360735

Battle of Sheriffmuir, near Dunblane,
Stirlingshire
0870 7200613 (tourist information
centre)
OS grid reference NN 827027

Skara Brae, near Stromness, Orkney
01856 841815
www.historic-scotland.gov.uk
OS grid reference HY 231187

Stirling Castle, Stirling
01786 450000
www.historic-scotland.gov.uk

Tay Bridge, Firth of Tay,
Dundee
OS grid reference NO 392268

Whithorn, Dumfries & Galloway
01988 500508
www.historic-scotland.gov.uk
OS grid reference NX 444402

Picture Acknowledgements

1. Abbotsbury Swannery in the 1860s (photograph courtesy of Abbotsbury Swannery)
2. The great Roman Bath, Bath, 19th-century photograph (Private Collection/ Bridgeman Art Library)
3. Lansdown Tower (photograph courtesy of the Beckford Tower Trust)
4. Interior of the Bunk Room at Clouds Hill (National Trust Photo Library/ Dennis Gilbert)
5. *Roofs of Lacock Abbey* by William Henry Fox Talbot, paper negative, June 1840 (photograph courtesy of the W. H. Fox Talbot Trust, Lacock)
6. Joseph Priestley's chemical apparatus at Bowood House (Wellcome Library, London)
7. Aerial view of Chysauster village (Skyscan)
8. Maiden Castle (Collections/Peter Thomas)
9. The Abbot's kitchen, Glastonbury Abbey (Bridgeman Art Library)
10. *Stourhead, The Temple of Apollo* (The Art Archive/Nicolas Sapieha)
11. *Cornish Mining Scene,* English School, 19th century (The Royal Cornwall Museum, Truro/Bridgeman Art Library)
12. *The floating of the last span of the Royal Albert Bridge,* English School, 19th century (Ironbridge Gorge Museum/Bridgeman Art Library)
13. Statue of Thomas à Becket in Canterbury Cathedral (© Ric Ergenbright/ Corbis)
14. Interior of Exeter Cathedral (Collections/Peter Thomas)
15. *The Battle of Hastings* from 'Mirouer historial abregie de France' (Bodley 968 folio 173f. Bodleian Library, Oxford/The Art Archive)
16. Aerial view of Portchester Castle (© Jason Hawkes/Corbis)
17. The *Mary Rose* (Magdalene College/The Art Archive)
18. Royal Pavilion, Brighton (Edifice)
19. Stained-glass window at The Grange (photograph: Clive Boursnall)
20. *Charles Darwin and his wife at the piano,* anonymous painting (Down House/ Bridgeman Art Library)
21. *The Goldfish Pond* by Winston Churchill (Chartwell Manor/Bridgeman Art Library)

22. *Vanessa Bell at Charleston* by Duncan Grant (Private Collection/Bridgeman Art Library)
23. *Visitors to Broadlands,* photograph possibly by Graham Vivian, 1859 (National Portrait Gallery)
24. Margate c.1900 (London Stereoscopic Company/Getty Images)
25. Autochrome of Munstead Wood by Gertrude Jekyll (*Country Life* Picture Library)
26. Roman mosaic of Cupid riding a dolphin (photograph courtesy of Fishbourne Roman Palace/Sussex Archaeological Society)
27. *Interior of Fleet Street Sewer,* watercolour by Fred Shepherd, 1845 (Guildhall Library, London/Bridgeman Art Library)
28. Arnos Grove Underground Station (London Transport Museum)
29. *The Beheading of King Charles I,* Dutch School, 17th century (British Museum/Bridgeman Art Library)
30. *View of the King's Grand Staircase, Kensington Palace,* English School, 17th century (Kensington Palace/Bridgeman Art Library)
31. *A Shilling Well Laid Out* by Robert & George Cruikshank (Private Collection/Bridgeman Art Library)
32. *Chiswick House,* English School, 18th century (Victoria & Albert Museum/Bridgeman Art Library)
33. *George Frideric Handel* by Philippe Mercier (The Viscount Fitzharris/The Art Archive)
34. *Interior of the Soane Museum* by Joseph Gandy (Courtesy of the Trustees of Sir John Soane's Museum, London/Bridgeman Art Library)
35. Design for the Arab Hall at Leighton House, by George Aitchison, 1880 (RIBA/Bridgeman Art Library)
36. The Penguin Pool at London Zoo designed by Lubetkin (Nick Dawe/Arcaid)
37. Stained-glass window at Michelin House (Richard Bryant/Arcaid)
38. *The Execution of Wat Tyler* from 'Chronicle of English History' (British Library/The Art Archive)
39. *An Ideal Lord Mayor's Show* (Coram Foundation/Bridgeman Art Library)
40. *Sigmund Freud at his desk,* 1914 by Max Pollack (Freud Museum, London/Bridgeman Art Library)
41. *Alexander Fleming* by Ethel Gabain (Private Collection/Bridgeman Art Library)
42. Aerial view of The Monument (Skyscan)
43. Trellick Tower (Etienne Clément/arc blue)
44. Winston Churchill in Sidney Street, 1910 (Getty Images)
45. Westminster Hall by T. Rowlandson and A. C. Pugin (Stapleton Collection/Bridgeman Art Library)
46. The Drawing Room at Linley Sambourne House (Linley Sambourne House, photograph: Martin Charles)
47. *Battle of Barnet,* illuminated manuscript MS.236,f2r (Universiteitsbibliotheek Gent)
48. *Burning of Hugh Latimer and Nicholas Ridley* (The Art Archive)
49. *William Cowper,* English School, 19th century (Private Collection/Bridgeman Art Library)

50. *Andrew Marvell visiting his friend John Milton* by George Henry Boughton (Bonhams, London, UK/Bridgeman Art Library)
51. Detail of the Hoover Factory building (Edifice)
52. Neville Chamberlain at Heston Aerodrome, 1938 (Corbis)
53. Greenham Common (© PA Photos/Empics)
54. *David Garrick and his wife by his Temple to Shakespeare at Hampton*, c.1762 by Johann Zoffany (© Yale Center for British Art, Paul Mellon Collection/ Bridgeman Art Library)
55. *Strawberry Hill* by Thomas Rowlandson (Victoria & Albert Museum/Bridgeman Art Library)
56. *Swan Upping* by Stanley Spencer (Tate Britain. © Estate of Stanley Spencer. All Rights Reserved, DACS 2005)
57. Bowthorpe Oak (Alamy Images)
58. Uffington White Horse (Getty Images)
59. Darwin's collection of dry crustacea (Museum of Natural History, Oxford)
60. Noel Olivier, Maitland Radford, Virginia Woolf and Rupert Brooke, unknown photographer, 1911 (National Portrait Gallery)
61. Chart of Orford Ness by Ananias Appleton, 1588 (British Library)
62. Drainer's Dyke, Wicken Fen (National Trust Photo Library/Joe Cornish)
63. Lincoln Cathedral, east window, north aisle, showing John the Baptist (© Sonia Halliday and Laura Lushington)
64. Medieval pilgrim badge (Museum of London/Bridgeman Art Library)
65. *Portrait of Olaudah Equiano*, English School, 18th century (Royal Albert Memorial Museum, Exeter/Bridgeman Art Library)
66. *Thomas Coke inspecting his South Down sheep with Mr Walton and the Holkham shepherds* by Thomas Weaver (Collection of the Earl of Leicester, Holkham Hall/Bridgeman Art Library)
67. *Willy Lott's House, near Flatford Mill*, c.1811 by John Constable (Victoria & Albert Museum/Bridgeman Art Library)
68. The 'Roman' staircase at Burghley House (Bridgeman Art Library)
69. Tilbury Fort (English Heritage Photo Library/Skyscan)
70. Rushton Triangular Lodge (English Heritage Photo Library/Skyscan)
71. Engraving of Berkeley Castle by Johannes Kip (Private Collection/Bridgeman Art Library)
72. Tomb of Edward VII, Gloucester Cathedral (Collections/David Mansell)
73. *The Country's Complaint Recounting the Sad Events of the late Unparalleled Rebellion* from 'Mercurius Rusticus', 1685 (Private Collection/Bridgeman Art Library)
74. Spaghetti Junction, Birmingham (Skyscan)
75. The Baptistery window of Coventry cathedral by John Piper (Bridgeman Art Library)
76. *Iron Bridge at Coalbrookdale*, c.1790 by William Williams (The Art Archive/ Ironbridge Gorge Museum)
77. *Richard Arkwright's Cotton Mill*, 1763, by Joseph Wright of Derby (Derby Art Gallery/The Art Archive/Eileen Tweedy)

78. *Portrait of Matthew Boulton* by Carl Frederick von Breda (Birmingham Museums and Art Gallery/Bridgeman Art Library)
79. *A Bar at the Folies-Bergère, 1881–2* by Edouard Manet (Samuel Courtauld Trust, Courtauld Institute of Art Gallery/Bridgeman Art Library)
80. The Chatsworth Lion, Chatsworth House (Fay Godwin/Collections)
81. The summerhouse in Edward Jenner's garden (Wellcome Library, London)
82. *Interior of Ruskin's study, 1893* by Joseph Severn (Russell-Cotes Art Gallery and Museum, Bournemouth/Bridgeman Art Library)
83. Aerial view over Grasmere (Alamy Images)
84. Shadow of the Blackpool Tower (Alamy Images)
85. Aerial view of Calder Hall Power Station (Corbis)
86. A. C. B. Lovell at Jodrell Bank (Corbis)
87. *O the Roast Beef of Old England, 1748* by William Hogarth (Tate Britain)
88. *Manchester Heroes, 1819* (British Museum/Bridgeman Art Library)
89. Band of Hope Workers Rally, Free Trade Hall, Manchester (Manchester Library and Information Service: Manchester Archives and Local Studies)
90. Interior of the cellarium, Fountains Abbey (National Trust Photo Library)
91. Lindisfarne Castle (Collections/Roy Stedall-Humphryes)
92. Clifford's Tower, York (English Heritage Photo Library/Jonathan Bailey)
93. *Alnwick Castle* by Canaletto (Private Collection/Bridgeman Art Library)
94. *View of Cragside House* (National Trust Photo Library)
95. View across the nave of Durham Cathedral (Alamy Images)
96. Launch of the *Zetland* Lifeboat (RNLI Zetland Lifeboat Museum, Redcar)
97. *The Wealth of England: the Bessemer Process of Making Steel, 1895* by William Titcomb (Kelham Island Industrial Museum, Sheffield/Bridgeman Art Library)
98. *The Kneeling Slave*, English School, 18th century (Wilberforce House, Hull City Museums and Art Galleries/Bridgeman Art Library)
99. *The Opening of the Stockton to Darlington railway*, engraving c.1830 (The Art Archive/Marc Charmet)
100. William Gladstone at Hawarden Castle (Getty Images)
101. Roman amphitheatre at Caerleon (Skyscan)
102. Beaumaris Castle (Britainonview)
103. Manorbier Castle (Alamy Images)
104. Rhossili Bay, Gower Peninsula (Alamy Images)
105. Detail of St David's Cathedral, Dyfed (Britainonview/Rod Edwards)
106. The Boathouse, Carmarthenshire (Alamy Images)
107. *The Menai Bridge* by George Arnald (Julian Simon Fine Art, London/Bridgeman Art Library)
108. *The Grant of the Diwani*, c.1818 by Benjamin West (British Library)
109. *The Battle of Culloden, 1797*, engraving by Laurie and Whittle (The Art Archive/Eileen Tweedy)
110. *The Hall at Abbotsford House, 1834* by David Roberts (Private Collection/Bridgeman Art Library)
111. Portrait of Robert Burns at Burns Cottage (Britainonview)

112. *Queen Victoria on horseback with John Brown* by Charles Barber (Forbes Magazine Collection, New York/Bridgeman Art Library)
113. *The Affray in the High Church* by Felix Philippoteaux (Private Collection/ Bridgeman Art Library)
114. Calton Hill, Edinburgh (Britainonview)
115. Interior of the Glasgow School of Art (Arcaid)
116. St Martin's Cross at Iona Abbey (Britainonview)
117. St Ninian's Chapel, Isle of Whithorn (ePic Scotland)
118. Glencoe (Getty Images)
119. Pictish Round Tower, Abernethy (ePic Scotland)
120. *The October Meeting*, 1862 by Thomas Hodge (The Royal and Ancient Golf Club of St Andrews)
121. The model set for the film about the Tay Bridge Disaster (Getty Images)
122. Lord Kitchener Poster, 1914 by Alfred Leete (The Advertising Archive)
123. Wreck at Scapa Flow (Lawson Wood/Corbis)
124. Detail of the Scottish Parliament building (Keith Hunter, arc blue)

Index

Entries for the five hundred landmarks appear in **bold**; in some of the longer entries, folios for the main references appear in **bold**.

Bovington Camp 1, 9,
19–20
Bovington Tank Museum
8–9
Bowness-on-Solway 389
Bowood House 9–10
Bowthorpe Oak x, 255–6
Boy's Own Paper, The 450
Bradford 374, 391
Bradwell-on-Sea 256
Bragg, William 172
Bramham Moor, Battle of
(1408) 382
Brantwood 356–7
Branxton Hill 387
Brasher, Chris 235
Brawne, Fanny 151
Brawne, Mrs 152
9 Brechin Road,
Kirriemuir 471–2
Brereton, Sir William 344
Bridego Bridge 208–9
Bridei, King 452
Bridge Street 118–19
Bridgwater 38
Brighton 6, 45, **52–3**
Bristol 1, 10–13, 30, 365
Britain, Battle of (1940) 45,
86, **95–6**, 147, 359
Britannia Bridge 37
British Broadcasting
Corporation (BBC) x,
122, 371
British Empire Exhibition
(1924) 306
British Library 119–20, 121
British Museum 116, 119,
120–1, 186, 290
British Telecom 124
Britten, Benjamin 251, 285
Brixham Harbour ix, 13–14
Brixton 138
Broad Court x, 123–4
Broadcasting House x, 122
Broadhalfpenny Down x,
73–4
Broadlands 53–4
Brock, Sir Thomas 127
Brocket Hall 209–10
Brompton Cemetery 150
Bromsgrove Guild 127

Brontë Parsonage 391–2
Brontë, Anne 379, 391–2
Brontë, Branwell 391
Brontë, Charlotte 379,
391–2
Brontë, Emily 379, 391–2
Brontë, Rev. Patrick 391–2
Brooke, Rupert, 270–1
Brough Castle 358
Brougham Castle 358
Brown, Charles Armitage
151–2
Brown, Ford Madox 51
Brown, John 373
Brown, Lancelot
'Capability' 243, 355
Brown, Louise ix, 373–4
Brownsea Island 14–15
Bruce, Sir Edward 444
Bruce, Robert (grandson of
Robert I of Scotland)
397
Brummell, Beau 149
Brunel Engine House, The
124–6
Brunel, Isambard Kingdom
x, **12–13**, **36–7**, 105, **125**
Brunel, Marc Isambard
105, 112, **124–5**
Brut y Tywysogion 434
BT Tower 126
Buchan, Countess of 384
Buchanan, George 485
Buckingham, 2nd Duke of
136
Buckingham, James 376
Buckingham Palace 126–7
Buckland Abbey 15–16
Buckler's Hard 54–5
Builth Wells 410, 419
Bullen, Sir Geoffrey 75
Bullen, Sir Thomas 76
Bunhill Fields 127–8, 206
Bunyan, John 127, 201,
205–6
Bunyan's Baptism Pool
205–6
Burbage, James 144
Burford 201, 210–11
Burghley House 257–8
Burghley, William Cecil,

1st Marquis of 220,
257–8
Burlington, 3rd Earl of 60,
134–5, 169, 243, **274–5**
Burlington House 135, 169
Burne-Jones, Edward 51
Burns Cottage x, 441–2
Burns Monument 459
Burns, Robert x, 437, 440,
441–2, 467
Burns, William 441
Burton, Decimus 77, 158
Burton upon Trent 311
Butchers' Company 145
Bute, John Stuart, Earl of
76
Butterfield, William 337
Byrhtnoth 280
Byron, Lord 7–8, **162**, 210,
333–4, 385

Cabinet War Rooms ix,
128–9, 362
Cabot, John 10
Cadbury Castle 1, 16–17
Cade, Jack 200
Caerleon 93, 411–12
Caernarfon Castle 407,
412
Caerphilly Castle 407, 413
Caesar, Julius viii, 45,
65–6, 89, **97**
Calder Hall ix, 351, 357
Calderdale 391
Calleva Atrebatum see
Silchester
Calton Hill 458–9
Calvin, John 454
Cambridge 258–62
Cambridge University 228,
251, **258–60**, 261
Camelot 1, 16–17, 349
Cameron, Sir Ewen 470
Campbell clan 465–6
Campbell, Colen 135, 275
Campbell, John 466
Campion, Edmund (later
St) 338
Camulodunum see Colchester
Canary Wharf 130, 140,
167

Chipperfield, Jimmy 28
Chiswick House 60, **134–5**,
243, 312
Chorley 362, 364
Christ Church, Oxford
234, 260, 329
Christ's College,
Cambridge 259
Christchurch Priory 18–19
Christie, James (father) 136
Christie, James (son) 136
Christie's 135–6
Chubb, J. 150
Churchill, Clementine 61–2
Churchill, Sir Winston vii,
ix, 1, 9, 14, 20, 45,
54–5, **61–2**, 64, 129, 181,
184, 208, 217, 290, 362,
367
Chute, Chaloner 96
Chute, John 244
Chysauster Ancient Village
1, 19
Cibber, Caius Gabriel 312
Cistercian Order 388, 434
City of London 105, 128,
130, **145–6**, **158–9**, 167,
278
Civil War, English (1642–9)
35, 101, 135, 159, 176,
179, 210–11, 275, 277–8,
295, **308–9**, **319–20**,
332–3, 358, **342**, **344**,
410
    Battle of Edgehill (1642)
    176, 295, **319–20**, 344
    Battle of Naseby (1645)
    vii–viii, 176, 295, **332–3**
    Stow-on-the-Wold (1646)
    210, 295, 319, **344–5**
    Saracen's Head, **The**
    (1646) 342
Claremont House 432
Clarence, George, Duke of
(nephew of Edward IV)
343
Clarence, Lionel, Duke of
(son of Edward III) 240
Clark, Sir James 443
Clark, Kenneth 162
Claudius, Emperor 89, 265

Claydon House 212
Cleckheaton 384–5
Clee Hill 326
Clement, St 176
Clement VII, Pope 329
Clergy House, The 45, **48**
Cleves, Anne of 348
Clifford, Lady Anne 358
Clifford, Lord ('Butcher',
'Bloodsupper') 403
Clifford, Roger 419
Clifford's Tower 405–6
Clink Prison 199–200
Clive, Edward, Earl of
Powis 432
Clive, Robert 431–2
Cliveden House 201, 213
Clothworkers' Company 145
Clouds Hill 1, 19–20
Clyde, river 465, 476
Cnut, King (Canute the
Great) 176
Coal Mines Act (1842) 183
Coalbrookdale 295,
313–14
Cobbett, William 425
Cobham, 1st Viscount 243
Cockerell, C. R. 231, 459
Coggeshall Abbey 264–5
Cogidubnus, chieftain 72
Coke, Thomas *see* Leicester,
1st Earl of
Colchester 265–6
Coldstream 387, 445–6
Coldstream Guards 446
Coleridge, Samuel Taylor
360
Collingwood, Admiral
Cuthbert 256
Colman, James 282
Colman, Jeremiah 282
Colman, Jeremiah James
282
Colman's Mustard Works
x, 282–3
Colston Bassett & District
Dairy 289
Colt, Samuel 276
Columba, St 404, 437,
469, 477
Columbus, Christopher 215

Commons Preservation
Society 48
Commonwealth (1649–60)
137, 206, 210–11, 224,
255, 279, 281
Compleat Angler, The
(Walton) 339
Compter Prison 199
Comyn, John 437, 444
Conan Doyle, Arthur 450
Congleton 369
Coniston 357
Coniston Water 356
Conran Roche Co. 160
Constable, John 251, 269
Constantine, Emperor 56
Contrasts (Pugin) 271
Conway 326
Conwy Bridge 424
Cook, Captain James 77,
379, 400–1
Cook, Robin 350
Cookham 213–14
Cooks' Company 145
Co-operative Movement
351, 375–6
Coopers' Company 145
Coppergate, York 404–5
Coram, Captain Thomas
142–3
Corbridge 389
Corn Law (1815) 371,
427–8
Cornell, George 117–18
Coronation Street 371–2
Cosin, Dr John 259
Cotton, Charles 339
Cotton, John 255
Cotton, Sir Robert 119
Coty Co. 236
Council for the Protection
of Rural England (CPRE)
418
Countess Pillar, The 358
Country Life 80, 261
Courier Building, The
449–50
Covenanters 437, 456, 468
Coventry Cathedral 170,
295, 314–15
Coward, Noël 109

de Valois, Katherine (wife
of Henry V) 85
De Winton, H. 260
de Worde, Wynkyn 139
Debatable Land 483
Deben, river 289
Debenham & Freebody Co.
182
Debenham, William 182
Declaration of
Independence, Scottish
437, 442
Deene Park x, **316–17**
Defoe, Daniel 127, 288
Deheubarth 414, 423, 434
Delabole Wind Farm 20–1
Denmark, Anne, Queen of
James I of England 485
Derby 369, 447, 462
Derby, 12th Earl of 70
Derby, Edward Stanley,
14th Earl of 223
78 Derngate, Northampton
335–6
Descent of Man, The
(Darwin) 68
Descriptio Cambriae
(Giraldus) 423
Despenser, Hugh (father
and son) 300
Devonshire, Deborah,
Duchess of 313
Devonshire, William
Cavendish, 1st Duke of
312
Devonshire, 6th Duke of
312, 355
Devonshire, 11th Duke of
313
Devonshire, 2nd Earl of
325
Devonshire, 3rd Earl of
325
Devonshire, 4th Earl of *see*
Devonshire, 1st Duke of
Devorgilla, Lady 475
Dewar, James 172
Dickens, Catherine 73
Dickens, Charles, 63,
72–3, 115, 199, 345, 449
Dickens, Fanny 199

Dickens, John 63, 72–3
Dickins and Jones Co. 182
*Dictionary of the English
Language* (Johnson) 295,
330
Digby, Everard 317–18
Discovery, RRS 448–9
Disraeli, Benjamin (1st Earl
of Beaconsfield) 223–4
Disraeli, Mary Anne 223
Dissenters 128, 150, 206,
211, 255, **360–1**
Dissolution of the
Monasteries 1, 15, 18,
23, 25–6, 30, 35, 101,
102, **133**, 134, 189, 220,
239, 244, 265, 250, 291,
292, 310, 311, 389, 434,
435
Dissolution, Act of (1536)
133
District Line (Railway) 112
Dixon, Reginald 147
Docklands, London 130
Dodgson, Charles 234
Dolbadarn Castle 407,
415–16
Domestic Cookery (Rundell)
162
Don Juan (Byron) 162
Donne, John 339
Dorchester 29
Dorn, Marion 171
Dornberger, Walter 148
Dorney Court 214–15
Double Helix, The (Watson)
262
Douglas, 'Black' Earls of
478–9
Douglas, Earl (1388) 382
Douglas, George 473
Douglas, 8th Earl 478–9
Douglas, 9th Earl 479
Douglas, Earl (1402) 341
Douglas, J. N. 22
Douglas, Lord Alfred 237
Douglas, Sir James 475, 479
Douglas, Sir William
(1296) 383–4
Douglas, Sir William
(1567) 473

Douglas, Willy 473
Douglas-Home, Sir Alec
213
Dove Cottage 359–60
Dover 65–6
Dover Castle 66–7, 267
Dover, Treaty of (1670)
285–6
Dover, White Cliffs of 45,
65–6, 97
Down House ix, 67–8
10 Downing Street 128–9,
136–7
Downing, Sir George 137
Doyle, Arthur Conan 162
Drake, Sir Francis 1, **15–16,
32–3**, 169, 290–1
Drapers' Company 145
Dreadnought, HMS 481
Dream of Gerontius, The
(Elgar) 232, 331
Druidism 41, 164–5
Drumossie Moor 447
Dudley, Lord Guildford
245
Dugald Stewart Monument
459
Dunbar, Battle of (1296)
482
Dunbar, Battle of (1650)
446
Dunchurch 317–18
Dundas, Lord 399
Dundee 448–50, 486
Dunfermline 437, 450–2
Dunfermline Abbey 437,
450–1, 475
Dunlop Tyre Co. 160
Dunmore House 215
Dunnichen 452–3
Dunnottar Castle 458
Dunrobin Castle 453–4
Dunstan, St, Archbishop of
Canterbury 6, 26
Durham Cathedral 379,
386–7, 394, 395, 397,
451
Dust Hill viii, 332
Dwyfor, river 421–2
Dyers' Company 4, 214

James II also known as
James VII of Scotland
(1685–88) ix, **13–14**, **38**,
44, 141, 172, 206, 224,
231, 274, 281, **285–6**,
312, 466, 468, 469–70,
483
James II, King of Scotland
(1437–60) 478–9
James III, King of Scotland
(1460–88) 480, 486
James IV, King of Scotland
(1488–1513) 379 **387–8**,
458, 480, 482, 486
James V, King of Scotland
(1513–42) 376–7, 454,
455, **461–2**, 485, 486
James VI, King of Scotland
(1567–1625) 384, 440,
454, 455, 456, 462, 473,
482, **485**; *see also* James I
of England
James VII of Scotland *see*
James II of England
James, Henry 91
James of St George, Master
410, 412
Jane Austen's House 63–4
Jane Eyre (C. Brontë) 391
Jarrow ix, 379, 393
Jedburgh Abbey 450
Jefferies, Richard 128
Jeffreys, Judge George 1,
38, **44**, 151
Jekyll, Gertrude ix, 45, 48,
79–80
Jellicoe, Admiral John 475
Jenner, Edward viii, 301–2
Jerusalem Chamber 105,
193–4
Jessop, William 177
Jew's House, The 251,
278–9
Jews in Britain 105, 116–17,
142–3, 278–9, 405–6
Jhabvala, Ruth Prawer 162
Joan of Arc 347–8
Joan of Navarre (Queen of
Henry IV) 194
Jockey Club 281
Jodrell Bank 365

John, King (1189–1216) viii,
67, 90, **238–9**, **267**, 271,
279, 327, 340, 414,
415–16, 430
John Milton's Cottage 211
John XXII, Pope 442
John, Barry 414
Johnson, Amy 64
Johnson, Dr Samuel 99,
219, 246, 295, **330–1**
Johnson, Elizabeth (Tetty)
330
Johnson, Michael 330
Johnston, Archibald 456
Johnston, Edward 113
Jones, Herbert 71
Jones, Inigo 6, 40, 96,
114–15, 135, **165–6**, 221,
281
Jones, John Paul 378
Jones, William 428
Jonson, Ben 307
Jordans Meeting House
201, 211, **224**
Joseph of Arimathea 1,
25–6
Joyce, William ('Lord Haw-
Haw') 132
Julian of Norwich 281–2
Julius II, Pope 458
Jungle Books, The (Kipling)
55
Just So Stories (Kipling) 55
Jutland, Battle of (1916) 481

Kamal-ud-Din, Khwaja 104
Kay, John 315
Keats, John 151–2, 345
Keats House 151–2
Keble, John 232
Keeler, Christine 213
Kelham Hall 342
Kelham Island Museum
399
Kenilworth Castle 295,
300, **327–8**, 413
Kennel Club 42
Kensal Green Cemetery 150
Kensington Palace 152–3
Kent, William 135, 137,
153, 243

Kettering 328
Kew x, 76–7
**Kew Bridge Pumping
Station** 224–5
Keynes, Geoffrey 175
Keynes, John Maynard 59
Killiecrankie, Pass of
469–70
'Killing Times' 456, 468
Kim (Kipling) 55
King Lear (Shakespeare)
144
King's Arms, Southwell *see*
Saracen's Head
King's Bench Prison 199
King's College Chapel 23,
259
King's College, Cambridge
215, 259, 260
King's Oak 333
Kingsley, Charles 268
Kinneff church 458
Kipling, Rudyard 9, 45,
55–6
Kirkcaldy 470–1
Kirkgate Market 394–5
Kirriemuir 471–2
Kitchener Memorial 474–5
Kitchener, Field-Marshal
Lord 474–5
Knight, John Peake 118–19
Knight, Laura 113
Knights Hospitallers 189,
271
Knights Templar 188, 264,
271, 429, 478
Knox, John 437, **454**, 455,
473
Knox, Lt.-Col. Thomas 416
Komisarjevsky, Theodore
147
Kray, Reggie 117–18, 132
Kray, Ronald 117–18, 132
Kyrle, John 434

Lamb House 91
Lacock Abbey 26–7
Lady Lever Art Gallery 375
Lady Windermere's Fan
(Wilde) 237
Laguerre, Louis 312

Newton in the Willows
334–5
Newton, C. H. 150
Newton, Sir Isaac 116,
179–80, 294
Newton, Rev. John 227
Ney, Marshal 431
Nicholas II, Tsar 284
Nicholas, Jemima 417
Nichols, Colonel 182
Nicholls, Arthur Bell 392
6a Nicolson Street,
Edinburgh 459–60
Nigg Parish Church x,
477
Nightingale, Florence 67,
182, 212
Nightingale, Parthenope
212
Ninian, St 437, 477, 487
Nolan, Capt. 316
Norden, John 25
Nordenfelt, Thorsten 354
Norfolk, 1st Duke of 49,
310
Norfolk, 3rd Duke of 49,
377
Norfolk, 4th Duke of (Sir
Philip Howard) 49
Norfolk, 5th Duke of 49
Norfolk, 15th Duke of 49
Norham 379, 397, 472–3
Norman Conquest *see*
Hastings, Battle of
Normandy, William Duke
of *see* William I
1–3 North Parade,
Grantham x, 272
Northampton 335–6
Northampton, the Battle of
(1460) 241
Northampton, Treaty of
(1328) 445, 473
Northanger Abbey (Austen)
64
Northolt 95
Northumberland, John
Dudley, Duke of 244–5,
269–70
Northwich 372–3
Norwich 278, **281–3**, 369

Nottingham 299, 315, 342,
369, 385, 426
Nunhead Cemetery 150
Nyren, Richard 74

O'Connor, Fergus 304
Observations on the River Wye
434
Observer 140
Offa, King of Mercia
(757–96) 6, 239, 429
Offa's Dyke 428–9
Offa's Dyke Path 429
Okey, Colonel 333
Olaf (Olave), St 177
Old Bailey 131–2, 187
Old Grammar School,
Huntingdon 275–6
Old Lifeboat Station, The
398–9
Old Palace, Hatfield vii,
220
Old Pretender *see* Stuart,
James Francis Edward
Old Sarum 31–2, 210
Old Vicarage, The 270–1
Oldham 373
Olmsted, Frederick Law
226
Olney 201, 226–7
Olympia & Yorke Co. 130
Omega Workshops 59–60
On the Origin of Species by
Means of Natural Selection
(Darwin) ix, 67–8, 233
Operation Overlord 55, 218
Ordnance, Board of 222
Ordnance Survey 222
Ore, river 284
Orford Castle 283
Orford Ness 254, **283–4**
Orkney 437, 473–4, 481,
484
Orwell, George 216
Osborne House 81–2
Osborne, John 371
Osterley Underground
Station 113
Oswald, King of
Northumbria (605–642)
404

Oswy, King of
Northumbria (d.670)
256, 393–4, 404
Otterburn, Battle of (1388)
382
Our Mutual Friend (Dickens)
73
Owen, Robert 43, 375, 476
Oxford 201, **227–35**, 326,
342, 344
Oxford Archaeology Unit
247
Oxford Botanic Garden
230, 233
Oxford Circus 163
Oxford Movement 232
Oxford Museum *see*
Museum of Natural
History
Oxford Street 182, 187
Oxford University 230, 231
Oxford, Earl of (1461) 205

Palace cinema, Southall
147
Palladio, Andrea 96, 134–5,
166
Palmer, Roger 214
Palmerston, 1st Viscount
54
Palmerston, 3rd Viscount
53–4, 140
Panizzi, Sir Anthony 120
Pankhurst, Christobel 226
Pankhurst, Emmeline 71
Panmure, Lord 102
Paradise Lost (Milton) 201,
211
Paradise Mill 369
Paradise Regained (Milton)
211
Paris, Matthew 267
Parker & Unwin Co. 226
Parker's Piece 260–1
Parkes, Alexander 305
Parliament Act (1911) 422
Parr, Catherine 348–9
Parsons, Robert 338
Paterson, William 113
Paulett, Frances 288
Paxton, Joseph 354–5